GOVERNMENT AND LABOUR IN KENYA 1895-1963

Anthony Clayton
Royal Military Academy, Sandhurst

and

Donald C. Savage
Executive Secretary of the Canadian Association of University Teachers

FRANK CASS : LONDON

First published 1974 in Great Britain by
FRANK CASS AND COMPANY LIMITED
67 Great Russell Street, London WC1B 3BT

and in United States of America by
FRANK CASS AND COMPANY LIMITED
c/o International Scholarly Book Services, Inc
P.O. Box 4347, Portland Oregon 97208

ISBN 0 7146 3025 X

Library of Congress Catalog Card Number 73-82525

Made and printed in Great Britain by
The Garden City Press Limited
Letchworth, Hertfordshire
SG6 1JS

In Memoriam

T. J. M.

TABLE OF CONTENTS

MAP

KENYA, 1954
Ethiopia
Sudan
Lokitaungo
Lake
Rudolf
Lodwar
Moyale
NORTHERN
Marsabit
Wajir
Uganda
Somalia
Mt. Elgon
Kapenguria
Mbale
Kitale
RIFT VALLEY
Maralal
Uasin Gishu
Lake Baringo
Baringo
Tororo
Jinja
Eldoret
Kabarnet
Laikipia
Isiolo
Kakamega
Rumuruti
Nanyuki
Meru
NYANZA
Eldama Ravine
Kisumu
Thompson's Falls
CENTRAL
Mt. Kenya
Tana
Aberdare Ra.
Nyeri
Kericho
Nakuru
Karatina
Embu
Garissa
Lake Victoria
Kisii
L. Naivasha
Ft. Hall
River
Thika
Narok
Nairobi
Ngong
Kitui
SOUTHERN
Machakos
Magadi
Kajiado
Makueni
Lake Natron
Lamu
Tanganyika
COAST
Mount Kilimanjaro
Malindi
Arusha
Moshi
Voi
Indian Ocean
Kilifi
Mackinnon
'White Highlands'
Uganda railway
Provincial boundary
Mombasa
Kwale
0
Miles
150
Kms.
Tanga
eac

ACKNOWLEDGEMENTS

It is a pleasure to acknowledge the debt we owe to many who have helped us in East Africa, the United Kingdom and in Canada. We are particularly grateful to those who allowed themselves to be interviewed or who discussed the issues with us, especially to the late Mr. Tom Mboya who gave freely of his time and arranged for us to see certain documents and to interview other trade unionists. We must, perforce, list the remainder with gratitude but without specifying the nature of the assistance: Messrs. J. D. Akumu, J. M. Gachago, B. M. Kaggia, J. K. Karebe, C. Kibachia, P. Kibisu, A. Kutahi, C. K. Lubembe, O. O. Mak'Anyengo, S. Muhanji, A. A. Minya, D. J. Ngethe, A. A. Ochwada, S. T. Omar, H. A. Oduor, W. D. Ogutu, Makhan Singh and many other past and present officials of the Kenya trade union movement; Messrs. S. Cockar, R. Damerell, E. M. Hyde-Clarke, K. D. Harrap, J. I. Husband, Sir Richard Luyt, M. A. O. Ndisi, W. R. C. Keeler along with many labour officers and other officials of the Labour Department; Captain G. R. Williams and other officials connected with the port of Mombasa; Messrs. T. Bavin, J. Bury, A. Hammerton, P. de Jonge, D. Taylor, E. K. Welsh and others serving the I.C.F.T.U.; Mr. W. Hood and Miss Marjorie Nicholson of the T.U.C.; Rev. A. Hake and Rev. D. Taylor of the Christian Council of Kenya; the late Mr. I. Duthie and Mr. D. Richmond of the F.K.E.; Professor B. A. Ogot, Dr. G. Muriuki, Dr. G. S. Were, Mr. W. C. Rodgers, Mr. R. E. S. Tanner, Dr. R. van Zwanenberg and many other academics including those associated with the African History seminars at the Institute of Commonwealth Studies; and Archbishop L. R. Beecher, Messrs. C. Chalfin, T. C. Colchester, S. V. Cooke, Sir Walter Coutts, Sir Derek Erskine, S. H. Fazan, G. Foggon, W. G. S. Harrison, M. Hill, C. Legum, J. Johnson, Sir Francis Loyd, R. Luckett, C. V. Merritt, R. G. Ngala, P. Odero Jowi, A. Pandya, the late P. Pinto, A. Riddell, C. Sanger, Mr. Humphrey Slade and Shirley Williams. We wish particularly to thank Mr. J. A. Murumbi both for discussing the theme of this book and for the use of his personal library. Many of those interviewed did not, in fact, share our views and conclusions but nevertheless gave generously of their time. The mention of an interview in this book should not be taken to imply any agreement with our interpretation.

We are indebted to Mr. A. T. Matson for reading the entire manuscript and for his valuable suggestions, and for the comments of Mr. E. M. Hyde-Clarke, Mr. F. M. Goldsmith, Mr. T. C. Colchester, Sir Francis Loyd, Mr. N. Hyman and Sir Frederick Pedler who read sections of it.

Especial thanks is due to Mr. N. W. Fedha, the Kenya Government Archivist, and to his staff at the Kenya National Archives, to Mr. D. Simpson and his staff at the Royal Commonwealth Society, to Lieut.-Col. G. A. Shepperd and his staff at the Royal Military Academy Sandhurst Library, and to Mr. G. W. Trowsdale and Mr. J. Prinz and their staff at the

Vanier Library, Loyola of Montreal. We are also grateful to the librarians in the Public Record Office, and in the British Museum as well as to those in the libraries of the Foreign Office, the Colonial Office, the Department of Labour (Canada), the International Confederation of Free Trade Unions, and the Institute of Commonwealth Studies in London. We also wish to thank the librarians of Rhodes House, the Church Missionary Society, Edinburgh House, Edinburgh University, the National Library of Scotland, Nairobi University, Makerere University, the MacMillan Library, Northwestern University, and the National Library of Canada. We were also helpfully assisted by the authorities at the Royal Mint who answered questions concerning East African currency. We are indebted to Miss Pamela Scott for access to the papers of Lord Francis Scott, to Mr. J. Bury for private papers in his possession, to Dr. J. Weeks for the loan of a microfilm in his possession, to Mr. Makhan Singh for papers in his possession, and to the Hamlyn Publishing Group for permission to quote from *My African Journey* by Sir Winston Churchill.

Quotations taken from Crown-copyright records in the Public Record Office appear by permission of the Controller of H.M. Stationery Office.

The first chapters of this book are based on a doctoral dissertation by Anthony Clayton for the University of St. Andrews. We would like to thank Dr. G. Seed and Mr. S. McDowell of the university for many helpful suggestions, and also Professor G. A. Shepperson of the University of Edinburgh both for valuable criticism and the suggestion which resulted in this work. We would also like to thank Mrs. H. R. Savage and Mrs. Judith Clayton for their work on the proofs and the Index.

Finally we wish to acknowledge the financial support of the Canada Council and of the C. D. Howe Foundation without which it would have been impossible to undertake the field research.

ANTHONY CLAYTON
London

DONALD C. SAVAGE
Ottawa
March 1973

INTRODUCTION

The history of a country can be likened to a rope composed of strands of several different colours, at any one section of the rope one or two strands may appear on the surface, a third and fourth may lie below to reappear a little distance away. In Kenya's colonial history three strands form the rope—land, labour and the action and reaction of races to one another, expressed consciously in politics. All three strands are necessary for a complete understanding of Kenyan history, but while the land and racial-political strands in various periods have been the subject of close study, the study of labour has not yet received the same attention.

The subject merits study on its own, as an examination of the circumstances under which many thousands of men lived for a period of their lives, and for the importance of labour in the growth of nationalism. But labour also merits study for the light it throws on colonialism in its very broadest sense, as an examination of the evolution of colonial labour policy in Kenya leads into widely varied fields. The repercussions of a small number of employers, mostly white men, endeavouring to obtain the service of Africans for hire were profound, both for the people involved in Kenya and elsewhere; policy and consequent action might one year be determined in response to local needs at a provincial or district level, but the next year be determined in London in response to very different pressures.

For example Kenya's labour conditions were one of a relatively very small number of problems in British Africa which on several occasions attracted considerable public attention in Britain in the pre-1939 period when colonial rule was unchallenged. The Secretaries of State for the Colonies, the responsible British Cabinet ministers, were normally prepared to leave African colonies largely alone, accepting the advice and recommendations of the governor, the 'man on the spot', for the day to day running of the country, and only occasionally seeking parliamentary consent for minor change of policy or a development loan. Colonial Secretaries changed frequently and the Colonial Office officials were organized into regional departments; until 1925 the Office also dealt with the dominions. Resident permanent advice and interest on a specialist subject such as labour was not available to a Colonial Secretary until the late nineteen-thirties. But labour matters in Kenya, however, were to lead to pressure, in and outside Parliament, from a very large number of interested people and organizations in Britain, and sometimes from other countries as well. In Britain anti-slavery and missionary societies had begun a close watch from the earliest years of colonial rule; they were followed by other church and political organizations, and the Trades Union Congress. Beyond Britain, South and Central Africa on the one hand and the International Labour Organization and the International Confederation of Free Trade Unions on the other were later to exert almost contradictory pressures. The influence of these groups on policy was to be considerable, and often at variance with the ideas of the 'man on the spot', who ceased to be entirely trusted by British public and political opinion.

The need to induce Africans to work, to leave their tribal societies and customs and to hire themselves to immigrant, largely British, employers also produced the very widest consequences at the local level. The size of the tribal land units, known as reserves, was the subject of early controversy, European farmers pressing for small reserves with limited funds spent on their development in order to maintain a supply of men who were obliged to work elsewhere. Taxation, instituted initially as a normal feature of administration, was used as a tool to increase labour supply. Personal identity documents were framed with labour retention and discipline as their aim. African education for many years was planned only to equip men for the semi-skilled labour market, and for a long time social services of various types existed primarily to assist the labour supply. The degree of compulsion retained by the government for the supply of its own labour needs was on occasions planned with an eye to indirect assistance to the local private employer. Trade union, minimum wage and workmen's compensation legislation were all introduced later than in other British African territories. Even relatively minor matters, the size of a proposed coinage, railway freight charges, restrictions on African dances, pass laws, and the appointment, promotion or transfer of Colonial Service officials were often influenced by the politics of the labour market.

The importance of labour throughout the history of colonial Kenya cannot be over estimated. It was at work, and not as in most other British African territories as a governed public, that a very large number of Kenya people first met the white man; they met in the relationship of employee to employer. Sometimes this was a kind relationship, sometimes one of fatigue, impatience and irritation, often one of plain insensitive stupidity and misunderstandings. The European claimed to speak of 'employer' and 'employee'; the title of his early legislation, the 'Master and Servants' Ordinance, and his usual reference to African employees as 'boys' reflected his real attitudes. To the African 'employer' in Swahili was for almost the whole colonial period either *bwana* (master) or later in industrial negotiation, *mtajiri* (the rich man), while 'employee' was *mfanyi kazi* (the one who does the work) or *mtumishi* (the servant). In Kikuyu the nearest word to 'employer' is *mwandikali* (the one with the lists, the one who puts you to work) and 'employee' *mwandikwo* (the one who is listed, and put to work). These uses of African words, evolved in the relationship, indicate its appearance to both parties. A second major consequence of an economy based on migrant labourers, one not fully apparent until late in the colonial period, was that it was at work, on the farm, in the factory, and in the town that men of very different ethnic origins normally resident hundreds of miles apart met each other, began in some measure to think of themselves as all inhabitants of an area called Kenya and formed associations and unions of Kenyans, political and occupational, for their mutual benefit.

The concept of work was natural to the nineteenth and twentieth century Briton. Most British people worked for a wage, the man who did not might be suspect as an idler; to work was a moral obligation to the community. The less intelligent or sensitive settler or official found it impossible to understand why Africans could not fall in with this concept, nor could they understand the consequences for traditional societies. For the African worker whatever his ethnic group, came from a very closely knit set of communal and family obligations of which manual work, if necessary for very long hours, formed a part of the overall pattern, but a pattern in which there was no division between 'hours of work' and 'time off', for which no one was paid by coin for demarcated periods of time, and where the reward from labour was an immediate benefit for the whole family, or for the whole clan or community. Ideas of hours of work, payment by coin per month and the useful purchases which coin could effect, ideas of the foreman or overseer, the small family and its home, of higher salaries for special skills or of notice, were in the early years almost entirely alien and unintelligible concepts, and explanation of them through double translation (English to Swahili, Swahili to vernacular) immensely difficult. Mission and later government schools helped to convey these new ideas, and it is noticeable from early in Kenya's history that the better educated the man, the more he regarded wage employment as the norm and the greater was his appreciation of consumer goods. But the cost of starting a farm or plant in Africa meant that the wages an employer could pay had to be, by British standards, very low. The result of these factors was a reluctance by Africans to leave their traditional societies for this new and unusual mode of life, with an absence of interest in the work, absenteeism, a high rate of turnover and much waste of manpower, particularly in large undertakings. Until the population increases of the inter-war period the monthly employee had his land for his daily livelihood. He came to work to earn a specific sum to purchase a wife or a second wife, to pay his tax, to buy a bicycle or clothes. The target achieved, he left, with or without notice. The employer lost interest in his ever-changing and unreliable labour force, and made no effort to raise productivity with the reward of a higher wage.

The fit young or youngish man had, for very necessary reasons, been the pride of many African tribes, cared for, served and sometimes spoilt by the women. They were the standard of the tribe, proof of its virility and guarantee of its continuing identity. To the newly-arrived European, however, these were young men 'lolling about' in 'bestial idleness' while the unfortunate women carried the loads and worked in the gardens, and even the most enlightened and intelligent officials could feel that western habits of industry must somehow be learnt if Africans were to advance. A number knew little of the very real duties which, in fact, had to be performed by the men of the tribe.

Even less understood in the early years, and only partially understood as late as the nineteen-fifties, were the consequences for traditional societies which arose from the introduction of wages and the beginning of a long process of economic individualization. The employed labourer left his home area, the provisions, disciplines and restraints of his clan elders, and, provided he kept fit, he earned by his work a personal benefit, coins. He could spend some or all of these without thought for his communal or family duties. In the early years, low though the wage rate was, many labourers suddenly found themselves able to acquire for themselves new goods on an undreamed-of scale. They could however also acquire new problems, such as changed and uncomfortable climate and diet, disease and difficulties with strange laws. Later the position changed to their disadvantage, particularly when the pressure of population increase began to destroy the land security on which the whole low wage system rested. In the late nineteen-thirties and forties this problem became exacerbated to crisis point, violence erupting in 1952.

Uncomfortably situated between the employer and the Colonial Office, early colonial governors tried awkwardly to ride the storms. Their Royal Instructions, their oaths, their traditions, enjoined them to protect the possessions and liberties of the natives of the territory. But for many years the realities of power in colonial Kenya lay elsewhere; '. . . neither Kenya's Governor nor Downing Street itself has power in the last resort to control that very British community [the Kenya Europeans]', wrote one governor in the nineteen-twenties on the position as it appeared to him.[1] The Colonial Office, which might be a friend, was far away; the European settlers were at his front door on occasions quite literally. Some governors gave way and yielded to pressures, some failed to keep the Colonial Office properly informed of their actions, or even their legislation; another device of a weak governor was to receive a policy from London and subtly to alter its emphasis locally. Even a strong governor had often to minimize or conceal work undertaken for Africans. For historical reasons, colonial governors had long been permitted a very great measure of autonomy of which some took full advantage, particularly in the early years when in addition communication was more slow. So too, would various provincial and local officials sometimes implement policy in a way adjusted to their own or local views or pressures. However, in the very early years the calibre of the provincial and district Colonial Service officials was very poor and although by the nineteen-twenties the standard was greatly improved, no permanent Labour Department existed in Kenya until 1940.

Labour fell broadly into four categories. Firstly there remained, at the outset of British rule, the legal status of slavery within a ten-mile strip of land at the Coast. This status was abolished in 1907, and thereafter slavery very quickly disappeared. Secondly, in varying stages of evolution in 1895, was communal labour, where men of a tribe or clan combined their efforts for a social purpose, path-making, hospitality or bush-clearing. Comparisons can be made with the *corvée* in France and statute labour and team duty in Britain. This concept was taken over and developed by the early colonial administration for a variety of purposes, road-making under district officers, porters for the district commissioner and his family or staff when on tour or transfer, the laying out of *bomas* (district headquarters) and similar tasks. The chief or headman (in Kenya a government nominee) would be told to produce the men, and few would examine his methods. The quality of the work produced by the tens of thousands of men recruited in this way varied very greatly according to the nature of the work and the tribe. Sometimes, particularly with road and path-making in the first years and when it was seen to be of benefit to the community, men would turn out willingly once or twice a year and work with enthusiasm to repair bridges, clear ditches and mend roads—providing they remained within the tribe's area. The Kamba could work communally with particular enthusiasm, the

Kikuyu more often with reluctance. Communal porter labour duty was universally much less popular. Communal work of this type was usually unpaid, and never moved a man from his home district. Under an intelligent district commissioner the work involved no hardship, it could be a ritual, almost social occasion with communal singing by day and an *ngoma* (or tribal dance) in the evening. Under a thoughtless administrator, with work too severe and at an inconvenient season, communal labour might be onerous. At certain periods in Kenya's history, when added to other burdens, it was severe oppression. The system survived for many years (the concept survives today in communal self-help schemes), but changes came with the need for improved motor roads when the disadvantage of the communal labourer in comparison with the paid labourer became clear, although the difficulties associated with the use of unpaid porters was already fairly well known in administrative circles.

Compulsory labour was at first thought to be a reasonable development of communal labour; it became in fact very different. Here a chief or district would be directed to produce a certain number of fit men to work for urgent state purposes, for example railways, docks and major roads, the work usually taking place away from the man's home area, and being rewarded by wage payment. The men nominated faced penalties if they refused to work. It was a system widely used in colonial Africa, and a system liable to severe abuse. Its origins can be seen in the pre-1918 period, though the numbers remained small; the system only developed fully after the First World War when it became one of the factors leading to the political crisis of 1921. At its worst, compulsory labour was made available at this time to private contractors involved in a state enterprise, enabling them to tender low and grossly neglect the conditions of work. Plans were also prepared to link compulsory labour, to be paid at a rate below current rates, to increasing the supply of voluntary labour for private employers who would pay a higher rate. These abuses led to an attempt by the Colonial Office to assert a reform policy, an attempt successful on paper and increasingly so in reality, although on occasions disobeyed by Kenya authorities, both central and provincial. Finally, following further British pressure and much I.L.O. activity, peacetime compulsory labour had almost disappeared by 1939, but it was to be revived to meet the needs of food production in the Second World War.

The fourth and most important category was voluntary contractual labour, the general legal status of the large majority of workers in colonial Kenya. Since Africans could only be ordered to work for state purposes, and since in the early years they were self-sufficient in respect of their simple needs at home, they had to be induced or 'encouraged' by the government to work for private employers, and when at work to stay working. Pressures reasonable enough in themselves, the advice of administrators and chiefs, taxation, the lack of room for increased family sizes in the reserves, in totality quickly became coercive to the point of oppression as the expanding economy developed the demand for labour. The disinclination of Africans to remain in work became reflected in penal provisions in employment legislation and in the *kipande* identity document system, designed primarily to combat desertion.

Throughout Kenya's history, one further theme is as important as economic or administrative issues, the psychological factor, the real nature of the various different white employer-African employee relationships on the farm or at the construction site or town factory. Ferocious views expressed throughout the colonial period by local European politicians and farmers, so different from their liberal kinsmen in Europe, appear a disturbing example of the way environment may affect values, the demand for labour warping ideals of justice and humanity. The fervour of the cries for increased taxation, reduction of the reserves and 'encouragement', seem to support this; and the conditions of work and treatment of labourers in the pre-1914 period, when the South African settler element dominated much of Kenya's life, is convincing evidence for the early years.

Laurens van der Post, writing of Kenya's Europeans in the nineteen-fifties noted that they appeared to live '... in a permanent state of agitation, of frenzy, rage, rebellion and resentment, against various facts and circumstances of their daily lives.'[2] He thought this not explicable simply by the difficult circumstances of their lives, but caused perhaps by an attempt to live in a fantasy, a nostalgic dream of English country life no longer existing or relevant to the times. He noted the ease with which they became excited, the eccentricities of their dress and behaviour, and their lack of inhibitions in morality and crime, which they themselves explained by the altitude, but which he attributed to their environment and their contact with tribal Africans around them. This study will include summaries of a number of spectacular examples of harsh treatment and legal cases arising from uninhibited and vicious behaviour by European employers which reinforce this view, particularly as in the early years physical insecurity added an element of fear. Even in later years appalling cases occurred from time to time and created little sense of real outrage among the majority of European employers. Further, in the building of stereotypes the process over the years was cumulative; the 'daily operation of exacting work from wage-paid labourers does involve a severe output of nervous energy' wrote William McGregor Ross, Kenya's Director of Public Works, of the white farmer in the nineteen-twenties.[3] He went on to add that the isolated life of the farmer led to a 'strange evaporation of humility and the easy substitution of arrogance and self sufficiency in its place', an arrogance not unmixed with paternal kindness and affection for the children—in their place.[4] The highly intelligent and well-educated writer, Llewellyn Powys, wrote of the effect of the 'terrible penetrating tropical sunshine which rendered any continuous thought or action impossible', and of himself as a farm manager 'Brutalised though I had become by these devilish tropics ...'[5] One of the keenest observers of the white farmers, and one herself, the Danish writer Karen Blixen added that to many white people there was frequently something vexatious and mortifying in the attitude of Africans. 'It is indeed the same what you do to them, you can but do little, it disappears, it will never be heard of again. They neither thank you nor bear malice. You can do nothing about it. It is an alarming quality, it seems to annul your existence as a human being and to inflict upon you a role not of your own choosing, as if you were a phenomenon in Nature, as if you were the weather'.[6] The ordinary less sensitive farmer in day to day terms expressed this 'I give up, I just can't understand the native'.

The early African reaction to the employment situation, too, was by no means simple. At first, among the inland peoples came stunned bewilderment, a conscious feeling that the whole pattern of life was changing in ways unpredictable and inexplicable, together with subconscious feelings of insecurity and inferiority. But for Africans too the process of racial interaction was cumulative; as anxiety deepened a search for adoption and protection entered into the employee side of the relationship, first through porter labour and domestic servants, later and much more significantly, in the resident labour system.

The search for adoption, and the apparent contentment of Africans in the service of the better, kindly, paternal employers whose numbers increased greatly after the First World War led many Europeans to believe in an indefinite future of paternal employment. And in truth in the years before the Depression large numbers of Africans found an emancipation from the restrictions of traditional societies and an opportunity for first ventures into the modern world through such employment. The relationships, being personal, provided psychological satisfactions to both sides; very often European employers, particularly farmers, could provide real help to employees in times of sickness, distress or old age and took pleasure in so doing. However not all employers were good employers, and absenteeism, desertion, carelessness and destruction of property were frequently incoherent forms of resistance to harshness and oppression.

But the apparent contentment could not last, nor could paternalism, essentially rural, ever provide any real form of security or comfort for the unskilled migrant town labourer. By the late nineteen-twenties, on the land and in the towns alike, the system was beginning to crumble. The key factor was population pressure in the African reserves, aggravated by poor farming practice and the impossibility of expansion into the White Highlands; the reserves most seriously affected were those of the Kikuyu. However, a series of accidents and fortuitous events masked for most of the European community the true nature of this pressure until the full gravity of the situation became clear in the late nineteen-fifties.

In the nineteen-thirties it was natural to assume that unemployment and hunger were caused by the Depression and that a return to healthy economic growth would solve these problems; voices who pointed to the destruction of land and the increase of population were lonely and disregarded. Then came a series of economic booms which considerably increased the capacity of the European community to hire African employees. The advent of the Second World War opened up jobs in the army, in the service corps and in local construction work, while the Colonial Office ensured that the horrors of the First World War were not repeated. East Africa was also seen as the food supply base for the Middle East which in turn resulted in incessant demands by the European farmers for more labour. Eventually the government, with some reluctance and insisting on certain safeguards, acceded to their insistence on civil conscription.

It was widely believed that this prosperity would collapse after the war. In fact Kenya entered into a building and manufacturing boom in the late nineteen-forties and early nineteen-fifties which resulted in the transformation of Nairobi and which greatly increased the importance of light industry, particularly that catering for the new African market which had grown during and after the war. This boom, emphasizing the shortage of skilled African labour, further concealed the worsening population realities. The eruption of the Mau Mau rebellion in the early nineteen-fifties did not depress the boom; it even accelerated it for a short while, partly because the British government was spending so much money to suppress the insurrection. Furthermore the arrest of so many Kikuyu created another shortage, albeit short-term, in the labour market as well as some important changes in the market's ethnic complexion. It was only with the decision of the British government to commence African participation in government and then full-scale decolonization in the late nineteen-fifties and early nineteen-sixties that the European business and farming world began to stagnate. And it is in this period also that the reports of district commissioners throughout the colony first begin to warn of that large-scale unemployment and population problem which would become a staple of post-independence economic and social commentary.

Despite the boom and expansion, serious labour problems arose long before the eve of independence—problems to which most of the European community were blinded by the prosperity of the nineteen-forties and fifties. In the countryside the system of resident labour was rapidly breaking down as European county and district councils at differing speeds in different areas attempted a reduction of the plot and stock-owning resident labourer, or 'squatter', to a rural proletariat of smaller numbers. The government's hope that agricultural and land tenure reforms in Kikuyuland and African land development elsewhere would absorb the large numbers of rural unemployed proved vain as the drift to the towns gathered rather than lost momentum.

Population pressure, new agricultural systems, the growth of manufacturing, and the lure of the city had all attracted increasing numbers to Nairobi and Mombasa from the nineteen-thirties onward, a trend accelerated by the location of post-war industrial development. Urbanization, however, could not be squared with the European vision of the paternal white farmer and the obedient and illiterate African retainer. The first reaction of the Europeans was to look the other way—to ignore the shanty housing, the filthy conditions, the inadequate sanitation, the limited and expensive water supplies, and the diseases such as tuberculosis which increased in the slums of Nairobi and Mombasa. Paternalism meant nothing in these slums except to a few major employers such as the Railway, and discriminatory practices against the emerging African elites of junior civil servants and teachers soured the channels of communication. Alternatives were slow to emerge. The vast majority in the cities were unskilled workers with a smattering of primary education. They drifted from job to job and were dismissed by the Europeans as idlers and loafers, the despised mission boys. They were, in fact, the forerunners of the army of the unemployed of the late nineteen-fifties and sixties.

First the Depression and then the Second World War had excused inaction on these fronts. Gradually, however, the Colonial Office forced the creation in Kenya of government agencies such as the Labour Department to deal with some of these problems; it later arranged for the investment of British government money and obliged the European community to accept a modicum of responsibility for labour conditions and for their rectification. In particular, money was invested in housing and in the rehabilitation of African land. But the amount was never enough as the events of the nineteen-fifties were to show.

After the Second World War the Labour Department also began to make operative some of the ideas of the nineteen-thirties, many of which had been imposed on the colony by Whitehall as a consequence of Britain's adhesion to various I.L.O. conventions. The most important of these were effective laws concerning minimum wages, safety, workmen's compensation and the protection of juvenile and female labour. For the first time the Labour Department began to acquire a sufficient staff to implement such legislation. But inflation combined with a disastrously ineffective policy of price controls and subsidies undermined much of this protective work and created the conditions which facilitated the spread of Mau Mau from the farms to the towns in the nineteen-fifties. The most controversial of the decisions of the Colonial Office and of the local Labour Department was to encourage the growth of trade unions in order to re-create in Kenya the system of industrial relations prevalent in the western world. Later critics have argued that this was divisive and irrelevant to the needs of the Third World. Such criticisms imply that trade unionism was created in Kenya by the British. But while there can be no doubt that the colonial government ultimately provided the forms for industrial action, labour protest was equally certainly an indigenous growth.

These policies were also controversial at the time because they involved the government, and more particularly the Labour Department, with groups frequently allied to nationalist or proto-nationalist movements. There had been, of course, labour protest since the beginning of colonial rule, but it was not until the nineteen-thirties that it began to take on a permanent form in the shape of trade unionism. The pioneer in this was the son of an Asian printer, Makhan Singh, who formed the Labour Trade Union and hoped to create a general labour protest which would include both Asians and Africans. Although Makhan Singh remained a figure of some consequence until the late nineteen-forties, he was only partly able to fulfil his dream and then only for a very brief period.

In Mombasa, for instance, there grew up a local tradition of labour protest which was first formulated in terms of tribal conflict but culminated in the general strikes of 1939 and 1947 as well as a series of minor stoppages during the Second World War. It was only after 1947, and then only for a brief period, that the leaders of the Mombasa workers were significantly involved in nationalist politics or had other than the most tenuous political connection with developments in Nairobi. In the capital there was a rapid growth of African trade unionism after the war, formalized in 1949 by the formation of the East Africa Trade Union Congress. The congress was both a federation of trade unions and a ginger group within the dominant nationalist political party, the Kenya Africa Union, led by Mzee Jomo Kenyatta. It took a militant position both industrially and politically which culminated in the attempt to boycott the Duke of Gloucester's visit to Nairobi in 1950, and later that year in an attempted general strike, after which the colonial government destroyed the congress by arresting most of its leaders.

With the rise of Mau Mau in the early nineteen-fifties, the colonial government imposed severe restrictions on African political life and organizations of a political flavour. However trade unions were largely exempt, and the decade saw the rise of Tom Mboya as general secretary of the Kenya Federation of Labour and as the leading labour spokesman in East Africa. Mboya delicately balanced industrial and political considerations in his strategy. He secured his reputation and his ongoing labour base by two remarkably successful industrial actions in 1955, the victory in the dock strike in Mombasa and the gaining of recognition for his former union by the white-dominated municipal government of Nairobi. On the other hand he more and more became one of the leading voices of African nationalism in the colony. In the middle nineteen-fifties Mboya could justly claim that '... the K.F.L. became the voice of the African people, in the absence of any other African organization to speak for them'.[7] Mau Mau also shocked both the colonial government and the major British commercial firms. Whitehall insisted that reform had to go hand in hand with repression in the attempt to defeat the uprising, a policy which ensured that the trade unions survived the difficulties of the Emergency. It also meant that the attempt of most of the settler leadership to arrest the development of western-type industrial relations finally came to an end and senior colonial government officials came increasingly to consult and respect, if not always to agree with, the views of Mboya and the Kenya Federation of Labour.

By 1956 the major expatriate firms, too, had realized that they could no longer trust their survival to the local European politicians and small businessmen. As a consequence they formed their own organization, later to be known as the Federation of Kenya Employers, to safeguard their own interests. This they conceived, in part, as coming to terms with the rise of trade unionism by recognizing its inevitability and working with it. Mboya was able to exploit this to ensure both a wide advance of the trade union movement in the late nineteen-fifties and also the creation of a sound base for his own political career. This industrial relations system created by expatriate business, the trade unions and the Labour Department proved durable enough to survive independence essentially intact and to become one of the cornerstones of the Kenyatta system. For an understanding of that system and to view from a new perspective the story of British rule and the reaction and resistance of the Africans, we claim that a study of labour policy in colonial Kenya is indispensable.

NOTES

1. Lord Altrincham, *Kenya's Opportunity*, 1955, 88–9.
2. L. van der Post, *Venture to the Interior*, 1952, 51.
3. W. McGregor Ross, *Kenya from Within*, 1927, 120.

4. *Ibid*, 125.
5. Llewellyn Powys, *Ebony and Ivory*, 1929, 78 and *Black Laughter*, 1925, 106. In *Black Laughter* Powys was here writing specifically of his attitude to an employee.
6. Karen Blixen (Baroness Karen von Blixen), *Out of Africa*, 1937, 137.
7. T. J. Mboya, *Freedom and After*, 1963, 35.

CURRENCY AND EXCHANGE RATES

Until 1906, the currency of the East Africa Protectorate consisted of annas and rupees, 16 annas equalled 1 rupee, annas were themselves divided into pice. The number of pice to the rupee fluctuated for various reasons, such as too many having been minted. In 1900, for example, 64 pice equalled 1 rupee, by 1902 the rate was 80. The rupee itself also fluctuated, it was only Shs. 1/0½d. in 1897 but by 1906 it had become stable at a value of Shs. 1/4d. The currency pattern from then until the end of the First World War was:

100 cents = 1 Rupee
15 Rupees = £1

For convenience a table of equivalents is set out:

25 cts.	=	4d.
50 cts.	=	8d.
1 Rupee	=	Shs. 1/4d.
2 Rupees	=	Shs. 2/8d.
3 Rupees	=	Shs. 4/0d.
4 Rupees	=	Shs. 5/4d.
6 Rupees	=	Shs. 8/0d.
7 Rupees	=	Shs. 9/4d.
8 Rupees	=	Shs. 10/8d.
9 Rupees	=	Shs. 12/0d.
10 Rupees	=	Shs. 13/4d.
11 Rupees	=	Shs. 14/8d.
12 Rupees	=	Shs. 16/0d.
13 Rupees	=	Shs. 17/4d.
14 Rupees	=	Shs. 18/8d.
15 Rupees	=	£1

1d.	=	6.25 cts.
3d.	=	18.75 cts.
6d.	=	37.50 cts.
9d.	=	56.25 cts.
Shs. 1/–	=	75 cts.
Shs. 2/–	=	1 Rupee 50 cts.
Shs. 3/–	=	2 Rupees 25 cts.
Shs. 4/–	=	3 Rupees
Shs. 5/–	=	3 Rupees 75 cts.
Shs. 6/–	=	4 Rupees 50 cts.
Shs. 7/–	=	5 Rupees 25 cts.
Shs. 8/–	=	6 Rupees
Shs. 9/–	=	6 Rupees 75 cts.
Shs. 10/–	=	7 Rupees 50 cts.
Shs. 15/–	=	11 Rupees 25 cts.
£1	=	15 Rupees

Chapter 1

THE EARLY YEARS, 1895–1901

... and we want every freed slave to be turned not into an idle vagrant but into a free labourer working for a recognised wage.

The Under-Secretary of State for Foreign Affairs, G. N. Curzon, House of Commons, 10 February 1898.

The earliest years of British colonial rule are notable for three entirely separate labour issues, slavery and its abolition, the labour needed for the construction of the Uganda Railway, and the state of porter labour.

Slavery and its Abolition

The abolition of slavery had been an aim of British policy in East African waters for very many years, an aim pursued by both the British government and the Imperial British East Africa Company. The aim had not been fully achieved by 1895 when the British protectorate was declared and could not be immediately implemented on account of one major difficulty. A strip of land at the Coast ten miles wide remained under the authority of the Moslem Sultan of Zanzibar and many of the inhabitants were Moslems whose law permitted slavery. This permission was qualified; the slave should not be a Moslem (though a number were), the Koran taught kindness to slaves, their liberation was an act of piety, house-born slaves could not be sold, nor could families be split by sales. A further complication to abolition was that Islam would not permit borrowing money from infidels, which made a change to wage payment difficult as capital to start a business could not be borrowed.

As a legacy of previous British pressure on the sultans of Zanzibar, the first British administrator of the protectorate, Arthur Hardinge, inherited a complex legal situation. On the hinterland side of the ten-mile strip, slavery had no legal status. Within the strip, earlier decrees had declared all who entered the sultan's dominions before 1 November 1889 and all born after 1 January 1890 to be free; that the status of slavery was totally abolished at Kismayu; that members of fourteen hinterland tribes were under I.B.E.A. Company protection and could not be held as slaves; that slaves of a master who died without child were free and that slaves could both purchase their freedom and complain to the courts in case of ill-treatment. These legal limitations, however, were disregarded in many coastal areas where the company's authority lacked reality.

The slave, man or woman, was the absolute property of his master. He could neither own nor dispose of property, nor give evidence in a court of law, nor sue his master or any other person. He could neither marry without his master's permission nor engage in trade. Theoretically there was no legal restriction on either the work or the punishments a slave-owner might impose. Many female slaves were concubines, a practice permitted by the *sharia*. Children of such unions were legitimate and when children arrived the concubine became in effect an extra wife.[1] The slavery status, severe in law and in practice in Zanzibar and Pemba was by this time very much moderated on the mainland. The administration believed that the mild Coast slavery of 1895 was dying a natural death with the majority of the slaves content with their lot, and past abuses checked by the work of the missions, the Royal Navy and the general presence of Europeans. Officials asserted there was little real demand for emancipation as many slaves had entered slavery as a result of earlier famines and had therefore no particular envy of freedom; they also pointed out that any slave had only to cross the ten-mile border to be free.

This claim appears generally true, particularly in the area around Mombasa, but at Malindi and in Tanaland some estates were owned and slaves supervised by harsh Arab landowners, as in Zanzibar, and there some demand for emancipation existed. Hardinge stated the total number of slaves in 1897 to be 26,259, out of a total population of 275,000 for the region.[2] The work performed varied greatly. A certain number were purely domestic retainers, cooks, messengers and carriers; these in general were the most content with their lot, though for a few the status could be precarious with a capricious master. A much larger number were agricultural slaves, living partly for protection in villages of 50 to 300, the property of several absentee masters whose patches of land they tilled. Some masters had no idea of the number of slaves they owned and their hold on the slaves was often very weak. The crops were divided between slave and master. In a coconut plantation the slave might give the coconuts to his master but keep all else he grew, or elsewhere keep the maize and give the millet to his master; such slaves usually tilled a patch they called their own for two days a week.

Another large category of slaves was the petty artisan or non-agricultural labourer—the dhow captain, sailors, tailors, masons, carpenters, small traders and porters. These paid to their masters a percentage of their earnings or profits, between one-third and two-thirds depending on the cost of their tools which the master had to supply. A large percentage of porters in caravans of the eighteen-nineties were slaves; they might pay their master one-half of their earnings for the journey. Lastly there was a special category of military slaves, armed retainers of the Arab chieftains.

Tolerable though these conditions may have been the institution of slavery was a pernicious one. The master was demoralized, little interested in efficient work or development and the slave lacked ambition, any real pride in his work, or enterprise. Further, its continued survival gave encouragement to wishful thinking that the great days of slavery might return, an encouragement reflected in occasional illicit enslavement. The company and its officials had made some physical efforts to reduce slavery. Inland slaving caravans and raiding parties had been dispersed; at the Coast a number of slaves had been assisted to purchase or gain their freedom. The company's work, however, had aroused suspicion and hostility among the Arabs, which led Hardinge, who came from a landowning family and had some sympathy for them, to a belief that abolition must be an aim to be approached slowly and with caution, and must be accompanied by compensation.

Such a view was highly unfashionable in Britain where the Anti-Slavery Society, missionary and other interests were constantly exerting parliamentary and other pressures on the Foreign Office for immediate abolition. Their chief spokesman was Bishop Tucker of Uganda, who immediately after the proclamation of the protectorate directed his missions that since they were now on British territory, they were no longer to return runaway slaves either to the authorities or to their owners, a move resented by the Arabs.

The new administration was almost immediately faced with a military crisis, the revolt of the leading Mazrui chiefs. This revolt had as its aim the breaking of the British administration, resented and feared for its views on slavery and its association with the missions, before it became too powerful. The revolt, in which large numbers of slaves both military and agricultural supported the Mazrui, was put down in the following year, but it served to strengthen the views of both sides in the controversy. Hardinge saw his preference for caution confirmed and Tucker the reverse.

The next four years saw a spectacular series of battles, fought in the House of Commons and the courts, over the status of slavery. Each year abolitionist Members of Parliament headed by Sir Charles Dilke mounted a full-scale attack on the protectorate administration during the supply debates, moving a reduction of Hardinge's salary; the government found its position of an apparent defence of slavery both embarrassing and confusing.[3] The Foreign Office tried to urge Hardinge to abandon his caution, Salisbury and Curzon taking him to task on certain individual cases and local court judgements. In one of these cases, that of Heri Karibu, a runaway slave girl, Bishop Tucker successfully conducted the defence himself; in another the court ruled that three runaway slaves who had taken refuge ten years previously at the Ribe mission station should be returned to their master, a ruling which aroused passionate debate in the House of Commons.[4] With much courage considering the harm such unpopular views might do to his career, Hardinge continued to assert that slavery as an institution was in any case dying, and repeated his forecast that abolition of slavery and concubinage would reduce aged slaves to destitution, concubines to prostitution, and their children to illegitimacy. The views of Sir Charles Eliot and Sir Donald Stewart, who followed Hardinge, were identical to those of Hardinge, and the evident reduction in both numbers and hardship as the system died served to reduce parliamentary criticism after 1900.

On the return of the Liberal government in 1905, however, the new Colonial Secretary, the Earl of Elgin, and his Under-Secretary, Winston Churchill, both decided that the status of slavery must end. The Colonial Office, to which the protectorate had been transferred in 1905, held a more critical view of slavery than the Foreign Office. The Liberals had been criticizing conditions in the Congo and felt that slavery in a British possession weakened their case, and there was a general feeling that slavery should be ended in the hundredth anniversary year of 1807. Perhaps most important of all the government feared defeat on the issue from a rebellion of its own back-bench supporters; Stewart's estimate of the cost, an average of £4 per head for the 10,000 slaves was one that could reasonably be met.[5]

Elgin decided that in general the pattern of Zanzibar should be followed—initially the abolition of the legal status of the slave, which he thought should be followed by a more complete abolition in four or five years, though what he meant by this is not clear. The purpose of the abolition of legal enforceability was two-fold. Firstly it confined argument to relationships that could be ascertained, and secondly it provided for gradual adjustment, as often neither slave nor master wished for hurried change, although the slave under the ordinance was free from the moment the ordinance became effective. As a final garnish it was decided the Abolition of Slavery Ordinance should be the first to be debated and enacted by the protectorate's new Legislative Council.

The ordinance abolished the legal status of slavery from 1 October 1907 and provided for district or special courts to decide compensation for the owners, subject to a maximum of 100 rupees and with penalties for fraudulent claims.[6] Sick or aged slaves could also claim and receive compensation, the master receiving none in these cases as they had lost no labour. Concubines were specifically exempt from the ordinance to the fury of Bishop Tucker and of the missions; their legal status was preserved though they were given rights to appeal to the courts in cases of cruelty.

The Arabs, resigned to their fate, made not even a show of resistance. The Governor, Lieut-Col. J. (later Sir James) Hayes Sadler, addressed a meeting of Coast Arab dignitaries and explained to them that he had been instructed to legislate for abolition, but that compensation would be paid. The meeting indicated that the Arabs were content with the arrangements. A circular was issued by the government on the procedure to be followed in the courts—the average compensation for a fit slave was to be 64 rupees, with additions or deductions for age and poor health. The maintenance procedure for old slaves was set out, and if a slave could prove cruelty by a master no compensation was to be paid. Slaves could then work for anyone on any basis they chose.[7] A register of freed slaves was kept, each slave being given a brass badge with a registered number on it as proof of his freedom.

The process began slowly but accelerated later. For the period from 1 October 1907 to 31 March 1908 the total sum paid in compensation was only £938 and in the next twelve months again only £8,378, against the £34,000 estimated. But in the next financial year, 1909–10, for which £6,000 had been estimated £13,595 was in fact spent; thereafter the amounts declined each year, with Stewart's estimate of £40,000 proving to be very nearly the correct sum at his valuation of a slave.[8]

In 1909 the Abolition of Slavery Ordinance was amended to provide a terminal date, 1 January 1912, for the payment of compensation claims, and its scope extended to cover concubines.[9] These women were now to be free, but they and their children could continue to enjoy their rights and privileges under Islamic law unless they left their master without his consent. This satisfied nearly all the abolitionists except Bishop Tucker in Uganda who regarded it as shocking.

The Arabs kept their best slaves to the end if they could, and appeared passively to give up as their slave labour departed. They either let the land revert to waste or sold the land; some were ruined and many suffered severely. There does not seem to be any evidence to suggest that the liberated slaves replaced their former loyalties with any new or wider one, though some remained on their former masters' land paying a small rent in kind.

So ended a form of labour in East Africa, one with a terrible history but made mild in its latter years. The end had two consequences. A substantial number of men, possibly 20,000 between 1895 and 1912, were released for the labour market where many must have wished for the old days. Their liberation for men like Elgin, Churchill and Tucker was a matter of principle, but a wise observer later remarked, 'The sudden substitution of slavery by freedom seldom benefits the first generation of freed men'.[10] Secondly, affairs in the East Africa Protectorate came under close parliamentary and mission scrutiny, a scrutiny often hostile to the local officials, but establishing a British interest in the territory. This interest served to alert these groups to future developments.

Fifty years later the word *huru*, meaning a liberated slave, formed the basis for the word *uhuru*, political freedom.

Porters

East Africa contains no navigable rivers. At this time flies killed donkeys, the wheel had never been seen inland, oxen were not used and horses were known only to the Somalis. Merchandise was transported on the heads and shoulders of porters. Porter labour had had a miserable history of bad preparation, overloading, incompetent and cruel headmen and enforced recruitment.

Hardinge, newly arrived in Zanzibar in 1894, had established a registry of porters and had issued regulations for their welfare, which technically applied to the ten-mile strip but were neither enforced nor observed there. In 1894 some badly prepared caravans had met with disaster due to famine conditions inland, and in 1895 a Uganda government caravan under two incompetent Swahilis returned with 44 out of its 111 porters dead or missing, most of the latter apparently abandoned sick. This scandal led to a parliamentary question in 1896 but by this time a worse disaster had occurred. A very large government caravan of about 150 Swahilis and 1,200 Kikuyu was returning from moving food from Fort Smith (near the present Nairobi) to Eldama Ravine. The journey up had passed peacefully. On the return journey in the Kedong Valley, Maasai elders warned the porters to leave the women and cattle of the local Maasai alone. The warnings went unheeded and Maasai warriors massacred 90 of the Swahili and nearly 550 of the Kikuyu. The protectorate authorities handled the political side of the catastrophe with remarkable tact but the labour side threw into sharp relief an already serious problem, which through criticism from Bishop Tucker, was arousing concern in London.

There were in 1895 about 1,100 regular porters in the Mombasa area; casuals could also be obtained at certain seasons. In addition, the I.B.E.A. Company had experimented successfully with the local use of Teita porters recruited inland, and some caravans went into German territory to recruit Nyamwezi men who excelled at porterage. But for the needs of the Uganda and East Africa Protectorate administrations, the expanding demands of Mombasa and the Coast plantations, and the new demands of the railway and the military the supply was woefully inadequate. The survivors of the Kedong massacre arrived at different times, each bringing a new story of death and suffering.[11] Although the missionaries did what they could by organizing a relief fund for widows and educating the orphans free, the administration could not face a loss of confidence among porters, and one of Hardinge's earliest instruments of local legislation in 1896 was therefore the Regulations for the Registration and Protection of Porters.[12] These regulations covered every aspect of porterage. They required an official registration of porters for all journeys over ten days, with a deposit for each porter for any journey over three months; unregistered porters were liable for detention and were placed beyond the protection of the law for unpaid wages. Porters were to be paid the balance of wages due within six days of the end of their journey. The loads of a porter including his own kit, were not to exceed 75 lb. Caravan leaders were to report desertions, deaths and punishments to district officers who might investigate and listen to complaints; punishment could only be inflicted after enquiry with written evidence, it was to be limited to thirty strokes with a light stick and in more severe cases the offender was to be brought to a government station. Any balance of pay due to deceased porters was to be given to the Registrar of Porters for their families. Caravans were to take a supply of medicines, every porter going beyond Ndii was to be given clothes, singlet and a water bottle and if the caravan went beyond Kibwezi one or more blankets were to be supplied as well. Porters falling sick were to be taken to the nearest station even if a load had to be abandoned, and before any caravan could set out the Registrar or his agent had to issue a certificate certifying that the provisions of the regulations had been carried out.

These complicated regulations were at first frequently disobeyed. But within a few years and after a number of prosecutions, conditions greatly improved; the improvement was assisted by the extension of administration into the hinterland, enabling caravans to be inspected more frequently. Among certain tribes and always provided it was voluntary and not compulsory, porter work became very popular, and by the turn of the century very large numbers of men had worked as porters. Some men, particularly among the Nyamwezi, devoted their lives to portering.

A well run caravan could develop a regimental *espirit de corps.*[13] An early protectorate official wrote '... the stir created by the fitting out of a big caravan... was terrific. It was the one topic of conversation in the native quarter, and the recruiting agents combed the town persuading men to engage... The Indian shops did a good trade; the Swahili ladies all appeared in new clothes and the vendors of palm wine flourished exceedingly.' The key appointments were those of the *nyapara,* or headmen, usually one or two for each fifty porters. The headmen, usually Swahili but sometimes Somali, had neither to be too familiar nor too oppressive with the ordinary porters. The fact that headmen came from a different ethnic group, however, prevented the emergence of spokesmen for rank and file porters. Many headmen had worked their way up from being kitchen-boy to porter and under-headmen; they could probably read and write Swahili, and talk a little Kikuyu and Maasai. Good headmen would assist in recruiting the porters and *askaris*. Caravans in the early days usually included *askaris* on the basis of one to ten porters, equipped with ancient rifles whose defensive value was largely a deterrent; in practice their duties usually included pitching tents, stacking loads, and building the *zariba*. They earned a rupee or two more. The good caravan owner with good headmen had little difficulty in recruiting, the bad were known and avoided.

In order, so it was said, to provide for families while the men were away for a long time, porters of a long safari received three months' pay as an advance, plus a ration allowance from the time of engagement to the actual departure. Some of the money might be spent by the porter on small comforts for the journey such as salt or tobacco, and experienced porters would take a handful of beads and wire with them as small change for local purchases on the journey. Sometimes this money was not so well spent, and the first day out was usually marked by desertions, objections to loads and protracted farewells. This and the general danger arising from porter desertions led to special regulations issued later in 1896 inflicting a heavy penalty (a fine not to exceed 60 rupees with six months' imprisonment and twenty-five lashes) for desertion after an advance of wages; the porter could also be ordered to fulfil the agreement.[14] Sometimes employers adopted their own methods, sending headmen back to Mombasa to round up deserters.

In general the wise employer chose porters from several tribes thus guarding against a mass desertion and introducing a competitive element. Men of different tribes could not, however, be put in the same tent of five men. The employer would try to learn names and crack little jokes, preferably bawdy, and would ensure that the loads were fairly distributed, though quite often the best porters sought out the heaviest loads with pride. A well run caravan had little recourse to corporal punishment, reserving it only for extreme cases such as looting or insulting the headman. Minor offences were best punished by an indignity, the addition perhaps of some small item to the load. But portering was a hard occupation, and without doubt in a very large number of less well run caravans corporal punishment was regularly used for laziness or bad conduct. In such cases the regulations' requirement of a light stick was often disregarded and the hide whip, or *kiboko*, used. Many of the early district commissioners saw no reason to disapprove and did not prosecute for this type of offence. Porters also had their own code of ethics, particularly among a group of men of the same tribe; a good porter would neither abandon his load nor pilfer, and he would often share his food and water.

On the march the day began early, perhaps at 3 or 4 a.m., to the beat of drums. After breakfast, probably only a bite of cold maize meal, loads would be picked up and the day's march begun in the cool of the morning. The march would be lightened by whistles, gongs and drums beating, or improvised music, often obscene and sung in strophe, anti-strophe and chorus. Marches varied in length according to season, terrain and the load, but were usually between twelve and twenty miles per day with a 75 lb.

load; well-trained porters could, with a 60 lb. load, accomplish over thirty miles. The march would end in the early afternoon, when tents would be pitched and parties sent out for water and firewood. In the evening different parties, usually by tribe, would gather round the fires. The master would have his evening meal at a camp table and if he was wise listen to the talk or watch the dances.[15] *Posho*, the staple ration, literally meant maize meal, but the Nyamwezi preferred rice and the Kikuyu porters beans. Meat was enormously popular, its distribution needing discipline or the excitement could lead to disorder. Raw meat or venison would be cut in long strips and warmed over the fire.

The evening would also give the master a chance to see the crafts of his labour force. Some of the Nyamwezi would make lace caps, other craftsmen would grind tobacco to make snuff. A shoemaker would make sandals from animal skin, a barber would cut hair in circles with a sharp hunting knife and a safari 'doctor' would dispense herbal remedies. Most caravans included at least one or two small boys, *totos*, who somehow attached themselves as cooks' assistants.

Wage rates remained steady for many years, the usual being 10 rupees per month for an ordinary Coastal porter, plus *posho* or rations to the value of 4 rupees. Headmen might receive between 20 and 50 rupees, according to their experience. Men from the inland tribes who often were reluctant to go far from their own area received much less, perhaps at first only 5 rupees plus *posho*. Loads came to be slightly reduced; by 1902 they were usually only of 60 lb. The porter, though, had to carry his own kit, sleeping mat, spare sandals, part of his team's cotton shelter-tent and food, his water bottle, knife and probably blanket, this latter forming a turban to support the load. Early on the journey a porter would cut himself a stout stick which served to prop up the load, to cross fords and, by notches cut each night, to record the length of the journey. On their return '. . . their chief reward, to which they look forward during the whole journey, is the proud moment when they enter Mombasa decked out gaily with flowing red cloths (their customary perquisite) and march through the streets with their glistening white burdens showing off before the admiring crowds'. Later red cloth was replaced by a liberal cash tip from a good master.[16]

The work was hard, the terrain, thorny thickets, malarial swamps, or lava-strewn stretches made worse by tropical sun. A badly planned or unlucky caravan could suffer severely. If for example waterholes happened to be dried up, a caravan might be forced to march on with porters in a weakened condition. If a porter could no longer march, four others had to carry him in addition to their usual loads, a burden which might cause them also to collapse, so worsening the problem. The early caravans suffered frequently from desertions, mutiny and disease.

But the nature of the work had a fascination for many inland Africans at this stage when a world outside the tribe was being dimly seen for the first time. Portering for a European filled a need felt by some, a need to travel and see for themselves the unknown lands, together with the security a well-ordered caravan provided. The presence of a European owner seemed to safeguard the caravan against the evil consequences of, for example, a jackal crossing the route, or the breaking of an earthenware jug, which in the past had brought misfortunes. Another more practical attraction was the frequent provision of meat. These attractions, together with the protection of the law, assured a supply that usually met the demand, a demand which sporting safaris were to maintain after the railway took over the movement of goods. The Nyamwezi so based their lives around portering that their children practised carrying tusks from an early age; it is probable that the unusual 'joking relationships' of Nyamwezi custom evolved through the association of men on the march, and their humour was also evident in the names such as 'Bandika' (load-up) or 'Nyumba ya ulaya' (the European's mule) they chose for themselves on enrolment.[17] The craftsmen, usually Swahilis, often preferred the free life of a caravan porter to permanent work at their trade. The Teita took to portering with enthusiasm so long as it was voluntary, even abandoning their own agriculture, though later they resisted compulsory demands for porters. In the early years they would be brought to Mombasa clad in skins and armed with bows and arrows for their work. The Kamba reacted similarly. The Kikuyu, however, although often good at portering in hilly country, carrying their loads on their backs, always disliked porter work—known to them as 'the work of leather strips'; they viewed it as women's work and in times of difficulty they would desert. The Kikuyu also believed with some increasing justification that travel spread disease. Porter numbers were also augmented as a result of violence in the Congo, a number of men from the Manyema district deciding to earn their living as porters in British East Africa, where despite frequent truculence in manner some travellers held them to be second only to the Nyamwezi.

Military operations called for large numbers of porters.[18] In 1897 a number recruited at the Coast went to serve in Uganda, and in 1900 about a thousand from Mombasa and others from Zanzibar sailed for the Gold Coast to serve at the usual 10 rupee rate in the Ashanti Field Force. The *Gazette* recorded 'The men are said to have been much pleased with the accommodation and the food provided for them'. In the Gold Coast they were regarded very highly, being superior to both the local porters and others imported from Nyasaland and Sierra Leone. They marched fifteen miles a day with a 60 lb. load and eight days' rations despite the very difficult Ashantiland conditions. A few were killed, but most returned just in time to be used again in the 1901 Ogaden expedition. H. R. Tate, the Officer in Charge, attributed their success to careful selection and their 'unusually liberal' daily ration of 1 lb. of rice, 1 lb. of fresh meat and dates twice a week. At the other end of the protectorate 1,500 porters were required for the 1900 Nandi campaign.

In 1902 new regulations replaced those of 1896, the new ones covering all forms of labour and being entitled the Native Porters and Labour Regulations.[19] These in fact varied little from the earlier ones in respect of porters, the chief differences being a reduction in the maximum load to 70 lb. including personal food and gear and more specific paying-off procedure and listing of equipment and food—one *kibaba* (approximately 1¼ lb.) of rice or similar grain per day, one good flannel shirt or thick jersey, loin cloth, blanket and water bottle, together with tents, medicines, and bandages, and a cooking-pot for every ten men. The new regulations also specifically forbade the punishment of porters by caravan leaders unless so authorized by the provincial sub-commissioner. But there seems little doubt this section of the regulations was frequently broken. The regulations remained in force until the second Master and Servants Ordinance became law in 1910.

Wages at first rose little (porters recruited in Nairobi were still only earning 7 rupees per month in 1907), but the work when voluntary remained very popular due to the psychological factor, the meat, the clothing provided, higher wages and the tip. Further, wages and the tip were paid in Mombasa and Nairobi where they represented real purchasing power. Sadler wrote that one of the causes of the 1908 labour shortage was the numbers recruited by the safari firms, of which Newland and Tarlton was the largest. The safari organized by this firm for Theodore Roosevelt, for example, included 500 porters, all issued with blue jerseys, shorts and a pair of boots, the latter frequently remaining unused. But even the smallest sporting safaris needed at least twenty porters and retainers. District officers, too, would often be more prepared to assist in the provision of men through chiefs and headmen for the shorter periods of time spent by sportsmen on safari in preference to the longer periods required for farm work. With the completion of the railway, the porter market moved to Nairobi where men of different tribes could be recruited with little or no difficulty.[20] An increasing number of men preferred a few weeks portering to earn their tax money; they reinforced the rather smaller number of regular porters, men who spent the earnings of one safari so quickly that they were soon back on the march. The non-permanent porter was of course not so strong as the regular, and could usually manage a load of 60 to 65 lb. only. From Nairobi, too, the caravan would sometimes be entrained for a day's journey to the safari starting point, a journey which could be unpleasant in an iron-covered goods van under the African sun with only occasional halts. But conditions improved later and porters sometimes travelled third-class; on the march some of the heavier loads were carried by donkeys. Occasionally porters were killed by game, when it seems a cash payment was made by most sportsmen to a next-of-kin if one could be traced.

By 1911 the introduction of the motor-car had begun greatly to reduce the number of porters required. But porter labour had played an important part in the process of introducing Africans to the concept of a cash payment in return for manual services. Very large numbers of men, including many who had been slaves, participated. When portering was voluntary and well-managed it was popular, and government regulations had greatly improved conditions for porters by the turn of the century. The evil reputation that still clings to portering lay not in the pre-1914 free porter market but in peacetime compulsion and later in the appalling conditions of the First World War.

The Construction of the Uganda Railway

The official approach, British and local, to both slavery and free porter labour included a genuine belief that the man doing the work had real interests which deserved concern and protection. No such concern was evident among parliamentarians, missionaries or administrators for those at work on the construction of the Uganda Railway. It was decided to build the railway as quickly as possible; its construction was viewed almost as a military attack—casualties were inevitable and might be large if the objective was to be attained and momentum not lost.[21]

Construction was under the direction of the Foreign Office Uganda Railway Committee, and the whole cost was paid by the British government as an imperial undertaking promoted to safeguard the upper Nile. The Foreign Office decided that Asian labour would be necessary, a decision reached on the grounds of local underpopulation and British engineers' experience of Asian labour. The Indian government, who were obliged to amend legislation to permit labour to travel, insisted on the men's choice of remaining in East Africa or repatriation.

The presence of Asian coolies necessitated many special arrangements. Railway employees were in 1896 placed simply under the Indian Penal Code's penalties for desertion, and then in March 1898 under the whole of the code probably with the intention of retroactive effect; a travelling magistrate was seconded from India with jurisdiction in the two-mile wide railway zone. In May 1898 further 'urgent' regulations permitted Railway officials authorized by the Commissioner to sentence labourers to a whipping of a maximum of thirty strokes with a light cane or twelve strokes with a *kiboko*, one month's imprisonment or a fine of 50 rupees, for petty larceny, desertion or insubordination. These penalties were increased by regulations in 1899 which also permitted certain Railway officials to hold a court for a wider range of offences.[22] These special arrangements came to an end in 1901 after the line had reached the Lake.

There were obvious dangers in providing an employer with judicial powers in his own causes. The Protectorate Court set aside several convictions and sentences by Railway officials, notably cases where proper enquiries were not made by the officials or where men engaged as semi-skilled workers had been ordered to undertake manual work.[23] But there must have been many cases which were not so reviewed.

The coolies were of almost the poorest class the Indian sub-continent could offer, illiterate and uncouth in the mass. The first batch, some 2,000 labourers plus a number of masons, smiths, clerks and carpenters arrived at Mombasa in January 1896 and began work on houses and stores. The original survey had estimated 7,500 coolies would suffice but the numbers rose as follows:

Date	Total	At work
December 1896	3,948	
March 1897	4,269	
December 1897	6,086	
March 1898	7,131	
December 1898		13,003
March 1899	15,593	
December 1899		18,030
March 1900	23,379	18,720
March 1901	31,646	19,742
March 1902	31,983	

After 1901 the numbers began to fall, by March 1902 only 13,646 Asians were at work; a year later their replacement by Africans was proceeding so fast that only 6,704 were still employed.[24]

The conditions of work were appalling and the apparently slow progress led to inquiries by two special experts sent out from Britain, the first in 1899 and a second in 1901. The former, Sir Guilford Molesworth, wrote of the problem as a '. . . combination of difficulties . . . quite unique in the whole history of railway construction' . . . involving the '. . . maintenance of an alien army amounting now to about 15,000 men, in a practically waterless country devoid of resources and of all means of animal or wheeled transport'.[25] The provision of labour from India was slow in 1897 because of plague; this in turn delayed other works. The first 250 miles were tsetse-infested, and there were the added hazards of attacks by lions, heat-exhaustion, thirst and disease of many types. The behaviour of the Asian coolies towards the African tribes through whose land they passed was often bestial. Wherever possible the coolies inveigled African women, girls, Somali prostitutes and small boys into the squalid camps to the disgust of the protectorate officials who were powerless to intervene in the railway zone. The spread of venereal disease (but not its introduction which dated from Arab slaving days), among the Maasai and the Kikuyu was another far-reaching consequence of this behaviour.

Rough men and rough conditions were worsened by rough overseers and camp-commanders, the better ones were ill-educated Englishmen like Turk, the Cornish sailmaker turned caravan-master, the worst were Boers, Anglo-Indians, or Asian *jemadars*.[26] Many were incapable, some were inebriates, and their disciplinary methods were not often closely supervised by the senior engineers. Judge C. Cracknell, in a criminal appeal case brought before him in 1897 in the British court of Zanzibar commented on the 'painful picture of oppression and injustice in the railway camp'; the case concerned an overseer who had tried to extort a confession from a labourer by a succession of beatings.[27] This case was by no means exceptional; later as conditions worsened Moslems and Hindus fought each other, several being killed.

In 1898–9 the attacks of lions on the labourers' camps at Tsavo, in the course of which twenty-eight coolies were eaten, led to plots to assassinate the engineer, J. H. Patterson, and following pay stoppages to a mutiny. Labourers lay on the line to stop a train; the majority clambered aboard and normal work was considerably delayed.[28] Shortly afterwards, early in 1900, parliamentary criticisms of the cost and a reduction in privileges (tobacco, servants' allowances, hardship money, and additional leave) led to unrest. This began with a series of small local strikes by the Europeans. Crowds of coolies soon joined and rushed through Mombasa's streets, destroying stores and pulling up some line. George (later Sir George) Whitehouse, the Chief Engineer, acted very firmly, arresting the ringleaders and settling some of the grievances.[29]

On the construction sites feeding seems to have been reasonably satisfactory, but the accommodation and hospital services were deplorable. In 1901 Colonel T. Gracey, the second of the two special inquiry experts, noted that while the housing for superior staff was excellent and for subordinate grades such as drivers was suitable or fairly easily made suitable, the large corrugated sheds erected for the workmen were uninhabitable, full of fleas, and insanitary.[30] Conditions in the tents used in the earlier stages of construction had been no better, particularly in the rainy seasons.

From the first health had been one of the major problems, a wide variety of ailments filling hospitals with cases of jiggers, tick fevers, malaria, diarrhoea, dysentery, blackwater fever, abscesses and ulcers and heat-exhaustion together with simple thirst and accidents. In January 1897 half of the coolies were sick from malaria. By March 1898 340 coolies had died from various causes and a further 705 had been invalided home. By 1899 the hospitals contained 2,306 coolies, and a year later some 17,000 patients per year were passing through the Railway's four hospitals. At the dissolution of the Railway Committee in 1903 it was recorded that of the 31,983 coolies brought from India, 6,454 had been invalided home and 2,493 had died.[31] Diseases of the respiratory system, diarrhoea and dysentery, and fevers were about equal in proportion as major groups of causes. The hospital conditions were most unsatisfactory; on account of plague in India there was often no doctor at a hospital, much work being left to unqualified assistants, and with fever patients lying overcrowded on the wet grass floors of tents. In 1899 there were four hospitals, at the railhead, at Makindu, Voi and Kilindini, but in addition there were a large number of men sick in the camps. Administrative muddles over feeding, admission, discharge and treatment made matters worse.

Labour was divided into sections—permanent works, platelaying, surfacing, mountain survey, advance survey and the preparation of the base—advancing in average conditions one mile per day, less in difficult terrain. The methods were of the simplest, scores of coolies carrying small baskets of earth being used, for example, to construct an embankment. The unskilled Asians' contract rates of pay were 12 rupees per month, craftsmen receiving up to 45 rupees; in addition a small efficiency premium was paid for good or quick work but financial penalties for laziness or absence were also levied. Despite the hardship and the low wage many coolies willingly re-engaged; in 1899 Whitehouse proudly noted that 219 out of the first 1,030 who had completed the three-year contract had elected to remain another year.[32]

While the Asians formed the regulars for the construction work, Africans formed the auxiliaries. A few Africans, mostly from the Coast and some being runaway slaves, were semi-permanent employees of the Railway; for temporary labour the Railway tried to recruit casually from the area through which it was passing. The semi-permanent Coastal men formed a portering service, a few engaging also in woodcutting and bush clearance. Men locally recruited, chiefly Kamba and Teita and a few Giriama, were also put to dig and to work as porters and by April 1898 a large number had made a brief appearance at work. Payment in coin at a rate of a quarter of a rupee per day or 4–5 rupees per month began to replace beads, cloth and wire, but the unfamiliarity of coins, of the concept of labour for hire, or of the simplest European-patterned tools prevented any large increase in numbers. The supply too was most erratic. Famine in the Kamba country did not produce any lasting interest in regular employment and attempts to persuade the Kikuyu to work at Kibwezi were a failure, the distance and different climate leading to desertion. Seasonal variations also affected the supply. By January 1899 African numbers had risen to only 2,650, which dropped to an average figure of 2,000 for the next four years. The Kikuyu, however, proved less unwilling to work when the line advanced across their own country. A small number of Africans must have died in the construction of the railway but indifference was such that no records appear to have been kept.

Details of the Asian sick and death rolls were included in parliamentary papers, but the British parliament seemed most concerned with the cost of the railway. Occasional parliamentary questions on sickness and mortality began in 1899, but became only slightly embarrassing for the government in 1900. Mission interest was absent, although the *Anti-Slavery Reporter* occasionally queried recruitment without pursuing its enquiries.

The Asian trader with his store full of goods followed the line. As a consequence payment in the interior changed from beads and wire to rupees. But, on balance, from a labour point of view the interests of Africans suffered as some 6,500 of the 31,983 coolies brought from India decided to remain. Little official thought was given to their future, and there was no significant attempt made to integrate them into the country's life. Some remained in unskilled labour, but the majority entered the small-store trade either as proprietor or shop-assistant, or moved up the labour scale to the artisan, carpenter, mason, fitter or clerk levels, with a small number, chiefly Goans, in hotel and domestic service. They were to continue in these craft or clerical occupations, in numbers reinforced by large families and immigration, throughout the colonial period; by the end of this period only in the building and construction field were a large number of Asian unskilled labourers still to be found, though a few 'untouchables' remained as office sweepers as late as 1940. The consequences of this 'middle level' Asian presence have been obvious in terms of politics and African advancement. Less well known is that organized trade union activity in Kenya began in this community after the First World War.

Other Labour

The number of men employed in other activities in these early years remained very small.

At the Coast the I.B.E.A. Company as part of its anti-slavery work had introduced paid labour in its plantations, and paid labour had also been used for the laying of a local light railway and for road construction parties. In Mombasa itself a small number of men were hired casually for the unloading of ships, and another even smaller number were employed drawing trolleys through the streets, there being no public transport system. There was a shortage of such labour, and attempts were made to increase numbers by recruiting in Zanzibar, which in 1896 the Zanzibar government decided to limit by restricting numbers and prohibiting altogether any employment beyond Mombasa Island. The protectorate government on Foreign Office instructions retaliated in 1901 by refusing the Zanzibar government's desire to recruit men from the mainland to work for three years on the island clove plantations.[33] The shortage of labour was reflected by governmental regulations limiting *ngomas* for which a fee was charged and for which after 1901 permission from a government officer had to be first obtained.[34] Vagrants, too, were liable to imprisonment from which they might be sent to work.

Inland the beginnings of both the concepts of communal labour for the state and of paid labour can be seen. Communal labour, with a calico or occasionally a small cash reward, was the only possible method at this time, the government having no resources for wage payment and Africans no desire to work for reward in a commodity which they did not understand. But at Machakos John Ainsworth was able to supply a small but steady stream of Kamba porters, *askaris* and construction teams.[35] He met only occasional obstruction; in general he was held in such esteem that he could ensure a voluntary supply even for road work. At first payment for even 'regular' labour was beads and wire or calico, but early in 1895 Ainsworth induced two Asian traders to come and open stores at Machakos. These, followed later by others in the wake of the railway, assisted the change from barter to cash payment. For the larger tasks, road, bridge or camp construction, men were engaged in batches from a group of villages, sometimes choosing their own headman.

The very few pioneer farmers found the greatest difficulty in engaging men to work on farms, only succeeding through appeals to curiosity and the reward of a string of beads or wire, and then never enjoying the services of any men for more than a few days.[36] In time, a regular arrangement was made with an African community of a particular area or ridge, and the employment of Africans as domestic servants began though on a very limited scale due to the total unfamiliarity of the Europeans' ways and the consequent fear of them. Where wages were paid in cash, chiefly at the Coast, a kitchen boy would earn 8 rupees and a sweeper or water carrier 10 rupees with *posho*—usually maize meal only, or sometimes maize meal supplemented by occasional meat or vegetables. A pattern of Coast wages at a higher level than those inland was emerging due to the greater familiarity of the Coast peoples with European ways, which appeared to employers as greater skill. The calendar year of 1897 saw forty-nine court cases described as 'Wages', presumably government prosecutions for non-payment by employers, so at the Coast at least there does seem to have been redress for the employee whose master defaulted.[37] On the other hand the problem of desertion, to cause so much trouble later, had also appeared and a case in 1901 showed a hardening attitude. In this case a Mombasa hospital servant gave a month's notice of departure but did not stay to complete it. The Town Magistrate rejected the government's claim for recovery of a month's wages, but on appeal Judge R. W. (later Sir Robert) Hamilton reversed this verdict saying severely that the contract carried the intention of both parties to observe English law which the servant then broke.[38]

As administration spread inland the practice grew up of the new district administrative officer appointing a chief or headman on a first, often unreal, semblance of authority, and telling him that he must provide men to help build rough houses, stores, and offices, to cut timber, to make bricks and clear paths or tracks. A certain measure of compulsion was introduced to secure porters for officers' tours which became a rapidly increasing burden.[39]

Lastly, the earliest limited efforts to train African labourers to skilled and semi-skilled work had been begun at the Church Missionary Society's (C.M.S.) mission at Freretown, where in 1895 six carpenters and three metal workers were under instruction, a number which was increased slightly in the next few years, and was followed by similar beginnings at the Church of Scotland mission at Kibwezi.[40] The missionaries at the Coast later sponsored a small firm, East African Industries, which took over the C.M.S. plantations and the C.M.S. craft teaching at Freretown, continuing to teach a few men brickmaking and carpentry. It was here at the turn of the century from 1899 to 1901 that the short-lived African Workers' Council of freed slaves led by a small number repatriated earlier from India organized demands for improved salaries and status for Africans working at the mission in capacities such as pastors, catechists, evangelists, priests and deacons.[41]

In 1902, in order to place the Uganda Railway under the administration of one protectorate government rather than two, the former Eastern Province of Uganda was transferred to the East African Protectorate. For reasons quite unconnected with labour the protectorate received two heavily populated areas with profound consequences for their inhabitants. Later, when demands for labour from Nyanza became ever more clamant, Africans came to believe the change was made to supply labourers for European farmers, but nothing in the papers and documents of the time suggests that such a possibility was even considered.

NOTES

1. 'We had slaves but no racial prejudice. An Arab slave would marry a Negro slave girl or take her as his legal concubine, and her children had just as much rights as any by his Arab wife'—remark made by the daughter-in-law of Tippu Tib, the great Arab slave trader of the nineteenth century, J. A. Hunter and D. Maddix, *African Bush Adventures*, 1954, 12.
2. *Report by Sir A. Hardinge on the Condition and Progress of the East Africa Protectorate to the 20 July 1897*, C.8683 of 1897. This report provides much information on slavery at the time. See also Sir C. Eliot, *The East Africa Protectorate*, 1903, xvi.
3. The position, for example, of slave porters who crossed the ten-mile strip was particularly difficult to define. G. N. Curzon told the Commons in 1897 that such men were free, but his successor, St. J. Brodrick stated that they were not.

   The Attorney-General in 1897 ruled that if British officials returned runaway slaves who were proved not to be criminals their act would have been contrary to British law, but he refused to condemn E.A.P. officials for what might be their only legal action against criminals who happened to be runaway slaves. The Foreign Office on the strength of this advice told Hardinge that the Attorney-General had ruled that any British official returning a runaway slave to his master was breaking British law. Hardinge was much disturbed by this ruling and arranged for it to be modified in practice.

   More parliamentary time was spent on slavery than any other aspect of Kenya's affairs until Mau Mau; see, for example, *Parliamentary Debates, Commons*, 28 May, 24, 25, 28 June 1897, 10 Feb, 6 Aug 1898, 10 Feb, 13 Feb,

20 June 1899; also *Correspondence respecting the Abolition of the legal status of Slavery in Zanzibar and Pemba*, C.8858 of 1898; *Correspondence respecting Slavery and the Slave Trade in East Africa and the Islands of Zanzibar and Pemba*, Cd. 593 of 1901. For a more detailed examination of this subject see A. Clayton, 'Labour in the East Africa Protectorate, 1895–1918', unpublished Ph.D. thesis, Univ. of St. Andrews, 1970.

4. For the official account of the Heri Karibu Case see *Zanzibar Gazette*, 4 May 1898; the Ribe Case is described in the *Church Missionary Intelligencer*, Feb 1899. Hardinge nevertheless wrote afterwards, 'I always entertained a strong feeling and regard for my African Thomas à Becket.'
5. C.O. 533/36 contains a minute by the Parliamentary Under-Secretary, Churchill, warning Elgin of a possible parliamentary defeat at the hands of the government's own back-benchers. C.O. references are to the Colonial Office series in the Public Records Office.
6. The Abolition of Slavery Ordinance, Ord 7 of 1907, *Official Gazette of the East Africa Protectorate* (hereafter *E.A.P. Gazette*), 15 Sept 1907.
7. C.O. 533/43, Sadler to Colonial Office, 2 Apr 1908 and enclosure.
8. These figures of estimated and actual expenditure are taken from the annual statements published in the *E.A.P. Gazette*.

   The government's financial year at this period ran from 1 Apr to 31 March.
9. The Abolition of Slavery (Amendment) Ordinance, Ord 6 of 1909, *E.A.P. Gazette*, 6 July 1909.
10. A. G. Church, *East Africa, A New Dominion*, 1928, 163. The racial attitudes of Coast Arab property owners appears to have lasted for many years. J. Okello, *Revolution in Zanzibar*, 1967, 61–3, notes that there Arabs addressed African labourers as 'mtumwa', or slave, as late as 1958.
11. J. J. Mbotela, *The Freeing of the Slaves in East Africa*, 1956, 79.
12. *East Africa Protectorate, Ordinances and Regulations up to March 31 1899*, 1899, 26.
13. A very large number of sportsmen's books and memoirs throw some light on porters. Among the most useful are A. H. Neumann, *Elephant Hunting in E. Equatorial Africa*, 1898; C. W. Hobley, *Kenya from Chartered Company to Crown Colony*, 1929; C. W. Hobley, *Notes on Caravan Equipment, Organisation and Procedure*, 1894; C. Lestock Reid, *An Amateur in Africa*, 1926; S–E White, *African Camp Fires*, 1913.

    Some caravans were very large, that which carried the first consignment of parts for the Lake steamer *Sir William Mackinnon*, for example, required 350 porters.
13. *Ordinances and Regulations*, 1899, 32.
15. C. Lestock Reid, *op. cit.*, describing the evening talk observed 'You will be perfectly certain to hear "bloodee fool" followed by shouts of laughter.'
16. Sometimes there were difficulties on their return, as a porter might have used his father's name on enrolment, or chosen a new and exciting European one. If the man then claimed his wages on his normal name he might not be recognized.
17. By 1905 there was a settlement of about 1,000 Nyamwezi outside Mombasa; they elected their own chief and maintained contact with the German consul. A number returned at the request of the German authorities at the time of the Maji-Maji Rising.
18. The value of Nyanza men as porters seems to have been noticed for the first time in one of these minor operations, Colonel Ternan's Kamasia expedition of April-May 1897. Ternan wrote, 'The Wa Kavirondo had never carried loads in their lives before; they could not however resist the sight of the beads in which they were to be paid, and some hundreds came forward and proved themselves quite good porters.' *Some Experience of an Old Bromsgrovian*, 1930, 289.
19. *E.A.P. Gazette*, 1 March 1902. Lieut.-Col. H. C. Lowther, *From Pillar to Post*, 1911, 246, alleges the government's own caravans frequently broke these regulations. A bad Uganda scandal occurred in 1899 when the porters serving an

Indian Army battalion returning from Uganda arrived in the protectorate with numbers of Baganda and Basoga dying or sick.

20. A vivid account of what is obviously a free labour market appears in S–E. White, *African Camp Fires*, 152–7.
21. The construction, for example, of the 100 miles of railway between Lagos and Ibadan took four years; the construction of the 527 miles between Mombasa and Lake Victoria took only one year longer.
22. *Zanzibar Gazette* Notices, 17 Nov 1896, 2 March 1898, 25 May 1898, 5 Apr 1899.
23. *E. A. Law Reports*, I. 1906, 8, *Dunjibboy Postwalla v. Secretary of State*, and 14, *Fakir Chand and Duni Chand v. Regina.*

    For many years the Protectorate Court or senior judges sitting in chambers reviewed magistrates' court proceedings and sentences in a form of appeal, setting aside verdicts which the judges felt to be erroneous. But this form of appeal often took many months and were of little help where a sentence of imprisonment or corporal punishment had been awarded.
24. This table has been compiled from M. F. Hill, *Permanent Way*; *Report of the Uganda Railway Committee*, 1898–9, C.9333 of 1899; *Report on the Uganda Railway* by Sir Guilford Molesworth, C.9331 of 1899; *Report on the Uganda Railway* (1901) by Colonel T. Gracey published in *Correspondence respecting the Uganda Railway*, Cd. 670 of 1901; *Final Report of the Uganda Railway Committee*, Cd. 2164 of 1904.
25. Molesworth Report, C.9331 of 1899.
26. For a description of Turk and other supervisors see R. Hardy, *The Iron Snake*, 1965, *passim*, although this account should be treated with caution.
27. *Zanzibar Gazette Supplement*, 24 Nov 1897.
28. Lieut.-Col. J. H. Patterson, *The Man Eaters of Tsavo*, 1907, 72.
29. M. F. Hill, *op. cit.*, 203–4, and R. Hardy, *op. cit.*, 264.
30. Gracey Report, Cd. 670 of 1901.
31. These figures are taken from M. F. Hill, *op. cit.*, and the Molesworth and Gracey Reports.
32. *Zanzibar Gazette*, 12 Apr 1899, letter from G. Whitehouse.
33. F.O. 2/443, Foreign Office to Eliot, 25 July 1907 and *Parliamentary Debates, Commons*, 18 June 1901. F.O. references are to the Foreign Office series in the Public Record Office.
34. 'The regulations have had a salutary effect, for while an *ngoma* is going on the natives dance all night and sleep all day'. wrote an official report in 1902.
35. John Dawson Ainsworth, 1864–1946. Educated privately; served in the Congo 1884; joined the staff of the I.B.E.A. Company; Sub-Commissioner, Ukamba Province 1895; Sub-Commissioner, Naivasha Province 1906; Sub-Commissioner, Nyanza Province 1907; Military Commissioner for Labour 1917; Chief Native Commissioner 1918–20.
36. An interesting account of an early attempt to persuade inland Africans to work for Europeans appears in Mrs. Stuart Watt, *In the Heart of Savagedom*, (n.d.), xvi, xviii.
37. *Protectorate Annual Report 1897–98*, C.9125 of 1899.
38. *E.A. Law Reports*, I, 41, *Secretary of State v. Mahomed bin Abdulla.*
39. Sir C. Dundas, *African Crossroads*, 1956, 20, describes the methods of James Ainsworth (the younger) an early D.C. at Kitui. His porters having absconded in the middle of a journey, Ainsworth told the elders of the area that he wished to dance. 'That evening there were hundreds of dancers in our camp, youths and girls and Ainsworth in the midst of them, arrayed in gumboots and pyjamas, capering with zest.' At the end of the evening he announced the dance would be resumed at the next camp, the men might take their girls with them and incidentally also Ainsworth's loads. The next day he had four times the men he needed and no further problems on the journey. In early colonial Africa a man with personality, official or private employer, could often achieve the seemingly impossible.

As time progressed, however, and administration became more associated with labour requirements, such happy arrangements became rare.

40. 'A Visit to Mombasa', *Zanzibar Gazette*, 13 May 1896.
41. 'Workers' in this context refers to lay or social workers and not manual labourers.

For an account of this council see A. J. Temu, 'The role of the Bombay African on the Mombasa Coast, 1874–1904', *hadith 3*, (Proceedings of the 1969-70 Conference of the Historical Association of Kenya), 1971.

Chapter 2

THE ESTABLISHMENT OF THE LABOUR SYSTEM, 1902–1914

'The natives,' says the planter, 'evince a great reluctance to work, especially to work regularly.' 'They must be made to work,' say others. 'Made to work for whom?' we innocently ask. 'For us, of course,' is the ready answer; 'what did you think we meant?'

The Under-Secretary of State for the Colonies,
Winston S. Churchill, 1908.

With the decision of the protectorate's second Commissioner, Sir Charles Eliot (1901–4), to permit and encourage white settlement, the employment pattern hitherto coastal and railway begins a total change. Settlement involved three major labour problems: to obtain men either by recruitment or compulsion; to retain them, in the local context to prevent them from deserting; and to make them work diligently. All three problems were to lead to incessant conflicts and to crises in 1908 and 1912–13.

In economic terms white settlement meant an injection of white capital, or capital in the form of skills, for development. This capital was spread over a large number of small projects, most of which in themselves were without sufficient cash capital. Apart from market-gardens around Nairobi large-scale farming was necessary if profits were to be made. To clear the ground, in the absence of skills and equipment, the farmer was obliged to seek a sizeable labour force of several score, sometimes several hundred men to work with their own rudimentary implements. But the capital necessary for such a labour force was beyond the reach of most of the new settlers, whose difficulties were worsened by the high interest rate charged by banks on loans. The situation was neither an economic climate in which the interest of labour was likely to flourish nor the labourer likely to receive a wage which genuinely and permanently attracted him. The attitudes of the settlers themselves to their labour reflected these difficulties.

Master, Servant and Government

The early settlers included a moderate number from British upper-class families, usually with a certain amount of capital; the large majority, however, were roving men, adventurers at first, more genuine planters later, without or with very limited capital. These latter were hard men with hard prejudices, some from Britain and Europe, but a very large proportion from South Africa. Of these latter an Acting Governor wrote that many '. . . were not of a very good glass and left their previous homes with a record in some cases doubtful and in others distinctly unsatisfactory'.[1] The numbers increased rapidly. By April 1903 the dozen or so farmers of 1901 had swollen to over 100; numbers rose again in 1904, and by 1905 the total lay between 500 and 600. The figure then grew more slowly until 1908, the peak year, when 280 Boers arrived from South Africa complete with wagons and ploughs but with no capital at all. Most of these Boers trekked up to the Uasin-Gishu plateau, where for the first few years little was cultivated.[2] Government departments also increased in number bringing new demands for labour, and recruitment became very early on a major government concern. Further, as already noted, the territory's sporting reputation led to an increasing demand for caravan porters.

For several decades few Europeans saw anything wrong in a pattern of development in which the African was to be converted to a worker, and a study of European attitudes is an important introduction to the actual events. Europeans saw their qualities, ideals and institutions as superior to those of Africans and believed that they were performing a service to humanity by replacing them.[3] The pre-1914 world believed that as the world population rose so more food would be needed, and Europeans who provided it were serving humanity and an expanding world, at the same time offering Africans an opportunity of instruction in general civilization, particularly in simple economics, ploughs, wheeled transport, stock-breeding and manuring. Doubts rarely disturbed this self-confidence.

The early settlers, sturdy, self-reliant individualists, carried these views several stages further under the pressure of the difficulties of the environment, the uncertainties of the time, and the shadow of disease. They argued that the government had arrived before them, had encouraged them to settle in the territory and join this white civilizing mission and that it lay with the government to see they did not fail through want of labour. Labour, they claimed, would teach the native that idleness was wrong and work the basis of prosperity, that he would learn new skills in working, and that anyway he had now nothing else to do since tribal warfare had ended and work should be his thanks to the British for this blessing. None paused to consider that the more labour was coerced artificially the less would any concept of 'dignity' of work carry conviction. The pattern of African life in reserve areas was not understood at all, and the apparent lack of visible work in the 'lying off' periods concealed from the settler the tasks of African men at harvest time. Finally it was argued that work improved Africans physically. Settler arguments often gained an added bitterness from the fact that when reward appeared at last in their grasp it was jeopardized by lack of manpower. Their remote loneliness added an element of insecurity and fear, almost unjustified, but reinforced by memories of the Rhodesian and Maji Maji risings. This fear led to assertion of a dominant status—and also to extremist provocations to test their own strength, or as Ainsworth believed, to provide an excuse to take further native land and cattle by provoking a rising and then suppressing it.

There were many settlers particularly those of South African origin, therefore, who stood with Ewart Grogan, one of the most famous of the early pioneers when he wrote '. . . the African native . . . is fundamentally inferior in mental development and ethical possibilities . . . to the white man . . . On principle he never tells the truth and consequently never expects to hear it.'[4] Grogan regarded leniency and kindness as either weak or suspect, and recommended that '. . . a good sound system of compulsory labour would do more to raise the native in five years than all the millions that have been sunk in missionary efforts for the last fifty. Work was the keynote to the betterment of the African.' It might have to be called 'education' to pacify critics in Britain, pay would have to be fixed at a 'rational' level—'three shillings give him as much satisfaction as three pounds'—but restrictions on the number of lashes that might be given were 'ridiculous'. The South African Boer settlers mostly took their national view that the native (whom they usually referred to as a 'nigger') was intended by the Almighty to work for the white man, and if he did not work almost any disciplinary measure was justifiable; if a thrashing resulted in death the only reaction was likely to be that there appeared to be many more Africans and perhaps the victim was due to die anyway.[5] Some settlers also argued that the employee accepted corporal punishment of his free will, knowing he had done wrong and agreeing that the punishment was just. While many other farmers, perhaps a majority, did not go to these extremes all were prepared to see a considerable measure of coercion in labour supply, and most accepted corporal punishment (though not always the lash) as a regrettable necessity despite the fact that its administration by a private employer was totally illegal.[6] In December 1911 the *Leader*, a local settler newspaper, claimed knowledge of and sharply criticized a secret Colonial Office circular instructing that the lash was only to be used in extremely serious cases. Lord Cranworth's writings reveal the attitude of another typical employer in this period.[7] The Kikuyu, he said, was 'sly, cunning, deceitful, cowardly, and devoid of all sense of honour', he was a liar, thief and poisoner, and in addition 'intensely lazy' and 'callously cruel'. Other tribes were only relatively superior, Nyanza men earning some faint praise for superior strength, and being as individuals more 'cheery . . . trusting and trustworthy'. After saying wages should be paid promptly when due, proper feeding and housing supplied and that fines were undesirable unless shared, Cranworth goes on to say a 'thorough' beating with the whip was 'the best and kindest preventative and cure for lying, petty theft or cruelty to children and animals'; for domestic servants, too, he advocated periodic inspection of kitchens and cooking pots, 'an unpleasant task and the result usually ends with a feeling of soreness on the part, the posterior part, of your cook'.

The settler farmstead could vary considerably, and there remained a wide gap between the best employer, with sufficient capital to pay wages regularly, a civilized home, and a patriarchal approach to his labourers, and the large majority of rougher adventurers characterized by greed and the 'look of cheap debased vulgarity of the colonist type', described by Llewelyn Powys. Often living by themselves, their standards fell, clothing became invariably dirty, comfort being found in cheap tobacco, cigarettes and liquor. Their homestead of mud and wattle walls and corrugated iron roof might have only apertures as windows and a mud floor. The furniture would be rough, of the camp type, deck-chairs and tablecloths being soiled with sweat, food prepared and served on cracked china or chipped enamel platters, with the room's only interior decoration being horned skulls of game on the walls. For relaxation this type of settler would have dogs, probably tick-infested mongrels, his packs of cards and his alcohol.[8] Sometimes also he might order his staff to produce a woman, and a few labourers' wives or daughters were not averse to the chance of prestige or gain, with or without their menfolk's approval.[9] The house would be characterized by flies and unpleasant smells. For such settlers, and there were many, recourse to the whip was instant and on the slightest provocation for farm and domestic staff alike. The *East African Standard*, another settler newspaper, in a series of articles on 'The Native' in 1913 devoted two to the desirability of maintaining discipline by corporal punishment, elaborating at length the theme that any form of kindness would only be derided as weakness. Other articles advocated low wages, the need for registration, and that district commissioners should arrange labour indentures with chiefs.[10] The lessons learnt by labourers on such farmsteads were not healthy, either socially or medically.

A further factor working to the advantage of the settler was the jury system; this led to considerable abuse when the government tried to prosecute employers for assault or homicide. White juries preferred to acquit such employers and only very rarely indeed convicted without some qualification or recommendation for leniency.[11]

The reality of the labour shortage in the whole of the pre-1914 period in general terms is difficult to assess. It was never the very real shortage of Southern Rhodesia. One farmer, a former Director of Agriculture and more liberal than the majority, wrote perceptively, '... The subject of labour is almost inexpressible in definite terms, in fact there is and there is not a scarcity of labour. The supply of labour depends on the individual temperament of the person receiving labour, on the part of the country where settled, on the reasonable or unreasonable demands made on hand labour by purely manual labour employing farmers and on the action of the Government.'[12] However to many settlers there appeared to be a labour shortage sometimes appearing acute, while Africans appeared to be idlers, and even the good employer had occasionally to engage in tedious recruiting. We shall examine later the particular situations in critical years.

The missions in the pre-1914 period were not able to soften the harshness of these attitudes in any real degree. Most missionaries had arrived in up-country East Africa after the settlers from whom they tended to keep aloof. They were much divided among themselves and since many (except the Roman Catholics) were of Low Church or Presbyterian creeds, they often lacked influence among the class which furnished settler leaders; nor were they particularly influential in Britain except in the matter of slavery. Many of austere views even subscribed to local attitudes on the civilizing effect of work.[13] Most advised Africans to pay their taxes regularly, sometimes an important factor in obtaining acquiescence. Some missions, too, were employers of a labour force of several hundred which they needed to grow their own food and stock to survive; the poorer missions were poor employers.[14] Further, in time, the larger missions became increasingly dependent on government funds for some of their medical and educational work, and settler pressures might be brought on the government.[15]

Missionaries tempted to protest had to consider whether Africans might not in fact be the losers.

These then were the European attitudes, sometimes in extreme cases turning to cruelty and crime. The inland Africans' earliest attitudes in this situation need now an exercise of imagination to comprehend. Their life and beliefs were so unprepared for the European economic and cultural assault that their general reactions in the first years were passive to a degree we may now find surprising. There were, however, from the beginning certain Africans who had a shrewd awareness of the value of association with the strangers, and far from being intimidated used the white man to advance their own political and economic ends. Such were adventurers like Kinyanjui and chiefs like Mumia.

The world, as most inland tribesmen saw it, despite the existence of a creator God, was moved in practice by unseen and cold spirit forces, in some cases ancestral, and identifiable by their works such as a good harvest, famine, locusts, a male heir.[16] They could to some extent be controlled by ceremony and magic, but were more often held in check by rules and purifications. The new aliens were without understanding of these forces but appeared impervious to them, irresistible, and immensely wealthy. The strangers preached of a God who lived in an empty house and taught the merits of a single wife; this appeared a heavy domestic burden for one woman. Their dress, their houses, their personal possessions and family customs, their means of transport appeared totally strange and illogical, at times dangerous. Pencils, soda-syphons, lawn-mowers, even lamps could appear to be the habitations of spirits. The work required by the strangers seemed completely purposeless. Why stretch wire between poles over miles of country? What were the extraordinary loads a porter had to carry to the new farm—a gramophone, a sewing machine, a plough, or a mattress? What were the plants the settler was trying to grow? Sometimes the work was not just incomprehensible, it was criminal folly and likely to leave fearful consequences from enraged spirits. What could be more dangerous than manuring a garden with cow dung? Or building a road so straight that attack was invited? Or boiling milk, or killing a cow, to a Nandi not only wasteful and cruel, but a serious risk to the future milk supply.

Further on his arrival the stranger announced that a new law and custom had come. He would stop the attacks of the Maasai and in return the warriors should help him with his work. One man was selected to be his friend, for no particular reason, and all were expected to obey him.[17] Sometimes being the stranger's friend went to the chief's head, and he became rapacious over land, wives, stock and the rewards for supplying labourers. At the end of a day's work the stranger gave out a piece of metal saying that it was worth a goat, but no one would give a goat for it, and later the stranger returned and said he wanted it back. Sometimes the strangers differed over exactly what they wanted. Finally labour involved contact with other tribes, many of whom were believed to be notoriously evil.

The stranger on his farm seemed quite unable to understand some of the necessities of life that might force an African to leave abruptly, however loyal he might feel to his employer. A crack might have appeared in the cooking-pot, or a kite flown overhead, his wife's bed might have broken, or a member of the family might have trodden on a human bone, a baby might have been born feet foremost, or a caterpillar have walked in the family group of huts. These were believed to be evidence of someone's ill-will or a curse, and purification after a compensation payment had to be arranged urgently before disaster struck. Or some family business, or illness, death or a marriage might require a man's presence at a council, perhaps some distance away. The stranger, too, always required men to work at traditional planting times and at harvest time. These reasons were to the Africans urgent and compelling, but they quickly learned the Europeans would never understand them, and some in turn advanced reasons which they thought the Europeans would understand. These to the Europeans often lacked credibility. But conversely if the European owner killed a servant or beat his men harshly, few Africans immediately felt any great sense of injustice at a time when they themselves punished cattle-thieves and other offenders extremely cruelly.

The Africans did not think of themselves as idle, as there were specific tasks, mostly seasonal, which the menfolk had to do—clearing new ground, harvesting, craftwork and the building of huts. With the absence of warfare their days may not have been full, work perhaps taking only two or three hours a day in certain seasons but who was to do this work if the men went away? But, apart from interest in the new marvels, why should a man leave his family, homestead and the security of his tribal custom? There was enough land for all to live on comfortably so no question of subsistence was involved. What was to be gained? Why work without a break for thirty consecutive days?[18] Nor was work for the foreigner seen at first by the Africans as providing any of the non-cash incentives which may motivate the Europeans—a sense of belonging or a sense of value and achievement.

Misunderstandings inevitably multiplied. The European would give his orders in broken Swahili, often confusing present and future tenses.[19] Failure of the non-Swahili speaking labourer to understand either English or Swahili led to ill-temper. The Kamba thought it respectful to turn their back to a superior; the European thought this surly. The European considered Africans cruel to the dying, to their wives, and to their animals. On many farms Africans would practice horrible cruelties on animals for purification ceremonies, for entertainment, or to announce to the farmer that the animal was 'sick' or had 'died', with a view to eating it. Revolted employers reacted sharply. But many African peoples thought the practice of yoking oxen criminal. The European brought effective medicines; the African felt they dealt only with the superficialities rather than the spirits that caused the ills. The African thought the European so wealthy that a little pilfering was no more evil than taking honey from a beehive, and gifts a mark of adoption rather than occasions for particular protestations of gratitude. Indeed, a man might follow up one gift by asking the European for another and express concern if it was refused. In different degrees by different tribes, Africans thought plain speaking or full answers to a question to be either rude or dangerous. The ideas of individual thrift and of personal responsibility, too, were not strong ones in the old communal societies, but they were strong ones in the minds of the employer who looked down on employees who exhibited no appreciation of their virtues.

These misunderstandings daily reinforced the European's conviction of the superiority of the white man. The apparent ability of the African labourer to live and work on a diet of maize meal porridge appeared proof of an essential physiological inferiority rather than one main cause of his inefficiency as a worker. Proposals for better feeding and treatment encountered therefore a psychological as well as an economic resistance. Similarly in the matter of housing a benevolent employer might go to some trouble to build a good hut. An employee's relative would then die in the hut which no one would then use again, proof to some employers of the uselessness of good quality housing, ingratitude, and of African preferences for old dirty tumble-down shacks. The foremost of the only two recognizable African spending patterns in these early years, cattle with which to purchase an additional wife or wives—for reasons as much or more economic than sexual—led the European settler to take a moral tone not always in accord with his own practices. The other African preference, for cloth, met with greater approval. But even the exasperation provoked by labour told the European what he most wanted to hear, the absolute rightness of his civilizing work from his position of crude dominance, at this time very different from the more benevolent paternalism of later years. But even in these early years it is possible to see the beginnings of paternalism.

At the outset work was too transistory and exceptional to yield any coherent pattern of reaction. But by 1910 there was a closer acquaintance of the European and his new ways, leading for some to a stimulated appreciation of the benefits of spending power but for others an increased fear of the new order and a reluctance to participate. Dr. Norman Leys noted that large numbers of men recruited or 'encouraged' to go out to work deserted on the journey. Others hid in strange villages. African reaction to work for Europeans was ceasing to be passive; many of the faults such as petty theft, carelessness, insubordination, negligence or desertion, about which European employers complained were in fact the earliest and simplest forms of African industrial protest. European employers almost without exception failed to understand the real significance of these gestures.

The significance lay deep. A psychological transition was under way caused by the twin processes of individualization and the erosion of tribal societies in those areas producing numbers of labourers. The white man, the settler employer, had power and material success undreamed of; in contrast the old magical and animistic processes of the past were taught by parents and elders themselves beginning to doubt them to a young generation which started inevitably to lack the integration of the old societies. Signs of this disintegration can be seen in several spheres. Chiefs continued profitably to build up their land, their stock, and their sometimes very large number of wives, but the younger men began to ignore both them and also their traditional elders.[20] The local press is full of reports of cattle stealing, both from farmers and from other Africans in the reserves, and of petty crime in Nairobi.[21] Heavier drinking was taking place both in towns and in the reserves. Some of the social evils consequent upon the absence of menfolk from their families for the longer periods of contract labour were just beginning to appear. Sometimes, too, old family customs such as a family paying together for the bride of a young man were sapped, the young man being expected to pay himself. This process was exacerbated by the missions who taught that only one complete payment constituted a moral marriage, rather than any instalment payment system; so young men turned to borrowing, with a number of consequences in terms of a need to return to work or the mortgaging of land rights.

The more obvious signs of change, particularly drink and crime, were seen by European settlers as added evidence that many young men were idlers. Equally, the partial acceptance and emulation of some of the new ideas were seen by the Europeans as progress and complete evidence of the civilizing effect of work. And so to some limited extent it was—for example the hygiene of the better European homes led some Africans for the first time to wish to make their own more clean and neat. By 1912 a number of town workers were adopting such European customs as shorts, shirts, and trimmed hair in emulation of the police and military. But the farm or construction workers usually retained their long hair, small leather waist-cloaks, traditional charms (bracelets, goats horns, little cylinders of powdered leaves and rattles), and blankets worn over the shoulders as an outer garment. Africans were beginning to purchase goods such as cups, saucers, matchets and hoes, cutlery, rice, tea, sugar and blankets. Sometimes African families or small communes decided together to send one or two of their members out to earn tax money for them all while the remainder looked after his interests at home. On receipt of his pay, having now a much better idea of its value, the labourer would usually bury it under the floor of his hut, or spend it on a wider range of consumer goods in addition to wives or clothes. The development of the resident labour system also made a certain appeal to Africans, reflected in their attitudes to work; these attitudes will be considered later.

The third point in the triangle to examine is the attitude of government officers themselves. In these early years the great majority were of mediocre quality, concerned with matters of sport, sex, drink and status more than with a real understanding of their communities.[22] All were in some sense employers of Africans as domestic servants, and might often find themselves in some sympathy with the frustration of a farmer. Only a very few officers, led by John Ainsworth, queried the general view that Africans would produce and learn more when in settler employment, though a number had differing views on the degree of 'encouragement' to be given to enter employment. Some thought work and acquaintance with the outside world a step of progress; others, contemplating ochred and befeathered warriors, or Nyanza men with neither ochre nor feathers, or a party of shy and giggling girls clad only in beads and leather aprons, felt that more time should pass before such people were required to leave their houses for work, a view often reinforced by the condition in which some workers returned. Sometimes they urged farmers to pay higher wages, but more often they found the settler the only congenial social company and did not. Only a very few officials took any action against the farmer who used the *kiboko*, and the press and law reports indicate that a number of district officers as magistrates imposed, quite illegally, corporal punishment sentences for desertion and other labour offences. In general settlers held those officials who appeared pro-native in contempt, resenting their 'interference' and ostracizing them socially.

Four chief weapons were used to coerce Africans to work: taxation, the size of the land areas to be reserved for them, the attitude of the administration and legislation.

The first of these, taxation, had an innocuous origin in the need to pay for the cost of administration in the years before labour had become a serious problem—an origin common to many colonies. Collection at the rate of 1 rupee per hut began at the Coast very late in 1901; the rate was raised to 2 rupees the next year. As the rate in Uganda's former Eastern Province had been 3 rupees, the rate was raised to 3 rupees in the Kisumu and Naivasha provinces in 1903; payment might be in stock or labour for the government.[23] As fresh districts were brought under administration the district commissioner introduced taxation, usually only at the 1 rupee rate at first, increased to 2 rupees in the second year.

In 1904 and 1905 settler pressure for the use of taxation to stimulate labour supply is evident. Lord Hindlip writing in 1905 expressed a general settler feeling that payment in kind should cease and that Africans should be obliged to work in order to earn coin; he favoured also a tax on wives and a poll tax to discourage 'loafers and general riff-raff'.[24] By 1906 payment in kind was dying out, the Africans themselves becoming sufficiently familiar with coin to prefer it. In 1905 the rate was raised to 3 rupees in the Mombasa area, and in 1906 to 3 rupees in Kikuyuland and Ukamba, these latter being reserve areas near settler farms, clearly with labour supply as a cause. There followed in 1907 a Colonists' Association demand for a poll tax, a tax on African cattle and action against tax evasion. In reply in 1909 the government began the extension in certain labour supplying areas of the hut tax levy to all adult males living under one roof, a measure which accorded ill with African custom. The methods of collection were unsatisfactory, often being left to illiterate chiefs and headmen who operated in the early years on a 3 per cent commission system, later raised to a permissible maximum of 10 per cent. The government in collecting tax, therefore, worked parallel with the settler demand for the increase in number and rate of Africans taxed; more revenue pleased the government, more labour pleased the settler.

Hut tax, the cash rate of which was not excessive in comparison with other colonies, might have been no imposition if at least a fair percentage of it had been spent on development of African areas.[25] But almost from the very start of settlement it seemed accepted that development in agriculture would be the role of the European, and that the African areas were to be reserved on the basis of the existing population density, any surplus arising from natural increase being available for future labour requirements. The protectorate government had existed for so short a time and been so preoccupied with Coastal problems that there had been neither experience of nor thought given to the development of inland peasant economies. Eliot had vaguely thought in terms of a close inter-penetration of settler farms and reserves so that labour could be easily available, an arrangement similar to that in Natal. But the prevailing European feeling of insecurity led to European demands for native reserves few in size but large in number, far from European farms, with for labourers small villages on the farmer's land. Another demand was for a pass system for all natives living in the European areas to ensure the return to the reserves of those not in employment; if there was an overflow the general labour supply would be so increased. On this basis the government delineated a number of reserves for the larger tribes in the years 1906 to 1912. But several demands for the reduction of the reserves and tribal areas were made in the 1908 disturbances, and within six years of large-scale settlement land allocation policy was becoming conditioned as much by settler demands for labour as by white expansion.[26]

Within the reserves the day to day detail of administration was seen as the task of chiefs and headmen. Since almost all Kenya peoples were acephalous these men needed to be selected and appointed, and at their inception chiefs and headmen were provided with certain powers, *inter alia* in respect of communal labour. Under the Village Headmen Ordinance of 1902, headmen could be directed to keep any public road in condition and repair, and could also be used for the raising of a communal fine.[27] But with settlement, chiefs and headmen came quickly to be viewed by the settlers as the key both to labour recruitment and discipline. A pattern of demands emerged that the government should direct the chiefs and headmen to urge the desirability of work upon their communities or physically supply the men, and should even be responsible for their industry at work, in particular by punishing deserters and stock thieves. A system grew up by which the small settler in a district was expected to recruit his own labour, with perhaps contacts with chiefs arranged by the district commissioner (if he approved of labour), while the government would help more positively by telling the chiefs or headmen to produce a certain number of men for large employers or farmers far from the reserves.[28] These employers came quickly to insist on the government's obligation to provide men and should they desert replacements. In particular, the government often gave this positive help both to contractors engaged in work for the railway or other public needs and to its own departments. Many of the contractors, particularly the Asian ones, lacked the necessary capital for their tender with unfortunate results for the labour. To most chiefs or headmen, new and unversed in their authority, a request from a district officer to try and assist one settler by 'encouraging' men to volunteer, and a direct command to produce labour for another or for the government were indistinguishable. Frequently the settler might supply a *douceur* either in cash or in kind and many chiefs, some in all honesty, saw nothing wrong in accepting such reward for the supply of men.[29]

The chiefs' difficulties and confusion were worsened by the emergence in 1906 of the professional labour recruiter. These men went into the reserves and obtained manpower, sometimes by bullying or bribing the chiefs or even posing as government officers; they were often unscrupulous characters who wielded great power in a particular area without any proper check. The men they recruited were taken in gangs escorted by mercenary retainers to the nearest railway station. The recruiters then charged employers a *per capita* commission. Chiefs and headmen were therefore very early linked with duties and conditions which made considerable demands on their time and energies, and led their communities to view them with apprehension rather than confidence. On the other hand the colonial government made no conscious attempt to destroy an existing African social structure for labour purposes as happened in Southern Rhodesia.

The weapon of legislation was used principally to retain Africans in employment rather than to coerce men out to work by any direct legislative compulsion.

In 1903 all labour except domestic servants was governed by the servants section of the Native Porters and Labour Regulations of 1902. These required contracts of more than two months to be prepared before a registering officer, who had to explain the wages and duration of work to each employee; the regulations also required the employer to return the servant to the place of engagement at the expiry of the contract. The regulations were later extended to men from certain areas on contracts of less than two months, but they were obviously unsuitable for the labour problems of larger scale settlement. The form of replacement legislation became a matter in which settlers were to take a great concern. The association of government officers with attestation of contracts originally planned as a safeguard acquired a new aspect, and settlers came to demand penal provisions against employees who departed from work without warning.

A preliminary examination of these four weapons—taxation, the reserves, chiefs and the administration, and legislation—is necessary if later the increases of pressure, often gradual and not apparently very great *per se*, are to be seen in their full strength. In total their coercive effect amounted to compulsion in certain areas and at certain times.

Lastly the total effect of these measures was worsened by the method of payment of wages. From the earliest days of settlement farmers had tried wherever possible to establish the system of payment at the end of the month, this being seen as the only effective way of ensuring that an employee remained in service for a month without deserting. Many Africans in consequence preferred to work for Asians who paid by the day; this avoided the problems of the first month at work and facilitated any sudden departure.[30] In 1905–6 the ticket system began in the protectorate; this was an alternative system of South African origin but with no legal status designed to make and keep the labourer at work. A man engaged on a contract the remuneration for which was monthly was given a piece of paper ruled into thirty squares. Each square was ticked at the end of a day's work and payment only made on completion of the ticket. The system was defended by the settlers on the grounds that Africans could not understand a month, or why they were expected to work for six consecutive days but not seven. But the system led to exhaustion and abuse as many employers began to pay only when thirty working days were recorded on the ticket, and also to inefficiency as the completion of the thirty days work might last two or three months.

Sadler, Hollis and Churchill, 1903–8

The administration felt the pressure of the first settler demands for labour in 1903, at the same time it was being asked if men could be supplied for work in the South African mines. A *Report on Slavery and Free Labour in East Africa* was produced to assess the situation.[31] The report, written by a protectorate official, stressed the need for supervision recommending payment by piece work rather than time, but warned of the absence of thrift and skills; it noted most wages were paid in cash and were spent chiefly on cattle with which to purchase extra wives, with small amounts on beads and wire and other clothing. At the Coast labour was still only barely sufficient for local needs, men going to Zanzibar and Pemba for clove picking of their own free will despite the ban on open recruiting. Inland the report observed the pastoral tribes were unsuited for labour. The Railway took the majority of the available Kamba. The Kikuyu refused to work far from home and the Nyanza people, some affected by sleeping sickness were unwilling to move away at harvest time. In so far as South Africa was concerned the report said that East African labour would be unwilling to migrate and should be kept for local needs. The protectorate Commissioner, Stewart, wrote in 1904 that there was 'considerable local feeling . . . that the Administration should apply pressure in some form or another to the natives to increase the supply . . .', a feeling which he rejected. He thought labour bureaux might meet the need—as a form of labour exchange at the principal government stations where settlers could engage labour at a rate fixed by the government, but he admitted the whole question was 'hedged about with difficulties'.[32]

Difficulties of all types were appearing indeed. For general security reasons, movement of Africans of one tribe into areas peopled by another had been controlled by pass regulations, but these had had to be amended very quickly to enable labour to move. More officers were given powers to register contracts; employer practices of attachment on labourers' wages as punishments for negligence were forbidden but most serious of all were problems of recruitment and desertion, of which complaints were beginning to appear in the *East African Standard*.

The administration extended its service of attesting contracts to promoting in Ainsworth's words, 'mutual agreements between the settlers and the natives whereby the former arrange with the latter to portion off a part of their holding for a native settlement'; in these early years the relationship was however more one of 'Kaffir farming' tenancy than labour.[33] In addition a Land Committee appointed by Stewart reported in 1905; this committee recommended the demarcation of reserves on the basis already noted and a system of labour resident on European farms, paid a low wage, but with a small plot for private cultivation in return for periods of employment. For towns the committee recommended a strict pass system and racially separated locations which they justified on health grounds, with some reason in the absence of any effective measures to improve African health standards. The committee also marked the first unofficial demand for a reorganization of the government machine to assist with labour problems; one recommendation called for a Commissioner for Native Affairs to concern himself with labour supply, discipline and wages.[34] The committee made a number of other political recommendations, partly as a result of which Elgin at the Colonial Office agreed to the establishment of a Legislative Council with nominated unofficials, four European and one Asian.

These unofficials, of course, were on land issues settlers and on labour issues employers. On labour Elgin said he would await the views of a new Land Commissioner. This officer advised significantly that in his view the good employer had no fear of a shortage of labour, and Elgin therefore approved a change in the administration rather different from that envisaged by the committee; he agreed to the provision in 1906 of a Secretary for Native Affairs and three assistants whose task was 'the regulation and protection of native labourers'.

On Stewart's death in 1905, Lieut.-Col. J. Hayes Sadler was appointed Commissioner, a title changed to Governor in 1906. Sadler was a man of courtly charm and manner but was to prove too weak and conciliatory to discipline the harsh, bitter South African element in the territory; at the outset however there seemed little indication of the trouble to come. Sadler in 1906 noted with satisfaction the number of Kikuyu and Nyanza men already at work and believed the attraction of consumer goods would increase the supply. He added, though, that he thought the Native Affairs Department (which he called a 'labour bureau') would help by obtaining labour for the needs of government and assisting also the private employer, a significant change of role.[35]

Before examining the actual establishment and work of this department, we must note another example of the effects of settler pressure on a weak governor which occurred at this time in the field of legislation. At their January 1905 meeting the Colonists' Association following a number of demands to make contracts more binding appointed a sub-committee to consider labour legislation. As a result in 1906 a new Master and Servants Ordinance came into force, an ordinance prepared locally and only sent to the Colonial Office several months later.[36] It had been modelled on Gold Coast and Transvaal labour legislation, many (but not all) of its more severe features deriving from the latter. It permitted payment in kind, and provided for fines or in practice imprisonment for a variety of offences constituting breach of contract by the servant and one or two similar employer offences; it also stopped for a while the practice of employers imposing their own fines. Penal clauses for breach of contract were a stock feature of colonial labour legislation; they were considered indispensable where dismissal was neither an effective economic nor moral threat. Employees had little chance of civil procedure redress, so some sanctions were applicable to employers. The Colonial Office decided that little could be done though Lord Elgin minuted 'I adhere to my opinion that this is a doubtful Ordinance'.[37] The protectorate government was told they should have consulted the Colonial Office on its provisions, and particular anxiety was expressed over the permitted maximum length of contracts of three years, the payment for services in kind, the principle of imprisonment for breaches of contract, the number of offences for which a prison penalty was liable, and the addition of the duration of a prison sentence to the contract. To emphasize their disapproval the Colonial Office requested a full report on the reasons for the provisions and the incident reinforced doubts on Sadler's competence. The settlers however were pleased, the secretary of the Colonists' Association claiming with some justice that the ordinance had been enacted as a result of their representations.[38]

Despite Sadler's modification of its role, the Native Affairs Department did not prove the success the settlers hoped, due very largely to the character of its head, A. C. (later Sir Claud) Hollis.[39] The government's original plan had been for a Superintendent of district commissioner's rank, with five 'assistants', but this was changed to a Secretary for Native Affairs with assistants to be attached to the secretariat, and in this form the Colonial Office approval was given. Following unofficial criticism in the Legislative Council the number of assistants was reduced to three; their duties were to correspond on labour matters with the Secretary sending copies to provincial commissioners. This led to confusion, and in 1907 at the time of Churchill's visit the assistants were re-styled 'assistant district commissioners' and given the status of full district commissioners, but placed below the provincial commissioner of the area in which they were working. Normally they were to correspond with the provincial commissioners on labour matters sending a copy to the Secretary for Native Affairs when important, an arrangement which caused some friction but still re-reflected Churchill's insistence on a certain measure of autonomy.[40] Armed with these powers, Hollis's staff began a survey of labour conditions and quickly became shocked by much of what they found.

But before the new Native Affairs Department could make any real impression on the labour scene, the protectorate was shaken by a noisy and significant incident in Nairobi. Captain Ewart Grogan, president of the Colonists' Association, had led a public flogging of three Kikuyu employees in front of the town magistrate's office, brushing aside the magistrate and a police officer. Grogan asserted that the men had been disrespectful to his sister and another lady, an assertion magnified by S. C. Fichat, the association's secretary, to a rumour of sexual assault. Each employee received twenty-five lashes and a government medical officer said later that two had suffered simple hurt, and one severe hurt nearly amounting to grievous hurt. Grogan and five others were charged with assault, a charge very quickly reduced to unlawful assembly. They were all released on bail and the charges against one dropped. The Colonial Office firmly supported the government; a cruiser was despatched to Mombasa and the incident and trial then became a political question. But it is important from a labour point of view for several reasons. It is a vivid illustration of the attitude of the South African settler element; W. Russell Bowker, one of the defendants, at his trial stated 'it has always been a first principle with me to flog a nigger on sight who insults a white woman', and the local press wrote in sympathy. The incident attracted some attention in the House of Commons, the government eventually producing a parliamentary paper of despatches outlining the events; these undermined the wide claims for self-rule the colonists were making and again alerted a few sections of British opinion to conditions in the protectorate. The incident also added force to the fear and concern of the most intelligent of the officials such as Ainsworth and Hollis. The Acting Governor wrote to the Colonial Office of the growing tendency of the European population 'to deny the native any rights whatever', and that 'the labourer shall be not a labourer but a helot, not a servant but a slave'.[41]

With the controversy in full spate, Hollis's small department unexpectedly received massive on-the-spot support from Churchill, then Parliamentary Under-Secretary. Churchill, greeted by demands for a poll tax, pass laws and a labour recruiting board had on arrival seen at first hand a shocking example of bad labour conditions. He had found a large party of some 300 labourers walking back from a site over 150 miles away and demanded an explanation; he wrote of them later as 'skinny scarecrows crawling back to their tribe after a few weeks contact with Christian civilisation'. Hollis ascertained that the men had originally been recruited for work on a farm not far from their homes near Nairobi, but the farmer had transferred them to a railway ballast contractor who did not have the money to feed or house them. At the end of the contract the contractor had been unable to pay the men off, telling them to wait, without food, for five days until a train with the money arrived. But the labourers had had enough and had begun to walk home. The contractor, a European, was prosecuted, no doubt at Churchill's instigation, and ordered to pay immediately or face imprisonment.[42]

The incident led to the strengthening of the status of the Native Affairs Department and to the publication of a notice drafted by Hollis in the *Official Gazette*, defining the terms under which the government was prepared to assist private employers in search of labour.[43] The terms, based in part on the 1902 regulations, required employers to provide suitable accommodation, a good blanket, a modest food scale with proper cooking arrangements, and clean water; they prescribed medical arrangements and procedures in the case of sickness or death, and equitable arrangements for the labourer's journey home. Cash deposits for the men's food and as a security for their pay were also required. Hollis further wrote a general memorandum on labour conditions in which he stated that the worst employers were the Railway and the Public Works Department (P.W.D.) along with their contractors. Churchill's views, Hollis's memorandum, the *Gazette* Notice and the text of a circular to administrative officers instructing that chiefs were not to be permitted to compel labourers to work were all sent by Sadler to the Colonial Office with the approval of Elgin. But neither Churchill nor Hollis at this time saw anything wrong in the principle of government recruiting for reputable private employers. Hollis's staff were assisting in this work, and during his visit Churchill several times spoke in favour of the government supplying settlers with labour providing conditions at work were satisfactory. Both were later to change their views, Churchill's revised opinions only becoming effective in 1921 on his return to the Colonial Office.

Early in 1908 tension mounted. The Labour Rules—as Hollis's *Gazette* Notice was described—were bitterly criticized as 'pampering' by the settlers and local press; the *East African Standard* argued that the blanket should remain the property of the employer, Africans should pay part of the attestation fee and the government should prosecute all employees who deserted after engagement on the terms of the Labour Rules. In the Legislative Council Lord Delamere asked why labour, when it had been paid, should be given food for the return journey.[44] In addition the difficulties experienced by some farmers in obtaining labour were greater than usual since a good harvest in certain reserve areas had led men to decide to remain at home. The Kisii (Gusii) military operation, German demands on the Nyamwezi, clove picking on Pemba and safari portering were making large demands on the supply, over 3,000 being engaged in clove picking and 4,000 men employed by the safari firms at a rate of 10 rupees per month with *posho* and meat; at Mombasa stevedore wages had been doubled reinforcing the attractions of the Coast.[45] Many farmers too were changing from stock to grain farming which needed more men. Furthermore there were allegations in the press and at meetings that Hollis and his assistant were discouraging labour. This was certainly not so; in the five months prior to March 1908 the government had received applications from settlers for 1,346 men, of whom 696 were supplied. The government had also recruited 2,042 men for its own departments and 2,893 out of 3,589 requested for private contractors to the government. At least one assistant in Kikuyuland was however telling people that the chiefs had no power to compel them to work if they did not wish to, and this may have appeared to ordinary Africans as a government statement that if they did not wish to work they could stay at home. Hollis's assistants would sometimes ask men recruited by chiefs whether they really wished to work, and on receiving a negative reply the assistants sent the men home. Hollis's staff also inspected work places and listened to labourers' complaints, which led Delamere to protest angrily against 'secret enquiries . . . and in fact men being encouraged to tell tales about their masters'. There was, therefore, slightly more appearance to the usual settler complaint of a labour shortage; although throughout the crisis there were two or three hundred work-seekers in Nairobi these were men who did not want rough work on strange and isolated farms.

In March, a hot and trying month before the rains arrive, the explosion took place in the form of a march on Government House.[46] On the morning of 23 March a meeting of settlers took place to consider the labour situation, Sadler out of mistaken kindness taking the chair. In an opening speech he said he thought that the labour problem would eventually be solved by creating 'wants', by moral suasion and by good conditions. He agreed that details of the Labour Rules, such as the provision of blankets and food to natives who returned home at night might be discussed perhaps by local boards, but he refused to depart from the main principles. He pointed out the existing government help in recruiting which he said would continue; he rejected a maximum wage but promised to examine the legal issues over desertion. Settlers at the meeting then put forward a variety of views; these included demands for 'a strong man . . . who could make the natives work' in the government, compulsory clothing, pass laws, increased hut and poll tax, reduction of wages and reserves, and registration to prevent desertion. They spoke angrily of mass desertion after payment of advances, of P.W.D. rates being higher than farm rates, and of the advisability of recourse to the *kiboko*. Several speakers claimed chiefs who formerly helped them now no longer did so and some also spoke of their resentment at Government 'interference' and the sympathetic hearing of African complaints; others alleged that the cost of labour had been doubled by the rules. The Rev. Dr. H. Scott favoured legislation to encourage the African to work by means of a tax equal to one month's wages, with a tax of two months' wages for those who did not work. Delamere concluded by demanding legalized methods to force Africans to work. The meeting finally agreed to a long resolution which demanded that: (1) the Labour Rules be withdrawn; (2) new ones should be formed by a central board, with employer representation, and be alterable by district boards; (3) contracts should entail obligations and a minimum term of service; (4) 'luxuries' (blankets) should be paid by the employee on a hire-purchase basis; (5) Labour matters should be removed from the Department of Native Affairs; (6) the rate of wages should not exceed that of 1906; (7) government departments should observe the new rules; (8) all officers should be strictly commanded to 'encourage' labour; and that the central board should discuss further means of 'encouragement'; and (9) a Native Commissioner 'of tried Colonial experience' (a code-word for South Africa) be appointed to head the Native Affairs Department. Sadler, winding up, rejected charges of lack of sympathy and promised to consider the points. He weakly said he could not be responsible for what one officer in Kikuyuland was saying, but he reiterated that he could not support any forcing of labour, and affirmed his view that any rise in wages was due to the safari firms rather than to the Labour Rules.

All then adjourned for refreshment, Delamere having called a further afternoon meeting at which in an excited state he presided. He urged the settlers to demonstrate for a reply to the morning resolution. About a hundred headed by Delamere then set off for Government House. One of Delamere's principal supporters was a South African unofficial member of the Legislative Council, A. Baillie, another was Bowker of the flogging incident. Bowker was apparently wearing his customary headgear, 'a battered felt hat on which was mounted a small leopard's head, the two yellow canines bared by the snarling lips'. In the grounds of Government House, this apparition, with Lord Delamere shouting 'Tomorrow, tomorrow, tomorrow. It is always tomorrow. We are sick of tomorrow. We are not schoolboys, we demand an immediate answer on the spot and nothing else', must have created a remarkable impression.[47] The settlers refused to send a deputation indoors to see the Governor, so Sadler appeared amid cries of 'Resign' and a disorderly shouting match ensued.

The next day Sadler met the deputation which offered no apology for the march. Sadler refused to withdraw the rules, but said they might be modified in detail and agreed to a board of inquiry to consist of a number of senior officials with six unofficials. In detail and in reply to the specific points of the Association resolution, he said that: (1) a central board must await the success of his projected local boards; (2) the Master and Servants Ordinance contained obligations for both parties, but that the proposed giving of judicial powers to headmen might help the apprehension of deserters; (3) payment might be asked for a blanket; (4) labour must remain an administration matter; (5) he would try to check any rise in wages but he could not fix legal maxima; (6) government departments would conform to the new rules; (7) 'encouragement' was the government's policy but that he would issue a further circular; (8) local boards might discuss legal measures if they wished, and (9) he refused to consider appointing an outside official. He then proceeded to suspend Delamere and Baillie from the Legislative Council. The Colonial Office fully supported his actions, emphasizing that though details of the rules might be discussed in Legislative Council, the main principles must be observed. Further settler meetings of protest inevitably followed and Delamere and Baillie both demanded an impartial inquiry.

Sadler reported to the Colonial Office that in his judgement the Labour Rules were only a pretext by which Delamere had been able to appeal to the feelings of a number of people discontented for political reasons, and to some poorer settlers 'on their beam ends' for whom the labour question was an expression of general bitterness. He maintained that the good employer had still no labour supply difficulty but admitted that the supply had been reduced by the correction of abuses by chiefs and by the rival attraction of safaris, and he added another memorandum by Hollis on the work of his department.

This second memorandum provides the best evidence now available as to the extent of the abuses of the whole labour system at the time. Hollis stated that his attention was first drawn to the need for protection by the discovery at Londiani of a number of dead Kikuyu on a road leading from an Asian railway contractor's camp of 'miserable grass huts neither windproof nor watertight'. The labourers were frequently given no blankets, strange food and uncongenial work. He proceeded from this discovery to a general inquiry, and exposed the steadily worsening system of forced labour for government and for a number of private employers. At first only goats of reluctant men had been confiscated, but soon armed force was resorted to in 'scores of cases', men being seized and sent to work for any contractor or settler who applied, often not being told where they were going. As late as April 1907 he had found a whole gang of men illegally sentenced to fourteen days' hard labour for refusing to work for an unpopular employer. Asian contractors had proved the most disgraceful employers and recruiters, with frequent beating, poor feeding and housing, and ill-treatment generally leading to many deaths. Pay promised was often not given. Sometimes workers had tried to run away, those successful dying in large numbers of hunger and fatigue. Sadler on learning of this state of affairs had issued a circular prohibiting coercion, and his department had begun the work of reform. The worst contractors had been replaced, the P.W.D. and other employers had been told to feed and house their men which the P.W.D. was now doing commendably, the High Court was insisting on the provisions of the Master and Servants Ordinance, the police were ceasing to arrest any native on the chance he might be a deserter, inquiries were begun by Hollis's assistants if they suspected an injustice, and the Labour Rules had led to an improvement in conditions in many places. Hollis graphically summed up this side of his work by saying that now 'natives are no longer flogged or imprisoned for a breach of contract unless they are guilty'. He did not however add that such flogging was illegal unless the employee had absconded with his master's property. On the labour shortage itself Hollis noted the African preferences for work at the Coast, portering and growing their own crops. He thought good management was still the key to recruiting, noting some considerate employers could still pay a low wage and have no shortage.

The Colonial Office was shocked as the memorandum had arrived at a time when the Foreign Office were busy taking King Leopold's Congo to task, Sir Edward Grey demanding reserves large enough for considerable population expansion over two generations. One official minuted 'It must on no account be published' on Hollis's memorandum and commented 'One might almost say there is no activity in the Congo—except mutilation—which cannot be matched in our Protectorate' and 'King Leopold would, I think, give a large sum for this document in answer to our representations'. The new Colonial Secretary, Lord Crewe, decided to wait for further information before he acted.

In Nairobi Sadler was precariously trying to please everyone. The labour inquiry board had not been a great help. It had recommended an adult male poll tax to replace the hut tax, the receipt for which was to act both as a pass and an identity document, with a remission of tax for work done for a month for a European or other approved employer. It gave approval to the revised Labour Rules, agreed that improvement in camps and living conditions were to be desired and it requested that government officers should remove the impression that government did not want the natives to work. It also recommended that heads of departments co-operate with the settlers in preventing wage increases. Lastly the board recommended land areas in the reserves be limited to the needs of the tribes at the time.

The revised rules were published in April.[48] The chief differences were that employees had now to pay for their own blanket which would only be provided if the employee or a district officer specifically asked for it; the requirements to provide food and cooking utensils were less specific, and the general phrasing of the requirements in respect of water, food for a return journey, medical aid and sureties were less exacting though the principles remained unaltered. The small differences between these rules, approved by the settlers' own representatives, and the earlier rules, is a measure of the general excitement and hysteria.

After attending several meetings in different parts of the country, Sadler recommended to the Colonial Office that a poll tax be introduced for males not paying hut tax, with arrangements for remission; he thought this system would provide in the main a solution to the farmers' problems, though he was obliged to add that Hollis, Ainsworth and two other provincial commissioners had opposed a poll tax. At the Coast he recommended the importation of two to four thousand indentured Asians. He thought these measures along with the inclusion in the letters of appointment to chiefs and headmen of a duty of impressing on the native the desirability of working for a wage, would solve the problem.

Sadler also restated the policy of providing direct government assistance for the private employer. Hollis was now disturbed by it; and in London questions were being asked in Parliament, with allegations of forced labour for private employers and government alike, with men seized in night raids on villages. In August 1908 the Colonial Office sent Sadler a reply in which he was told that it was not the duty of government to recruit for private employers, a practice which Crewe had 'no hesitation in condemning', the task of government being to lay down regulations for the proper treatment of labour, and then 'to stand aside, leaving the settlers to make their own arrangements'. On the other detailed proposals of Sadler, a selective poll tax not to exceed 2 rupees was accepted, as in principle was remission, 'it being clearly understood that exemption arises from work done irrespective of the race or status of the employer' or work done on a self-employed basis. The request for Asian labour was refused, but the Colonial Office agreed that Nyasa labour might be imported under certain conditions. Sadler's despatch of 19 May and the Colonial Office reply were both tabled in the Legislative Council.[49]

But neither for the first nor the last time, Colonial Office policy, set out in a despatch and incorporated in a government circular to officials, remained only a partial success. The force of the Colonial Office view was weakened by Sadler's circular, as although it banned coercion, the text had also called on chiefs to advise men to go out to work. Further, the duties of headmen appointed under the Village Headmen Ordinance had been already set out formally and publicly in the *Official Gazette*; these duties included *inter alia* the specific charge 'to encourage and advise his people to work for the current rate of wages'.[50]

In December 1908 the Executive Council, faced with this conflict between earlier promises and local pressures which were in direct contradiction of the Colonial Office instructions, considered the question of help for the private employer again and produced an ambiguous compromise decision: that settlers should be encouraged to make their own arrangements but that until new legislation had been prepared, it 'would be better to adhere to what has already been stated'.[51] To the district officer in the field this policy at best was vague and left him with neither clear guidance on what he should do nor defence against charges by the settler of obstruction. Nevertheless, unsatisfactory though the various instructions may have been, overall the work of Hollis and his staff and the evident concern behind the instructions appear to have eliminated the worst abuses. For the rest of Sadler's governorship 'encouragement', no doubt practised in most if not all the more densely populated areas, seems to have operated more humanely.

The Colonial Office could therefore justly claim a partial success, with Sadler a weak but by no means totally ineffective ally. Hollis wrote in his April 1908 memorandum perhaps to stiffen the resolve of his master, 'I have no hesitation in saying that by the abolition of forced labour His Excellency has done more to render the natives of this Protectorate happy than any of his predecessors'. Certainly the triangle of a reforming Colonial Office, a governor perhaps weak but nevertheless when alerted concerned with the welfare of his people, and a senior official with the necessary zeal achieved some temporary reform. No comparable improvement was to be repeated for many years to come and then only after much hardship.

The real benefit to the ordinary man can be well seen in a further report by Hollis on labour conditions in July 1909.[52] Hollis, reviewing two years work of his department (to which three more assistants had been added), contrasted the conditions of 1907 and 1909. He said that in most camps he had had no complaints either from employers or employees, the men were now well-fed and contented, with increased wages and with contractors receiving more for their contracts so enabling proper payments to be made and better overseers to be employed. Hollis recommended that the government should now withdraw from all forms of recruiting.

The provincial labour boards were set up in 1908–9; they included strong unofficial representation. Their chief functions became on the settler side to ensure that the government continued to 'encourage' labour and even more important to peg wage rates; and on the government side to ensure 'encouragement' did not lead to abuse. Hollis's activities in the labour field incurred the wrath of the local press; 'the pious fooling of Mr Hollis' and the 'fatuous Exeter Hall ridden policies of the government' were contrasted with 'the first impulse to civilisation . . . given by the Good God himself when he drove Adam and Eve from the Garden and forced them to work'.[53] Sadler also received his share of abuse, and his apparent weakness led the Colonial Office to transfer him elsewhere in 1909.[54]

Girouard and Belfield, 1908–12

The arrival of Sadler's successor, Sir Percy Girouard, coincided with increased economic development due to a number of factors, the chief of which were the improved world trading conditions producing further public and private United Kingdom investment, and locally a rise in the world price of coffee at a time when many plantations were maturing. Sisal production, too, expanded in quantity and more settlers began to grow maize. The number of settlers increased slowly but steadily; more small processing industries were started, and in 1911 the imperial government authorized loans for the improvement of the railway system and the provision of piped water for Mombasa. By 1910–11 this expansion required a labour force of some 70,000 men at certain peak periods, a figure which rose to over 85,000 by 1912.

Girouard was an extremely able, clear-thinking administrator of the very greatest energy, but his character was at times brittle and unstable; he had a short temper made hastier by prolonged work in Africa, and like many compulsive workers he was impatient of those who did not work as hard as he did. Difficulties in his private life led him to close social contacts with Delamere and other settler leaders, an arrangement foreshadowing the post-war 'government by agreement'. Despite real ability and success in other fields Girouard never faced up to the full social consequences for labour of development by settlement. Indeed he wished to follow the South African pattern of a Native Affairs Department actively 'encouraging' men to work for settlers, thinking in terms of a 'Recruitment of Native Labour Ordinance' and a 'Masters Union' of employers for recruiting. The Colonial Office offered no support for this latter proposal and it found little favour locally. Nevertheless Girouard personally urged chiefs to recruit labour, and his administrative officers returned to the old practices of 'encouragement' with few questions asked, even giving chiefs quotas of men which their areas were to produce. Girouard's views on land, taxation and policy in the reserves also coincided with the views of the more moderate of the settlers and served their interests. His work included a general improvement in the efficiency of the administration, measures to strengthen the authority of the chiefs, instructions to administrative officers on their duties which for example included a requirement that provincial commissioners were to include notes on where labour might be obtained in their handing-over reports, and increases in the number of these officers in the more heavily populated reserve areas to tax and perhaps 'encourage'; these actions all greatly helped the settler and his labour supply. Girouard further viewed without enthusiasm the work of Hollis's staff, Hollis's post being abolished in 1912 and the staff merged with the field administration shortly afterwards.

Girouard proved a disappointment to the Colonial Office and he resigned in 1912 for a mixture of personal and official reasons. He was replaced immediately by H. C. (later Sir Henry Conway) Belfield, an elderly official from Malaya. Belfield remained Governor until 1917, a capable desk administrator whose despatches reveal little sympathy or understanding of African problems and who easily succumbed to settler pressures.

The changed style of the administration is noticeable from a number of sources, the best, to be examined later, being the evidence to the Barth Commission.[55] Leys alleged that officers unpopular with local settlers because of low labour returns were already being posted to remote stations with diminished chances of promotion. As early as February 1910 a farmer's letter to the *Leader* noted that Ainsworth, now provincial commissioner in Nyanza, had by sending an officer out on tour with him enabled the writer to recruit over 250 labourers.[56] But Ainsworth almost certainly only helped employers he trusted, as the next year he sent a spirited circular to farmers in his area bluntly putting the blame for a labour shortage on to bad employers in the area who held the 'idea that even work oxen are to be treated far better than natives', and alleging poor food, thin blankets, beatings, wretched huts and very long hours.[57]Ainsworth's circular was to lead to a furious reaction from the local colonists' association and the central Convention of Associations in Nairobi.

'Encouragement' was applied when new areas came under administration for the first time. Belfield's view on the subject can be seen in his November 1912 speech to the Legislative Council, where he stated that it was the duty of the native 'to contribute something either by means of labour or pecuniary equivalent towards the development of the Protectorate'.[58]

The views of Girouard and Belfield on taxation were identical, expressed for example at their clearest by Belfield in 1913: 'We consider that taxation is the only possible method of compelling the native to leave his reserve for the purpose of seeking work . . . Only in this way can the cost of living be increased for the native.'[59] The 1908 proposal for a 2 rupee poll tax was therefore changed to one for 3 rupees; it was to be paid in coin by men not liable to hut tax and collection was begun in 1910. As in general the 'hut' was the mark of the adult married man, poll tax was thought particularly suited to 'encourage' the younger man to work and it was applied at first to 'labour-producing' areas. In special circumstances where commutation was allowed, labour was acceptable at the rate of one month's work for the government for each 3 rupees due, the first example perhaps of the linking of the government's coercive powers for its own needs with those of the private employer by making the former less attractive. At the same time tax collection was made more efficient, a number of officers were given powers to demand the production of tax receipts, and more severe penalties for non-payment were prescribed.[60] In general, although the chiefs' commission was now abolished, the system by which district officers both collected tax and 'encouraged' labour to earn the tax money was liable to abuse, and taxation accelerated the trend to individualization already noted.[61] By 1913 some evidence was beginning to appear that taxation was having the reverse effect to that intended, reducing rather than increasing the number of work-seekers, and just before the outbreak of war in 1914 Ainsworth was appointed by the Governor to inquire into native taxation.[62] If settler leaders had had their way, taxation to recruit labour would have been extended to indirect taxation, demands being made that freight rates on *amerikani* cloth and blankets be increased and the African liquor and *ngomas* be taxed heavily. Hints were also dropped to chiefs that if they failed to produce labourers direct taxation would increase.[63]

Whether an appreciable amount of the money paid in tax should be spent in the African reserves became in these years as great a matter of controversy as the reserves themselves. The controversy centred chiefly around the work of Ainsworth in Nyanza. He set about a deliberate and planned policy of improving African agriculture in his reserves, a policy extending to the distribution of free seed. His general views were throughout his career entirely consistent—Africans must work harder if they were to advance into the twentieth century, but the choice of work in the reserves for themselves or outside for a wage was to be a free one, views foreshadowing the 'Dual Policy' of the nineteen-twenties. Ainsworth's ability to foresee the long term effects of government policies was strictly limited, but he had a warm human concern for African peoples and saw no objection to working for a wage for a farmer if the conditions of employment were satisfactory; indeed he thought such work could only benefit race relations. But he believed that in the reserves African peasant proprietorship should be encouraged as the basis for advancement, and under his guidance Nyanza province quickly became a large producer of maize, simsim and hides, though an attempt to grow cotton was a failure.[64] Ainsworth's work, derisively called his 'zoo policy' by the settlers, came early under fire for discouraging labourers. Ainsworth justified his views in a letter to Delamere: 'I am convinced that the more industrious the natives become in their own areas the more likely they are to labour outside . . . an industrious native is always wanting something; his wants extend to luxuries . . .[65]

But it is an open question whether this view remained entirely correct in the last pre-war years when the total numbers required at work each year were still increasing. Settlers and the local press complained that from 1911 onwards diminishing numbers of Nyanza men were coming out to work, for which Delamere personally blamed Ainsworth. The whole issue is complicated by the emotional factor as some impoverished farmers sought to discredit Ainsworth's policy by producing irrational criticisms rather than careful assessments of the labour supply. Also Nyanza men were used under varying degrees of coercion by the government and its contractors for some of the hardest work in the country with the express object of leaving the Kikuyu available for farmer employers.[66] The hard public work, in addition to removing Nyanza men from farmers' notice, may well have discouraged many from life outside the reserves. Ainsworth himself claimed the figure of 28,496 men who registered for work in Nyanza Province in 1913–14 represented an increase as great as 57 per cent on the previous year. But the extended family system of tribal societies could support the subtraction of a surprisingly large percentage of their adult and most enterprising men (the former warrior age-groups) relatively easily, provided the subtraction was not for periods much longer than six months, and providing the percentage did not exceed a figure which could vary by tribe, but in general probably lay between 15 per cent and 25 per cent. These two provisions largely operated at the time, the P.W.D. for example in 1912 employed some 40,000 men each year but only 6,000 at any one moment. Ainsworth however did not appear to recognize these qualifying conditions in defending his policy as a basis for the future.

Furthermore, the fact that Ainsworth's Nyanza policy was not wholly successful ensured that if they wanted to do so or found it necessary, an appreciable if not entirely sufficient number of Nyanza men still preferred to come forward to work to earn cash. They worked for a particular target such as tax, a consumer article or stock, or to see the world, or because the earning of money was easier by labour than by cultivation at home. But in sum it cannot either be said with certainty that peasant production was prejudicing seriously the labour supply, or that the labour requirement even artificially stimulated was seriously if at all retarding the contemporary level of peasant production, although a future divergence of interests was discernible. No comparable effort to develop resources in other tribal areas was made at all, although despite settler demands the size of these areas was not further restricted.

The last of the major weapons, legislation, was also strengthened. A new Master and Servants Ordinance came into force in 1910.[67] Only two of Elgin's major objections to the 1906 ordinance—the maximum length of contracts, reduced from three years to two, and the abolition of payment in kind—received attention and the number of offences for which an employee was liable to a heavy fine or imprisonment was increased, though employer penalties were reduced. The provisions of the revised Labour Rules (which had provided for food and housing only if the employee could not return home at night, and fixed no standards for food, housing or medical care) were included in the ordinance, as was a firm obligation on the employer to provide the cost of the return journey and food for its duration to a man's place of engagement. Two new features were introduced—a statutory requirement that labour agents and their staff were to be licensed before they might operate, and provision for apprenticeship. Apprenticeship had had an evil reputation in South Africa where it had often become abused as cheap juvenile labour, and certain provisions of this ordinance, that 'apprentices' might be children aged nine to sixteen or mature men and that the trades for which they might be employed and trained could include domestic service, seem to indicate a similar intention. In the event, however, the apprenticeship provisions appear to have been little used by private employers other than mission industrial schools, perhaps the requirement for a magistrate's approval proving an effective deterrent. Provision was also made for some magisterial powers, initially only the attesting of contracts other than apprenticeships and the issue of warrants for arrest, to be shared with newly created justices of the peace. The intention was that the J.P.s should be local European farmers or businessmen, and that these evolving powers would therefore pass into settler hands. Government officers continued to inspect work-places, but such inspection was necessarily limited by the number of district officers available, the accessibility of the sites and the priority that an individual district commissioner gave to the work, a factor which suffered considerably after Hollis's departure. From the employee's point of view, they had been better placed with the 1906 ordinance, the first Labour Rules and Hollis's department than under Girouard or Belfield and the new ordinance.

The government continued to try to meet its own needs to the irritation of settlers by a greater degree of coercion for work outside the reserves and by an extension of the communal labour system within. In 1910 compulsory labour or roads or other works in lieu of a communal fine for offences such as harbouring criminals was permitted; in the same year was also passed the Roads in Native Reserves Ordinances by which men of an area might be directed to turn out and work for not more than six days per quarter.[68] In 1912 under the Native Authority Ordinance, the purposes for which men could be called out for six days a quarter was extended to 'communal projects', which could include water courses, minor irrigation and dams.[69] The measure of compulsion applied by officials to chiefs for the provision of government safari porters also increased.[70] Some ambitious officials trying to develop an area began to require men to leave their homes for communal labour, on occasions not observing the legal limit of six days per quarter. A hard-pressed chief might turn to women and juveniles for communal work; a visiting Scots minister found a girl of twelve obliged to work eighteen days as a tribal police hut-cleaner away from her home in the Nyeri district.[71] For the large number of men required for work in the service of the two big employing departments outside the reserves, the Uganda Railway and the P.W.D., the shortfall of voluntary labour, between 10 per cent and 20 per cent for the Railway and 50 per cent for the P.W.D. was 'procured by District Commissioners' in the words of Ainsworth.[72] Prison labour, too, was used at this time for work such as draining marsh land and light railway construction.

The conditions of work for the Railway's contractors and in the P.W.D. remained very far from satisfactory, though valiant attempts were made to improve them by the latter's director, W. McGregor Ross. It was in the service of a railway contractor in August 1910 that there occurred Kenya's first organized African industrial strike.[73] One thousand red-blanketed Nyanza labourers working for a ballast contractor at Sultan Hamud stopped work and marched to Nairobi where they complained of excessive work to the district commissioner. This officer tried in vain to pacify the men and then marched them to the town gaol where all were charged with offences under the Master and Servants Ordinance. The next day the town magistrate heard both sides, but remained unsympathetic, sentencing the strikers' leader to twelve lashes and two months' imprisonment; the remainder then promised to resume work. A second strike, this time of direct employees of the Railway, took place in 1912 being settled equally drastically. The majority of railway goods shed workers in Nairobi went on strike because an extra hour had been added to their work. The Railway rejected the men's claim for overtime; those who refused to work on the existing terms were dismissed.[74] An indignant letter to the *Leader* in April 1913 described the thrashing and imprisonment by a district commissioner of some P.W.D. labourers who had come to claim their unpaid wages, conduct which the writer contrasted with the 75 rupees fine of a farmer who had thrashed his cook.[75] Some settler evidence to the Barth Commission noting leaking huts and thin blankets revealed examples of failure of the P.W.D. in remote areas to implement McGregor Ross's reforms which included the banking of earnings, proper train accommodation to work sites, and adequate food. The known sympathy of McGregor Ross for Africans began to attract settler criticism to his department. Settlers complained that the government paid wages at the end of a month if the ticket showed twenty-five or twenty-six days work completed—i.e. if Sunday had been left a free day; they demanded thirty working days be required for payment, a demand resisted by the department. As late as 1914 settler criticism, the 'standard rates' system and compulsory recruitment enabled the department to employ in Nyanza large gangs of labour on road work at a rate as low as 2 rupees, despite all its director's good intentions.[76]

Up to the end of the 1910–11 financial year the Railway carried the labourers of its own contractors free; in 1910–11 this had amounted to 28,635 men. From April 1911 contractors had to pay rail fares with no doubt consequent pressure to oblige their labour to work for a longer period. From 1907 the Railway also offered concession rates for labourers in batches of ten or more, its 1911 advertisements noting these men might have to travel by goods trains. To the Railway however should perhaps go the credit for the first attempt at the provision of some form of superannuation arrangements for permanently employed Africans. The Uganda Railway Provident Fund, established shortly before the war and intended chiefly for Asians, seems to have included a number of Africans among its contributory members.

It was decided in 1911 to exploit the soda ash deposits at Magadi for which the building of a special railway line was necessary. By March 1912 the work was engaging some 50 Europeans and 3,500 Africans; at first the Africans were mainly from Nyanza. As the work progressed the supply became reduced and problems mounted despite the relatively generous wage of 8 rupees. The food supplied was very poor—2 lb. of maize meal per day and beans, with rice after three months—insufficient to maintain work in the conditions of extreme heat relieved only by torrential rain. Leys commented that 'a considerable number of them [the labourers] could hardly crawl along the road', and noted complaints of sickness, long hours, the *kiboko,* bad food and sour water.[77] The Embu district commissioner found that 500 men had receved two months' wages for three months' work. Only a part of the labour force, too, was housed in iron huts, many were in miserable grass ones. Labour began to desert 'by the hundreds', and progress slowed down. Two thousand men were to be imported from Mozambique, but a plague outbreak along the Coast prevented the arrival of all but a hundred leaving Paulings, the construction company, and the protectorate authorities with the problem unresolved. Harcourt refused to sanction the importation of Asians and recruiters using various methods were engaged to secure men for the railway wherever they could do so. Rumours about the conditions acted as a deterrent to the labour supply. One of the many reasons why men would not volunteer for any work was fear of being sent to Magadi. At the end of 1912 the Magadi line works were engaging over 4,000 men, but even at this figure they were 25 per cent short. Despite the appointment of a government inspector the conditions did not improve greatly in 1913; during the first eight months there were over 1,000 admissions to hospital from an average strength of less than 3,000, and at least 157 deaths of which 111 were caused by dysentery. Many others must have died unrecorded, with yet others returning sick and emaciated to Nyanza. In early 1913 there was one doctor with no trained help for the 3,000 men spread over ninety-two miles of railway line work. 'Some wretched huts with hopelessly inadequate accommodation did duty for hospitals', they were severely overcrowded (one hut designed for 50 held 140), the sick lay on the bare ground with neither blankets, mats, pure water nor latrine buckets. In mid-1913 the contractor appointed another two doctors and made some improvement, but at Magadi itself conditions remained lamentable, men 'living under sheets of iron in holes and corners all over the place'.[78] Conditions on the Thika railway extension were only a little better, the supply of labourers being assisted by the use of prisoners and tax defaulters, these latter in material conditions superior to the paid labourers. A small number died in the rainy seasons, with the likelihood that an unknown number perished later from malaria on their return home. In addition to illness, railway work was liable to accidents, a few men being killed or injured each year. On the Magadi line in one such accident a train ran away killing eighteen men and injuring twenty-nine, and a small number were blinded in a blasting accident. It is very doubtful whether the relatives of the nine Africans killed or even those blinded received any compensation at all.

It is at first sight surprising, in view of these conditions on the Railway and in contrast to McGregor Ross's efforts to improve conditions in the P.W.D., that the former had the better voluntary recruiting rate. Pure railway work (as opposed to construction) had however a fascination for Africans once their fears of smoke-belching monsters were overcome, and men used literally to walk along the railway line to join.[79] Further for an intelligent man the pay was usually better.

The search for tractable manpower led to demands for foreign labour, attractive for its prospect of long contracts, as well as attempts to retain any foreign labour already at work in the protectorate, and where possible discouragement of protectorate men going to Zanzibar and Pemba to pick cloves. Some of the Mombasa Nyamwezi returned to German East Africa, a loss regretted by settlers and only partially offset by the limited E.A.P. employer recruiting permitted in German territory. About 500 Baganda had worked in Kisumu from 1903 to 1906; other Uganda labour were working in the Lumbwa. In 1911 the Uganda government permitted 2,000 men to work on a sisal estate at Voi, but all had returned home two years later. This gain was more than offset by many Nyanza men preferring to go to Uganda for work. After the 1908 troubles the Nyasaland government was approached for labourers, but the 11.50 rupee rate of pay proposed was unacceptable to the settlers.[80] Inquiries were made in Aden for 'Arab coolies' but only a very few ever arrived. A further effort to find foreign African labour for which the Colonial Office was partly to blame was the recruiting of over 250 homeless Somalis, with their families, for work on Coast sisal estates at 8 rupees per month in 1913. These Somalis were brought to Mombasa in a filthy and overcrowded ship; a number deserted on arrival, being imprisoned on recapture. On the estates there were faction fights, complaints and a riot when the police had to open fire, killing two Somalis.[81]

For many, particularly at the Coast, the Asian coolie still appeared the simple answer, 500 being brought for railway work in 1906. Of these many were of such poor physique as to be useless. A further 900 were brought in 1907–8, but 300 of them went on strike over pay almost immediately. Following the recommendations of the Sanderson Committee on Asian emigrant labour, the British government forbade any recruiting for the private employer, only permitting recruitment for government work. On this basis the protectorate government resumed recruitment of Asians for work at Kilindini. The indentures provided the same terms as the Railway, a three year contract at a rate of 45 rupees for artisans, free passages, rations, housing and medical facilities. The war intervened before many men were actually engaged, but British government apprehensions were confirmed by a strike in July 1914 of nearly all the railway workshop Asians, together with many from the P.W.D. and some in commercial firms over the new requirement to pay non-native poll tax at the heavy rate of 15 rupees. The Asians claimed their terms of service had contained no reference to taxation; the strike lasted for over a week and was only terminated by substantial concessions.[82]

Asian labour was most needed in the skilled and semi-skilled labour spheres, where only a handful of Africans were available. Until 1911 African education lay in mission hands. After the publication of Professor Frazer's report on education which noted *inter alia* that skilled African labour would be cheaper than skilled Asian, some missions received from 1909 a small subsidy for craft courses. The Church of Scotland had from 1903 been offering training in masonry and carpentry and other missions followed this example. In 1912 the C.S.M. opened a new workshop at Kikuyu. The numbers rose to 50 in the following year. The Nairobi St. Austin's Mission trained some 25 building apprentices in a three year course, and other missions in Nyanza, at Nyeri and at Kijabe also offered similar technical education to small numbers. A P.W.D. Industrial Training Depot opened in 1911, and by 1914 it was training 30 boys as carpenters. Further expansion was prevented by a shortage of space, but the P.W.D. claimed in addition that a 'considerable number of African handicraftsmen more or less thoroughly trained' were earning 35 rupees (without rations) in various offices of the department.[83] The Railway trained men in a number of crafts, the postal authorities established a small training school, and in 1913 the Government Industrial School at Machakos began producing a small number of artisans. But the total numbers in training remained very small;

the P.W.D. examined 101 mission boys, passing 79, in 1913–14, and the protectorate's dependence on Asian semi-skilled and skilled labour became greater.[84] The presence of settler representatives on the protectorate's Education Board ensured that government support for African education would favour craft curricula.

Conditions for workers in the larger towns in these early years also reflected the need for labour at the cheapest possible rates. Although purely African reserve areas were nearer to Nairobi, Mombasa and Kisumu than later, so enabling many labourers to return to their own society and homes at night, conditions for those who dwelt in the towns were very poor. Since conveniently most town workers returned each night to the reserves, the African areas of the large towns remained unplanned for some time. Nairobi's early African areas were scattered villages of huts of mud or flattened paraffin tins with thatch or tin roofs, around which chicken and goats wandered, or the long lines of tin huts of the Railway and P.W.D., with no windows and only one door through which little sun or air penetrated. The most important of the villages was Pangani which provided lodgings of the very roughest type, *hotelis* and brothels described by the Principal Medical Officer as 'an unwholesome medley of native restaurants, dilapidated pedlars' shops, filthy latrine buckets and ill-laid drains'.[85] These *hotelis* were the first of the rapidly increasing number of lodging-houses which sprang up to serve Nairobi's migrant labour population in conditions which were unsatisfactory both materially and morally. The town committee also owned a few blocks of rooms known as *landies* which they either used for their own staff or let out at 5 rupees per month. Many employees of Asian traders slept on the floor of the shop or store, in a draughty corridor or a tumble-down shack in the garden. A centre at Pumwani for Africans working in the city was planned in 1911 but not opened until 1921. A small number of Africans and Asians died from periodic plague epidemics in Nairobi and other towns. Conditions in Kisumu and Mombasa were even more unhealthy than Nairobi, being exacerbated by the climate.[86] Sanitation in towns, camps and labour lines was to remain a problem for many years. Water-closets were too costly, all other types proved offensive and had to be situated some distance from sleeping spaces. Many workers did not care to traverse the distance, particularly in the bush at night. The latrines themselves required either deep pits or frequent digging and covering of shallower trenches, both varieties needing a daily washing down, supervision and some expense to be satisfactory. More often than not the arrangements were neglected by overseers and employers. In towns the problem was complicated by space and land values. The result was enteric fever and malaria, caused by soil contamination and inadequate surface drainage.

The Nairobi municipal committee, a wretched employer, was faced in January 1913 with a demand from its African employees, led by one described as 'extremely aggressive', for a wage increase of 2 rupees on their wages of 5 rupees plus *posho*. One councillor talked of 'the thin end of the wedge of trade unionism' as a joke, and the committee grudgingly granted an increase of 1 rupee to all employees with more than twelve months' service.[87]

In general though wage rates played a relatively small part in the supply of labour; the requirement that the labour remain cheap prevented any operation of the laws of supply and demand in a number of ways. One was simply that the government was so large an employer in relation to the rest of the country that the rates which it and its contractors paid became in practice minimum wages. The contractors and the government were anxious for a cheap supply and used varying degrees of coercion to gain it; this 'minimum' rate therefore became a low one. Furthermore the fixing of these rates came under settler influence which aimed at making them also into local maximum wages. Employers generally could either not afford to pay more, or resented the paying of higher wages to labour they regarded as inefficient, or consciously or unconsciously feared a larger pay packet might affect their position of domination.[88] Demands were also made that where the government was paying by piece rates, these should be adjusted so that work should neither finish early in the day nor should the total earned be appreciably more than the current local rates. The table below shows how very little cash wages rose during the period 1903–14, although despite the real difficulties of consumer goods distribution the expanding economy should have yielded a greater rise.

MONTHLY WAGE RATE IN RUPEES TOGETHER WITH RATIONS TO THEIR APPROXIMATE RUPEE VALUE (shown as + RV)

Date	Unskilled labour			Domestic servants		Porters
	Coast	*Nairobi and Central Kenya*	*Rift Valley and Nyanza*	*Coast*	*Inland*	
1895–1901	10 + RV 3–4					10 + RV 3–4
1902–3	10–15 + RV 4–5	3–5 + RV 2–3	3–6 + RV 2–3	10–25 + RV 4–5	8–10 + RV 3–4	10 + RV 3–4
1904–6	Local: 10–15 + RV 6–8 Inland: 4–5 + RV 2–3	3–7 + RV 3–7	3–7 + RV 2–6	10–25 + RV 4–5	8–10 + RV 3–4	10–12 + RV 6–8 (Inland rate 6–10 + RV 4–7)
1908–11	Local: 12 + RV 7–8 Inland: 5–8 + RV 2–3	4–7 + RV 3–7	4–7 + RV 2–6	12–15 + RV 5–7	8–10 + RV 3–4	10–12 + RV 6–8 (Inland rate 8–10 + RV 4–7)
1912–14	Local: 12–14 + RV 7–8 Inland: 6–9 RV 7–8	5–8 + RV 3–8	5–8 + RV 3–8	12–15 + RV 5–7	10–15 + RV 4–6	10–12 + RV 6–8 (Inland rate 8–10 + RV 4–7)

Notes

1. There were considerable differences in engagement rates, hence the two figures noted. Construction and government contractors' rates, where labour was coerced, were frequently below the rates shown in this table. Often labour would be engaged at a low rate and receive a 1 or 2 rupees increase after a month or two months' work. Some employers would make adjustments in respect of blankets, fuel or hut-building materials supplied.
2. Men of proved reliability or skill received a higher rate, as did Swahilis at the Coast.
3. Juveniles often received a lower rate, as did very temporary labourers who could live at home.
4. Rations would only be provided when the employee lived away from his home.

In 1907, to endeavour to establish a common practice for government labour whether voluntary, coerced or compulsory, a meeting was held of senior government officers in Mombasa to discuss wages.[89] At this first meeting they could neither agree on a rate, nor whether to pay cash only, or cash with *posho* which latter the labourers preferred as they then had a minimum food supply. A second board was set up for inland labour. In May after further meetings rates of 2–4 rupees with *posho*, the exact sum being dependent on physique, were agreed for Kikuyu labour, and hours of work from 6 a.m. to 5 p.m. with one hour free at noon. Headmen received 1 cent per day extra for each member of their gangs, usually twenty-five. For the Coast a rate of 10 rupees for the first six months and 12 rupees thereafter, neither with *posho,* was fixed for Swahilis, and 4 rupees with *posho* for Kikuyu. Coast cart-pullers, called *hamalis,* were to receive 25 rupees. A rate of 4 rupees was fixed by the Railway for their Nyanza men.[90] These rates became known as the 'standard' or 'local' rates; they seem to have been unrealistically low at least for Mombasa. One irritated letter to the *East African Standard* observed that everyone knew that the effective engagement rate there was 12 rupees plus *posho*. Another of the settlers' accusations in the 1908 troubles was that some government departments were paying in excess of them—presumably made necessary by Hollis's checking of recruiting abuses and a consequent limited operation of the laws of supply and demand.

After the 1908 troubles, the new provincial labour boards with settler representation inherited the role of 'standard' rate wage-fixing from the purely official boards. Thus settlers were able to impose a fairly effective check against any rise both in wages and food in kind. The check was backed up by strong social pressures against any employers who wished to pay more; as these might amount to ostracism they could sometimes be very effective. The commercial safari firms, no doubt arguing that their work was casual, virtually ignored 'standard' rates. In 1908 the Colonists' Association objected to government departments giving rice to their porters, insisting on the cheaper and less nutritive maize meal. It is hardly surprising therefore that there was no official objection to a paragraph in the *Leader* in November 1911 which asked all employers to insert wage rates on testimonials so as to prevent labourers' seeking a higher wage on changing their work.[91] Both Girouard and Belfield also spoke out against any increase in wages.

Coinage presented problems for the labourer. When cental currency replaced annas and pice at the rate of 6 cts. for 1 anna in 1905, the change only yielded 96 cts. per rupee; employers could pass on their 4 per cent loss to employees in their pay packets. A new 1 cent coin disintegrated when in contact with perspiration, a fault only corrected after a number had been issued. Some men paid a wage fixed at a round sum in rupees were reluctant to change them into smaller coins until they had returned home. Cases were reported of men dying of starvation on their journey home, with 4 or 5 rupee pieces on their persons.[92]

One form of employment which was nearly always popular, often paid wages considerably above the general level and occupied very large numbers of male Africans of presentable appearance was domestic service. Domestic work connoted a degree of personal adoption for which many Africans were looking, it provided instruction in the new ways, it was paid better than manual labour, it offered perquisites unauthorized or authorized, and it was frequently near markets where wages could be spent. The servants at this time usually lived in mud or thatch huts at the end of the employer's garden. At work the house servant, in his long white *kanzu* and fez, or white or khaki drill suit and apparently in a trusted relationship with his master, carried great status. Even at times of labour shortages there were domestic work-seekers to be found outside government offices where in the larger towns a government Asian clerk ran a small labour exchange. In Nairobi there was also a private exchange. But not all those who so offered their services were suitable, and as early as 1903 Ainsworth in Nairobi tried to institute a system of official 'Service Books' designed to recommend the good servant and protect the employer from the bad; the scheme was not a success.[93] After a similar local attempt early in 1910, the Legislative Council passed an ordinance establishing a national scheme of domestic servants registration and reference to be applied by areas.[94] No area proclamations were made and the ordinance was repealed in 1924. Wages rose perceptibly despite a variety of attempts to peg them; these included the efforts of private exchanges, the abuse of testimonials written by irritated employers, either by a *double entendre* phrase (for example 'this cook is the absolute limit, just try him') or the deliberate insertion of the wage paid to warn any future employer to pay no more.

Three final points concerning domestic servants deserve note. For an increasing number of European and Asian town dwellers, particularly wives who might otherwise have held more liberal views, domestic servants would be the only Africans they met. The presence of male African servants when European house owners were out at work led to tensions and a need for public show by the European housewife.[95] The experiences of European householders and their wives, experiences of misunderstandings, of apparent negligence by the servant, of ignorance and occasionally of dishonesty, confirmed the Europeans' sense of superiority, particularly if in return they remained in their own eyes kind employers. Magistrates continued to award erring domestic servants ten strokes of the cane or six months or a year imprisonment for offences such as the theft of small sums of money. For African men also, domestic service stimulated the desire for personal household goods, sometimes producing the first signs of dissatisfaction with womenfolk at home in the reserves who knew nothing of tea, or shorts and shirts, or torches or bicycles. Lastly, the worst employers of domestic servants were the wealthier Somalis, who 'sold' their servants to each other leaving arrears of wages unpaid, or took Kikuyu juveniles into Jubaland province and thence on into slavery in Arabia, a practice stopped by the protectorate administration when it was discovered in 1916.

Labour needs progessively broke down the movement pass system, but in conjunction with the Vagrancy regulations they were periodically used in police inspections of villages and labour lines, when men without work or a pass would be returned to the reserves.[96]

By 1911 farm employers had begun to realize that the only way to keep a cheap labour force, particularly over the harvest seasons, was by the resident labour or 'squatter' (a South African term) system, as the labourer with his own plot on the employer's land would then not wish to depart. As a system it was inefficient, but it provided the labourer with a chance to live with his family and also with land on which to keep stock and grow food, which meant more to him than earning a wage. The system made a particular appeal to the Kikuyu, a number of families already finding that their home areas in Kikuyuland could not support their increased stock. Another appeal was that resident labour status led in some areas to instruction in bullock ploughing and in general the chance to learn about and perhaps acquire greatly superior types of animals and poultry; certainly bullock ploughing was first noticed in the Kikuyu Reserve in the years just before the war. The tenancy aspect of the relationship also had some similarity with the traditional Kikuyu *ahoi* system of tenure. As farms were opened up in the upper Rift Valley, some Nandi and Kipsigis also took to squatting. In their turn planter employers soon came to value the manure of squatter stock. When abuses had been removed, the system in the majority of cases provided both sides with psychological satisfaction and a sense of security to last overall until the late nineteen-twenties. To the employer, seeking dominance rather than efficiency, a client or protégé was preferable to an industrious worker, a client poorly paid in cash but often rewarded in kind more reassuring than the well-paid worker who might have his own independent ideas. However, by the very fact that master and squatters were working together in this relationship, farmers learnt to become a little more tolerant and understanding of their men and their personal problems. This understanding was facilitated by the presence of the squatter's family which often became the concern of the farmer's wife. The more intelligent farmers learnt that some respect for human dignity might ensure a good future labour supply.

This bond between resident labourers and farmer could sometimes evolve to the most profound depths, in which the labourers took immense pride and personal concern in the farm-owner's well-being, local standing, and even spiritual happiness. Karen Blixen's accounts show how involved this feudal relationship could become—the gesture of her labour force all appearing with a variety of injuries for her to treat after she, in despair, had burst into tears on finding her careful bandaging of an injured boy had been replaced by cowdung, and her help to those in great pain by the loan of a letter from the King of Denmark believed by her labourers to have immense pain-relieving powers.[97] Although a number of farmers and labourers, particularly before 1918, abused the trust placed in them, the change in the relationship from the harsh texture of the first decade of the century to the paternal regard of the third and fourth decades had nonetheless already begun in small measure by 1914.

For Africans, too, aware that times were changing fast and inexplicably, the resident labourer status at its best provided not simply an economic refuge in terms of land but also a psychological one in terms of adoption by a patron. This patron was one easily identifiable man who might be liked or disliked personally but was responsible for them as individuals. Resident labourers, for example, very rarely learnt individual farmers' surnames, the name given by the squatters indicating their personal opinion and esteem. A good farmer might be 'The Bwana who laughs', a hard worker might be 'Bwana the blacksmith', a greedy or bad employer 'Bwana Pig' or 'Eater of beans'. As patron or protector if the squatters were happy and scapegoat if they were not, the farmer acted as the long-stop for breaches of custom caused by the changed pattern of life; in his turn the farmer willingly accepted his requirement for responsibility and dependence, and saw this and any emulation of his personal habits as tribute to his greatness. However such little evidence as exists tends to suggest that after an initial period of marvel Africans became quickly less and less impressed by European science and technology and at the domestic level more concerned with human issues.

But initially the status was not always an easy one for the African squatter whose plot might be very different in geographical terms from his homeland, a fact not understood by the employer. Familiar crops which grew well at home might not grow at all, or grow to a fantastic size due to different seasons, altitudes, soil and rainfall. The European farmer might insist on a compulsory purchase, at a poor price, of the squatters own produce. Other squatters on the farm or the headman might be uncongenial or from different tribes. A Kikuyu squatter's wife, for example, might at first be miserable away from the communal life of Kikuyuland, in constant fear of spirits that shrieked from strange trees, fearful animals, icy cold nights, birds that could not be prevented from eating her millet, with all her efforts to grow bananas, beans and sweet potatoes in vain.[98] The Uasin-Gishu and Molo areas had particular difficulties in attracting squatters in the early years. Changes to new foods might lead to ill-being or illness, and make the period of adjustment a most trying and unhappy one before the relative prosperity in terms of cash and stock which many squatters attained was finally reached. On the other hand the resident labourer saw himself freed from his communal labour, his chiefs and tribal retainers, and from the magic or evil influences that many believed were directed against them at home. Instead, almost as pioneers, they were moving into areas where sheep and goats were both cheaper to purchase and freer from disease, and living primarily as a tenant rather than a labourer, a view which led to disillusion in the nineteen-twenties.

Another serious disadvantage of the resident labour system was the difficulties facing squatters who lost their job for accidental reasons such as the sale of the farm. The longer men worked the more were their ties with the reserve severed and the more difficult was it to move or to find land anywhere for their stock. The administration foresaw some of these problems; some officers feared also a loss of tax revenue from their districts, and in general supported the chiefs who tried to discourage resident labour.[99] The Barth Commission recommendations marked some guarded change in government attitudes, but official luke-warmness prevented the change-over of the majority of farm labourers to resident labour status prior to 1914, although the minority increased in size each year after 1909.[100]

As the numbers increased and more squatters and their wives came to know something of the European and his environment, past fears of his machines and belongings became replaced by curiosity, a desire to possess the smaller belongings, and a real pride in knowing their mechanism and purpose. On many farms women and juveniles began to assist with the lighter work at harvest seasons, in particular with coffee-picking; they would receive 2–5 rupees per month, or, with coffee, piece rates per bag. As they were usually either living at home in the reserve or with squatter husbands and farmers, food in kind was not usually given.

On the farm normal work would begin early, perhaps shortly after 6 a.m. when the farmer, speaking through his headman, would allocate the tasks for the day. The headman might be a Somali or a Swahili, later, as inland African men gained sufficient experience to be promoted, the headman might be of the same tribe as the majority of the labour force, and a local entrepreneur in his spare time. Certain tribes exhibited particular aptitudes, the Kikuyu for bullock ploughing, the Kamba for their intuitive grasp of machinery and, later, the Nandi for coffee-pruning. The Swahili had a reputation for adaptability, cheerfulness and honesty, the Somali for haughty arrogance. A Somali headman was expensive, not only in the cash wage he had to be paid, but also in the clothes and goods such as plates, knives and tea which he demanded partly for his comfort but also to show his superiority over the Africans. Some crops presented particular problems for an untrained labour force; sisal necessitated cross-ploughing before planting, and workers at the processing plant had to be supervised carefully. Scratches from the spiked ends of the leaves were liable to cause serious injury or to fester, which made sisal plantation work particularly unpopular. Work would continue to 4 or 5 p.m., having included a midday break. The *posho* or maize meal ration would usually be distributed weekly, but some farmers preferred monthly or daily distributions. A small number of farmers would supplement *posho* with meat from game animals of their own shooting, always a very important factor in the retention and recruiting of labour.

The system of labour recruiting by professional agents, many of dubious character and method, expanded under Girouard and Belfield. The government became concerned over abuses reported by chiefs and district administrators and in 1910 issued rules to control professional recruiters.[101] These rules were in effect a tightening up of the requirements of the Master and Servants Ordinance; they required a labour agent to inform provincial commissioners of their recruiting plans, to report to local district commissioners, and to supply free food to any men they might engage for their journey to the site. The recruiters' names were published in the *Official Gazette*, together with the duration of their permits, most of the names being European with a small number of Asians or Swahilis; the issue was by no means automatic and cases of refusal to issue permits occurred. But the local administrative staff was usually too small to enforce the requirements or supervise recruiters' activities at all, and the abuses continued. Recruiting was an expensive system; the farmer had to pay the recruiter his *per capita* fee, the cost of the rail fare and, if it was supplied, food. The cost might be equivalent to three months of the man's wages for a six months period of work. If the men deserted, the cost of fee, fare and food was lost. To add to the confusion sometimes labour recruits were decoyed by other labour agents on their journeys.

The 1912–13 Native Labour Commission

With the return to 'encouragement' and increases in taxation, together with closer administration to make both more effective, and a larger number of professional recruiters, it is not surprising that the years 1909 to 1911 saw little or no outcry claiming a labour shortage; the protectorate annual reports even noted that in some areas of the country labour was plentiful and cheap. In 1912, however, the signs of a labour supply difficulty reappeared. The early weeks passed with only a few complaints from the Coast, but the January meeting of the Convention of Associations revived demands for tax increases with remission for periods at work, and a labour bureau. In the second quarter of 1912, when simultaneously, new farmers were arriving, the railway system was being extended to Thika and Magadi, the Mombasa piped water delivery system was under construction, Mombasa harbour works were in progress, and near Nairobi, Muthaiga was being built, there was once more an apparent labour shortage although again the good employer suffered little difficulty.[102] To exacerbate the increased demands of the expanded economy, a very severe epidemic of cerebro-spinal fever was beginning in Kikuyuland, greatly reducing the number willing or able to work. In this situation the government's failure to accept the Convention's January resolutions came as a slap in the face, to which the July session of the Convention replied by demanding a commission of inquiry which the government accepted. On 1 October the commission's terms of reference were published. These were drawn in the widest terms covering all aspects of labour—the attitude of the administration, wage rates and methods of payment, the reserves, accommodation, food, medical facilities and transport, taxation, 'Kaffir farming' and recruitment of all types. The commission was specifically instructed to take evidence from employers and employees.

As originally appointed the commission's chairman was Judge J. W. (later Sir Jacob) Barth, the most able of the protectorate's judges, with as members A. F. Church, the Chief Engineer of the Railway; F. G. Hamilton, a district commissioner; B. G. Allen, a Nairobi solicitor; G. Williams, a farmer and chairman of the Convention; and two missionaries, Father G. Brandsma and the Rev. Dr. John Arthur.[103] Delamere was originally nominated; he declined on business grounds but was appointed again in May 1913. An additional official C. C. (later Sir Charles) Bowring, the Chief Secretary, and an additional unofficial, M. H. Wessels, a land agent and farmer were appointed in October and November 1912. The commission published an itinerary and called for evidence; the press and the Convention demanded that a new Native Affairs Department be established with a South African head, registration, lashes for employee offences and, lastly, that an end be put to the 'pampering of natives by the government' by allowing them any choice as to whether they should work.[104] In May 1913, probably as an alarmed reaction to scandalous conditions discovered at two Coast plantations, the government issued an extraordinary official communique on labour offering employers two pieces of advice.[105] The first was that when a gang of men were dismissed, the few who for sickness or other reasons had not worked the full period should be paid their entitlement with the others, to avoid difficulties in the reserve if a batch of men returned home with some members missing. The second was for a varied diet of properly cooked food, with one member of a large gang being appointed cook. The amateurishness of this communique, after ten years of settlement, stands in striking contrast to the detailed material on other contemporary matters filling the *Official Gazette*.

The *1912–13 Native Labour Commission Report* (hereafter referred to as the Barth Commission Report) is one of the major documents in Kenya history; the volume in which it was published contains also all the written and oral evidence submitted, much of it in the words of McGregor Ross, a 'concerted display of negrophobe malevolence'.[106] It is perhaps most convenient to examine first this evidence and the commission's findings before proceeding to their recommendations and the actions taken thereon. It is a measure of the virtual domination of the political and economic scene by the labour question that a labour commission took evidence and made recommendations on almost every aspect of the territory's affairs. Over two hundred European and over sixty African witnesses gave evidence. All spoke freely, the Europeans needing little encouragement to do so; some of the Africans, one suspects, were carefully prepared by sympathetic administrative officers or missionaries.

Hollis, giving evidence prior to his departure, estimated the total manpower requirement to be 100,000 men. The evidence of farmer and other witnesses indicated that when the farm could so afford, large numbers were often still preferred.[107] It was noticeable, though, that the Rift Valley ranchers complained less, sometimes not at all, of a labour shortage as often their needs were fifty men or fewer. The loudest complaints came from the large plantations, particularly over difficulties at harvest time. The commission agreed in general terms that the rapid development of the economy was one of the major causes of the difficulties and listed the other specific causes as they appeared to them—ambiguity of instructions to district officers; the wealth of certain tribes in terms of land, stock and trade; the methods of recruiting agents; 'the Insufficiency of Administrative Staff' preventing officers familiarizing themselves with their districts, its peoples, languages and its sources of labour supply; and, lastly, bad conditions such as poor monotonous food, bad housing, active employer ill-treatment, and hardship on journeys.

Hollis claimed that the conditions of labour, in general, were still a great improvement on those of 1907, and he reiterated his belief, which he regarded as vital to every aspect of labour including its supply, that the task of the administration was to look after the natives rather than 'exploit the native for Europeans'. He then left the protectorate to the undisguised joy of the local press. The evidence which followed, however, leaves a painful impression of bad conditions, malpractices, little concern for African welfare or the preservation of an African society or economy, and is relieved by the concern of only a few missionaries and officials, and even fewer farmers.

The commission found that the actual diet of many labourers seemed limited to maize meal or beans, the latter being often mouldy causing diarrhoea; salt, leaf or root vegetables and meat were mostly absent.

Occasionally farmers improved the diet but very many did not nor was it supplemented in the construction camps. At home men had had varied meals including some protein perhaps twice or thrice a day; at work the labourer had one meal per day only, perhaps only of beans or maize meal, often cooked badly after the labourer had himself fetched the wood and the water. Housing, too, remained in many cases flimsy grass huts incapable of keeping out the cold of a Highland night.

It was not surprising under these circumstances that large health problems were again revealing themselves, particularly among inland labourers working at the Coast. In theory these men were supposed to be examined medically before they were recruited but many were not. McGregor Ross stated that on the Mombasa piped water works the death rate was 176 per thousand per annum, chiefly from malaria and dysentery. Early attempts to use local Arabs and Swahilis had been an expensive failure.[108] Experimentally, Meru labour from inland was then tried, 500 men being sent, of which between twenty-five and thirty died on the road alone with a slightly smaller number dying near the site. These Meru had to be repatriated, more dying on and after the journey, and their further recruitment at the Coast was forbidden; even among the Kikuyu the sickness rate was 33 per cent and the death rate for 1911 14 per cent. A further harmful factor was the powerful local Coast coconut beer which weakened men's resistance to malaria, dysentery, and hookworm (ankylostomiasis).[109] Nyanza men fared better. They were in any case in smaller numbers at the Coast as in 1912 Ainsworth had refused to allow them to work east of Nairobi, ostensibly to prevent the spread of sleeping-sickness though very likely with their protection also in mind. The Kikuyu chiefs were already objecting to recruiting for the Coast. The compilation of death figures could never be accurate since deaths from malaria very frequently took place ten or fourteen days after a man's return to his own home area, but the medical staff at Embu and Meru had to be given extra funds and drug supplies.[110] Work in towns was also creating problems, one chief believing that the labour shortage was largely caused by the deterrent effect of thin, syphilitic men on their return to the reserves, or men not returning at all, a view shared by many administrative officers.

Dubious or plainly crooked employer practices, too, were exposed by the evidence. Some employers frankly admitted witholding part of the wages of their labour force as a surety that men would work another month. Sometimes pay was simply late; one witness admitted that the Railway paid its Nairobi labour thirteen days and its Kisumu men nineteen days after pay was due. Sometimes a deliberately impossible task was set, or an incident staged to provide a pretext for witholding pay; African witnesses and two district officers told of men being driven off after twenty-five days when pay-day was approaching.[111] Leys noted 'though illegal the power to fine and flog is supported by public opinion', and gave an example of a servant suspected, probably justifiably, of theft who was given no less than fifty lashes necessitating three weeks in hospital, for which the employer was not prosecuted. One witness spoke of the men returning with weals on their backs, and another of men harassed and beaten like oxen. The commission accepted that poor labour conditions were partially responsible, but took the optimistic view that these often lay only with a small minority of bad employers.

Almost all employers agreed that increased wages would not attract more labour, a view shared by a number of administrative officers who feared the process of 'individualization'. Ainsworth and a few of the more liberal officers disagreed, Ainsworth arguing that any increase in African purchasing power would help the labour supply. McGregor Ross confirmed that in 1912 he had increased the hinterland wage rate for P.W.D. labour from 4 to 5 rupees (with daily rations of 2 lb. of grain, food and quarters), and in Mombasa, following a partial suspension of work, from 8 to 9 or 10 rupees (with neither food nor quarters), but he was criticized by settlers for so doing. Leys and other witnesses commented that cash payment had little value for the lack of trade goods had devalued the rupee; this in turn had led to an increase in the cash price of stock, already inflated because more men were looking for wives than in the days of tribal warfare.[112] Parents could demand higher prices both in and for stock. But witnesses noting African purchases of consumer goods led the commission to a view that African labourers were well paid both for their period at work and for their future.[113]

The commission found that instructions to administration officers on 'encouragement' were too vague, and the evidence of the officers themselves supports this, widely differing attitudes being revealed. One officer, for example, admitted that he told his chiefs their efficiency might be judged by their success in recruiting, while others adhered to purely voluntary principles and even checked whether those professionally recruited were true work-seekers. The vast majority of employers demanded a policy of positive 'encouragement', some favouring compulsion, or the alternatives of compulsion at very low remuneration in the reserves to attract labour by better rates to work outside.[114]

Chiefs and headmen in general followed the attitude of their local administrative officer. If the district officer believed in 'encouragement' they would act accordingly either from loyalty or self-interest, but the means they used were often deplorable. Leys summarized their impossible position by saying ' "Encouragement" by District Officers means compulsion in practice or it means nothing. The whole basis of Government in a reserve is that every wish of the District Officer is law.' Leys went on to state he had seen frequent cases of gangs recruited by chiefs appearing before the district commissioner as perfectly willing to go to work at the Coast, but malingering at his medical examination. When he made enquiries he discovered compulsion. A large majority of the African witnesses alleged inescapable pressure from chiefs, now assisted by tribal retainers and headmen, often to supply labour to professional recruiters in response to a bribe.[115] The evidence contained examples of a chief burning down the huts of reluctant workers, imposing curses and stock fines, and confiscating land and accepting bribes. Chief Muraru admitted that he had recruited fifty labourers by sending his spearmen out for 'volunteers'; and no doubt others settled personal vendettas in the same way. Some chiefs were apparently using powers to order communal labour for their own purposes, others possessed unnecessarily large numbers of retainers. The chiefs in some cases undoubtedly found it difficult to distinguish between one white man and another but the result in total, was a deterrent for labour and a hardship for many individuals. Equally, a number of responsible chiefs tried to take their unfamiliar responsibilities seriously, sending recruiters to the district commissioner before allowing them to recruit, or convening a council of elders to decide on whom it would be fairest to lay the burden of work, and expressing concern at the state of labourers on their return.

The commission accepted that the methods of the professional labour recruiters discouraged the flow. Some we have already seen, but to these must be added the not uncommon practice of replacing recruited young men who had failed their medical examination or had run away by older and less fit men. Recruiters often failed to make any real provision for the journey of their men to work, and the commission noted that men who had never perhaps seen a train before were 'packed tight into third class coaches, even iron-covered goods vans' for three days.[116] Such trains might be side-tracked for more important ones to pass along the single track; the men would be locked in, with fearful conditions of heat and cramp and only occasionally let out for water and a brief stroll. Most administrative officers disapproved of these practices and tried to rectify them where possible, sometimes taking the view it was better that they, as district officers should supervise recruiting, or at least administer clean, healthy labour transit camps.

The commission heard many conflicting views over taxation. A large majority of settler witnesses urged an increase in native taxation with remission for months out at work. This view was opposed by many of the official witnesses, McGregor Ross observing that a high tax rate as a target merely lessened the interest and efficiency of the labourer in his work, and both he and a district officer pointed out that poll tax collection from men at work had the effect of making men stay at home.[117] But it was on the question of how the money from taxation was to be spent, linked with the development in and size of the reserves that the sharpest divisions of view appeared. About half the settler witnesses including Delamere favoured a reduction of the native reserves, arguing that Europeans were more efficient at development than Africans who should play their part in development as labourers. Attacking Ainsworth, Delamere discounted the argument that Africans were producing more at home, and asserted that Ainsworth had discouraged labour to foster peasant production when he had been in Ukamba, 'with the result that the Kamba were now to be found drunk from one end of the country to another'. Ainsworth, in reply, denied any reduction in Nyanza work seekers and said that he thought a reduction of the reserves would be 'highly immoral'. One of the missionary witnesses spoke of the deterrent effect on the supply of men caused by the disruption of family and social life, and McGregor Ross suggested that population pressures were already beginning to be felt; he claimed that in some parts of North Kavirondo the density was already 700 to the square mile, or less than one acre per head. A missionary teacher, A. R. Barlow, drew the commission's attention to the obligations expected of men in tribal societies, attacking settler pre-conceptions on idleness. He listed these duties as breaking new ground, assisting with the weeding and cultivating, planting sugar cane, yams, bananas and sweet potatoes, taking duty to guard ripening maize from night attacks by animals, the pruning of trees, the building of huts and stores, and for the boys and young men, the herding of sheep and goats. Men had also to make tools, beehives, stools and other domestic utensils, and of course participate in communal councils.

Many employer witnesses favoured a development of the emerging resident labourer system, but both they and the officials complained that the system was running into difficulties, chiefly caused by large numbers of 'Kaffir farmers', Africans living virtually unsupervised on farms, paying the landowner part of their crop or a rent of 8 to 30 rupees but not specifically working for him. Hollis said he had found no fewer than 1,200 on one farm, a figure which, with the number of absentee landlords at the time, was by no means unusual.[118]

A large majority of the employer witnesses asked for an identity card system or an extension of the pass system to serve the same purpose—the apprehension of deserters, so permitting contracts with penal sanctions to be enforced.[119] Some witnesses recommended that the new J.P.s be given powers to try desertion cases. Ainsworth disagreed with registration neatly pin-pointing two of the main causes of desertion— pressure to work outside a man's home area and bad treatment.

One or two individual items of evidence merit mention on account of their remarkable views. An Indian contractor, Ahmed Khan, asked for legalisation of the *kiboko*, compulsory labour for a quarter of the men in any district, and a legal requirement that employees buried their fellows' corpses, which otherwise the 'poor employer' had to do. One European witness proposed that each chief should supply two hundred men to Kiambu settlers each month, adding 'this would not lead to any trouble'. Another proposed the purchase from Uganda of young girls whom he claimed were sold there very cheaply by their parents. The cumulative corrosion of working a reluctant labour force on European patience and equanimity can be gauged by some of the very real irritations, the sudden desertion of the great part of a labour force often on the day following pay or before the tax collector's visit, the absence, demand for more pay or intoxication of labourers at critical moments, the posting of sentinels to alert labour gangs not at work, the apparent lack of supervision and bad conditions of the government's own labour, or an agreement to reckon days worked by the tying of knots on a piece of string being frustrated by the African putting two knots for one day. These frustrations, primitive forms of resistance, were put forward by many witnesses; their significance was not understood.[120] Furthermore Beech observed that the European owed to the African far more than he realized, and that despite land grievances many Kikuyu still felt it their duty to work for a white man.[121] Repeated evidence showed that the personality of the employer was usually decisive in obtaining and retaining men.

The commission considered that the evidence indicated that the labour burden was not being divided equally among the tribes, the Kikuyu and the Nyanza peoples bearing the heaviest burden, while the Kamba had largely disappeared from the labour scene, the Giriama contributed little to work, appearing in very large numbers to be taking to alcohol.[122] It was generally agreed that the Maasai, Galla and Somalis would never work for a European, regarding such work as a helotry suitable only for Bantu and Nilotic people.

Lastly, a few employer witnesses, including two or three from the Coast, recommended importing Asians for large works and plantations there with compulsory repatriation when the project was complete; only a small minority of settlers favoured granting the coolies any right to remain.

The commission, faced with this mass of evidence, nevertheless produced an almost unanimous report both in its findings and recommendations, these latter covering all the main matters of controversy. In respect of 'encouragement' they recommended that district officers be given specific instructions 'in unequivocal language' to ensure the maximum possible number of men came out to work for Europeans but they rejected any form of direct government recruiting as amounting to compulsion. They recommended a reorganization of administration in the reserves so that these areas would be cared for by special officers responsible to a new official, a Chief Native Commissioner, while the settled areas remained under the Chief Secretary; the reserves were to be demarcated on the basis of their adequacy for the present population, if necessary some were even to be reduced. The commission judged the African population could afford to pay a higher tax but that the imposition of a higher rate purely to coerce labour would not be justifiable, though increased taxation could be justified to pay for a system of identification and the other recommendations of the commission. A system of identification they saw as 'absolutely essential' to deal with desertion; they recommended a document to include a man's personal particulars but no record of employment. The commission strongly felt that the practice of 'Kaffir farming' should cease and the resident labour system under certain conditions and in limited numbers be encouraged. On recruiting, the commission recommended the abolition of the professional recruiter and that properly supervised labour camps should be built at government centres to which district officers might direct work seekers. The commission also recommended that the government take immediate steps to improve the condition of labourers who travelled by train and to provide transit camps for gangs who travelled by road. For conditions of work at the larger sites, legislation to provide for a system of inspection was recommended, the commission noting that considerate treatment had an appreciable effect on the labour supply.

On the question of importing indentured labour from India the Commission was in general critical for economic and political reasons, only a minority of members favouring free immigration. The commission made a number of interesting but less important recommendations on matters of detail. They thought, for example, that the Kamba and the Giriama were 'very large potential suppliers of labour'. They felt labour might be used a great deal more efficiently and had no hesitation in taking the government to task for its own labour shortcomings. They recommended the expansion of agricultural and technical education, with also a limited development of literary education to the primary level to increase the supply of African clerks. They sought more encouragement for the provision of clothing and restrictions on liquor, and recommended the abolition of unpaid communal labour in the reserves.

It is easy to condemn the commission for failing to make firm positive recommendations to end 'encouragement', to prohibit the increase of taxation, to foresee the oppression the identity document system would create, or to castigate other abuses in round terms. In fact, within the conception of the pre-1914 world in which its members operated and particularly within the pressures and unhealthy atmosphere of the protectorate at the time, the commission, perhaps with the exception of 'encouragement' and taxation, made a generally honest and sincere effort to come to grips with the problems and put them right where possible. The report aimed to correct particular abuses and hardships but did not nor could not judge how far the system itself was responsible for these; it could hardly be expected that the commission should have criticized the whole rationale of the protectorate at the time, ever-increasing white settlement. But its members yielded to no pressures, they took evidence from any who wished to give it to or were encouraged to do so; all the evidence was published and their comments and recommendations were outspoken.

Among the European population the report was viewed at first with favour as a fair commentary on the labour situation, and the January 1914 meeting of the Convention of Associations approved the recommendations. Demands were voiced for a speedy introduction of the necessary legislation and it was thought that the Native Commissioner would be a suitable representative for Africans in the Legislative Council.[123] The report was completed and signed early in August 1913 but it did not reach the Colonial Office until March 1914, Belfield wishing first to learn the views of the Convention. Belfield then forwarded the report, supporting almost all the recommendations except that concerning communal labour and despite all the previous correspondence adding that he was giving his own personal authority to 'encouragement'.[124] In Britain however the report once again aroused alarm. The recently amalgamated Anti-Slavery and Aborigines Protection Society wrote anxiously to Lewis Harcourt, the Colonial Secretary, the letter receiving wide publicity as it was printed as a pamphlet; it was followed by an article written by the society's secretary in the *Contemporary Review.*[125] There followed a number of parliamentary questions and observations, and on 28 July 1914 in the debate on the Colonial Office Vote the report was raised again. Probably briefed by Leys, T. E. Harvey, a Quaker and Liberal M.P., demanded assurance on compulsion, taxation and the size of reserves, while, following the insistence of the Anti-Slavery Society, W. Joynson-Hicks sought a specific assurance that the Colonial Secretary regarded forced labour for private purposes as the equivalent of slavery. Harcourt in reply cautioned members not to confuse the evidence with the recommendations and gave assurances on the reserves, taxation, conditions of work and recruiting. On 'encouragement' he stated 'Our officers . . . though it is their proper duty to afford information as to where employment may be available, do nothing which savours of or suggests Government compulsion in the matter of recruitment. It is sometimes difficult to discriminate nicely between advice, persuasion and compulsion in this matter.'[126] In other words Harcourt reiterated Crewe's position of 1908. A promised parliamentary paper and further House of Commons debates or wider public concern were however precluded by the outbreak of war.

Between January and July feelings had strengthened in the protectorate where the apparent labour shortage had worsened; a sisal estate at Voi had shut down through want of labourers and had complained to the government and the Colonial Office. At the July meeting of the Convention the report was seen as 'ancient history', the government was supporting 'useless parasites, doing nothing and paying little for protection', and demands were made for increased taxation, a 'good labour law' and a definite policy. A summary of Harcourt's views including a certain amount of detail were laid before the Convention serving only to add to their resentment.[127] The summary was sent in the form of a letter rather than a verbatim statement, the letter being actually signed by W. J. Monson, the Assistant Chief Secretary, but without doubt after preparation with Belfield. The process is significant, the protectorate government conveying views on a major political subject to the Convention rather than insisting on the pre-eminence of the Legislative Council, and even more significant, the government failing to publish Harcourt's actual despatch as Sadler had published that from Crewe in 1908.

The letter added a different gloss on a number of points made in Harcourt's despatch, and a comparison of some subjects discussed makes interesting reading. Harcourt agreed in general with the proposal for the division of the country into native areas under a Chief Native Commissioner and European areas under the Chief Secretary, but he stated he wished to see specific plans before agreeing to the actual division, a point which received less emphasis in the summary letter. He approved the proposals for improved rail travel conditions and for labour transit camps as an experiment, providing that the operation of the camps gave no impression that the government was using undue influence in the collection of labour, a provision omitted in the summary. He agreed to consider an identification system but warned of the need for 'careful watching to prevent hardship and abuse'; he affirmed taxation should not be related to labour supply. He foresaw difficulties over a greater development of the resident labour system and said he would want to make a careful examination of the type of agreement planned. On the vital issue of the reserves, the protectorate government's summary noted that the Secretary of State 'hesitated to accept' any proposal that the reserves might never be increased and totally rejected any reduction; but it did not convey the full emphasis with which Harcourt, noting that the report itself contained evidence that some reserves were full, had firmly stated 'it is impossible to lay down that any increase in the native population must be provided for by service under Europeans'.

In 'encouragement' the discrepancy between Harcourt's despatch and the protectorate government's summary was glaring. The despatch set out in some detail the clearest ruling on 'encouragement' provided by the Colonial Office. Harcourt forbade any form of compulsion, adding that he thought similar compulsion had been at least partly responsible for the second Matabele war. He thought any advice to work must be very carefully limited and defined, as Africans could not easily tell official advice from compulsion and as the chief function of the government was the protection of the labourer. Advice to work should be limited to where work might be found and assistance 'to realise the advantages to be derived from any form of industry', avoiding either any 'systematic invitation to work' or anything suggesting pressure in any form. The protectorate government's summary simply recorded that the Secretary of State had ruled that it was of the utmost importance that government officers should take no measures suggestive of compulsion, which simplification was then followed by an addition, presumably drafted by Belfield:

> Definite instructions have been issued by His Excellency to Provincial and District Officers to the effect that they are to lose no opportunity of explaining to the natives the advanages of going out to work and are to refrain from making any observations which may leave the people under the impression that Government is not anxious that they should do so. The Governor has himself taken the opportunity of expressing to the Chiefs of the various tribes with whom he has from time to time been in contact his desire that they should give their personal support to labour emigration, and he has been at pains to explain to them the precautions which are being taken to safeguard the health of their people and to provide for all their daily requirements.

The Convention appointed a standing committee to give the report further consideration, noting that there was 'little hope of a satisfactory solution of the question unless he [the Secretary of State] is prepared to go much further than the reply indicates'. In particular the Convention rejected Harcourt's views on taxation and the reserves. On 1 September Belfield sent the Colonial Office detailed plans for the reorganization of the administration which were in line with opinions expressed at the July Convention meeting.[128] He envisaged the division of the country into settled areas where administration would lie in the hands of a district commissioner or a magistrate responsible to the Chief Secretary and into native areas administered by 'Native Commissioners' responsible to a Chief Native Commissioner assisted by 'Travelling Commissioners'—the latter to inspect work sites and farms. A more serious part of the scheme was a proposal for 'licensed labour bureaux' at the principal sources of supply; four bureaux were envisaged, to be nominated by 'the principal firms interested in the exploitation of labour, and associated with a Government Labour Officer'. The bureaux were to receive estimates of the number of able-bodied men in each location prepared by the native commissioners, and the officers in charge of the bureaux were 'to do everything possible to encourage men to seek work either through the bureaux or recruiters. The Colonial Office ruled that such a scheme must be left for post-war reconsideration.

The stage appeared to be set for conflict between a Colonial Office under an active reforming Secretary, supported by public opinion in Britain and by some senior protectorate officials (if not at the level of Governor) versus the East Africa Protectorate settlers, a conflict which might have led to another Colonial Office 'assertion' had not the protectorate and its problems become engulfed by the needs of the war.

Conclusion

By 1914 many thousands of men had worked for Europeans, the majority for only short periods at a time. The government employed some 3,000–5,000 in the P.W.D., and some 7,000 on the Railway (including contractors). The private sector raised the total employed at peak seasons to approximately 110,000. In terms of percentages of men away in employment this requirement amounted at the most and in certain hard-pressed areas such as Dagoretti and in South Nyanza, to 32 per cent; in the other large reserve areas to about 24 per cent, often less.

The fact that men, pre-1914, changed over frequently contributed to the preservation of the peasant sector even where percentages were high. Subtractions from societies which had kept their adult men under-employed, or even in concealed unemployment, over long periods of time for military reasons were not great enough to destroy either peasant economies or tribal societies; indeed, under careful administration as in Ainsworth's Nyanza, peasant economies appear to have been flourishing. It is very doubtful whether they would have flourished even better with the missing 25–30 per cent given the available land. Certainly in Nyanza the signs of future conflict between the labour market and peasant agriculture had appeared; the nature of the conflict was concealed by a number of local factors but any harm to the labour market if harm there was, was at least offset by a generally increased appreciation of the value of coin and consumer goods, which led many to work.

The keynote of the pre-1914 period was not, therefore, one of large-scale labour exploitation but one of large-scale harshness, particularly in the construction and contractor fields though lessening on the farms, and the creation of a pattern of labour arrangements to last for nearly forty years. By 1914 the territory was for almost all purposes divided into white settled areas where economic development, even if unsound or in debt, was to be protected; along with closely-administered, efficiently-taxed African reserves, the more densely populated of which were spoken of as the 'labour-producing areas'. In the settled areas Africans were to work as contract or as resident labourers or else they were to be 'repatriated''. In the up-country towns the majority of Africans lived not for craft or marketing reasons but as the inhabitants either of labour lines or 'the boys' quarters'; they were controlled by pass regulations and municipal by-laws. In the reserves economic development was at best only taking place under criticism and obstacles, more often it was not taking place at all for fear that the labour supply would be reduced. There was no determined national effort to create peasant proprietor production with inter-tribal trade; on the political side the African was thought of less as a man to be ruled, directly or indirectly, but as a lotus-eater, part of a pool of manpower or as a feudal retainer on a squire's estate.

The pattern was only tolerable because excesses were periodically held in check by the Colonial Office, the pre-1914 withdrawal of adult males from the reserves was not excessive in either numbers or duration, and because the pattern of dependence established was one acceptable at this contemporary stage of African evolution. It could only be perpetuated without destitution so long as the economy supported the labourers' families by the possession of a piece of land either in the reserve or on the settler's farm, conditions which because of the abnormally reduced size of the African population at the time remained feasible.

The system of the labourer with only a transitory or target interest in his work led to waste and inefficiency though it can be said that the concept of regular work for wages, if not its actual achievement, had by 1914 become implanted in many African minds; this concept was reinforced by mission education extolling the moral virtues of work and teaching an appreciation of consumer goods and the status which work could bring. A man's period in employment was a gamble. For some the new experience of work brought disease or death, for others hardship and poor reward. But for a large number labour was not without attraction as it brought real wealth to the labourer himself personally, and a chance to spend this wealth in a variety of attractive ways, again of the labourer's individual choice.

Strikes against this emerging pattern of society were rare; only one further example to those already mentioned merits note, a strike of Mombasa boatmen in 1912 against a new police licensing system. The boatmen jeered the boat company's manager and hauled down the company flag. The strike began to spread to the town, but the administration then took firm repressive measures.

One small tribe revolted against the new pattern of life, the coastal Giriama. The government and settlers had felt for some time that the Giriama should come out to work but they had refused to do so. Belfield therefore began to make plans in the autumn of 1912 to bring the Giriama under closer administration, plans endorsed by the Barth Commission's recommendations; in particular some 15,000 were to be moved south of the Sabaki River for more convenient control and in general hut tax was to be collected more efficiently, communal labour obligations imposed and men encouraged to work in Mombasa and on the plantations.[129] But Belfield in his various reports to the Colonial Office was careful neither to suggest that labour supply in any way might have been a cause of the violence which followed, nor to report the pressures on the Giriama which followed the Barth recommendations. Tension rose in the summer of 1914, violence breaking out in August and necessitating a punitive expedition during which 400 Giriama were killed. Eventually in September the Giriama agreed to surrender terms which required their evacuation of the fertile area north of the Sabaki on which much of their self-sufficiency had rested, the provision of 1,000 military carrier recruits and a fine of 100,000 rupees, this latter mostly taken within a year by seizure of goats, crops and ivory. Leys, commenting on the revolt, adds his view that the real cause was the intention 'to increase the supply of labourers.'[130] This view was endorsed by the reports of local administrators at the time and a post-war inquiry.

The Giriama rising was a revolt essentially different from other conflicts of the decade, although the difference was not seen at the time. The Giriama were not engaged in primary resistance to an extending colonial administration. They were in revolt as a people, trying to resist the imposition of an order in which they saw dimly that Africans were to be labourers, and the activities of the administration increasingly devoted to coercing them to enter the labour market.

NOTES

1. C.O. 533/28, Jackson to Colonial Office, 27 March 1907.
2. These Boers employed virtually no Africans in their first years in the protectorate. They did much of their work for themselves, running an ox-wagon transport service, building their own houses, making their own shoes and harness from hides, boiling their own candle-fat, making their own harrows and implements, etc. Some prospered but many remained permanently without capital and were poor employers. A government Labour Office, E. J. Scott, wrote in his diary for 6 Dec 1950, 'I admire the Afrikaans for their independence and amazing obstinacy; they vary from the tidy and thrifty to the dirty and drunken—and poor—in which class I put the farmer of this morning'. Rhodes House papers.

   A few brought one or two Coloured servants with them from South Africa. Two of these were arrested for house-breaking in 1913, when the courts ruled that although they might be part-European in ancestry they were 'natives' for the purposes of East African legislation. *E.A. Law Reports*, V, 1914, 32, *Rex v. Peter and Jim.*
3. For example, 'the dignity of labour seems to me to be the first lesson to be impressed upon the natives', wrote *The Leader of British East Africa* (hereafter *Leader*), on 13 Apr 1912, adding that 'respect for their betters and respect for themselves' should be the second. See also Elspeth Huxley, *White Man's Country*, 1953, I, 81. 'To suggest that the interests of the natives were paramount would have seemed to that generation a mere contradiction in terms. The idea that the interests of an assortment of barbaric, ideal-less and untutored tribesmen, clothed in sheep's fat, castor oil or rancid butter—men who smelt out witches, drank blood warm from the throats of living cattle and believed that rainfall depended on the arrangements of a goat's intestines—should be exalted above those of the educated European would have seemed to them fantastic'. The local press quite frequently openly referred to the African population as 'niggers', the term in common speech usage.
4. E. S. Grogan, *From the Cape to Cairo*, 1900, xxiv.

   Ewart Scott Grogan, 1874–1964. Educated Winchester and Cambridge; arrived E.A.P. in 1903 and acquired considerable land and property interests; military service in both World Wars; M.L.C. at various times. For a romanticised biography of this famous Kenya political leader see N. Wymer, *The Man from the Cape*, 1959.
5. For an eye-witness account of these extreme views, see W. Lloyd Jones, *K.A.R.*, 1926, 103.
6. Under Indian legislation applied to the protectorate, a servant could be whipped for theft of his master's property; in German East Africa employers were legally entitled to inflict a maximum of fifteen lashes. These examples, the general climate of the times, and a belief the native 'understood' corporal punishment but did not understand prison or fines led a large number of employers to beat their employees, and on a number of occasions for magistrates to award quite illegal beating sentences.

   The early settlers were, of course, the product of societies which believed that to spare the rod was to spoil the child.
7. Lord Cranworth, *A Colony in the Making, or Sport and Profit in British East Africa*, 1912, *passim.*
8. For an illuminating description of a pioneer's home see L. Powys, *Ebony and Ivory*, 1929, sketch entitled 'Black Parasites'. This sketch narrated the story of a settler of the coarsest type who rode out after a deserting labourer; the labourer had stolen a sheep. The settler punished the man by tying him to a tree and setting the surrounding bush on fire, an incident only too likely to have been recounted from Powys's' observations of his neighbours.
9. L. Wilkinson, *The Letters of Llewelyn Powys*, 1943, 92, provides an example.

'Their maidens even weary me,—the old trouts would if they could pox me. For three months I have not been to bed with any of them—how they all lie and steal and deceive you—what duplicity behind their dusky skins...' (Letter written 15 July 1917). Settlers' relations with African women generally and those of their labour force in particular were never discussed or written about at the time. It would however present an incomplete picture of the labour scene at the time to omit all reference to the question. A number of farmers, particularly in the early years, used African women. The practice continued on a smaller scale throughout the colonial period. E. J. Scott, a government Labour Officer, wrote in his diary for 16 Nov 1950, '... to a farm in the Turbo-Kipkarren area, its owner, apparently, regularly sleeps with a Nandi girl...' Rhodes House papers. Nandi women were particularly attractive to Europeans; some established a semi-permanent mistress relationship with, in addition, virtual farm-manager status.

10. *East African Standard* (hereafter *E.A.S.*), 31 May, 7, 14, 21 June 1913.
11. Comparisons can be made with Ireland, both North and South, at a slightly ealier date and also with Rhodesia, South Africa and the United States of America.
12. C.O. 533/4, Jackson to Colonial Office, 6 Sept 1905 attaching the views of A. D. Linton.
13. The Rev. C. Johnston for example observed: 'His idea with regard to improving the labour supply was to preach the dignity of work; being a missionary he believed in preaching the Gospel which advocated work. *Native Labour Commission 1912–13, Part I. Evidence and Appendices, Part II. Report*, Nairobi, 1913 (hereafter Barth Commission Report). As late as 1919 the 1918–19 Annual Report for Kiambu District observed 'Canon Leakey writes strongly advocating compulsory labour for men between the ages of 18 and 40 as being greatly to the advantage of the Gikuyu'. All references to provincial administration reports are to the series in the Kenya National Archives.
14. The American Friends Africa Mission at Lumbwa, for example, employed a labour force never less than 200, sometimes as much as 500 in the 1906–8 period. W. R. Hotchkiss, *Then and Now in Kenya Colony*, 1937, 99. In C.O. 533/74, Girouard to Colonial Office, 11 June 1910, the Governor complaining about an Italian mission, wrote 'I fear that in many of these small stations, labour has been used in a manner with which we cannot entirely agree'. For another interesting comment see *Harry Thuku, An Autobiography*, 1970, 7, 'Funnily enough, if a circumcised man or youth took on work with the [Gospel Missionary Society] mission he got a rupee for six days' work, however small he was; and an uncircumcised boy received a rupee for eight days' work whatever his size!'
15. An example of this occurred in Jan 1921, at a time when the missions were disliked by the settler community for their defence of the interests of labour. An unofficial member of Legislative Council, in a violent attack, demanded the reduction of their subsidy.
16. For contemporary records of African attitudes, see Elspeth Huxley, *Red Strangers*, 1939, a work of fiction based on her own conversations with Kikuyu people); Sir C. Dundas, *African Cross Roads*, 1955, and W. McGregor Ross, *Kenya from Within*, 1927, (hereafter McGregor Ross).
17. Sir C. Dundas, *op. cit.*, 28, '"Is he then my father?" was a remark occasionally heard when someone was exhorted to obey the chiefs or headmen we had appointed.'
18. Sir S. Olivier, *White Capital and Black Labour*, 1910, 82–3, wrote of the African worker: 'Half a dollar may be worth one day's work to him, a second half dollar may be worth a second day's work, but a third half dollar will not be worth a third day's work. A third day's work may seem to him worth two dollars', a wise observation quoted by a D.C. in his evidence to the Barth Commission but otherwise little understood.
19. Barth Commission Report, evidence of M. W. H. Beech.

20. *Ibid.*, evidence of M. W. H. Beech, 'they disobey the orders of the Elders and think only of themselves'.
21. The indirect repercussions of labour demands were sometimes to blame. Hollis cited an example of Kikuyu stock theft from Somalis because the Kikuyu concerned had had their own stock confiscated by a chief for refusing to work for a European. C.O. 533/61, Jackson to Colonial Office, 27 July 1909 and enclosure.
22. Tables of official precedence for example appeared with surprising frequency in the *E.A.P. Gazette*, and one governor gloomily wrote to the Colonial Office, which had taken him to task over the behaviour of a D.C. cohabiting with African women, that the majority of his officers so behaved. The Minutes of Executive Council for 18 May 1908 recorded 'Officers of the Administration have openly kept native women as a matter of common usage'.
23. Payment in labour was often necessary in early stages of development as Africans had no access to a cash market and coins might be in short supply. Sheep, goats, ivory, grain and even crocodiles' eggs were accepted. Labour payment could not be mandatory and had to be for state or communal purposes, it enabled many early roads and tracks to be made. Its severity depended on the chief. The initial African reaction to taxation seems not to have been unduly critical. Coast people regarded payment as a fair charge for protection against slave raiders, and many appreciated the benefits of peaceful travel on the new tracks and roads.
24. Lord Hindlip, *British East Africa, Past, Present and Future*, 1905, vii.
25. Comparative direct tax rates in other territories were as follows:
    North-West Rhodesia: Poll tax of Shs. 5/- to Shs. 10/- with an additional Shs. 5/- to Shs. 10/- for plural wives, the exact amount varying by district.
    North-East Rhodesia: Hut tax Shs. 3/-
    Uganda: Hut tax 3 rupees.
    S. Rhodesia: Poll tax Shs. 20/-
    Nyasaland: Hut tax Shs. 6/-
    Swaziland: Poll tax Shs. 20/-

    In other British territories the taxation system differed so greatly that no useful comparisons can be made. In the Gold Coast, for example, taxation was indirect, and in North Nigeria the emirs were given sums to collect through the traditional structure.
26. There is no evidence to suggest that where land belonging to a hinterland tribe was alienated the alienation was made as a specific response to a demand for labour from that tribe. Where such land was alienated the cause was sometimes 'pacifying' as when the Nandi surrendered some land to facilitate supervision, or sometimes simply that the land was attractive, as for example, Laikipia. The case of the Coastal Giriama is examined later.
27. The Village Headman Ordinance, Ord 22 of 1902, *E.A.P. Gazette*, 7 Nov 1902. *E.A. Law Reports*, II, 1909, 134, *Mathendu v. Masenti and Others* gives a remarkable example of the way in which, under Sadler and Hollis, British justice could still very occasionally reach out to the ordinary man. In 1908 some villagers were acquitted of a conviction for refusing communal labour. The Machakos D.C. instructed a headman that a road should be cleared; the headman ordered a number of men to do the work. Some refused, and were convicted by the D.C. for a breach of the Village Headmen Ordinance, being fined a goat and sentenced to one month's rigorous imprisonment. Judges Bonham Carter and Hamilton held that while the ordinance imposed the responsibility for the road's condition on the headman, it neither gave the headman the power to enforce the work without pay on particular individuals, nor the D.C. the power to levy a fine, except collectively on a whole area. The judges ordered the conviction to be quashed, the men released, and the goats to be returned.
28. 'If the planter had to find his own labour, he would do his utmost to keep it, because he wishes to profit by it,' wrote the Ukamba P.C. in his 1907–8 Annual Report.

Private employers who recruited on their own adopted some interesting methods. The most effective if the employer was a humane man was to send a trusted man to bring in his friends. If a farm was near a reserve a lamp fixed to the top of a pole was found successful; lamps were a matter of intense curiosity to Africans, and bargaining could soon begin with awe-struck observers. Free ostrich feathers were offered by some farmers.

In the Kiambu area (but almost certainly only in the Kiambu area) settlers found some of the land of their farm under cultivation, and the resident Kikuyu were told that they could only remain if they agreed to work for their new masters.

29. A remarkable account of 'encouragement' at work, the offering of *douceurs* and a D.C.'s abuse of his powers to help a friend appears in Bror von Blixen-Finecke. *African Hunter,* 1937, 19–29. Blixen decribes his negotiations with an Embu chief whom he refers to as 'King Kater' admitting attempts to bribe him. Eventually he persuaded the D.C. to support him '. . . giving King Kater a bit of a fright and that worked—fifty per cent at least. The next morning I had two hundred men . . .'

    In March 1909 the government forbade gifts to chiefs from private employers, a move sharply criticized in the *Leader* of 13 March 1909. The ban was, in any case, generally ignored. Some farmers who lived near certain reserves established a semi-permanent relationship with particular chiefs, the 1920–1 Annual Report, Kenya Province, speaking of 'affiliated chiefs'. Elspeth Huxley, *The Flame Trees of Thika,* 1959, 32, describes her parents' arrangement with a local chief of a goat for each ten men recruited by him; this type of arrangement was forbidden by government instruction in 1920.

30. The settlers disapproved of daily payment of wages, the *E.A.S.* from time to time observing that it was a custom which contributed to 'loafing'; but at the Coast, particularly at Mombasa, wages were often paid at the end of the day, a further reason for the Coast's popularity.

31. *Report on Slavery and Free Labour in the East Africa Protectorate,* Cd. 1631 of 1903. The report was written by W. J. Monson, Assistant Secretary of the Government at the time.

32. *Protectorate Annual Report, 1903–4,* Cd. 2331 of 1905.

33. *Report by Mr Ainsworth on the Progress of the Ukamba Province from July 1895 to February 1905,* Cd. 2740 of 1906, 20. From later evidence it appears that these Africans were in practice, and certainly thought themselves to be, more tenants than wage-paid labourers. They sold their own produce either at a reduced price to the farmer who resold at a profit to himself, or sold their produce direct paying a proportion of the profits to the farmer.

34. C.O. 533/2, Stewart to Colonial Office, 23 June 1905, and *House of Lords Paper 158* of 1907.

35. *Protectorate Annual Report 1905–6,* Cd. 3285 of 1907.

36. The Master and Servants Ordinance, Ord 8 of 1906, *E.A.P. Gazette,* 15 Apr 1906.

    This ordinance followed by certain test cases established a basic principle of Kenya law, that no unwritten contracts were to last longer than a month, so that each month (where wages were paid monthly) it came to an end. If a servant remained, the contract by implication was renewed.

    Written contracts, not to exceed three years, were to be attested and explained by a magistrate.

    A servant could be fined a maximum of a month's wages, or imprisoned for a maximum of one month for any of the following offences: failure to work; absence or intoxication in working hours; carelessness or work improperly performed; using the employer's horse, vehicle or property without leave, or using insulting language to the employer, or to his wife. A servant could be fined a maximum of two months' wages, or imprisoned for a maximum of two months for wilful breach of duty or drunkenness leading to the loss, damage or risk to his employer's property, or leading to a refusal or an omission to do his work with proper care; or if the servant were a herdsman, failure to report the death or loss of animals, and preserve parts of their carcasses necessary for proper inquiry as to their cause of death (unless the Court decided the circumstances were entirely beyond his control); or if he departed from service without lawful cause; or if the servant alleged loss of employer's property, which the employer could show must have been lost through the servant's negligence.

Interpretation of the Master and Servants Ordinance led to certain confusion and some revision cases. When the ordinance came into force, the Principal Judge sent a circular to all magistrates advising that the ordinance was only 'quasi-criminal', and saying a defendant need not go into the dock, and also that he could give evidence. There were to be no court fees, and the magistrate was to stand primarily as an arbitrator, awarding penalties only when necessary or when adjustment was impossible and after very careful enquiry into the causes of dispute.

Difficulties arose also over verbal contracts. In a case in 1907, a man employed on verbal monthly terms who had not resumed work one month was taken before a district commissioner who ruled that he must return to work and give one month's notice before he could leave. When the case was reviewed by a judge, the requirement for notice was set aside, the judge holding the contract became invalid unless renewed, at the end of the month. A less happy conviction for desertion was a case in 1905 at Mombasa, where a planter had engaged labour at 10 rupees per month with food to go and work on a plantation at Shimoni. On the day the gang were due to depart, all demanded an advance of one month's wages. When this demand was refused the men refused to go. The magistrate fined them 2 rupees each, ordered them to complete the contract, and without any legal authority or enquiry into the cause of desertion sentenced them in addition to fifteen strokes of the *kiboko* each. At one of the March 1908 meetings the Secretary for Native Affairs said that verbal contracts providing for pay at the end of the month held good for that month, and the employee who deserted during the month could be punished. But employers replied that whenever they took such a case to the courts they were told that unless there was a written contract employees could leave at any time in the month, demanding payment of wages earned up to that day; this ruling was both irritating and inconvenient to employers, who continued to complain. In March 1909 the Executive Council recommended that when no period of contract was defined, and wages were paid monthly, the engagement should be held to be for one month. This appears to have ended the employee practice of demanding the payment of wages earned to the date before the end of the month on which he decided to terminate his services, but it afforded no practical safeguard to the employer faced with desertion without such a claim.

37. C.O. 533/16, Jackson to Colonial Office, 20 Aug 1906 and attached papers and minutes.
38. *E.A.S.*, 26 Jan 1907.
39. Alfred Claud Hollis, 1874–1961. Educated Switzerland and Germany; E.A.P. civil service 1897–1912, from 1907 Secretary for Native Affairs; Colonial Secretary Sierra Leone 1912; Secretary and later Chief Secretary Tanganyika 1916–24; Resident Zanzibar 1924–30; Governor Trinidad 1930–6.
40. C.O. 533/33, Sadler to Colonial Office, 26 Nov 1907, and attached papers.
41. *Correspondence relating to the Flogging of Natives by Certain Europeans at Nairobi*, Cd. 3562 of 1907; C.O. 533/28, Jackson to Colonial Office, 16 (telegrams), 23 and 27 March 1907; N. Wymer, *Man from the Cape*, 1959; and McGregor Ross all recount this incident.
42. C.O. 533/33, Sadler to Colonial Office, 26 Nov 1907 and enclosures and papers, and *E.A.S.*, 30 Nov 1907.
43. *E.A.P. Gazette*, 1 Dec 1907.
44. *Minutes of the Proceedings of the Legislative Council of East Africa,* (hereafter *E.A.P. Debates*), 9 Dec 1907. Delamere's question is another revealing illustration of the attitude of many employers, who were quite willing to

see a sizeable percentage of a man's earnings spent on his journey to his home from which the employer had recruited and transported him. Delamere in fact resigned from Legislative Council shortly afterwards in protest against the Government's handling of expenditure, land, surveys and labour. He later withdrew the resignation.

Hugh Cholmondeley, 3rd Baron Delamere, 1870–1931. Educated Eton; travelled in East Africa from 1891 onwards, first arriving in Kenya, (EA.P.), 1897. Returned as settler 1903; leading farmer and European politician 1903–1; M.L.C. and M.E.C. at various times.

45. The Gusii had been punished by a stock levy calculated to force them on to the labour market.
46. *Correspondence relating to Affairs in the East Africa Protectorate*, Cd. 4122 of 1908; Sadler's despatches in C.O. 533/42, C.O. 533/43 and C.O. 533/44; Elspeth Huxley, *White Man's Country*; and *E.A.S.*, March–April 1908 provide accounts of this demonstration, its causes and consequences. Hollis's memorandum is attached to Sadler's despatch of 8 Apr 1908, C.O. 533/43.
47. Elspeth Huxley, *White Man's Country*, I, 227.
48. *E.A.P. Gazette*, 15 Apr 1908.
49. C.O. 533/44, Sadler to Colonial Office, 19 May 1908, and attached papers which include the text of Crewe's reply of 27 Aug 1908. These documents were published in *E.A.S.*, 21 Nov 1908.
50. *E.A.P. Gazette*, 15 Aug 1908.
51. Minutes of Executive Council of 23 Dec 1908. The ambiguity is made more difficult by the poor English in which the council's policy was formulated. Council 'advised under the circumstances that it would be better to adhere to what has already been stated, that direct recruitment of labour would follow the introduction of the legislation referred to. In the meantime it would be well to instruct District Officers in view of the opinions already expressed by some Labour Boards, that pending the introduction of legislation on the subject, the recruitment of labour by settlers and private individuals should be encouraged as far as possible to make their own arrangements to procure the labour they require.'

    By 'direct' recruitment the council meant recruitment direct by the private employer. In the last sentence, the council evidently meant that a warning of a future policy change would be prudent in view of views, presumably adverse, put forward by district labour boards.

    Executive Council resolutions were sent to P.C.s so this confusing statement could easily be interpreted in different ways by different officials to add to the confusion.
52. C.O. 533/61, Jackson to Colonial Office, 13 July 1909, and enclosure. The 1908–9 Report of the Principal Medical Officer 'noted a considerable improvement in the care of these moving or stationary gangs of labour since the beginning of the year'.

    It is also noteworthy that when in Aug 1908 Sadler wished to go on tour he was unable to do so as men could not be recruited voluntarily at a wage the government was prepared to offer, and compulsion was not applied.
53. *Leader*, 20 Feb 1909.
54. Sadler had come under criticism in Britain. An M.P. had asked what the Governor had been doing in the chair at a settlers meeting. The Government House demonstration had once again aroused the concern of humanitarian bodies. Sir F. Buxton, presiding at an Anti-Slavery Society meeting, had said the settlers possessed the motives of slave drivers using the methods of suffragettes.
55. The *Protectorate Annual Report 1911–12*, Cd. 6007 of 1912–13, for example recorded the 'natives of Meru show considerable progress. Thousands have been induced to go to Nairobi and Mombasa for work', and the 1913–14 Annual Report, Nyeri District, noted 'demands [for labour] have often led to bloodshed'.
56. *Leader*, 26 Feb 1910.

57. *Leader*, 25 Nov 1911 and Barth Commission Report, evidence of J. J. Drought, who quoted from this plain-speaking circular: '. . . so long as there continues an idea that any wretched hut and a minimum amount of mealie and matama meal is good enough for a native, and where as is the case in the Highlands, a black man from hot Kavirondo is turned out in the early morning and worked nearly all day, then has to sleep in a leaky or wind exposed hut with possibly one thin blanket to cover him, with no one to cook his food or bring him wood or water after the day's toil is done, and with no one to take an interest in him, then the labour must naturally suffer.'
58. *E.A.P. Debates*, 25 Nov 1912.
59. *E.A.S.*, 8 Feb 1913. N. Leys, *Kenya*, 1924 (hereafter Leys) wrongly attributed these remarks to Girouard.
60. The new hut and poll tax rates were supplied to Embu, Fort Hall, Nyeri, Ukamba, Naivasha and all the Coast except Jubaland. Probably thanks to Ainsworth, it was not at first applied to Nyanza, but it was extended to the Nyanza districts later. The reader may need to be reminded that at this time the Europeans and Indians paid no form of direct tax at all, though a non-native poll tax at the rate of 22.50 rupees (Shs. 30/-) per adult male was instituted in 1912. The administration officers in the areas clearly saw in 1912 the tax increases as a labour producing device, a number commenting in their annual reports that this aim was only achieved in part.

   The increased size of the administration enabled the more densely populated districts to have three or four assistant D.C.s, a great part of whose time and energy could be devoted to tax collection. The following table indicates this trend:

	1905	1909	1915 (approved in 1914)
Provincial Commissioners	6	6	6
District Commissioners	15	15	44
Assistant District Commissioners	28	40	67 *Colonial Office Lists.*

61. One such abuse, for example, was that if an African could produce a 10 rupee note, either for himself or a group of two or three, change would not be given. Another is described in the Sept 1912 Quarterly Report of the Ukamba P.C.: '60 men were obtained for the Telegraph, they were not exactly volunteers as being Poll tax defaulters. They were given the choice of being prosecuted and sent to Gaol for two months or doing one month's work. A good report was received of their work.'
62. The likelihood of being taxed twice—hut tax at home and poll tax at work, appeared to be the cause.
63. The 1912–13 Annual Report, Ukamba Province, noted this threat.
64. The reasons for this failure are examined by H. Fearn, *An African Economy, A Study of the Economic Development of the Nyanza Province of Kenya 1903–53*, 1961, 70–2. Labour demands were at the most only one of a number of contributory causes. By producing maize and sim-sim, an African producer could earn 10 rupees per month with little difficulty at this time.
65. F. H. Goldsmith, *John Ainsworth, Pioneer Kenya Administrator, 1864–1946*, 1955, 86–7 notes the text of this letter. See also Ainsworth's evidence to the Barth Commission for elaboration of his views.
66. Barth Commission Report, evidence of the Rev. W. Chadwick.
67. The Master and Servants Ordinance, Ord 4 of 1910, *E.A.P. Gazette*, 1 Apr 1910.

   Offences under the ordinance were again divided into two classes each with separate penalities.

   For Class I offences a servant was liable to a fine not to exceed one month's wages or in default of payment, imprisonment with or without hard labour for a maximum of one month if he failed to start the agreed employment or absented himself without leave; if he were drunk at work; if he neglected to perform his work, or performed it carelessly or improperly; if he used his employer's horse, vehicle, or property without permission; if he used insolent or insulting language to his employer; if he refused to obey a lawful command; and if he gave a false name and address in order to enter employment. The last two offences were not included in the original draft of the bill, being added after Legislative Council debate.

For Class II offences a servant was liable to a fine not to exceed two months' wages or in default of payment, imprisonment with or without hard labour for a maximum of two months if by wilful breach of duty or by intoxication, he committed any act tending to the loss or damage of any property of his employer in his care; if he refused or omitted through wilfulness or drink to protect his employer's property; if a herdsman he failed to report the loss or death of any animal of his employer; or failed to preserve any part of an animal having been so directed by his employer; if he alleged loss of property and the employer could show the loss was due to his default; and if without lawful cause he departed from service with intent not to return.

It is interesting to note the two additions to the list of Class I offences related to 'respect'. The penal provisions were evidently well used, the *Protectorate Annual Report 1912–15*, Cd. 7050 of 1914, noting 'large numbers were proceeded against under the Master and Servants Ordinance'.

68. The Roads in Native Reserves Ordinance, Ord 12 of 1910, *E.A.P. Gazette*, 1 May 1910.

69. The Native Authority Ordinance, Ord 22 of 1912, *E.A.P. Gazette*, 1 Nov 1912.

See also Sir C. Dundas, *op. cit.*, 18–19. Dundas wrote of the common practice of the Kamba to slink into the bush abandoning family and cattle on the approach of a European. 'The habit of absconding was due not only to shyness but the fear of being conscripted for porterage'. Dundas went on to describe a file of unwilling men brought into Kitui under police escort tied together with string through holes in their ear lobes, which were pierced and distended by Kamba custom.

70. In some stations where labour was scarce, either for local reasons or because it was all required for farms, D.C.s were permitted to maintain a permanent station gang, sometimes Swahilis from the Coast.

71. *Scotsman*, 16 Aug 1913, article by the Rev. N. Maclean, reprinted in the Rev. Maclean's book, *Africa in Transformation*, 1913, 181. See also the evidence of Dr. H. R. A. Philp to the Barth Commission 'girls and even children were constantly commandeered'.

72. 'Labour for the Government was in cases ordered out by the chiefs, he estimated that the Railway engaged from 80 to 90 per cent and the P.W.D. 50 per cent (before the war); the balance was procured by District Commissioners', evidence of Ainsworth to the Economic Commission, 1917; *Economic Commission Final Report, Part I. 1919*. A copy of this is attached to a despatch by Northey to the Colonial Office, 5 June 1919, C.O. 533/210.

73. *Leader*, 2 Aug 1910. The *E.A.S.* of 28 March 1908 makes an obscure reference to a strike at the government farm at Mazeras of which no details survive.

74. *E.A.S.*, 14 Dec 1912. These men were paid 44 cts. per day for a five and a half day week, weekend duty being paid overtime.

75. *Leader*, 12 Apr 1913, letter signed 'Disgusted'.

76. *1913–14 Annual Report, P.W.D.* Sometimes men on engagement only received 1 rupee.

77. Barth Commission Report, evidence of Dr. N. Leys.

78. For accounts of Magadi and its railway construction see M. F. Hill, *Magadi*, iv, the evidence of Leys and E. W. Hickes to the Barth Commission and the Report on Public Health and Sanitation prepared by Professor Simpson, of King's College, London for the E.A.P. government. A copy of this latter report is in C.O. 533/168.

Paulings employed some poor characters as supervisors. One of these, an Italian named Fenoglio, kicked a labourer in the stomach for refusing to work at 5 p.m. on a Sunday. The kick touched the man's spleen which was enlarged from malaria, with the result that he died in agony. The case attracted parliamentary attention.

79. The *1915–16 Annual Report, Uganda Railway* noted this customary practice.
80. *E.A.S.*, 13 March 1909 observed that the government should concentrate its efforts on making local men work before importing Nyasa men at this expensive rate.
81. C.O. 533/133, Belfield to Colonial Office, 2 March 1914. The Colonial Office appear originally to have proposed this scheme in order to resettle certain Somalis made homeless as a result of fighting in Somaliland.
82. *E.A.S.*, 25 July 1914, and C.O. 533/140, Belfield to Colonial Office, 10 Sept 1914. The cause of the strike was without doubt primarily political, the first prosecution for refusal to pay non-native poll tax.

    The strike was engineered by L. W. Ritch, an Anglo-Indian lawyer, who had been associated with nationalist politicians in India and South Africa. There were however contributory industrial claims made by the strikers. The Railway General Manager conceded most of the industrial demands without reference to Belfield, to the latter's annoyance. He also promised strike pay and no victimization as an appreciation of the loyal response to the outbreak of war. Ritch was however deported by the military almost immediately after the war began without reference to the Governor, although Belfield later approved their action. The strike involved nearly all the Railway's Indian employees with the notable exception of the Goans. The P.W.D. Asians, in the majority, supported the Railway employees a day or two later as did Asian employees of one large commercial firm.
83. *1913–14 Annual Report, P.W.D.*
84. The P.W.D., for example, employed 201 indentured Indian artisans in Apr 1913, at a rate of 50 rupees per month; by March 1914 the number had been reduced to seventy-eight. The reduction, although offset by a large increase in the number of locally recruited Asians employed, proved too great and in 1914 attempts were made to recruit 200 Asians on indentures from India on three-year contracts. A large number of these were found on arrival to be totally devoid of the skills for which they had been recruited (masons, glaziers, carpenters, smiths, and painters); many had to be repatriated at once. Acrimonious correspondence with Mackinnon's, the government's agents in India, suggests the protectorate government had been the victims of substitution practices prior to embarkation. C.O. 533/152.
85. C.O. 533/102, Girouard to Colonial Office, 6 Feb 1912 and attached papers.
86. Professor Simpson in his report on sanitation described Mombasa as a 'huge insanitary area . . . defective building arrangements with absence of light and ventilation, presence of vermin and uncleanliness and nauseous smells'. He further noted it was impossible for employers to fulfil their housing obligations under the Master and Servants Ordinance.
87. *E.A.S.*, 1 Feb 1913. The 1914–15 Annual Report, Machakos District noted that sixty-eight municipality employees deserted, 'the majority of whom were caught and punished'.
88. Belfield's views, for example, were as sharp as his opinions on taxation; 'To raise the rate of wages would not increase but would diminish the supply of labour . . . A rise in the rate of wages would enable the hut or poll tax . . . to be earned by fewer external workers . . . it follows that if we increase the rate of remuneration of the individual we decrease the number of individuals necessary to earn a given sum.' *E.A.S.* 8 Feb 1913.
89. The meeting included the Coast P.C., the Director of Public Works and Transport, and representatives of the Uganda Railway and the Native Affairs Department.
90. *E.A.S.*, 9 March, 4 May 1907.
91. *Leader*, 25 Nov 1911.
92. A general account of the one cent coin appears in McGregor Ross, 199–200.

The Royal Mint, in a letter to the writers, confirmed that the coins were defective, tests conducted at the time leading to the conclusion that 'the corrosion was due to the action of animal secretion such as perspiration'. *E.A.P. Gazette, passim*, records coinage issued. Evidence to the Barth Commission noted African reluctance to 'break in' to rupee pieces on a homeward journey; several witnesses remarked on this reluctance in particular a D.C., R. G. Stone, a labourer, Kogi wa Manyingi, and a farmer, T. Hewitt.

93. *E.A.S.* (at that time *African Standard*), 5 Sept 1903.
94. *Leader*, 12 March 1910. The Registration of Domestic Servants Ordinance, Ord 24 of 1910, appears in the *E.A.P. Gazette*, 1 Oct 1910.
95. The study of Swahili phrase-books for new European arrivals in East Africa makes interesting reading. Phrases are peremptory, always in the imperative and usually prefaced by 'Boy'. For very many years 'there is no Swahili word for please' remained a European stereotype.
96. *Leader*, 23 May 1914, described one such operation, '. . . these nocturnal raids on the boys' quarters of suburban residences are likely to yield a rich harvest of lazy black wasters . . .'
97. Isak Dinesen (Baroness Karen von Blixen), *Shadows in the Grass*, 1960, 41–76.
98. Elspeth Huxley, *Red Strangers*, vi, provides a valuable fictional account of the experiences of a resident labourer's wife in a strange area.
99. Most of the chiefs who gave evidence to the Barth Commission were opposed to resident labour. Their opposition was based on the more people left the heavier tax burden for those remaining, disputes over land and stock among those absent and those who returned, and the education of children away from tribal custom.
100. It is impossible to assess the number of true squatters in the pre-war period, as the numbers are inflated by Kaffir farmers. But in general witnesses to the Barth Commission appear to have had only small percentages of their labour, properly speaking, resident with their families.
101. *E.A.P. Gazette*, 1 May 1910. Labour agents also occasionally advertised in the press. For example, on 4 Jan 1913 W. G. Parker and Co. advertised in the *E.A.S.* 'Strong boys in batches of 50 to 1000 supplied.' This particular advertisement was repeated for many months. Parker recruited largely in Meru, where the 1911–12 Annual Report for the district observed he collected some 1,400 men in two months. As in that year only 3,000 men (excluding porters) went out to work from Meru district this represents a very large proportion; only in post-war years do the district reports assert with confidence that all labourers were examined medically. One or two other agents also advertised in 1912, 1913 and 1914.

    For a remarkable photograph of a labour agent, his staff and a gang of recruited labour see Rev. N. Maclean, *op. cit.*, 177.
102. It is also noticeable that one W. S. Bent, operating a private labour exchange (one purpose of which was to keep wage rates low) in Nairobi, advertised each week in the *E.A.S.* that men could be supplied. This exchange, probably intentionally, also assisted the replacement of Asian domestic staff by Africans.
103. John William Arthur, 1881–1952. Educated Glasgow Academy, Glasgow University; arrived Kenya, (E.A.P.), as missionary and doctor 1906; organized Kikuyu Missions Volunteer Corps 1917–18; M.L.C. (for native interests) 1924–6; M.E.C. 1928–9; retired 1937.
104. *Leader*, 15 Feb 1913.
105. The two estates were the E.A. Estates Ltd. and the Gazi Rubber and Fibre Estates, both at Shimoni. The conditions were so disgraceful that Belfield forbade both estates from engaging more labour and on 18 Aug 1913 reported his action to the Colonial Office. C.O. 533/121. The Coast P.C., Hobley, reported that neither estate had even a medical dresser, though both were in unhealthy areas. At the time of his visit, Hobley was told that a Swahili dresser had formerly been employed but had departed and not been replaced. At the Gazi estate dysentery sufferers were being given maize

meal porridge, a very dangerous diet for a dysentery victim. Many employees were suffering from ulcers and the rations of all sick were cut by a half. The estate had failed to report twenty-eight deaths. Hobley judged the manager to be a 'weak character' and to his labour apathetic to an 'astonishing' degree. On the E.A. Estates plantation, Hobley found over 100 sick, including fifteen dangerously ill. There was no hospital, the medicine was limited to zinc ointment for septic ulcers. Hobley judged the camp to be 'scandalous', adding 'the whole camp stinks, it is, I believe, thoroughly septic and swarms of flies rise up from the ground as one walks around'. After his visit fifty-three men were admitted to the local hospital, seven dying almost immediately. Between 18 per cent and 29 per cent of the labour, mostly Nyanza, on both estates were sick. E.A. Estates Ltd., maintained discipline with the *kiboko* but the government considered the only breach of the law by either estate was the failure to report deaths and possibly also to provide medical facilities. The Governor reported a few weeks later to the Colonial Office that conditions at the two estates had been greatly improved, C.O. 533/124. But the whole incident did not apparently suggest to Belfield any immediate measures stronger than the communique.

Harcourt minuted 'A horrible account' on the file.

The communique was published in full in the *Leader*, 3 May 1913 and in part in the *E.A.P. Gazette*, 15 Apr 1913.

106. McGregor Ross, 98.

107. A few examples illustrate the numbers: a Limuru mixed dairy farm, 150; a Kiambu sisal, coffee and wattle farm, 135; Lord Delamere's farms, 550; a sisal plantation at Punda Milia, 500; an Asian railway ballast contractor, 200–500; the Magadi railway works, 4,200; the Thika railway, 2,600; a Coast rubber plantation, 150–200; an Njoro fuel cutter, 800.

108. *1913–14 Annual Report, P.W.D.*

109. The situation seems in no way to have improved after the commission took evidence. The *1913–14 Annual Report, P.W.D.* noted an outbreak of plague in addition to the other diseases, necessitating the dispersal of the camps; thirty-one men died in the 1913 14 year, including thirteen plague victims.

The Mombasa water supply was by no means exceptional in respect of health hazards for the Kikuyu. Sadler had forbidden goverment officers to recruit or assist the recruiting of Kikuyu for the Coast in 1907, but this prohibition had not prevented private recruiting and was largely ineffective by 1912. The Nyeri P.C., in his evidence, noted that of 220 Embu recruited for work at the Coast in Apr 1912, fifteen had died and sixty were sick at the time, and forty Kikuyu had died in the Vanga District in four months of 1912 alone.

110. In this respect, according to the evidence of Dr. H. R. A. Philp, work on the Fort Hall and Naivasha-Baringo roads, was the most dangerous. He described this work as 'constant murder', saying he could not classify deaths he regarded as preventable in any other way.

111. McGregor Ross, 91, describes this practice as common.

One of the district officers was M. H. W. Beech of Dagoretti, who cited in his evidence an example of an employer who gave a chit for each day's work but never issued more than twenty-eight, after which he set about beating the men. Beech investigated the case and reported a whole crowd of men came in with calabashes of chits but that none could produce thirty.

After the publication of the report the system of inspection of camps and work-sites was improved. Administrative officers were instructed to report under the following headings: Contracts of service (to cover each contract, medical examination, labour agent, period of contract and wages, food, blankets and cooking utensils), Numbers resident, Housing and Sanitary Arrangements, Water Supply, Sickness (covering medicines, food for the sick, hospital arrangements and the number of men invalided home), Desertions, Deaths, Punishments, Crediting of Unfinished Work, System of Records,

Complaints and General Observations. Deficiencies were followed up by correspondence with employers and reference to Nairobi.

But in view of the small number of officers available for inspection work abuses of all types continued virtually unchecked.

112. At the beginning of white settlement, a man might pay, in Kikuyuland, twenty to twenty-five goats, in Kamba country ten goats, for a wife. The price was now at least thirty to forty if not more, and in some areas a sheep or a goat were costing as much as 8–12 rupees, making a minimum bride price of 240 rupees in cash terms, though it must be remembered the labourer would have owned some goats before he went out to work. The inflationary rise in price was exacerbated by Somali traders, who bought cheaply from the pastoral tribes to sell at a profit in Kikuyuland. A number of consumer goods had also risen in price.

113. The evidence revealed interesting African spending patterns. Tax money for himself or his family was the chief target, but stock to purchase a wife or wives was popular, and a number of African witnesses stated preferences for consumer goods, cups, saucers, cutlery, tea, sugar, rice, peppers, hoes, matchets, axes, clothes and blankets. Reference was also made to beer and women in the towns.

114. One witness favoured, quite simply, that the natives be told it was the government's wish that they should work, and any who objected should be given twenty five lashes for insolence.

115. Tribal retainers acquired a sinister reputation, often being sent around homesteads to threaten men to work in one form or another. The 1910–11 Annual Report, Kikuyu District, described their work as 'serving summonses under the Master and Servants Ordinance (for desertion) and other offences'. They received no pay and so almost inevitably were quickly to turn to corruption. The evidence of M. W. H. Beech is once again of particular interest. He cited two bottles of whisky as an example of a bribe, stated he had seen forged contracts and a faked request to a chief purporting to come from himself for 300 men, and added his own experience of sick men being left to die by the roadside. McGregor Ross added a variety of bribes in his evidence, these included a shot-gun, whisky, a mule with saddle and harness and other consumer goods. Beech's evidence was selected for a specially critical article in the *Leader* of 16 Nov 1912, which commented that the evidence showed the 'kink of officialdom'. He was already notorious for having deposed a headman for forcing labour.

116. The Railway appeared to have no sense of shame over their practice. The *E.A.P. Gazette* in Nov 1911 published a notice announcing a reduction of 25 per cent or more in 3rd Class Railway fares, with for batches of not less than ten an even greater reduction, providing the batches were proceeding to work on farms, plantations, mines or the Railway, and with the reservation that if the Railway administration so required, the men must travel by goods train.

117. One government officer, J. Pearson, expressed his belief that tax so nearly equating a man's monthly pay led a labourer to borrowing money which he found he could never repay. He then deserted taking work elsewhere under another name.

118. 'Kaffir farming', which usually took place near Nairobi or the railway, had a further implication unacceptable to the majority of settlers, that the African could grow and sell his own produce, contrary to one of the major tenets of the settlers' self-justification. It is not surprising, therefore, the practice was frequently and strongly condemned by the Convention of Associations.

Sometimes 'Kaffir farmers' even further abused their position by forcing sales of their tenants' crops. The December 1910 Quarterly Report, Ukamba Province, noted sixty-seven villages of 'Kaffir' tenants on one farm in the province.

119. Ainsworth operated a voluntary pass system designed to help the work-

seeker and curb desertion, a system that seems to have been used widely by Africans from Nyanza. In his evidence Ainsworth emphasised that his system was in no way compulsory.

120. See also Lord Cranworth, *op. cit.*, 55, which gives as typical examples of this type of irritant the careful digging of a tunnel under a shed to steal a calf, the removal of the interior of a woodpile carefully preserving the exterior façade of piled logs, and similar purloining of maize cobs piled on a platform within thin wire walls. L. Powys, *Black Laughter*, 1925, 95, gives others. Such irritants added to the employer's sense of moral superiority, appearing to justify harsh penalties.

121. Beech was probably over optimistic. More likely reasons for loyal work were a belief that the Europeans' occupation was only temporary and that it would be an affront to past and future generations of the tribe to leave the land uncared for. See, for example, a fictional Kikuyu's reaction in J. Ngugi (Ngugi wa Thiong'o), *Weep Not Child*, 1969, 35.

122. The Kamba were often small employers; there were some 2,000 Kikuyu working for them at a wage which varied from a goat to 4 rupees per month. The Kikuyu considered this work easier than work for Europeans. The Kamba avoided the labour market for many years except in uniformed tasks such as police and the K.A.R.

123. *E.A.S.*, 31 Jan 1914.

124. C.O. 533/134, Belfield to Colonial Office, 9 March 1914.

On encouragement he wrote: 'It is of the utmost importance that all officers entrusted with duties of native administration should impress upon the people the desire of the Government that their young men should go out to work, and should keep the fact always prominently before them. I am taking steps to see that more attention is paid to the subject than has been the case in some instances in the past. While among the Wadigo people at the Coast, and more recently among the Kavirondo in the Mumias District, I alluded to this subject at every *baraza* I held, not only telling the people that it is my desire that they should supply as large and regular a labour force as possible for outside employment and pointing out the advantages accruing therefrom, but adding particulars of the steps which have been taken to ensure the health and comfort of labourers at their work, and assuring them that the establishment and maintenance of such conditions was a matter which was engaging my personal attention'. He noted also that he had written a circular to administration officers in similar terms.

125. J. H. Harris, 'Making the "Lazy Nigger" Work', *Contemporary Review*, June 1914, denounced as 'selected taradiddle', *Leader*, 18 July 1914. The society's interest once aroused was to continue in the nineteen-twenties and thirties. Harris, for example, helped Jomo Kenyatta with his expenses in London in 1930.

126. *Parliamentary Debates, Commons*, 28 July 1914. British press reporting of this debate on 29 July was limited, events in Europe no doubt over-shadowing the parliamentary scene. *The Times* for example offered only a few lines under the heading of 'E.A. Land Commission', and the *Scotsman* noted 'Debate ranged over a field as varied as it was wide. It concerned the situation in Somaliland, native reserves in East Africa, the recent constitutional crisis in Tasmania.... On all these points Mr Harcourt took an optimistic view. He declared that there was no ground for the alarmist reports as to Somaliland, and he expressed his determination to see that the natives were not imposed upon either in respect of their land or of labour conditions.'

127. *E.A.S.*, 4 July 1914 and *Leader*, 4 July 1914 both carried the text of the summary letter and reported the debate. C.O. 533/134, Belfield to Colonial Office, 9 March 1914 and attached papers contain the draft of Harcourt's reply, which appears to have been sent on 20 May 1914.

128. C.O. 533/140, Belfield to Colonial Office, 1 Sept 1914.

Further details of the scheme provided for Native Affairs Department representatives in towns; complete registration; labour officers at the principal points of labour 'exit or entrance' with magisterial powers to check registration complaints, wage rates and travelling arrangements; the government to recruit for its own purposes exclusively through the bureaux, the government to maintain camps to house men delayed by the medical examination requirement; a labour camp at Nairobi; and the bureaux to run other reception camps if required.

Belfield and Ainsworth both reiterated the importance of avoiding direct recruiting by government officers, but it is hard to see how they imagined African peoples would distinguish between the bureaux and the government.

129. *E.A.P. Debates*, 25 Nov 1912. In opening the session of the Council, Belfield referred to labour and noted 'some tribes which declined to come out to work. He referred to the Giriama tribe, who would be able to supply a large proportion of labour required at the Coast and yet absolutely declined to come out of their country and do a hand's turn for anybody. He was hopeful however that this disinclination might be dispelled by the appointment of additional officers to administer such tribes.'

130. Leys, 131.

Chapter 3

THE FIRST WORLD WAR, 1914–1918

You shenzi* of prolific race
Of lazy action, hard old case
With one life's work, to feed your face
It's good we had you handy . . .

And midst the burst of a 4.1
Mid the patter of feet of the porters who'd run
You have joked at the aim of a German gun
When I didn't quite like it myself.

East African Standard,
8 February 1919

Oh! The Lindi road was dusty
And the Lindi road was long
But the chap w'at did the hardest graft
Was the Kavirondo porter, with his Kavirondo song.
It was 'Porter, njo hapa'†
It was 'Omera, hya! Git'
And Omera didn't grumble
He simply did his bit.

Wartime verse, quoted F. H. Goldsmith, *John Ainsworth, Pioneer Kenya Administrator, 1864–1946*

The First World War imposed infinitely more severe burdens upon the African population, while the political and economic demands of the European settlers were at the same time greatly increased in both scope and pressure. The four years of the war were years of almost unrelieved, incomprehensible, and seemingly interminable suffering for the African population, to whom even the consolation, if it were such, of knowing other peoples in other lands were also suffering was denied.

It is clearest to examine separately the recruitment and service of African military labour and the efforts made to keep at least some settler farms in production, efforts which continued to require a sizeable number of men. Both operated against a background of officials increasingly overworked but decreasing in number and quality and of the wartime preoccupations of London politicians and Colonial Office officials against which the voices of humanitarian pressure groups, themselves muted by the war, could make little impression. Equally important, both military and normal labour were employed in the context of an end of prosperity and the rapid accumulation of public and private debt.

* Shenzi—a slatternly individual.
† Njo hapa—come here.

Military Labour

The war came as a surprise and when it began the protectorate shared the belief that it would be settled quickly in Europe. Little prior thought had been given to any African campaigning; the few manuals were 'practically silent on that speciality of African warfare, carrier transport on a large scale', an inexperience to prove extremely costly.[1] But the demand to make the African work now became invested with patriotism when both military and other labour was required. Previously the native was a 'shirker' by his reluctance to work, in war he was a 'traitor', and only a very few Europeans, a number which decreased as the casualty lists in Europe lengthened, saw any remaining objection to overt compulsion. At the outset and except for the Giriama, the African response was generally one of loyal support, those chiefs requested to produce labour doing so without much difficulty, all in the belief that the war like African wars would be short.

The military authorities first requested carrier labour in August 1914 and two district officers, of which O. F. Watkins was the senior, were told to organize the men.[2] Hasty improvization led to great confusion, men despatched to Nairobi deserting or changing their names or groups en route and with muddles over food and camps. To improve the organization and to impose discipline it was decided to give the carrier units military status with young district officers or farmers as officers. The name first selected was the Carrier Corps.[3] But none of the officers, not even Watkins for some considerable time, carried any rank higher than captain. In these early units African labourers participated in the operations against the Giriama and in the disastrous Tanga expedition, suffering a number of casualties in open lighters.

The numbers required and the confusion quickly led to an end of the supply of willing volunteers. By early 1915 even the high wages paid were failing to attract men while annoying settlers seeking agricultural labour. Martial law and the Native Authority Ordinance were both wrongly used to impress men and chiefs were given large quotas to provide, their methods being supervised less carefully. As 1915 progressed pressures became more severe, co-operative chiefs and headmen being rewarded by favourable reports and promotion, and others punished. The least scrupulous chiefs sent tribal retainers for little or no reason to arrest men; these along with others convicted of minor offences in court and Gusii and Luo followers of the Mumbo cult were all sent forward to the carrier depots. Sometimes raids at night were organized to round up men; others either in normal regular employment or on a brief vacation might be seized and vagrants and other offenders against pass laws would be regarded as 'loafers' and sent for service.[4] Sometimes ruses were carefully prepared to attract a crowd when the menfolk would be seized by guards or soldiers and herded into a pen.[5] At the front desertions began.

Other factors combined to the disadvantage of the carrier. Carrier Corps service, lacking glamour, failed to retain its best officers; these became replaced by Rhodesians or South Africans, or British Army sergeants, all less concerned with the men's welfare and more inclined to harsh discipline. More men became needed for the Turkana punitive force, for expanding operations against the Germans and for military railway construction.[6] Different categories of carriers began to appear—the aristocrats such as uniformed machine-gun porters and stretcher-bearers being better paid, while officers' servants and carriers from other territories who were also reasonably paid and administered formed a middle class, and the lowly E.A.P. carrier or construction labourer lay at the bottom of the scale where he was a general target of abuse.

The needs for more and more men, a minimum of 3,000 per month, led to the enactment of the Native Followers Recruitment Ordinance in September 1915. This ordinance gave district commissioners powers to instruct chiefs and headmen to supply any numbers of recruits under thirty-five years of age for carrier service under threat of severe penalties.[7] The ordinance was greeted with warm approval by the settlers. Letters to the *Leader* earlier in the year had demanded action against 'loafing Niggers' in Nairobi, the paper now commenting that 'under the Ordinance our idle, irresponsible natives will at last be compelled to do their duty towards the Empire . . .'[8] The Colonial Office, to whom the ordinance was sent more than two weeks after its passage by the Legislative Council, accepted the justification of urgent action.

The ordinance gave clear legal authority to the district commissioners to order men to enlist, which of course many were in fact already doing, through chiefs or elders, these now reinforced by new unpaid retainers known as *capiteni*; the result was a large increase in the numbers of men conscripted. Rules made under the ordinance in April 1916 laid down that liability for service was to extend for the duration of the war, but that if military exigencies permitted, the unskilled carrier was to be relieved after nine months. At the same time and to reflect the changed work, the Carrier Corps organization gave way to the Military Labour Bureau (later Corps) and a new organizational system provided some measure of specialist care with two officers and four non-commissioned officers for each thousand men. From July 1916 pay also passed to the Military Labour Bureau which introduced, significantly for the future, a proper documentation system based on fingerprints and identity discs known as the *kipande*.

The conscription of large numbers of men brought the question of the payment rate to a head. At the outbreak of war the carriers were engaged at the current Coast rates. These varied between 10 and 15 rupees with rations, a rate considerably above that of farm labour to the alarm of up-country employers. In July the government instructed that the 10 rupee rate be paid only to men in the firing line and others be paid at 'local rates', a successful protest against this change being lodged on behalf of Mombasa men. The newly formed War Council with its strong European settler membership took up the matter of carriers' rates almost immediately, arguing both that it was an expense heavy in itself and that the 'high rate of pay was bound to affect unfavourably the industrial conditions of the country both now and in the future'.[9] The Council recommended rates of 5 to 6 rupees with rations, and at a settler Defence Force dinner Belfield announced these reduced rates to enormous applause. From this time carriers were paid 5 rupees with rations for the first three months, 6 rupees with rations thereafter, a rate lower even than that of the P.W.D.

The carrier, once recruited, was issued with one, very occasionally two blankets, a knife, waterbottle, haversack and identity disc, and according to the stores situation one or more jerseys and pairs of shorts. If he was lucky he lived in a thin tent, if unlucky under any shelter he could find. On being enlisted he might be put in a cattle or goods-wagon, given a handful of maize meal and sent on a two day journey to the front or to the Coast. From the Coast he might be sent to the front by ship, a terrifying experience for an African who had never seen the sea. In the forward areas conditions worsened as the Allies advanced in 1916 and 1917. Difficulties of strange climates, heat by day and cold by night, were worsened by exceptionally heavy rains in late 1916 and early 1917 and the almost total exhaustion of the supply of oxen. The terrain was everywhere difficult—dry hills, waterless wastes of thorn, jungle and high grass, rivers with their terrors for non-swimmers, and the animal hazards of lions, leopards, rhinoceros, elephants, crocodiles, leeches and insects. Nor did the enemy draw a distinction between carrier and soldier; the carrier suffered from enemy raids (particularly on construction parties), artillery fire and many of the hazards of battle. Occasionally when troops were short, commanders used carriers as a decoy force. Carriers taken prisoner were often left foodless to wander and die.

The work required of the men varied from port construction, railway repair, and camp and road construction, to the simple carriage of heavy loads of food, stores or the sick; in theory loads were limited to 45 lb. per man for ten miles per day, but the needs of the campaign often led to overloading and longer marches. On the march the carriers' issue of clothes quickly wore out and were replaced by purloined red blankets, loin cloths or kilts made of reeds or straw. By day the carriers struggled on, singing if energy and the absence of the enemy permitted. At night loads would be dropped, if possible near water, and any exhausted ox or horse consumed with the *posho*. Discipline was enforced by corporal punishment, fines or stoppages of pay being almost meaningless in the circumstances.[10] In the early days desertions were few, but by 1917 the situation had so deteriorated that a special Carrier police had to be formed to prevent wholesale desertions.[11]

Food was unsatisfactory for most of the campaign. If carriers were near the enemy, cooking might be impossible; heavy rain or staff confusion might prevent the delivery of supplies and priority was always given to soldiers rather than carriers. The issue of an adequate ration was one of Watkins's chief concerns throughout the war, but he found himself opposed by the Central Committee of Supplies, composed almost entirely of East African businessmen and farmers and reflecting their prejudices.[12] In October 1914 the authorized ration was only $1\frac{1}{2}$ lb. of maize meal or beans, $\frac{1}{2}$ lb. of meat and $\frac{1}{2}$ oz. of salt per day, though these rations were slightly improved late in 1914 and again early 1915, with some real improvement in 1916 when the quality of maize was improved and sugar and oil or fat provided. Only in July 1917 was a soldier's ration scale at last conceded. The rations at all stages posed distressing problems, the issue of maize or beans to men unaccustomed to them causing diarrhoea and dysentery, particularly as in the early years of the war poor quality maize unevenly ground was issued uncooked to gangs of carriers to prepare as they wished. The men, unaccustomed to winnowing, often worsened matters by careless food preparation. The use of better ground South African maize meal only partially improved the situation, many Africans afflicted with internal troubles still developing a death wish only too easily attained. In 1917 it was decided that all food would be prepared by trained cooks, a decision that led to one or two small strikes but quickly resulted in a marked reduction in sickness and death.

It was never possible to select men for work and life in climates for which they might be best suited nor to plan operations with carriers' welfare to mind; it is not surprising therefore that carriers became quickly worn out and diseased. It was soon found that the percentage of sick men increased out of all proportion to the increase in total numbers, a condition exacerbated by severe rains in 1916–17. In September 1916, wrote Watkins:

> ... when they were called upon for a supreme effort on short rations, the men were already debilitated and overworked. As a final torture, the rains broke early and converted large areas into swamp, throwing still more work on the carrier, who in one stretch of the Dodoma-Iringa road had to carry nine miles mostly waist deep in water, much of it on raised duck walks made of undressed poles laid side by side, whilst the Mikesse line was little better ... The sufferings and casualties of this period from September 1916 to March 1917 will never be fully known.[13]

The medical problems were almost overwhelming. Fevers, dysentery, malaria, pneumonia and bronchitis, anaemia and valvular heart disease killed men on the march, in hospitals, and after their return home where diseases were distributed wider. Some tribes became inflicted with diseases hitherto little known to them (for example the war spread malaria among the Nandi for the first time). Enteric fever, too, spread as carriers polluted streams. Once again the carrier rated low, Watkins freely admitting that many doctors were not greatly interested in the carrier, who came a poor third after the white officer and the black soldier.[14] Urgent requests were made for more doctors from England and India and a separate carrier medical service was built up in 1916. By the end of 1917 there was an Assistant Director of Medical Services (Carriers), 110 doctors, 2,000-bed hospitals for carriers all along the line with a total of 15,000 beds, and a variety of staff operating first-aid centres or hospitals every few miles. Increased supplies of motor-vehicles eased the transport of sick carriers, and from mid-1917 carriers began to return from the front in slightly better shape and the death rate was lowered.

But the harm had been done in 1916, the tales of horror or even more sinister the silence of the small number of gaunt men, skin stretched tightly over ribs and shoulders, hair unshaven and eyes sunken who had returned to the reserves made others there seek any refuge possible to avoid enlistment. Rumours abounded about those who did not return. Thousands deserted immediately they could, hiding in the bush or with friends; some fled to Uganda and others took the easy option of volunteering for the army. Those who fled to the bush risked punitive expeditions such as one at the Coast described in the local press early in 1916 as 'exciting sport of the "fox and hound" description'; the hunters set the bush on fire and 'shirkers' were driven by the fire towards *askaris.*[15] Chiefs were bribed to enable some to be spared and others to be collected or to facilitate desertion. Some men sought sanctuary by offering themselves to the various missions but by 1916–17 the missions were refusing to accept fit adult males. Others sought the lesser evil of employment on a European farm. One local paper cheerfully reported 'so many boys are coming forward to escape the kamata [grab] that . . . shamba [plantation] owners would probably meet with little difficulty in reducing wages from the present high standard', and a 'threat of dismissal and Sirkali [Government] kamata is settling all sorts of labour trouble'.[16] Chiefs actually prevented men going out to farm work in order to retain them for Carrier Corps recruitment, which led to a renewal of settler criticism of Ainsworth and the administration for obstructing 'encouragement'. Although the full overall consequences of the war and Carrier Corps recruitment were only reached in 1918, even as early as 1916 Dr. H. R. A. Philp wrote that 'probably up to half' the adult men in the Kenya Province were sick and that the reserves were being combed for men who were not there. He noted that the hut tax receipts recorded a drop of 7,000 in Nyeri District alone and protested vigorously against the practice whereby men who were rejected on medical grounds for the Carrier Corps were compelled to work on farms.[17]

Even worse burdens, however, were to befall the African population. As the campaign advanced deeper into the remote areas of German East Africa, the army asked for the services of Ainsworth to recruit extra carriers and in March 1917 he was nominated Military Commissioner of Labour with the rank of Colonel. Ainsworth was instructed to produce 42,500 men almost all from the protectorate and over and above the 52,000 on the books at March 1917, with monthly drafts of 3,000 for April and May and 1,600 per month from June onwards; Ainsworth later reported he had raised 50,000 East Africa Protectorate men from 1 April to 1 October.[18]

To provide this drastic toll of men, the chiefs were no longer the principal agents; the method was simple enforced recruitment by the district officers, frequently by armed raids leading to fights on farms and in the forests and reserves, together with the closing of the previous escape routes.[19] In these raids men who had already served and were resting, men on leave from farms, personal enemies of tribal retainers and others busy or idle were all caught indiscriminately. Except for the Maasai, no tribes were any longer exempt by virtue of any other work, nor were men at work on European farms from whom a certain percentage was taken. The African reaction to such conscription was widespread desertion, with important political consequences to be noted later. The missions, faced with the threat of the forcible conscription and indifferent administration of their adherents, decided to form their own unit and in April 1917 the Kikuyu Missions Volunteers Corps was formed by the Rev. Dr. Arthur, assisted by other mission staff.[20] The total strength reached 1,500; there was also a Catholic Labour Corps. These mission carriers were protected from the worst of the horrors befalling the majority and proved very successful. A post-war law case provides some idea of conditions at this time. A sisal estate refused to pay two labour agents for labourers recruited by them in 1917, stating that some had been between nine and twelve years old and others sick or partial cripples; the evidence of medical and administrative officers affirmed that the very large majority were under thirteen and a number were sick.[21]

Recruiting at this pace could not last long and in August 1917, somewhat suddenly, compulsory recruiting stopped. Although there is insufficient evidence definitely to assert that the protectorate was near a rebellion, both Ainsworth and Watkins were disturbed at the general distrust and resentment and feared violent consequences.[22] Demobilization began in March 1918; between 1 April 1918 and 31 March 1919 73,057 men were returned home mostly in need of convalescence. There appear however to have been no incidents and no evidence on the surface of the later political restlessness.

The easing of the pressure came in the nick of time as a series of natural disasters struck the reserves. The short rains of November 1917 failed and maize had to be brought from South Africa. It was then sold to those, for example, such as returned carriers who could pay, or to employers at cost price to feed their labourers, or issued in return for public works performed by adult men. Disaster was exacerbated by the sacrifice of stock in prayer for rain, fire destroyed much African grazing, malaria and dysentery brought by returning carriers spread, and stock animals died from rinderpest, heartwater or plain exhaustion. Llewelyn Powys in a vivid passage described this period:

> Famine stalked through the land with Pestilence galling his kibe. Week after week the country lay prostrate under the blank stare of a soulless sun. Month after month the waters of the lake sank lower and lower ... It was as though the earth itself was undergoing some appalling process of putrefaction. The air was tainted, the flaked dusty mould stank. Everywhere one came across the carcasses of animals dead from exhaustion, carcasses with long muddy tongues protruding ... The vultures grew plump as Michaelmas geese ... The sun rose and sank in a blinding heaven, and under its hideous presence all sensitive life trembled and shrank.[23]

Lastly a virulent influenza epidemic struck the diseased and distracted African population. As if these catastrophes were not sufficient, 1918 also saw a great increase in hookworm and tuberculosis, two frequent products of African labour camps.[24] Ainsworth estimated the total African deaths to be approximately 155,100, the largest proportion of these deaths being among Kikuyu. Some missionaries gave an even larger total; settlers wishing to justify labour coercion, however, argued that the African population was increasing fast.

The government passed Famine Relief Ordinances giving power for the direction of labour and compulsory food growing for famine relief. The ordinances were much criticized, the *East African Standard* commenting that attempts to increase food growing in the reserves would only decrease settler production, others arguing that famine relief should only be given to those who worked for Europeans.[25] One correspondent to this paper actually wrote 'I feel most strongly that the world would not be rendered poorer by the elimination of those members of society ... who would rather starve than work.'[26]

By mid-1918 the overall state of the reserves, both socially and economically was ruinous. In the major reserves the call on fit adult men had drawn away not less than 75 per cent, in some areas 85 per cent or more.[27] Many men were still absent on service, old people were dying, women listless and children pot-bellied. Tribal occasions such as circumcision and dances were not held. Grain prices had risen, other goods were often short in supply. Drinking seemed for many the only consolation, others turned to theft. The returning carrier, bearded, with unkempt hair and only partially recovered in health, often fell to such temptations.

It is difficult to assess overall the numbers of actual soldiers and carriers killed or deceased in the war. The protectorate government in a despatch to the Colonial Office estimated that of the total of 201,431 military labourers 26,193 were known dead, and a further 14,000 deserters were presumed dead, to which should be added a large number of men who died on their homeward journey or at home.[28] Leys gives a figure of 366 porters only killed in action; the deaths of the remainder were due to disease or overwork.

What was the impression of all this suffering on Africans? Labour for the European in peacetime had been alien, his warfare totally incomprehensible.[29] Why march endlessly to disappear in a strange, evil country, rather than fight a brief quick campaign to seize women and stock and then return home? At the same time simple peasants came into violent contact with the twentieth century. Watkins wrote in his report:

> Men who a few years ago had never seen a white man, to whom the mechanism of a tap or a doorhandle is still an inscrutable mystery, have been trained to carry into action on their heads the field wireless or the latest quick-firing gun. Men of tribes which had never advanced so far in civilisation as to use wheeled transport who a few years ago would have run shrieking from the sight of a train, have been steadied till they learned to pull great motor lorries out of the mud, to plod patiently along hardly stepping to one side while convoy after convoy of oxcarts, mule carts and motor vehicles grazed by them, till they hardly turned their heads at the whirr of passing aircraft.[30]

The cost was greater than the mere toll of death. The British soldier, in the mud of the Ypres salient, knew that death would at least bring peace and if he were religious also very probably spiritual salvation. To the African carrier, however, there were fears beyond the grave. Much of the work he was called upon to do was not simply unpleasant, it was a painful and recurrent eternal evil—life in the same hut or tent obviously cursed as shown by the number of dying men, the carrying of corpses or the wounded from whom blood was flowing, the strangeness of the country and of other carriers from other tribes, the pain and incomprehensibility of poisoned water, wounds and disease, and burial with strangers in a common ditch. These evils might kill a man, but far worse, what would then become of his spirit (who was believed to play a part in the life of a man's children) lost for ever in these terrible foreign lands? Some sought death deliberately; others swore never to discuss matters which they felt at the time must excommunicate them from their own home societies. A deafness seemed to affect the Nandi and Lumbwa men, and a dumbness the Kamba, the Medical Department judging these to be hysteric conditions comparable to shell-shock. Both the Medical Department and the mission doctors commented on a temporary insanity which affected many in Kikuyuland. Without doubt the Nyanza peoples stood the strain the best, creating a lasting memory of cheerful good humour among Europeans. In Nairobi the *Leader* noted as early as 28 October 1916 that men feared to venture out in the dark lest white men cut them up to restore the wounded, and the strains led to occasional inter-tribal brawls.

Return to the reserves brought small consolation since social life and marriages were disrupted and war widows and aged parents destitute. Returning men found themselves dispossessed and obliged to take legal actions for recovery. The chiefs, rewarded by medals and promotion, had become '. . . in native eyes, the paid labour agents of the Government', in both recruitment and the recapture of deserters.[31] Some chiefs were disturbed by these duties, the majority appear not to have been. Some simple men arranged tribal sacrifices in vain, believing the gods were angry that young men had allowed themselves to be taken away to die in the Europeans' war. One perceptive observer noted as a further consequence that 'a Kikuyu who came out of his reserve lost caste, and on his return he could not get a wife, but was made to do Government work before the others', another adding that some chiefs feared the escape of young men from their control.[32]

The general disillusion and the limited inter-tribal contacts made on active service found expression in an awakened sense of racial consciousness, many Africans beginning to blame the Europeans for their misfortunes. For the majority this pattern of thinking remained semiconscious, a condition in which the bad could quickly be forgotten in prosperity, but equally quickly be remembered in further adversity. Many administration reports of the time comment on the 'surliness' and 'indiscipline' of labourers at work. But for a minority, the grievances, reinforced by the inspiration of Asian and Baganda political activity, led to a decision for action. A number of Africans engaged in the early political activities of the nineteen-twenties and thirties were former carriers who had learnt the power of discipline and organization.[33] Africans had seen a European tribal conflict in which the British had suffered severe reverses. Individually many Africans had seen astonishing examples of both European bravery and weakness, physical and moral. Individually, too, many thousands of African survivors were left with greatly awakened appetites for new foodstuffs and consumer goods.

The war experience also left an emotional impression on the other two parties in the employment situation, the employers and the government. A number of farmers who had fought in the campaign returned with both an admiration for and a resolution to make life easier for their labour in future. 'I cannot get away from the feeling that where even a Kikuyu is called upon to make the supreme sacrifice it is but common justice that acknowledgement of that sacrifice be made', wrote Lord Cranworth.[34] In a country where the employment situation was so much a psychological one such words were important, for they marked a step in the realization by some employers that their labourers were human beings with lives to lead or lose. A number of government officers had served with the carriers or had seen the state of the reserves in 1918; both experiences led some to protest at the further impositions of the immediate post-war period. More tangible than these general attitudes was the direct knowledge of labour acquired by government administrative officers, in particular Watkins, a knowledge which he incorporated in regulations for the care of the government's own labour, and which he published in the *Official Gazette* for the attention of everyone with all the authority, considerable in Kenya, of experience gained in the war.[35] On Ainsworth himself the effect was severe; contemporary photographs of him show a man who had aged and tired, a factor of importance in the controversies of 1918 and 1919. Lastly, some government officers with First World War experience were to rise to senior positions in the late nineteen-thirties, and by proper planning well in advance to ensure that military labour in the Second World War had never to suffer the miseries of their predecessors.

There remain a few miscellaneous points which need a brief examination to complete a study of military labour in the First World War. Some attempts were made to protect carriers against disease by inoculations, of which the most ambitious was the distribution of various types of anti-dysentery vaccine. The results were of only limited value some vaccines causing complications later if the patient became reinfected with dysentery of a different type. Conditions in camps, hospitals and ships often left a great deal to be desired; 2,100 men died at the Nairobi carrier camp in 1917 alone due, it would seem, to the poor site and absence of drainage.[36] From the start of the war Ainsworth made great efforts in respect of welfare, inaugurating a welfare fund.[37] On his appointment as Commissioner in 1917, he initiated plans for convelescent camps, personally inspected carrier camps, ships and hospitals; he also arranged tax exemption for life for the disabled and exemption for carriers while on service, together with some easement for the worst affected reserve areas.[38] The value of Ainsworth's work was noticed in the field. Captain Lenox Murray of the East African Service Corps writing home to his family on 11 September 1917 noted '. . . since the rains have stopped, and with better organization and good feeding, the losses have been reduced considerably, and they are also not recruiting from the tribes which died so much'. On 26 October 1917 Captain Murray wrote further 'Everything that can be done is being done for the porters now, and that department has improved wonderfully.'[39]

Ainsworth also tried to introduce order into the difficulties of the pay question, carriers were only being paid a proportion of their earnings on the march, the remainder being kept for their return. Many changed names for reasons good or bad or simply used that of their father on some occasions, to the confusion of the records system. Most difficult of all was the question of pay due to missing or dead carriers, which the government tried to solve by legislating a distribution according to tribal custom, with monies unclaimed after three years to be spent for the benefit of the community. In 1921 when the Kenya government proposed to spend the balance of unclaimed pay for African benefit it was forbidden to do so, the British War Office ruling that unclaimed carriers' pay was to be treated in the same manner as that of soldiers and retained by the imperial government. This ruling may at the time have been inspired by fears of shell-shocked claimants subsequently presenting themselves, but its prolongation was obviously unjust and the subject of frequent pressing requests from the Kenya government, missionaries, and settler leaders. The refusal of the British government to pay became a scandal. Sir W. Morris Carter, chairman of the 1931–3 Kenya Land Commission, and S. H. Fazan, the secretary, both of whom had seen at first hand the work of carriers in the war, arranged for the report of the commission to mention in strong terms the outstanding sum, approximately £50,000, although such a matter was outside the commission's terms of reference. Belatedly the British government provided £50,000 to assist to meet the costs of adjustments to land areas recommended by the commision in 1935.

In July 1918 it was decided to call up a small number of Maasai; until 1918 the Maasai had been regarded as unsuitable for any military purpose. The decision was made in the belief that the *moran* or young men needed discipline, but the measure was mishandled by the administration, a military column in error killing some Maasai women. The Maasai, enraged attacked first the column and then Asian stores in a wide outbreak of violence in September and October. The Maasai incident, like its pre-war counterpart the Giriama Rising, is of importance as an early example of secondary resistance to the colonial power, a resistance occasioned principally by a labour requirement.

In conclusion, in contrast to the increasing British anxiety both in Parliament and in the country as a whole, over the welfare of African labour evident in the summer of 1914, the years of the war saw virtually no effective concern for the African military labourer expressed in Britain. The Anti-Slavery Society sent a deputation to the Colonial Office to protest against a project to send African labour battalions to France where they would probably have been better treated than in German East Africa. The society made one ineffective protest about porters' conditions as did P. Molteno, the Liberal M.P. for Dumfries on the basis of information sent him by his nephew, Captain Murray. As the hardships of the war increased in Britain, the more were Africans expected to 'do their bit' and the fewer and less effective were the questions on the conditions under which he served. The E.A.P. Africans in their worst experience with the European were deprived of such limited political support that had been theirs in times less difficult.

Labour Within the Protectorate

The war years saw a great increase in the direct power and indirect influence of the local European community which in the context of employment meant employers, effectively organized, against employees, dispersed and disunited. This political influence reasserted the strident bitter tones of pre-war years amid the difficulties of mounting debt.

The early months of the war brought a short-lived peace to the internal labour scene since many farmers were away. The Hon. G. Cole, Delamere's brother-in-law who had been deported for failing to report that he had killed an African who had stolen one of his sheep, was readmitted to the country, a measure welcomed by the European community.[41] Ainsworth's inquiry into African taxation led to an increase in hut and poll tax rate to 5 rupees; the increase however only became effective in 1916.[42] The Barth Commission's registration recommendations were embodied into an ordinance which was approved by representatives of the Convention and applauded by the local press. The registration system provided for a certificate for all adult males which was to record personal particulars and fingerprints, employers, wages and discharges; employers were forbidden to engage men without a properly completed and endorsed certificate. The government was to keep copies of certificates so deserters could be traced—the real purpose of the measure which was reinforced by stiff penal provisions. The ordinance became law in mid-May 1915, but, significantly, was only sent to the Colonial Office in June.[43] The Colonial Office directed that the scheme be postponed until after the war, but their officials were not able to foresee the full degree of oppression which this innocently titled Registration of Natives Ordinance was to produce.[44]

In September 1915 the changed balance of power in the protectorate was formalized by the formation of the War Council, a body of settlers representing different areas and including many South Africans which was set up by Belfield to further the war effort. Once established the War Council immediately reduced carriers' pay. The Nairobi Defence Force dinner where the reduction was announced to great applause was arranged by Major Grogan and Captains Bowker and Fichat, the three principal defendants in the 1907 flogging incident; the protectorate Chief Secretary and Treasurer figured as a corporal and private respectively.

With the strengthened European voice, the government began to employ a variety of methods to assist the employers. For its own labour needs it did not hesitate to take men gathered under the Native Followers Recruitment Ordinance (although paying them more than carriers). A limited number of prisoners-of-war came to be used by farms and road gangs in the Rift Valley, occasionally authority was given to officers directly to recruit for the private employer, and the Nairobi municipal committee was provided with prison labour.[45] Any labour deserters found in the reserves were sent to the Carrier Corps. Employers visited Carrier Corps depots camps and procured medical rejects. Well-meaning district commissioners, faced with the problem of a group of pre-war farms looked after by one elderly farmer or a farm run by an absent farmer's wife, would often on their own authority direct chiefs to produce labour. In sum, although conscription was not applied directly to farm labourers the pressures fell only a short distance from it.

Following a War Council resolution and again without prior reference to the Colonial Office, the Master and Servants Ordinance was rapidly amended early in 1916 to make desertion and other employee offences cognizable to the police who were givn powers to arrest without warrant.[46] Many deserters had previously effected a get away before a magistrate or J.P. could be found. To some extent, therefore, the disciplinary powers lost when London deferred the Registration Ordinance were nevertheless enacted as the Crown was now obliged to prosecute whether the employer complained or not; equally important, the powers were on the statute book for the moment when the Registration of Natives Ordinance would make them really punitive. A year later, as difficulties mounted, Belfield openly stated work for Europeans to be highly desirable in itself, with pressures to ensure such work entirely proper, and not a temporary expedient made necessary by the war. Opening the February 1917 session of the Legislative Council, he emphasized the importance of 'encouragement' in the strongest terms, and called on district officers to see that their areas supplied the necessary men:

> It cannot be too well and too widely known that it is the declared policy of the Government to give the fullest encouragement to the settlers and natives alike to arrange for the introduction and maintenance on farms of a supply of labour sufficient to meet the varying requirements of different proprietors ... I am prepared to state definitely that we desire to make of the native a useful citizen, and that we consider the best means of doing it is to induce him to work for a period of his life for the European ...[47]

This speech was warmly applauded by the local press. The application of these instructions however became involved in the arguments in 1917 about post-war policy. These controversies were embittered by the desperation of many settlers as their farms ran deep into debt and the physical and numerical exhaustion of the available African manpower. The desperation was made worse by the African reaction to the 1917 grand levy of men; those found unfit for military work and sent to the farms quickly deserted, while others followed when they saw desertion would no longer be followed by compulsory drafting to the Carrier Corps. Farmers' associations saw only government incompetence as the cause and demanded the extension of martial law to the increasingly truculent farm labourers. Some district officers acting as magistrates awarded illegal *kiboko* sentences for desertion. The local press became violently negrophobe in tone with demands for forced labour, even proposing that 'the idle tribes will have to go to the tune of the Maxim guns'.[48] Local settler district associations provided a practical outlet to emotion by resolutions designed to keep the rate of wages low. Another less openly emotive argument saw work as necessary to re-settle demobilized *askaris* and carriers who might otherwise cause trouble, an argument that convinced a number of administrative officers and was also used to justify increased white settlement. In November 1918 a Legislative Council resolution called for the introduction of registration; 'even the Honest Nigger will rejoice' wrote a correspondent to the local press.[49] Once again some administrative officers, either fearful of the future or despairing of their ability to pay returned carriers without some proof of identity, supported early registration.

It was in these unpropitious circumstances that the protectorate government in March 1917 appointed an inquiry known as the Economic Commission to consider post-war commercial and industrial policy. On this commission and on a later one to plan increased settlement, Europeans were strongly represented, with no one to speak for employees other than a small number of officials not connected with African affairs. Settler witnesses to the Economic Commission repeated many of the suggestions given to the Barth Commission in respect of labour—demands for labour bureaux, resident labour legislation, registration, movement control, restriction of *ngomas*, the extension of magisterial powers to justices of the peace and rather less forcibly than previously, some reduction of the reserves. Ainsworth recommended the division of the country into segregated white and black areas, a division which he thought essential for African protection.[50] In his evidence he warned of a serious post-war labour shortage, and favoured state-regulated labour bureaux in place of either a state-run bureau or private recruiters. In a subsequent letter to the Acting Governor Ainsworth defended the chiefs and headmen, affirming that criticism of them was designed to portray the reserves as evil places which good men should leave for work.[51] He also publicly defended his reserve development policy. But to a debt-laden farmer, a senior official suggesting that Africans should be assisted to develop their own lands was intolerable; there followed attacks on both the size and development of the reserves, with yet further demands for 'encouragement'.

In January 1918 both to alleviate the existing famine and for future policy needs Ainsworth instructed administrative officers to develop reserves to the maximum, but this instruction and the famine relief controversy aroused further settler suspicions. These produced stormy criticism when Ainsworth went on to introduce a bill providing for the compulsory development of the reserves and then financial estimates which for the first time made budgetary provision for technical assistance of less than £2,000 for African agriculture. An unofficial member in November 1918 opposed the objects of the bill commenting '... it gives the Government the right to force the native to work within the reserve while the right to force the native outside the reserve is denied'.[52] The local press even more bluntly wrote of 'misplaced sentiment of the Little Grey home ... in the reserves' suitable only for 'the old women in Exeter Hall', and the government tamely withdrew Ainsworth's bill. Delamere commented how undesirable it would be if the large majority of Africans were not at work.[53] In September at a *baraza* at Kisumu Ainsworth, increasingly weary and concerned at African misfortunes, returned to his pre-war position and told chiefs that men should work, that they should use all possible 'encouragement' but must refrain from force, but if men wished to stay in the reserves and work on their own plots they should be left alone to do so. The chiefs replied saying that their menfolk were hungry and wished to work on their own land; they said they offered 'encouragement' as far as they could, and many of their men were away at work. Several complained of the behaviour of recruiters. The meeting was reported in the local press, arousing angry letters from farmers.[54] A full press onslaught on Ainsworth then gathered force increased by the announcement in October 1918 of his appointment to the new post of Chief Native Commissioner. He became portrayed as the one old-fashioned, prejudiced official who stood between the hard-pressed settler and a labour supply. This widened in 1919 into a largely successful attempt to undermine his policies in the eyes of the new Governor, Sir Edward Northey, with far-reaching consequences. But until Northey's arrival in February 1919, the only concession by Ainsworth was the publication of the demobilization arrangements of returning carriers to assist farmers seeking labour.[55] Northey in an arrival speech said his policy would include the encouragement of natives to work on plantations'.

Against this background of debt and controversy the ordinance recommended by the Barth Commission to control resident labourers finally reached the statute book. The war saw an enormous increase in the trend to the resident labour system; in addition to the basic reasons already outlined wartime supervision of many farms was very difficult, with a greater need for labour continuity. More and more Africans thought that resident labourer status provided stability and security and that a resident labourer's chances of avoiding carrier service were much better. Economically squatter labour was cheaper for the employer and profitable for the labourer who had his own plot, and furthermore the labourer's family could earn money at various seasons of the year. Wives and children could, for example, pick coffee at some 12 cts., per day or earn a similar sum in the protectorate's short-lived flax boom. In sum, if the change-over had not taken place, the protectorate's farming would almost certainly have collapsed; the change, was also blessed by mission opinion which saw the system as preserving family life and countering prostitution.

The first Resident Natives Bill was prepared in 1916, but as it proposed to limit the numbers of families normally permitted to fifteen it immediately met sharp opposition.[56] The local press observed that farms needed more than fifteen men and that the government was discouraging enterprising work-seekers.[57] The government argued that the settlers themselves had earlier requested a limit on numbers, but it is clear the government had other reasons in mind as at the time work-seekers without passes were apparently being arrested.[58] These reasons may have been carrier recruitment, or support for the chiefs who disliked absent men or veterinary fears of squatter stock spreading disease. Under pressure the government deferred the bill and permitted free movement of work-seekers.

In 1918 a new bill was prepared; this stated unambiguously that 'it is desirable to encourage resident native labour' and its most important clause was a requirement that adult men living on farms under the provisions of the ordinance should work for not less than ninety days per year for that farmer, a period doubled to 180 in the final text of the ordinance. Powers were provided for the return of natives to the reserves unless they were employed either as resident or other contract labourers, so the full division of the country into settled areas and reserves was virtually completed. Magistrates were to allow farmers to have as many resident labourers as they needed and district commissioners were only to allow men to work as resident labourers on production of such a permit from the magistrate. This bill became law in December 1918.[59]

Amid the mounting difficulties many officials turned to outright compulsory labour for state purposes as the solution even in peacetime. The Executive Council approved the preparation of a bill in December 1917; it then appears to have occurred to the protectorate government that the Colonial Office should be consulted. Accordingly in October 1918 Bowring cabled the Colonial Office to obtain approval for the measure 'to regularise the position arising from actual facts . . .' The Colonial Office reacted sharply, demanding an explanation with which it was not satisfied, and directing the protectorate government to end compulsory labour practices pending the arrival of the new Governor. The Colonial Office officials were motivated by their fear of parliamentary criticism.[60] Northey on his arrival and by his own initiative, however, permitted compulsory labour recruitment for certain purposes (chiefly railway maintenance and the cutting of timber for engine fuel by private contractors), and then repeated his predecessor's request, seeking legislation permitting the government to call out men for six months work per year.[61] The post 'khaki election' Colonial Office then sanctioned compulsory labour, though the obligation was reduced to three months in line with the similar *kasanvu* system at that time being introduced in Uganda.

The trend towards compulsion can also be seen in the wartime extension and abuse of the communal labour system. Sometimes men were made to work outside their districts on tasks other than portering. As the fit adult manpower supply dwindled, more women came to be used, quite illegally. If the work was light and near their homes, for example light planting or the cutting of grass by girls who received a pinch of salt at the end of a day's work, no great harm might result. But when women and girls were transported away from their homes at night and left to the mercies of junior headmen or tribal retainers they were liable to interference; they often found, also, that their work would be protracted.[62] Once again misunderstanding rather than malevolence was often the cause, with inexperienced district officers anxious to make a reputation for progress, or believing that communal labour taught habits of industry. An inquiry in 1916–17 revealed a minor example of such abuses when it was found that the Embu district commissioner had called out 250 men for 150 days for clearing local roads and paths, the *boma*'s camp area and grounds, and the laying out of a golf course.[63] Such obligations were obviously unpopular, produced inefficient work and led to dissatisfaction with the chiefs.

The government made some effort to control labour recruiters, following the Barth Commission's criticisms, using the war as a pretext not to renew licences and tightening the legislation, but the system remained oppressive. The communal labour inquiry, which arose from allegations made by a recruiter, noted that a number of recruited men who had deserted were 'far from willing recruits' coerced for work by the headman with the cognizance of the local district officers.[64] The Colonial Office maintained its objections to labour bureaux which Belfield again requested in 1916.

One beneficial result of the war was the provision of better railway carriages for labour. The Railway continued the practice of offering reduced rates for batches of men, but to improve travel conditions the 1918–19 Estimates provided for eight temporary labour rest camps on the main routes. The real solution to bad travel conditions, however, arrived with the motor lorry which reduced the duration of the journey to tolerable lengths.

The war worsened urban problems, but Nairobi and Mombasa now partly equipped with electric light increased their magnetic appeal and their populations rose continuously. In 1917 and 1918 there was a wave of burglaries, evidence of the increased attraction of consumer goods. The burglars were sometimes returning carriers who stayed briefly in the towns, sometimes urban migrant workers or visitors. In addition the carrier depots created public health difficulties. Nothing was done to improve housing conditions by the Nairobi municipal committee. Domestic servants' huts under Nairobi by-laws were supposed to provide a compartment floor area of 50 sq. ft., a height of at least 10 ft., and a window one-eighth of the floor area; many failed to do so. In the African locations blocks of land were divided by tribe and community into plots called 'stands' which employers could rent and on which they could build wattle, daub and thatch huts; these were supposed to provide 100 sq. ft. of floor area and a minimum of 500 cu. ft. per adult. One door and one window were supposed to be compulsory and huts were to be at least 7 ft. from their neighbours. Where drainage was limited to public open drains employers were required to provide pail closets; there were also a few communal cess-pit latrines.

Although in 1915 a small camp for the destitute was opened in Nairobi, these individuals performing work in lieu of rent, the numbers of homeless rose with the arrival of the curious, the returned carrier, and the famine stricken. Relatives crowded into servants' quarters or hopelessly wandered and died around the African locations. The municipal committee remained a poor employer, its employees again providing one of the very few examples of labour unrest during the war. In August 1918 after refusing a request for an increase in pay the committee found they were losing their night soil collection staff, some of whom were apparently eating garbage from bins.[65] These night staff men were receiving only 7 rupees without food, a rate some way below those of the railway and P.W.D.; the committee grudgingly granted an increase to an average of 10 rupees, and sold 1 lb. of maize meal per day to the staff at a rate very slightly below cost price.

In Mombasa the most important event to notice is the first attempt to establish a control system for the port labour force. The traditional method of recruiting port labour had been for men to assemble at various gates and trees to bargain with the foremen of the stevedoring companies or to join labour gangs operated by Asian contractors. But war conditions led employers to outbid each other, and the general shortage of labour led to inflated rates. The town employers complained of 'two days work and five days idleness' at the port; feeling was further inflamed by suspicion that the labourers who mainly came from German East Africa were being supported by the Asian contractors. Women were even at work carrying baskets of coal from barge to stack, receiving 1 ct. per trip. In 1915 Belfield refused to permit the formation of Carrier Corps units for the docks. In 1916 the situation worsened; many men apparently were working only two days each month, and the army's supplies were delayed by refusal to work at night. The *Glenart Castle* took four weeks to unload at a time of acute shipping shortage. As a result of representations by the shipping companies and the military authorities, casual labour registration was introduced in August 1916, the cost of the scheme being met by the employers. Some 1,600 *hamalis* and 800 stevedores were registered, each receiving a metal badge. Employers under threat of severe fines were directed to employ only registered casual labourers engaged at the official exchanges and to pay men at carefully laid down piece-work rates; these varied according to the weight of the load and the length of the journey.[66] Employers then urged the government to withdraw the badges of labourers who failed to work a sufficient number of days; by 1918 the total force was reduced to some

2,000, working seven to ten days per month at an average of 2/55 rupees per day.[67] In 1918 the port was also placed under martial law and the district commissioner given powers to order any unemployed African to work. But casual labour control and registration was abandoned shortly after the end of the war.

The financial crisis of the war years led to an early cost-reducing Africanization programme in the Railway and other departments, a programme which dovetailed neatly with European anti-Asian political feeling. A number of Asians assisted this process by resigning from the Railway probably mostly because they could earn more in one or other form of self-employment. This led to a serious shortage of skilled men. Some Asians' contracts were extended under emergency legislation, and fresh recruitment in India was attempted with only partial success. An increasing range of semi-skilled artisan work passed to Africans. As early as 1915 there were 183 Africans, more or less skilled, employed in the main workshops operating cranes, lathes and drills, and riveting boilers; in other departments Africans were learning printing, caulking and elementary seamanship. By 1918 practically all the trackmen, 16 drivers and shunters, over 170 firemen, 13 pump-staff and 180 workshop apprentices were all African, and training of signallers had begun.[68] The 1918–19 Railway Report noted reluctance among Asians to teach Africans, and collective self-preservation was certainly a chief reason for the formation in 1918 of the Railway Indian Staff Association. Several hundred Asians of the Railway went on strike in December 1918, a belief they were to be replaced by Africans being one of the major causes (the other grievances relating to housing, residential areas and time-machines for clocking-in).[69] The Railway promised to investigate and discuss these claims and work was resumed.

Elsewhere, African craft education suffered during the war, mission schemes and the P.W.D. Depot work were reduced or closed down, and only medical orderly and motor-transport driver training expanded.[70] Financial stringency led to a reaffirmed European-first education policy, and plans made for improved services for Africans came to nothing.[71]

The Master and Servants Ordinance was amended again in 1918 to provide for the legal recognition of thirty-day ticket contracts; at the same time punishments for Class I offences under the ordinance were increased to one month rigorous imprisonment or a fine of 50 rupees, or both.[72] The recognition of ticket contracts, either oral or in writing, required that the thirty days of work be completed within forty-two days (a maximum fixed to prevent the abuse of a man engaging with two employers); a safeguard was provided for the employee in requiring that the employer pay him for days of work completed if he fell ill, or could not complete his forty-two days for other justifiable cause. Nevertheless the overall result of the ticket system was the preservation of cheap and inefficient labour.

One odd feature of the colonial system was occasional legislative preoccupations with the totally irrelevant. At a time when hundreds of labourers were dying through lack of elementary necessities, the protectorate government in 1917 enacted a Boilers, Prime Movers and Machine Ordinance protecting workers in boiler houses and factories. Previously boiler inspection had been taking place with no legal backing and in the face of settler criticism. The numbers involved in the protectorate at the time must have been small, particularly as the government exempted itself and the Railway and the ordinance was not in any case proclaimed as operative until after the war. But elsewhere accidents were common especially on farms where raw labourers injured themselves in a variety of ways. Compensation depended on the attitudes of individual farmers. Between six and ten African employees were killed and others injured each year in railway accidents; no record of compensation appears but it is likely some private informal collection would have been made. The difficulties of a formal payment were great. It needed apparently the sanction of the Executive Council to pay 30 rupees in June 1915 to a P.W.D. African employee whose thigh was broken while at work.[73] A larger payment of 150 rupees to another P.W.D. African who lost a leg in 1917 was referred to the Colonial Office, where an official minuted the casualty was the 'first case of the kind I remember'.[74]

The protectorate's record for occasional spectacularly brutal labour crimes continued throughout the war and indeed for many years to come. In 1915 a European farm manager whipped an employee so severely with a thong whip that he died. The farm manager was charged with culpable homicide; his defending lawyer pleaded guilty to simple hurt. The judge accepted the plea and sentenced the manager to a fine of 75 rupees, a deliberately low sum as the defendant promised to enlist. In April 1918 an even worse case occurred when a Lumbwa farmer and his Swiss assistant sadistically tortured and killed an employee from a neighbouring farm caught stealing. Both cases were reported in *Truth* and representations made in Britain to the Colonial Office. Such cases and some scandalous conditions found in 1918 at government labour camps underlined the urgent need for an inspectorate, but this remained one of the Barth Commission's recommendations not implemented during the war, partly because of the impossibility of recruiting staff, and partly because of settler opposition. Provision was, however, made in the 1918–19 Estimates for four labour inspectors in the new Native Affairs Department.

The acute shortage of labour in the last two years of the war led to a small increase in wages which even the system of 'standard' rates, the resolutions of farmers associations and the low rate of pay of the Carrier Corps could not entirely prevent. Unskilled farm labour on monthly terms was generally receiving at least 5 rupees on engagement and often 6 to 8 rupees after two months, an increase of at least one rupee, sometimes two, on 1914 rates. Railway or private wood-cutters were earning 6 to 10 rupees, and cart drivers 20 rupees, but sweepers and road gangs in the country, often being conscripted, were still at a 5 rupee rate. Resident labourers were usually engaged at a 3 rupee rate, with 2 lb. of maize meal per day plus their own plot and grazing area. Domestic servants, if obtainable, appear to have been earning 11 to 12 rupees for a garden worker and up to 20 rupees or more for a house servant, both with maize meal and a hut. But the purchasing power of these cash wages was declining rapidly. The increased wartime prices of simple consumer goods made them unattainable for

Africans, and such goods ceased to provide an incentive to work for some considerable time.[75]

Nyanza remained the largest labourer producing region, the majority of men there being recruited by labour agents or employers direct on six month contracts. The Kikuyu were the next largest producer usually going to known employers for shorter terms. Embu and Meru worked irregularly in small batches. The Kamba remained averse to working for Europeans except occasionally in the semi-skilled field, the pastoral tribes were similarly opposed to any work other than herding, and with the return of peace the coastal Giriama and Teita resumed their former unwillingness to enter a labour market. On employment generally Ainsworth noted most employers refused to answer questions on the numbers of men they needed, preferring instead to raise a 'constant but indefinite cry' for labour.[76]

The labour situation, then, was by the end of 1918 as dark and unpropitious as possible. At the Colonial Office the former Liberal concern had been replaced by preoccupation with the war and Conservative indifference, and there was in consequence virtually no parliamentary criticism. With the appointment of Lord Milner as Colonial Secretary and Leopold Amery as Parliamentary Under-Secretary in 1919, any chances of amelioration seemed to recede still further. Amery at this time was quite willing openly to support 'encouragement':

> It is not enough for the Government merely to try and hold an even balance between the desire of the planter to get plenty of cheap workmen and their duty towards seeing that the native is well treated and remunerated. More than that, we want to see that production is not hampered by the absence of willing, understanding and wishful workers in that field.[77]

The new Governor, Northey, saw the future of the country as one based on increasing white settlement; he had little time for Ainsworth's work and would not hesitate to compel labour for state needs in such a manner that voluntary labour for the private employer might appear the lesser of two evils to Africans.

In the Legislative Council the demarcation of European constituencies, weighting the rural areas against Nairobi and Mombasa was decided in part to provide platforms for different types of employers: '. . . the labour policy of the government' wrote the Acting Governor, 'will always be in the foreground and for that reason alone it would appear desirable to have as many different interests as possible represented from the first'.[78] Official representatives, liable to violent press and political attack, were an inadequate counterpoise for the defence of African interests.

On the farms improved pay and conditions were the last thoughts in the minds of debt-ridden farmers returning to overgrown plantations, rusted implements and buildings half-devoured by white ants.[79] The civil service was described by the Principal Medical Officer as 'an under-staffed overtaxed body of war-stale Government servants'; the railway, roads, bridges and Kilindini port were all badly in need of repair. Owing to a deficit on the civil account for three years and also to war expenses the protectorate's finances were exhausted.[80]

The future was seen as development by increased settlement with an imperial grant-in-aid or loan for reconstruction; the protectorate government preferred a grant in order to avoid the increased taxation necessary to repay a loan. Little thought was given to the implications for labour of either new settlement or of public works, still less thought to the burden of both at once. The African population, who had passed through two bewildering decades of change and a fearful war leading to famine and disease, were thought to have been well rewarded by the relative safeguarding of their reserves, the protectorate government's preference for a grant rather than a loan, and the provision of the first small visible returns for tax paid, chiefly in the medical field.[81] But even these medical services were seen as necssary as much for the provision of a fit labour force as for any other reason.

NOTES

1. 'Report on the Period from Aug 4 1914 to Sept 15 1919 by Lieut-Col. O. F. Watkins, C.B.E., D.S.O., Director of Military Labour to the B.E.A. Expeditionary Force', 9a. Enclosure to C.O. 533/216, Monson (Governor's Deputy) to Colonial Office, 31 Dec 1919 (hereafter Watkins Report). It was treated as confidential at the time and has never been published officially. For a detailed examination of the military recruitment measures, see D. C. Savage and J. Forbes Munro, 'Carrier Corps Recruitment in the British East Africa Protectorate, 1914–1918', *Journal of African History*, vii, 2 (1966).
2. D.C.s were told to recruit for the K.A.R. in Nandi and Ukambani where the races were thought to be martial; elsewhere other peoples were to be drafted to the Carrier Corps.
   Oscar Ferris Watkins, 1881–1943. Educated Marlborough and Oxford. British Army 1900–1; S. African Constabulary 1902; Uganda government service 1904; E.A.P. service as Assistant D.C. 1908; Director of Military Labour in First World War; Acting Chief Native Commissioner 1920; Principal Labour Inspector, then Deputy Chief Native Commissioner 1921; Senior Commissioner 1928.
3. The nomenclature used changed several times, but the Carrier Corps remains the one remembered. The Kariakor district of Nairobi marked the site of the Corps' Nairobi Depot camp. In Aug 1915 after the return of the Uganda carriers for operations west of the Lake, the Corps became the East African Transport Corps (Carriers Section); in 1916 the Military Labour Bureau and later, in 1918, the Military Labour Corps with in 1917 Ainsworth as Commissioner. Until 1917 Watkins was always in charge rising from captain to major, and on Ainsworth's appointment he remained as Director although subordinate to Ainsworth.
4. *Final Report Part I of the Economic Commission*, evidence of C. R. Watson; also occasional irritated letters to the press, for example one from a Naivasha settler to the *Leader* of 4 Nov 1916. The *Leader* of 29 Jan 1915 under the heading of 'Grand Scoop of Thieves and Loafers' noted that district commissioners were 'up to their eyes in the work of bringing the necessary influence of the kamata of boys'. The *Leader* saw this work as 'a blessing in disguise asserting the Gospel of Work and clearing the Coast of enormous numbers of thieves, loafers and vagabonds'.
5. Elspeth Huxley, *Red Strangers*, 272–3, gives the example of men being called to a great law case. On their arrival the men were seized, and divided into 'Fita' [i.e. fit] who were sent to Nairobi; 'Shamba' [i.e. 'farm'] who being less fit were sent to work on settlers' farms, and 'Rotha' [probably 'return to home area'], who mainly old or infirm were set free. See also Rev. Dr. H. R. A. Philp. *God and the African in Kenya*, 1935, 41–2. Dr. Philp wrote '. . . when the military requirements were at their height I sat inside a wire fence at

Karatina Government Camp . . . into the wired enclosure the local chiefs were pouring their men.'

6. The Turkana force was engaging 3,000 labourers in 1915 and 6,000 by 1916.
   At first men were used very wastefully, each Indian soldier of the 13th Rajputs, for example, was given five porters to carry his rifle and equipment. Col. R. Meinertzhagen, *Army Diary*, 1960, wrote in disgust 'And the miserable brute who wears uniform drags himself along behind carrying nothing . . . there is no term in the English language for such men. They certainly are not soldiers'.
7. The Native Followers Recruitment Ordinance, Ord 29 of 1915, *E.A.P. Gazette*, 8 Sept 1915.
8. *Leader*, 21 Aug 1915. For another consequence see H. Thuku, *op. cit.*, 1970, 16 'It was at the *Leader*, from about 1915, that I first began to think seriously about some of our troubles as Africans—especially this question of forced labour'. Thuku was at the time employed by the *Leader* as a compositor at a salary of 46 rupees per month.
9. *Leader*, 13 Nov 1915.
10. M.L.B. Circular 38, 25 Jan 1917, restricted the number of lashes to sixteen or twelve, reduced the number of officers who could authorize a beating and ordered that no man should be beaten twice in a fortnight.
11. Watkins Report, 14. The final establishment of the Carrier police was 1,500 men.
12. 'The Ration at first issued based on the practice of the country was wholly inadequate and far below that allowed to African Troops, nor was public opinion, which in the absence of an expert native affairs department, largely guided the newly arrived Military Officers, sufficiently educated to consider the extension of the troop ration to the carrier . . .', Watkins Report, 20.
13. Watkins Report, 4–5. See also the despatch from Lieut.-Gen. A. R. Hoskins, G.O.C. East Africa, covering the period 20 Jan to 31 May 1917, published in the *London Gazette* of 27 Dec 1917. General Hoskins commented that the Dodoma-Iringa route was so precarious that the Kilosa-Iringa line had to be used 'though it involved heavy casualties among the porters and donkeys'.
14. Watkins Report, 21–2. Conditions at the rear and at depots were eased by the provision of the carrier hospitals, but at the front-line the priorities did not alter.
15. *Leader*, 15 Feb 1916. The report continued, 'Thus all the natives, including the conscripts, find added zest to their lives and are enjoying such incidents, laughing as only the Bantu can laugh.'
16. *Ibid.*
17. C.O. 533/193, Acting Chief Secretary to Colonial Office, 6 July 1918, attaching the Medical Department Report and a special typescript report by Dr. Philp. Dr. Philp regarded the compulsion of the medically unfit to work on farms as immoral as the sinking of the *Lusitania.*
18. C.O. 533/182, Bowring to Colonial Office, 20 June 1917, contained a report on Ainsworth's first eight weeks of work. The latter figure appeared in a despatch on health problems in C.O. 533/185, Monson to Colonial Office, 15 Oct 1917, enclosing letters from Ainsworth.
19. *Ibid.* Arthur Papers, memorandum Dr. S. E. Jones, 27 June 1917, noted 'the native police forcibly took all on whom they could lay their hands'. Some D.C.s were reporting that chiefs and elders were becoming afraid to select men, as if they subsequently died, their relatives claimed compensation from the chiefs.
20. The Arthur papers, in Edinburgh University Library contain letters and articles written by Dr. Arthur about the Corps, and the manuscript diary he kept in a field note-book while on active service. Arthur laid down the most precise orders governing daily routine, food, sanitation, tents, equipment, cooking, clothes and pay. Punishment took the form of extra drill, light drill or heavy drill according to the offence, with the *kiboko* for only the worst

crimes. The Corps had prayer in the morning and evening, with services on Sundays, and catechumen, communion and other classes in the evenings when possible. Sports were also organized in the evenings and at Christmas each man received a present. It was scarcely surprising therefore that the Corps casualties were very low, only 100 (5 per cent), and other protectorate Africans encountered on their travels asked if they might join, one group of Kamba expressing pleasure that they were 'not kibokoed unjustly'.

The last pages of Dr. Arthur's field diary contain paragraph headings, evidently for a sermon preached on his return. Arthur saw the Corps as a continuation in action of the oecumenical spirit of the 1913 Kikuyu missionary conference, 'a Divine Movement with a Divine Purpose', of duty, training and witness.

21. *Leader*, 8, 29 March, 5 Apr 1919. The 1916–17 Annual Report, Kenya Province. wrote, 'Villages are denuded of men between the ages of sixteen and thirty-three almost to a man.' At least however the women were spared; in German East Africa the Germans conscripted women when the male labour supply was inadequate.
22. Early in Aug 1917 Ainsworth firmly told the Army Command 'we have undoubtedly come to the end of our resources in this connection'. C.O. 533/183, Bowring to Colonial Office, 13 Aug 1917, enclosing a letter from Ainsworth. Watkins, writing in 1919, observed that the E.A.P. and Uganda Government were agreed in believing further demands would lead to a rising. Watkins Report, 6.

    One exception was North Nyanza, which was directed to produce a further 3,000 porters for the Turkhana force.
23. L. Powys, *Black Laughter*, 1925, xxi.
24. C.O. 533/214, Bowring to Colonial Office, 2 Oct 1919, enclosing the Medical Department Report for 1918. The report noted 'One condition which the progress of medical work during the war has demonstrated very clearly is the enormous liability of the African to helminthic infections. Fully three quarters of the native population is infected and the question of ankylostomiasis alone must have a marked bearing on the labour market. In fact it is possible that the African lethargy inherent in this tropical region is largely dependent on this cause.' This view is perhaps exaggerated but helminthic infections were a most serious question at the time.

    Professor Simpson's report noted 77 per cent of the Magadi Soda Company's labourers from Mombasa suffered from hookworm, while those from Nyanza were free from this disease.
25. *E.A.S.*, 19 Jan, 22 Apr 1918.
26. *Ibid.*, 1 Feb 1918.
27. Leys, 179–80, gives a breakdown of figures for Fort Hall which he states were given him by a district officer. Out of an estimated 33,000 adult males, 8,711 were on Carrier Service, 3,001 on Government Transport, 10,900 at work on farms, 2,009 at work elsewhere, 870 on the P.W.D. or Railway works, and 1,417 in mission schools and service.

    Not the least of the consequences of this massive subtraction was that family huts, normally rebuilt every six or eight years, became verminous as they were not reconstructed.
28. C.O. 533/216, Bowring to Colonial Office, 31 Dec 1919.
29. *Red Strangers*, Elspeth Huxley's fictional work again provides the material for a reconstruction.
30. Watkins Report, 24.
31. Rev. Hooper to Dr. Oldham, 27 Dec 1920, a copy of which (dated 29 Apr 1921) is in the Oldham papers.

    The King's Medal for African Chiefs, a much esteemed colonial decoration appears to have originated from a suggestion put forward by Ainsworth, who proposed a medal for chiefs who had performed especially loyal service in the war, for example the recruiting of carriers; this medal was to be continued in time of peace.

32. *Final Report of the Economic Commission Part I*; this body, unlike the 1912–13 Native Labour Commission, heard only European and occasional Asian witnesses.
33. For a very valuable examination of this relationship see C. G. Rosberg and J. Nottingham, *The Myth of Mau Mau: Nationalism in Kenya*, 1966, which notes that J. Kangethe had been a sergeant in a machine-gun bearer unit, P. J. Karanja later secretary of the Kikuyu Association had been one of the Mission Volunteers headmen, Johanna Karanja, later chairman of the Karinga Education Association had been one of the Church of Scotland's contingent, M. N. Karatu, later a Kikuyu Central Association leader had served in the Catholic Labour Corps, and Johnathan Okwirri, later first president of the Young Kavirondo Association had been a Carrier Corps headman.

    The *1917 Annual Report, Medical Department* comments on the impression created by camp discipline and personal and clothing hygiene rules.
34. Lord Cranworth, *Profit and Sport in B.E.A.*, 1919 ed., 47, 75–6. Cranworth wrote, in these significant additions to his pre-war work, 'Many an officer will long retain a warm spot for the despised Kavi'. [Kavi = Kavirondo or Nyanza porter.]

    Officers of the post-war administration noticed that experience of carriers in the war led to a marked improvement in attitudes among farmers who had served as officers, and also among a number of other farmers in general.
35. See *infra*, p. 252.
36. *Leader*, 13 Oct 1917. The Nairobi municipal committee said the camp's poor food, given to 'sick men' was the cause, but one Dr. Radford argued the cause was the siting of the camp in Nairobi's African area. It is likely that conditions in the transport ship *Wong Hai* in which thirteen men died in one voyage, may have been more common than the press were allowed to report. These deaths are recounted in F. M. Goldsmith, *op. cit.*, 98.
37. The fund was to supply beds, medical comforts, wound bonuses, convalescence expenses, grants to widows, snuff, cigarettes, tobacco and other comforts. Transport difficulties, however, prevented any large distribution of goods and the balance of the fund was made over to the Alliance of Missionary Societies after the war. It was used for the foundation of the Alliance High School, Kikuyu.
38. If a carrier deserted he was to lose all his pay due to him up to the time of desertion, a very severe and questionably legal penalty agreed by Executive Council, Bowring dissenting, in May 1918. Minutes of Executive Council, 23 May 1918.
39. Chronicle of the Family, Molteno papers.
40. R. L. Tignor, 'The Maasai Warriors: Pattern Maintenance and Violence in Colonial Kenya', *Journal of African History*, xiii, 2 (1972) states on the basis of testimony of Masai he interviewed that the revolt was not occasioned by recruiting but by opposition to a proposed new school. The recruiting obligation seems the more probable cause, as no new school was planned for the Maasai in 1918, although a school was opened in 1919 out of the profits of the collective punishment fine.
41. M. Elwin, Llewelyn Powys's biographer quotes from a letter of Powys which describes Cole as a 'vicious high bred horse or like some f—— aristocratic snake'. Elwin continues, evidently on the basis of other letters of Powys, to say that Cole 'would waste no words on an offending native, but knock him down with a blow of his fist in the face'. M. Elwin, *The Life of Llewelyn Powys*, 1946, 126–7. One of Cole's favourite sayings was 'You will find no virtue under a black hide'. L. Powys, *Ebony and Ivory*, 46.
42. C.O. 533/134, Belfield to Colonial Office, 26 May 1915, enclosing the report, notes Ainsworth's view that most of the more densely populated 'labour supplying' reserves could afford to pay higher tax.
43. The Native Registration Ordinance, Ord 15 of 1915, *E.A.P. Gazette*, 19 May 1915. The text of the bill was first sent to the Secretary of the Convention before it was published in the *E.A.P. Gazette* to the approval of the local

press. *Leader*, 9 Jan 1915. The local press also approved of the measure proposed '... it will help build up the stability of the labour supply'... 'we should see less of the elusive Kamaus and Karanjas who for one brief spell flit from one house to another, one employer to another'. *E.A.S.*, 8 Jan 1915.

44. The innocence of the title may have allayed any anxieties. One who was not deluded was McGregor Ross who opposed the ordinance from the start, earning the description of himself as a 'public servant with the views and principles more suited to a mothers' meeting in a rural Welsh Methodist Bethel', *Leader*, 16 Nov 1918.
45. The 1915–16 Annual Report, Kenya Province, for example, notes 2,000 men supplied to private employers.
46. *Leader*, 11 Dec 1915, notes the resolution; the ordinance (Ord 1 of 1915), was published in the *E.A.P. Gazette*, 26 Jan 1916. It provided that all Class II offences be cognizable and increased the penalties from a fine of two months wages to a fine of 75 rupees, and the prison maximum from two months to six.

    In fact during the war lashes were on occasions awarded quite illegally for desertion. The 1917–18 Annual Report for the Nakuru District records such sentences of ten to fifteen lashes.
47. *E. A. P. Debates*, 12 Feb 1917.
48. *E.A.S.*, 30 March 1918. The *Leader*, 30 July 1918, published a poem entitled Jack Nigger, of which two verses ran as follows:

    Jack Nigger you're as cute's can be
    Five beans to you make ten
    You drink and scrounge and sleep and laze
    And laze, scrounge and drink again!
    Your bibis do domestic jobs
    They sow and plough and reap
    And mend your pants and mind the kids
    While you lie fast asleep.

    In fact they live for you alone
    You gay and lazy dog
    They make and fetch your pombe and
    They feed you like a hog
    And with it all but one thing can
    Disturb your lordly rest
    And that, Jack Nig, you likewise know
    Is twenty of the best.
49. *E.A.S.*, 5 Oct 1918.
50. *Final Report of the Economic Commission Report Part I.* Its theme, as far as labour was concerned, was that 'one white immigrant into East Africa may galvanise a thousand economically dead Africans...' The commissioners said they saw no evidence of any exploitation and that labour was free enjoying a 'complete absence of economic pressure'.
51. Ainsworth to Northey, 30 Sept 1919, sent by Northey in a general despatch on policy but with neither support nor comment to the Colonial Office on 31 Oct. C.O. 533/214.

    The 1918–19 Annual Report, Ulu District, however, provides a different point of view by saying 'the system of bribery to obtain exemptions, fines for the evasion of service in the Carrier Corps and the appropriation thereof by Headmen and Native Councils on the cessation of Carrier Corps recruiting gradually crept into the ordinary course of Native administration'. The Ulu D.C. had imprisoned some headmen, fined others and replaced all his tribal retainers. A number of other reports speak of the petty extortions of tribal retainers and their wartime counterparts, the *capiteni.*
52. *E.A.P. Debates*, 5 Nov 1918.

53. *Ibid.* One or two of the original opponents of the bill became converted to Ainsworth's views and did not support the withdrawal.
54. *E.A.S.*, 21 Sept 1918, a report almost certainly written to inflame opinion. The P.C., C. R. W. Lane, was reported as saying that chiefs should give their men so much communal labour that they would prefer to go out to work for a wage.
    Ainsworth said that a circular would be issued prohibiting compulsion. His own report of this meeting is in C.O. 533/273, Ainsworth to Bottomley, 20 July 1921.
55. *Ibid.*, 14 Dec 1918.
56. *E.A.P. Gazette*, 6 Oct 1916.
57. *Leader*, 14 Oct and 4 Nov 1916.
58. *Ibid.*, 13 Jan 1917 makes this charge.
59. The Resident Natives Ordinance, Ord 33 of 1918, *E.A.P. Gazette*, 31 Dec 1918.
    The ordinance gave magistrates these administrative powers. Settlers hoped to replace district commissioners by magistrates in the settled areas, and then eventually to provide for the magistracy amongst themselves.
60. C.O. 533/198. Sir G. Fiddes of the Colonial Office minuted 'The House of Commons would never stand it, and rightly in my opinion', to which W. Long, the Colonial Secretary replied 'I concur'.
61. C.O. 533/213, Northey to Colonial Office, 30 Sept 1919.
62. Miss Marion Stevenson to Dr. Oldham, 13 Oct 1921, recorded in 1915 that it had been proved one girl had had to work for twenty-six days in three months, involving a total stay away from home of thirty-three days. Miss Stevenson also noted that men's communal labour was often 'a month at a time' and some D.C.s felt such labour necessary to uphold the prestige of the chief. Oldham papers.
63. C.O. 533/184, Bowring to Colonial Office, 24 Aug 1917 and attached papers.
64. *Ibid.* The 1918–19 Annual Report, Kenya Province, writes of the suspicion still aroused by the labour recruiter, 'He is known to sell the people (in their own words) . . .'
65. *Leader*, 17 Aug *E.A.S.* 7 Sept 1918.
66. K.N.A. file Coast 38/603 contains the papers relating to the introduction of this scheme, later legalized by the Defence (Hamalage) Regulations, 1919, *E.A.P. Gazette*, 5 Feb 1919. Examples of the rates for import cargo are as follows:

Bags of Rice, Mombasa Customs to Railway Station	12 cts. per bag.
Bags of Flour, Mombasa Customs to Railway Station	18 cts. per bag.
Cases of Beer, Mombasa Customs to Railway Station	20 cts. per case.
Bales of *Amerikani*, Mombasa Customs to Railway Station	20 cts. per bale.

    Rates for export cargo were similar but slightly lower, presumably as the porters and coolies moved their loads downhill; night work earned an extra 10 per cent. At Dar es Salaam the problem was solved by the temporary employment of Chinese labourers recruited in Shanghai.
67. *1918–19 Annual Report, Native Affairs Department*, hereafter Annual Reports, N.A.D.
68. *1914–15*, *1915–16*, *1916–17*, and *1917–18 Annual Reports, Uganda Railway.*
69. *E.A.S.*, 7 Dec 1918.
70. For reasons largely linguistic the Baganda proved the Army's ablest trainees; they were to form a very high percentage of the African motor vehicle drivers in Nairobi after the war.
71. Work was still thought even by the highest in the land to be the most valuable education. An astonishing example of this attitude is to be found in a 1917 law case where revision judges upheld a magistrate's decision that a contract of service for six months was enforceable upon a boy of ten. The boy had been engaged for domestic service at a rate of 3 rupees per month with food and clothes, the contract had been attested before a magistrate but the boy wished to end it. The judge held that an infant could contract for personal

service without the protection of the apprentices sections of the Master and Servants Ordinance, and since it was 'clearly for the benefit of the boy that he should earn his livelihood', he should be held to his contract. *E.A. Law Reports*, VII, n.d. 37, *Isaji Mamuji v. Mzee bin Ali.*

72. The Master and Servants Amendment Ordinance, Ord 30 of 1918, *E.A.P. Gazette*, 31 Dec 1918.
    The ordinance also provided that the employer was liable for the feeding of a resident ticket contract employee if he were sick for the duration of the forty-two days. The bill proposed an amendment that under penalty of a fine of 50 rupees no employee on a thirty day contract could be compelled to work on a Sunday, but following consideration by a Legislative Council committee this proposal was discarded.
    McGregor Ross tried in vain to insert a clause providing for a maximum of six consecutive working days.
    The amendment led to difficulties, as the High Court subsequently ruled that a ticket employee was entitled to leave his employer at any time during the contract without notice and to claiming payment for the days worked. The ordinance had to be further amended in 1925.
73. Minutes of Executive Council, 28 June 1915.
74. C.O. 533/186, Bowring to Colonial Office, 18 Dec 1917 and attached papers.
75. *1918–19 Annual Report, N.A.D.* notes the majority of these rates, others are taken from administration and press reports.
76. *Ibid.*
77. *Parliamentary Debates, Commons*, 30 July 1919. This statement merits comparison with the remarkable defence by Bowring, as Acting Governor, of the introduction of compulsory labour in Legislative Council on 3 May 1920. '... The object of the measures is thus ... not to force the natives to work, but to see that the work is done.'
78. C.O. 133/185, Bowring to Colonial Office, 14 Aug 1917.
79. Elspeth Huxley, *White Man's Country*, II, 50.
80. A War Bonus, a form of cost of living allowance increase, was paid to all European and Asia government officers, but the only Africans to receive the bonus were the small number earning more than 30 rupees per month, and the uniformed staff of the Police, Prisons, Customs and Forest Departments. It was held that the bonus was necessary to cover the increased prices of goods which the immigrant communities needed and Africans did not, but the discrimination aroused resentment.
81. The 1918–19 Estimates provided eight new medical officers of health for work in the major reserves, together with seven new sanitary inspectors and an increased subsidy to the Kikuyu medical mission.
    Most unofficial members supported these provisions, some in accordance with the opinion of J. Brumage, president of the Ruiru Farmers Association; 'In a sentence of cold business meaning, if a native is worth taxing he is worth dosing.' *E.A.S.*, 4 Feb 1919. The Jan 1919 meeting of the Convention also demanded that better medical facilities be made available for labourers.

Chapter 4

CRISIS AND CONSEQUENCES, 1918–1930

We cannot possibly handle a local question of this kind without remembering its relations to those larger theories, those wider principles which ought to have been, and I think, have usually been governing principles in our action to other races especially the backward and the child races.

Dr. Randall Davidson, Archbishop of Canterbury, House of Lords, 14 July 1920.

Complaints by labourers: NIL. All quite satisfied. Employer ... does not seem to be beating his labour now. My cautions seem to have been effective. Labour Inspection report on the camp of H. H. McPhee, a railway track maintenance contractor, 3 July 1925.

The immediate post-war years were crowded with events. Numerous pressures, some of them seemingly innocent were applied simultaneously to Africans, creating the worst peacetime labour oppression in the history of the territory.

The most evident of the events, particularly in 1919–21 were a great economic expansion interrupted but not halted by a slump, and increased European settlement which to some extent altered the nature of previous controversy over the size of the reserves. Asian immigration also increased. The overall result was a demand for larger numbers of men for work, to be obtained by renewed 'encouragement' or by open compulsion for the state sector. Tax increases were to be a further goad to oblige men to seek work; the introduction of registration and an expansion of the resident labour system were to ensure that men remained at work. Yet further burdens imposed on the African population were currency and coinage changes which produced demands for the reduction of African wages incorrectly believed by settlers to have become inflated, and a number of labour scandals. These events seemed to return the protectorate to the pre-1914 position; on the political front they were spearheaded by vociferous European demands for self-government argued chiefly in an anti-Asian context,

Less evident but more fortunate were other processes before long to prove more important which were to lead the territory in a different direction. These processes derived from the changing views on the duties of a colonial power brought about by the League of Nations and the concept of trusteeship. In Britain these new views were expressed to the Colonial Office by organizations such as the International Labour Organization, the mission and a better informed and more powerful British Labour Party. In Kenya, as the East Africa Protectorate was renamed in 1920, the expression took the form of a better-trained and more experienced administrative service and a partially effective labour inspectorate. The harshest of pre-1914 settler attitudes were already diluted by the fact that almost all of the new settlers were British rather than South African; in addition some older settlers had acquired a sympathy for Africans through the shared experience of active service in German East Africa. In the late nineteen-twenties and thirties two further powerful new influences appear. The first was the British-owned, adequately capitalized commercial enterprise unconcerned with settler pschological attitudes and thinking simply in terms of cost-effective labour, notably the Magadi Soda Company and the Nyanza tea plantations. The second influence was through the Colonial Office's first official studies of labour and social problems.

But perhaps the most significant of the new processes was the emergence of an ill-co-ordinated but clear African protest, part-political part-industrial, in the most densely-populated and therefore the largest labour supplying areas of Kenya. All these more liberal processes led first to political controversy in Britain over Kenya's labour conditions, and then to the Devonshire statement and the Dual Policy, which together may be seen as a partial return to the assertion of Colonial Office power that had been abandoned in 1914.

Northey, Coryndon and Grigg

The economic expansion began with post-war reconstruction and was followed by the extension of the railway system from Nakuru through the Uasin-Gishu to Uganda. While the Uasin-Gishu work was still in progress, a further extension from Thika to Nyeri was begun and also at the same time the expansion of Kilindini harbour. Rather later, further extensions took the railway to Nanyuki, Solai and Thomson's Falls. In the private sector the large, officially backed 'soldier-settler' and other schemes to recruit more settlers greatly increased the number of European farmers both in areas already settled and in new areas, notably the Trans-Nzoia.[1] Many argued that the soldier-settlers had a particular call on government support and that if they did not receive it they would become a dangerous political element. Numbers continued to increase throughout the nineteen-twenties as young Britons arrived, often to work a few years as a manager until they could afford a farm of their own. By 1929 over 2,000 Europeans were recorded as occupying agricultural land. A further source of supply was the retiring civil servant and business man with his family, increasing numbers of whom remained to farm, later being officially encouraged to do so.[2]

The rise in the number of settlers led to repeated demands that fresh land be alienated for settlement. These expressions dovetailed neatly with the previous settler demands for a reduction of the reserves to oblige the surplus population to come out to work. Some land was ceded in the Nandi and Lumbwa areas about one-half of which was later returned; but elsewhere the demands, repeated by a Land Tenure Commission Report in 1922, were resisted by the government in accordance with the original Colonial Office comments on the Barth Commission Report.[3] The chief opponents to alienation of reserve land were Ainsworth and his successor, Watkins, who acted as Chief Native Commissioner after Ainsworth's departure in 1920. Watkins also repeated Ainsworth's warning on the dangers of a labour shortage through over-ambitious settlement plans. Controversy over the reserves as labour producing areas then finally moved from their size to the amount of money to be spent on their development, an amount which remained small and which also, in conjunction with the fall in African reserve production and increase in population, ensured an adequate labour supply from 1927.

In 1919 and 1920, however, while the reserves were still facing the consequences of war, famine and epidemic, the settled areas were receiving a large increase in Europeans and capital both requiring labour to take full advantage of the post-war boom. Increasingly clear government warnings of probable difficulty went unheeded (except by the Uganda Railway, which purchased coal from Britain on the assumption there would be no men for wood-fuel cutting) and there was an immediate crisis. As we have noted Northey on his arrival was met by numerous demands for 'encouragement', registration, increased African taxation and bitter personal attacks on Ainsworth for his 'zoo' policy. The Convention even passed a resolution criticizing Ainsworth's appointment as Chief Native Commissioner. Northey's personal views, stated on several occasions, were almost identical with those of settler leaders; he saw the duty of himself and government not to allow the 'natives to remain in uneducated and unproductive idleness in their so-called Reserves . . .' but to 'encourage voluntary work in the first place, but to provide power by legislation to prevent idleness'.[4]

Northey, a soldier with little experience of politics, apparently saw nothing contradictory between these views and those of his Royal Instructions which stated that he was not to assent to any legislation which discriminated against non-Europeans, and that he was 'especially to take care' of the native inhabitants 'in the free enjoyment of their possessions, and by all lawful means to prevent and restrain all violence and injustice which may in any manner be practised or attempted against them'.[5] These instructions, repeated with little alteration for successive governors, also laid down that certain bills affecting natives were to be referred to the Secretary of State and were not to take effect until the Secretary of State's approval had been given, a procedure which in these post-war years of controversial legislation was frequently neglected. At lower levels a number of provincial and district officials sincerely felt that 'encouragement' might be justifiable in view of the demoralized state of the reserves. This attitude was to some extent shared by Ainsworth on whom the strain of the war and the mounting criticism of his policies were telling; he came to favour a Native Labour Association for supervised recruiting. The government's overall position had been greatly weakened by the return of European members to the Legislative Council, the undeclared but general policy of 'government by agreement' (agreement in the labour field being agreement with employers), and the contemporary practice of allowing official members to vote as they wished. Sometimes for one reason or another they allied with settlers to defeat government proposals.

In one bewildering year 1919, therefore, the registration scheme was introduced, the Resident Natives Ordinance was applied, and an ordinance drafted to increase the rates of hut and poll tax. Worse was to follow before the year ended.

In an attempt to make this coercion physically humane and following the recommendations of the Barth Commission, the protectorate government made a simultaneous attempt to improve work conditions by an amendment to the Master and Servants Ordinance.[6] This amending ordinance gave a new official, the Principal Labour Inspector, and his staff powers to inspect work places and to ask to see all employees, housing, food, water and medical equipment, and power to prosecute with the Chief Native Commissioner's permission. Medical officers were given the same inspection powers along with the right to order sick natives to enter hospital or return home at the employer's expense, to condemn food and accommodation, to order the supply of food, and to order at the cost of the employer recoverable from the employee the provision of one or more blankets or clothing. A second section of the ordinance gave the governor powers to make rules for minimum standards of rations, housing and medical attendance; criticism in the Legislative Council led to this section being amended to require the governor to table such rules in the Legislative Council. A third section prohibited the employment of natives recruited by a labour agent unless there had been a free medical examination by a government medical officer, any rejected at a medical examination to be returned home at the recruiter's expense; it further prohibited the employment of boys under sixteen in heavy manual work. Severe penalties of a 1,000 rupees fine or six months' imprisonment, or both, were set out for breaches of this section. A final section defined a government medical officer to include assistant and sub-assistant surgeons, which in practice gave powers to some thirty-five partially qualified Asian officers.

Opposition to the bill in the Legislative Council led to the insertion of a provision making private homes free from inspection and stipulating that inspections were not to interfere with work. It also required the Chief Native Commissioner's permission before prosecution, and an undertaking by the government only to use the Asian surgeons when no medical officer was available which in practice limited the effectiveness of the medical inspection provisions. Settler members of Legislative Council argued that the bill added to the obligation of the employer only and not to the employee and moved it be deferred until registration was introduced. Ainsworth insisted that the bill be passed quickly adding 'if things were to go on much longer in this irresponsible manner there would soon be no labour. There would be no natives left to work.' He spoke of men recruited by recruiters often quite unfit to work, some 'in a starvation condition'. the provincial commissioner at Mombasa, Hobley, agreed adding that a number of labourers recruited in Kisumu without a medical inspection had recently arrived at the Coast sick, having infected the railway with enteric fever on the way.[7]

For reasons of staff shortage and the preoccupation of its inspectors with registration, the Labour Section of the N.A.D. made only very limited impact in its first years. But by the later nineteen-twenties, the Labour Section, slightly increased in size, had in various ways checked many of the more glaring abuses of the pre-1914 period; the very fact of its existence enabled the district commissioner or the good farmer to have someone with whom to discuss any local bad farmers and action usually followed in time. The Labour Section could only rarely create ideal conditions, but it did before long prevent most conditions where men died or suffered unduly.[8] H. W. Gray, who had had wartime experience of labour, became the first Principal Inspector with the status of a district commissioner; he and his successor, Watkins, recruited a small staff initially of men such as former police or health inspectors. In later years recruits tended to be men whom it was thought would command the respect of the settlers through prowess in other fields such as a good war record or sport—a necessary approach in the Kenya of the nineteen-twenties and thirties.

The establishment and achievements of the Labour Section have been somewhat overlooked because of its initial failures, and the controversies aroused at the end of 1919 by the amendment of the Native Authority Ordinance to provide for paid compulsory labour for state purposes coupled with the issue of the famous Northey circulars on 'encouragement' for private purposes. These were prepared at the height of the post-war labour shortage and were accompanied by an increase in the rate of tax from 5 to 8 rupees. At the same time insecurity was created by fluctuations in the currency, the coin value of which began to rise against sterling greatly to the disadvantage of the new investor of capital. This currency factor added to the already clamorous demands for positive government action and led to a vociferous and partially successful demand for the reduction of wages by one-third.

The first and most important circular, dated 23 October 1919, was a directive to 'encouragement' in terms far stronger than ever before, linking 'encouragement' with satisfactory relations between natives and settlers, development being seen as the sole concern of the latter.[9] District officers were to do 'what they can to induce an augmentation of the supply of labour' for farms 'by every possible lawful influence, in particular by addressing meetings with employers and their agents present'. Chiefs and elders were to do the same and be 'repeatedly reminded that it is part of their duty to advise and encourage all unemployed young men . . . to go out and work on plantations'. The names of those chiefs who were notably helpful or the reverse were to be reported to the Governor. Women and children who lived near farms were to be encouraged to go out to daily work. Employers and their agents were to be assisted to recruit in the reserves and the circular concluded with an ominous threat to introduce 'other and special measures' if necessary. The circular was published in the press.

The first draft of the circular had been prepared by Ainsworth on instructions from the Governor, but this draft was apparently strengthened by Northey himself who sent it to print without reference back to Ainsworth.[10] Officers in the secretariat and in the field received it with very mixed reactions. Some, sympathizing with the prevailing view that if the country was ever to develop the demoralized African must be cajoled into working, welcomed the circular saying they now at last knew where they stood, and acted upon it vigorously with the help of their district chiefs.[11] Some from poor areas where men could not pay tax saw it as right to encourage Africans to work for the development of the country. These officers saw little wrong in directing men sometimes at harvest time in hundreds or thousands to work for the European planter, there being no other method by which schools or medicine could possibly be paid. But as in pre-war years others felt they were being instructed to use compulsion but not be found out and objected to operating thinly disguised forced labour for private employers as a consequence of political pressures which had overridden their advice and that of Ainsworth, the latter still favouring state regulated labour bureaux.[12] Yet others held their Africans in paternal regard and refused to encourage men to experience strange climates, foods, separation and strange new human relationships. Of these latter a few voiced their objections to the missionaries or their superiors; Ainsworth, Bowring and Tate, the Kenya Province provincial commissioner, also strongly expressed their concern to church leaders at a special meeting in October 1919 in Bowring's office.[13] Northey reacted adversely to such criticisms. Arthur noted later that the Governor '. . . seemed to want to get rid of all men who would in any way oppose his policy. We are extremely sorry that men like H. R. Tate should be retired this year. We understand that he himself does not want to, and he is not an old man'.[14]

Concurrent with the issue of the circular and adding to the anxiety of its critics, the Legislative Council was debating the Native Authority Amendment Ordinance creating an obligation of sixty days' paid work for certain state purposes for men apparently not in employment.[15] This legislation will be examined in detail later.

Both of these policies had origins already noted. The government was to argue somewhat flimsily that compulsory labour was only an extension of the obligations previously imposed for government transport and in any case comparable with the *kasanvu* compulsory labour system in Uganda. It also argued that the Northey 'encouragement' circular was only a clearer definition of previous policy designed to remove discrepancies caused by different interpretations. Added to these, moreover, were the planned increases in the already high hut and poll tax and the introduction of the registration system. The total pattern conformed to the plans of the settler leaders as advocated in their campaigns for election early in 1920—the alternatives of portering or forced labour for the state's rough contractors to act as a stimulus to the supply of men for the private employer, mostly as resident labourers. After a demand for tax which Africans could not meet, those not compelled or 'encouraged' were likely to fall victims to the labour agent working in varying degrees of collusion with the local chief.

In contrast to their pre-war ineffectiveness the missionaries were now able to speak with much greater force, partly as the majority had formed the Alliance of Protestant Missions, and partly because of the generally changing conditions of the post-war world. The two Anglican bishops of East Africa and Uganda and Arthur as the senior representative of the Church of Scotland drew up a statement known as 'The Bishops' Memorandom' criticizing the Northey Circular, though more in detail than in principle. The text appears to have been finalized at the October 1919 meeting with Ainsworth, Bowring and Tate, and the memorandum itself was typed by Bowring or his staff; a Chief Secretary concerting a protest against his Governor's policy represents a remarkable event in colonial history.[16] They accepted that in the circumstances of East Africa at the time 'some forms of pressure must be exerted', pressure which they even accepted for private employers though they thought compulsion should be directed primarily to state work. They forecast that leaving pressure to chiefs must lead to abuse as 'to the native mind a hint and order on the part of the Government are indistinguishable'. They thought that when compulsory labour was necessary it should be legalized openly, confined to able-bodied men with no pressure whatever on women and children, that the work should be primarily for the state and done under properly administered conditions, and distributed fairly among tribes and individuals for a reasonable time with reasonable exemptions granted and each man free to choose his own employer. They also dissented from the prevailing view that the native was idle in the reserve, noting that he too had '. . . his months of strenuous work, cultivating and planting, harvesting and building, etc'.

The memorandum leaves the impression of a compromise document. It never questioned the right of the settler to the labour of the Africans. Its concluding paragraph began 'The Missions welcome His Excellency's general policy . . .', but in the text they noted that although 'technically there is no compulsion; practically compulsion could hardly take a stronger form'. A circular from the Kiambu district commissioner arranging child labour for coffee picking was quoted with stern disapproval, and the memorandum warned of the dangers of such an arrangement continuing for both women and children and operated by headmen under fear of dismissal. Further social consequences of the migrant labour system were also clearly portrayed: 'To leave his own plantation, perhaps at a critical time, for the benefit of someone else's plantation; to leave his house unthatched, his crops unreaped, his wife unguarded perhaps for months at a time, in return for cash which he does not want on the "advice" of his chief—which he dare not disregard—is not a prospect calculated to inspire loyalty . . .' The more critical passages probably reflect the influence of Arthur who acted as spokesman at a meeting with the Governor early in 1920.

In general most local missionaries supported the Bishops' Memorandum and also the subsequent protest in June 1920 of the Alliance of Protestant Missions against the increase in African taxation. Even Archdeacon Owen later to be the most outspoken defender of the Africans and Arthur both thought properly and fairly administered compulsion preferable and more honest than coercion by chiefs or taxation; the comment of Leys '. . . even the bishops could not escape from the mental atmosphere that surrounded them' must remain the verdict on the year 1919 in Kenya.[17]

One radical critic who regarded the Bishops of Mombasa and Uganda as 'traitors' was the Bishop of Zanzibar, Frank Weston, whose diocese included sections of mainland Tanganyika.[18] To alleviate the labour shortage the protectorate government had been attempting to recruit labour in Tanganyika whose government had been reluctant to help until overruled by Milner, the Secretary of State. Weston went to see Milner to protest. At the meeting both apparently irritated each other. Milner in particular annoying Weston by quoting the Bishops' Memorandum as supporting compulsion. A furious Weston thereupon played an important part in arousing public concern in Britain; he wrote a pamphlet called *The Serfs of Great Britain* in which he charged the Kenya government with introducing a new form of slavery. He described this as both anti-Christian and political and moral madness. Less polemically he argued that the recruiting, medical examination and feeding were all abused, the medical staff being inadequate, the recruiters callous, and 'always the lash is used freely in such circumstances' making Milner's promises meaningless.

Following the pattern of the anti-slavery movement of the first decade of the twentieth century, with on occasions some of the same people and societies at work, the battle then moved to London where attention was secured by Bishop Weston's activities, the further protest of the Alliance on the increase in taxation which they correctly saw as another coercive measure, letters from individual missionaries expressing increasing concern, and anxiety expressed by a few officials on leave. The non-Roman churches, the Anti-Slavery Society, the Labour Party, other organizations along with the *New Statesman* and the *Contemporary Review* all appealed to public opinion. In the mission field the principal figure was Dr. J. H. Oldham, the Secretary of the Conference of Missionary Societies in Great Britain and Northern Ireland.[19] Oldham's papers at Edinburgh House record his indefatigable energy, patience and tact in drawing together men from many different walks of life. He was continually supplied with fresh evidence from missionaries, Leys, McGregor Ross and sympathetic administrators such as G.A.S. (later Sir Stafford) Northcote. Some of the abuses reported included chiefs compelling boys and girls to work on farms on occasions with the approval of the local district commissioner, the seizing of men on the roads and paths by tribal retainers sometimes including those returning home after a period at work and the striking of women by native supervisors. Oldham prepared memoranda for different Protestant missionary societies, corresponded with the Archbishop of Canterbury and determined to mount an effective nation-wide protest campaign. Other well-known critics included Sir Sydney Olivier, Lionel Curtis, Sir Frederick Lugard, and, although less well known at the time, Leonard Woolf. Missionary societies arranged special meetings, and the Church of Scotland stated it would not approve any form of compulsory labour at all to the embarrassment of Arthur.

Parliamentary attention in both Houses in consequence grew in force in the early months of 1920, culminating in a major debate in the Lords in July when Lord Islington, the Archbishop of Canterbury, and other Lords spoke in sharp criticism of Northey's policies.[20] The Secretary of State replied that a new circular was to be issued by the government which would make it clear that only encouragement and advice and not force or compulsion were to be used, but he reiterated the old view that men in the reserves were living in idleness and vice against which 'habits of steady industry' were to be encouraged. His despatch, sent to Nairobi in July and published on 1 September turned out to be very largely a further defence of Northey.[21] Milner rejected compulsory labour for the private employer as totally opposed to the traditions of the local administration, arguing that criticism had overlooked that the government was not obtaining labour for any particular employers. But he stated he approved of encouragement and advice, provided adequate safeguards remained for workers, for which he regarded the Kenya legislation as comprehensive. He argued that the native profited from working, and it was therefore just to use 'all lawful and reasonable means' including the maintenance of records of those chiefs who co-operated and those who did not. He also approved further recruiting in Tanganyika for a period of six months, despite the Archbishop of Canterbury's defence of an official who had refused to assist in this recruiting.

Although defended at this juncture the protectorate government was already finding its position increasingly embarrassing. At the 1920 New Year meeting of the Convention resolutions had been passed which approved the original circular and in particular the acceptance of the principle that settlers' labour needs were the legitimate concern of the government, and the hope had been strongly expressed that no pressure would lead the government to relieve district officers of their 'lawful' task. In reply the Acting Governor had promised that the policy would be maintained and possibly strengthened and a second circular in affirmation had been issued making two points, that while officers and chiefs were not to become recruiters of labour, they should 'induce the men by all lawful means to seek work', and that the tribal elders should be 'induced to adopt an attitude of refusing to allow their sons to remain idle'. Officers were also to be ruthless in tax collection. The Colonial Office subsequently cancelled this circular.[22]

On his return to Kenya after medical treatment in Pretoria and armed with a knowledge of Milner's views obtained in London, Northey issued a further circular on the day of the Lords debate.[23] This circular was said to be necessary because of 'misconception'. It instructed that officers were to supervise chiefs who were not to abuse their authority, that labour was to be administered fairly, and district officers were to enforce the protective legislation. Men needed for useful work in the reserves were to be left alone, children were only to work if they could return home at night, and women employed only if their husbands were at work and resident on the same farm. Subject to these safeguards unemployed young men were still to be advised and encouraged to work on farms. In yet another circular issued at the same time the district administrations were also advised that Africans should only grow cash crops on alienated land and that on their own land Africans should concentrate on their own food supplies.[24]

Milner's defence of Northey, Ainsworth's retirement and the subsequent circular did nothing to reassure public opinion in Britain.[25] A deputation waited on the Secretary of State on 14 December with a memorandum entitled 'Labour in Africa and the Principles of Trusteeship' signed by a number of exceptionally weighty names, including all the non-Roman church leaders, influential members of both Houses, and some notable academic figures.[26] The memorandum, drafted with care largely by Oldham, queried both 'encouragement' and compulsion in the context of the Covenant of the League of Nations and of the new concept of trusteeship; it warned against indirect compulsion and objected to any form of coercion for private employers; it expressed doubts on what were 'public purposes' and sought assurances that a healthier independent native life would immediately be fostered in the reserves. It finally called for a royal commission to examine overall native policy.

So significant a step, a rare and important example of British public concern over an African question in the inter-war period, could not fail to have major consequences. Milner, anxious to resign for some time, finally left the Cabinet early in 1921 and was replaced by Churchill, who was far more sensitive to post-war ideals and in addition was personally acquainted with the Kenya problem. Under Churchill and his successor from October 1922, the Duke of Devonshire, two important consequences appear—firstly a fresh despatch on the subject of labour, and secondly the growth of doubts about Kenya policy, caused by the extravagant European political and economic demands and their anti-Asian activities. The consequences of these doubts can be seen first in the replacement of Northey, later in the Devonshire Paper and the Dual Policy, and lastly in the criticism of the Closer Union proposals.

After further severe parliamentary criticism including a renewed demand for a royal commission, and discussions with Northey in the summer of 1921, Churchill issued his despatch considerably modifying labour policy.[27] In this despatch he rejected the more 'ill formed allegations . . . that the Government is exploiting the natives' though he accepted the desirability of 'inculcating among the natives habits of industry' but significantly 'inside or outside the Reserves'. He also upheld the principle of communal labour. On the major issue of compulsion he stated that except for government porterage the practice was only to be used for essential purposes after permission had been obtained from the Secretary of State for each specific task. On 'encouragement' he returned to the positions of Crewe and Harcourt, that the government was to provide information facilities for work-seekers and employers alike but to take no part in recruiting. This despatch was published in the *Official Gazette* in October 1921; Tate, now moved to the less controversial Nyanza province, described it in his annual report as a great '. . . Emancipation Act for which the administration had fought long and persistently'. An amendment to the Native Authority Ordinance was prepared to give legal authority to its requirements.[28]

Although on paper this despatch was a substantial change in policy in Kenya, it remained one thing for a despatch to be issued and quite another for it to be obeyed immediately and in all details. In respect of open compulsory labour away from home the despatch was very largely successful. As will be noted later the Kenya government only sought the Secretary of State's permission to recruit compulsory labour once prior to 1939. In late 1924 permission was requested in rather general terms in order to expedite railway and harbour construction work, but the government was so closely examined on its precise needs and so closely controlled in the permission given that the experiment was not repeated. 'Encouragement', as will be seen later, remained an ambiguity for several years to come. Farmers' associations and elected M.L.C.s objected strongly to the policy of 'neutrality' and many district officers still felt they did not know what they were meant to do when a farmer asked them for labour.

Meanwhile two parallel political developments were forcing a succession of crises, firstly the ever more vocal European political demands for self-government expressed as a refusal to provide equal rights for Kenya Asians, and justified among other reasons by the charge that the Asian was a bad influence and employer from whom Africans should be protected; and secondly, the reaction to the totality of pressures at work on the Africans, the mismanagement of construction labour and communal labour particularly in the use of women and children, and the proposal to reduce African wages by one-third as a result of currency changes.

The issues of the Asian controversy were almost exclusively racial-political with origins as far back as the early years of the century, and brief mention only need be made to expose the hollowness of the labour arguments. At this time there was relatively little Asian opposition to African advancement in the labour field as the Asian had virtually no competition in his principal occupations—craft trades, the retail trade, and clerks; only very occasionally did Asian work-people object to employment of a skilled African. Equally, however, there was very little positive Asian effort to train the Africans, and when a training or skilled vacancy occurred, they preferred to see their own race selected unless there was substantial profit to be made by employing an African at a lower wage. Europeans opposed to Asian political aims and continuing immigration argued that the Asians were obstructing African advancement, setting a corrosive moral example and preaching communism to those Africans in Asian employment. More valid both before and for long after these years of controversy was the charge that the Asian trader overcharged the African labourer and sold him short-weight. Both European and Asian employers were replacing Asian by cheaper African labour in spheres such as domestic service; store boys and watchmen. An organization emerged called the European and African Trades Organization, promoted by Nairobi European businessmen; they and others issued demands for a training college for African artisans, the end of Asian immigration, and opened a small employment bureau for skilled Europeans and Africans.[29] A boycott of Asian shops was attempted, and the importation of cheap Italian or Seychellois labour studied until the few genuine European workers objected. In 1923 a representative of the European Workers' Association' was even sent to try to gain the support of the British Labour Party.[30] Feeling rose so high that a conspiracy was formed to kidnap the Governor and declare independence, and a certain measure of political support was obtained from South Africa. One practical consequence was the founding in 1924 of the Native Industrial Training Depot.

In advancing their case the settler leaders repeatedly affirmed that local employers were particularly concerned with the welfare of tribal Africans and African employees. It was, however, the absence of this concern in practice which among other reasons eventually led the British government to reject settler demands. The years 1919 to 1922, in addition to the pressures we have already examined, contained a number of labour scandals caused by both government and by settler alike. In 1920 one farmer, Captain Hawkins, over a three-day period intermittently flogged one man to death, supervised the flogging of a pregnant woman so that she later suffered a miscarriage, and tortured two more men by screwing their fingers in a vice, a case widely reported in the local press, a European public subscription being launched to meet the cost of the trial.[31]

More grave was the wretched administration by the contractors, Messrs

Norton Griffiths, of the labour on the Uasin-Gishu railway extension where in May 1922 the death rate had reached 83 per 1,000 per annum, the overall figure for the year being 436 or 51.32 per 1,000. The government appointed inspectors with magisterial powers and a doctor, but the death-rate remained large, 35.28 per 1,000 in 1923 (in May 1923, 17,426 employed), and 14.28 in 1924 (about 5,000 employed).[32] The Secretary of State, the Duke of Devonshire, later ordered an enquiry. At the time the deaths were said by the government to have been caused by the cold and rain of the high altitude camp, overcrowding, and the natives' 'ingrained habits' in respect of sanitation; the P.M.O. added that pneumonia was probably able to strike so disastrously due to earlier dietary deficiencies. These deficiencies were in no way remedied by the contractors' early ration issue—2 lb. of maize meal per day, plus 1 lb. of beans and a small ration of dried fish per week.[33] It is noticeable that one sub-contractor who supplied meat in addition had one death only among his large labour force. Men brought from Tanganyika, mainly Nyamwezi and Sukuma, about 1,800 in total, suffered particularly severely, as some of these had not been medically examined and others had been rejected at their medical examination, but nevertheless allowed to 'volunteer'; a considerable number died. Tanganyika men were also at a disadvantage as sometimes foremen or supervisors withheld their pay believing that the offence would not be discovered, and the hazards of the journey had to be added to those of disease and employer indifference.[34] Only the reduction of farm labour requirements caused by the post-war slump, together with the continuing necessity to work to pay taxation maintained a voluntary supply for this project for as long as two years.

Abuses in 'encouragement' and communal labour mounted. 'The 'encouragement' of women and children had already been noted, but in the unhealthy psychological climate of the period communal labour, originally only an obligation on men but subsequently extended not unreasonably to women and children for very light tasks, became distorted to severe tasks no longer of benefit to the community. Men past working age were directed to work on roads. McGregor Ross on tour in 1922 found a number of young women and girls conscripted to fill the water tank of the house of a government officer, a task involving their staying overnight 'in their daytime lack of costume' in a ramshackle outhouse with neither food nor blankets. He complained to the Chief Native Commissioner who issued orders that the practice must stop. The orders quoted another example that had come to light, of women and children being obliged to carry heavy loads of grass for a long distance for which they received no food and a very low wage.[35] As a consequence of these malpractices rules were also issued in March 1923 under the Master and Servants Ordinance, by which no woman worker was to remain on a farm at night unless accompanied by her father or her husband, proper accommodation was to be provided for single women, and farm owners who failed to provide this accommodation were not to employ any woman at a distance greater than three miles from her home. But these rules were not universally obeyed.[36]

African reaction to this sum of compulsion, coercion and taxation became apparent as early as 1920.[37] Since pressure on the African population was industrial, reaction then developed in great part through organizations of employees with aims partly political and partly industrial, and Nairobi's first African political riot in 1922 was also very largely a general strike. Domestic servants, employees and labourers had been meeting on Sunday afternoons mostly in Pangani where they formed the East African Association, largely Kikuyu but open to all. In 1921 during discontent over the proposed one-third reduction of wages, the association threw up its first effective spokesman in Harry Thuku who also organized the Young Kikuyu Association composed mainly of office boys and domestic servants in Nairobi. Harry Thuku was a Treasury telephone operator who had earlier in life been in prison for issuing a forged cheque, and then worked as a compositor for the *Leader*, whose editorials and prejudices he had found offensive and disturbing. He had been, by the standards of the time, well-educated at a mission and further possessed gifts of oratory and administration. His association represented the young men who through employment had started to leave the fold of tribal society, disregarding its customs and its leaders. He seems to have formed a purely tribal association for reasons of communication and in emulation of the vocal and effective Young Baganda Association. He worked with the assistance at first of A. R. Barlow, a Scots missionary, and later with Asian political leaders who assisted him with translations, transport and publicity. He began to address meetings which drew large crowds to the annoyance of some of the chiefs. His speeches were a mixture of attacks on African conditions which he compared to slavery, political and land issues, and effective protest against the most oppressive features of the labour scene, all confused with Messianic personal claims.

At a large meeting at Dagoretti in June 1921 Africans, including a number of chiefs, complained of the forced labour of women and girls, alleging that some had been sent because the district commissioner whom they named had ordered their fathers to send them.[38] They cited sixty who had been taken to a European farm to work, listing those who had been raped there. Other complaints alleged that goats were taken from families who objected, and that headmen who did not produce their quotas were made to carry heavy loads as a punishment or were detained. Further grievances included tax, communal road labour obligations upon old people, sometimes for private roads, and the *kipande* system on which Chiefs Munyua and Koinange and the young Josiah Njonjo spoke. A number of chiefs and elders spoke as strongly as the younger men. Thuku himself asked for government action to prevent the reduction of wages by refusing to reduce those of its own staff. The Chief Native Commissioner replied that he and his officers would examine specific grievances, denying not entirely convincingly some of the charges, and stating that the government only approved of women and children working when they returned to their homes at night. On the wages reduction question he argued ambiguously that 'local' rates would be paid by the government.

Thuku followed up the meeting by sending a list of grievances to the Colonial Office for which he lost his job. The Colony Treasurer was not unsympathetic, giving Thuku leave and a good discharge certificate, but McGregor Ross who offered to take him was not permitted to do so. Free from employment Thuku began touring the country addressing a series of meetings, at which more demands to repeal the Registration Ordinance or suspend it for five years, to stop the wage reduction and to discard hut tax were mixed with ever more ambitious political and Messianic messages. In one such speech Thuku challenged: 'I desire if the Europeans tell you to do any sort of work at all that you tell them Harry Thuku has refused to allow you to make camps, or to make roads, or to work in the station or for the Public Works Department, or to give out food for porters or firewood.'[39] He called for a plan to collect all *kipandes* in a lorry and deposit them at Government House and sent telegrams to Lord Islington and Colonel Wedgwood in Britain. Parallel with Thuku's activities, a series of meetings called by the Young Kavirondo Association and attended by several thousands of people were taking place in Nyanza at which labour grievances received the same emphasis as issues of land and political power.[40] A protest leader, Ndonyo wa Kamiti, also emerged among the Kamba; he again demanded an end to forced labour and taxation.

The crisis came in March 1922 when Thuku was arrested and detained in a Nairobi police station. A crowd growing in size assembled outside. The following day parties of young men toured offices, stores and homes calling men away from their work, achieving an almost total stoppage in the city centre, and building up a hostile crowd of over 7,000 outside the police station.[41] The Chief Secretary interviewed a deputation while other government officers appealed for the crowd to disperse, promising a fair trial for Thuku, but in the excitement of seeing his inspector manhandled a police *askari* opened fire others joining in. At least twenty-one people were killed (including four women), and a number of arrests were made of 'ringleaders' who received prison sentences while Thuku was detained without trial in a remote area until 1931. Some who joined in the strike were dismissed or fined a month or two weeks' salary. The Europeans chose to see the hand of the Asian agitator behind the riot, and the Asian controversy received new heat. The East African Association collapsed without its most effective spokesmen. The riot had two further consequences—tax was reduced from Shs. 16/- to Shs. 12/- and was never raised again with labour recruiting as a primary purpose, and the worst labour transit camps were closed. This real evidence of African discontent, despite attempts by Northey to suggest the crowd assembled out of curiosity, confirmed the views of liberal and mission sentiment in England which were to play a vital part in the policy decisions of 1923. Lastly the riot was another factor shaking Churchill's confidence in the impartiality of Northey who was replaced in the summer.[42] Thuku was seen as a national hero in Kikuyuland; an immensely popular girls' song ran:

> Filipu aromakoguo
> Nio matwarithirie munene wa Nyacing'a
> Nyacing'a ituire Kahawa-ini.[43]

Under Northey's successor, Sir Robert Coryndon, although much noise continued to be made the texture of Kenya life improved slightly. For the first time since Crewe, Sadler and Hollis, the triangle of an informed and watchful Colonial Office with a governor and officials mindful of African interests is partially repeated, reinforced additionally by the influence of the new and more progressive British elements among the settlers replacing the old South African ideas. Although the brave affirmation of policy in the Devonshire Paper that 'Primarily Kenya is an African country . . .' was an overstatement if taken literally, it served as a check to European political ambitions, and in the labour field the paper was an assertion that Africans in their own country were not simply helots but individuals with certain rights. In execution the new or Dual Policy as it was called was defined by Coryndon as the 'complementary development of native and non-native production'; theoretical debate centred round whether or not the trusteeship of the native lay solely with the colonial government or was to be shared with the local Europeans. If judged in terms of positive achievement and immediate practical steps to develop African areas there was little to show for many years, but new perspectives were set, and by the nineteen-thirties a number of European leaders had accepted the desirability of the development of services in the reserves beyond the 'labour' needs of health and industrial education. Plans were made for further reserves to be demarcated reducing partially the sense of insecurity. The Local Native Councils (hereafter L.N.C.s) formed slowly in the middle and late nineteen-twenties, provided a channel in which a number of grievances including some affecting labour could be aired and put right. By the late nineteen-twenties administrative and professional officers who spoke up for the African or refused to countenance malpractices ceased to be retired, transferred or lose promotion as Tate, McGregor Ross, Ainsworth, Leys and others had been, though inevitably a minority could not resist the social temptations of popularity among the settlers to the disadvantage of Africans.[44] Occasional direct attacks were still made on the administration, one was mounted by Delamere in the 1925 and 1926 sessions of Convention; at the former speakers talked of the combing out of officials who were not encouraging labour. Unco-operative junior officers were described as inspired with anti-white ideas and bolshevist tendencies, and at both sessions Maxwell, the Chief Native Commissioner was severely criticized.[45] Amery's unqualified support for Maxwell in face of parliamentary questions convinced European politicians of the futility of this course.[46]

The recommendations of the Barth Commission concerning the reorganization of the government had been only partially carried out in the post-war years. It proved unrealistic to replace district commissioners by magistrates in the settled areas. From 1920 to 1929 the district commissioners were renamed resident commissioners in these areas and except for Kiambu and Machakos they were initially removed from the provincial structure, corresponding directly with the local Colonial Secretary, though later provincial officers were reintroduced. The remainder of the country was divided into provinces each under a Senior Commissioner, with the Chief Native Commissioner above and district commissioners below. In August 1922 an economy committee on which settlers were strongly represented sought the abolition of the post of Chief Native Commissioner, a move seen by Archdeacon Owen as an attempt to deprive Africans of representation on the Executive and Legislative Councils. Northey approved of the proposed economy but the Colonial Office insisted that the Chief Native Commissioner's post be preserved in the interests of a consistent native policy.[47] In 1929 the Chief Native Commissioner's status was slightly reduced but overall these structural changes *per se* reflected little on labour. The closeness of the administration in the context of tax collection and 'encouragement', however, played a much greater part. A Kenya native district might have half the population of a Uganda district or a quarter that of a Nigeria district but the same number of administrative officers. The belief in the desirability of varied experience and personal reasons of health and leave led to frequent moves by these officials. Throughout the inter-war period it was in no way unusual for one district to have ten changes of commissioner in seven years; these changes, too, mitigated against a proper understanding of the people of an area.[48]

Debate and politics still centred around familiar themes with one new addition, Closer Union. Those of the European settler community who supported Closer Union hoped thereby that control over general native and labour policy would pass to them. Critics of Closer Union in Britain and East Africa were often men with a record of protection over African labour, land and racial issues; in opposing any union which devolved power to Europeans they had the interests of African labour in mind.

A few other attacks on the administration with the object of recovering lost ground in the labour field are noteworthy: a demand for labour bureaux in 1921 and a request to be allowed to pay wages in kind in 1924 were both rejected.[49] Settler leaders also from time to time expressed the traditional opposition to agricultural development in the reserves as endangering the labour supply. They claimed this development was the cause of a labour shortage in 1924 and 1925, on this occasion a very genuine one but whose real cause was the returning prosperity which led to the opening of new farms and expansion of old ones. Once again the old arguments of the idle native 'carousing in the reserves' leaving all to his women were heard, and attacks on the 'neutrality' of administrative officers renewed, placing the district officer in his old dilemma. Their difficulties were increased by an old-fashioned statement to the Convention by E. B. (later Sir Edward) Denham, Acting Governor after the sudden death of Coryndon early in 1925, that the government expected all district officers to give 'all possible encouragement' to labour.[50] Allegations were also made in the Legislative Council that some chiefs particularly in Nyanza were advising men not to work. Demands were made that administration in the reserves be tightened up, that natives should not be allowed the full profit from their own farming, part being taken away for their own good to discourage idleness. The Council's Economic and Finance Committee judged that the whole country was concerned with the supply of labour for development and production—by which they meant European production. Other ideas aired at various times in 1925 and 1926 included: the timing of hut tax to coincide with the harvest, that African children be taught double-handed picking of coffee, a revived demand for the reduction of the reserves, increase in tax rates, the opening of closed areas for recruiting, the importation of indentured Indian or Chinese labour, or Italian peasants (seen additionally as a racial reinforcement), or labour from adjoining territories, and the increase of the minimum number of obligatory working days required of a resident labourer. A call was also voiced for the importation of Mozambique labourers who were thought to be more tractable, and a private attempt was made to recruit Egyptians which the Kenya government forbade.[51] One Legislative Council member even argued for open compulsion, but he carried little support and was criticized in the press. The renewed demand for self-government sought control of labour among its first objectives.

Periodic apparent or real labour shortages, the prospect of obtaining labour at an even lower wage rate, and their suitability for certain light seasonal work led to a considerable increase in the number of employed juveniles and children in the nineteen-twenties. Women too were used for seasonal work. In 1925 5,477 women and 11,315 children had been at work at some time or another in the year.[52] Where this work consisted only of tea or coffee picking or light domestic work, the educative and economic value was possibly beneficial, but a number of boys were at work often unsupervised by employer or family, in shops or on errands in the towns. Also in the early nineteen-twenties the less scrupulous railway fuel and ballast contractors were using boys under the age of ten for heavy fuel and stone cutting tasks despite the provisions of the 1919 amendment to the Master and Servants Ordinance. These practices were stopped when they came to the notice, sometimes belatedly, of the Labour Section staff.

The overall shortage throughout most of the decade led many Africans from Uganda and Tanganyika to come to Kenya to work; although specific recruiting (with certain exceptions) was no longer permitted by either government, no restriction was placed on the free movement of voluntary labour. In 1923 there were over 8,000 Baganda at work in Kenya chiefly as clerks or domestic servants, and over 5,400 other East Africans from Uganda and Tanganyika; by 1929 the figure had increased to monthly averages of some 10,000 Uganda and 7,000 Tanganyika adults at work.[53] Despite the Kenya pressures, however, the traffic was not all in one direction. Sizeable numbers of Kenya labourers still departed for seasonal clove picking in Zanzibar and Pemba where an unskilled labourer could earn as much as Shs. 30/- per month by hard work. Other Kenya men almost entirely drawn from Nyanza went to Kampala, Namasagali and Jinja to work on sugar estates, in the building industry or for the Railway.[54]

The shortages also led to a number of commissions and committees. A Legislative Council committee examined the resident labour system in 1926, noting that employers neglected the supervision of their labourers and their stock and also the maintenance of employment registers; it recommended a special inspectorate to ensure enforcement. A Labour Commission sat in 1927 as a result of a Convention motion; in general this body judged that the shortage was temporary and that with improved efficiency and the use of labour saving devices even larger labour requirements in the future could be met. Its recommendations included greater use of juvenile labour and machinery at harvest time, improved food scales and permanent settlements of labourers and their families in the European areas.[55] Consideration was also given to the control of casual labour and the abolition of professional recruiting by Labour Agents; legislation for both subjects was drafted but not enacted, apparently on account of the difficulties of supervision.

In 1925 the government also appointed a Native Punishment Commission to inquire into punishment for minor offenders, many of whom had been convicted under the Registration or Hut and Poll Tax Ordinances, the Resident Labourers Ordinance or Pass laws, or for Master and Servants offences such as desertion or negligence. This commission thought fines for such offences the best penalty, but in default, a period in a detention camp (not mixed with the hard-core prison criminal) with unpaid public work would have 'a reformative effect'. An ordinance to effect their recommendations was passed, and camps opened shortly afterwards.[56]

The number of men engaged in the unproductive work of domestic service continued to increase with the arrival of fresh Europeans, adding to the periodic shortages of labour. In 1926 over 22,000 Africans were in domestic service, approximately one employed man in seven. The very large majority of these servants were men; only a small number of Baganda girls and even smaller number of Nandi and Kikuyu girls worked as *ayahs* (nannies). Despite the *kipande* system the control of domestic servants was still seen as a problem, and following a 1926 Convention of Associations resolution a new Domestic Servants Registration Ordinance was drafted and enacted in 1929.[57] Fear of assaults on the increasing number of European women and girls had led to this reintroduction of special registration. The ordinance was similar to that of 1910; it provided for the issue of pocket registers which would note fingerprints, a complete employment history, causes of termination of agreement, character references, and by subsequent rules, wage rates. The ordinance was first applied to Nairobi in 1930; its consequences became apparent in the nineteen-thirties and will be examined in the next chapter.

The beginnings of liberalization under Coryndon received a set-back with the appointment of Sir Edward Grigg as Governor in 1925. Like his predecessors Girouard and Belfield so in his turn did Grigg subtly modify specific Colonial Office instructions against 'encouragement'; and from the Governor's chair he directed the last major attack on the neutrality of the administration. District officers were again instructed to 'do their utmost to promote the flow of labour'.[58] The East African Governors' Conference expressed the apparently innocuous opinion that where natives could not produce in the reserves they should be definitely encouraged to go out and labour though in the event of both alternatives being open the choice was to be free, an opinion easily misconstrued in Kenya. Grigg apparently even permitted certain sisal estates to import Mozambique labour late in 1925; throughout his tenure he repeatedly disagreed with those, including the Missionary Council, who felt that further settlement should await an adequate labour supply. A circular under the signature of G. Maxwell, Chief Native Commissioner, but clearly inspired by Grigg, was sent to all administrative officers in January 1927. This circular noted the E.A. Governors' Conference statement and observed that in some parts of Kenya 'young men who should be usefully employed are giving themselves up to idling, drinking, immoral dancing and unrestrained licence, so that their manhood is wasted'. The Governor directed that *barazas* be held to ensure that all those not at work in the reserves be reminded of their responsibilities towards, and opportunities for learning in, the settled areas of the colony.[59]

Forces in England and elsewhere, however, were now sufficiently well organized to limit the regression of a governor such as Grigg who was in any case receiving decreasing support from Amery, the Secretary of State. Oldham continued to supervise and co-ordinate mission pressures, gaining the approval of the 1926 conference of all non-Roman missions working in Africa. His work received further support from Lugard, whose authority had been enhanced by appointment in 1922 to the Permanent Mandates Commission. Other humanitarian societies such as the Anti-Slavery Society maintained their watch. From a different angle the interest and concern of the Labour Party also grew; a number of members asked questions or spoke forcefully on East African affairs, as occasionally and with poor knowledge the Trade Union Congress began also to do. In 1925 the Temporary Slavery Commission of the League of Nations decided indirect pressure on labour for private employers was equivalent to compulsion, and shortly afterwards the International Labour Organization began its studies on forced labour. The separation of the Colonial Office from the Dominions Office in 1925 and the beginning of special subject studies rather than purely regionally based desks led also to a greater and more knowledgeable official attention and less susceptibility to South African prejudices. The Secretary of State in the 1924 Labour government, J. H. Thomas, rejected Lugard's odd proposal to divide Kenya and appointed a commission to study policies in East Africa in the context of possible 'Closer Union' under the chairmanship of W. Ormsby-Gore.[60] Parliamentary attention was still maintained after the return of the Conservatives, Amery having to face questions on the Mozambique labour project and suspicion that the principles of the Churchill despatch were not being upheld.[61] Conditions requiring 'fair conditions of labour' were included in the 1926 East African Transport Loans Act and the 1929 Colonial Development Act.

In Kenya itself the Kikuyu Central Association was emerging as the most representative Kikuyu political and industrial voice although of course not recognized as such by the government. Its requests to the Ormsby-Gore Commission included the abolition of registration, an end to further land alienation, tax exemption for women, and a guarantee that, provided natives paid tax and produced crops on their own *shambas*, they would not be compelled to leave their land and go out to work for Europeans.[62] In Nyanza the Young Kavirondo Association evolved under the guidance of Owen into the Kavirondo Taxpayers Welfare Association, and began to raise a wide range of political and social questions. This association spoke with such effect that Nyanza labourers on far distant farms were asking to join which McGregor Ross described as hopeful and 'a development in the direction of trade unionism'. Another such development was the emergence, following the example of European officials, of the Kenya Asian Civil Service Association and the African (B.E.A.) Civil Service Association.. The former was in being as early as 1921, addressing the Secretary of State on house allowances and income tax. In 1922 the association in conjunction with the Railway Asiatic Union, held a mass meeting to protest against a government proposal to reduce Asian salaries; they sent a further petition to the Secretary of State and gained their point.[63] The African association successfully petitioned the Secretary of State in 1920 complaining against a reduction of war bonus and house allowance and asking for pensions; they repeated the process in 1921, again seeking a pensionable 'Native Civil Service' and a general improvement in terms of service, but they received only a promise of consideration.

In the last years before the Depression the close watch on Kenya affairs continued. Although Grigg supported the local European demand for association in trusteeship (a lever for participation in formulating native policy) which Amery conceded in the July 1927 White Paper, the feeling of unease over East African affairs prevented Amery from creating the East African federation which he wished, and led to another commission to examine the question under Sir Hilton Young with Oldham as a member. The commission received evidence from organizations such as the Kavirondo Taxpayers Welfare Association and the Kikuyu Central Association representing the younger generations, and the Kikuyu Association representing the elders and chiefs. All opposed federation arguing that a European majority, the settlers' condition, would lead to increased settlement, reduction of the reserves and labour compulsion; all also once again asked for the abolition of registration. Other pressures at work on the Colonial Office in these years included a resolution on labour compulsion passed by the International Missionary Council in Jerusalem in April 1928, and more critical resolutions on compulsion, native land areas, taxes, recruiting and penal provisions in labour legislation passed by the 1928 Labour and Socialist International Congress at Brussels. This congress also recommended that the International Labour Organization should prepare a code for native workers to be enforced by the League of Nations. The books of Leys and McGregor Ross, the revised edition of Lord Olivier's *White Capital and Coloured Labour,* and occasional British press articles by Leys, resulted in the concern noticeable in parliamentary questions.

The Hilton Young Commission Report, published in 1930, reflected the impression made by these views, in general stating that while immigrant communities might justly claim partnership they could not claim control, and in particular returning to the Crewe-Churchill position on labour. The report affirmed that Africans could never be 'a mere accessory to the immigrant community', and, even more strongly that 'the foundation on which the protection of native interests must be based . . . is a policy which would make available for every native for his own cultivation sufficient land to maintain himself and his family, and to provide him with the cash required for the taxes which he has to pay'. In detail the commission recommended the regulation of new settlement to match the labour supply and the health of native societies, the limitation of 'encouragement' to the provision of information and ensuring that the flow of labour was entirely voluntary, and that a specialist survey of labour conditions be undertaken, a recommendation abandoned on account of the Depression.

Having recorded the sequence of the principal events in the labour field in the nineteen-twenties, a number of particular subjects need closer examination.

The Resident Labour System

The 1918 Resident Natives Ordinance was brought into force throughout the protectorate other than certain Coastal areas in November 1919; rules at the same time laid down the permit forms for the farmer and the squatter. District administration officers were appointed as magistrates for the purposes of the ordinance in areas where none were available. Soon afterwards, early in 1920, the first gazette notices appeared warning named farmers that on plots not under development, natives were living illegally and were to be removed.

Thus legalized, the resident labour or squatter system became the relationship by which farmers in the nineteen-twenties engaged the largest proportion of their labourers, and the relationship by which, in consequence, immense numbers of Africans first came into close contact with a white man and his farming methods. The Kikuyu migration of the war years continued in the early nineteen-twenties. But resident labour status also provided the pastoral tribes with a not altogether uncongenial introduction, and new men from all tribes with a further stage in their adjustment to some concept of regular employment. In general men and their families preferred to work as squatters on farms near to their own districts. By the end of the decade the total number of squatters was in the neighbourhood of 120,000 of which some 35,000 were adult males. After the ordinance was passed farmers began legalizing the status of men already at work or engaging large numbers on the new arrangements. While the men were working their 180 days, their wives with their babies left in the shade of a tree sometimes tended by an older child had the task of breaking the ground of their plots—often a hard and unfamiliar experience in terrain very different from that of their former homes.

As we have seen, the status at its best could provide a material security and preservation of family life, together with a paternal relationship that was for a period of time desired by both sides.[64] In the improved psychological climate of the inter-war period many farmers provided a number of small services for their squatters. The farmer's wife would often look after the sick. A large farm or a group of small farms might run a small school at which squatters' children received instruction by day and, sometimes also the adults in the evening. The teacher was usually a man who had completed a mission primary school course. The results of such enterprise varied considerably, many farmers complaining that the schools they provided were poorly supported. The education was almost invariably limited to that which the farmer thought necessary for a future squatter—literacy, elementary mathematics and hygiene. A kind farmer might allow former labourers too old to work to live out their days on a corner of the farm land. The practice grew up on many farms of a *kiama*, or council of the older and more responsible farm labourers settling minor differences and feuds that sprang up between squatters.[65] The wise farmer watched his *kiama* closely lest the old men used fines from the young to their own advantage, or he might allow a few younger men to join on payment to the elders of an entry fee in goats. *Kiamas* imposed small fines, though not legally entitled to do so. They would often meet in long sessions under a tree, the older men on stools, the younger squatting on their heels, speakers emphasizing their points by throwing twigs on the ground and raising their voices. Wage rates rose little, but the rental value of the squatter's land, often quite high, rose by virtue of the increased knowledge and skill of the owner passed on to some extent to his labourers. The good employer, too, would often supplement his squatters' cash wages and *posho* with meat and assist with the provision of materials for the construction of huts. On some farms an employer might from time to time organize games or permit an *ngoma*, asking the district commissioner to grant a temporary brewing licence, and watch the dances with fascination—his labourers covered in red chalk with the star performers in ostrich feathers, shouting, jumping, stamping and gyrating towards the oiled womenfolk in their traditional bead-embroidered leather skirts and mantles. Sometimes, however songs sung at such *ngomas* were anti-European or seditious songs which had been banned in the reserves.[66]

Many employers were not good and the squatter could still suffer severely at the hands of the bad farmer. The winding-up or sale of a farm or the death of the farmer could involve the squatter in formidable difficulties, particularly if he had lost touch with his reserve and another man was now farming his land there, the chief supporting the other man and all common land now allotted. Some squatters guarded against this by keeping one of their wives at work in the reserves. The farmer employer rarely took the trouble to provide for his labourers in such circumstances and squatters returning home who created any form of disturbance were liable to become unpopular with the local administration. At least one district commissioner kept a black list of returned squatters.[67] Although the farm labourer was perhaps protected against famine or food shortages that might affect his reserve, his prosperity might almost as nearly depend on that of the farm as a whole, in turn dependent on world trade at the time. Many squatters were to suffer along with their masters at the time of the Depression. Most farmers believed in mixing squatters of different tribes to form their labour force, partly so that no one tribe should gain a dominant position and partly to utilize different aptitudes. This could lead to disputes, theft, and occasionally to violent inter-tribal clashes.

Many squatters in these early years became very wealthy in the traditional terms of wives, sheep, cattle and goats, though the value of the stock could be very quickly lost if the squatter had to leave his land and work. A number developed a considerable petty entrepreneurial skill when selling their own produce, a skill often passed on to their children. Others however remained in poverty. On a large number of farms women and children were employed at harvest time, often picking coffee, tea and later pyrethrum and earning a few cents an hour; the 1925 figures recorded over 11,000 children so employed. A few trusted squatters' children would be trained from an early age in domestic work inside the farmer's house. In general the squatter came into much closer contact with his employer at home than did the non-domestic town labourer, and from the early nineteen-twenties this contact began to be reflected in dress and habits—squatter huts began to have furniture modelled on that of the European, men arrived with long hair and then had it cropped short, and some discontinued the practice of piercing ear-lobes. Machines, tractors, engines (the *tinka-tinka*), gramophones, lanterns, European food, the printed word, lost their magic and passed into every day use.

The 1918 Ordinance was amended in 1925 following a ruling by the Supreme Court that a squatter was a tenant, and not a servant under the Master and Servants Ordinance and that therefore the desertion and disciplinary provisions of the Master and Servants Ordinance did not apply. An attempt was made in 1923 to place the whole resident labour system under the Master and Servants Ordinance by an amendment to the latter ordinance with various additions such as five-year written contracts; this amending bill appeared in 1924 as an ordinance with the further additions that the feeding of sick servants on ticket contracts would no longer be the employer's responsibility and that work might take place on Sundays.[68] However this proposed amendment which was also to repeal the 1918 Resident Natives Ordinance was disallowed by the Labour Secretary of State, and the Resident Natives Ordinance had hurriedly to be revived.[69] In the following year a new ordinance, this time clearly entitled the Resident Native Labourers Ordinance, was passed and not disallowed by the Conservative Secretary of State.[70] The 1925 ordinance added almost identical penal provisions to those of the Master and Servants Ordinance and provided for the grant of contract attestation powers to local farmers, which largely negated the previous safeguard whereby a magistrate could refuse to attest a contract where he judged the wages to be below the local level. In the debate on the ordinance, Delamere said that resident labourers wanted long contracts of as much as twenty years for security of tenure, but the Chief Native Commissioner replied that the Colonial Office forbade contracts longer than three years.[71] Many squatters objected to re-attestation on the new terms, and as they came to see that the relationship was evolving from one of tenancy to one of poorly paid labourer disillusion increased. In 1929, at the time of the Kikuyu unrest over the female circumcision issue, Kikuyu squatters in considerable numbers refused to work further, and tried to return to their homes in the reserves. Some were persuaded against this by their employers or the administration and went back to squatting, others found little or no land left for them in the reserves and a return to squatting the only alternative to destitution.

Other more fundamental problems began to appear in the late nineteen-twenties. The inefficiency of the system became more clear; in 1926 the Convention of Associations first demanded that the number of obligatory working days be increased from 180 to 270.[72] Squatters were found not to be working their contract days or other agreed periods of time and stock thefts increased. As the African populations in the reserves began to grow, more and more families were obliged to seek work as squatters, or went out to visit kinsmen on farms, sometimes settling in substantial numbers on the more remote and undeveloped areas of a farm. Employers, too, failed to keep their registers properly which facilitated illegal squatting. Perhaps most serious of all, squatter stock multiplied at a time when for external market reasons European farmers were tending to change from maize to dairy products; some farmers reacted to this simply by shooting their squatters' stock without proper compensation. These problems were to come to a head in the following decade but the unrest noted in 1929 was not appreciated as a warning by the colonial administration.

Registration: The Kipande *System*

The Registration of Natives Ordinance as passed in 1915 was amended by a bill which became law in 1920 providing for a numbered metal case (the number being the same as his certificate) to be given to each male African so that his certificate could be protected.[73] Penalties of a fine of 15 rupees or a maximum of three months imprisonment, or both were provided for people who destroyed, damaged or disposed of their certificate or its case, and replacement charges for a lost certificate were laid down.

In the course of the two-hour political tirade with which Grogan greeted Sir Edward Northey at a banquet of welcome in February 1919, he said the settlers demanded the immediate introduction of the registration scheme. The first post-war session of the Convention in January 1919 had made the same demand as did local farmers' associations throughout 1919, sometimes supported by certain civil servants whose views on the desirability of work we have already noted.

Late in 1919 the first proclamations were issued applying the ordinance to Nairobi, Kisumu, Kakamega and Kiambu, and early in 1920 to Fort Hall and Mombasa, followed in April by extension to the whole territory. 'Natives' were ordered to the local administration offices to receive their certificates and tin canisters. Rules issued at the time of the first proclamation set out the form of the certificate which recorded a man's name, district, location, registration number, father's name, tribe, sub-location, clan, approximate age and district, together with name of the employer, date and nature of employment, rate of wages last paid, and if supplied *posho*, the date of discharge and the employer's signature; sufficient space was provided to record a whole employment history and a man's left thumb-print.[74] The registering officer on a separate form recorded a man's name, all his tribal particulars and all ten finger-prints and sent them to the Chief Registrar of Natives in Nairobi. Blocks of serial numbers were allotted to different areas, and district commissioners and labour inspectors were gazetted as registration officers. Later the district clerk, usually a Goan, was frequently granted registration officer powers.

The 1920 amendment had also strengthened the ordinance by the addition of a number of severe provisions. One laid the onus of obtaining the endorsement of discharge entirely on the employee who had to be a brave man to attempt to use the only safeguard, a right of complaint to the local registration officer. Other provisions tightened the requirement that an employer had to check that the certificate of a man whom he wished to engage had been signed-off in respect of previous employment, confirmed that finger-prints might be prima facie proof of identity in criminal proceedings, and required employers to notify district commissioners of all engagements and discharges even to the extent of *nil* returns monthly under threat of severe penalty for failure to do so. A re-enactment Ordinance in 1921 affirmed clearly that it was illegal for an employer to engage a man whose *kipande* had not been 'signed off' in respect of previous employment, and added a requirement for an employer to notify changes of wage-rate paid on the certificate at the time of discharge; it also lowered the age of males to which the ordinance might be applied to sixteen, and increased the penalties for employers who disregarded the ordinance.[75] These new offences were also made cognizable to the police.

Minor alterations to the rules, forms of the certificate, and changes in the penalties were made at various times but these original measures constituted the machinery of the system, legally required of all Africans but generally only applied to those outside their own reserves (although required of Africans at work in townships in the reserves). The ordinance was in error applied to a few reserve areas at the outset, an error which increased its unpopularity, and its scope extended to registered casual labourers in 1927. Prisons and reformatories were to notify the Chief Registrar of admissions and to record discharges on a man's certificate.

The effect of this system, ostensibly one of identification, was in fact to restrict both a man's freedom to leave his work and his freedom to bargain with an employer for a wage not necessarily related to that of his previous employment. The certificate was used in courts of law as evidence of an oral contract of one month, and in the early years there is some evidence to suggest men cultivating their own land in the reserves were fined (which probably meant they had to work for Europeans) if they had no certificate. A central registry was established using experience gained in the Carrier Corps which served to check fraud and impersonation. Sheets of tear-off forms entitled 'Complaint of Desertion of Registered Native' were supplied by the government free to employers. When a man deserted the employer filled in the form (addressed to the Chief Registrar in Nairobi), after which the government would trace and arrest the deserter through the reserve chiefs and headmen, once again putting these men in an impossible position. If the employer was required to appear as a witness at the prosecution he could claim expenses.

McGregor Ross provides an account, perhaps only slightly exaggerated, of the system at work and rightly draws attention to the fact that at its inception it was accompanied by large-scale prosecutions for desertion; he states that of 2,790 reported desertions by the end of 1921, 2,364 were traced.[76] Leys provides figures of 77 per cent of the 3,595 deserters being traced and punished for 1921, and Ross notes that desertions had fallen by 1922 to only three per thousand.[77] Ross comments that statistics of the system, including a total of 8,377 prosecutions 'involving tens of thousands of detentions and interrogations' conducted up to the end of February 1922, were given to the local press on the day of the Harry Thuku riots of which the certificate was one of the major causes. Figures showing Africans actually convicted are included in Appendix I, Table 1.

The *kipande* and its metal container worn round the neck (like the badge on a dog's collar, as some Africans observed) struck deep at the African sense of self-respect, as well as providing him with a number of justifiable employment grievances; a demand for the abolition of the *kipande* formed from then on a principal item in the platform of African 'protest'. Thuku voiced African objections to the system at his Dagoretti meeting in June 1921 and his Thika meeting in November 1921; the meetings of protest in

Nyanza argued similarly, Northey's comparison of the *kipande* to a passport carrying little conviction. As we have already seen one of Thuku's plans immediately prior to his arrest was a call on Africans to deposit their certificates from a lorry at Government House, and resentment again found expression in the K.C.A. request for abolition to the Ormsby-Gore Commission. Almost every statement of African political associations in the nineteen-twenties, thirties and forties demanded the abolition of the *kipande*, and the system was criticized in the House of Commons from time to time. The tribes of the northern frontier refused to have anything to do with it, a small section of the Gereh people moving across the frontier to Ethiopia to escape from it.

Apart from the sense of discrimination and the indignity of the taking of all ten finger-prints, the system led to a number of abuses. Whenever an African was outside the reserves, working, resting, or travelling, he was liable to arrest and prosecution on a criminal charge if he could not produce his *kipande*. The ordinance provided that an African must produce the certificate on demand by a police officer of assistant inspector rank or above or other authorized official. A cook without a *kipande* crossing a road after 10 p.m. to see a friend might be liable for a month in prison. Sometimes with reason, sometimes without, police would say of a man whom they wished to arrest but about whom they could not obtain sufficient evidence, 'We will get him on a *kipande* charge.' Obtaining a *kipande* for a member of a pastoral tribe wishing to make an occasional visit to a city might involve a long journey to the nearest district office. The court proceedings might be slow; Ross gives the example of the reduction by the Supreme Court of a sentence for desertion by one month, a reduction made after the accused had already been in prison for two months.

There were also abuses of their power by malevolent employers. Some, in the early years of the system wrote unpleasant comments on the *kipande* about men they did not like, comments which could not be erased. When this practice was stopped groups of farmers or employers in an area might have a private understanding that men signed off in, say, red ink, were unreliable and not to be employed again in the locality. Sometimes to keep a man at work an employer would refuse to return or to sign-off an employee's certificate; the chances of an employee being able to obtain redress were limited. Some employers even gave their employees long periods of leave with a *kipande* not signed-off as a surety for their eventual return, a court case in 1935 revealing one employer's practice of one month work followed by three months' leave.[78] A few notorious employers even kept on their books in this way two or three times the numbers actually at work, and sometimes professional recruiters would destroy the *kipande* of a man who had deserted from his previous work and purchase a replacement for him. We have already noted some of the urgent reasons which might lead an African to desert; the *kipande* system took no notice of these, it simply placed a punitive power in the hands of the employer which could stretch far into the reserves. Because of this power the settler community clung tenaciously to the system despite its considerable cost, even in periods of acute economic difficulty.

The severity of the system was a little eased by a relaxation effected in

1925 when desertion was removed from the list of offences cognizable to the police.[79] The government had, according to Ross, attempted to achieve this in 1922 but the unofficial members of the Legislative Council had objected so strongly that the attempt was abandoned. Leys states that the Colonial Office then directed the Kenya government to amend the procedure, after which desertion was only cognizable by a magistrate after the employer had taken out a summons. Employers were generally reluctant to do this, partly because of the work involved and partly because it gained them a bad reputation as an employer. The value of the concession was also weakened by a considerable increase in the number of prosecutions of men for failing to request an endorsement of discharge from employers, a procedure used to serve as an alternative to prosecution for desertion.[80] However although the legislative force had been removed and in the nineteen-thirties a proportion of employers, mostly Asians, ignored the regulations altogether, the deterrent value the *kipande* had achieved was in large part retained.

As a system the *kipande* assisted and strengthened the position of the bad employer so weakening the effect of improved employment conditions which might be offered on the labour market. To the good employer the *kipande* meant more paper work, police enquiries, raids in labour lines to look for other people's deserting labourers, and expense. McGregor Ross states that many good employers were opposed to the *kipande*, some refusing to operate the system in the hope that it would then break down. But few signs of breakdown were to be seen in this decade.

Compulsory Labour

As we have noted the concept of compulsory labour developed from that of communal labour, arising from the needs of government transport, from the free use of compulsion for state purposes in the war leaving a feeling that compulsion for urgent state purposes in peace might not be unjustifiable, and by analogy with the Uganda practice of *kasanvu.* The expansion of the economy, in particular the need for roads for the motor car and for extensions to the railway led to a requirement for men to work both for periods far longer than communal labour could provide, and in areas far from a man's home; such compelled labour had therefore to be paid.

Although compulsory labour was common in other African territories, in Kenya it had one distinctive feature—its relation to the 'encouragement' of labour for the private employer. One commonly held view, for example, was that labour from the remoter areas should be the subject of compulsion, leaving the labour nearer at hand available for the private employer. This view was then taken a stage further by the payment of a lower wage for the compulsory worker, it being thought that as a consequence Africans would prefer to work for three months (the minimum to secure exemption from compulsory labour) at a higher wage in relatively congenial work rather than two months of hard construction work at a lower wage. The choice before Africans would appear as one of free options. This Hobson's choice, made acute by the Northey circulars, aroused the opposition in Britain which we have already examined.

Another factor which led to abuse was that although compulsory labour was intended only for state purposes, this definition extended to private contractors working for the state; these contractors were capable of neglecting their labour to a scandalous degree, or on occasions threatening to prosecute them for 'desertion' if they did not 'volunteer' to remain after their compulsory period was completed. Owen, for example, discovered that men who had been recruited under the compulsory labour procedure were then being forced to sign six-month contracts.[81]

The government, foreseeing the future labour needs of railway construction, other post-war reconstruction and road-making passed the Native Authority Amendment Ordinance which became law in February 1920 at the height of the controversy in Britain and Kenya over the Northey circulars.[82] Both the circulars and the ordinance were heavily criticized, although the latter was in some respects less onerous by itself than comparable legislation elsewhere. The ordinance in fact provided for the compulsory requisition via the chiefs and headmen, of paid porters for the tours of government officers and the Transport Department, and of paid labour for the construction or maintenance of railways, roads, and other public works. The work was not to exceed sixty days per year and was not to be required of men fully employed or who had been fully employed for three full months (excluding travelling time, in some cases as much as ten days each way) out of the preceding twelve. It was not specifically stated but was nevertheless clearly intended that the employment should be wage labour for an employer, though Milner in the House of Lords stated he thought three months work on a man's own land should be a proper exemption. Communal labour provided no exemption, so a man who did not work for an employer might find himself obliged to work for the government for eighty-four days per year, sixty paid and twenty-four unpaid locally. Controversy aroused by the burden of these twin policies upon Africans led Milner in his published despatch of July 1920, although supporting the compulsory labour provisions of the 1920 ordinance and noting they were not at variance with the conditions of the Bishops' Memorandum, to warn Northey that the system could neither be extended nor commuted in return for increased tax.

Milner's despatch was published in September 1920, and was followed, in March 1921 by a circular instruction over the signature of Watkins as acting Chief Native Commissioner on the care of government native labour, significantly also published in the *Official Gazette*. The circular contained the most precise statement of the requirements of African labourers that had yet appeared from the territory's government and was clearly intended for the private employer as much as the public. The instructions required a medical examination, blankets and rations (or an allowance) for a journey to work, proper tentage or an adequate hut, a working day of eight hours beginning in the cool of the morning, loads for untrained porters not to exceed 50 lb. and to be distributed under supervision, diet to be varied and including specified quantities of carbohydrates, proteins, vitamins, fats and salt, and clear instructions on food preparation, sanitation, water, procedure for sickness and discipline, discharge and death. The text included a number of 'home truths' taken from the wartime *Military Labour Bureau Handbook*, e.g. 'a native cannot work or walk all day after being kept awake all night by rain or cold', 'it is a popular fallacy that the native likes the sun to work in. He does not', and 'There are two common misapprehensions with regard to food . . . that a native can keep well and work steadily on a 24 hours fast followed by a heavy gorge . . . (and) that a coarse mealie porridge is all he requires . . .' On discipline Watkins wrote 'You have no authority to inflict corporal punishment. If you flog a man you do so at your own risk and the amplest justification will be demanded. Aim at securing a hold on your men by accessibility, justice and good temper . . .'[83] Although an important step forward the instructions were not properly observed even by government departments for some considerable time. Two weeks later the *Official Gazette* contained a further instruction from Watkins on compulsory labour in which district commissioners were directed to follow certain documentation procedures for men called out, to ensure that any department extending the men's work beyond sixty days would be reported to the governor, and defining sixty days as sixty calendar days not sixty working days.[84] Yet another instruction was published in the *Gazette* in August 1921 for a public wider than those immediately affected; this was the Native Labourers Diet Rules which required fuel contractors to the Uganda Railway to provide their employees with rations almost identical to those set out in the March instructions.[85]

However the dissatisfaction in Britain with Milner's despatch led his successor, Churchill, to attempt even stricter control of compulsory labour. In his September 1921 despatch Churchill supported a maximum of six days communal labour per quarter in the reserves subject to supervision against abuse, but stated that conditions had changed since Milner's approval of the compulsory labour arrangements and he wished it to be placed on public record that it was the declared policy of the government of Kenya to avoid recourse to compulsory labour for government purposes except when this was absolutely necessary for essential services.[86] Churchill permitted compulsory labour legislation to remain on the statute book provided that the governor first sought the permission of the Secretary of State to use the powers of compulsion for any work other than the provision of paid porters for government officers on tour or for the transport of urgent government stores. Permission would only be given for 'specified works for a specified period'. Churchill directed the existing legislation to be amended accordingly and emphasized that compulsory labour for contractors must, too, receive the Secretary of State's approval. This despatch was also published in the *Official Gazette* in the following month, and a bill to implement Churchill's instructions, defining the essential services as roads, railways, wharves, harbours or other works of a public nature was published in August 1922. European unofficials objected to reference to the Colonial Office arguing that it was derogatory to the authority of the governor, and emergency procedure had to be used to secure its passage through council without delay. The *East African Standard*, reporting the gazetting of the Bill asked 'Who Rules Kenya? Another triumph for Messrs Harris and Wedgwood'. Criticizing as irrelevant 'the moral aristocracy of the British party system, the charms of slumdom and the leisured culture of the Staffordshire potteries', the article concluded by saying, 'We have got to free Mr. Churchill from the tyranny in which he is at present bound.'[87]

The ordinance went somewhat further, telegraphs and telephones were added to the list of essential services, and urgent repairs for unforeseen damages were added to the portering work for which the governor could call out labour without reference to London. The definition of work of a public nature carried the additional phrase 'provided for out of public monies' to cover contractors, and the procedure clearly required the governor to obtain the prior approval of the Secretary of State, which was to be requested only for a short period and to be notified in the *Gazette*. The ordinance also added a ban on meetings of natives which in the opinion of the district commissioner might be subversive, an important factor where there was no other outlet for labour discontent.[88]

From the first it had been intended that there should be certain exceptions to the compulsory labour requirements, but these too became a matter of controversy with European settler opinion trying to reduce the exemptions to the smallest possible number. A bill published in August 1920 provided for exemption from compulsory labour and registration for ministers of the Christian and Moslem religions, teachers, skilled employees, men in regular employment and self-employed men with a Standard VI level education.[89] This exemption was only to be granted following a letter of application to the Chief Native Commissioner, the letter being renewable annually; a fee was to be paid on issue and renewal each year and an oath of allegiance was also required. The exemption certificates had to be produced on demand and a late application for renewal could lead to disqualification. This bill was modified in the Legislative Council, the skilled and semi-skilled men being removed and exemption limited to barristers, advocates, chemists, druggists and engineers (of which there were none), and natives who had attained a standard of education approved by the settler-dominated Board of Education together with 'natives specially exempted by the Governor in Council'. So modified the bill became Ordinance No. 25 of 1920.[90] In practice the severity of the ordinance was mitigated by a section in Watkins's March 1921 instruction to district commissioners in which the latter were told to exercise 'a careful discretion' and exempt 'any who in their opinion shall show good cause for remaining in the Reserve'.[91] In 1923 the Governor issued on his own authority an administrative order exempting in addition headmen, camp caretakers, market masters and other local supervisors, members of councils, hospital dressers, chief's clerks, all contract employees and natives approved by their district commissioner as being 'steadily engaged' in trade, business or agriculture as well as the aged, the infirm, and ministers of religion.[92]

In December 1924 an acute labour shortage on the construction of the Uasin-Gishu and Thika-Nyeri railway lines led Coryndon to request approval for the call-out of men for this work as well as Kisumu dock where the contractors were falling behind their schedule.[93] The labourers were to be paid at a rate lower than the voluntary labourers as a 'lesson'. The Colonial Office reluctantly granted approval in January 1925 for the compulsory recruitment of a maximum of 4,000 men at any one time for work on the two railway extensions, refused permission in respect of Kisumu docks, insisted that wages be not less than Shs. 2/- below voluntary labour (this lower rate being equivalent to farm labour in the area), and reminded the Governor of British pledges to the African population. Amery added that he hoped the selection of labourers would be made from men who had neither worked for hire nor produced a cash crop. In the event the only men called out by the Kenya government were just over 1,500, mainly from Nyanza for the Uasin-Gishu line, plus a further 1,138 for the Thika-Nyeri line, the Kamba here being preferred to the Kikuyu as the former had 'only thirteen per cent of the available labour [to be] working'. The Kikuyu were however later called upon for a small number of men. The Uasin-Gishu proved unhealthy for the minority of labourers called out from the Kamasia, Elgeyo and Suk tribes despite a medical examination of individuals prior to their departure. Chest diseases and influenza proved rife. But the death rate, in contrast to (and no doubt as a consequence from) the early years of work on this line, was low fewer than twenty dying of which seventeen were caused by an outbreak of pneumonic influenza leading to purulent pericarditis. The number called out for the Thika-Nyeri line, where conditions were subject to close supervision, technically exceeded the Colonial Office's specific permission for this branch but fell within the permitted total of 4,000 overall, though with no more fatal casualties than, at the worst, 16.48 per thousand.[94] The cash wage paid to voluntary labour on the lines varied between Shs. 18/- and Shs. 14/-; the compulsory labourer received for the most part Shs. 14/-, or even as little as Shs. 12/- in areas where volunteers were receiving Shs. 14/-. Almost all the labourers were repatriated by the end of June 1925, the remainder shortly afterwards.

The compulsory labour appears not to have been of a high physical standard, and since the men did not see any economic benefit to their own community, it was also inefficient; but its recruitment does not seem to have aroused resentment, at any rate on the surface. Denham, the acting Governor, reported to the Colonial Office in June 1925 that on tour in Nyanza he had heard no complaint and that the provincial administration officers confirmed 'there was no feeling on the subject of any kind'. But he later admitted some resentment and large numbers of deserters among the Kamba. Denham claimed that compulsion had led to some increase in the number of men coming out to work voluntarily but the claim has an appearance of self-justification.[95] The controversies aroused previously by compulsory labour and conditions on the Uasin-Gishu line led the Kenya government to take the most careful steps to supervise the conditions of railway construction work and contractors were no longer employed; in addition the staff of the Labour Inspectorate was reinforced and officers were specially posted for this purpose. McGregor Ross states that some labourers appealed against their selection for compulsion, took their cases to court with success and were released.[96]

The gravity with which the Colonial Office viewed the calling out of compulsory labour in Kenya and the detail of the control and reporting which the Colonial Office required, appears greatly to have impressed the Kenya officials. Furthermore with the virtual end of railway construction, the improved labour supply caused by an increasing population and the emerging interest at the I.L.O. in forced labour, permission for compulsory labour away from home was not again requested in peacetime. Amery's summary of the system as not only unjust but economically unsound was correct. In his February 1925 despatch authorizing compulsion for the railway, Amery added:

> The standard of work under any system of compulsion will naturally be inferior to that of voluntary workers; and in addition the fact that compulsory labour is available tends to discount enterprise and progress by diverting attention from the possibilities of labour-saving machinery. Moreover I fear that the results of any widespread association of labour with the sense of oppression caused by resort to the compulsory system may outweigh any educative influence which might otherwise be effected by inducing the natives to offer their labour upon terms sufficiently attractive to them.

an interesting modification of his 1919 views.

The milder form of compulsory labour however remained—the old communal labour obligation which, in face of the competition from paid work and sometimes at the request of the new local native councils, now necessitated payment at 'local rates'. The tasks continued to be portering, track and road clearing, and minor irrigation or terracing works. In 1925 for example 15,240 men were ordered out for 76,264 work days.[97] Tighter discipline reduced the number of abuses of the type examined earlier but these nevertheless continued; a parliamentary question in 1929 revealed that gangs of girls aged between ten and sixteen in South Nyanza were being compelled to collect thatching material involving a daily walk of thirty miles, a task forbidden by the local district commissioner as soon as he heard of it.[98] Sometimes chiefs or elders imposed these tasks on women and girls to try and strengthen their powers or because the men refused to do them. In order to regularize and strengthen the power of chiefs peremptory imprisonment for refusal to obey a communal labour order was provided by an ordinance in 1928, and the former tribal retainers were placed on an official footing as tribal police in 1929.

All these associations with 'encouragement', compulsory and communal labour and the recapture of labour deserters, however, were to prove one of the main reasons why the chiefs could never become a fully effective channel of communication between government and governed in Kenya. But paradoxically much African political expression called for paramount chiefs, whom it was evidently hoped would be sufficiently powerful to stand up to the government.

Currency, Coinage, Wage Reduction and Taxation

The question of Kenya's currency in the years 1919–22 is one of great complexity, made even more confused by statements from political leaders who either did not understand or deliberately obscured the issues.[99] Kenya's currency was the Indian rupee fixed at the rate of 15 rupees to the pound or Shs. 1/4 by the 1905 Order in Council. Plans were in preparation in 1914 to change the currency to the pound but these were interrupted by the war.

As a consequence of the war and the suspension of the gold standard the value of the rupee, a silver coin, began to rise towards the end of the war and with it also the value of rupee notes. Martial law regulations were issued in 1917 prohibiting the melting down of coin. In June 1919 the *Gazette* commenced publication of notices setting out the increased conversion rate of sterling. By September the rate had increased from Shs. 1/4 to Shs. 1/10; in December it rose first to Shs. 2/2 and then by Christmas to Shs. 2/4 at the official rates. Unofficially it appears at times to have reached rates of Shs. 2/6 and even Shs. 2/10 after the Indian government fixed the value of the rupee at Shs. 2/- in gold. Attempts were made early in 1920 to legalize English notes at the rate at first of 8.50 rupees and then later 9.25 rupees to the pound.

The rise in value of the rupee gravely affected European business and European employers. The new settler found he might only have received 11.50 rupees for each pound of his capital in respect of accounts he had to pay in local currency such as wages, tax, food and provisions, loans and overdrafts fixed in rupees. The older settlers on account of the war were often heavily in debt; if any of their income (either fixed from an extra-protectorate source, or from the export of produce) came from Britain their difficulties increased almost two-fold at the worst period. Badly needed new capital was similarly reduced if the source was Britain. Local costs including wages remained unaltered.

Many farmers only survived because of the good prices their produce, in particular sisal and coffee, were fetching in Britain in the immediate post-war trading boom which was to prove short-lived. They received some assistance from the fact that imported consumer goods in the shops cost slightly less, but so many Kenya farms being at the time financed by loans this assistance was a great deal less than the difficulty caused by the lower exchange rate on sterling credits. To the less perceptive, it began to appear that the real value of wages was rising, a theory vigorously argued by settler politicians. In terms of the African labourer's pattern of spending, little changed from that of 1914, his gain if any at all was small, and before long more than offset by the increase in taxation. At the level at which the African bought and sold where two or three rupees were formerly required, the Asian trader selling blankets, tea or cloth, or the Somali selling sheep wanted the same quantity of rupees, or the new unit, florins which were to replace them and in fact were still called 'rupees' by Africans. The settlers' argument, however, was one factor precluding any rise in wages that the labour shortage might otherwise have occasioned.

This economic disturbance led to considerable political agitation for stabilization, opinion being divided as to whether the rise was temporary or permanent. Local settler opinion held, as it later transpired correctly, that the rise was temporary, and opposed stabilization at an increased rate, arguing that local services and labour would thus be artificially enhanced. The Colonial Office on the best advice and in good faith judged the rise to be permanent, and the decision was taken to stabilize at Shs. 2/- (sterling) in March 1920. This new rate represented an increase of 50 per cent on sterling debts, loans, overdrafts and interest, a very serious matter for Kenya farmers, forcing a number to bankruptcy; on a loan of £5,000 the new farmer now found he had an extra £2,500 to repay and to service, but without development to the value of £2,500 with which to do it. To make matters worse, railway and ocean freights were increased to match the new rate. The new railway charges then led to an increase in the price of many goods, particularly those purchased by Africans which offset the previous price reductions. The only class of people relatively unscathed were officials whose salaries were fixed in sterling but converted at the old rate of rupees.

Having stabilized the rupee at Shs. 2/- (for which florin notes were issued as a temporary measure) the government considered a return to the old Shs. 1/4 rate when by the second half of 1920 the Indian rupee's value had fallen; at the request of the unofficial members it even introduced a motion in January 1921 in the Legislative Council to this effect. Under the influence of the bankers who would have had to face the loss of Shs. 6/8 on every £1 loaned between March 1920 and January 1921, the proposal was rejected by the same unofficial members after a remarkable volte-face; but the belief of settler opinion that the rupee coin or note, many of which were still in circulation, was really only worth Shs. 1/4 persisted. Some Asians too were sufficiently astute and unscrupulous as to import Indian rupees in order to exchange them profitably for the florin or local East African rupee notes, or to pay their labour in coins of apparent if not real value. The importation of these Indian rupees was forbidden, and then the actual rupee notes and coins demonetized, the former being recent importations without redemption and the latter redeemable during a brief period only.

From currency the issue changed to coin. The new florin coin was minted; its value was to be two English shillings or one rupee for the period of redemption of East African Currency Commissioners' rupee notes. The coin was of 1.181 in., approximately the same size as the old Indian rupee coin, and over 7 million of them were sent to Kenya. A second coin, inscribed Fifty Cents—One Shilling was also struck with a diameter of 0.829 in., approximately the same size as the half-rupee; but it does not appear to have been despatched. European opinion however pressed for a coinage system to be based on a one shilling unit so that Kenya's coinage could ultimately be one of pounds, shillings and cents. There were some acceptable arguments for this, the chief ones being rationality and that a lower-valued coin might reduce local prices. Less acceptable however were local views argued from the questionable premise of the value of the East African florin and rupee, on the size of the actual coin and the future of the existing cental coins (cents of the old rupee, and now cents of the florin). The government appears to have accepted the argument that since the proposed shilling lay, in 1918 terms, half way between the value of the old rupee, Shs. 1/4, and the old half-rupee, Shs. 0/8, the new shilling coin if it was to be the basis of the currency system should be of an intermediate size. Otherwise it was argued Africans would have expected the new coin to be worth only one-half of the old basic rupee unit whereas by local political reckoning it was worth three-quarters. The Fifty Cents—One Shilling coin, of 0.929 in., the same size as the half-rupee coin, did not meet this requirement and an entirely new shilling coin of size 1.092 in. diameter was prepared instead on the recommendations of a committee on which settler opinion was strongly represented. A 50 cts. (half-shilling) coin 0.825 in. was also prepared, this was larger than the old 25 cts. piece, 0.710 in. The committee intended that florins and the old larger cental coins (largely in the hands of Europeans and Asians and certainly the overwhelming proportion of such of their wealth as was expressed in coin or note) should be changed to the new shilling unit at the rate of one florin to two shillings. The small cental coinage (much of which lay in the hands of the Africans and formed a very high proportion of that part of their wealth as was expressed in coin) was to be devalued from 'cents of a florin' to 'cents of a shilling', an action thought to be justifiable as representing the Africans' part of the sacrifice caused by the changes since 1918 and the economic difficulties caused by the post-war slump which at this time, 1921, was seriously affecting the colony. Banks and firms who had large stocks of cental coins were, however, to be allowed to redeem them at full value by a further special proposal. If this measure had been adopted employers who paid their employees wholly or partly in cents would have been gaining their labour at half the previous wage, a fact seen by the less reputable as a sensible step to reduce the 'costs of production'. A Privy Council Order effecting this devaluation was in fact prepared and signed in August 1921, but not published for action.[100] At this stage the Colonial Office officials appear to have been totally bemused by the issues.

Once again public opinion in Britain, alerted by the missionary societies and questions in Parliament and reinforced by an angry reaction from members of all communities in Uganda (which used the same coinage) in October 1921, led to closer Colonial Office examination. McGregor Ross corresponded with Leys throughout these manoeuvres. Leys raised the issues with Oldham, and was probably responsible for an article in the *New Statesman*. But the most effective pressure on this occasion seems to have been brought by the Alliance of Missionary Societies corresponding directly with the Colonial Office, sending copies to Steel-Maitland, Wedgwood and other sympathetic M.P.s.[101] Intervention followed in the form of a firm government statement that cents were to remain 'cents of a florin' until replaced, a decision that was highly unpopular and greatly resented by the settler population. The old cental coinage remained until its replacement by new coins of a different colour, Africans having to remember that the actual value of the old coins were double the face value until the change-over process was complete.

The change-over took place at a time when the prices of Kenya's produce were falling, for major crops such as coffee and sisal by as much as 50–57 per cent, while flax which had enjoyed a wartime boom had totally collapsed. Many farms as a result of the boom had been over-producing with too large a labour force. The difficulties led many settlers in their desperation to accept readily the apparently logical argument that African wages had risen by 50 per cent and should be reduced by one-third. Following demands from various local farmers' associations, the Convention of Associations passed a resolution recommending that African wages in respect of newly-engaged men be reduced by one-third from 1 June 1921 (a time when tax was being collected); this was construed at the time as an opportunity for Africans to co-operate in the development of the country and as an educative process which the European would be failing in his duty if he were not to administer. The co-operation of the government, by far the largest employer in the country, was to be obtained by the 'local' rates procedure to which the government apparently raised no objection on principle, leaving it to individual departments to determine.[102] Some departments including the Railway agreed, though the cut was later cancelled by the General Manager on his return from leave. The opposition was led by McGregor Ross, who as Director of Public Works not only flatly refused to cut wages, but also refused any 'compromise', such as longer hours or payment by thirty-day ticket, an opposition which was to lead to the victimization of himself and his department.

Overall the attempt to reduce wages had only a limited success despite the fact that on some occasions district officers apparently assisted farmers and farmers' associations in explaining the purposes of reduction. Sometimes the Africans accepted the arguments advanced, or if they did not do so left farm work, which accounted for the relative ease with which the Uasin-Gishu railway extension obtained its labourers in 1922 and 1923, men being paid Shs. 10/- to Shs. 14/- per month, while the farm labourers' former starting wage of Shs. 10/- was reduced to Shs. 7/-. Farmers again complained bitterly of the labour shortage. Sometimes employers, by no means all of whom approved of the reduction, either refused to implement it, or if they feared their neighbours, concealed the reduction by an increase of food given in kind. Some employers noted the crowds attending meetings to voice discontent and decided not to add fuel. A number of labourers who left their farms took the precaution of working for a few days before deserting and then arguing that they were 'on leave' on their return to the reserves, an argument not always successful in view of the *kipande* system.

In addition to the general difficulties and confusion which currency and coinage created for the African labourer at this time, inevitably there were also particular cases of hardship. In February 1921, for example, quite suddenly and in order to stop the activities of smugglers bringing Indian coins and notes into Kenya, the government declared Indian notes were to be no longer valid. The proclamation was published in the *Official Gazette* of 8 February 1921 and made immediate. Large numbers of employees had been paid wages in whole or in part for their month's work at the end of January. McGregor Ross alleged that a number of men returning from government work in Tanganyika were thus deprived of substantial earnings earned over a longer time, only a minority being paid again in silver coins. No doubt a substantial number of employees in the private sector similarly lost their earnings, perhaps in some cases saved in boxes or wrapped in cloth and buried under hut floors for some considerable period. It was also noticeable that the government found it necessary to include a notice in the *Gazette* on 2 March that any employer who paid his labour in the demonetized rupees would be liable for prosecution. The Indian rupee notes, no longer legal tender from February were declared on 20 July 1921 to be no longer redeemable after the 22nd; the period allowed for Africans to change Indian rupee coins was extended to five months. Africans who had mistakenly retained the notes would have found them suddenly to be valueless and men in remote areas or on six-month farm contracts found difficulty in changing even the coins in time.[103]

Problems of currency and coin were worsened by increases in taxation. At the end of the war African hut and poll tax stood at the rate of 5 rupees maximum, a number of areas in fact being permitted to pay a lower rate. Pressure again began from local European employers for another increase, the chief purpose being labour supply but also with the general development of the country as a second financial purpose; such development was of course to take place almost entirely in European areas but was to be paid for by all. One project suggested was the institution of an African stock tax for which a bill was prepared but not enacted. The previous method of increasing hut and poll tax was instead used. In December 1919 another bill was prepared increasing the maxima to 7/50 and 10 rupees respectively for hut and poll tax, the government in the Legislative Council stated that the majority of Africans could easily meet the new rates and that the remainder could do so with a little effort. It also promised to spend a proportion of the revenue on services for Africans in the reserves. European elected members proposed an increase of the maximum for hut tax to the same rate as that for poll tax as, otherwise they argued the heavier poll tax rate penalized the single working native, which they felt might deter more than it encouraged.[104] They supported expenditure in the reserves on services such as medical facilities which might assist a labour supply. The government accepted the proposed tax rate of 8 rupees for both types of tax, retaining legal maxima of 10 rupees in the ordinance for the purpose of the special payments required from the Maasai whose wealth lay in stock.

In June 1920 the new 8 rupee rate was proclaimed with concessions of 1 or 2 rupees for poorer Coastal areas. McGregor Ross stated that the introduction of the new rates led to 'a rain of remonstrances' from district officers over the addition of this burden to those of the *kipande* and state labour obligations; once again Tate was notably outspoken even expressing a wish to resign.[105] As a result some of the poorer areas in the Rift Valley and Central Province were quickly afforded a relief of 3 rupees, though those so relieved in the Central Province suffered an increase in the following year.[106] The protest of the Alliance of Protestant Missions has already been noted. Once again Oldham's information and intervention were important; a manuscript note in the Oldham papers records on the evidence of Arthur that this heavy tax rate obliged some families to send young boys out to work to earn the necessary money, and a note in Arthur's handwriting observes 'the schools were depleted practically of all their young men and many boys'.[107]

A further factor adding to the hardship of the tax burden at this time was the decision of the government to change its financial year to correspond with the calendar year. An ordinance was passed in 1921 to effect this from 1 January 1922, the ordinance at the same time prescribing a full year's rate of taxation for the period from 1 April 1921 (the end of the 1920–1 financial year) to 31 December, a very severe measure for the African taxpayer, the large majority of whom were still dependent on wage earning for several months to gain even the small amount necessary to pay tax.

A condition of Colonial Office approval for the new rates had been that 'non-natives' should also pay an increased tax, and simultaneously with the 1919 Bill to authorize the new maxima, the government tried to introduce a bill for income tax applicable to companies and individuals, together with a land tax bill. The latter measure was so altered by European opposition as to be unworkable and was disallowed by the Colonial Office. The proposal for income tax aroused the most violent objections and some poorer farmers conducted a form of passive opposition. It was applied after delay for one year, 1921, and collected from people, on fixed salaries, chiefly town-dwellers. Asian business men found evasion simple. After intense political activity income tax was abandoned in May 1922 by the government as too difficult to operate, the government using its abandonment as an argument for the reduction of African taxation, which was proclaimed in August.

The main reason for the reduction of African taxation, however, was the March 1922 Thuku riot and the widespread discontent voiced at *barazas* throughout the country. Hut and poll tax were both fixed at Shs. 12/- with a reduction to Shs. 10/- for Taveta District, and the Maasai left at their old rate of Shs. 20/-. Tax was collected at the time of year thought most likely to be rewarding bearing in mind the ability of peasants and labourers to pay—for example after coffee picking near Kiambu—and avoiding the wet seasons.

The lowering of the tax to Shs. 12/- is of importance not only as a political victory for African protest, but also as the end of attempts to coerce more and more men out to work by simply increasing the cash rate men had to pay in tax. Never again was tax raised for the deliberate single purpose of filling of the labour market. And from 1922 onwards controversy over tax and labour supply was to centre not on the cash rate but on the manner in which the money raised was to be spent—for 'general' development, a great deal of which seemed to be of more immediate direct assistance to Europeans, or for development in African areas, feared by some employer interests as likely to prove detrimental to labour supply, but more generally opposed by Europeans as an unproductive way of spending revenue.

Africans who lived in towns were exempted from paying rates (as distinct from rent), but those who lived in the reserves were liable for payment of rates to L.N.C.s when these were formed in the late nineteen-twenties. Technically, migrant workers were also liable but they were frequently not obliged to pay, though sometimes they were met with a demand for arrears on their return to the reserve. Evidence in respect of later decades indicates that chiefs and headmen sometimes met the Nairobi trains, particularly during the Christmas holidays, to demand payment of arrears of rates from returning workers; this practice is likely to have had earlier origins.[108] Commutation of tax payment into labour for the government was abolished in 1921, being considered as too easily identifiable with compulsory labour in African minds. After 1925 persistent refusal to pay tax led to imprisonment for one to three months in a detention centre where light work might be set. In 1935 some 8,700 were sentenced to periods of detention. The name detention centre does, however suggest a greater degree of harshness than the very light restriction on movement imposed—usually restriction to the general area of the district headquarters together with communal labour tasks.

To preserve government revenue against the loss of income tax and the fall in African tax, customs duties were increased, the intention being to raise the charges on goods purchased by non-Africans. The duties on tobacco and cigars were increased to 90 per cent *ad valorem*, wines and spirits to 60 per cent and motor cars to 30 per cent with this in view. However those on cigarettes, a large percentage of which were smoked by Africans, were also increased to 90 per cent and those on bicycles to 30 per cent, as were the duties on tea and sugar, and later for different reasons wheat, also all much used by Africans. In 1927 European taxation was increased by Shs. 30/- per head to pay for education, but this measure established the debatable principle of racial payment for racial education. The imbalance between European and African incomes and taxation was justified by some settlers as a loan by the Africans to the country ultimately for their own benefit, but as late as 1929 the Director of Agriculture commented that little had been done for African agriculture.

A limited amount of money was, however, devoted to African education, European opinion being willing to support African technical and craft training and a small measure also of literary education as a move to displace Asians. Overall, though, the government's policy remained that of educating Africans for inferior positions in society—which the government believed to be their academic ceiling and future station. After stimulus from the reports of the Phelps-Stokes Commission and a Colonial Office education committee some small steps were taken. Mission schools received grants, particularly for craft instruction, and the government opened a trade school for institute level work at Kabete in 1925; this school concentrated on the building and tailoring trades and in 1927 already had 443 students. In addition a small number of government African schools were begun and the Jeanes School, for village school teachers, was opened. There were 1,121 boys in apprenticeship in 1927, and government departments offered training to African boys or men as laboratory assistants and hospital orderlies, clerks, typists, interpreters, telegraphists and linesmen, printing craftsmen, firemen, engine cleaners, fitters and coach-builders, blacksmiths, stokers, sailors, painters and workshop hands of all types, survey staff, entomological staff, masons, carpenters and bricklayers. The four departments with the largest training schemes were the Medical, Agriculture and Public Works Departments and the Railway, but other smaller departments and some commercial firms, chiefly in building, furnishing and printing also trained men for their own needs.

One feature of the evolving educational pattern for Africans that accorded well with the employment future planned for them was the late introduction of English into the literary curriculum; primary teaching was in tribal vernaculars, with instruction in Swahili in the fourth year, English only following at the 'Intermediate' level. Kenya's linguistic problem was an exceptionally difficult one and it would be incorrect to assert that the late introduction of English was deliberately repressive. But equally a large number of employers at this time preferred their employees to speak Swahili as a mark of their status; Africans speaking English were viewed with great suspicion.

Conclusion

Despite the tribulations of the early years the latter half of the decade brought some measure of progress to the African labourer. The age of harshness involving large numbers of deaths and much suffering, had evolved to one essentially of taut economic exploitation managed paradoxically in an increasingly humane way. The exploitation was not seen as such by many of the administration's most intelligent and humane officers, nor did these officers see themselves as supporting white racialism. Most saw settlement and labour as necessary evils in the absence of any other more speedy way to promote African advancement. 'Government by agreement' and strong settler representation on the Legislative Council, its important Estimates Committee, the 1922 Economic and Finance Committee and other government bodies prevented any effective questioning of the settler position and the essentials of the economic system protecting it; there seemed no easy crop for Africans to grow for quick prosperity and no more land for population expansion. When therefore men in increasing numbers, or from fresh tribes such as the Kamasia appeared on the labour market, many honest administrators saw this as progress.[109]

With the improved conditions for labourers their claim was not without all justification. By the end of the decade the cruelty and abuses of labour agents and recruiters had been checked although professional recruiting continued.[110] Medical examination procedures had become more efficient and a number of rest camps and rest houses properly inspected and administered had been established on labour routes, though the unwitting labourer could fall a prey to thieves or tricksters in these camps. The routes themselves were shortened in time by the use of motor lorries replacing long train journeys. The Master and Servants Ordinance (now referred to as the Employment of Natives Ordinance) had been amended and used in a number of respects to the advantage of the employee. As we have already noted, desertion ceased to be cognizable to the police in 1925. In 1923 rules made under the ordinance gave medical officers powers to order men to cease work and if necessary to be returned home or enter a hospital at their employers' expense.[111] In 1926 further rules prescribed medical stores to be kept by large employers and made the employer of contract (but not resident) labour liable for any hospital expenses of an employee for the duration of the contract.[112] Attempts with only very limited success were also made to reduce corporal punishment; in 1922 a farmer received a small fine for giving his cook ten lashes. To try and replace private administration of corporal punishment. 'insulting behaviour' to an employer was added in 1925 to the list of penal labour offences; for these offences the penalties were at the same time increased to a fine of Shs. 100/-, imprisonment for a month, or both. But farmers' recourse to stick or *kiboko* still remained common. Further amendments to the ordinance prescribed punishments for decoying and harbouring the servants of others.[113]

The Labour Section of the N.A.D., although still only a Principal Inspector with between three and five inspectors for the whole territory, were managing over 800 inspections a year in the latter part of the decade;

they also produced some useful and influential publications on labour matters of which the most successful was *Straight Talks on Labour*, written by Dr. V. Fisher, a government medical officer who subsequently became the Principal Inspector. *Straight Talks* were published first in the local press and then as a government booklet.[114] They were based on Fisher's study of labour conditions elsewhere in Africa with which he indicated Kenya compared unfavourably. In January 1930 a four day exhibition on health, a section of which was devoted to the health of labourers, was shown in Nairobi. In addition to inspection work the Labour Section successfully pursued a number of injury compensation cases, 400–500 each year in the middle nineteen-twenties; the payments they obtained were not large but are noteworthy as the private employer was under no legal obligation to pay at all.[115] They also pursued annually a large number of cases of non-payment of wages, recovering considerable sums of money for employees. The procedure of formal notices addressed to employers demanding compliance in respect of legal requirements for food, housing and medical and sanitary necessities, followed if necessary by a visit from an inspector established the section's authority among the majority of employers. The staff also advised where appropriate on suitable tasks for men employed on piece and task rate, thus increasing both efficiency and the labourer's cash earnings, and reducing employer abuses such as impossible tasks, though that could never be entirely abolished.[116]

The general level of labourers' cash earnings rose only very slowly, and then only in the latter half of the nineteen-twenties; the 'local rates' procedure and the *kipande* system both acted as brakes with, particularly in the early years, direct coercion also restricting any operation of the law of demand. Unskilled labour in 1921 was being engaged at Shs. 9/- to 11/- with a maize meal ration; by 1923 the cash element had risen to Shs. 12/- to 14/-, and at the end of the decade the rate was between Shs. 16/- and 18/-. In some areas, notably the Trans-Nzoia, and on some types of farm, particularly maize, the rates would be lower; the Railway, P.W.D. and the sisal estates (whose work was unpopular) would pay the higher figure. Although a substantial minority of workers were earning rather higher rates overall, those of unskilled labour represented little or no increase in purchasing power when the increased prices of African consumer goods and increased taxation were taken into account. On the other hand with the end of wartime requisitioning the price of native cattle and stock required for bride-price did in fact fall. But it was never possible after the war to finance any general reserve development on the cash earnings of labour.

African employer housing for farm and estate labour remained very poor in standard—mud, wood and grass huts providing inadequate shelter against cold or wind at night, necessitating hearth fires with neither chimneys nor ventilation and creating a number of health problems; on the worst estates insanitary conditions and overcrowded labour lines still led to worm infections and epidemics.

The worst housing conditions of all were in Nairobi and Mombasa. In Nairobi several of the old porter villages were pulled down and Pumwani location built, some 250 houses of six to eight rooms each, built of mud and wattle with thatched or corrugated iron roofs. Pumwani with the older and even more insanitary location of Pangani (approximately 300 houses of four to eight rooms) and a small number of Nairobi Municipality dormitories, constituted the housing for most African labour where this was not provided on the site by employers or the employee did not live in the Kikuyu Reserve. The Railway and P.W.D. owned their own labour lines, these providing cramped cells in which families could reside; the Medical Department commented very unfavourably upon them. The large majority of domestic or shop staff slept on or near the premises. In 1923 before Pumwani was completed and when conditions were particularly bad, the government had been obliged to open a hostel for the use of labourers but this was later closed. Conditions in Mombasa and Kisumu hardly improved upon the pre-1914 state which we have already noted. In general town employers, led by the majority of government departments and the town authority, either ignored the housing requirements of the Master and Servants Ordinance or paid a small house allowance well below the rents actually charged. Employers argued righteously against any system of 'tied housing' but such arguments usually concealed either indifference or a preference for sub-economic housing financed by someone else.

There were in addition a number of other factors that slowed progress. The major of these was disease. Although as we shall see great improvements were made in the provision of medical facilities in the African reserves, the very fact that men were being obliged to work in climates still strange and upon diets often unfamiliar, ill-cooked and inadequate, led to frequent disease. The sickness, if not actual death, rates therefore remained high among men at work and in their villages on their return. Malaria, dysentery, tick fever and hookworm increased considerably and syphilis to a lesser extent among men whose early years had in any case been marked by nutritional deficiencies. The majority of employers refused to supply the supervised latrines and mosquito-nets necessary for protection. The development of the Uasin-Gishu and Trans-Nzoia areas led also to an increase in chest and lung diseases, and the early use of Nyanza labour on the tea estates brought malaria to the Kipsigis. It is true that labourers on a well-run farm, estate, or well-supervised railway works could and did improve in health and physique, but the medical balance is definitely adverse.

A second factor was the social consequences of the disturbed family life of the migrant labourer, now away from home for longer periods. Many in towns availed themselves of the services of a prostitute or took a temporary wife, sometimes even on a monthly contract and perhaps shared with others, to prepare their food. For farm and estate labourers on six months or longer contracts the temporary wife could become semi-permanent, with the 'real' wife maintaining the labourer's holding in the reserve and looking after the children. In societies in which polygamy was permitted and girls rarely remained single, most men saw no harm in these liaisons, but as time passed many men paid decreasing respect to tribal commitments and customs to the harm of their children, legitimate and increasingly illegitimate.

A third factor was the essential indifference of a system in which labourers were recruited in batches, perhaps under pressures from a bribed chief or headman, paraded before a medical officer, attested by a district commissioner or magistrate for a three or six months' contract with an employer they had never seen and had no choice in selecting, transported and supervised by men often callous, and fed on an issued diet which even when satisfactory was dully monotonous. It is small wonder than labourers would often travel long distances freely to volunteer their services to a kindly employer who took an interest in his men's welfare, or that the Magadi Soda Company was able to dispense with its labour agent's services at the end of the decade despite its remote location. The company's official responsible for labour was W. H. Billington, one of the new Kenya Europeans; severely wounded in the war that he was determined must not have been in vain, Billington made Magadi now strengthened financially by becoming a subsidiary of Imperial Chemical Industries into the colony's leading large employer with good African housing, welfare services and hospital. He himself made it his business to tour the reserves to know something of the area from which his labour came. But Magadi and at the end of the decade, the tea industry where the leading estates had been advised by Billington and were able to draw on experience in India were the exceptions; the rule was indifference. The camps of the railway contractors and the large Coast sisal estates, where over 500 men might be at work, remained the worst. Tough tasks, beatings and the withholding of rations and wages led to strikes and desertions at the camps of the two worst contractors, H. H. McPhee and Akbar Ali Khan in 1925 and 1927 respectively, and other Coast camps required frequent inspections to preserve barely tolerable standards.

Lastly the migrant labour system was one of the factors that prevented any great expansion of the peasant sector of the economy in the reserves. The labour system cannot, however, be asserted to be the only factor; others equally important were the protective features of the settler-dominated economy—the routing of the new railway extensions, the lack of land for African expansion, and taxation and expenditure policies. In the reserves the continuing restrictions on the growing of certain crops, and the absence of others visibly profitable enough to attract the peasant grower or sufficiently simple for him to grow and sell in the light of his agricultural methods and tenure at the time were severe hindrances. The state of world markets also played some part in restricting development.

The total population in the major reserves, as already noted, fell in the war and probably continued to fall in the early nineteen-twenties; by 1925 numbers were beginning to rise again. During the years of the fall, the subtraction of adult manpower varying between 45 per cent and 60 per cent, at times greater, for periods of six months or more inevitably weakened initiative and enterprise; native crop production overall rose relatively little and in most areas was declining by 1929. The later nineteen-twenties showed no improvement. The Chief Registrar of Natives recorded the percentages of adult males at work in January 1927 as 72 (Lumbwa), 72.28 (Kikuyu from Kiambu), 64.45 (Nandi), 50.30 (Kikuyu from Fort Hall), 48.22 (North Nyanza), 44.91 (North and South Nyeri) and 42.53 (Teita). Only the Maasai (25.28) and the Machakos Kamba (20) remained at percentages comparable to those of 1914.[117] In terms of total numbers employed, the difficulties of

1920 reduced average monthly totals to some 90,000, but by 1923 the figure was at least 129,000, rising to 152,000 in 1925 and 169,000 in 1926.[118] Thereafter the number declined slightly to 160,000 in 1929 due to improved efficiency and changed crops; this slight decline set against the population increase approximately balanced supply and demand for the rest of the decade, and despite the apparently compelling instructions of Grigg lessened the element of coercion from 'encouragement'. In 1927 160,435 men were at work, they were employed as follows:

Agriculture and Pastoral Holdings	76,838
Railway Construction	4,000
Maintenance, Railway	11,203
Maintenance, Marine	428
Railway Fuel Cutting	1,013
Magadi	880
Government Departments	12,890
Domestic Servants	22,400
Timber Industry	5,658
Firewood	278
Building Trade	750
Wharfage and Harbour Work	2,270
P.W.D. Contractors	500
Prisoners	2,527
Missions	3,000
Townships (i.e. office messengers, shops, etc.)	15,800

in addition some 30,000 women and children were employed seasonally.[119]

It is not surprising in all these circumstances of mounting difficulties in the reserves but improved employment conditions outside that many Africans volunteered, apparently quite freely, for a few months at labour. By the end of the nineteen-twenties, new problems of over-population or excess stock were beginning to arise in the reserves; district commissioners could well believe work away from such reserves to be the only way to prosperity for an individual or his community and 'encouragement' no longer undesirable. In addition to these goads there were also the carrots of the new ways of life in towns—consumer goods, cinemas and electricity, clothes, freedom from restrictive and in some cases declining tribal societies, or an equally real attraction, the agricultural and veterinary methods, the machines, superior grain and the cattle, poultry and vegetables of the settlers. Further, except for an increasing number of squatters the reserves in the nineteen-twenties were still large enough to provide a piece of land even if inadequate for almost all men away at work; this land supported a man's wife and perhaps his family, and it constituted his old age pension. In this period the possession of such land gave Africans a limited bargaining power when deciding on a particular employer, the moment to seek work, a minimum acceptable wage rate and the ability to avoid the worst employers; it was one of the causes of the small wage increases already noted.

In the reserves themselves the chief item of progress was the great expansion of medical facilities. One of the main reasons for this social service continued to be the maintenance of a fit labour supply; arguments on this theme were used to justify the cost to a critical settler public, but other humanitarian aims were also present. By the end of the decade there were twenty-five medical officers and ten nurses at work in the reserves and a great increase in the number of native hospitals and dispensaries in addition to subsidized mission staff and facilities.[120] These facilities provided some return for the tax paid from the labourer's wage, particularly in the treatment of diseases of rural life such as yaws. But overall the Medical Department could only attempt to cure rather than to prevent the diseases caught from deplorable accommodation, supervision and sanitation at many estates on which its officers were still commenting unfavourably as late as 1930.

The Dual Policy of parallel development of native and settler economies in their respective areas was, then, being very considerably undermined, if not entirely negated by the general dominance of the settlers' position in particular their labour requirements. Social services reflected inferior status; the work of the British agricultural officers and African instructors posted to the reserves was largely confined to increasing the efficiency of subsistence economies or the production of small quantities of cheap maize meal and vegetables for town or estate labour forces. The settler still believed Africans were best educated by work on European farms where hard work would also bring them prosperity; though most settlers, particularly the new arrivals also believed that the government's duties should extend to the provision of medical and technical education facilities and the inspection of work places in addition to the administration of reserves as labour recruiting areas. For the future the settler wished to see Africans develop at the subsistence level, in craft not in literary skills, speaking Swahili not English, knowing little of British dress, customs or ideals and never challenging authority in government or at work—a status many settlers emphasized by personal affronts to Africans in day to day contacts. In sum, an African had no place outside his reserve except as a worker.

The African labourer became increasingly preoccupied with the preservation of his own land. Work outside might be a useful means of earning tax, or purchasing a wife or consumer goods; otherwise it was of no particular moral obligation to the community and the government's attempts to persuade him to the contrary aroused his increasing suspicion. The impact of the European occupation was still so great as to preclude much effective questioning of the economic structure or industrial action; the 1929 squatter resistance was significant but short-lived and not understood at the time. Storm signs were, however, clearly seen in the reserves. The Native Affairs Department reports annually commented on the one hand on the attitude of suspicious watchfulness in the reserves and of growing antagonism between generations; on the other and in the same volume the Labour Section reports commented on the generally happy relations between employer and employee. No conclusion applicable to the latter was drawn from the former, and government officers continued to confuse acquiescence in an exploitative situation with acceptance of that situation; the least happy feature of the Dual Policy was its obscuring of the issues.

APPENDIX I

Table 1

AFRICANS CONVICTED UNDER THE NATIVE REGISTRATION ORDINANCE

1920	206	1925	2,277
1921	2,220	1926	2,956
1922	2,494	1927	4,114
1923	2,335	1928	3,121
1924	2,240	1929	4,244

Source: *1931 Annual Report, N.A.D.*

Table 2

REGISTERED ADULT MALE AFRICANS IN EMPLOYMENT (MONTHLY AVERAGES)

1922	119,170	1926	169,000
1923	138,330	1927	147,893
1924	133,890	1928	152,274
1925	152,400	1929	160,076

Source: *Annual Reports, N.A.D.*

Table 3

COMPULSORY LABOUR (EXCLUDING RAILWAY CONSTRUCTION)

Year	Numbers ordered out	Days worked	Average number of days per man
1922	10,547	124,855	11·73
1923	25,501	241,196	9.45
1924	19,323	151,064	7.80
1925	15,240	76,264	5.00
1926	13,228	56,781	4.29
1927	12,809	95,975	7.49
1928	12,897	86,587	6.71
1929	9,663	64,657	6.69

Source: *Annual Reports, N.A.D.*

Table 4

INSPECTIONS CARRIED OUT BY LABOUR SECTION STAFF

1921	156	1926	884
1922	443	1927	1,104
1923	421	1928	872
1924	532	1929	883
1925	430		

Source: *Annual Reports, N.A.D.*

NOTES

1. In July 1925, 734 of the 1,031 farms allotted under the soldier-settler schemes were being worked, of which between 519 and 545 were being farmed by the original allottee. *Parliamentary Debates, Commons,* 277 July 1925.

   In 1914 some 500–550 farms were being worked; by 1938 the approximate 1925 total of 1,250 had risen to an approximate total of 1,800.
2. Even before official encouragement, a large number of European government officers sought Colonial Office permission to acquire a financial interest or land in Kenya. For a list of such officials, which included Northey himself, the Commissioner of Police, a Senior Commissioner and a number of other responsible officers, see C.O. 533/276, Northey to Colonial Office, 9 March 1922. Later when officers had to be retrenched for economy reasons, they were offered plots of land on favourable terms.
3. The Colonial Office very firmly instructed Northey to provide and demarcate reserves 'sufficient not only for present needs but also for any probable increase of the population'. C.O. 533/265, Northey to Colonial Office, 18 Nov 1921 and attached papers.
4. These opinions of Northey are taken from his opening speech to Legislative Council in 1919 and a letter, dated 21 Oct 1919 to the Convention of Associations, R. L. Buell, *The Native Problem in Africa*, 1925, I, 333. Similar views of Northey were quoted by Milner in the July 1920 House of Lords Debate, *Parliamentary Debates, Lords,* 14 July 1920.
5. *The Official Gazette of the Colony and Protectorate of Kenya* (hereafter *Kenya Gazette*), 29 Nov 1920, Instructions passed under the Royal Sign Manual and Signet to the Governor and Commander-in-Chief of the Colony of Kenya.
6. The Master and Servants Amendment Ordinance, Ord 27 of 1919, *E.A.P. Gazette*, 22 Oct 1919.
7. *E.A.P. Debates*, 7 July 1919. In 1920 European unofficial members protested against the expense of labour inspectors and sought in vain to limit their activities to government camps and only those farms from which a specific complaint had been received.
8. An example of the type of improvement the section could effect is to be found in the *1923 Annual Report, N.A.D.*, which noted improvements at the Powysland Sisal Estate at Kilifi following inspections. At this estate thirty-two men had died in 1923 from dysentery and pneumonia brought on by bad conditions. The management was threatened with prosecution and obliged to improve its conditions.

   The inspecting officers used initially printed inspection books noting information under headings generally limited to those instituted in 1914 (see *supra*, p. 77 footnote). Carbon copies of the inspection reports were sent to the Chief Native Commissioner and the Principal Medical Officer.
9. The text of this circular can most conveniently be found in McGregor Ross, 103, or Leys, 395.

   It stands in marked contrast to the previous circular instruction issued on 13 Jan 1919 under the signature of Barth, as Acting Chief Secretary, which clearly forbade any form of compulsion, noting with disapproval abuses of power by chiefs and foreseeing a future labour supply dependent on a free market stimulated only by official support for native 'wants'—better clothing, housing, consumer goods and improved standard of living.
10. Goldsmith, *op. cit.*, 102, records Ainsworth's own description of this procedure. Although Ainsworth's name appeared in the circular it is misleading therefore to attribute authorship to him; Northey himself wrote later 'I personally take full responsibility for the Labour Circular, I do not want Mr. Ainsworth blamed'. Northey to Arthur, 5 Nov 1919, Arthur papers.
11. The exact methods varied. A. de V. Wade, the Kiambu D.C. wrote to his superior on 29 Jan 1920 describing his approach, 'no compulsion force or

pressure was used other than repetition that it was H.E.'s wish that no one should remain idle, coupled with a direct order to all Headmen to bring to me for a personal interview anyone who refused to work himself or who refused to allow his family to work'. Each headman was made responsible for a group of farms. Wade added that he had received no complaints from lawyers and only a few addressed to him directly, which he considered to reflect African acceptance. The Fort Hall district commissioner operated a system of immediately meeting settler requests with all the men they required 'by means of direct pressure from this office'. D.C. Fort Hall to P.C. Kenya Province, 3 Apr 1920.

The Kenya Province provincial commissioner, Tate, commented that '... in our effort to force labour out of the Reserve by Administrative pressure unbacked by force of law we are compelled to follow the line of least resistance, which results in the same male adults going out time after time owing to their being too poor or friendless to escape the Headman's levy. The rich native or the Headman's relative or favourite gets off each time'. Tate to Chief Native Commissioner, 13 Jan 1920. All three letters in Elspeth Huxley papers, Rhodes House.

12. For an explanation of the former, sincerely held, view we are indebted to S. H. Fazan, interview 1968; an example of the latter view appears in Sir P. Mitchell, *African Afterthoughts*, 1954, 98–9. District administration reports reflect the same wide divergence of views.
13. A document marked 'Private and Confidential' in the Arthur papers in Edinburgh records this meeting. The document is undated but appears to have been written for the missionaries' own use and reference shortly afterwards. It records Tate's strong desire that the missionaries should make an effective protest. Tate was later to protest as strongly against the increases in taxation, see *infra*, p. 270; he also tried to keep professional recruiters out of certain areas for which he was responsible.
14. Arthur to Oldham, 10 Oct 1922, Oldham papers.
15. Ord 3 of 1920, *E.A.P. Gazette*, 11 Feb 1920.
16. The text of the Bishops' Memorandum is printed in Leys, 397 Arthur's record of the meeting notes 'I am hardly at liberty to say more than that both of them [Bowring and Ainsworth] were obviously in entire agreement with our protests and our suggestions as embodying some of their own which had not been listened to. The Memorandum was typed for us by the Chief Secretary ...'
17. Leys, 195.

    Ven. Archdeacon W. E. Owen, 1879–1945. Educated St. Enoch's School, Belfast and Islington Theological College; ordained 1904; Rural Dean Budu 1915; Chaplain B.E.A. Forces 1916; Archdeacon of Kavirondo 1918–45.
18. For an account of Bishop Weston's activities see H. Maynard Smith, *Frank Bishop of Zanzibar, 1871–1924*, 1926, xiii. Of his fellow bishops Weston wrote 'I am heart-sick with Christian institutions, though you find Christ riding on such asses'.
19. Joseph Houldsworth Oldham, 1874-1969. Educated Edinburgh Academy and Oxford; Secretary of the World Missionary Conference 1908 and of its continuation Committee 1910 and of the International Missionary Council 1921–38; Administrative Director of the International Institute of African Languages and Cultures 1931–8; Member of the Advisory Committee on Education in the Colonies 1925–36.

    Oldham papers, boxes labelled 'Kenya Native Labour' and 'Kenya, Correspondence' with Dr. Arthur, Rev. Hooper, Archdeacon Owen and McGregor Ross.
20. *Parliamentary Debates, Lords*, 14 July 1920. At the time of the Lords debate Milner seemed unaware of the existence of the second circular noted below.
21. *Kenya Gazette*, 1 Sept 1920. The text can also be found in *Despatch to the Governor of the East Africa Protectorate relating to Native Labour and Papers connected therewith*, Cmd. 873 of 1920.

22. Cmd. 873 of 1920. The Colonial Office officials felt alarmed by the strong terms of the circular but judged that amendments under discussion with Northey would render it void.
23. *Ibid.*
24. McGregor Ross, 100. A manuscript note in the Oldham papers records a protest against this circular by a district officer, and a protest to the Governor by Archdeacon Owen.
25. On the occasion of Ainsworth's retirement, Northey had attempted to secure the services of a South African official with experience of labour in the Union as Chief Native Commissioner. He suggested two possible candidates, both so qualified, to the Colonial Office. The Colonial Office feared the criticism that such an appointment might arouse and wished in any case to make an appointment from within the service. C.O. 533/238, Northey to Colonial Office, 17 Dec 1920 and attached papers.
26. The Deputation included Principal A. B. Garvie, The Marquess of Salisbury, Sir Samuel Hoare, the Rev. Donald Fraser and Dr. Oldham. J. H. Thomas and Gilbert Murray stated they would have liked to be present but had been prevented.

    The names included the Archbishops of Canterbury and York, the Moderator of the Church of Scotland, the Primus of Scotland, the Archbishop of Armagh, and the various Heads of almost all Methodist, Baptist and Congregational Churches in the United Kingdom, nine members of the House of Lords, eleven members of the House of Commons including J. R. Clynes, Walter Elliott, A. Henderson, J. H. Thomas, Sir S. Hoare and the Hon. E. F. Wood, and many other public names such as G. Murray, Beatrice Webb, C. K. Webster and R. H. Tawney. A full list, with the text of the memorandum, appears in *E.A.S.*, 19 Feb 1921, and there are copies in the Oldham papers.
27. See *Parliamentary Debates, Commons*, 14 July 1921, Speeches by Sir A. Steel-Maitland, Colonel J. Wedgewood, Sir S. Hoare and Lord H. Cavendish-Bentinck all expressed profound concern and dissatisfaction with the situation. Steel-Maitland, carefully briefed by Oldham, quoted cases of compulsion and violation of women and girls, and he and Wedgwood expressed anxiety over taxation.
28. *Kenya Gazette*, 19 Oct 1921.

    The amending Ordinance, passed in 1922, was The Native Authority (Amendment) Ordinance, Ord 26 of 1922, *Kenya Gazette*, 30 Dec 1922.
29. *E.A.S.*, 28 July 1923.
30. For a description of these synthetic 'labour' movements see McGregor Ross, xxi. P. C. Green of the European Workers' Association accompanied the European delegation to the talks in London. By 1937 he had become a building contractor and was one of the employers involved in the strike of May of that year, see *infra*, p. 182. A remarkable letter from one Maj.-Gen. P. Wheatley, the settlers' nominee for appointment as 'Commander-in-Chief of the Forces of Kenya Colony' if they were to seize power, dated 28 Feb 1923, is published in Earl of Lytton, *The Stolen Desert*, 1966, 75. General Wheatley wrote: 'It is said that adversity makes one acquainted with strange bed-fellows . . . A man I am working with constantly is Ward, a Labour agitator from South Africa. In that country he has both done time and is also a deportee. Well he is turning up the Labour Party at home in K.C.'s [Kenya Colony's] interests. The chief point he is making is that the Indian has a seventy-hour week. This of course is anathema to the Labour Party with its forty-four hour week. Also the Indians have no trade unions—so he calls a meeting of the white labour in Nairobi. This meeting cables home to Ramsay Macdonald, Sidney Webb & Co. pointing out the grave danger to the Labour Movement throughout the Empire . . .'
31. McGregor Ross, 114, and *E.A.S.*, 12, 19 June 1920. The case was raised in Parliament.

    An equally unpleasant case occurred in 1923. An African stable hand rode a mare in foal contrary to his master's instructions on a journey to a distant railway station. His employer, a farmer named J. Abraham, flogged him for some considerable time and then after kicking him, bound him tight in a store where later in the night the man died in agony. Abraham received only two years' rigorous imprisonment for grievous hurt, but the case came to the notice of Devonshire, the Colonial Secretary, who wrote to say that there appeared to be no extenuating circumstances and that the verdict should have at least been that of manslaughter. The case was widely reported in the local press but aroused little or no sense of shame among the settler community. Of this case Leys observed 'the brutality ... is ... due ... to the economic system in which all are equally involved ... Europeans who murder and Africans who are murdered are equally its victims'. Leys, 164–65 and *E.A.S.* of 4 and 11 Aug 1923. A parliamentary question also drew attention to this case in Britain.

32. *1923, 1924 Annual Reports, N.A.D.*
33. This ration scale is an example of the deliberate ignoring of the government's instructions set out in March 1921. The ration scale is reported by A. G. Church, *op. cit.*, 182, and the *1922 Annual Report, Medical Department*; the latter report also describes the contractors' initial total indifference to the health of their labour. By August 1922 1 lb. of meat per week supplemented by vegetables, *ghee*, sugar and salt was being given to most employees following pressure from government inspectors, conditions in camps and hospitals improved and more reasonable tasks set. As a consequence of this scandal, the Principal Medical Officer sent an officer on tour in other areas of Africa to study labour conditions and needs, and, on his leave, to study dietetic requirements. The results were the articles 'Straight Talks on Labour' noted *infra*, p. 148. Other abuses and disregard of government instructions included those of sub-contractors in charge of recruiting who would provide only one day's food for a three- or four-day journey to labourers returning home, or who would hire as 'volunteers' men conscripted but rejected by the medical examination, the cutting of wages and the setting of unfair tasks.
34. Eighty-eight Tanganyika men died between Jan and June 1922. The Tanganyika labourers were however protected by the insistence of their Governor, Sir Horace Byatt, that they should be repatriated at the end of their contract and not permitted to remain in Kenya. Northey opposed this measure unsuccessfully.
35. McGregor Ross, 110. Ross's correspondence suggests that it was he himself who discovered and reported this incident. The government's orders were set out in Circular 89, 14 Dec 1922, quoted R. L. Buell, *op. cit.*, 370. The second incident is in Owen to Oldham, 21 Oct 1922. Oldham papers.
36. The Native Women Workers Protection Rules, *Kenya Gazette*, 2 March 1923. Northey opposed this measure but was instructed by the Colonial Office to ensure that proper accommodation for single girls was provided on European farms.
37. The *E.A.S.*, 26 June 1920, for example, notes a strike of Nairobi railway porters which even the Chief Native Commissioner could not call to order.
38. *E.A.S.*, 15, 16 July 1921 report the views aired. Leys, 203, and McGregor Ross, 225-6 also provide accounts of this meeting; and a full report including the lists of girls raped is included in the Oldham papers. Northey ordered an investigation into the complaints and alleged to the Colonial Office that the girls had been willing accomplices rather than the victims of rape, and that in general although 'in certain instances Headmen have with the best intentions gone rather further than Government would have approved', the complaints were either false or exaggerated. C.O. 533/264, Northey to Colonial Office, 31 Oct 1921.
39. *Papers Relating to Native Disturbances in Kenya*, 1922, Cmd. 1691 of 1922. Thuku also sought the advice of Marcus Garvey.
40. An account of a large meeting held at Lundha, in North Nyanza, in Dec 1921 is included in Oginga Odinga, *Not Yet Uhuru*, 1967, 25–8. Of the ten major grievances recorded in a note for the D.C., two dealt with communal

labour, one with compulsory labour, one with 'encouragement' and one with poll tax.

41. J. Kenyatta, *Kenya: The Land of Conflict*, n.d., describes this event under the heading of 'The First General Strike'. For a further interesting general account see H. Thuku, *op. cit.*, ii.

42. The measure of discontent evidently came as a surprise to the Colonial Office. On 23 March, Wood, the Parliamentary Under-Secretary, in answer to questions from Wedgewood and Lord H. Cavendish-Bentinck said 'I strongly deprecate the suggestion that there is any discontent in Kenya'.

43. Further verses began with Kionange, Josiah and Kinyanjui respectively.

The text of this song was sent by Dr. Arthur to the Chief Native Commissioner on 17 Nov 1922. Arthur translated it as 'Filipu (or one of the other named Kikuyu chiefs) let him be cursed. It is they who have caused to be taken away the chief (Thuku) of the girls who live in the coffee'—a reference to the coercion of girls and woman to work on coffee farms. The government forbade the singing of the song but a new one in similar terms was quickly composed. The Oldham papers include a copy of Arthur's letter.

The breakdown in communication is clear when the words of the song are compared with the views of Northey after the Dagoretti meeting, when he wrote to the Colonial Office'... it is clear on the evidence of the Chiefs themselves that no force whatever has been employed in sending girls to the plantations'; Northey also denied that headmen had been punished for refusing to allow their womenfolk to go to work. C.O. 533/264, Northey to Colonial Office, 1 Oct 1921.

Thuku in his autobiography notes that the nickname 'chief of women' remained with him all his life ... 'and do you know, even today, Kenyatta and others still call me that name when we meet.'

44. For a description of the hazards of service in Kenya at this time, see McGregor Ross, xvi.

McGregor Ross had been the most notorious and outspoken of all, in addition he was, as head of the Public Works Department, a very large and unconforming employer. Bitter attacks on him veiled as criticisms of departmental inefficiency were mounted from 1918 onwards leading to a commission of inquiry in 1920. McGregor Ross routed the commission's criticisms in Legislative Council, but his triumph was short-lived and he fell victim to an 'economy measure' in 1923. He narrates the story of Shirley V. Cooke, an outspoken Irish district officer who on appointment to Kiambu district had released a boy aged fifteen detained without trial by his predecessor. The boy had been detained because a local farmer, C. K. Archer who was also the Chairman of the Convention, had written to complain that he was lazy, suggesting a period of compulsory labour. The boy had apparently left Archer's employment normally at the end of a month. Cooke also freed another man who, following a similar complaint, had been obliged to do thirty-five days' unpaid communal labour as a porter, and had publicized this action by writing in plain terms to Archer. There was a great settler outcry, the governor appointed a commission of inquiry headed by the Chief Justice. Cooke was vindicated, but his next posting was on the Northern Frontier while his predecessor received an agreeable hill station.

Ross gives a further example of the transfer of an assistant D.C. who sentenced a farm headman to prison because the headman had locked up a number of women as hostages following failure to recruit men. Local opinion condemned the officer. Ross also claims that an unusual Kenya Civil Service rule that an officer might be retired after twenty years was a concession to settler opinion in respect of unco-operative officers.

45. *E.A.S.*, 14 March 1925, and McGregor Ross, 174. The *New Statesman*, 25 Apr 1925, in a report on the Convention notes W. MacLellan Wilson, a former missionary who had become a farmer, as saying 'Nowadays the service was being recruited from college men in whom was a seething spirit of

Socialism, all men-equal, brotherhood-of-man views, which made them unbalanced and erratic in their actions'.

46. *Parliamentary Debates, Commons*, 2, 8 March 1926.
47. Owen to Oldham, 21 Oct 1922. Oldham papers. Owen asked Oldham to raise the matter with the Colonial Office, which Oldham considered unwise. Owen stated that the economy proposal recommended a board for native affairs, the secretary of which was to be a junior official unable to defend African land or labour interests. The *Report of the Commission Appointed to Enquire into and Report on the Financial Position and System of Taxation in Kenya*, Col 116 of 1936, (hereafter Pim Report), 63, notes Northey's support for the economy despite the strong objections of the Chief Native Commissioner and the Colonial Office decision.
48. This condition was to persist. See, for example, the *Report of the Commission of Inquiry appointed to Examine the Labour Conditions in Mombasa, 1939*, (hereafter Willan Report), Appendix V, where the acting Coast P.C. complained of the consequences of continual movement of officers.
49. The demand for labour bureaux had led in 1921 to the appointment of a special commission to examine the question. The commission had included farmers, a missionary, businessmen and McGregor Ross with Watkins as Chairman. The commission firmly rejected any labour bureau system, recommending only closer supervision of existing procedures, the erection of transit and rest camps, improved medical and craft education facilities, the enforcement of the Resident Natives Ordinance and free movement of labour throughout East Africa. *E.A.S.*, 25 March 1922.
50. *E.A.S.*, 15 March 1925. Coryndon, just prior to his death, had addressed meetings in Kikuyuland saying that 'he heard with regret that European coffee picking and the Nyeri railway line extension were both held up due to labour shortages, and urged his listeners to remember the two roads' (Dual Policy), by which the territory was to advance. The chiefs present said wage rates were too low; some apparently offered to supply any number of men required if they were allowed to use a little pressure. *E.A.S.*, 17 Jan 1925.
51. This attempt was noted in a speech to the Autumn 1926 meeting of the Convention of Associations, *E.A.S.*, 30 Oct 1926. The speaker said the attempt had been made in the early post-war years and that the Egyption government had given approval to the project, assembling men at Suez.
52. *1925 Annual Report, N.A.D.*
53. *1923, 1929 Annual Reports, N.A.D.*
54. A possible reason for this is that generally the diet of Nyanza peoples, in particular the Luo, was better balanced, giving them superior physical strength.
55. Cmd. 4903 of 1932 (Lord Moyne's report on taxation in Kenya) comments adversely on the estimates of African reserve production noted in the 1927 Labour Commission Report, and states that the estimates were strongly contested by the administration at the time as being too optimistic.
56. The Detention Camps Ordinance, Ord 25 of 1925, *Kenya Gazette*, 9 Dec 1925. There does not seem to be any evidence to justify the contemporary fear of the *Anti-Slavery Reporter* that the Ordinance would lead to heavier sentences in order that D.C.s could obtain a labour supply. In 1928 the following sentences for detention were awarded: Native Registration Ordinance offences, 757; Employment of Natives Ordinance offences, 638; Resident Native Labourers Ordinance offences, 227. *1928 Annual Report, N.A.D.* A comparison of prosecution totals with other territories makes interesting reading. The Colonial Labour Committee Papers 1931–41 record: '. . . number of charges and convictions under the Masters and Servants (or similar) Ordinances in East and West Africa Territories . . . during the year 1929.

	No. of Charges	*No. of convictions*
Kenya	2,105	1,492
Nyasaland	771	755
Tanganyika	666	500
Uganda	238	190

Zanzibar	115	67
Gold Coast	7	4
Nigeria	180	154

57. The Registration of Domestic Servants Ordinance, Ord 11 of 1929, *Kenya Gazette*, 23 July 1929. Rules made under the ordinance required a judge or magistrate to endorse any court convictions on the register.
58. Colonial Secretary to Legislative Council, *E.A.S. Supplement*, 23 Oct 1926.
59 C.O. 533/480, Brooke-Popham to Ormsby-Gore, 16 Oct 1937 enclosing N.A.D. Circular, No. 4, 20 Jan 1927.
60. William George Arthur Ormsby-Gore, 1885–1964. Educated Eton and Oxford; M.P. Denbigh 1910, Stafford 1918; Parliamentary Private Secretary to Lord Milner and Assistant Secretary to the War Cabinet 1918; Under-Secretary of State Colonies 1922, 1924; Chairman East African Parliamentary Commission; Postmaster General 1931; First Commissioner of Works 1931; Secretary of State Colonies 1936; High Commissioner, South Africa 1941; Chairman the Midland Bank and Bank of British West Africa; Pro-Chancellor, University of Wales; 4th Baron Harlech.
61. *Parliamentary Debates, Commons*, 8, 22 Feb, 29 March, 9, 14 June 1926, deal with the Mozambique labour project. Amery first stated he would make inquiries and then denied that permits had been issued. The *E.A.S.* however named the individual estates; these may well have abandoned the project in view of the criticism.

    Parliamentary Debates, Commons, 5 July 1926 records Amery's assurance that there had been no change in policy. The *E.A.S.*, 1 Jan 1926, noted that Grigg had issued licences to import foreign labour.
62. Kenyatta, *op. cit.*, 14, quotes from the text of this memorandum.
63. The Asians claim was a highly complex issue related to the change in currency (see *infra*, p. 139). The Kenya government was proposing that their pay (which they argued with some justification had already been unfavourably revised) should be reduced as an Asian contribution to the colony's weak economy. It was proposed that the Asian salary scales, worked out in florins, should be converted to shillings at the rate of 20 shillings to 15 florins, and a small local allowance paid on the new scales. The main reason behind the Kenya government's economic argument appears to have been to preserve the differences between European and Asian salaries.

    The Colonial Office felt that civil servants engaged on permanent terms could not have these terms reduced in this way, though they saw no objection to reduced scales for new recruits or for officers seeking promotion.

    The Railway Asiatic Union later protested again to the Colonial Office against new rules concerning leave.
64. A number of memoirs provide European accounts of farm life at this time. Karen Blixen's *Out of Africa*, 1937 and *Shadows on the Grass*, 1960 are classic; also illustrative is E. D. Bache, *The Youngest Lion*, 1934. From an African point of view J. M. Kariuki, *Mau Mau Detainee*, 1963 and R. M. Gatheru, *Child of Two Worlds*, 1964 provide happy and unhappy accounts respectively.
65. The administration sometimes ran tribunals for disputes among squatters that could be settled by tribal custom; one such tribunal for the Kikuyu sat in Nakuru.
66. The Minutes of Executive Council for 19 Feb 1930 note in particular a song called 'Mambo Leo' or 'Mutherigo', 'a varying seditious and often obscene commentary upon prominent missionaries, officials and Government generally . . . peculiarly associated with the Kikuyu Central Association . . . and it was not sung amongst the pagan Natives in the Reserves'. This song in fact attacked those who were trying to suppress female circumcision.
67. 1921–2 Annual Report, Ulu District. For a very candid description of the type of personal records a D.C. might keep, see C. Chenevix Trench, *The Desert's Dusty Face*, 1964, 5; in this case the records took the form of a 'Noted Blokes Book' maintained by successive D.C.s over the years.

68. The Master and Servants (Amendment) Ordinance, Ord 7 of 1924, Kenya *Gazette*, 22 Feb 1924.
69. The Resident Natives Ordinance, Ord 19 of 1924. *Kenya Gazette*, 16 Oct 1924.
70. The Resident Native Labourers Ordinance, Ord 5 of 1925, *Kenya Gazette*, 6 May 1925. An amendment to the Master and Servants Ordinance enacted at the same time provided for 'special contracts' under which an employee could engage himself to an employer for a period of time not to exceed one year, with the obligation to work for at least five-sevenths of the total number of days of the contract. Food was to be provided for the employee by the employer. This extended form of ticket contract in theory provided for men who might be committed to a form of short-term squatting, but it does not seem to have been generally used as such.
71. *E.A.S. Supplement*, 18 Apr 1925, quoted R. L. Buell, *op. cit.*, 326. Farmers were arguing that squatter labour was skilled and that, therefore, engagements of more than two years were necessary for the labour to become valuable. There is some evidence to suggest a number of employers had tried to inveigle squatters into contracts for life.
72. *E.A.S. Supplement*, 6 Nov 1926, quoted R. L. Buell, *op cit.*, 327. The resolution also proposed that employers should collect their squatters' tax, endorsing their *kipandes* to that effect and retaining the employees' official tax receipts to prevent their departure.

    Rumours of the longer obligations and exaggerated talk of enslavement or 'tenants for life', may have been the cause of the 1929 unrest among Kikuyu squatters.
73. The Native Registration Amendment Ordinance, Ord 19 of 1920, *Kenya Gazette*, 18 Aug 1920.
74. *Kenya Gazette*, 5 Nov 1919.
75. The Native Registration Ordinance, Ord 56 of 1921, *Kenya Gazette*, 4 Jan 1922.

    The Ordinance was even extended to boys of the apparent age of twelve or over as a disciplinary measure in the Nakuru district in 1923.
76. McGregor Ross, xi. Ross errs in dating the re-enactment Ordinance as 1920, not 1921. Other information in this section has been supplied by administrative officers of the period.
77. Leys, 198.
78. An earlier test case, *Rex v. Glassford* in 1923, *Kenya Law Reports*, ix, 94–7, had ruled an employer was obliged to sign off an employee's *kipande* at the lawful termination of a contract.
79. The Master and Servants (Amendment) Ordinance, Ord 4 of 1925, *Kenya Gazette*, 6 May 1925. This ordinance also made an effort to deal with the problem of 'indefinite leave' by requiring five-sevenths of the total number of days contracted to be worked in the cases of long written contracts.
80 *1925 Annual Report, N.A.D.* records this alternative procedure with satisfaction, adding 'Altogether action has been taken either by the employers or by this Department against about 50 per cent monthly of the natives reported as deserters'.
81. Note of a conversation between Arthur and Oldham, 9 Dec 1920 in which Arthur reported the discovery of this practice by Owen. Oldham papers.
82. Ord 3 of 1920, *E.A.P. Gazette*, 11 Feb 1920.
83. Instructions for the care of labour by Government Departments, *Kenya Gazette*, 2 March 1921.
84. Instructions to Govern the Application of the Native Authority Amendment Ordinance, *Kenya Gazette*, 16 March 1921.
85. Rules made under the Master and Servants Ordinance, *Kenya Gazette*, 24 Aug 1921.
86. *Kenya Gazette*, 19 Oct 1921.
87. *E.A.S.*, 25 Aug 1922.
88. The Native Authority (Amendment) Ordinance, Ord 26 of 1922, *Kenya Gazette*, 30 Dec 1922.

89. Bill—Native Exemption Ordinance, *Kenya Gazette*, 11 Aug 1920.
90. The Native Exemption Ordinance, Ord 25 of 1920, *Kenya Gazette*, 29 Dec 1920.
91. *Kenya Gazette*, 16 March 1921.
92. *Kenya, Compulsory Labour for Government Purposes*, Cmd. 2464 of 1925.
93. *Ibid.*
94. *1924 Annual Report, N.A.D.* This figure was seen as 'normal'. The Department in 1923 judged the death rate in the reserves of males of these age groups to be 32 per 1,000.
95. Denham enlarged on the apparent contentment of the Nyanza labourers returning from railway work in three reports sent to the Colonial Office in 1925, and published as *Kenya, Tours in the Native Reserves and Native Development in Kenya*, 1926, Cmd. 2573 of 1926. He reported that all the men he met said they were content with their conditions and nearly all carried a wooden 'chop' box containing possessions amassed at work, chiefly shorts, coat, hat, stockings, mirror, etc. He had received no complaints against compulsion in Nyanza. But he reported that the women of Kitui District had refused to work their gardens in protest at the number of absent young men, a protest apparently as much against *ngomas* without partners as anything else.
96. McGregor Ross, 109.
97. For figures covering the years 1922 to 1929 see Appendix I, Table 3.
98. *Parliamentary Debates, Commons*, 24 July 1929.
99. For a generally reliable account of this incident see McGregor Ross, xii, xiii.
100. This Privy Council Order, together with a subsequent amending order, were both published in the *Kenya Gazette* of 16 Dec 1921.
101. Oldham papers; *New Statesman*, 14 May 1921.
102. The Kenya government reported this view to the Colonial Office where one official minuted 'the Govt., while not stimulating a reduction of wages reaps the advantage of the movement where it is successful. There is nothing wrong in this'. This view was shared by senior officials and the Parliamentary Under-Secretary. C.O. 533/263, Notley (Acting Governor) to Colonial Office, 26 Sept 1921 and attached papers.
103. 'It seems very probable that not half the rupees in circulation have yet been presented for exchange, because natives have not appreciated the necessity for redeeming them until they ceased to be accepted as legal tender. Strong objections have been raised from outside to this change of currency, on the grounds that it is proving a great hardship to the natives . . .' wrote the Colony's Treasurer to the Currency Officer, Mombasa, 12 Aug 1921; C.O. 533/263, Notley (Acting Governor) to Colonial Office, 19 Sept 1921 and attached papers. See also Thuku, *op. cit.*, 20, 'The new rate was one old rupee equals two shillings, but many people tried to give Africans one shilling for one rupee.'
104. *E.A.P. Debates*, 14 May 1920. Ainsworth denied that the bill had anything to do with labour supply but the support given to the bill by the European unofficials was clearly based on its possibilities of increasing the number of men at work.
105. '. . . a tax repugnant both to our feelings of justice and to the paternal relationship which we bear to the natives . . .' wrote Tate to the Chief Native Commissioner, 16 Jan 1920, adding 'Speaking for myself I feel so strongly on the injustice of increasing at present the native hut and poll tax that if the proposal becomes law I shall, because I am unable financially to leave Government service, be compelled to give effect to a measure which neither I nor I believe the majority of my colleagues can defend in any way'. He insisted that his views be sent to the Colonial Office. Elspeth Huxley papers, Rhodes House.
106. This pattern, already established of the gradation of tax by prosperity of a district rather than the income of an individual could also entail an indirect form of 'encouragement'; for example a poor district not far from an area requiring labour might be judged capable of earning money for tax while

other districts, remote but marginally less poor, received a reduced tax rate.

107. Manuscript memo by Arthur, 29 Dec 1920, Oldham papers.
108. Interview Sir Francis Loyd, 1970.
109. This conviction was reinforced, for example, by the practice of many farmers of giving the Kamasia a week of rest and food after engagement, to build up their strength before setting them to work.
110. The recruiters were private individuals or small two- or three-man businesses and, in certain areas, associations of employers such as the Fort Hall Recruiting Association.
111. The Master and Servants (Medical Inspection) Rules, *Kenya Gazette*, 22 Aug 1923.
112. *Kenya Gazette*, 25 Aug 1926. On remote farms, however, it was generally not possible for an employer to arrange hospital treatment for sick employees.
113. The Master and Servants (Amendment) Ordinance, Ord 4 of 1925, *Kenya Gazette*, 6 May 1925.
114. *E.A.S.*, 12, 19, 26 June, 3, 10, 17, 24, 31 July, 7, 14, 28 Aug and 4 Sept 1926.

    The articles emphasized humane treatment, balanced diets, simple medical treatment, the merits of permanent housing and concern for the children of labourers. For total numbers of inspections carried out each year see Appendix I, Table 4. The Labour Inspection report form, too, was modified so as to ask more specific and detailed questions on rations supplied and statistics of health and illness.
115. The Labour Section recommended a payment, for example, of Shs. 250/- for the loss of a leg, and two years wages as compensation to relatives in cases of death.
116. The only category of workers to enjoy special legislative protection in respect of tasks and hours of work were shop-workers. Shop-hours legislation had been discussed in Kenya for a number of years; European commercial employers were unusually willing to champion protective legislation as it would impede the competition they faced from the enormous majority of Asian owned shops. The Asian employers objected and another very early Asian industrial organisation, the Indian Employees Federation, protested against the employers' attitude and alleged victimization of its members. A bill was drafted in 1920 but this only reached the statute book in 1925 when (subject to reservations for certain particular trades, seasons and areas), maxima of a fifty hour week and a nine hour day were prescribed in the Shop Hours Ordinance (Ord 24 of 1925). The ordinance also provided for meal breaks, a weekly half-holiday and an annual holiday of at least twelve days. This ordinance was then applied without much success to Nairobi and later to a few other towns but not Mombasa.
117. 'Labour Statistics and Tribal Progress', *E.A.S.*, 26 March 1927 quoted Buell, *op. cit.*, 345–6. The article was based on figures supplied by the Chief Registrar; it quoted from the previous year's N.A.D. Report to explain the absence of the Kamba—'I regret to have to record that the Akamba are still addicted to immoderate drinking and to excessive and immoral dancing.' More accurately, the Report noted the 'spurious prosperity' of stock accumulated by the tribe.

    The 1929 Annual Report, Nyeri District, estimated that some 13,600 men out of a total of 42,700 adult males were at work; the D.C. added that one man in three was at work at any one time usually for six month spells, and that two men out of three went to work on this basis per year.
118. *1923, 1925, 1926 Annual Reports, N.A.D.* For figures covering the whole decade see Appendix I, Table 2.
119. *Memorandum on Native Progress*, 1928.
120. A useful summary of the progress made from 1920 to 1932 appears in the *1932 Annual Report, Medical Department.*

Chapter 5

DEPRESSION AND UNREST, 1930–1939

> ... the policy of Government which I may be asked to approve and which I have to defend in the House of Commons, must be like Caesar's wife, above suspicion.
>
> The Secretary of State for the Colonies, W. Ormsby-Gore, to Lord Francis Scott, 22 February 1937.

The next decade was governed by Depression and population increase. The growth of population in some areas ran parallel with a great increase in stock, together leading to clear acts of political unrest and to increases in burglary and produce thefts, the latter being sometimes the only way a man could satisfy hunger. But the colonial and settler establishment had no real fear of African politicians, many had never even heard of them and all believed that European rule and settlement would continue for the foreseeable future. As Philip Kerr, later Lord Lothian, wrote to Oldham in 1927:

> The central fact about the vast area included in the highlands of South and East Africa ... is that except for the coastal belt along the Indian ocean and certain low-lying valleys in its central portion, the whole of it seems inevitably destined to be colonised in greater or less degree by the white race. People often talk as if this were still a matter of policy, and as if it were possible for Parliaments or peoples to decide whether or not these areas are going to be colonised by white men ... I do not think it is a question of policy at all. It is a matter which has already been decided by the facts.[1]

But if all Europeans were agreed that the white man should rule, disagreement over precisely which section of the white community the white farmers, the business community, or the Colonial Office officials in Whitehall or in the field continued. The answer was bound to have considerable effect on the problems of labour.

The White Farmers

The most clamorous section remained the white farmers. Their main preoccupations in this decade were the definition of the White Highlands, the securing of control over finances, increasing the number of Europeans, and the settlement of the squatter problem. The first of these was of prime importance; the debate over land, particularly during the hearings of the Kenya Land Commission (hereafter Carter Commission) dominated the thinking of European and African leaders through much of this decade, thereby relegating labour problems to a secondary although none the less important position, population increases having virtually removed the question of supply. Furthermore, except for the question of squatters, the Colonial Office, so far as East and Central Africa was concerned, was more interested in the problems of the copper-belt and of migratory labour in other colonies.

With the death of Lord Delamere settler leadership passed into the hands of Lord Francis Scott, although he did not establish his authority firmly until the late nineteen-thirties.[2] He was aloof and frequently ill from war injuries, but he had been a Guards officer and through the Duke of Buccleuch was related to the Royal Family. He had many connections in the British upper classes; the letters beginning 'Dear Billy', to Ormsby-Gore when the latter was Secretary of State testify to this. But in the early part of the decade, settler leadership had to contend with a tough and suspicious Governor, Sir Joseph Byrne, whom one of the officials at the Colonial Office called 'the first real attempt at a Governor which Kenya has ever had...'[3] However, with the appointment of Air Chief Marshal Sir Robert Brooke-Popham as Governor in 1937, the settlers acquired a man much more to their liking.[4]

In general the settlers still hoped to develop Kenya along the lines of Southern Rhodesia and of South Africa. General Smuts told Kerr that he expected the Union and the Rhodesias to form a kind of league which would guarantee local control but would ensure that certain problems would be dealt with jointly. Kerr was certain that this would eventually include East Africa as well: 'The more you examine it the more obvious it is that it is the experience of the Union which gives the most valuable information about policy and that it is the policy of the Union which is most likely to set the pace in determining the relations between... white man and black.'[5]

Although the Kenya settlers in the nineteen-twenties had failed to create a white dominion along South African lines, these notions were not entirely dead. During this decade the Joint East Africa Board continued to press for Closer Union. In March 1935 there was a meeting of Kenya and Tanganyika settlers to Arusha to revive this demand.[6] Some like F. S. Joelson, the editor of *East Africa and Rhodesia*, dreamed of a truly British white dominion in Africa which would embrace both East Africa and the Rhodesias.[7] In a letter to Ormsby-Gore in 1936 Lord Francis Scott told him that 'Rhodesia is the nearest country on similar lines to ourselves...'[8] Others looked to South Africa. Even Scott in the same year that he wrote to Ormsby-Gore about Rhodesia, accepted an invitation to South Africa from the Governor-General, Lord Clarendon. *The Times* correspondent wrote, 'His visit is expected to strengthen the links recently created, by mutual desire, for the purpose of providing a greater understanding and an opportunity for fuller co-operation between North and South through the unofficial communities.'[9] Two years later Brooke-Popham told Malcolm MacDonald that the unjust criticism levelled at the white settlers was driving them to look south—'to adopt the ideals and traditions of South Africa rather than those of England'.[10] While it is true that the more brutal and eccentric of the pro-South African party remained out of power in this decade and that the Colonial Office refused to accede to demands for

Closer Union or for the formal devolution of power, none the less the main lines of development in Kenya were patterned on the Union and the Rhodesias.

The settlers' first instinct, having been denied home rule, had been to secure a *de facto* influence within the structure of government particularly on financial matters.[11] The settler leaders already sat on the Executive Council and had a majority on the Standing Committee on the Estimates. There was constant pressure to increase settler influence in the executive, preferably by the grant of responsible government. In the early thirties the settlers had lost some ground when Byrne stifled the Board of Agriculture with its settler chairman and postponed the creation of an economic committee for two years. In 1932 they had to content themselves with a parity of officials and unofficials in the newly-formed Standing Economic Committee. Furthermore Byrne appointed only one unofficial member, Lord Francis Scott, to it. Two years later the Governor created a Standing Finance Committee in which the settlers secured three members, the Asian community one, and the administration four, thereby denying the settlers the majority they wanted. There was nevertheless a general impression among officials not only that the Standing Finance Committee was the real seat of power but also that, whatever the numerical balance on the committee, the people who really counted were the settlers.

In September 1935 the Convention of Associations urged its representatives to 'take such action as is required to bring about the grant to the European colonists of adequate and effective responsibility for the control of their affairs'. Malcolm MacDonald replied the next month by refusing to reopen the question of Closer Union and by declaring his opposition to increased unofficial control of finance and administration.[12] This period was the nadir of relations between the settlers and the administration during this decade. Already four unofficial members had walked out of the Legislative Council protesting against the economic policy of the government, and the Convention had created a Vigilance Committee reminiscent of the drama in 1922.[13] The committee wanted the settlers to have the power to nominate the secretary and unofficial members of the Economic Development Board. At one meeting Grogan made the position perfectly clear by analogy with the War Council in the First World War. He told the executive '. . . that in that Committee also, the Government had attempted to nominate a personnel which was distasteful to the unofficial community, and which the Elected Members at that time refused [sic] to accept, with the result that the nominations desired by the European Elected Members were forced on Government'. Petitioning, Grogan told another executive meeting of the committee, was a waste of time—'. . . the only thing the Home Government ever took notice of was clamour'.[14] The Vigilance Committee gained its point about the unofficial members, but the board was successfully emasculated for the next three years by the use of the economy axe. As a counterpoint to this intrigue, there was also a violent public uproar about the decision of the government to apply income tax to the white community.

However by 1936 Lord Francis Scott had decided that such tactics were unproductive. Although he and Major F. W. Cavendish-Bentinck resigned from the Executive Council in March 1936 because they had not been consulted concerning changes in defence policy, he was already thinking of a settlement with the imperial government.[15] Both he and Captain H. E. Schwartze, another unofficial member, visited London in 1936 for discussions with the Colonial Office. They did not demand self-government but instead urged that the Kenya government should 'take the settlers into closer and more effective consultation'.[16] Schwartze called on Lord Plymouth at the Colonial Office and '.... urged that much could be done to ease the position between the Government and the unofficial Europeans if they could be given an active responsibility in the administration, for example by the appointment of one of them as a Minister of Agriculture...'[17] Although the Colonial Office refused to sanction such a move, the settlers and the administration came to terms later in the year, the settlers accepting income tax in return for an increase in their numbers in the Executive Council. 'Whatever the details of the new constitution may prove to be', wrote *East Africa and Rhodesia,* 'it is already clear that the settler and commercial community will be given a much greater share in the framing of Government policy...'[18] The following year the Council was reconstituted with proportions exactly the same as in the Standing Finance Committee thereby increasing settler power but denying them parity. With the appointment in the same year of Brooke-Popham as Governor, the winds of change were beginning to blow. 'I know', said Brooke-Popham in a letter to the Colonial Office in 1937, 'the idea is to give unofficial members more responsibility...'[19] As a token of this a prominent settler, R. E. Norton, formerly Chairman of the Coffee Board was nominated in 1938 as the first full-time secretary of the Economic Development Board. The Colonial Office specifically approved Norton rather than an administrative officer in order to secure the co-operation of the settler leaders.[20] The settlers also, of course, secured a majority on the Highlands Board which was created as a consequence of the Carter Commission and which protected white interests in the matter of land.

The settler power in such financial and economic committees was, so far as labour problems were concerned, largely negative. They could and did prevent the abolition of registration and they held up or emasculated much of the labour legislation suggested by the Colonial Office and by the International Labour Organization. They also constituted an important influence in the allocation of scarce resources between the various racial communities, and they conducted a long and partially successful attack on the remuneration and the morale of the colonial civil servants who were working in Kenya, thereby hoping to make them more amenable to the settler point of view.

For the white farmers taxation policy was the key area, and it remained very much under their influence. The most notable exercise of their power was the defeat of Byrne's proposal for the institution of an income tax in 1933. Although the white community was forced in 1937 to accept a light income tax modelled on Rhodesia, the price of this had been the reconstitution of the Executive Council in their favour. Any fully detailed assessment of the taxation system in the inter-war years is beyond our scope involving matters such as the African contribution to defence costs, debt repayment, central government costs, and pensions on which the weight of argument may differ.[21] The general pattern remained overall the same. The cash rate of the taxes on Africans was not unduly high compared with other territories in East and South Africa. Neither the Ormsby-Gore nor the Hilton Young Commissions criticized African taxation as too great, but Lord Moyne in 1932 thought that the 'natives [were] bearing relatively the greater burden', with 'heavier individual sacrifice than that at present imposed upon the non-native population!'[22]

The European farmers insisted that the costs of white settlement should come as far as possible from the general revenue of the colony, while in African areas development costs should be paid by Africans through the rates levied by the local native councils. The clearest example of this lies in roads policy. In European areas they were built by the European district councils or with cheap private farm labour. For the best part of twenty years European local government in the Highlands was 99 per cent financed by the central government's road grant. Some European district councils never rated themselves in their whole history, and most did not do so until the mid nineteen-fifties.[23] In African rural areas the costs fell on the L.N.C. rates or were absorbed through communal labour. The Hilton Young and Joint Select Committee Reports, Sir Alan Pim and Lord Moyne all recommended that the L.N.C.s should receive a rebate, but this was not permitted before the Second World War. Another major grievance was the differential investment in education. Many Europeans still seemed to hold to the view that 'ignorance is a form of security and a guarantee of subservience . . .'[24]

Although the rate of taxation seemed low, the Depression made payment more and more difficult for Africans. On a Depression cash income of Shs. 80/- to Shs. 100/- per annum (supplemented by some food, huts and often firewood, water, perhaps blankets and the produce of his own plot, perhaps Shs. 40/- to Shs. 200/- per year, and the plot rent free) a resident labourer would have to pay Shs. 12/- in tax, more if he had a number of wives.[25] In addition to his direct tax and possibly his L.N.C. rate of Shs. 1/- to Shs. 2/-, a labourer would also have to pay high import charges on some of his preferred purchases, charges aggravated by a high railway import rate. For education, of increasing importance in African eyes in the nineteen-thirties, an African would have to pay mission school fees with only some limited prospect of an L.N.C. grant in return for his rates—Shs. 60/- to Shs. 160/- per year for a boy's primary education and Shs. 200/- for secondary.[26]

The return for these taxes remained not very high. The social services continuing to be limited to those fitting Africans to be labourers, of which the most important was medicine. Although these medical services remained inadequate for the total population, they nevertheless served a large number of Africans free. The reserve development services improved slightly in the nineteen-thirties. Most Europeans had come to accept that a certain measure of prosperity in the reserves was desirable, some arguing that the alternative of a black proletariat must lead to unrest, others that the cost of an economic wage for a labourer and his family away from the reserves would be ruinous. The government policy first set out in 1928 that revenue from public native taxation should be spent in the reserves, therefore, met with little direct criticism. However, there was a good deal of argument about the division of the public revenue on the basis of who paid what—a fruitless game played for many years. In the early nineteen-thirties as taxes became more difficult to pay receipts in consequence dropped.[27] In some twenty areas the cash rate was lowered by amounts varying from Shs. 2/- to Shs. 9/- but these were exceptional. Reduced taxation led to some reduction in expenditure on education and medical services which in turn led to parliamentary questions in Britain. In 1935 Pim still felt an absence of any real policy for African agriculture or veterinary services, but by the late years of the decade the staffing and advisory services had improved with demonstration plots, seed farms, new and improved crops, grading and marketing arrangements.

In 1934 impoverishment became a legal ground for tax exemption. At the same time women owners of huts were made to pay tax if they could do so. Powers were given to chiefs and headmen to collect taxes, a measure that quickly led to abuse. In 1937 following a commission of inquiry the government grudgingly raised the age from sixteen to eighteen at which taxation commenced, but postponed Pim's recommendation of a lower tax rate for additional huts; Moyne's general comments on the obsolescence of the hut tax concept in view of changing African social patterns remained unheeded until 1942.

Another major area of concern for the European farmers was the encouragement of white settlement. The prime mover in this regard was Cavendish-Bentinck who suggested various schemes throughout the nineteen-thirties, in particular one to lure retired British officers of the Indian Army to the colony. But neither the settlers nor the Colonial Office were particularly keen on the one obvious source of white immigrants in this decade—the Jews fleeing from Nazi Germany. The class basis was also open to easy self-caricature. Scott wrote in the preface to *Retirement—Why not Kenya?*: 'Europeans of every class have settled in Kenya, but in the country districts of the Highlands they are for the most part of the service and public school type. Social amenities are to be found all over the settled areas and include provision for riding, shooting, polo, tennis, golf and bridge ...'[28] Nevertheless Italian P.O.W.s of all classes were accepted as immigrants after the Second World War. In 1939 Cavendish-Bentinck surveyed the situation in relation to white settlement in a memorandum which not only urged more settlers but drew the necessary conclusions in terms of the racial stratification of the labour market which would follow the success of such a programme:

> 6. I am leading up to this: If we are to support a large European population, we shall have amongst other things to make timely provision for the employment of young people ...
>
> 7. I therefore consider that in the interests of the future generations of all races, we should now begin to earmark (perhaps not rigidly, and of course by statute) certain lines of employment for white people, others possibly for Asians, and fit the native into this picture as best we can.
>
> 8. Such a policy has had to be adopted in the Union of South Africa during the last few years, and at the time of its inception was bitterly

opposed by all who considered themselves spokesmen for the Asian and native peoples. All have now changed their views, and consider that the policy is justified and was the correct one . . .

9. . . . The truth of the matter is, that throughout British East and South Africa, from the Abyssinian border to the Cape, there should be some form of—within limits—agreed and co-ordinated policy in these matters.[29]

The Depression effectively prevented any large-scale increase in the numbers of the European community.[30] But Cavendish-Bentinck's memorandum set the tone for the post-war period when there would be a large increase in European immigration and a consequent heightening of racial tensions. It also indicated that the racial nature of employment had been and would continue to be fixed by common understanding in the European community rather than by legislation which was likely to be vetoed by the Secretary of State. Three years earlier Scott had been pressing the Secretary of State for a native policy, including a labour policy, suitable to East and Southern Africa. The Colonial Office was unsympathetic, largely because the situations in the two regions were not analogous as there was little competition as yet between black and white for jobs in Kenya, but concluded that the problem could not be prevented from arising. Racial discrimination in middle class jobs was more of a problem for Asians than for Africans in this period, but the shabby treatment by the Kenya government of Peter Mbiyu Koinange when he finished his studies in the United States was a hint of things to come.[31]

Both for European farmers and for Africans of all classes one of the most emotional labour issues remained that of registration. The *kipande* system stayed on the statute book throughout the nineteen-thirties, and many of the abuses described in the previous chapter continued. The system was nevertheless beginning to break down. Large numbers of men were finding work without *kipandes*, particularly at the Coast; literate friends would sign off the *kipande* of an illiterate deserter, and fewer questions came to be asked by employers, particularly those employing small numbers, on engaging men. Temporary certificates which did not have to be signed off and did not record wage rates came into increasing use by men who had decided to lose their original *kipandes*. When Pim came to survey the structure of the government in order to try to effect economy, he suggested that the registration system was becoming ineffective and that it should be abolished thereby saving some money through the disappearance of the Native Registration Department.[32] Pim, however, failed to recognize that the *kipande* was more than a system of control. It was also a symbol of European domination as the much more spectacular debate over abolition in the nineteen-forties would show.

Pim's proposals were shelved and in 1937 an ordinance was introduced to tighten up procedures. It abolished the temporary certificate procedure and prevented the granting of indefinite leave. A considerable storm was raised over a clause which provided for fines of Shs. 400/- or three months imprisonment for harbouring those who had deserted without getting their *kipandes* signed off.[33] Vincent (later Sir Vincent) Tewson wrote on behalf of the T.U.C. to MacDonald protesting that the effect of such a clause would be to prevent strikes by appearing '. . . to command the co-operation of the entire population in the interests of any employer, however reactionary, for the victimisation of any worker who leaves his employment without permission'.[34] Archdeacon Owen, fresh from his attack on juvenile labour, joined in as did McGregor Ross who took up the cause in Geneva. Since 1931 the Colonial Office had favoured the exclusion of desertion and harbouring from the penal code. Great pressure was put on the Kenya government to amend the legislation. Ultimately an amending ordinance was passed which specified that the offending clause was to be directed exclusively at employers who enticed labour from another firm. But the penal sanction for harbouring remained although reduced to £10 or one month imprisonment. In March 1939 MacDonald told the House of Commons that it was his hope to separate identity registration from labour records.[35] But this remained a hope until after the Second World War and registration continued to be one of the major crosses both of the Africans and of the Labour Inspectorate.

The system was undoubtedly oppressive but it had a few useful by-products. With a *kipande,* an African had proof of employment and salary as well as identity which could be useful in matters such as small loans or credit from Asian traders. He did not suffer the risk, which had earlier been a real one, of being mistaken for a criminal, and in the event of sickness or death relatives could be notified and property or earnings returned to the next of kin. The system also played an important part in converting the tribal African to the concept of regular wage employment. But this took place at a considerable cost. Each year between 3,000 and 5,000 Africans were prosecuted for *kipande* offences, the principal charges being failure to carry the *kipande,* mutilation and alteration, and the carrying of someone else's *kipande.* A letter to *The Times* from Owen in June 1938 stated that no fewer than 50,000 Africans had received prison or detention camp sentences since 1920.[36] The Native Affairs Department reports note convictions averaging 4,500 per year for the years 1935 to 1938, the figures for each year of the decade are noted in Appendix II, Table 1. Not only were the mass of the people oppressed, but the new African middle class although tiny in numbers especially resented the *kipande* which was a symbol of their perpetual inferiority—the sign that they would never be admitted to the club. As a consequence the *kipande* received special attention in African nationalist political oratory throughout the next decade as the new élite began to grow in numbers.

Allied to the question of the *kipande* was that of the registration of domestic servants. The Domestic Servants Registration Ordinance was applied to Nairobi in 1930, to Nakuru and Trans-Nzoia in 1934, and to Nairobi District and the Uasin-Gishu in 1935, thereby imposing one more obligation on the African communities. As the ordinance was applied *kipandes* were checked and offenders prosecuted. Pim suggested that this was not a particularly useful form of registration as it really duplicated the *kipande,* but he noted that it was strongly backed by the East Africa Women's League. Once again the register, known as the Red Book, was as much a symbol of authority as a purely economic device. What else could explain the incredible ferocity of the female leaders of the European community in defence of this system? On the economic side, it may have done something to protect the employer from unqualified domestic staff making exaggerated or false claims of experience, but its noting of wage rates restricted opportunities for legitimate increase and the requirement for an employer's testimonial led to much abuse. An African writer, Mugo Gatheru, has vividly described an example of such abuse, relating how one domestic servant was delayed on his return to his employment by police inquiries over his *kipande*. On his arrival he found his employer, a European woman, exceedingly angry. She said, 'Bring your Red Book right away. You have no job now. You are entirely unreliable, a lazy, untrustworthy African. I hate you bloody niggers.' In the Red Book she wrote, 'He is quick in his work; he likes sweet things and may steal sugar if he has a chance; sometimes his thinking is like that of an eleven-year-old child.' The servant burnt the book but he had to wait a month before he could obtain a new one.[37]

For the settler community as a whole, however, the main labour question was the securing of agricultural workers and their efficiency whether as squatters, seasonal labour or as ordinary full-time workers. Most white farmers in Kenya still believed in a paternalism by which they would treat their employees as they treated their personal servants; they would protect and look after them in return for labour and obedience. The colour bar was both a consequence of these attitudes and was reinforced by them. The opinion of the time remained that Africans were children, devoid of all history and incapable of looking after themselves. It was necessary therefore for the employer to look after his own workers; only a cad would mistreat servants and children, but only a fool would fail to be firm with them. Lieut.-Col. J. G. Kirkwood, the member for Trans-Nzoia, perfectly expressed this view in a speech to the Legislative Council:

> I always treat my natives the same as I treat children. I try to be kind to them, and to advise and direct them, but when kindness has no effect you have to do the same as they do in the public schools at home and throughout the empire—use the cane.[38]

Many did play the part of the enlightened and paternal employer. But persisting in the belief that black men were different in nature from white and fitted for an inferior status only, they frequently and deliberately cultivated an authoritarian and impersonal manner. As a consequence, white farmers could genuinely believe that they took a deep interest in and had a profound knowledge of their African employees when, in fact, they often did not. Dr. Julian Huxley, walking through groups of labourers on one of the better farms in the Highlands, noted 'no signs of hostility or glumness, but just a curious remoteness, an indifference to any possible human relationship between black and white . . .'—a relationship that was almost entirely economic, a comment also made frequently in the N.A.D. reports.[39]

The N.A.D. seemed to believe that if only farmers lived up to the ideals implicit in the doctrine of trusteeship then all would be well. The authorities tended to judge the success of labour relations by the flow of workers from the reserves to the European farms. The government hoped that by exhortation, common sense, and inspection the white farmer would be led to see the virtues of generous treatment. In the annual report for the colony in 1937 it was maintained that '...employers who were willing to take a personal interest in their employees and to feed and house them well obtained labour with ease'. But the Depression made it ever more difficult to be enlightened and paternalistic. Coffee prices fell from £115–£120 per ton to £65–£70, maize from Shs. 12/- per bag to Shs. 3/-, sisal from £40 per ton to £14, and butter from Shs. 143/– per cwt. to Shs. 58/–. The collapse of prices combined with the large amounts owed to the banks brought many of the farmers to the edge of ruin. Nor did the traditional economic wisdom of the time allow the government to do much to assist in these circumstances. As a consequence unskilled farm labourers' wages fell rapidly: from Shs. 14/- to Shs. 7/- or Shs. 8/- per thirty-day ticket, sometimes as low as Shs. 6/-; unskilled town labour fell from Shs. 18/- or Shs. 19/- to Shs. 15/-. Some farmers felt a loyalty to their labour force and tried to keep and feed them on reduced wages and rations but with increased plots of land. Small profit margins, however, discouraged most farmers from improving the housing and general living standards of their labour and led to a decline in their concern for their welfare. Each year the N.A.D. annual report commented on unsatisfactory and primitive housing constructed with little or no supervision, poor sanitation and the lack of personal interest, vainly pointing out that the employer who paid, fed and housed his labourers well received real returns in contentment and efficiency.

The impersonality of the system, the lack of checks on the exercise of the authority of the white farmers, and the strains of the Depression continued to lead to occasional cases of violence, chiefly on the more remote farms. These testify to the problems of unrestrained authority and to the difficulty of running what amounted to a near-feudal system in the twentieth century. A particularly unpleasant case in 1934 attracted considerable publicity. A European woman and four Africans were convicted of manslaughter after having beaten five Africans so severely that one died. After the beatings the four Africans were locked in a *posho* store for the night; the next day the farm owner said, 'I cannot allow baboons to be placed in my car', and the men were obliged to walk to Kitale some seventeen miles away, arriving in a state of collapse. The European woman was ill and her husband dying; in consequence she was awarded a light sentence of one year. The husband, a former Indian Army major, had arrived in Kenya in 1920 and the years since then had been ones of financial struggle and of declining health; the violence was the outcome.[40] A Kenya doctor observed at the trial that the *kiboko*, was still in common use for punishment; other evidence points to the continuation of heavy corporal punishment by certain farmers, now a minority, of the old school.

In 1937 two cases attracted the attention of the Colonial Office. In the first, Raymond Letcher, who later became an elected member of the Legislative Council, was sentenced to one year imprisonment for deliberately running down and crippling for life an African whom he incorrectly suspected of stealing maize.[41] The second concerned a farmer, Jacobus Paulus Englebrecht, who savagely and repeatedly flogged a boy of fifteen with a *kiboko*. Englebrecht's summing up gives the full flavour of this type of settler:

It is my duty to civilize these uncivilized natives, practically called vermin. If I find them doing wrong whilst in my employment I should think I am in the same right as a schoolmaster or a father to learn them civilization.

Further, he appealed to the jury: 'If a matter like this is encouraged, where will it end? How many settlers will be brought up for an assault.' It was a sign of the changed times that not only did the judge consider this '... a mere appeal to uphold a form of lawlessness ...', but the jury convicted although it stipulated that flogging was not brutal.[42] Even more remarkable was the case of a young Dutchman at Kitale who in 1937 pleaded guilty to injuring an African employee and accepted a sentence of birching administered by the local European prison officer.

Violence, however, could beget violence particularly when there was no effective redress of grievances. In 1938 a young European farm manager, Jack White, reproved, quarrelled with and struck one of his employees, Wakahu wa Kihenya. Kihenya then rushed to the farm slaughter-house which was a few yards away, took a butcher's knife, stabbed and killed White. The Supreme Court reduced the sentence from murder to manslaughter owing to White's provocative language and actions.[43] Kihenya would have hanged under Girouard or Northey.

Nor were such incidents confined to the relations of white employer and black labourer. There were wider repercussions involving some Africans who held authority as a consequence of the economic system. For example, in 1936, two Africans were accused of killing a fellow African headman:

It was part of Kamenju's [the headman] duties to see that two accused did their work properly at night; they were employed as guards to look after the farm nurseries at night and protect the nurseries from buck and wild animals. Kamenju had been employed on the farm only a short time, during which he had been very zealous in supervising the two accused at night. He had on several occasions reported them for neglect of duty and had caused their working days to be docked on their work-tickets on this account, and had also taken, no doubt illegally, chickens and other things belonging to them by way of penalty. The accused therefore disliked Kamenju and made up their minds to avenge themselves upon him.[44]

Although most farmers did not perceive it at the time, there was an important change in terms of the labour market taking place—the most significant in the history of the colony. This change was the consequence of the rapid increase in population in the reserves which was caused largely by improved medical and agricultural facilities. The overcrowding led for the first time to substantial categories of men whose land-holding in the reserve was reduced; their holdings could neither any longer adequately support them and their families nor provide the revenue for taxation. Others had no land at all, as some resident labourers of long standing had been finding in the late nineteen-twenties. Among the Kamba the problem took the differing form of a vast accumulation of stock creating erosion and reduced carrying capacity. There are no reliable statistics to measure the African population increase, but overall from 1925 to 1939 it is likely to have been at least 500,000, quite possibly more, an increase principally among the large tribes whose reserves were already carrying a full population. In addition to the sheer pressures of humans upon land, the reserves suffered severely from locusts in 1929 and several years of poor rainfall in the early nineteen-thirties.

The Depression severely aggravated the problem. Wages fell; major employers such as the P.W.D. and the Railway reduced their African staff by several thousands, and many estate and processing plant employers were obliged to do likewise. Others failed completely and frequently involved the labour inspectorate in the difficult task of recovering wages; in 1938 the failure of the Mazongoleni Sisal Estate '... scattered throughout the reserve Natives with Labour Department chits stating the amount of wages owed them'.[45] Overall the average number of men employed fell sharply from 160,435 in 1927 to 141,000 in 1931 and to 132,000 in 1932. By 1933 the numbers had begun to rise again to 141,000 and thereafter annual increases brought the total up to a monthly average of 182,964 in 1938.[46] But this slow rise failed to match the increased population and throughout the decade supply exceeded demand which, in the Kenya context, meant small parties of lean-looking men presenting themselves hopefully at the settlers' farms asking for work. For almost all, the problem of finding the few shillings necessary to pay the annual tax became one of the greatest difficulty and unhappiness. No longer would conscription and similar pressures be necessary to force Africans to work for Europeans. Population pressure and the demand for consumer goods would be sufficient, but the settlers, imprisoned in the outlook of the early part of the century, continued to complain about shortage in the nineteen-thirties and to demand during the Second World War the long-denied right to conscript African labour for private enterprise. Settlers always complained about labour shortages; when there was a genuine shortage, they demanded forced labour.

The squatter problem added to the acute pressures on the rural African community. But for the white farmer the future of squatting was the most important labour question of the decade. The resident labour system was breaking down; it no longer served the interests of most of the European farmers owing to its inefficiency, the increase in illegal squatting as a consequence of the growing population in the reserves, and the rapid multiplication of squatter stock. These factors all led the settlers in the Rift Valley to demand firm government action to decrease the number of squatters, thereby, of course, aggravating the problems of the reserves and of the labour market. This demand grew as a consequence of the Depression when in any case farms could not be expanded to absorb more labour, and instead there was an acceleration of the change from maize to dairy farming. The dairy farmers saw large squatter herds as a source of general anxiety and a future commercial challenge, though the Kiambu and Thika planters still valued the manure. In 1934, for example, squatter cattle were estimated to total over 100,000 in the Uasin-Gishu and 40,000 in the Trans-Nzoia—the less advanced European areas.[47]

The anxiety of dairy farmers was generally expressed in terms, valid but also convenient, of disease risks; this anxiety was heightened by wider fears for the future as farmers contemplated a labour force far larger than they needed, the labourers often with big families but with no links with the reserves and nowhere to go on dismissal. Squatters were also seen as an impediment to closer settlement. The demand for a reduction of squatters and their return to the reserves met with some sympathy from administrative officers and the more conservative tribal authorities who saw large numbers of children growing up removed from and ignorant of traditional customs. But the fact that, on account of the pressure of land shortage, many Kikuyu were now once again begging for resident labour status was taken by many, both official and unofficial, as evidence that they liked squatting, preferring it to life in the reserve, and also that the European engaging a squatter was granting a favour which could if necessary be withdrawn. This view, or self-delusion, in turn induced a feeling of complacency which prevented many Europeans from seeing the increasing hardship which reduction would cause.

The removal of goats and reduction of squatter stock began in the Rift Valley, and early in 1930 was followed by the beginning of a reduction in the number of squatters themselves, notice procedures being generally observed. Some of those owning little or no land in the reserves began to turn to politics but without much effect at this time.

The Carter Commission, and also a special committee composed of three officials, one missionary and four settlers which reported in 1935, both emphasized the desirability of a change from any form of tenancy contract to a purely labour contract. The Carter Commission recommended an increase in the size of the reserves so that surplus squatters could return to a plot of their own, but the land proposed was inadequate in area and for the most part also in quality. The committee's recommendations formed the basis of new legislation which made the individual squatter legally into an employee in the place of being the head of a tenant family, and permitted contracts up to five years but reduced the period of notice from six months to three. It linked engagement to production of the *kipande*; squatters might engage in other occupations after completion of the employer's agreed period of work, which the employer was now statutorily required to provide. The powers of inspection were widened to enable police inspectors to count squatter stock, and stock regulations were tightened. Perhaps most significant of all, local district councils in the settled areas (on which Africans were not represented) were given powers to prohibit or limit squatter stock, order the removal and limit the number of squatters and to increase the number of days to be worked for a farmer to 270.[48] This legislation was drafted as a bill in 1937 and after some slight modification was passed later in the same year, but the Secretary of State's approval was held up until late in 1939.[49]

The Colonial Office found itself much embarrassed by the new ordinance, and the office files reveal considerable correspondence with interested parties in Britain and with the newly appointed Brooke-Popham, who had been sent to Kenya with a personal appeal from the Secretary of State, Ormsby-Gore, to find some humane solution to the problem.[50] Ormsby-Gore's successor, Malcolm MacDonald, was even more anxious to achieve this, but Brooke-Popham's despatches generally reflected the views of local European unofficial leaders and at times, as for example in one dated 8 June 1938, furnished information far from accurate; Brooke-Popham wrote, '. . . normally a native on the termination of his contract as a

Resident Labourer will experience no difficulty in finding a home for himself amongst his own people'. In defence of African interests, Arthur Creech Jones, the Labour Party colonial spokesman, wrote of the lack of land for repatriated squatters, the reduction of tenants to servants together with the denial of any African land rights in the white areas and the restrictions on crops and stock without any compensating increase in wages except by longer periods at work; Creech Jones favoured the Nyasaland system of native tenancy which enabled an African to work or to grow his own food, whichever he preferred, reinforced by a minimum wage.[51] Professor W. M. Macmillan, one of the very few British university Africanists of the time, also urged the Nyasaland pattern and wrote of Kenya 'following closely the disastrous South African precedent'.

The Colonial Office was anxious to avoid a parliamentary debate and appalled at any re-opening of the general question of the reservation of land in the White Highlands. Further its officials noted that certain conditions among indigenous workers, in particular contracts involving entire families, had recently been discussed at an I.L.O. conference at the instigation of McGregor Ross who had acted as an adviser to the British workers' delegation. Overall the Colonial Office officials saw the solution to the problem as an improved inspectorate rather than a minimum wage policy. The officials' minutes reflect great concern, knowledge of and attention to the details of the contracts squatters might have to sign. But on the vital question of the availability or otherwise of equitable land to resettle squatters, the Colonial Office staff lacked the necessary local knowledge. Nevertheless the questions of the obligations of members of squatters' families, squatters past working age, penal provisions, land for repatriated squatters, the situation created by a change of ownership of a farm and the conditions under which, and by whom, a squatter's removal might be ordered were all raised with Nairobi. The Colonial Office also objected to the removal of squatters who might refuse to sign new contracts on the new terms unless land was made available to them, and required that implementation of the ordinance be delayed until suitable land was ready.

In consequence, an amending ordinance was prepared early in 1939 which permitted each male member of a squatter's family, on attaining the age of sixteen, to enter or to terminate at any later time any contract he chose with the farm owner. The powers of magistrates to order removal of squatters were limited to breaches of the peace; no removal order powers were left with the farm owner at all and increased protection was given to squatter families on a change of farm occupancy. In addition the new complete Resident Labourers Ordinance was not implemented until August 1940 when the government had earmarked a small resettlement area.

But the safeguards did not really strike at the root of the problem which, despite the assertions of Scott and of Brooke-Popham that removal would be gradual and painless, remained that expressed by the Kiambu chiefs in 1935: 'It should be remembered that 110,000 people who are living outside of the native lands will be turned off in the near future. Where will such people go?'[52] A further complicating factor was found to be that of difficulties arising from cattle disease. Squatter stock dipped and inoculated in order to live in disease-free areas was discovered to succumb quickly to other diseases on return to the changed environment of the reserves. The majority of the surplus stock could not be returned to the reserves at all on account of quarantine rules or the difficulty of transport and had to be sold, usually at a poor price.

Some of the evicted squatters went to live in the Maasai Reserve; of these a number were accepted but others were forced to move on either by the Maasai or by the administration. The government's plans provided for the resettlement of others at Olenguruone, on the south side of the Mau, but the land was remote and unsuitable. Other landless Kikuyu were also to be settled there; Olenguruone quickly became an area of major disaffection and unrest in the next decade.

By 1939 the total number of Africans resident on European farms had dropped by over 30,000 from the figure of 150,000 thought to have been the peak, although even this considerable figure may nevertheless have been an underestimate. Raids to find and remove illegal squatters and excess stock occupied a great deal of the time of the small Labour Section field staff. Moreover this reduction did nothing to solve the essential weaknesses of the system which, with the problems of reserve population and squatter stock, was to worsen in the war years.[53]

The Business Community

As noted in the previous chapter a second group of Europeans, the business community, was beginning to exercise an influence in Kenya. These included the managers of the local banks, owners and directors of large commercial undertakings in Nairobi and Mombasa, and the managers of the major plantations particularly those owned overseas. In 1936 Byrne told one of the officials at the Colonial Office that he relied on people such as the head of Barclay's Bank in Kenya whom he had put on the Expenditure Advisory Committee. He also pointed out that the leaders in the plantation industry and those in commerce and mining preferred to deal directly with the government rather than through the settler politicians. He urged the Colonial Office, therefore, not to take the settler claque as representative of the European economic interests in the colony.[54] This view was endorsed by the influential London Joint East Africa Board, representing in London the large commercial interests in East Africa.

The businessmen differed from the settler community in certain important aspects. Some were less committed to the system of white settlement since they represented companies which were commercially successful in colonies where there were no settlers. Some of their personnel were more transitory, and, therefore, could take a more objective view of their economic interests than those committed to stay in the colony. Some represented companies such as Brooke Bond which had a history of successful paternalism elsewhere and had the capital to support such policies. On the whole they tended to be less militant than the settlers. In the great debate over income tax, the Nairobi Chamber of Commerce, while reluctant to see the new taxes come into force, recognized that some credible alternative had to be put forward.[55] They were, as well, more willing to listen to the Colonial Office and to the Labour Section when it urged modern labour legislation, minimum standards and the like. For instance in 1926 the Mombasa Chamber of Commerce told the Association of Chambers of Commerce that it was '... the opinion of this Chamber that it is essentially a matter for the Administration of this Colony to devise means for solving the labour difficulties'.[56] This was not creeping liberalism but a matter of self-interest; international experience had persuaded some to try to kill labour discontent by kindness, a view which dovetailed with that of many Colonial Office officials who, therefore, found more of a similarity of view with the businessmen than with the settlers. F. J. (later Sir Frederick) Pedler, for instance, who assisted Lord Hailey in his famous survey and who co-authored an influential memorandum on wages in Kenya in 1939 subsequently left the Colonial Office for the United Africa Company. This point of view would grow in strength over the next decade but only become completely triumphant in the nineteen-fifties. It is not possible however to differentiate completely between the settler and the commercial communities. Cavendish-Bentinck, for instance, was a director of Equator Saw Mills, Kenya Consolidated Goldfields and other companies.

The tradition of business paternalism established at Magadi continued in the nineteen-thirties. The tea companies at Kericho which had been expanding since the mid-twenties patterned themselves after Magadi and provided good housing, reasonable wages and amenities although they fell foul of the redoubtable Owen on the use of juvenile labour as pickers. The N.A.D. reports continued to comment on the excellence of the tea estates as employers, the major estates producing houses of permanent concrete, well lit and ventilated, with glazed windows and bunks, and adding hospitals despite the Depression conditions.[57]

Another area of economic expansion was gold mining. Gold was found near Kakamega in 1931, and amid violent controversy reaching the House of Commons over the government's mineral rights in a native reserve, a mushroom mining industry was able to employ as many as 450 Europeans and 10,000 Africans by 1933. Conditions in the mines were, by the standards of the time, mostly satisfactory. The larger companies, following the example of the Kericho tea estates and Magadi, offered good terms—decent food and adequate housing of good mud and wattle huts in clean and supervised labour lines, though the supervision might vary in quality. On the smaller mines less satisfactory conditions were partially eased by the number of casual employees who were able to return to their homes at night. Some of the mines had their own hospital or dispensary, others shared one. The accident rate was small, much of the work being on the surface, and there was no mining disease risk. The administration, acutely aware of the scandal over mineral rights, was determined not to have a second storm over labour conditions.[58] The peak year for employment was 1935; thereafter the numbers employed fell as production declined.

But the majority of employers in the mid-thirties were oblivious to such considerations. In Mombasa, for instance, the companies operating the port made profits throughout the decade but none the less reduced the pay of the dock-workers and were unwilling to consider any improvement in their condition until the general strike in 1939.[59] Since the conventional wisdom of the time held that the urban African was only a temporary worker who would return to the reserve and since the urban slums were less obviously the fault of one employer as they would be in the rural areas, most business concerns chose to ignore the problem. In numbers, moreover, the business community was pre-eminently one of small businesses owned and operated by local Europeans and Asians. The profit margins were small and the temptation to oppress the labour force consequently large. Such small European businessmen usually allied with the settlers and attempted to use the chambers of commerce, particularly in Nairobi, as their vehicle of expression.

Overall labour usage remained inefficient. Some limited efforts were made during the Depression to use men less wastefully, but the underlying belief in cheap labour prevented any effective attempt to cut the circle of low wages, migrant labour, low purchasing power, little incentive and low productivity. Some changes did occur, notably the increased use of sisal estate machinery, the motor lorry, and of tractors which on a well-run farm could reduce the labour force by half. At the root of labour inefficiency, though, was the migrant system; a man with one foot albeit precariously in the reserves coming out to work for six or nine months in the year and paid accordingly would not develop any lasting interest or pride in his work or see his personal efficiency as his own road to prosperity; the N.A.D. in 1937 estimated that on average it required two and one-half men to fill an employer's requirement of one man throughout the year.

One issue, however, brought all European businessmen together. That was the challenge of Asian commerce and of the Asian artisan. The Asian businessman invariably undercut the European. One way to strike back was to employ cheaper African labour rather than Asian artisans. This had been the object of the private labour exchange noted in the previous chapter. But cheap labour was not really cheap because it was not skilled. Most Africans did not possess the necessary skills to replace the Asian artisan. This in turn brought some European employers to support technical training for Africans. Shell, Texaco and the Kenya Bus Company all started programmes of their own. The Railway had its own training school. Another source was the Native Industrial Training Depot. In the late nineteen-twenties the number of students increased, and the standards were improved. Pim noted in his report that '... the school has filled a useful purpose; it supplies Native artisans for work in the European areas on wages considerably lower than those paid to Indian artisans ...'[60] This was particularly important for companies such as George Blowers, Ltd. and W. H. Lewis and Son in the building trade where the pressure of competition was very severe.

The nineteen-thirties also saw the rise of radical trade unionism among the Asian artisans in the building trade. Thus support for African technical education could both encourage competition between African and Asian in the labour market and also strike a blow at Asian trade unionism. In 1922 there had been a brief confrontation between European employers and Asian artisans which foreshadowed the events of the thirties. When the government and the Railway decided to reduce the salaries of their Asian staff by 10 per cent there was an immediate reaction. The Railway Artisan Union came into existence to defend these workers, but the Railway, by dismissing or deporting many of the executive, finally broke the union in 1923.[61] Meanwhile the private employers had decided to follow the example of the government. They formed an employer's committee and agreed on joint action 'to bring the country into line with the Government and Railway workshops'. George Blowers explained that the employers were seeking either longer hours or lower pay because the artisans worked for more than eight hours for the Indian contractors, thereby giving them a 22 per cent advantage over their European rivals. He appealed to the white community to support the European contractors and urged a clause in all building contracts to forbid sub-contracting. About 200 *fundis* went on strike, but they could not prevent a 10 per cent reduction in salaries.[62]

In 1931 the Asian employees of W. H. Lewis and Son went on strike, thereby delaying construction of the Nairobi Municipal Market. They formed an organization called the Workers' Protection Society under Bhagat Singh. W. H. Lewis countered by importing Africans, Arabs and Coast Indians to break the strike. This, combined with the economic circumstances of the Depression, broke the strike and caused the collapse of the union.[63] Some years later a large contractor was interviewed by the *Kenya Weekly News* and said that he was not very alarmed about the future. He added that '... more and more he was using African artisans, and if the Indians started to play up in a few years time he would not be employing any Indians at all. And he gave me some hair-raising figures of the sum that he had paid Indian fundis in his time.'[64]

In the mid nineteen-thirties Makhan Singh, who was to become the best known trade unionist of the late thirties and forties, formed Kenya's first durable mass trade union—the Labour Trade Union.[65] In 1937 he called a protracted strike, first of the Asian contractors, then of the European. The strike was aimed particularly at George Blowers Ltd. who promptly hired Africans in training at the Native Industrial Training Depot as strike breakers.[66] Towards the end of the month, W. H. Lewis came to the aid of Blowers by locking out its artisans. The firm joined the lockout because it believed that it had to '... support the affected employers in their efforts to counter the activities of the "Labour Trade Union of Kenya"'. But it went on to say that it had 'no objections to the stonemasons forming a body of their own and presenting any grievances they may have...'[67] B. G. Moulton of the Motor Service Company, another victim of the strike, probably spoke for most of the larger European employers when he wrote to the *East African Standard* that the real exploiters were the Asian contractors. He charged that the strike was designed 'to confirm the authority of the Union as the dictator of the relationship between employers and employed' and that recognition of a 'semi-political organization' would inevitably lead to confusion. That was the rhetorical part of the letter; the reality was the revelation that the employers had offered higher pay and the recognition of a properly constituted trade union. Moulton went on to say that the employers would welcome both an employers' federation and trade unions 'devoid of all political tendencies' and composed of 'men of standing in the trades concerned'.[68]

The *East African Standard* was also in favour of legislation along these lines. It first cast a nostalgic eye backwards: '... it has always been believed that relations between employers and employed were sufficiently good to avoid recourse in an African country to methods which have become part of industrial life in the older communities'. It recognized, however, that those days were passed:

> ... Trade Unionism should be recognized and properly established by legislation ... all those who are responsible for the welfare of the community ... should make it part of their business to see that their functions and responsibilities are properly developed within the framework of a structure to which the whole country has agreed ... what is important is that before the movement spreads, its future progress should be properly visualised and regulated giving full opportunity to bodies legitimately formed to look after legitimate industrial and social interests ...

It believed that the African should not be introduced to labour agitation '... by the slogans and methods which are now being put before him by a group of people competing with him for a living'. Nor should recognition allow for general unions, irresponsible sympathy strikes or the dishonouring of agreements. Three days later the paper welcomed the introduction of trade union legislation which would guide such bodies along proper lines and prohibit political involvement.[69]

Later in May Moulton wrote a second letter to the *East African Standard* in which he said that the employers had already offered to negotiate but that the most important obstacle was the lower pay offered by the Asian employers and accepted by the union.[70] Some of the European employers were beginning to realize that either trade union action or minimum wage legislation might go some way towards improving their competitive advantage. Early in the strike one correspondent had written to the *East African Standard* saying, 'personally I believe many employers would welcome a properly constituted organization which would regulate rates of wages among all employers which would certainly put them in a fairer and better position to avoid uneconomical price cutting ...'[71] In May Percy C. Green, a Nairobi contractor, wrote that a minimum wage was necessary as the 25 per cent increase demanded by the union would favour the employers paying the lowest wages.[72] Finally in early June the two major contractors offered 10 per cent and recommended that the Minimum Wage Ordinance of 1932 be put into effect and that arbitration machinery be set up.[73] All in all the strike showed that some Nairobi employers were prepared to step gingerly into the modern world of labour relations. They were not prepared to go any further than they thought they needed to, but they seemed prepared to accept company unions or perhaps more accurately some form of arbitration procedure within their companies. They also seemed willing to accept that wages to some extent would have to adjust to market conditions. As the *East African Standard said*, '... the principal cause [of the strike] being the increasing cost of living and the feeling that the profits of prosperity should be shared'.[74]

But there still remained that most persistent of European views—that all could be put well if only the government would act firmly. Even those who recognized that living conditions were not all they might be wished the government to suppress agitation, and only then to make right the things that were wrong. The important point was for the action to be undertaken on its merits, not because the Africans or the Asians demanded it. It was essentially a matter of face. During the Mombasa strike in 1939 the *East African Standard* freely admitted the appalling conditions in the city and recommended an inquiry to settle the grievances. But it also saw the strike as the result of government weakness. 'Agitation', it stated, 'it allowed to proceed without firm official retaliation.'[75] It continued the next day:

> Behind movements of this kind there is always irresponsible agitation and whatever may be the rights or wrongs of the various claims which are put forward in a wrong atmosphere, the State cannot remain indifferent to inflaming influences or neglect to take firm and prompt action to discourage those who see in disturbing conditions an opportunity for exploitation.
>
> We hope that those responsible for its [policy] application are not unaware of the relationship between Government firmness and prestige and the picture of mobs of illiterate and irresponsible Africans careering about Mombasa and threatening to invade the colony's main port to prevent peaceful citizens from working.[76]

The principal difficulty of the major employers was a lack of organization. They preferred to work individually and privately—the casual chat in the club rather than the public pronouncement. This procedure, together with the weighting of Legislative Council seats noted earlier, had its liabilities as it allowed the representatives of the white farmers completely to dominate the local political scene. When J. A. Cable, formerly editor of the *Times of East Africa,* complained of this to the Colonial Office, an official, Flood, minuted:

> When he talks about the 'foolish politicians' of Kenya he is probably right, but the trouble is that the people in Kenya who are not 'foolish politicians' and do not see eye to eye with them remain absolutely silent. As a result, the settlers of Kenya are represented by the politicians and there is a complete absence of any indication that the politicians do not really count for as much as they pretend . . .[77]

The Civil Servants

The Colonial Office in London was served during the nineteen-thirties by a number of remarkable civil servants who wished to make the empire run efficiently and justly, who did not regard Kenya as the centre of their world, who viewed the activities of the settlers with some contempt, and who had a considerable amount of local knowledge at their command with which to deal with the problems of Kenya.

The most dyspeptic was J. E. W. Flood, an Assistant Secretary, who minuted in 1936 that '. . . Kenya is not of itself important in the scheme of things . . .' He did not think that the empire would have lost much if all Kenya's trade were to disappear and he suggested that 'the fact that a man goes and lives in Kenya does not *ipso facto* qualify him to be regarded as a superior being who must be assisted whenever he gets into hot water . . .'[78] He did not really believe that the Africans wanted the Europeans in Kenya and, as a consequence, he thought the most sensible policy was the one which interfered the least with the Africans.[79] Nor was he especially impressed by white settlement. 'My own private view', he minuted, 'is that white settlement is for economic and medical (they all go "nervy") reasons utterly hopeless and doomed to damnation.'[80] He was not however a friend of the liberals and of the humanitarians, and considered for instance the creation of an Africa Committee by the Anti-Slavery and Aborigines Protection Society as 'a distinct menace to good government'.[81] In other words, he believed that the Colonial Office and the colonial civil service, and they alone, could run the empire efficiently, profitably and high-mindedly. This point of view provided the background for much of the discussion of labour issues in London in the nineteen-thirties. Moreover, the civil servants were fortunate in their secretaries of state, particularly in the late thirties when Ormsby-Gore and Malcolm MacDonald had a considerable interest in policy in Kenya.[82]

A new pattern had been set by the Labour government in 1929 which included Lord Passfield as Colonial Secretary and Dr. Drummond Shiels as Parliamentary Under-Secretary. Passfield first curbed a number of settler political claims and then, in his 1930 Memorandum or Native Policy, re-asserted in theory the primacy of African interests and the British government's sole responsibility for them. He followed this up by appointing Byrne as Governor whose strong personality and attacks on the practice of 'government by agreement' we have already noted. On the labour front, both from its nature as a political party and from experience of labour unrest in India in the late nineteen-twenties, the new government determined on reform, the details lying initially in the hands of Shiels. A Colonial Office Labour Committee of specialist officials was established in 1929, and their work and the new political winds can be seen in Shiels's speeches to the 1930 Conference of Colonial Governors where labour problems were fully discussed. Shiels asked the colonial governments to review their labour legislation not only in the light of the new I.L.O. requirements but also in its general suitability with particular regard to penal contract provisions, protection for women and children, workmen's compensation and factory legislation, low wage levels and the possibility of minimum wage legislation, trade unions, and related subjects such as the enfranchisement of workers, taxation and provision for old age.[83]

This enthusiastic start was followed by a series of Colonial Office despatches, the first in September 1930 urging governments to pass simple trade union legislation protecting the right to strike and providing for the registration of trade unions. A despatch in 1931 emphasized the importance of I.L.O. conventions, and another in 1932 suggested simple legislation to prescribe minimum wages for areas or categories of workers. Throughout the remainder of the decade a steady flow of despatches, some enclosing model ordinances, repeatedly urged attention to the provision of workmen's compensation, factory inspection, statutory industrial disputes, arbitration and inquiry procedure, minimum wages for particular occupations and cost of living indices, low wage levels and minimum wage fixing. Most important of all, colonial governments were pressed to establish labour departments free from the provincial administration and staffed by trained specialist officers. On this latter subject both Ormsby-Gore and MacDonald, in their turns as Colonial Secretary, laid great emphasis, strong parliamentary pressures in Britain and industrial troubles in Northern Rhodesia, the West Indies and Mauritius adding to their concern.[84] To maintain and further this initiative, a Labour Adviser to the Colonial Secretary was appointed in 1938, a Social Services Department with specialist labour staff set up within the Colonial Office in 1939, and training courses in Britain for colonial labour officers begun in the same year.[85] Finally in 1940 the Colonial Development and Welfare Act stated that no development schemes would be approved in territories whose legislation failed to protect trade unions, ensured fair wages clauses in public contracts and forbade the regular employment of children under fourteen.

An important stimulus to this initiative had been the I.L.O. Apart from direct legal implications, the I.L.O. conventions or the rumours of impending conventions could be useful sticks with which Colonial Office officials could beat the local colonial governments. During the nineteen-thirties they also gave a handle to the colonial critics of the Labour Party, notably Arthur Creech Jones. From 1938 Sir Walter (later Lord) Citrine, much moved by his work on a royal commission in the West Indies of that year, used his power at the T.U.C. to advance the cause of labour reform within the colonial empire along the lines of the I.L.O. conventions.[86] Three Conventions concerning Women, Young Persons and Children adopted in 1920, 1921 and 1922, a Convention on Minimum Wages adopted in 1928, a Forced Labour Convention (the subject of an especially careful study by an I.L.O. committee of experts which had included Lugard) adopted in 1930, a Convention on the Recruiting of Indigenous Workers adopted in 1936 and two Conventions adopted in 1939, one concerning Contracts of Employment and the other on Penal Sanctions were all made, via the Colonial Office, the subject of Kenya legislation during the decade. Other conventions of more limited relevance also had an effect in Kenya through different legal procedures such as the British Orders in Council applying maritime conventions. The actions of the I.L.O. were much resented by the settlers. When C. J. Curtis of the Nakuru District Council visited the Colonial Office in 1938 to complain that it was '... much too ready to tie the hands of employers in our Colonies by undue subservience to Geneva ideas', he cannot have been very happy with the answer recorded by one of the officials:

> As regards the recent legislation, I told him that far from it being relaxed in the future there was every prospect that in various respects it might have to be tightened up as a result of the Conventions on contract labour and penal sanctions which will probably be adopted at Geneva next year.[87]

How far were these enlightened forces successful in improving the lot of a labourer in the Kenya of the nineteen-thirties? The answers vary greatly according to the field; overall the achievement is disappointing. Settler political power was used either to postpone or to emasculate most of the Kenya legislation. In 1937 Shiels complained that legislation was too often in a permissive form. 'Thus', he said, 'the Governor might be empowered to establish local committees for various purposes, which were, in practice, not appointed. For instance, the minimum wage convention [of the I.L.O.] was followed by general legislation in almost all the Crown colonies, but the local machinery to start such innovations functioning was created only in St. Lucia . . .'[88]

Furthermore the Depression weakened the fibre of the local government. Economy blighted practically every aspect of its operations. It seemed frequently as though administrative officers were engaged solely in raising taxes and cutting expenditure. Economic theory and colonial practice demanded that the budget be balanced, thereby ensuring that money could not be available for social services or other new departures. Instead the administration cut its services in the interests of economy, in particular reducing African medical services and closing some of the labour rest camps.[89] The *kipande* system, on the other hand, was maintained in full operation despite a recommendation for its abolition by the government's own Economic Advisory Committee. The emphasis on taxation and economy bred an arid and frequently oppressive atmosphere in the secretariat—a 'dismal thrift' in the words of Margery Perham.[90] In 1939 Elspeth Huxley called the local Kenya government ' . . . one of the most apathetic and unenterprising in the world'.[91]

The execution of the policy lay heavily on the district administration where an officer's reputation could still depend on the tax he gathered. In the collection some old or unfit, or others not far below the minimum apparent age, were often made to pay. The apparent or sometimes real lack of occupation in an area led to abuses of power by exasperated district officers with ruthless consequences such as the confiscation of stock until tax was paid, or occasionally, chiefs and tribal police physically beating people. The district commissioner in Kitui noted in 1938 that 'there is little doubt that much of the Hut and Poll Tax from this area . . . is obtained by questionable methods and will continue to be so until some method of obtaining cash such as cotton-growing can be installed'.[92] To a man who claimed he had no money to pay tax the answer was often the old exhortation to go and earn it.

Tax collection always involved an enormous percentage of the time and energy of the district administration—of a district officer's seven or eight safaris each year, five or six would be for taxation work. Tax came therefore to alienate the government, which was seen as a greedy institution, from the people who would tell a sympathetic listener that they did not want what taxation purchased—roads, railways or police. Confusion was increased by the use of the same Swahili word, *kodi*, for tax, rate and rent.[93] All this was one inevitable result of the taxation philosophy of the time; to even the more liberal government officers, Africans were thought of as tribal groups to be taxed as such, rather than as individuals to be taxed according to any ability to pay, without necessarily any provision of direct services equal to their contribution in return, and the money for the tax payment being earned by work for Europeans.

Flood attacked a report on the taxation of Africans produced by the Kenya government in 1936:

> Reading this report makes me think that some of the people in Kenya are far too unsympathetic towards the native population. I, myself, take the somewhat queer view that we owe more of a duty to the native population than to get work, money, and economic crops out of them. Forty years ago

no native in Kenya had any money at all, and at present they work for ridiculously small wages ... With people who receive low wages (even though their wants are few) it is not right to extract money without regard to the conditions under which they live. I do not believe they want us in Kenya, and the way to make them more resigned to white man's rule is not to extract money from them and endeavour to hem them in at every turn. The Kenya attitude ... sometimes strikes me as not, what is the least that we can interfere with the black man, but how much can we safely take away from him I do not like it.[94]

Furthermore the settlers used the Depression to step up their traditional attacks on the civil service. Arthur Bemister, unofficial member for Mombasa, wrote to Scott in 1932:

... The present policy of the education department is nothing but extravagant inefficiency and has nothing to recommend it at all. It is designed to tie on the necks of the taxpayers enormous commitments which they cannot support but which will produce a heavy crop of pension etc. liabilities without any advantage to the inhabitants of Kenya.

We must do away with these scientific demagogues who are guided by the exquisite language of philosophic dons who have never studied either the requirements or the limitations of the peoples they are alleged to be educating.[95]

The settlers hoped that the Depression would force the government to create an economy committee in which they could wield the axe on the civil servants as in the early nineteen-twenties. In this they were not successful for the economy commissions were administrative rather than settler bodies. Furthermore Byrne, after making an initial retrenchment of £500,000, refused to make any further substantial cuts in the budget, preferring to run a deficit until 1934. However, the civil servants had to pay a levy on their salaries for five years before income tax was introduced for the European community.[96]

The settlers also pressed for the creation of a local European civil service. This would simultaneously provide employment for the settlers' children in the future, bring the service more fully under local control, and save money because the salaries would be lower and the pension benefits curtailed. Local European and specifically Asian civil service structures duly came into existence in 1935, but they were largely filled, especially in the European service, by expatriate personnel.[97] The settlers' aims had created a great sense of bitterness in the civil service. For instance in 1936 E. B. Hosking, the President of the European Civil Servants' Association and a future Chief Native Commissioner, wrote anxiously to Major R. D. (later Sir Ralph) Furse at the Colonial Office complaining of lack of security and political attacks by the settlers. He also expressed his contempt for the local European candidates for the service.[98]

Byrne, who as Governor of Sierra Leone had attended the 1930 conference and was in full sympathy with the aims of Shiels, tried to ensure that the service was defended from settler attack and that his Colonial Office instructions were obeyed. When there seemed to be little relevance or cost to the employer, the passage of legislation was smooth. But where there was an immediate cost, either direct in an area such as workmen's compensation or indirect through taxation to pay for a labour department, legislation was delayed; employers argued that economic conditions prohibited the expense. In general, too, the level of development of the reforms proposed by the Colonial Office was not always needed by Kenya at this time; for example, arbitration in trade disputes procedure was a low priority for scattered estate labourers. Nor could purely labour reforms redress an economic balance loaded against the labourer. But one of the labourers' major needs, an expanded autonomous and specialist labour department, was planned for establishment in 1940, six Kenya officers, all of course European, being sent on the first colonial labour officers' course in London in 1939.

The Labour Section continued its limited but useful work in the nineteen-thirties. By and large it escaped the economy axe. Pim recommended no reductions since, in his view, the work was heavy and useful. However, the post of Principal Labour Officer (formerly Principal Labour Inspector) was not filled when Fisher retired in 1934.[99] P. de V. 'Digger' Allen was acting Principal Labour Officer for three years until finally in 1937 he became the permanent head of the section.[100] Moreover prior to 1940 Kenya had refused to set up a specialist labour department despite circular despatches from the Colonial Office in 1935 and 1937 and pressure from such bodies as the Anti-Slavery Society. An additional officer, however, was added in 1938. Staff shortages were sometimes overcome by borrowing administrative officers, particularly when labour inspectors went on leave.

The Labour Section was successful in establishing tolerable conditions in most contractors' camps and on large estates, if not on all the isolated farms and Asian secondary and tertiary industries. Improved inspection, medical examination procedure, and the plentiful supply of men extinguished the last abuses of the recruiting system. The number of inspections carried out by the three to five officers rose each year from 562 in 1931 to 863 in 1934 and 1,233 in 1938.[101] Medical examinations of recruited men however were still not the invariable rule. Examinations of men at Kisumu could only take place two days a week; on the other days the labour officer, in attesting the contracts, merely weeded out those appearing unfit. Labour recruited in North or South Nyanza was usually not examined at all.[102] Inspectors continued to recover wages and arrange for compensation for injury. In 1933, for example, the Labour Section recovered £2,337 out of £2,753 wages claimed; in 1938 £1,751 out of £2,787. In 1938 £491 18s. was rcovered from employers as compensation for injury.[103] The section's work was extended to assist trained artisans and clerks to find employment, but no proper labour exchange system was instituted. Conditions, in particular housing, on the Coast sisal estates were improved to reinforce the successful campaign waged by the Medical Department against worm diseases among the Digo. The section's failure, however, to post a labour officer to Mombasa, and the government's consequent lack of knowledge of conditions there was to prove a major error. The failure clearly indicated the primary orientation of the section towards rural labour. In general the time of effective inspection by men whose chief qualifications were character rather than any specialist training was over by the end of the nineteen-thirties. The fact that Kenya was almost the last major British colony to establish a labour department is a significant commentary on the political and economic conditions of a colony with so many men in wage employment.

In the late nineteen-thirties the Colonial Office was sometimes called on to resist regressive tendencies, particularly when Brooke-Popham took over from Byrne as Governor. Brooke-Popham wanted to reissue Grigg's labour circular of 1927. 'It expresses', he said, 'very nearly what my views are on the subject and I have drawn the attention of one Provincial Commissioner to the circular.' The Colonial Office was aghast. Ormsby-Gore wrote back tactfully: 'But, in any case, things have gone a long way since that circular was issued, and I have very grave doubts whether it could have received approval here if it had been put forward now.' The officials were more candid, Flood minuting, 'Does anyone really believe in the "educative value of labour" on a European farm?' Sir Cecil Bottomley noted, 'But we have got past the stage when we can preach the gospel of industry from the text of shortage of labour for the European farms.'[104]

The labour legislation of the nineteen-thirties was the result of the interplay of the forces noted above. It was of course one thing to pass legislation; it was quite another to enforce it. Gradually through the decade, however, a legal structure for protection, social welfare and the regulation of disputes came into existence. Although in practice it was frequently frustrated and sometimes over-ambitious, the structure was there and in 1939 and 1940 it became clear that MacDonald as Secretary of State wished to put some teeth in it.

Minimum wage legislation was one example of the problem. In 1932 this was pressed on the Kenya government by the Colonial Office, Britain having adopted the relevant I.L.O. convention of 1928 by which each ratifying member agreed to create or maintain minimum wage fixing machinery. The Kenya government resisted and urged on the Colonial Secretary that 'the creation of such machinery would be premature in Kenya at the present time and indeed for a large number of years, and that nothing in the present state of the Colony or its state in the immediate future so far as it is possible to foresee it, justifies the setting up of an elaborate system of trade boards and arbitration tribunals'.[105] In other words it was felt that minimum wage legislation would inevitably lead to legal structures for determining all wages—a notion that was unacceptable to the white farming community. The Colonial Secretary nevertheless insisted, and an ordinance was passed which gave the Governor-in-Council powers to fix minimum wages for any area or occupation and to establish advisory boards for that purpose.[106] Despite the pressure of some businessmen in the late nineteen-thirties in favour of a minimum wage order, none was made under the ordinance prior to 1939, and the government's description of the legislation as 'merely permissive', published in the *Gazette*, reflected the spirit as well as the letter of this law.[107]

Another problem was workmen's compensation. The mines under an amendment to the Mining Ordinance in 1934, and the Railway in respect of its permanent staff, were the only two occupations covered by any form of statutory injury or accident compensation scheme. Despite the work of the Labour Section the large majority of the colony's labour force enjoyed no statutory protection. The need for it in certain occupations such as the timber industry, building, and electrical power stations was great, and even in occupations of less hazard, such as sisal estate work or ordinary farm work with machinery, the inexperience of African employees led to many accidents. There is some evidence to suggest that safety devices fitted on machinery in Britain were removed from the same machinery when it was exported to East Africa.[108]

In the nineteen-twenties the government had several times proposed that an Employers Liability Ordinance be prepared, but settler opposition had led to its abandonment. In the mid-thirties the question was revived, and the Colonial Office circulated a model ordinance. In 1936 this was given general support by the Joint East Africa Board, the East African Section of the London Chamber of Commerce and by the Association of Chambers of Commerce of Eastern Africa, the latter remarking that the legislation would '... in all probability, be a safeguard to the employer'. A joint committee of the London organizations '... reached the conclusion that in the interests of employers and workmen alike, as well as of the economic advancement of the territories as a whole, uniform legislation in the matter is desirable, and that, in principle, the model ordinance should be accepted.'[109] There were, however, strong protests from the agricultural interests, particularly the Kenya Sisal Growers' Association. A year later the Joint East Africa Board received a revised version of the ordinance from the Colonial Office, and noted that '... many of the suggestions put forward by the joint sub-committee of the Board and the East African Section of the London Chamber of Commerce had been incorporated'. It praised the '... spirit of co-operation shown by the Colonial Office'. This draft was also sent out in 1937 to the colonial governments in Africa, legislation following quickly in West Africa but not in East.[110] By 1938 the Association of Chambers of Commerce had changed its views, and no action was taken in Kenya prior to 1939.[111] Throughout this period Makhan Singh repeatedly demanded legislation for minimum wages and workmen's compensation and these became staple items in the programme of the Labour Trade Union of East Africa.[112]

The first I.L.O. convention specifically concerned with colonial territories was that on forced labour adopted in 1930 and ratified by Britain in 1931. The convention forbade peacetime forced labour except for certain works of immediate need to a local community or work in an emergency, and it further laid down protective conditions for such work which it hoped would soon be abolished. The objects of the convention were translated into Kenya by a circular instruction that communal work could not take place in or near a district headquarters and, in 1932 by a new law, the Compulsory Labour (Regulation) Ordinance. This ordinance permitted minor local works and government porter duties, the latter being restricted in respect of loads, time and distance, but it laid down very specific conditions for any more onerous work. The governor's approval was required for work other than portering that took a man from his home, and never more than 25 per cent of fit adult males in any given area were to be called out. Market rates were to be paid, and special sections provided safeguards for workers in terms of injury, maximum days and hours, and work in unhealthy areas. Teachers and pupils were declared exempt, and the ordinance stated unequivocally that men were only to be called out when the work was of local benefit, when voluntary labour was unobtainable, and when the call-out would not lay too heavy a burden on the community.

The Convention of Associations unsuccessfully opposed this reform. Of the old system it claimed that if '... fairly administered [it] is of considerable advantage to the natives themselves ...' The Convention saw this as a purely altruistic resolution '... seeing that communal labour is never used for any purpose connected with European industry'. But Byrne was firm. He told the Convention '... that the whole question had been taken up by the League of Nations and that he was under definite orders to put an end to the practice. He agreed ... that it would take the form of a very gradual introduction forced upon us by the League.'[113]

In practice communal labour was even more inefficient than contract labour, the declining efficiency being one of the main reasons for its less frequent use. One administrative official made a survey of the output of communal labourers' production of bricks for a school; he found the average output to be two bricks per day. Some communal projects of obvious benefit to a community such as the Migwani Dam in Kitui district, and the road building to facilitate the sale of goods in Kikuyuland, could produce enthusiastic work. But the pastoral tribes saw less necessity for roads, and attempts to order them out for similar road construction met with hostility. Local Native Councils were given powers to order communal labour out for varying numbers of days per quarter; this labour was unpaid and individual chiefs were often unclear as to whether they were ordering men out as chiefs or as L.N.C. officials. Compulsory porter labour was now paid at local rates; in the worst conditions of the Depression both it and other unpaid communal labour were often actually welcomed by the majority of the men involved. At its best, too, it could still remain a community occasion of work, singing and dancing.[114]

But it appears that the numbers called out by the central government and its officers (i.e. excluding L.N.C.s) fell very rapidly; those recorded are set out in Appendix II, Table 3. In 1930 9,098 men were ordered out for 37,465 work days, an average of just over four days per man. By 1934 the figures were 3,534 men for 5,950 days, an average of 1.68, and by 1938 only 1,304 were called out for 3,071 days, an average of just over two days for each man.[115] But overall as an obligation communal labour, whether paid for the central government or unpaid for a L.N.C., had by 1939 ceased to be a serious burden on the African population; protests against it were inspired more by the past than by the present, and the works such as school buildings required by the L.N.C.s were generally of obvious value to the community as a whole.

New legislation for women and juveniles also became necessary as the number of women, juveniles and children in seasonal or occasionally full-time work grew, a growth accelerated by the Depression requirement for the cheapest possible labour, and by the expansion of the tea and pyrethrum estates. In 1938 a committee studying the question of juvenile and child labour estimated that about 36,000 over the age of ten were at work some time during the year, though there were fewer than 14,000 at any one time. The tea estates employed some 5,500 per month; 1,500 were at surface work on the Nyanza gold fields carrying pans of mud or sorting ore at a rate varying between Shs. 3/- and Shs. 7/- per month.[116] Sisal, coffee and pyrethrum estates employed large numbers seasonally, the building industry a smaller number. On tea estates conditions for juveniles, most considerably over twelve, were satisfactory; the work was light while food, housing and medical conditions were good, a few elementary schools were provided, and wages of Shs. 5/- to Shs. 7/- were offered for a prescribed number of tasks. An industrious juvenile could earn Shs. 9/- to Shs. 15/-. Conditions on the sisal estates were less good, in addition juveniles often had to make long journeys. The worst conditions, though, were in the towns where many juveniles worked in the building trades or as domestic servants, particularly for Asian employers.[117] Many of these boys were not under any parental supervision, drifting, homeless, and often turning to petty crime.

In 1933 the government passed the first Employment of Women, Young Persons and Children Ordinance.[118] It incorporated the requirements of the conventions adopted in the early nineteen-twenties. Restrictions were placed on the employment of women, young persons and children in ships and in industrial plants, in particular at night. Children under twelve were prohibited entirely from working both by day and at night, and women could only be employed at night in a family concern. In 1935 the ordinance was amended to prohibit night work by boys under sixteen.[119] A further amendment in 1936 prohibited underground work in mines by women, more as a result of a further I.L.O. requirement than any need in Kenya.[120]

In 1938 and 1939 Owen raised a considerable storm in England over the decision to sanction work at the age of ten in the new Employment of Servants Ordinance. He issued a pamphlet, *Child Labour in Kenya Colony*, spoke to various clerical groups, and wrote letters to the *Manchester Guardian.* Letters from M.P.s and other interested parties poured into the Secretary of State. He obviously considered the excuse of the Kenya government, namely an oversight in drafting, rather lame. He then ordered the government to raise the permitted age to twelve, to eliminate penal sanctions against employees under sixteen, and to set up a committee of inquiry which turned out to be the guise under which these proposals were eventually accepted in Kenya.[121] The committee duly reported as the Secretary of State had requested.[122] However, a new storm blew up in January 1939. Brooke-Popham tried to temporize on the matter of legislation by suggesting that the question of juvenile labour should be incorporated in a new consolidated labour law, which the Colonial Office rightly recognized as a stalling tactic. Meanwhile, the report of the committee had been made public. It was welcomed by both the incumbent and previous Bishops of Mombasa who felt that it vindicated the government, but it was denounced by Owen for failing to provide safeguards for children forced to work long distances from home and by the T.U.C. who believed that the minimum age of twelve was inadequate.[123] Finally in July the ordinance was published.[124] It included the clauses suggested by the Secretary of State, forbade the professional recruiting of juveniles and required the consent of parents for any juvenile recruited for work involving his absence from home at night. It was intended to enforce these provisions by an extension of the *kipande* system to juveniles at work. The outbreak of war, however, led to the deferring of the amending ordinance as staff were not available to extend the registration system. A new amending ordinance was prepared and enacted in 1943.[125]

The Employment of Servants Ordinance of 1938 dealt with other matters besides the age at which children could work. It incorporated the requirements of the 1936 I.L.O. Convention on Recruiting of Indigenous Workers.[126] This ordinance provided for stricter control of recruiters and labour agents. District labour officers were given powers to cancel juveniles' contracts. Medical and attestation procedures were strengthened for all labourers. Provisions set out requirements in respect of transport, necessities for the journey and for repatriation which could, by agreement, be extended to the labourers' families.[127] Despite the pressure of the I.L.O. the penal provisions of the old ordinance were retained, as they had been in the amended Registration of Natives Ordinance. Imprisonment, however, might only be awarded in default of the payment of a fine, an important option for the eight to nine hundred Africans prosecuted under the ordinance each year.[128]

In 1937, as has already been noted, a trade union ordinance was passed in order to meet the situation caused by the strikes of that year. In the years previous to 1937 Kenya had been frequently urged by the Colonial Office to enact such legislation but had refused on the traditional grounds that it was 'premature'.[129] The reluctance of the settler leadership to accept such legislation was reflected in the speech of Cavendish-Bentinck to the Legislative Council:

> I think when it was originally suggested a few years ago that a measure of this kind should be enacted, most members on this side of the Council at any rate, felt we were some way off the days of trade unions, that we did not want them, we had not reached that stage, and that it would be a pity to have an unnecessary Bill dealing with something we did not want and hoped would not happen for some years to come. For that reason legislation of this kind was not proceeded with. Latterly, and with regret, we have had occasion to see that some such measure is necessary. As a result, this model Bill has been produced.[130]

The intention of the government was made clear by the speech of the Attorney-General, H. C. (later Sir Harold) Willan, who introduced the bill by saying that it 'will only recognize trades unions which are run on proper lines and according to set principles . . .' He referred to the strikes of the Labour Trade Union remarking that '. . . it was apparent that there was an attempt to organize labour in Kenya under the guise of trades unions on a class basis. I am sure I have the support of all members of the Council when I say that it is repugnant to all right-thinking people, whether they are employers or are employees.'[131] The government feared that unregulated trade unionism would be politically subversive. This was emphasized in an editorial in the *East African Standard* welcoming the introduction of the bill:

...The debate on the introduction of the measure indicated some recognition of the fact that this Bill may in course of time, and in certain special conditions, play a very important part in the powers of the Administration for the maintenance of peace, order and good government. At the present moment, so far as we know, the Government has no specific powers, except the declaration of a state of emergency and the general statutory provisions which refer to seditious speeches and acts, which can be called into use against undesirable organisations and it is clearly important that in a country where so large a proportion of the population have still primitive standards of life and knowledge; the public and the state should be protected against unwholesome and dangerous agitators under the cloak of trade unionism.[132]

The ordinance guaranteed a registered trade union against actions on the grounds of conspiracy (when its objects were not criminal) and stated that a union was not criminal simply because it might act in restraint of trade, but this provided unions with only a vague defence against actions in tort or inducement to breach of contract. Later Cavendish-Bentinck stated that this was deliberate.[133] Unregistered trade unions might enjoy no such protection, and their members were also liable for prosecution under the ordinance. The ordinance neither safeguarded peaceful picketing nor guaranteed the legitimacy of subsidiary political objects, and it is doubtful, given the attitude of the Attorney-General whether by implication either would have been permissible. On the other hand it made no restrictions in respect of the language, education or any criminal record of trade union officers, nor did it closely restrict the range of subjects on which funds might be spent. It, however, remained general Colonial Office policy that although trade unions might be useful as a political safety-valve, unions must be primarily industrial and that workers of little or no education must be protected against abuse of power or funds by union officials.

The ordinance, therefore, included a procedure which gave the Registrar powers of supervision on first registration and later annually in respect of all the activities of any union and its officers, in particular in the matter of funds, their collection and expenditure, and the election of officers. Eligibility was limited to 'any combination' of workmen and others 'in any trade or business' to avoid the general union; in theory only people actually at work in the trade could join. There was provision neither for a federation, nor inter-territorial unions, nor probationary trade union registration procedure. Appeal against a refusal for registration could be made only to the governor and not to the courts. The I.L.O. conceded the registration requirement in 1939 provided than any refusals were limited to unions which failed to observe formalities 'not substantive' in character. But no trade unions led by Africans or with anything more than a small minority of African employees were registered under the ordinance.

The Secretary of State gave his assent to this bill but requested the Kenya government to make some provision for legalizing peaceful picketing and the protection of trade unions against actions of tort. A bill which would have safeguarded peaceful picketing was published in November 1939 but was not proclaimed until 1940. This included provisions on intimidation borrowed from the 1927 British legislation and much disliked by the British labour movement. It also laid down the manner in which unions could sue and be sued but which gave no protection from actions of tort.[134] The government also introduced in 1939 a Trade Disputes (Arbitration and Inquiry) Bill which provided for the creation of arbitration tribunals for a particular dispute, subject to the consent of both parties, and for boards of inquiry which the Governor might appoint without such consent. This bill also became law in 1940.[135]

MacDonald seemed determined to make 1939 a year to remember in terms of labour legislation in Kenya. It looked as though the Secretary of State was finally going to bring the policies of Shiels into operation and create the civil service paternalism which would, in the view of many officials, finally usher Kenya into the world of twentieth century labour relations. We have already seen how in January he refused to allow the Kenya government to temporize on the matter of juvenile labour. In March the government asked the Carnegie Foundation for a grant for an anthropological survey. 'The great service of the . . . survey', it said in its application, 'would thus lie in improving and strengthening understanding between the governors and the governed, the employers and the employees, the Europeans and the Africans.'[136] In May came the Trade Disputes (Abitration and Inquiry) Bill.

Two months later the Kenya government, alarmed by labour unrest in Nairobi and Mombasa, asked that the Nairobi corporation be empowered to secure a loan of £30,000 for the construction of African housing. The previous year *East Africa and Rhodesia* had welcomed Orde-Browne's report on labour in Northern Rhodesia, in particular the sections on housing; the paper had remarked, 'That drastic measures are needed for the improvement of the native quarters in and around many of the towns . . . of Eastern Africa and the Rhodesias will be denied by nobody.'[137] The Secretary of State immediately agreed to the housing proposal in principle, but in the next few months gathered information from his officials in London for a very full and significant despatch which went far beyond the immediate subject of housing in Nairobi.[138]

Meanwhile MacDonald dealt with one of the many complaints of Brooke-Popham that Africans and Asians circumvented the regular channels for hearing grievances by going immediately to Whitehall or to opposition M.P.s. In 1938 he had complained that the Railway Asian Union used V. L. McEntee, M.P. as a means of airing their protests. In July 1939 he was more than unusually annoyed with the Kikuyu Central Association for using this tactic in connection with the problems of the Kamba reserve. MacDonald sympathized but pointed out that colonial regulation, precedent and constitutional practice prevented him from ignoring either petitions or requests from M.P.s. The sting came at the end:

> The ideal solution would be for Africans to acquire such confidence in those who are appointed to represent their interests on Legislative Council and on such bodies as the Native Lands Trust Board that, when they feel like making appeals, they address them to that quarter. If a few sensible Africans could be nominated in course of time to places of responsibility in which they can constitutionally represent African interests, it might help divert the expression of political feeling into local channels.[139]

In the same month MacDonald wrote to Brooke-Popham to say that he hoped the trade union legislation of 1939 would help to decrease the ignorance of local trade unionists concerning the real objects of the government. 'The task of overcoming this kind of uninformed opposition and by degrees securing the confidence of embryo trade unions in the good intentions of the Government is one, he urged, 'which I am anxious should be undertaken by Colonial Labour Departments and Inspectorates, and in this connection I may instance the case of Trinidad, where a very unpromising situation was most successfully handled in this way.'[140]

War, however, was rapidly approaching. It was essential for the government to prevent serious unrest at such a time of crisis. But MacDonald, for more positive reasons as well, hoped to ensure that the outbreak of war would not be an excuse for dismantling or postponing social reform in the colonies. This was in marked contrast to the attitude of the Colonial Office in 1914. In a circular telegram on 15 September, MacDonald told the colonial governments:

> I am anxious to see existing social services and development activities disturbed as little as possible, both because serious retrenchment and consequential curtailment of services at present juncture might have very unfortunate effect on Colonial peoples and also because on grounds of policy it is important to maintain our reputation for enlightened Colonial administration. In particular I am anxious to avoid any retrenchment of personnel.[141]

A week later another circular telegram ordered colonial governments to increase the taxes on the wealthy and to impose an excess profits tax.[142]

Meanwhile the officials at the Colonial Office were preparing the response to Brooke-Popham's request concerning Nairobi housing. The minutes of three officials, F. J. Pedler, J. L. Keith and G. St. J. (later Sir Granville) Orde-Browne, suggested that the problem went far beyond this particular housing scheme, and Pedler set out the case for the high wage economy with settled urban workers with which Union Minière had begun to experiment in Katanga in 1927, which would become an article of faith with the Kenya Labour Department in the late nineteen-forties and fifties. Pedler's initial note said that 'the Nairobi Municipality is finding, as others have found before, that if you withhold political representation from the common people it costs you a lot to keep them contented'. In a longer minute he suggested that the Colonial Office should solicit more information on the reasons for strikes in Nairobi, and he considered the governor '... optimistic in expecting to calm the troubled waters with so little oil'. He was unhappy with the proposal to subsidize the housing. 'If wages are not enough to enable economic rents to be paid for decent accommodation, then wages will have to go up and Government should do all it can to assist the process, starting with raising its own rates for unskilled labour.' Two paragraphs dealt with the general question of wages in Kenya:

> 4. Many people in East Africa have very fixed ideas about the amount of money which ought to be paid to an African. There is sometimes a failure to recognize that the law of supply and demand may work in connection with African wages. Many people speak of it as rather shocking if an African is paid at more than the usually prevailing rate. The whole place still suffers

from a legacy of the time when African labour was usually more or less forced labour and when consequently a very low standard of performance was expected and given. My own feeling is that before very long East Africa will have to change over—probably very suddenly*—from low grade labour and very low wages to something much nearer the standard of European manual labour and the European labourer's wage.† The Government ought to be on the look-out for the beginning of that process and ought to boost it for all it's worth. I am afraid that it seems to me more likely that the Government of Kenya, with its present outlook, may range themselves on the side of those who try to resist this process.

* Suddenly, because once equilibrium is lost on the balance between low wages and low performance, there will be no stability until a new equilibrium is found on a different basis.

† It may be objected that it takes years for low-performance workers to improve their output. But the rapid increase in wages would probably bring rapid increase in output by (1) causing men who work for wages only a few months a year to be replaced by men who work permanently for wages, and therefore more efficiently. (2) enabling workers to live, and support families, on the wages instead of reserving their best energies for their independent cultivation, as they often do at present.

6. I may mention that I am convinced that the Governments in East Africa could go a long way in raising their rates for unskilled labour without spending any more money than they spend now. Of course it would have to be done on the basis of getting more work from each man, and that would mean that fewer men would receive wages.

From his experience with the municipal compound at Ndola Keith pointed out that 'attempts to increase the rentals of houses resulted in riots, but the outcry was not so much that rents were increased but that wages ought to be increased so as to allow the people to live under better conditions'. Like Pedler, Keith thought the fundamental problem was low wages and inefficient work. He hoped that there would be a general housing policy for he believed that *ad hoc* solutions such as that of Nairobi would not work. 'It aggravates the situation where evil conditions exist by dividing the African urban community into an upper class earning good salaries and a lower class living in slum conditions.' Pedler felt the same way. 'Moreover, it must be remembered', he minuted, 'that unrest is caused, not by absolute degrees of poverty but by the width of the gap which exists between the comforts people have and those they think they ought to enjoy. If the municipality provides really good housing for 902 Africans, will not the thousands of Africans who cannot enjoy the new houses become more restive when they see, by contrast, how wretched their own accommodation is?' Keith thought that a lot of money would be wasted until a coherent housing policy was enunciated, and he suggested that the Colonial Office had a good deal to learn from the Belgians in the matter of building decent urban communities.

Orde-Browne took a rather pessimistic view. 'I am interested to meet this problem again', he wrote, 'on a smaller scale it was acute when I first knew Nairobi, just thirty years ago.' He agreed with Pedler's views on wages but '... unfortunately, long advocacy of these in East Africa has so far had no appreciable result'. He also agreed with Keith that the housing was probably too little and too late. Nevertheless he supported the scheme—'any advance is better than doing nothing', and recommended the need for a comprehensive and far-sighted policy.

MacDonald's despatch grew out of these views. He reiterated the Colonial Office's support of the housing scheme. He recognized that it would probably be necessary to provide housing at less than economic rent, although he pointed out that '...it is unsound for public bodies to subsidize the wages of persons in private employment, particularly when, as in Kenya, those wages are very low'. He announced the formation of a common pool of experience in London concerning colonial housing and asked for the co-operation of the Kenya government in this regard. MacDonald concluded:

> 12. If for financial or other reasons it should prove impossible during war time to proceed with the housing scheme, it may be that the alternative of raising wages will have to be faced. At present there is a tendency for employers to acquiesce in a very low standard of performance by their native labourers, and the general wages level is correspondingly low. A change-over to a higher level should automatically bring a very great increase in performance by stabilizing labour, achieving increased discipline, and enabling workers to live and support families on their wages instead of reserving much of their energies for independent cultivation... I do not wish to suggest that either the Government or private employers can afford to pay higher wages for the same amount of work, but if the view is accepted that higher wages will pay for themselves in improved performance, this difficulty will not arise. If the exceptional conditions of war time should afford an opportunity for encouraging a general adjustment of wages policy in this direction, I trust that the opportunity will be carefully studied and not be allowed to pass.
>
> 13. At present the urban centres are probably unnecessarily crowded by large numbers of persons who are only intermittently employed. A policy of grading up wages and performance concurrently might so far reduce the number of African employees as to make it possible to ease the housing situation, through the return of large numbers to the native areas. It should also have the effect of alleviating any general shortage of labour that might exist in the colony.[143]

All that, however, was for the future. Meanwhile the nineteen-thirties had been a time of special trials for the African population since the Depression had combined with the moment at which population pressure began seriously to affect the labour market. As on many earlier occasions, the settler community found arguments to justify their economic superiority; this time it was argued that the Depression showed the 'interdependence' of the settler and his labour. When the former suffered, the latter must necessarily also, an argument elaborated to claim that Africans should be grateful to the European community for the employment opportunities they were offered. But the effect of this arrangement struck other eyes differently.

Dr. Julian Huxley wrote of one of the better Kenya estates in the nineteen-thirties: '...I could not help but be struck, in this my first glimpse of the white uplands of East Africa, by the contrast between the native conditions here and in the advanced Native Administrations I had just left in Tanganyika'. Huxley felt that the Africans had been removed from their traditional culture without any significant gain to themselves. 'It was the atmosphere rather than anything tangible.'[144] That atmosphere was bound to breed discontent in time.

Nor were all Africans oblivious to the economic realities of their situation. Dr. A. R. Paterson, the Chief Medical Officer, commissioned a poll of his African staff in 1939 on the relative merits of weekly or monthly salary arrangements. In his report he noted:

> One employee observes that unless the rate of wages is to be raised the monthly system should be retained as it has at least the advantage of concealing from the employee how small his wages actually are, and advances the suggestion that if a weekly wage system were to be instituted without a rise in rate it would result in a great scarcity of farm labourers, since in his view though a labourer might be satisfied while he got a lump sum of eight or ten shillings in his hand at the end of the month few full grown men would be willing to work from 6 a.m. to 4 p.m. for a week to get only Shs. 2/- or Shs. 2/50 at the end of it.[145]

Amid these general conditions of difficulty can be seen some open unrest; the sudden growth of religious sects such as the *Watu wa Mungu* and some revival of Mumboism, clan rivalries in North and Central Nyanza, the revolt of the Lumbwa *Laibons*, the rumoured Laibon-inspired disaffection among the Nandi, the slow growth in strength of the Luo *Piny Owacho* movement, the continuing activity of the Kikuyu Central Association, the formation of the Teita Hills and Ukamba Associations. All these were principally political, but most included a protest against the *kipande*, the boycotting of settler estates and of compulsory labour in their aims. The *Watu wa Mungu* was probably not alone in feeding on labour grievances. In 1937 the Native Affairs Department recorded that this movement was particularly strong among the Kikuyu resident labourers in the Naivasha area including among its 'peculiar rites' the instruction from God not to work.[146] For most Europeans these events, if understood at all, were but clouds on the horizon. Two strictly labour events—the rise of Makhan Singh and the general strike in Mombasa—indicated, however, that the age of confrontation was not far away.

APPENDIX II

Table 1

AFRICANS CONVICTED UNDER THE NATIVE REGISTRATION ORDINANCE

1930	4,697	1935	4,767
1931	5,293	1936	4,576
1932	4,610	1937	4,182
1933	3,092	1938	3,527
1934	3,605		

Source: *1938 Annual Report N.A.D.*

Table 2

REGISTERED ADULT MALE AFRICANS IN EMPLOYMENT (MONTHLY AVERAGE)

1930	157,359	1935	No figure available*
1931	141,473	1936	173,000
1932	132,089	1937	183,000
1933	141,085	1938	182,964
1934	No figure available*		

* Staff shortages prevented collection in 1934 and 1935.

Source: *Annual Reports, N.A.D.*

Table 3

COMPULSORY LABOUR

Year	Numbers Ordered out	Days worked	Average number of days per man
1930	9.098	37,465	4.12
1931	5,682	12,265	2.16
1932	7,381	13,779	1.86
1933	4,507	11,270	2.50
1934	3,534	5,950	1.68
1935	3,814	5,578	1.46
1936	2,791	5,620	2.01
1937	1,674	3,414	2.04
1938	1,304	3,071	2.35

Source: *Annual Reports, N.A.D.*

Table 4

INSPECTIONS CARRIED OUT BY LABOUR SECTION STAFF

1930	594	1935	1,010
1931	562	1936	976
1932	855	1937	1,195
1933	833	1938	1,233
1934	863		

Source: *1930 and 1938 Annual Reports. N.A.D.*

NOTES

1. Kerr to Oldham, 17 Feb 1927. Lothian papers.
2. Lord Francis Scott, 1879–1952. 6th son of 6th Duke of Buccleuch; educated Eton and Oxford; married daughter of 4th Earl of Minto; British Army 1899; A.D.C. Viceroy of India 1905; served South African War, First World War, Second World War (A.M.S. to G.O.C. E. Africa); M.L.C. and M.E.C. at various times to 1948.
3. C.O. 533/464, minute by Flood. Flood's view was not shared by Ormsby-Gore who wrote of Byrne '... quite frankly the present Governor, Byrne and his wife have given little satisfaction socially or in other capacities'. Ormsby-Gore to Brooke-Popham, 21 Oct 1936, Rhodes House papers.

Sir Joseph Byrne, 1874–1942. Educated St. George's College, Weybridge, Maison de Melle, Belgium, Lincoln's Inn; British Army 1893–1916; Inspector-Gen. R.I.C. 1916; Governor Seychelles 1922; Governor Sierra Leone 1927; Governor Kenya 1931.

4. Sir Robert Brooke-Popham, 1878–1953. Educated Haileybury and Sandhurst; British Army 1898; R.A.F. 1918; retired 1937 Air Chief Marshal; Governor Kenya 1936; C-in-C. Far East 1940; retired 1942. Two of the obvious reasons for his appointment as Governor were the need of a defence expert following the Italian occupation of Ethiopia, and patronage for the R.A.F. It is also possible that the appointment reflected some personal concern for Africans, particularly labourers, formed by Edward VIII during his visit to Kenya as Prince of Wales.
5. Kerr to Oldham, 17 Feb 1927. Lothian papers.
6. *The Times*, 12 March 1935; *Financial News*, 22 Feb 1935.
7. F. S. Joelson, 'East Africa and Rhodesia; Some Impressions of a Long Tour', *East Africa and Rhodesia*, 10 Sept 1936.
8. C.O. 533/463, Scott to Ormsby-Gore, 12 Dec 1936.
9. *The Times*, 26 Sept 1936.
10. C.O. 583/511, Brooke-Popham to MacDonald, 13 Dec 1938.

    Malcolm J. MacDonald, *qui vivit*. Son of Ramsay MacDonald; educated Bedales School, Petersfield and Oxford; member L.C.C. 1927; Lab. M.P. Bassetlaw 1929; Nat. Lab. M.P. Bassetlaw 1931; Nat. Govt. M.P. Ross and Cromarty 1936; Under-Secretary Dominions 1931; Secretary of State Dominions 1935, 1938; Secretary of State Colonies 1935, 1938; Minister of Health 1940; High Commissioner to Canada 1941; Governor-General Malaya, Singapore and British Borneo 1946; Commissioner General for U.K. in S.E. Asia 1948; High Commissioner to India 1955; Governor, Governor-General and High Commissioner to Kenya 1963; Special Representative East and Central Africa 1965; Co-Chairman, International Conference on Laos 1961; Chancellor Univ. of Malaya 1949; Chancellor Durham Univ. 1970.
11. For a more detailed account see G. Bennett, 'Settlers and Politics in Kenya', *History of East Africa*, II, eds. V. Harlow, E. M. Chilver, A. Smith, 1965 (hereafter *Oxford History East Africa*); George Bennett, *Kenya: A Political History*, 1963, viii.
12. *The Times*, 12 Sept 1935; *Manchester Guardian*, 26 Oct 1935.
13. *The Times*, 3 Aug, 14 Sept 1935.
14. Minutes of the Executive of the Colonists' Vigilance Committee, 13 Sept, 6 Oct 1935. By 'Elected' Grogan meant unofficial. Scott papers.
15. Major F. W. (later Sir Ferdinand) Cavendish-Bentinck, *qui vivit*. Educated Eton, Sandhurst, Germany; First World War (wounded, G.S.O. War Office); unsuccessful Liberal candidate South Kensington 1922; Vickers, Brussels Office 1923; Private Sec. Governor Uganda 1925; Hon. Sec. Kenya Convention of Associations 1930; M.L.C. and M.E.C. 1934–60; Member for Agriculture and Natural Resources 1945–55; Speaker Leg. Co. 1955–60.
16. *The Times*, 12 March, 7 May 1936.
17. C.O. 533/462, memorandum, 5 March 1936.
18. *East Africa and Rhodesia*, 10 Dec 1936.
19. C.O. 533/484, Brooke-Popham to Maffey, 4 Jan 1937.
20. C.O. 533/494, Wade to MacDonald, 26 Aug 1938 and enclosures.
21. For an examination of taxation in Kenya see Lord Hailey, *African Survey*, 1938, 570–5, and Margery Perham and Elspeth Huxley, *Race and Politics in Kenya*, 1955 ed., 105–123.
22. *Report of the Financial Commissioner (Lord Moyne) on Certain Questions in Kenya*, Cmd. 4093 of 1932, 22, 36.
23. Interview T. C. Colchester, 1970.
24. *Manchester Guardian*, 17 June 1939, letter from E. Gates.
25. These extra wives could sometimes contribute to the total production of the extended family either on the squatter's plot or at home in the reserves. Sometimes, however, they were inherited relatives or widows producing little or nothing.

Cmd. 4093 (Moyne Report) gives some interesting figures of the fall in price of certain African grown produce which created increased tax-payment difficulties in some districts.

26. L.N.C. expenditure was limited until the nineteen-forties by the concept that 25 per cent of their balances were to be kept as a famine reserve; famine relief had been the origin of some L.N.C. rates.
27. Pim Report '36: 'In the year 1933 148 persons were sentenced to imprisonment under the Hut and Poll Tax Ordinance and 8,561 to Detention Camp, in 1934 the corresponding figures were 1,357 and 8,520 and in 1935 they were 622 and 8,655. In the Kavirondo area a considerable proportion of the men were stated by the Chief Native Commissioner to be young and able-bodied men with a modern taste in clothes.'
28. Fabian Society, *Kenya: White Man's Country?*, 1943, 11.
29. Memorandum by Cavendish-Bentinck, 16 Feb 1939. Scott papers.
30. European population: 1926 —12,529
    1931 —16,811
31. C.O. 533/484. The Colonial Office attempted to prevent Kionange from con-
    1935/36—17,997
    tinuing his studies at Cambridge and when he had nevertheless completed them he was offered only a minor post in the Education Department.
32. Pim Report.
33. The Native Registration Amendment Ordinance, Ord 1 of 1938, *Kenya Gazette*, 3 May 1938. Offenders against the ordinance had the option of paying the fine open to them, peremptory imprisonment being replaced in the amendment. But not all magistrates offered the option and a circular had to be sent to magistrates reminding them of the option in December 1938. Somalis were removed from the jurisdiction of the ordinance, partly because the provisions concerning them had never been enforced. C.O. 533/483. For other details see C.O. 533/497, 533/510, 533/511.
34. C.O. 533/497, Tewson to MacDonald, 14 Nov 1938.
35. *Parliamentary Debates, Commons*, 15 March 1939.
36. Owen wrote in strong terms, bluntly stating that there was little freedom for Kenya's Africans, but *The Times* only printed his letter in the columns reserved for those of secondary importance. He had raised this matter in a visit to the Secretary of State in 1934, quoting the recommendation of the Report of the Joint Select Committee that sympathetic consideration be given to African views on the *kipande* but with no result.
37. R. M. Gatheru, *Child of Two Worlds*, 1964, 93. The *1935 Annual Report, N.A.D.* noted 25,145 books issued and 53,310 testimonials on record. The report commented that while most employers were generous in their remarks, a minority were not. The N.A.D. favoured the amendment of the ordinance to make voluntary the issue of a testimonial by the employer and asked for this legislation to be prepared; no change was made before 1939.

    By the end of 1938 37,454 Africans had applied for registration successfully, 1,730 were refused registration at the time of application on grounds of a criminal record, and 1,436 of those registered later lost their registration for misconduct. Of those debarred and de-registered, however, 1,731 were subsequently given provisional registration.
38. *Kenya Debates*, 28 Nov 1941.
39. J. Huxley, *Africa View*, 1931, 145.
40. *E.A.S.*, 4 Aug, 29 Sept, 6 Oct 1934.
41. C.O. 533/481 contains the typescript of *Rex v. Raymond Letcher.*
42. *Ibid.* contains the typescript of *Rex v. Jacobus Paulus Englebrecht and Kumutai arap Kibore.* Juries were more ready to convict Europeans in the thirties but usually with relatively light sentences. There were still cases, however, in which the Colonial Office thought justice was frustrated by the legal system, such as *Rex v. Stanley Deneby Watchman.* 'There are as you know great difficulties in administering justice in a county where the Jury accept the statement of one European against twenty natives.' C.O. 533/467, Harragin to Bushe, 9 July 1936.

43. C.O. 533/501 contains the typescript of the case of *Rex v. Wakahu wa Kihenya and Koine wa Rutinu,* before the Supreme Court of Kenya, July 1938.
44. C.O. 533/462 contains the typescript of *Rex v. Wesonga s/o Moya and Ndiwa s/o Rutinu*, Criminal Case 69 of 1936.
45. 1938 Annual Report, Kitui District, and *1938 Annual Report, N.A.D.* In November of that year the Kenya Sisal Company's estate at Mazongaleni went into liquidation, its directors in England making provision neither for pay nor for repatriation for its labour; 1,277 labourers were owed Shs. 11,722/- in wages and Shs. 7,862/- for repatriation. The government assisted as far as it could, particularly with repatriation and the filing of claims, but the assistance could only be limited. Another more responsible estate closed down, paid all its labour and allowed them to live on the estate until a new purchaser arrived.
46. For average monthly totals of Africans in employment in the years 1930 to 1938 see Appendix II, Table 2.
47. *1934 and 1938 Annual Reports, N.A.D.*
48. *Report of the Committee on the Working of the Resident Native Labourers Ordinance, 1925*, 1935.
49. The Resident Labourers Ordinance, Ord 30 of 1937, published as a bill *Kenya Gazette*, 6 July 1937.
50. One of the Colonial Office official's minutes notes the Secretaary of State's personal appeal.
51. C.O. 533/483 contains representations to the Secretary of State on squatters.
Arthur Creech Jones, 1891–1964. National Secretary, Transport and General Workers Union 1923–30; M.P. Shipley 1935–50; Under-Secretary Colonies 1945; Secretary of State Colonies 1946–50.
52. C.O. 533/466, Memorial of the Kikuyu Chiefs from Kiambu to the Secretary of State, 5 Nov 1935.
53. *The 1938 Annual Report, N.A.D.* estimated 104,154 squatters on European farms, with 456,934 head of cattle, sheep and goats. A memorandum to the Carter Commission had estimated 110,000 Kikuyu alone to be squatting and the total in 1932 to be over 150,000. Even this figure may not have taken full account of illegal squatting. *Report of the Kenya Land Commission*, Cmd. 4556 of 1934, 466. For Olenguruone see *E.A.S.*, 16 Aug 1945 letter from C. E. V. Buxton; 24 Aug letters from Kariuki wa Kamau, Louis Sykes; 31 Aug letter from C. E. V. Buxton; 14 Sept letter from J. S. Gichuru.
54. C.O. 533/464, Byrne to Bottomley, 4 May 1936.
55. G. Bennett, *Kenya: A Political History*, 82; The Mombasa Chamber, however, simply denounced the tax. Minutes of the Mombasa Chamber of Commerce, VII, 10 Feb 1933.
56. Minutes of the Mombasa Chamber of Commerce, VI, 4 Oct 1926.
57. There was a rapid increase in tea planting between 1924 and 1933 when it was checked by the International Tea Restriction Scheme. In 1936 8,600,000 lb. were produced. *Financial News*, 28 Apr 1944.
58. Interviews T. C. Colchester, 1968, 1970. Colchester was loaned by the administration to the Labour Section for work in Nyanza province in 1936. The *1933 and 1934 Annual Reports, N.A.D.*, print the reports of Shields, the labour inspector for the Kisumu area, who wrote in similar, generally approving terms. In 1935 the lowest wage rates were Shs. 12/- for underground workers and Shs. 10/- for men on the surface for a thirty day ticket, reasonable rations being provided. No indentured labour was employed; on the larger mines there was an understanding that a labourer who completed six tickets received a khaki suit and a blanket.
59. The net earnings of the port were as follows:

1928	£100,288	1931	£117,483
1929	£137,353	1932	£131,088
1930	£138,430	1933	£176,593

1934	£170,223	1937	£287,918
1935	£222,952	1938	£283,769
1936	£254,730	1939	£230,834

The financing of loan charges meant, however, that the port ran a deficit until 1935.

60. Pim Report.
61. Makhan Singh, *History of Kenya's Trade Union Movement to 1952*, 1969, (hereafter Makhan Singh), 40–2.
62. *E.A.S.*, 15, 16, 17, 18 and 21 Nov 1922.
63. *E.A.S.*, 10, 17 Oct 1931; Makhan Singh, 42.
64. *Kenya Weekly News*, 23 Apr 1937.
65. See *infra*, chapter 6; Makhan Singh, vii, viii.
66. *E.A.S.*, 24 Apr 1937.
67. *Ibid.*, 29 Apr 1937.
68. *Ibid.*, 14 May 1937.
69. *Ibid.*, 11 May 1937; Makhan Singh, 61.
70. *E.A.S.*, 26 May 1937.
71. *Ibid.*, 17 April 1937.
72. *E.A.S.*, 19 May 1937.
73. *Ibid.*, 2 June 1937. The Minimum Wage Ordinance was not put into effect.
74. *Ibid.*, 21 May 1937; Makhan Singh, 61–2.
75. *E.A.S.*, 2 Aug 1939.
76. *Ibid.*, 3 Aug 1939.
77. C.O. 533/462, Cable to Colonial Office, 9 June 1936 and minute by Flood.
78. C.O. 533/464, minute by Flood on memorandum by Scott, n.d. 1936.
79. C.O. 533/471, minute by Flood, n.d. 1936.
80. C.O. 533/484, minute by Flood, 4 Jan 1937.
81. C.O. 533/471, minute by Flood, n.d. 1936.
82. The Benthamite spirit can be seen in Ormsby-Gore's foreword to C. W. Hobley, *Kenya from Chartered Company to Crown Colony*, 1929, 5–6. 'The coming of civilization has brought its problems—and the curse of politics in England as well as Kenya. At times one gets sick and tired of Nairobi politics —of the catchwords and formulae that have had their little day and become superseded in rapid turn by the newest product of journalistic thought. There is so much real work to be done in Kenya, real constructive developmental work that gets held up by politics and constitution mongering.'
83. *Colonial Office Conference 1930, Summary of Proceedings*, Plenary Meeting, 8 July 1930, Cmd. 3628 of 1930; Colonial Labour Committee Papers, 1931–41.
84. *Parliamentary Debates, Commons*, 25 July 1935, 9 July 1936, 2 June 1937, 14 June 1938. All record Labour M.P.s' anxiety over labour conditions in Kenya. The three best informed spokesmen were Lunn, Morgan Jones and Creech Jones who asked for a systematic inquiry into colonial labour legislation, improved conditions and a trained inspectorate. Creech Jones in addition in both 1937 and 1938 expressed his disapproval of the new Resident Labourers Ordinance, and in 1938 asked why ratification of the I.L.O. Convention on Recruiting had been delayed.
85. *Ibid.*, 15 March 1939, and *Labour Supervision in the Colonial Empire, 1937–1943*, Col 185 of 1943.

    The adviser appointed was Major G. St. J. Orde-Browne who had served in the German East Africa campaign both as a regular and a political officer; he had then been Labour Commissioner in Tanganyika from 1925 to 1931. He published a book, *The African Labourer*, in 1933, and had been sent to Northern Rhodesia to report on labour conditions, negotiating machinery and legislation in 1938.
86. Margaret Stewart, *Britain and the I.L.O.*, 1969, 27–8.
87. C.O. 533/497. One curious feature of official thinking was a defence of penal sanctions by Orde-Browne and strong criticism of them by P. E. Mitchell, a future Kenya Governor. Memoranda Orde-Browne 26 July 1938, Mitchell 9 July 1931. Colonial Labour Committee Papers 1931–41.
88. *East Africa and Rhodesia*, 29 July 1937.

89. Only the camps at Nairobi and Kisumu were retained. Their value can be shown by the number using this facility. These fluctuated during this decade but in 1938 the totals were: Nairobi 7,529 and Kisumu 26,502. Improved communications lessened the hardship caused by the closure of the other camps at Kendu Bay, Yala and Mumias although the closure of the camp at Sagana created difficulties for men from Embu and Meru. Four small camps, two in the Aberdares to assist Kikuyu crossing to the settled areas, and two on Mt. Elgon were opened in 1935.

    Cmd. 4093 (Moyne Report) comments sharply on the reduction in African medical services.
90. Margery Perham, 'Kenya Revisited', *The Times*, 17 Feb 1937.
91. C.O. 533/515, Elspeth Huxley to Smith, 18 July 1939.
92. 1938 Annual Report, Kitui District. In 1941 the D.C. reported that the 800 Kitui Kamba who paid tax in Nairobi, Mombasa or other areas were invariably charged Shs 12/- instead of the legal rate of Shs. 9/-. '. . . the Collectors' zeal to increase the amount of tax collected outweighs their sense of legality'. 1941 Annual Report, Kitui District.
93. In 1936, the *kodi*, a voluntary system of monthly payments by stamps, was introduced, the purposes of which were to prevent the exploitation a poor man might experience on account of the need to pay all his tax at once, to increase revenue and also to prevent the employer losing his labour through inability to pay.
94. C.O. 533/471, minute by Flood on G. Walsh and H. R. Montgomery, *Report on Native Taxation*, 1936.
95. Bemister to Scott, 30 March 1932. Scott papers.
96. *The Times*, 24, 25, 27 Sept, 22 Nov 1935.
97. Africans at this time were to be found only in clerical and very minor executive posts. In 1935 Pim found only thirteen African clerks on Asian terms of service, seventy officers on scales of more than Shs. 150/- per month and fifty on scales from Shs. 95/- to Shs. 150/-. These totals covered all departments but excluded Moslem officials at the Coast. Pim Report, 54–5.
98. C.O. 533/467, Hosking to Furse, 29 Jan 1936:

    '. . . my own experience shows that though the locally born are, if educated overseas, as fine a type as you could wish for, the local article born, bred and educated in Kenya is useless . . . I consider that the local Kenyan starts with the grave disability of having been brought up on a "motor car standard". In after life he has neither the bank nor the mental balance to live up to this standard. Further he is of necessity brought up with an anti-native bias, due partly to fear and partly to superiority compex. By virtue of his colour alone, a European child from earliest youth orders natives about and is led to regard them as dangerous helots to be kept in their place. As to his knowledge of the native language being an asset, it is generally a distinct liability. He learns not the language spoken by the native, but only the language Europeans speak to the native (Kisettla) . . . And yet if we are to avoid a "poor white" problem we *must* find uses for them.'

    M. H. Cowie in the nineteen-fifties was to describe the Kenya European boy as holding a 'pongo' attitude (i.e. one of contemptuous superiority).
99. Pim Report; also C.O. 533/463, C.O. 533/466, C.O. 533/477, C.O. 533/487.

    In 1938 the budget for the Labour Section amounted to £5,717, and that for Native Registration £9,723. It was expected to secure an income of £2,800 for registration by means of the scale of *kipandes* and 'Red Books'.
100. Percy de Vere Allen, 1891–1971. Born Melbourne; educated St. Kilda and Xavier College; farmer and businessman East Africa 1914–25; joined government service: labour inspector: 1925; Labour Commissioner 1940–45.
101. For figures covering the years 1930 to 1938 see Appendix II, Table 4.
102. *1938 Annual Report, N.A.D.*
103. *1933 and 1938 Annual Reports, N.A.D.*
104. C.O. 533/480, Brooke-Popham to Ormsby-Gore, 16 Oct 1937 and attached papers. See *supra*, p. 233.
105. Mimeographed official memorandum, n.d. (probably 1932). Scott papers.

106. The Minimum Wage Ordinance, Ord 22 of 1932; the text (as a bill) and the explanatory note are published in the *Kenya Gazette*, 14 June 1932.
107. See *supra*, p. 345.
108. A. G. Church, *op. cit.*, 302, gives a Tanganyika example of this practice.
The Labour Section inspectors in an amateur way drew the attention of employers to plant that was unprotected, and they succeeded also in reducing the unhealthy dusty atmosphere in the brushing sheds of a number of sisal plants.
109. *East Africa and Rhodesia*, 19 March 1936.
110. *Ibid.*, 30 Jan, 13, 27 Feb, 1936, 21 Oct 1937.
An amendment to the Mining Ordinance passed in 1939 (Ord 17 of 1939) added the provisions of the Colonial Office model ordinance. In a note on the purposes of the amendment, the government stated that it was prepared to introduce a general Workmen's Compensation Bill 'at a later date'.
111. *Ibid.*, 16 June 1938.
112. The union was not entirely consistent. During the building strike in 1937, it called minimum wage legislation premature as 'this question is generally raised by the employers, whose intention is to fail the strike . . .' *E.A.S.*, 11 May 1937. See also Makhan Singh, 52, 54, 67–9.
113. Minutes of the Executive of the Convention of Associations, 5 Apr 1932. Scott papers.
114. Interviews S. H. Fazan, T. C. Colchester, Kenya administrative officers in this period, 1968–70. For an example of hostility from a pastoral tribe, in this case the Maasai, in 1935, see R. L. Tignor, *op. cit.*
115. As districts became divided into locations, men's portering work became limited to the area of their locations, so reducing the time spent on the march.
In 1938 869 were convicted under section 25 (2) of the Native Authority Ordinance 1937 for failure to perform communal services. The most severe punishments were in Nyanza and were Shs. 30/- or two months hard labour, C.O. 533/508, Wade (Acting Governor) to MacDonald, 10 March 1939.
116. *Report of the Employment of Juveniles*, 1938; *1938 Annual Report, N.A.D.*
117. One Asian hotel was found to be employing eight children aged eight to ten at a wage of Shs. 2/- to Shs. 3/- plus food. The Labour Section staff at once repatriated the boys. The inspectorate also stopped the practice of using 'small children for long hours on quite heavy tasks' in the building industry. *1938 Annual Report, N.A.D.*
118. The Employment of Women, Young Persons and Children Ordinance, Ord 14 of 1933, *Kenya Gazette*, 9 May 1933. Young persons were between fourteen and eighteen, children below fourteen.
119. The Employment of Women, Young Persons and Children (Amendment) Ordinance, Ord 6 of 1935, *Kenya Gazette*, 13 Aug 1935.
120. The Employment of Women, Young People and Children (Amendment) Ordinance, Ord 35 of 1936, *Kenya Gazette*, 8 Dec 1936.
121. C.O. 533/496, Pilling to Ormsby-Gore, 12 Jan 1938; Colonial Office to Brooke-Popham (draft), June 1938; MacDonald to Brooke-Popham, 3 Nov 1938; *Manchester Guardian*, 12 May, 7, 23 June, letter from Owen; *ibid.* 23 June, editorial. C.O. 533/497, representations to the Secretary of State on child labour.
122. *Report of the Employment of Juveniles Committee* and C.O. 533/497. Although on the whole the committee considered the allegations of Owen overstated, it did remark concerning the sisal industry, 'the only reason for employment of juveniles is that such labour is cheap'. One of the officials minuted this tribute to the work of the Archdeacon: '. . . I agree that Archdeacon Owen's previous allegations were somewhat far-fetched, they at any rate had the effect of focusing attention in public and in Parliament on this question and that had this not occurred, the Kenya Committee would not have been appointed and the very necessary requirements which they advocate would not have been formulated.'
123. C.O. 533/510, Brooke-Popham to MacDonald, 10 Jan 1939; MacDonald to Brooke-Popham (draft), 20 March 1939; International Department, T.U.C. to

MacDonald, 16 Jan 1939; *Daily Telegraph*, 2 Feb 1939; *Manchester Guardian*, 2, 22 Feb, 13 March 1939; *East Africa and Rhodesia*, 23 March 1939; *New Statesman*, 7 Jan 1939, letter from Owen.

124. The Employment of Servants (Amendment) Ordinance, Ord 16 of 1939, *Kenya Gazette*, 25 July 1939; C.O. 533/510, Harragin to MacDonald, 17 May 1939.
125. The Employment of Servants (Amendment) Ordinance, 1943, published as a Bill, *Kenya Gazette*, 9 March; see *infra*, p. 451.
126. The Employment of Servants Ordinance, Ord 11 of 1938, *Kenya Gazette*, 3 May 1938. The ordinance was passed in 1937 to enter into force in 1938.
127. Between 7,000 and 9,000 men were still being recruited annually by professional recruiters at the end of the decade. A number of the professional recruiters were Asians who were using a large cash advance of two to three months' wages as a bait. This practice was stopped by the 1937 Ordinance which limited advances to one month's wages.
128. The figures of Africans convicted in 1935, for example, were as follows:

Under the Employment of Natives Ordinance:	833
Under the Resident Native Labourers Ordinance:	945

Penal provisions for breaches of contract in legislation had been a feature of nineteenth century Britain. They were removed from Indian legislation in 1926, an example followed shortly afterwards in the British West African colonies, but not until after the Second World War in Kenya. The I.L.O. had already stated concerning its Regulation of Contracts of Employment of Indigenous Workers: 'Penal sanctions, which are necessarily derogatory to human dignity and liberty, are considered as an "ultimate remedium" to be used only very exceptionally in connection with contractual obligations. Their application to contracts of employment in particular is repugnant to modern legal conceptions...' *Manchester Guardian*, 7 June 1938; Colonial Labour Committee papers 1931–41.

129. *A Bill to Amend the Trade Unions Ordinance, 1937: Notes by Major F. W. Cavendish-Bentinck*, Circular No. E.M.O. 3/41, 22 Feb 1941 (hereafter Cavendish-Bentinck Notes); Makhan Singh, 105–6.
130. *Kenya Debates*, 10 Aug 1937.
131. *Ibid.*, 26 July 1937.
132. *E.A.S.*, 9 Aug 1937, quoted Makhan Singh, 64.
133. 'We excluded, however, any provision legislating peaceful picketing, and we also excluded any safe-guarding provision protecting Trade Unions against actions of tort.' Cavendish-Bentinck Notes, 22 Feb 1941.
134. Ord 1 of 1940, *Kenya Gazette*, 30 Jan 1940. 'In this Colony we eventually gave way over peaceful picketing, but the way our Amendment, which was passed in 1939, was worded, rendered it harmless, although I personally opposed it. But we refused to give way on the question of actions of tort.' Cavendish-Bentinck Notes; *Kenya Debates*, 3 Jan 1940.

The relevant paragraphs of the ordinance read:

'Provided that it shall not be lawful for one or more persons... to attend at or near a house or place where a person resides or works or carries on business or happens to be, for the purpose of obtaining or communicating information or of persuading or inducing any person to work or to abstain from working, if they so attend in such numbers or otherwise in such manner as to be calculated to intimidate any person...

(2) In this section the expression "to intimidate" means to cause in the mind of a person a reasonable apprehension of injury to him or to any member of his family or to any of his dependants or of violence or damage to any person or property...'

135. *Kenya Gazette*, 9 May 1939 (as bill); as Ord 5 of 1940, 7 May 1940. The act was based on British legislation—the Conciliation Act of 1896 and the Industrial Courts Act of 1919.

When first introduced in 1939 Scott moved that it be adjourned *sine die* since it was 'quite a new principle', was of 'no urgency', and required 'more time to study'. *Kenya Debates*, 5, 7 June 1939, 3, 5 Jan 1940.

136. C.O. 533/514. The foundation refused to make a grant on account of the outbreak of war.
137. *East Africa and Rhodesia*, 13 Oct 1938.
138. C.O. 533/513, Brooke-Popham to MacDonald, 31 July 1939; MacDonald to Brooke-Popham, 11 Aug 1939.
139. C.O. 533/493, MacDonald to Brooke-Popham (draft), 8 Aug 1939. The attached papers include a letter of Makhan Singh.
140. C.O. 533/506, MacDonald to Brooke-Popham (draft), Aug 1939.
141. C.O. 533/503, circular telegram, 15 Sept 1939.
142. C.O. 533/503, circular telegram, 22 Sept 1939.
143. C.O. 533/513, MacDonald to Harragin (acting Governor), 18 Nov 1939.
144. J. Huxley, *op. cit.*, 144.
145. C.O. 533/513.
146. *1937 Annual Report, N.A.D.*

Chapter 6

CONFRONTATION IN NAIROBI AND MOMBASA, 1937–1939

> ... but where you can help is by insisting that any complaint or petition shall be sent through the proper channels and no notice taken of it until this is done. As I think I have said before owing to the increased ease of communications there is a tendency now on the part of the native to ignore his District and Provincial Commissioner and even the Governor, and deal directly with Whitehall, whereas he ought to look upon his District Commissioner as his father and mother ...
>
> The Governor of Kenya, Sir Robert Brooke-Popham to the Secretary of State for the Colonies, Malcolm MacDonald, 26 July 1939.

> ... it seems that the father-of-all-fathers, like the fathers in Turgenieff's novel, is perplexed and disturbed by the behaviour of his children.
>
> Minute of F. J. Pedler, a Colonial Office official, on the above.

Makhan Singh, Conditions in Nairobi and the Labour Trade Union of East Africa

The focus on land and white settlement in the nineteen-thirties blinded most people to the problems which were arising in the cities. The African locations of Nairobi and Mombasa were singularly depressing places in which to live. The African population of Nairobi had grown from approximately 14,000 in 1920 to 25,000 in 1930 and 40,000 in 1938, of which between two-thirds and three-quarters were men. Depression conditions prevented any but the most limited expansion of housing facilities, the accommodation provisions of the Employment of Servants Ordinance being virtually ignored by most employers including the municipality and the government. A small amount of new housing was built but in numbers far short of the need. Blocks of single rooms for single labourers looked like prison cells and many of the two-roomed houses for families used a space between wall and roof as an enforced, often chilling ventilation. The houses had neither water nor light; charcoal fuel, and lamp oil had to be purchased. Water was provided at communal taps, where long queues formed three times a day.[1] A certain number of wives came to the city creating a very small semi-stabilized labouring class, and some employers allowed brief visits by servants' wives. But often a man saw his wife very infrequently.

The condition of domestic staff who lived on their employer's property was frequently little better. Two or three servants often had to share a room; many employees of Asians slept wrapped up in a blanket on the store floor or in a shed. Most employers paid an inadequate bachelor 'housing allowance' of Shs. 2/- to Shs. 4/- using arguments on the dangers of 'tied housing' or 'the African prefers to keep one foot in the reserve' to justify their position. The demolition of the last of the very insanitary old villages, Pangani, was begun but the acute shortage of new housing preserved many houses until 1939. In Pumwani and Pangani men slept on sacks or blankets on the floor, sometimes seven or eight to a windowless room.

A good but insufficient child welfare service and an excellent maternity hospital failed to compensate for the general inadequacy of the other municipal services. The worst of these were the communal latrines, where the bins and trenches became quickly over-full, spreading to the floor space of the sheds surrounding them. The municipal staff responsible for emptying and cleaning were often late, the sheds ill-lit or not lit at all, the water supply in the trench latrines not always reliable and quickly blocked. Flies, faeces, pieces of tapeworm and foul odours filled the latrines. The streets were at best poorly lit, muddy in the rains, dusty in the dry weather. There were no nurseries or children's playing fields. There was one under-staffed primary school and no secondary school. The Labour Section and the medical officers commented unfavourably on these urban conditions each year with little visible effect. The city fathers wanted a South African policy on the cheap—inexpensive labour without expensive housing and welfare programmes. The Depression merely reinforced this. Conditions in such up-country towns as Nakuru, Eldoret or Kisumu were only marginally better.

The sustained use of the strike along with ideas of class solidarity in order to protest against these deplorable conditions are first to be found in Nairobi with the rise of militant Asian trade unionism. The Asian community had one foot in the slums, the other in the respectable middle class. Its middle class used such bodies as the Indian National Congress or economic ones like the Indian chambers of commerce to defend their interests. The clerks working for the government or for the Railway formed protective associations at a fairly early date to negotiate through the established procedures, or occasionally by direct appeal to Whitehall, over matters such as salaries, pensions, leave and the like. In the nineteen-thirties such associations were mainly concerned to prevent a deterioration in the position of their members. Trade unionism appealed to the skilled and semi-skilled Asian workers, particularly in the building trades and on the railway. Artisans and labourers were not allowed to join the clerical staff associations. This, of course, deprived them of the possible leadership of the more educated members of the community, but it also ensured that when these workers organized, they were likely to be more militant than any staff association could afford to be.

The events of 1922 and 1931 showed the limitations of early Asian labour protest. In 1922–3 the Railway had been able to break the Railway Artisan Union by victimizing its leadership, and the European contractors successfully forced a 10 per cent reduction in wages. The latter case revealed the strength and weaknesses of communal organization. Since most of the artisans were Sikhs, the structure of the community allowed a certain communal solidarity, the strikers, for instance, meeting at the Sikh temple. They did not, however, seem to regard the issue as a class matter for they promptly appealed to the Indian Association to negotiate on their behalf. This negotiation was carried on by M. A. Desai, a local businessman and political leader, who failed to move the European contractors. The strikers also failed in their attempts to spread the strike to the Asian employees of the government or of the Railway. The *East African Standard* recognized that this was the turning point in the strike which collapsed shortly thereafter.[2] By 1931 there had been some changes in attitude. The strike at Lewis and Son and five other contractors was a partial success owing to the use of picketing. The strikers also formed a union, the Workers' Protection Society, to deal directly with the employers. At the heart of the strike, however, were the Sikh artisans who relied on their own communal protective society; the headquarters of the union was on Campos Ribeiro Street in the heart of the Sikh area of Nairobi. But the Asian community was divided, Isher Dass supporting the strikers and Councillor H. N. Malik opposing them for fear of provoking a European boycott of Asian workers. Again the union was broken, although Lewis later restored the wage cut which had provoked the walk-out. At the end of the strike, effigies of the strike leaders who had returned to work were burned on Campos Ribeiro Street by workers wearing black masks and chanting 'he's dead'.[3]

The effective pioneer of continuing organized labour agitation was another Sikh, Makhan Singh.[4] He had been born in India and had come to Kenya in 1927 at the age of fourteen. His father had first worked on the Railway where he had been dismissed for helping to lead the abortive Railway Artisan Union. He had then set up a small printing shop which was to sustain Makhan Singh throughout his career. After four years at the Government Indian High School, Makhan Singh passed the London matriculation examination. At about the same time he seems to have picked up Marxist terminology and perhaps the communist faith; his communism was an egalitarianism which was to be secured by trade union agitation rather than by violent revolution.

In 1934 there were attempts to found a general union called the Indian Trade Union. This type of structure was chosen because the Railway workers, who were the union's strongest backers, feared victimization if they created their own organization. Most of them, as a result of an economy move, had lost their permanent status with the Railway and consequently their welfare benefits. The other major area of support was in the building trade. The new union was not an immediate success, but in meetings of 12 March and 18 April 1935 it was transformed into the Labour Trade Union of Kenya with Makhan Singh as secretary. It was nominally multi-racial but remained a largely Asian organization until 1939.

The constitution of the union was adopted in June 1935. It listed five aims of a general trade union nature of which the first, 'To organize the workers of Kenya on a class basis', was not calculated to appeal to chambers of commerce. It then went on to list fifteen immediate demands including the eight-hour day and a minimum wage of Shs. 200/- a month. It wanted the abolition of overtime, full pay while sick, eighteen days paid local leave, and four months long leave after four years of service. It also insisted on the abolition of piece work and the replacement of hourly or daily wages by weekly or monthly payments. The influence of the Railway workers can be seen in the demands for the restoration of their permanent status. Throughout the nineteen-thirties and forties lengthy lists of grievances were a feature of Makhan Singh's strategy, but it would seem that wages and hours remained the issues in which the workers were most interested. Between August 1935 and January 1936 the union called a series of meetings to demand an eight hour day. The Indian Youth League, which had also come into existence in the thirties as the vehicle of protest for the shop assistants, conducted a similar agitation for the limitation of hours by demanding the enforcement of the Shop Hours Ordinance of 1925. As a consequence of this pressure the government in 1936 introduced amendments to the ordinance to remove some of the loop-holes in the original legislation.

Makhan Singh then went to India for some months, and union activity lapsed in his absence. He returned later in 1936 and called the union's first annual meeting in September; it was resolved to demand an eight hour day from the Asian contractors. The secretary sent out leaflets to forty-seven firms and enclosed a form which the owner was to sign over a shilling stamp as an indication of agreement to the eight hour day. Most were willing to do so, but a short strike was needed to persuade the recalcitrant. Somewhat later, however, a few of the contractors sent Makhan Singh another legal form repudiating their original agreement. The exchange of forms was necessary because there was no trade union legislation.

These successes encouraged the union. In December it decided to demand a 25 per cent wage increase by 1 April 1937, and Makhan Singh wrote in this sense to most of the employers in the building and motor service industries. Meanwhile the artisans in Dar es Salaam had struck successfully for higher wages—a strike supported financially by the Labour Trade Union. The Nairobi demands were then refused by the employers, and on 1 April the Labour Trade Union called out the workers in a number of Asian concerns. The strategy was to secure concessions from the smaller firms and then to attack the larger European and Asian contractors. By 17 April the *East African Standard* confirmed that the first phase had been a success with nineteen firms signing contracts for a wage increase as well as conceding the eight-hour day and recognition of the union. The next day the workers struck at George Blowers Ltd. and the Motor Service Company Ltd. These seem to have been test cases. The strike lasted sixty-two days. Lewis locked out its workers in sympathy with Blowers, but eventually the union won a wage increase and the promise not to victimize the strikers.[5]

By this two-month strike the union had secured a great deal of publicity, and it was now a force of some significance in the Nairobi building industry although the Railway continued to ignore its complaints about the Asian artisans. The most immediately significant effect of the strike was to force the government to bring in the trade union legislation already mentioned. Although the Labour Trade Union objected to the ordinance on the grounds that the government would use the power of registration to strangle the union movement, it successfully applied for registration in September 1937.

The next two years were relatively quiet. The union had to face communal splintering, with the registration of the East African Ramgarhia Artisan Union for the Sikhs and the Muslim Trade Union of Kenya and Uganda.[6] Makhan Singh, however, successfully maintained the non-communal nature of the Labour Trade Union. Another difficulty was the refusal of the press to print information about the activities of the union.

In 1938 Makhan Singh convened a conference of Asian organizations on the question of workmen's compensation. Representatives came from the East African Indian National Congress, the Federation of Indian Chambers of Commerce, the Indian Elected Members' Organization, the Indian Youth League, the Kenya and Uganda Railway Asian Staff Union, and even from the rival Asian trade unions. An invitation was extended to the Kikuyu Central Association, but it was refused. Makhan Singh had secured a copy of the model compensation ordinance prepared by the Colonial Office, and the meeting was designed, unsuccessfully as it turned out, to bring pressure on the Kenya government to implement it. In addition the union made representations to the Uganda Labour Inquiry Committee and sent a petition direct to the I.L.O.[7] Nor did Makhan Singh ignore the more traditional method of agitation through the Indian National Congress. In 1938 and 1939 the Congress adopted a number of resolutions proposed by Makhan Singh and his allies which reiterated the demands of the Labour Trade Union concerning labour legislation, minimum wages and the like.[8] For instance, in 1938 Makhan Singh successfully moved:

> 9. This Congress considers the Trade Union Ordinance, 1937, to be very restrictive for the organizations of workers and especially the Indian workers, and urges upon the Kenya Government to repeal all the clauses of the said Ordinance which place unfair and unjust restrictions on workers' organizations, and to amend it in such a way as to make the powers of the Registrar and the Governor-in-Council subject to an appeal to the High Court.

During the early months of 1939, Makhan Singh began to sound out the Kikuyu Central Association on the possibility of Afro-Asian trade union co-operation. The union's May Day rally for the first time attracted an African audience. At first the K.C.A. was suspicious, as its earlier refusal to come to the compensation conference had indicated. But eventually Jesse Kariuki and George K. Ndegwa joined the executive committee. The third annual conference was held in July, handbills were printed in Swahili as well as Gujerati, and a large number of Africans attended. It looked as though a new opening had been found, but it was undoubtedly utopian to think that Asian workers who were better paid than Africans often solely on racial grounds would back a truly multi-racial union. From this time on Makhan Singh was a lonely general unable to retain the loyalty of more than a section of the Asian working class and held at a certain distance by the African militants in Nairobi; these latter increasingly looked on trade unionism as part of the African nationalist struggle in which it was difficult for an Asian to participate and to be fully accepted.

Before the annual meeting, the executive had decided to overhaul the structure of the union. It was divided into ten industrial sections of which only three, printing, construction and the railways, had started to function when the events of the Second World War overtook the union. Classes primarily for Asian workers were organized. The texts were *Trade Unionism* issued by the Left Book Club and a pamphlet by Arthur Creech Jones. Makhan Singh was already corresponding with the British T.U.C., the South African Trades and Labour Council, and the I.L.O. For a communist he was always eclectic in his sources of information.

In June 1939 the union vigorously protested against the new Trade Disputes (Arbitration and Inquiry) Ordinance, on the grounds that arbitration structures might well in the eyes of the workers eliminate the necessity for trade unionism. Orde-Browne thought that this demonstrated a lamentable ignorance by the union, and MacDonald urged the Governor to set up a specialist labour department which could, in his view, dissipate this ignorance and misunderstanding.[9]

The two most difficult structural problems for the union, however, were the collection of fees and the founding of branches. In theory membership cost 10 cts. a month, but in fact regular dues were never collected and the very limited revenue came from appeals at public meetings. The only surviving accounts, those of 1938, show an income of Shs. 545/-, plus Shs. 253/- carried over from the previous year, making a total of Shs. 798/-. Payments came to Shs. 655/-, mostly for a part-time clerk, leaving a balance of Shs. 143/-. The union did not try to act as a benefit society nor did it supply strike pay as the members were supported during these emergencies either by communal organizations or by their families.

In 1939 the union was registered in Tanganyika and changed its name to the Labour Trade Union of East Africa; it never, however, operated in that territory. In Kenya it claimed a number of branches, but only the one in Mombasa seems to have had any real existence, it sent a delegate to the second annual meeting in 1938 and in August of that year it distributed a pamphlet to the 'Indian Artisans of Mombasa, Kilindini, and Makupa' advertising the annual meeting. At the end of the year a strike broke out in a construction firm. Makhan Singh hurried to Mombasa to take charge of the strike committee. Dr. M. A. Rana and the district commissioner also intervened and a settlement was reached after ten days. But the Mombasa branch seems to have remained purely Asian and to have become dormant after this episode. Most of these attempts to evolve a bureaucratic structure were abortive as the Second World War broke out before they became effective. The movement remained, therefore, throughout the period from 1935 to 1939, largely the personal creation of Makhan Singh.

It seems likely that the Labour Trade Union had a considerable effect in popularizing the strike technique among Africans. In the early nineteen-thirties there had been scattered protests by Africans in Nairobi and in the up-country towns against local conditions. There was labour unrest over tax abuses in 1935. The same year also saw a successful strike by the boatmen who were the employees of the Asian fish merchants at Kisumu.[10] The strike secured a Shs. 2/- wage increase, an example followed with equal success by the boatmen at Asembo Bay in 1936.[11] The success of the strike by the Labour Trade Union in 1937 and the widespread publicity it received inspired Africans to do the same. The clearest such case was the strike of the African quarry workers near Nairobi. Makhan Singh claims that the K.C.A. were involved, but this was not the view of the acting

Principal Labour Officer, Alec Nisbet, who settled the strike and who had not been unwilling in other circumstances to blame industrial unrest on political agitators.[12] There were also strikes of African workers at the Railway marine workshops in Kisumu, the Teita Concessions sisal estate at Mwatate, on the Victoria Nyanza Sugar Company's estate at Miwani, and at the Shell Company's installations in Mombasa. The Labour Section staff commented on the improved organization of these strikes and noted that representatives frequently spoke for the workers.[13] In 1938 the conductors and drivers of the Kenya Bus Company went on strike demanding a wage increase but without success.[14] The following year there was a rash of minor strikes in Nairobi. One such was the strike of African Railway apprentices which collapsed when the management abrogated the apprenticeship agreements and sent the strikers home; this particular strike was supported by the Labour Trade Union.[15] The technique of the strike was clearly spreading. Increased prosperity brought higher living costs and consequent demands for wage increases. There is little indication, however, that the African workers involved thought of their actions either in terms of a sustained labour organization or on class lines; it is significant that when Makhan Singh began to search for African allies, he found them in the middle class leadership of the K.C.A.

By 1939 the Kenya administration itself was alarmed by the situation in Nairobi. The Municipal Native Affairs Officer, E. R. St. A. Davies, estimated a shortfall of 6,000 places for Africans already in Nairobi, and the Chief Native Commissioner commenting on this report considered that 18,000–19,000 Africans slept in 'highly overcrowded and unhealthy conditions'. An unscheduled count in the location in 1938 had revealed 503 Africans living in the space built for 171. It was also estimated that 16,000 Africans earned less than Shs. 21/– and on that could not properly feed or house themselves or their families. It was these conditions that had led Brooke-Popham at the end of July to request immediate approval for the Nairobi municipality to raise a loan of £30,000 for African housing. His reasons were illuminating:

> The present situation regarding native housing in Nairobi is undoubtedly serious. The demand for houses greatly exceeds the supply, with the result that considerable numbers of private native lodging-house keepers are able to demand rentals which are beyond the capacity of the average native to pay without hardship. This profiteering has led to considerable native unrest which has manifested itself recently in a series of native strikes which, in the opinion of the Principal Labour Officer, arose largely by reason of the high rents prevailing. The Principal Labour Officer was only able to deal with the strikers by informing them that early action would be taken to bring about a reduction in rents. He considers the situation serious and expresses the view that unless early action is taken, a native general strike is not unlikely to occur.[16]

It is unlikely that the Governor would have listened to the Principal Labour Officer if spectacular events in Mombasa had not shown exactly what urban African unrest could mean.

Conditions in Mombasa

Conditions in Mombasa were probably worse than they were in Nairobi.[17] The municipality was run by an insensitive Anglo-Asian oligarchy whose powers were consolidated by the local government legislation of the nineteen-twenties. It also existed as something of a political backwater, alternately complaining that it was ignored by the central government and rejoicing that it was not subject to the same pressures as Nairobi. The health, sanitation and housing problems of the municipality had been consistently ignored since the start of the colonial period. The exigencies of the Depression merely reinforced this neglect. Unlike Nairobi or Dar es Salaam which were created by the European invaders, Mombasa had grown up around the ancient port town which did not, as the Medical Officer of Health noted in 1905, lend itself to western ideas of sanitation.[18] Three years later the M.O.H. regretted that the opportunity for planning the growth of Mombasa had been allowed to pass, 'probably for financial reasons'; in 1907 the M.O.H. noted that sanitary measures were not enforced owing to 'the peculiar political situation of Mombasa'.

Exactly the same types of complaints were made throughout the nineteen-thirties. In 1932 the M.O.H. and some of his staff resigned owing to the harassment of the municipal board demanding economy. Throughout the thirties repeated attempts by the health department to remove the Asian dairies with their foul stables were frustrated by the board. In 1932 the meat inspectors 'incurred no little odium and virulent attack' for condemning meat. Four years later the M.O.H. noted 'there is apparently a feeling in certain quarters that the standards (of meat and food inspection) demanded are rather on the high side . . .'. In 1937 Dr. R. W. Wiseman complained that his proposals of the previous year concerning the control of milk to prevent adulteration had come to nothing because '. . . these efforts have been hampered on several occasions by determined opposition from various quarters'. In 1934 the M.O.H. suggested that the municipality was more interested in paving roads, presumably for the motor cars of the upper class, than in instituting a decent drainage system. This latter had been recommended in the Bush Report on Drainage and Town Planning in Mombasa in 1917, but no action was taken until after the Second World War. Wiseman also complained that the building regulations were a farce in that no attempt was made to restrict the density of population. 'Any suggestion,' he remarked, 'to reduce overcrowding [in the Old Town] is met with the answer that funds are not available, that the problem is insoluble or more helpfully that the question will solve itself in time.'

When the municipal board was first constituted, the government seconded six sanitary inspectors. Later 'and contrary to advice' the board reduced the inspectorate to four which, in practice, meant three owing to long leaves. Some members wanted the inspectorate reduced even more. 'Successive Health Officers have from time to time advised the Board as to the possible consequences of such a parsimonious policy . . .' In 1937 malaria dramatically increased after the heavy rains and again in December; 'a depleted and overworked staff' could not cope with the situation. The board, suddenly realizing that disease was no respector of class, hurriedly called a meeting of the health committee and sanctioned the hiring of a malarial overseer who was then engaged by telegram.

The conditions in which the working class lived were revolting. In 1932 Dr. Ronald Hunter, the M.O.H., stated that '... half the population of Mombasa continues to dwell in hovels of a type which was regarded as archaic before the time of Vasco da Gama ...' African housing became the responsibility of the Health Department in 1935. Effective control was with the health committee of the board. The committee rejected proposed housing by-laws and gave a 'decided negative' to a plan for a municipal native location. It decided that the only possible solution to the housing problem was better inspection and exhortation to the owners to improve their premises. In 1938 Wiseman reported that 'practically no private individuals or firms provide quarters for their house boys or labour [despite the clear legal obligation to do so]. They live in what is euphemistically known as "majengo" [i.e. the buildings]. The employer as a rule neither knows nor cares where that is. His boys appear for work of a morning and disappear from his ken in the evening to that vague address.' But, Wiseman noted, a room could cost Shs. 5/- a month, and many could not afford that—'... [they] sleep in any kind of hovel they can find. In cattle or goat sheds, in ramshackle huts made of odd pieces of corrugated iron and flattened petrol tins, they are to be found in all the odd corners of the island, living under conditions of squalor that one hopes their employers are unaware of.'[19]

The land in Majengo had been leased in the early nineteen-thirties to Arabs and Coast Africans at Shs. 5/- to Shs. 25/- a month per plot. The lessees built houses which cost between Shs. 1,200/- and Shs. 2,500/- and which were financed by borrowing. These houses contained two to eight rooms which were let from Shs. 2/- to Shs. 10/- a month. It was almost impossible to collect rents regularly owing to the precarious nature of employment, and the lessees fell into arrears on the ground rent. When this occurred the houses were sold off to Asians at Shs. 100/- to Shs. 300/-. The new owners had no interest to pay but still charged the same rates. By 1939 some 30 per cent of the housing in Majengo had passed into the hands of speculators.[20]

Everything that Wiseman had said was borne out by evidence given to the Willan Commission set up after the strike. The Chief Native Commissioner told the inquiry: 'Yes; I think you may take it that the law making it incumbent on the employer to provide this [housing] has been generally disregarded by Government as well as other bodies.'[21] The quality of housing was, in the words of the report, 'deplorably bad' except for the railway, customs and municipal workers. In Majengo 'cleanliness is almost impossible, latrines adjoin kitchens, light and ventilation are almost absent'—words little different from those of Professor Simpson in 1914. 'The housing accommodation supplied to their employees by the dairy owners must be seen to be believed. It is not housing accommodation in any sense of the term, because the employees sleep on mats or pieces of corrugated iron, either above or amongst the cattle, and they have very little protection from the weather.'[22] The commission heard detailed reports from Father Lawless of the Macupa Catholic Mission and from the Principal Labour Officer. It concluded: 'The reasons for the overcrowding at Majengo and the occupation of huts which are not fit for human habitation is that, generally speaking, employers of labour at Mombasa have failed to appreciate their responsibilities.'[23]

In 1914 the M.O.H., in writing of sanitation at Mombasa had said 'roughly speaking there is none . . . All that a sanitarian can do is to deplore and deprecate.' Eighteen years later Hunter could report:

> No attempt has been made to supplement the natural resources for sewage disposal with which a kindly Providence has endowed this Island. The provision of sewers for drainage of waste matter from houses, and of surface water from roads and land, remains in abeyance in spite of the urgent need for these facilities. In the meantime the Island becomes more and more saturated with sewage and at the present rate of progression Mombasa will ere long hold the proud distinction of possessing more cess-pits to the acre than any other part of the civilised world.[24]

Although by the nineteen-thirties refuse collection was on a daily basis, there was no adequate disposal and it was dumped 'into any convenient hole'. In 1934 the M.O.H. complained of 'the promiscuous dumping of refuse and the production of litter'. The domestic animals on the island, particularly the goats, aggravated the problem for they became scavengers in the garbage dumps.

Chronic amoebic dysentery was common. Malaria was endemic although measures to control it were beginning to have a limited effect. There was a small but consistent number of typhoid cases each year. But the most deadly disease of all was tuberculosis, the dread killer in urban slums. Every year the reports of the M.O.H. commented on the prevalence of tuberculosis. Hunter pointed out that between 1922 and 1931, seven times as many people died of tuberculosis as of smallpox and plague combined. In 1933 Dr. Kenneth Martin noted that:

> The spread of Tuberculosis is fostered by overcrowding poverty and general insanitary conditions. Unfortunately, a large proportion of the inhabitants of Mombasa are forced by circumstances to live under conditions which are a reproach to those concerned with their welfare. So long as these conditions exist, so long will Tuberculosis and other diseases flourish.[25]

Wiseman lamented in 1938 that 'yearly in these reports Tuberculosis is referred to as "alarming", "grave", "most serious", but that is all there is to it. The conditions which favour its spread [overcrowding, etc.] are allowed to remain exactly as they were . . .'

The labour market in Mombasa was dominated by three major government or parastatal employers: the port, the railway and the municipality, of which the port was the most important. The Railways and Harbours Administration owned the port of Kilindini, the new docks built to replace the ancient harbour in the Old Town. The first deep-water berths had been completed by 1926, and by 1931 there were five berths and an oil jetty. There were three private stevedoring companies who were responsible for unloading the ships. Two of these, the East African Lighterage Company and the African Wharfage Company owned the Kenya Landing and Shipping Company which was created to handle all cargo after it had been unloaded from the ships. This arrangement had been created by contract with the Railway in 1927. It was a very profitable alliance:[26]

The Kenya Landing and Shipping Company had a capital of Shs. 500,000/- divided into 25,000 shares of Shs. 20/-. The call up was Shs. 4/- on each share for a total capital of Shs. 100,000/- (£5,000).

Year ending 30 June	Net profit	Half year profit
1928	Shs. 28,781/85	—
1929	—	Shs. 46,520/61
1930	—	—
1931	—	84,951/85
1932	124,478/40	—
1933	—	—
1934	73,829/64	9,947/25
1935	—	31,593/69
1936	—	—
1937	76,254/58	—
1938	176,487/62	46,335/64
1939	161,235/49	—

The blanks indicate years in which the figures are not available in the Minute Books.

Dividends on 25,000 shares

1928	Shs. 4/50	£5,625 0 0
1929	2/75	3,437 10 0
1930	2/-	2,500 0 0
1931	3/-	3,750 0 0
1932	3/-	3,750 0 0
1933	10/50	13,125 0 0
1934	3/-	3,750 0 0
1935	8/50	10,625 0 0
1936	21/50	26,875 0 0
1937	25/-	31,250 0 0

All the companies in the port relied heavily on casual labour. There had been unsuccessful attempts to decasualize the labour in the nineteen-twenties. Perhaps one of the reasons for the failure could be seen in this interchange before the Willan Commission in 1939:

Chairman: If you had a combine of all these three companies to work the boats that came here, would it be possible to put the boys on contract?
Mr Jackson [Foreman, African Wharfage Company]: And possibly do away with half of the European staff?
Chairman: Would it be possible to put the boys on contract?
Mr. Jackson: I would not like to say that, because I should probably be one of the people that perhaps would be disposed of.[27]

When a ship arrived in port, word was sent to the bazaar that work was available, and the *serang* or foreman engaged the necessary labour at the dock gate. The Principal Labour Officer told the Willan Commission in 1939 that 'the tendency has been for employers to encourage larger reserves [of labour] than necessary, in order to keep down costs, and to provide an ample labour margin for any emergencies'.[28] Underemployment inevitably led to corruption. Since the *serangs* had the power of hiring in their own hands, they had complete control over the labourers. A worker had to pay the *serang* in order to get work. He had to pay more to work on clean rather than dirty cargoes, and he had to keep paying in order to maintain his job which was, of course, on a daily basis.[29] This corruption, the Principal Labour Officer said in his confidential report, 'has been stressed by natives when discussing their grievances with me'.[30]

The Landing and Shipping Company paid Shs. 2/- for a nine-hour day until 1931; then, on account of the slump, it reduced the wage to Shs. 1/50. The stevedoring companies generally paid 50 cts. more but they attempted a wage cut in 1934. In 1939 after the general strike the hours were reduced to eight. However, the commission paid to the *serangs* ensured that the workers did not take home their full pay and furthermore it was rare to get more than a week's work in any given month. Employers also allowed the tax officers to attend their premises to collect taxes. As a consequence it was frequently impossible to live on the wages taken home from the port, and the workers either had to try to find a second job or sleep in some shack where they would have to pay little or no rent.[31] Furthermore there were no increments for the general labour. Evidence was given to the Thacker tribunal of men who had worked twenty years on the minimum wage.[32] In 1939 the Principal Labour Officer estimated that the absolute minimum cost of living for Africans (rent, food, tax, fuel) was Shs. 12/50 a month, and that a man could not live at less than Shs. 16/- a month if housing were provided and Shs. 20/- if it were not. 'In many cases,' he noted, 'this wage is not being paid . . .'

Nevertheless, ever since the new port of Kilindini had opened in 1909, it had attracted some Africans looking for the means of raising money primarily for taxes but also for bride price, land or consumer goods. They came both from the Coast and inland, particularly Luo and Kamba who worked in the port and Kikuyu who were employed by the Railway. The district commissioner noted for instance in 1926 and 1929 that, just before taxes were due, the Digo and Giriama came to work on the more highly paid but dirty jobs such as coaling and discharging oil.[33] Gradually during the nineteen-twenties and thirties the Luos began to drive the Coast people from the labour market. The Luos were cheaper, worked for a longer period of time, and were less disease-ridden than the Coast Africans.[34] However, this competition along with the ethnic mixture in the city had for a long time served to prevent any serious organization to protest against the conditions in which the working class lived. Most thought of themselves as Luo, Giriama, Swahili or Arab rather than as workers. The appalling conditions and the competition for work caused them to fight each other rather than to fight the employers. In 1923 the district commissioner had noted fighting between the up-country Africans and the Swahilis. He formed a tribal liaison council but the tensions continued none the less.[35] Some groups such as the Luos formed ethnic protective associations of their own, but these could do little to alleviate the main problems of work in the port.

The nineteen-thirties were a period of transition from ethnic brawls to the beginning of concerted class action. As early as 1921 the district commissioner was complaining that Mombasa presented 'the worst results of detribalized or semi-detribalized natives...'[36] By 1927 there was a feeling that the up-country African was becoming a dangerous problem owing to '... a spirit of truculence and undesirable independance [*sic*]', in particular among the Luo and the Kikuyu.[37] In 1934 the stevedoring companies decided to cut the wages of casual labour arguing that no cuts had been made three years previously when the Landing and Shipping Company had made its reductions without difficulty. The stevedores struck. An attempt was then made to use the labour of the Landing and Shipping Company to take the place of the stevedores, but they also went on strike, presenting a list of their own grievances. The walk-out lasted six days. Picketing was general, and there were a few cases of violence. However, the manager of the Landing and Shipping Company reported that '... on the whole the labour remained very orderly and good tempered, but it is extremely unlikely that they would have continued so had the strike been prolonged.' The master stevedores met with the elders and headmen and agreed that the strikers should return for a month at the old rates of pay while negotiations took place. The *hamali* labour of the Landing and Shipping Company, however, repudiated the agreement of the elders. The company made concessions 'where their rates of pay seemed to have been cut perhaps to a too fine point'. Further negotiations took place with the elders and headmen, and the *hamalis* agreed to return. The Landing and Shipping Company also made certain concessions to the casual labour. The port manager and the Harbour Advisory Board were not pleased at the results of the unilateral action of the stevedoring companies, and the manager insisted that the companies and the port management must in the future maintain the closest liaison when wage negotiations were taking place.[38]

In 1937 there was a serious riot involving Luos and Washiri Arabs. Throughout July and August of that year there had been incidents involving various communities.[39] Late in August they clashed in a wild mêlée in which fourteen Washiri and one Luo were killed. After the death of the Luo, senior government officers and the *Liwali* addressed the port and railway labour. This, however, did not prevent revenge by the Luos. The newspapers speculated that the riot was caused by job competition. Washiri pickets appeared at the port, and the Luo labour had to be escorted to work by the police. The Governor's Deputy told the Secretary of State that competition for work was not the cause but rather that the Luos resented the Washiri ownership of the shops and boarding houses in Majengo. So localized was the clash that the European community was unaffected, and both the Mombasa Exhibition and the Air Conference continued without interruption. The official public statement complacently reported that the riot was '... an inter-tribal quarrel, and in no way directed against the Government, the Europeans, or the Indians...' *East Africa and Rhodesia* complained of exaggerated press coverage by *The Times* and considered the riot and another at Isiolo as 'affrays ... devoid of real significance'.[40] The conclusion drawn by the government was the need for control rather than for reform, an approach that echoed the prevailing attitude of the up-country European community.[41] Brooke-Popham wrote to MacDonald in 1938:

> The disturbances which occurred at Mombasa last year revealed the inadequacy of existing powers to control an outbreak of disorder among non-natives.
>
> Mombasa is an old oriental town in which Indians, Arabs, Seychellois, Comorians and Africans live side by side. The relationship of these peoples is generally friendly, but communal feeling is strong and at any time a small incident such as a dispute over a woman or a petty assault can develop into a clash between the communities. There exist, however, a permanent condition of inflammability and the consequent possibility of major disturbances, with loss of life, resulting from small beginnings, unless prompt and effective action can be taken to check the spread of an outbreak.[42]

He then included with his letter a draft bill for emergency powers which the Secretary of State refused to allow. Most but not all Coast Europeans agreed. An exception was Shirley Cooke who stood successfully for the Coast seat in the Legislative Council in 1938 and who warned in his election address of '. . . the signs everywhere manifest amongst Africans of increasing suspicion of the *bona fides* of the white man, leading to agitation and unrest'. He thought there should be a commission of inquiry into the causes of the unrest—a wish that would be fulfilled in rather different circumstances in 1939.[43]

The 1939 Mombasa General Strike

Although 1938 was quiet, in 1939 the voice of protest was heard more stridently with strikes in the ports at Dar es Salaam, Mombasa and Tanga. The news of labour unrest travelled easily up and down the coast carried by newspapers, by slogans chalked in the holds of the ships, and by the easy movement of people. On 17 July the casual labour at Dar es Salaam went on strike and stayed out for eight days without much success.[44] About the same time unrest began to come to a head in Mombasa. The oil workers struck first. On 19 July most of the workers at the P.W.D. went on strike. The Principal Labour Officer came from Nairobi to meet them on the 24th and he ordered an immediate increase of Shs. 3/- in lieu of housing. Strikes then spread rapidly through the city, and the Principal Labour Officer dealt with nine.[45] 'I received information,' Allen reported, 'that the original intention had been to call a general strike of African workers for the morning of Monday July 31st. I also had information given me that the port would be affected, but I was assured by the employers at Kilindini that they were confident that their labour would remain at work.'[46] On 1 August the strike began at Kilindini where the port manager had earlier stated that labour was '. . . apparently contented and had no desire to strike'; the following day the port was closed with large gangs of pickets preventing the permanent labour from entering.[47] The following day the police protected those going to work, and by the 4th the port was back to normal. The strike was remarkably peaceful. Cooke, now one of the members of the investigating tribunal, called it 'not more than an orderly demonstration' but based on real economic grievances.[48] This peacefulness was in sharp contrast to the strike that erupted immediately thereafter in Tanga where there was rioting and the King's African Rifles were called in; they fired on the crowd, and in the mêlée four workers and two *askaris* were killed. The local district officer testified to the Scupham Inquiry that bands of labourers were shouting, 'We want the same wages as Mombasa'. The manager of the East African Lighterage and Stevedoring Company and the *Liwali* agreed that the example of Mombasa was the cause of the strike.[49]

Although *East Africa and Rhodesia* thought the causes of the trouble 'obscure', *The Times* reported that the strike was 'believed to be connected with the arrival of native agitators from Nairobi'—a view shared by the *Daily Telegraph*, the *Kenya Weekly News*, the police and many Europeans in Mombasa.[50] This was also the view of Allen who seems to have thought that the Kikuyus who acted as the spokesmen for the strikers were connected with the Kikuyu Central Association which had been active for some time in the Teita Hills, eighty miles north of the city. He reported to the Chief Secretary in Nairobi that he considered that the strike was organized by Makhan Singh with the assistance of the K.C.A. He believed that 'the native workers had not the slightest desire to strike, and would have much preferred to bring their complaints and grievances to their employers through other channels. At present these channels do not exist and the only means left by which the employees can air their grievances is through political agitators and by the use of the strike weapon.'[51] However, the subsequent Willan Commission rejected this view and considered that the strike was provoked by the undesirable living conditions in Mombasa. The commission found that the Africans had no organization and no recognized leaders who could appear before it.[52] Both the Principal Labour Officer and the commission interviewed groups of labourers whose spokesmen tended to be Kikuyu. Most urban Kikuyu must have been aware of the K.C.A., some were probably members and more would have been affected by its militancy. But no evidence was ever presented that the K.C.A. had any branch in Mombasa or was involved in the strike. The same seems also to have been true of Makhan Singh who was in Nairobi at the time. He organized a sympathy meeting and then dashed to Mombasa to testify before the Willan Commission. Neither at the time nor in his book does Makhan Singh claim that the Labour Trade Union was responsible for the organization of the strike, although he does suggest that the union's example, particularly at the annual meeting of 2-3 July, 'heartened' the Mombasa workers and had 'an electric effect'.[53] The strike seems to have been more of a class than a political protest—a tradition which would remain strong in Mombasa.

The events in the three ports caused a great deal of concern in Nairobi and in London. Brooke-Popham, as noted above, immediately pressed for a new housing scheme in Nairobi to prevent similar strike action in that city. Commissions of inquiry were set up to investigate the events in Mombasa and Tanga. Willan, the Attorney-General, headed the Mombasa inquiry on which there were no African members.[54] It unanimously complained of the incessant changes of administrative officers in the city and made an immediate interim recommendation that a labour officer be posted to Mombasa.[55] This was accepted by Nairobi. The Harbour Advisory Board agreed to the eight hour day.[56] The Colonial Office considered the events somewhat similar to those which had occurred recently in Trinidad and Northern Rhodesia and hoped that the Kenya government would be sufficiently frightened so that they could be forced to accept some of the labour reforms proposed by London.[57] It was a vain hope.

The *Mombasa Times* argued that reforms must come. It recommended machinery to discuss grievances so long as employers were not left at the mercy of agitators. It favoured the creation of an inquiry into labour conditions and feared that the situation might be hushed up by the Nairobi government. It argued that payment of the lowest possible salaries invited trouble similar to the West Indies and recommended a legal minimum wage of Shs. 20/-. It considered Mombasa's housing to be a 'disgusting proximity to animal conditions'. It suggested the appointment of a labour officer and the creation of a municipal native location with a social centre; in September it urged that better housing, better food and recreation should be instituted in order to produce a contented African working class. It also, however, claimed that the strike was caused by outside political interference. It feared 'the restlessness' of the African population. There was, it felt, a need to watch and control the many 'curious' African associations, some of them political, which had recently come into existence. It thought Mombasa overrun by 'idlers and stiffs' and considered that the administration should exercise much firmer control, possibly by pass laws, and certainly by compulsory repatriation.[58]

Commander Lunt of the Kenya Landing and Shipping Company, and Norton of the Railway were prepared to take the initial steps towards the creation of embryo African trade unions. They '. . . gave evidence [to the Willan Commission] to the effect that it would be very beneficial if the employees of each particular trade could form guilds which would be under the guidance of the Labour Department. By this means those employees would be able to discuss conditions of service and bring forward for consideration of the Labour Officer and their employers any grievances.' Norton added that he did not want European-style unions. 'I do not think the boy is ready for a trade union, he is still in a very primitive form.' Even these cautious voices were unique among the Europeans who testified before the Willan Commission; the Principal Labour Officer recommended a structure similar to the local native councils in the reserves:

> I am not in favour of Trade Unions for natives, the time is not ripe for this, the most suitable medium would be a committee of native workers with a sympathetic white Chairman who is also an employer. In this way touch would be maintained with employer and employee and a spirit of co-operation introduced which does not exist today.[59]

The workers of Mombasa did make some short-term gains as a result of the strike. The Willan Commission did recommend a wage of Shs 18/50 excluding housing for an unmarried labourer. Wages did go up but these gains were soon wiped out by war-time inflation. Since the Willan Commission stressed housing as the major source of the difficulties in Mombasa, housing allowance was more generally paid. The commission recommended the creation of a Labour Department with a Labour Commissioner and an increased staff. The Standing Finance Committee also stressed the need to keep the department at full strength during the war. However, nothing was done to improve the situation at the docks nor was municipal housing built. No negotiating machinery for labour disputes was adopted. The Minimum Wage Ordinance was not applied to Mombasa.

When the Willan Report was sent to the Colonial Office in 1940 the Governor Sir Henry Moore (who had replaced Brooke-Popham), recommended that the new Labour Department should have an increased staff and that the Department should be fully autonomous, which the old Labour Section had not been. The Colonial Office approved, stating that Labour Commissioner should be an officer of provincial commissioner seniority and status, and the Office noted with regret that the government and so many private employers failed to observe the colony's legislation in respect of housing for employees. The Colonial Office also regretted that the report made no mention of the desirability and use of machinery for settling industrial disputes. In a further despatch in July 1940 Moore lamely reported that the government's failure to observe the legislation in its capacity as an employer arose from changes made when the ordinance was being debated in Legislative Council, and that the Willan Commission had made no reference to industrial dispute legislation because they knew the government had plans to introduce a bill.[60] The Colonial Office felt reluctant to press Moore on the wider issues at a critical stage in the war, and in short, only the negative side of the *Mombasa Times*'s paternalism came about. In his annual report for 1939, P. P. D. Connolly, M.O.H. and a member of the Willan Commission, wrote that he hoped the war would not be an excuse for inaction 'if further labour troubles are to be avoided and a serious threat to the public health removed'. It was a prescient remark for if the workers had gained little real economic advantage from the strike, they had created a measure of class solidarity which would grow during the Second World War.[61]

NOTES

1. A vivid description of Nairobi's African locations at this time can be found in R. M. Gatheru, *op. cit.*, 73–7.
2. *E.A.S.*, 15, 16, 17, 18, 21 Nov 1922.
3. *Ibid.*, 10, 17 Oct 1931; Makhan Singh, 42–3.
4. For the section on the Labour Trade Union, we relied on an interview with Makhan Singh, the manuscripts in his possession which unfortunately are not large in number as the police seized many of them in 1950, and upon his book, *History of Kenya's Trade Union Movement to 1952* which is his autobiography. Many of the documents of the Labour Trade Union are printed in full in this book, and we have only occasionally duplicated them. In the section on the Labour Trade Union footnotes are only given if they do not come from the above sources.
5. *E.A.S.*, 3 Apr–2 June 1937, *passim.*
6. C.O. 533/493, Harragin to Pedler, 24 July 1939. According to the Kenya government, the Ramgarhia Artisan Union was composed of 700–800 members. It charged no fees and was managed by the East Africa Ramgarhia Board, '. . . the Union being a branch of this Society'. Most of the members were employed by the Railway or the P.W.D. 'The Principal Labour Officer informs me that this Union is at present regarded by him as a loyal and reasonable body which is in touch with him in the matter of certain grievances relating to labour conditions.'

7. C.O. 533/493, Weaver to Calder, 16 Dec 1938.
8. C.O. 533/490, minutes of the 1938 congress; C.O. 533/504, minutes of the 1939 congress; *E.A.S.*, 8 June 1937.

   It is significant that after the 1937 strike the Asian trade unionists involved met at the Playhouse Theatre, and among other resolutions passed one of thanks to the Indian Association.
9. C.O. 533/493, Harragin to MacDonald (draft), 4 July 1939 enclosing memorandum of the Labour Trade Union; MacDonald to Brooke-Popham (draft), 8 Aug 1939.
10. *1935 Annual Report, N.A.D.*
11. *1936 Annual Report, N.A.D.* The report also describes a strike by 800 Africans at a sugar estate near Nairobi. This latter appears to have been caused by a vendetta between two Europeans, one of whom incited the strike.
12. *E.A.S.* 21 May 1937; *Kenya Weekly News*, 21 May 1937. The workers went first to the D.C. who called in the Labour Section.
13. *1937 Annual Report, N.A.D.*
14. *1938 Annual Report, N.A.D.*

   The company's rates were:

Learner driver:	Shs. 50/-
Full Rate driver:	Shs. 70/-
Learner Conductor:	Shs. 30/-
Full Rate conductor:	Shs. 50/-

   Plus Shs. 10/- per month bonus, quarters at a rent of Shs. 2/- per month, free medical attention and fourteen days paid leave.
15. Makhan Singh, 79. The *Kenya Weekly News*, 11 Aug 1939 reported that there were isolated wage demands in Nairobi. It suggested that there was a danger in dismissing these leaders as hooligans or agitators and thinking of them in terms of twenty years ago. There was now a need for new approaches, in particular a Native Advisory Council which should include Africans and also a need for propaganda.
16. C.O.533/513, Brooke-Popham to MacDonald, 31 July 1939; *Report by the Senior Medical Officer and the Municipal Native Affairs Officer on the Housing of Africans in Nairobi, 1941* (hereafter Martin-Colchester Report); memorandum by Davies, 1939.
17. In 1931 the official figure given for the population of Mombasa Island was 43,252:

Europeans	1,132
Indians	11,841
Goans	1,077
Arabs	6,679
Others	446
Africans (Natives)	22,077

   In 1939 the M.O.H. estimated the population at 55,068 of whom 30,194 were Africans.
18. The reports of the medical officers of health were consulted in the offices of the M.O.H., Mombasa. Subsequent quotations are from these reports unless otherwise noted.
19. 1938 Annual Report, M.O.H. Mombasa.
20. Report of the D.O. Mombasa (P. de J. Bromhead); *Willan Report*, Appendix IV.
21. The municipal board of Mombasa deliberately ignored sect. 31 of the Employment of Servants Ordinance:

   'Chairman: Am I to understand that the Municipal Board of Mombasa came to that decision knowing full well the implications of section 31 of the Ordinance?

   Mr. MacIntyre (Municipal Engineer and Acting Town Clerk). That is the case . . .'
22. *Ibid.*
23. *Ibid.*
24. 1932 Annual Report, M.O.H. Mombasa.

25. 1933 Annual Report, M.O.H. Mombasa.
26. The figures come from the Minute Books, Kenya Landing and Shipping Company. The African Wharfage Company was owned by T. B. Davis Ltd. of Durban. The African Wharfage Co. held the stevedoring contracts for the British India Line, the Union Castle Line and the French and Italian lines as well as some of the coaling ships at Mbaraki. The East African Lighterage Company worked the ships of the Clan and Ellerman Lines, the Harrison combine, and the Japanese and German lines. The Tanganyika Boating Company was owned by Holland-Afrika.
27. Willan Report: 1927 and 1929 Annual Reports, Mombasa District.
28. *Ibid.*
29. A *serang* of African Wharfage testified to the commission that he received Shs. 12/- a month plus Shs. 3/- for each day worked. In September which was an unusually bad month, he had worked four days. He picked his own gang and charged each man each day. The average worker worked ten to twelve days. There was no official overtime but men sometimes paid 50 cts. Some worked 7 a.m. to 12, others 1 p.m. to 5 p.m. The workers were generally single, they slept where they could, i.e. with relatives, or in stores at Shs. 2/- to Shs. 3/- or in shop doorways, etc. Food cost the *serang* Shs. 2/- a day when he had money and 12 cts. when he did not. *Mombasa Times*, 5 Oct 1939.
30. C.O. 533/507, Rennie to MacDonald, 19 Oct 1939 enclosing P.L.O. to Chief Secretary, 9 Aug 1939 (hereafter Report of P.L.O.).
31. Willan Report; Harbour Advisory Board Minutes II, 24; III, 104. Kenya Landing & Shipping Company, Minute Book I, 128–36.
32. *Mombasa Times*, 1 March 1947. One of the sixteen grievances submitted by the Landing and Shipping Company employees in 1947 was: 'We think that a man who has worked some time and who knows his work should get more pay than a man who has just started work.'
33. 1926, 1929 Annual Reports, Mombasa District.
34. *Ibid.*, 1922. In 1939 the Willan Commission estimated the breakdown of the labouring population to be:

Arabs and Swahilis	3,000–4,000
Luo	5,000–6,000
Kikuyu	5,000–6,000
Kamba	2,000
Tanganyika Africans	3'000–4,000
Coast Natives	3,000–4,000

Willan Report, Appendix IV.
35. 1923 Annual Report, Mombasa District.
36. *Ibid.*, 1921.
37. *Ibid.*, 1927.
38. Kenya Landing and Shipping Company, Minute Book I, 128–36.
39. For instance on 15 July 1937, twenty Chagga were arrested for rioting, and sentenced to one month hard labour and deportation. *Mombasa Times*, 16 July 1937.
40. *Manchester Guardian*, 26–31 Aug 1937; *East Africa and Rhodesia*, 6 Jan 1938; *The Times, Johannesburg Star*, 26–31 Aug 1937. The British popular press exercised its imagination in its headlines: 'Blood-crazed Blacks', *Daily Herald* and 'Savage War-cries', *Daily Mail*, both 27 Aug 1937.
41. *Mombasa Times*, 26 Aug–15 Sept 1937; C.O. 533/486, Governor to Colonial Office, 29 Aug 1937; Governor's Deputy to Colonial Office (both telegrams), 24 Sept 1937.
42. C.O. 533/500, Brooke-Popham to MacDonald, 14 June 1938. There was also a strike at the Shell Company in 1937. Claridge of Shell called in the P.C., the D.C. and *Sheikh* Mbarak Ali Hinawy who settled the matter. After the strike, Shell changed from daily to monthly rates, agreed to payment for work on public holidays and Sundays and gave sick pay. The monthly rate was based on twenty-five daily rate days. Testimony to the Thacker Tribunal, *Mombasa Times*, 12 March 1947.
43. *East Africa and Rhodesia*, 28 June 1938.

44. J. Iliffe, 'History of the Dockworkers of Dar es Salaam', *Tanzania Notes and Records*, 71 (1970).
45. C.O. 533/507, Report of P.L.O. Mombasa Conservancy Department, Municipal street sweepers, Mombasa Electric Light and Power Company, Texaco Oil Company, Mombasa Aluminium Works, Mombasa Indian and Somali milk suppliers, Mombasa vegetable growers, Posts & Telegraphs Department, Bata-Shoe Company.
46. *Ibid.*
47. The Railway refused demands but agreed to negotiate, thereby avoiding a strike. The Mombasa Electric Light and Power Company signed off the strikers and engaged new labour. Stones were thrown at strike breakers at Texaco, and new workers were signed on at the D.C.'s office and sent in a truck to Texaco. Three hundred Kikuyu and Teita milkmen went on strike. The P.L.O. arranged an increase of Shs. 4/- and they returned to work on condition that negotiations should continue concerning housing and rail fare to and from the reserves. *Mombasa Times*, 27–31 July, 1, 2 August; C.O. 533/507.
48. *E.A.S.*, 27 June 1947, article by Cooke.
49. *Tanganyika Standard*, 11, 18, 25 Aug 1939; *E.A.S.*, 4 Sept 1939. *Report of the Commission Appointed to Enquire into the Disturbances which occurred in the Port of Tanga during the month of August 1939*, 1940. The strikers wrote to the D.C.; 'Basi hatuna zaidi twaomba neno hili juu ya Serikali ya King VI tupate kanuni ya mishahara kama wanavyopte wetu wa nchi nyingine. Waafrika wote tupate vilevile wala hatuna maneno mengi haja yetu ni kama wanavyopta mshahara Mombasa, Dar es Salaam...'
50. *The Times*, 3 Aug 1939; *East Africa and Rhodesia*, 17 Aug 1939; *Daily Telegraph*, 2 Aug 1939; *Kenya Weekly News*, 4 Aug 1939; *E.A.S., 3 Aug. 23 Sept* 1939. The *Telegraph* wrote of a '... widespread subversive organization throughout East Africa', the *Kenya Weekly News* saw '... foreign propaganda', also mentioning the activity of the K.C.A. in the Teita Hills. Neither the Colonial Office nor the Kenya government as a whole believed these conspiratorial theories, C.O. 533/507.
51. Willan Report; C.O. 533/507, Report of P.L.O., 9 Aug 1939.
52. Willan Report. This was also the view of the *E.A.S.*, 9 Aug 1939.
53. *Ibid.*; Makhan Singh, x, which includes the full memorandum presented by Makhan Singh to the Willan Commission. He recommended a minimum wage of Shs. 50/-.
54. The Colonial Office tried but failed to secure labour representation on the inquiries. The Governor of Tanganyika replied that no suitable labour organization existed to nominate members, that he was avoiding both labour and employer representatives, and that he would nominate two administrative officers with sympathetic understanding of the African position. Colonial Office to Governor of Tanganyika (telegram), 25 Aug 1939; Governor of Tanganyika to Colonial Office (telegram), 26 Aug 1939. The request to Kenya was worded slightly differently and suggested persons 'whom the native workers as a whole in the territory would regard as being entitled to represent native labour'. Colonial Office to Governor of Kenya (telegram), 25 Aug 1939. Citrine from the T.U.C. pressed the Colonial Office to ensure that the Labour Trade Union was heard. Citrine to MacDonald, 18 Aug 1939. C.O. 533/493; C.O. 533/507.

    The members of the Willan Commission were: H. C. Willan, S. V. Cooke, C. J. Wilson, W. G. Lillywhite, Dr. S. D. Karve, P. P. D. Connolly, *Sheikh* Mbarak Ali Hinawy, P. de J. Bromhead (Secretary), *Kenya Gazette, 22 Aug* 1939.
55. In the eighteen months prior to the strike Mombasa had had twelve D.O.s. In the first six months of 1939, there had been six changes. Willan Report; C.O. 533/507, Report of P.L.O.
56. *Loc. cit.*; Harbour Advisory Board Minutes, III, 104.
57. C.O. 533/493; C.O. 533/507.
58. The Mombasa Municipality (Control of Casual Labour) By-laws, 1930, were passed in 1932 but never put into effect. They called for registration at a fee of Shs. 3/- with the town clerk and the issuing of a brassard. The acting P.C.

told the Willan Commission that he was in favour in principle of the idea but opposed to fees. Inspector Overton testified that such controls worked in South Africa. The commission recommended registration, the issuing of brassards, and the repatriation of the unemployable and the unregistered, but was opposed to passes for travelling to Mombasa. Registration was not carried out, but during the Second World War passes were introduced for those travelling to Mombasa. Willan Report, Part V.

59. C.O. 533/507, Report of P.L.O.; *E.A.S.*, 23, 25 Sept 1939.

60. C.O. 533/519, Moore to MacDonald, 7 Feb 1940 and Moore to Lloyd 24 July 1940, and attached papers. Moore, a former Kenya Colonial Secretary and a career colonial service official wrote with a much clearer understanding of the problems than Brooke-Popham. The latter had planned only a limited expansion of the Labour Section and an increase in the P.L.O.'s salary.

Moore stated that the government's original bill (for the Employment of Servants Ordinance) had contained a requirement that all employers were to provide housing 'to the satisfaction of a Labour Officer or an adequate house allowance in lieu, except in cases where employees made their own housing arrangements. A select committee of Legislative Council which had considered the bill had deleted both the reference to employees who made their own arrangements and that to housing 'to the satisfaction of a Labour Officer'. The result had been that government departments and employers had been paying a wage part of which, if they considered the matter at all, they claimed to be a housing element, and felt themselves absolved from any further housing responsibilities.

61. *Mombasa Times* (editorials), 2, 3, 5, 10 Aug, 21 Sept, 9 Oct 1939, 1939 Annual Report, M.O.H. Mombasa; Willan Report, Part XII, 46–8; C.O. 533/503, Harragin to MacDonald and enclosure, 9 Jan 1940; *Report of the Standing Finance Committee on the Draft Estimates of Revenue and Expenditure for the year 1940*, 1939.

Harragin wrote: 'As you yourself have intimated, retrenchment of personnel in time of war is to be deprecated and I consider that any reduction in social services would be politically unwise . . .' The *E.A.S.* also thought that a clean-up was necessary to prevent further trouble. It referred to '. . . the appalling social conditions in the port town . . .'; 'wages paid . . . often below the subsistence line . . .'; and private housing 'a discredit to the country'. It also preached the need for firmness.

Chapter 7

THE SECOND WORLD WAR, 1939–1945

The Labour situation has been acute throughout the year and farmers have complained that labour is almost impossible to get and what there is is inefficient and careless.

1941 Annual Report, Nyeri District.

Conscription, like other bad habits, is easier to acquire than to shake off...

Colonial Office minute, 2 April 1943.

The impact of the Second World War was to prove very different from that of the First. East Africa was spared a major military campaign. Higher prices for African produce and soldiers' remittances created a temporary prosperity in some of the reserves. In 1943, for instance, the district commissioner at Machakos estimated that Shs. 2,073,652/- had been sent home to the district that year, a windfall which subsidized the reserve during the food shortages of 1943 and 1944. Increased prosperity meant that more funds were available to rehabilitate African land and to finance agricultural development. An increased demand and price for meat encouraged the destocking of excess cattle. Even in a district as remote as Elgeyo the district commissioner could report in 1940 that stock was being purchased by the Supply Board, groundnuts had been sold to the K.A.R., and food had been exported from the region for the first time in years. Moreover the 300 men enrolled in the armed services remitted some Shs. 2,000/- a month.[1]

Both military and civilian jobs were available for those who wanted them. The major military presence was in Mombasa, but in 1941 the provincial commissioner in the Rift Valley listed five army and air force stations plus three P.O.W. camps, all of which hired some Africans. In 1939 the district commissioner in the Uasin-Gishu noted the economic effects of the arrival of the Kenya Regiment.[2] Two years later thousands of Africans were imported into the Thika area to commence construction of a railway to supply the armed forces in the Somali and Ethiopian campaigns. Confusion on the project led to political unrest, but the speedy termination of the military campaign caused the project to be suspended and the Africans repatriated.[3] In 1942 C. A. Cornell, the district commissioner in Kitui, could report that 'the normal life of the people has not been interrupted by the war to any great extent... In some ways this has been a "good war" for the district.'[4]

This was undoubtedly a complacent view, but in so far as it was correct it stemmed, in part, from a determination on the part of London and Nairobi to ensure that the catastrophes of the First World War would not be repeated. The Colonial Office remained more in command than in

1914–18 and was especially sensitive to criticism in the British parliament concerning labour problems, but it had to take into consideration that East Africa was a vital source of food for the armies in North Africa and consequently deferred to the local view as to the best methods of production. This in turn led to a reliance upon European agriculture and the introduction of conscript labour for the white farms. Whitehall was able however to ensure that men would neither be recruited nor conscripted unless there was a reasonable apparatus of supervision to prevent abuse. It put up a stout defence against settlers who sought large increases in African taxation, though small increases were made in certain areas. In London Labour M.P.s exercised a careful watch on the wartime emergency legislation and led by Creech Jones obtained amendments in the Colonial Development and Welfare Act of 1940 which ensured that development funds would only be granted to colonies whose legislation protected trade unions and forbade the employment of children under fourteen, and whose governments undertook to include 'fair wages' clauses in contracts using the Development Act aid. Parliamentary and T.U.C. pressures together with those of events elsewhere in the empire ensured increasing Colonial Office attention to labour problems. The departmental Labour Committee was expanded to a wider Colonial Labour Advisory Committee in 1942; this committee included representatives of British employer organizations and of the T.U.C.[5]

The settlers tried to repeat the political advances of 1914–18, but no war council was established nor were any formal extensions of European power conceded until the last months of the war. However, if the settlers did not secure *de jure* political power, they certainly gained *de facto* power within the structure of government since the services of many of them were used on government committees and boards, notably Cavendish-Bentinck who became, in effect, a semi-official minister. This development was an essential prelude to the growth of militant white nationalism after the war. In particular these precedents led to the creation in June 1945 of a quasi-ministerial system under which Cavendish-Bentinck became Member for Agriculture and, as such, responsible for the agricultural development of both European and African communities. Since he had been for years one of the most vocal champions of white settlement, the appointment was bitterly denounced by Asians, Africans and Arabs.[6]

The government was particularly concerned about the manpower and labour situation. Since this war had come as no surprise in Kenya, it had already given prior thought to the probable military calls on manpower; the pre-war measures included an expansion of K.A.R. units and the training of 360 men as a nucleus for two Pioneer battalions. This meant that when large scale recruitment was introduced after the Italian entry to the war, the reception camp arrangements for Africans were adequate.[7]

War Service and Experience

Initially compulsory military service was applied only to Europeans although large numbers of Africans were recruited on a voluntary basis. In 1940 the Defence (Native Personnel) Regulations gave the governor power to order provincial commissioners to produce quotas of fit men for the army or the East African Military Labour Service, but men nominated were given a right of appeal.[8] The combat K.A.R. and specialist units fought in Somalia, Ethiopia, Madagascar (where they fought French African units) and Burma. The African Auxiliary Pioneer Corps served in the East African campaign and in the Middle East, in both campaigns distinguishing themselves; they suffered a number of casualties through being employed on road repair work near the front.[9] The East African Military Labour Service were engaged in local construction work within East Africa for the military and their contractors. All were under military discipline, '... they were askaries,' wrote Colonial Brooke Anderson, the Director of Pioneers and Labour, 'subject to all a soldier's privileges and discipline'.[10] Pay was high enough to secure a steady flow of recruits—Shs. 12/- rising to Shs. 14/- plus uniform, rations, and board. There were also posts for African N.C.O.s. In all some 97,000 Africans served in one capacity or another; the maximum total serving at any one time appears to have been some 75,000 in 1944.

The experience of the Pioneer Corps was far different from that of the ill-fated carriers of the First World War. Initially the rank-and-file was raised entirely from Nyanza. In the expectation of a war with Italy, they were placed in camps in the Northern Frontier District. There were some difficulties at first, partly over conditions but mainly because some of the men would have preferred to be *askaris* and may well have thought that they were joining the much more glamorous K.A.R. The result was a strike and riot at Garba Tula led by Sudanese N.C.O.s in which seventy pioneers were injured and one killed and which was put down by the K.A.R. The G.O.C. then decided to try the ringleaders, dilute the Nyanza contingent with men from other areas, and improve the quality of the officers.[11]

When the war spread to North Africa, pioneer labourers from every part of British Africa were sent first to a vast tented base depot camp at Quassassin near the Suez Canal. They were then posted in companies formed from men of the same colony to different tasks in Egypt, Palestine and Syria. Their tasks included loading and unloading of stores, construction work, and, later, guard duties protecting stores against Arab pilferers. Casualties were sustained in German air-raids.[12]

The East African pioneers were the lowest paid, but their rate of Shs. 32/- per month compared favourably with Kenya wages. From this rate, however, there were uniform upkeep and expenses and the generally high cost of beer and local cinemas to be deducted. In theory each pioneer received four weeks' leave per year, and African leave camps were opened at Beirut, Jerusalem and Cairo. If conditions permitted pioneers could return home after two years service. The Army authorities provided good medical attention with frequent inspections; venereal disease was however a problem in some companies.

Conditions varied greatly according to the camp and work. The initial ration issue, maize meal and second-grade meat, was improved in time. Some camps had canteens and recreation tents, others had a large dining tent with a single lamp, and no lamps in pioneers' tents. One officer commented that there was a considerable amount of minor disciplinary trouble, the usual causes of which were offended *amour-propre* rather than pay or conditions. Few of the pioneers' officers had any African experience.

Religion, church services and visits from missionaries and padres played a very large part in pioneers' lives, particularly missionaries known at home and African padres (these latter were given African sergeants mess status). Evenings were often spent in singing or in tribal dancing. African pioneers were accepted in some N.A.A.F.I.s (British Army clubs and canteens) but not in others and eventually special African clubs were opened in a few towns, where pioneers could sit at tables and purchase tea and cakes. At first Africans viewed men from other regions of the continent with suspicion, but in time the suspicions were overcome, individual friendships formed and views on current problems and the future exchanged.

The impact of this service on soldiers and the army's labourers was, again, quite different from that of 1914–18. There were the inevitable social problems arising from separation but none of the enormous active service death rates.[13] Conditions were much better and temporarily paternalism seemed to work. The war situation in which there were no profits to taint motives, shared danger and mutual dependence caused improved race relations within the forces. Each race saw a better side of the other. Africans were in a situation where they were not menials and could demonstrate capacity and courage; the Europeans had to provide effective leadership. Among other things the army forced its officers to learn Swahili. The war also provided definite rules for living and a clear hierarchy obviously related to the need to stay alive and to defeat the enemy, and therefore, more rational to those concerned than peacetime restrictions and regulations. Waruhiu Itote, who was then in the K.A.R. in Burma and who later became General China in the Mau Mau revolt, wrote of this period:

> Among the shells and bullets there had been no pride, no air of superiority from our European comrades-in-arms. We drank the same tea, used the same water and lavatories, and shared the same jokes. There were no racial insults, no references to 'niggers', 'baboons' and so on. The white heat of battle had blistered all that away and left only our common humanity and our common fate, either death or survival.[14]

But the long term results of the war experience for Africans were much more subversive than most officers realized at the time. Itote, for instance, has recorded how he entered the K.A.R. in 1941 without any feeling for politics and how, by the time he was demobilized in 1945, he had become much more concerned with nationalism.[15] Much thought was given by the authorities to medical and sanitary conditions. Very little disease, apart from a limited amount of venereal disease, was brought back to the reserves on demobilization. On enlistment each recruit had been carefully examined medically, large numbers being rejected, and each recruit was inoculated and dewormed as necessary. The 1945 Medical Department report commented on the war 'bringing about in the great numbers of Africans in the Forces an astonishing improvement in physique and a remarkable change in outlook'.[16] Not only were Africans well fed, clothed, shod and housed, but very large numbers had learned to read and write in English since the army wished as many soldiers as possible to be literate—a development not welcomed by some Europeans in the colony who reacted with rudeness. Many Africans also acquired a wide range of skills—driving, vehicle maintenance, metal and electrical work, signals work, despatch riding, clerical work, instructing, cooking and medical orderly work. By 1942 the Native Artificer Training Depot, which had been taken over from the P.W.D. by the Army Service Corps, was turning out 300 artisans every three months. From a society where pre-war conditions had kept the enormous majority of Africans at the unskilled labourers' level, the effect in terms of self-confidence, familiar contact with Europeans in small units, knowledge of the world, and desire for expression was profound. The acquisition of good health and simple technical skills from the army played a far larger part in the political awakening of the African masses than the occasional sight of militant nationalism in the Middle or Far East, although soldiers who served in India contrasted the sweepers who cleaned their barracks and boots with the humiliation they received from Indian shopkeepers at home. Clearly visible military success against white soldiers, too, played a part: 'Mussolini amekimbia, nakumbuka njaro ya Nairobi, nakumbuka njaro ya 5 K.A.R.' (Mussolini has run away, I recall the splendour of Nairobi, I recall the smartness of the 5th K.A.R.) sang the triumphant *askari*.

This increased pride and self-confidence, ensured that the returned soldier would not easily submit to the humiliation of life in pre-war Kenya. For instance, the military censors found that one of the most persistent themes of *askari*'s letters home was hostility to the *kipande*. The immediate period of demobilization seems to have avoided engendering bitterness and disillusion owing to the euphoria of victory and to the savings and remittances sent home to the reserves, the Kamba reserve, as already noted, being so saved from destitution. But bitterness followed quickly when the returned soldier found himself in increasing conflict with the political and economic restrictions of his country.[17]

The colonial government made some real effort to foresee the problems. As early as 1941 a committee of non-officials of all races was appointed to consider post-war problems; it was chiefly concerned with increasing white immigration and ensuring that jobs or land were available. This committee, however, did appoint a sub-committee including government officers, employers and a missionary to plan for the return of African soldiers and labourers. It is doubtful whether even this much would have been done had not many Europeans feared that the *askaris* would practise the arts of war at home as well as abroad. But once appointed, the committee issued a stream of recommendations: phased demobilization, further training for tradesmen, medical examination, a labour exchange system for ex-soldiers, a civil labour corps smartly uniformed and officered by Europeans for public works, and most remarkably, a government officer to be 'guide philosopher and friend' for trade union development. It also strongly recommended immediate African representation in the Legislative Council.[18] Action upon this was limited to the appointment of one African M.L.C. (Member Legislative Council), Eliud Mathu, in 1944 despite strong pleas for greater representation by Labour Party spokesmen in the British parliament.

The actual arrangements, which varied from the initial plans, were carried out under a specially appointed Director of Man Power and provided a series of courses of varying length over the years 1945 to 1948. Trade and craft courses for artisans of various types such as blacksmiths, carpenters, masons, tailors, turners, painters, etc. lasting on average nine months were provided at the old Native Industrial Training Depot at Kabete and at the former Jeanes School at Lower Kabete. Longer courses trained men as primary teachers, agricultural instructors, clerks and social welfare assistants. More men applied for these courses than the facilities could admit and administer. A further small training centre was also opened at Thika, and a labour exchange system established. The Director of Man Power noted, however, that a very large number of men tried with misplaced self-confidence to embark on commerce or other entrepreneurial activity often with calamitous results, and overall, that: 'As with other ex-servicemen the world over, conditions are not what they had looked forward to. There is a natural reaction and they are searching for a peg upon which to hang their discontents. So far as they can see, it is the Civil Government through its local representative, the District Commissioner . . .'[19]

Conscription for Agricultural Production

However, the main thrust of the war effort was within Kenya. The Secretary of State and the governors of the East African territories decided that the emphasis should be on the production of food and raw materials.[20] Nevertheless there was a demand for military manpower until the victory over the Italians in East Africa ensured that Kenya would not become a battleground. In November 1941 the Minister of State in the Middle East confirmed East Africa's role as one of agricultural production.[21] This policy, in turn, made the problem of labour supply and the possibility of labour unrest of even greater importance.

At the outbreak of the war all constitutional guarantees were suspended by the Emergency Powers Order in Council which was applicable to all the colonies. The government was given broad powers of requisition, control of movements, and censorship. Throughout most of the war government tended to be by decree through the Executive Council and the defence regulations rather than by legislation in the Legislative Council.[22] The lack of newsprint alone ensured that vernacular nationalist newspapers such as the K.C.A.'s *Muigwithania* could not survive. In order to ensure publicity for the official point of view, the government sponsored the foundation of *Baraza*, a Swahili newspaper, and initiated radio broadcasts in African languages. Censorship was imposed as were travel restrictions, which were particularly severe in the Coast Province. These became more rigid when Japan entered the war in 1941 and the port of Mombasa again became a potential target. These regulations on news and travel ensured that no political party seriously hostile to the government could exist for very long; and in any case the main African political parties, the K.C.A. and its offshoots, the Teita Hills Association and the Ukamba Members Association were all proscribed in 1940 at the time of threatened Italian attack as some of the K.C.A. officials were suspected of receiving aid and encouragement from the Italian consul. In the same year Makhan Singh was interned in India for the duration of the war, and the Labour Trade Union languished in his absence although it was never formally banned. As a consequence there was no effective political or labour vehicle of protest for the African worker no matter how bad his conditions came to be. The result was isolated and fragmentary protest, with no attempt to create a labour organization of any kind to secure common action on the part of the workers. This, in turn, led many Europeans to believe that conditions were reasonably satisfactory.

E. B. Hosking, the Chief Native Commissioner, had been made Director of Man Power in 1939 with Lord Errol as his deputy. Very quickly there came into existence a hierarchy of committees under the Director of Man Power. The Central Man Power Committee was responsible for policy decisions, with as adjuncts Indian and Arab Advisory Committees. In the white areas European Man Power Committees administered the call-up and it was expected that the Chief Native Commissioner would guard the interests of the Africans.[23] In 1941 Mrs. Olga Watkins won a by-election protesting in terms almost identical to those of Grogan in 1915 against 'complacency and apathy in high places'; in the following year she helped create the Total Defence Union to stimulate the defence effort of the colony. In March 1942 all the European organizations demanded a restructuring of government. This was carried out but no war council was conceded. The post of Director of Supplies and Production for East Africa was created, under whom there was the East African War Supplies Board and the East African Civil Supplies Board. In Kenya the government created the Kenya Civil Defence and Supply Council under which were a variety of boards, including man power, agricultural production, transportation, finance and supply, and Indian affairs. This bureaucracy was given great power over the administration of labour between 1939 and 1945; it had, however, none but the most rudimentary statistics and information to hand, one of the results of the financial restrictions of the previous decade. Another problem was the departure of many of the younger and more dynamic civil servants for the battlefield, and the impossibility of recruiting new blood from England. The government was left in the hands of those who had grown up in the system and saw no particular reason to change it. Although many of the colonists also joined the armed forces, there were still many in Kenya who were glad to press on the government conventional advice in the direction of more drastic controls over the Africans. Most sincerely believed that these were needed for the defeat of fascism and condemned African civilians for a lack of enthusiasm, pointing out that the Nazis and the Japanese would hardly be an improvement on the British as overlords. Victory, however, for the settlers meant a return so far as possible to the political and economic conditions prior to 1939 which were unacceptable to more and more Africans. Many Europeans were also prepared to secure their own economic interests from the war, the farmers, for instance, pressing for labour conscription and low wages. Nothing indicated the peculiar flavour of the colony better than the interminable correspondence in the newspapers about the servant problem, or the decision of the government to have a committee sit between December 1939 and March 1940 to consider the problem of the registration of domestic servants.[24]

There was the same myopia evident as in the nineteen-thirties. The complacency of the time can be seen in a pamphlet published by Christopher Wilson, for eight years the M.L.C. representing native interests, in which he remarks of the return of the *askaris*: 'But I believe it would be unwise to expect too great a mental revolution. The African often seems to enjoy strange experiences without noticeable reaction, and to show a surprising tendency to return to the *status quo ante* when abnormal stimulus has ceased.'[25] The majority of Europeans felt that the most serious domestic problems of these years were crime and insolence. The newspapers were full of attacks on the quality of African labour and the indiscipline of servants and employees. George Nicol, the M.L.C. for Mombasa, told the Legislative Council that 'the thing that worries me more than anything else is the fact that the natives in the towns are becoming more insolent every day'.[26] In 1941 the Labour Department reported that there were 'complaints of general slackness, insubordination and increasing laziness among native workers'.[27] Examples could be multiplied many times for Kenya Europeans have always had a facility for the particularly insensitive and cruel letter to the press, and the colonial situation never ceased from breeding its widely and firmly held myth of impossible rectitude on the part of the rulers and of singular depravity and laziness by the natives. In 1941, for instance, John Boyes wrote that '... the native is still a child and wants a master to make him happy'.[28] An anonymous woman said, 'What we ... deprecate is the greed, slackness, and insolence ... In households where there is a bwana to kick him in the pants the native may still be amenable to discipline'.[29] The Europeans were quick to blame the armed forces for overpaying servants and treating them too laxly, and there can be little doubt that the army created a more competitive market for servants, particularly as in certain units such as the Pay Corps and the Signals practically every British soldier had a servant. In 1942 letter writers to the *Mombasa Times* complained that servants were demanding Shs. 40/- from settlers since they could get Shs. 30/- from the army with much less work, and the editor wrote of the introduction by the services 'of an element of competition out of all proportion to the needs and commonsense of the situation'. Another correspondent wrote:

> The chief cause of it is the misguided, over-zealous friendliness and undignified attitude of the Forces. It is nowadays a common sight to see a European soldier or sailor arm in arm with a native, treating him as a blood brother; I have even seen them smoking the same cigarette and drinking out of the same bottle of beer.
>
> I personally like the native and have a great admiration for the many who have so nobly responded to the call of war effort. But you have to know how to treat him, and as a resident of many years it both pains and disgusts me to see what goes on. If only for the sake of the native this behaviour must be stopped.[30]

There was also great concern about the rising crime rate. In 1943 Nicol urged the substitution of the cat-o'-nine-tails for the cane, and in 1945 there was a full-scale debate in the Legislative Council on the crime position in Kenya in which Nicol attacked the army and bemoaned the lack of discipline, while Major A. G. Keyser called for collective punishments, flogging and the increased use of police dogs.[31]

These settler feelings focused on the question of labour conscription. The departure of large numbers of men for the armed forces together with some local prosperity in the reserves created by higher prices for African produce and through soldiers' remittances of pay had eliminated by 1940 the labour surplus of the previous decade. Late in 1940 the Nanyuki Farmers' Association unanimously demanded conscription for civil use because the Military Labour Corps had caused shortages and driven wages up. It was pressure such as this which kept the Kenya participation in the corps the smallest of the three East African territories. One speaker at Nanyuki wanted to keep wages down through a conscription scheme; another pointed out that this was 'a heaven sent opportunity to discipline natives who never had had, and, otherwise would never be likely to have, any sense of discipline whatsoever (applause)'.[32] In February the district association at Thomson's Falls voted for labour conscription.[33] In August 1941 the Settlement and Production Board declared that it was 'far from satisfied' with the position of native labour.[34] Two months later the Kenya Farmers' Association called a meeting at Nakuru to protest against the lack of action by the government. Although the feeling was hostile to the authorities on this issue, the resolution on civil conscription was withdrawn probably as the result of pressure from Nairobi. In December the annual meeting of the K.F.A. at Kitale voted for civil conscription.[35] The *East African Standard* urged that compulsion was no solution. It believed the government must guarantee decent wages and insist on high quality work but should control military hiring and improve its propaganda. It called for the suspension of military recruitment for the E.A.M.L.S., A.A.P.C., and the drivers of the Army Service Corps until 1942.[36] The East African Chamber of Mines met at Kisumu in January 1942 together with some representatives of the farming industry, and voted for selective labour conscription, in particular supporting the Coffee Board and the Trans-Nzoia district council.[37] All this agitation was closely related to the campaign of Mrs. Watkins which resulted in the creation of the Total Defence Union.

The campaign unleased a crescendo of letters to the *East African Standard*. Once again attacks were levelled against officials for hindering labour recruitment. Very few of the writers were concerned about the supposed injustice of restricting conscription to the European community. Most expressed the same point of view, namely that 'the natives are entirely irresponsible...' and that 'what is wanted is a law which will make the punishment for negligence, or for irresponsibility fit the crime'.[38] One anonymous writer summed up the widespread view that the Africans had deteriorated from the days when the Europeans first came:

> In these days of turmoil dust and noise, one looks back with regret to twenty and twenty-five years ago, when many of us left England full of hope and trust, to settle in what was then the pleasant land of Kenya. There were few roads in those days, and fewer bridges; our rail-heads had not reached so far as now—but native tribes were mostly pleasant, willing and wishful to learn, and to help us with our work. During these years, they have indeed changed for the worse. Not only do they work far less but they demand far higher

> wages. They have become lazy, dirty, dishonest and noisy. One is appalled to watch them, and wonders what it is all leading to. Their filthy habits are a danger to the whole community; their thefts are increasing daily, their lies have become the joke of the Colony. In my humble opinion they have been educated and civilised too soon; they were not ready for the freedom and lenient treatment they now enjoy . . .[39]

Some voices, such as that of the editor of the *East African Standard*, were raised against language like this.[40] But these protests were swept aside in the torrent of abuse which reached its peak in the first three months of 1941 and again in September and October of that year. The farming community was determined to get what had hitherto been denied them. As one writer from Limuru put it, 'What the farms want at times like these is a good, honest and plentiful supply of labour and a well-staffed Police Force—not gallons of ink and yards of paper. It is only work that counts.'[41]

Gradually the government succumbed to these pressures. In October 1941 it requested all employers to report their exact shortages of labour to the local district commissioner, who would pass it along through the provincial commissioner to the reserves. This was widely regarded as a formal application for labour. On 20 October, a few weeks after the settler meeting in Nakuru, Moore requested the Secretary of State to approve conscription for agricultural purposes in the event of the failure of voluntary methods. Although there was considerable division among the Colonial Office officials on this matter, approval was telegraphed eleven days later. Then late in November the government commissioned a special labour census and appointed a committee on which the settlers were represented but Africans were not, under the new Director of Man Power, Walter (later Sir Walter) Harragin, to consider labour conscription. By this time the authorities were already trying to assist in the recruitment of voluntary labour, but without much success since it merely revived all the difficulties and ambiguities associated with 'encouragement'. Moore reported to the Colonial Office that '. . . in Nyanza, inspired by the indefatigable Fazan, there have been certain incidents which have aroused the wrath of Archdeacon Owen . . . If there has been more pressure than there should have been it is due to the enthusiasm of the Chiefs, who at the best of times find it difficult to make a nice distinction between the exercise of persuasion and the giving of a direct order.' The Harragin Committee reported in February 1942 and concluded that in late 1941 the agricultural industry had been 10 per cent short of its needed manpower. As a consequence it recommended civil conscription.

The Defence (African Labour for Essential Undertakings) Regulations were drafted by the government, approved with significant modifications by the Secretary of State and then proclaimed. Conscription was also imposed in West Africa, Northern Rhodesia and Tanganyika. The Kenya regulations created an Essential Undertakings Board to decide which industries were eligible for conscripted labour. The Secretary of State insisted on parity of wages between conscript and voluntary labour, the reduction of fines for Africans which were originally the same as for European employers, and on the creation of a Central Wages Board under the Director of Man Power which would be the final authority on wages, rations and supplies such as blankets. In the European areas, farmers who wanted conscripted labour submitted their requests to the local district labour committee, composed of white farmers with a district officer in the chair. If the application was approved, it was passed on to the provincial commissioner and then cleared to the relevant African district selection committee within the province. The provincial commissioner could appeal to the Chief Native Commissioner for conscripts from other provinces but this was not expected to be a frequent occurrence. The African district committee chose the men although their decisions were subject to appeal, first before the district commissioner and ten elders of the tribe and then to a district exemption tribunal composed of the district commissioner, two Europeans and four African officials.[42]

Medical examinations, transit camps, length of service and wages were all prescribed. The starting minimum wage for light labour was Shs. 8/- to Shs. 10/- and for heavy work Shs. 14/- Orde-Browne was particularly insistent on the matter of rations. He cited his experience with the carriers in the First World War whom he considered 'the most unsatisfactory and inefficient' labour that he had ever handled until the arrival of the South African doctors who introduced the Rand scale of rations including meat and transformed 'the sullen sluggish conscripts into almost enthusiastic volunteers'. He was determined that proper diet would be one of the prices paid by Kenya for conscription, and he got his way despite the opposition of the Governor and of the Nairobi establishment. The ration scales were balanced diets of maize meal, meat, groundnuts, vegetables and salt. Although the rates of pay were low, and probably designed to prevent any general increase arising from war conditions, the ration scale was considerably more liberal than that previously supplied to farm workers; the scale obliged farmers relying on purely voluntary labour to improve their ration issues. The first list of essential services under the act was largely agricultural; cereals, sisal, flax, sugar, tea and rubber. It also included saw-milling, the supply of timber, and the production of wood fuel for the railways. Within two weeks seventeen more items had been added. It appeared that the flood gates were opening, but the worst was averted as a consequence of pressure from London. The conscription measure was necessary to maintain production in certain parts of the economy; for instance, it saved the unpopular sisal industry. It no doubt greatly assisted some bad employers to obtain labour they would not otherwise have secured. In 1941, for instance, the district commissioner for Tambach reported that '... on several occasions employers known to be unpopular with this tribe were assisted with labour for war purposes'.[43] It also gave government sanction to the continuation of a low-wage economy and postponed the need for employers to consider the use of highly paid, full-time skilled African labour.[44] According to Orde-Browne, the major complaint of the Africans concerned wages, particularly on the part of those who were engaged in their own production in the reserves, as owing to wartime conditions they could earn considerably more than by compulsory labour.[45] The combination of the threat of conscription and increased prosperity also caused a rapid increase in the number of those seeking voluntary employment. Others such as workers from Meru district were drawn into new occupations like coffee-picking for the first time. In Nyeri district employment figures rose from 6,202 in 1936 to 10,477 in 1941; in Meru 5,982 were in employment in 1938, 11,264 in 1943.[46]

The government was very sensitive to charges that it was supplying cheap compulsory labour for private enterprise, and Harold Macmillan, the new Under-Secretary of State, defended the settlers so vigorously in the House that the Secretary of State had to assure the Governor that it should not be taken as a change of policy. The regulations were strongly opposed by the *Manchester Guardian*, the Anti-Slavery and Aborigines Protection Society, the Society of Friends, the Fabian Society, the T.U.C. and by some Labour Members of Parliament, particular concern being expressed over the use of conscript labour for the production of tea and coffee. Creech Jones wrote: 'The European settlers have secured, under the cloak of war emergency, another concession at the expense of the Africans.' He argued that the Harragin Report refused to consider the possibility of increased African food production and enforced by law the system whereby European farms were subsidized by cheap labour and the labourer, in turn, by his dependants in the reserves. Margery Perham made the same point privately in a letter to Lord Cranborne, the Secretary of State. The *Manchester Guardian* believed correctly that parliamentary pressures modified the original draft regulations in the direction of a proper inspectorate, reform of the system of punishment by fines, the provision of return travel facilities, and control over the conscription of boys at school.[47] At times the colonists seemed anxious to provide as much propaganda for the Labour Party as they could. One month after the regulations were promulgated, the Total Defence Union, the European Elected Members' Organization, the Convention of Associations and the Nairobi Chamber of Commerce jointly complained that the rules were unnecessarily complicated. In April 1942 the Nakuru district council passed a resolution that it considered '... the increased scale of rations for conscripted labour ... uncalled for at the present time and is a direct obstruction towards the Colony's effort'. It concluded that existing rations were perfectly adequate.[48] In November the government brought charges against Major Clarence Buxton for using conscript labour outside the terms of his contract.[49] In general, however, employers treated conscripted labour reasonably well since the administration was able to threaten withdrawal if they did not.

In September 1942 the government issued a communiqué urging the need for the highest possible productivity, 'just and reasonably generous reward' for additional services, and making rules to nullify certain loop-holes.[50] Moreover early in 1943 the regulations were tightened up, and in February when the gravity of the Kenya food shortage became apparent, conscription was suspended.

The East African Production and Supply Council considered the failure of the maize crop that year to be 'the greatest economic crisis of the war', and the newly formed Labour Department thought that 1943 was the most difficult year in the colony's history. The basic cause was the failure of the rains although some of those who pressed for an inquiry hoped to put the blame on the Asian merchants or on the Chief Maize Controller. The Chief Native Commissioner testified that in his view the government had withdrawn too many men from the reserves and this shortage of labour in the reserves may well have had a deleterious effect on the production of food; this period is referred to as the 'panya kuu', or time of the rats, i.e. when rats were eaten, in some areas of Kenya. It was a serious blow that a colony which was supposed to export food for the war effort was having difficulty feeding itself. The Central and Nyanza provinces were the worst hit areas. The government set up a Food Shortage Commission and embargoed the export of food from the reserves. It also supplied free rail passes for urban Africans who would return to the reserves. Some 10,000, about 60 per cent of them women and children were returned from Nairobi although the officers had no legislative authority for such action. Restrictions were introduced to limit the distribution of maize in certain industries which were considered less essential and also wasteful in their use of manpower notably quarrying, construction and road-building. The government also began the registration of labour in Nairobi as a preliminary to the introduction of food rationing.[51] The lunatic fringe opposed all such measures using the same arguments, almost the same phrases as 1918: 'The Bible asserts,' wrote one settler from Kipkabus, 'that he that will not work shall not eat, and Christ himself confirmed that dictum . . . Why then do our Government feed starving natives in the reserves, during famine periods . . . Rather let them say: go out to work, then we will see that you get food.'[52] Rationing began in March 1943 through a national system of commodity distribution boards; in Nairobi rationing was administered by a system of individual registration, a system not extended to Mombasa. Registration was fixed to the reverse side of the *kipande*; use was also made of church, traders and tribal associations to reach all men, women and children. Maize, wheat, bread and rice were controlled.[53]

Although conscription was partly re-introduced in July for the sisal estates, the Secretary of State used the opportunity to reduce substantially the number of farm industries which could call on such labour. In 1943 and 1944 sugar, lime-burning, fuel for the railway, rubber and flax were sanctioned by London. In November 1943 conscript labour was permitted for the production of essential foodstuffs, coffee being specifically excepted. The Secretary of State also insisted on the abolition of the Essential Undertakings Board which was totally dominated by the local interests and substituted for it the authority of the Executive Council whose decisions had to be reviewed in London. These changes were incorporated in a new set of regulations which were gazetted in February 1944 and replaced those of 1942. More safeguards appeared in these rules. The control of the labour camps was removed from the district commissioners and given to the Chief Native Commissioner and detailed instructions were circulated concerning their operation. The Central Wages Board was no longer bound to consider, in making its decisions, 'the average rate of wages and conditions prevailing (at the date of the coming into force of these Regulations) in the district concerned . . .' But the provisions on desertion were also tightened up. The War Cabinet was very sensitive to charges of profiteering through the use of conscripts, and in November 1943 it ordered an inquiry which was carried out secretly by Sir Julian Foley of the Ministry of Supply the following year. Foley accepted the arguments of the Kenya government that taxation had to be lower in the colonies than in Britain but also concluded that excess profits were not being made. A visit by Orde-Browne to East Africa was originally conceived as part of the same exercise. Neither visit was much appreciated in Nairobi. 'See no alternative to Orde-Browne', Moore telegraphed London, 'but am doubtful as to whether he will carry the same weight here as in London'.

At the end of 1943, the number of conscripted labourers was less than half the number at work in December of the previous year, but it rose again in 1944 and 1945.[54] Conscription was unpopular; in Nyanza, Meru and Nyeri, it caused men to leave their homes and hide in fear of a return to the horrors of the 1914–18 carrier corps; the *Dini ya Msambwa* gained a few adherents. District commissioners throughout the colony reported the general dislike of civil conscription, particularly for work on the sisal estates. But it was nowhere violently resisted nor were there any reprisal attacks on European farms. Resistance took the traditional form of desertion. For instance, every year between 1942 and 1945 the district commissioner in Kitui remarked on the dislike of conscription for work on the Thika sisal estates. By 1943 P. S. Osborne, the then district commissioner, was contemplating the creation of a small force expressly hired to search for deserters. 'The unpopularity of conscript labour is so evident,' he wrote, 'that some deserters have been arrested and rearrested two and three times without in any way damping their intention to desert a fourth time'.[55] The following year this special force was created and dealt with 227 deserters out of a total of 1,113 conscripted workers. Nevertheless the district every year secured its quota of manpower.

Once again, however, conscription drew administrative officers from other work and men from their plots of land—two contributory causes of the 1943 food shortages. Percentages of men away from home in Nyanza and Kikuyuland once again rose to 50 and 55 per cent. J. H. Clive, the district commissioner in Fort Hall, complained in 1942 that 'in considering the labour supply there is a tendency to overlook the labour requirements within the Reserves'.[56] The previous year he had taken vigorous exception to a story in the *East African Standard* to the effect that half the labour force in Fort Hall was idle. Clive wrote in his annual report that year:

> There was much talk of labour shortage in September and letters to the press . . . informing the world in general that the Government official was a worm and no man. In actual fact when I toured the Thika area in the middle of November there was no complaint of shortage and the harvesting of the crop was well in hand . . . On the Labour Commissioner's figures throughout the year over 50% of the labour force of the Reserve has been out in registered employment and I estimate that a further 10% is in unregistered employment, in the Army or as 'Hangers-On' . . . At least another 10% are genuinely employed in the Reserve . . . and it leaves a very small margin of the so-called 'work-shy'. To farmers who have written us to turn out the 'work-shy' native, I have replied that Fort Hall is not a closed district, and I should be delighted if they could tour the Reserve and see if they can find this hidden source of labour.[57]

The administration claimed that the conscript labourers on the whole 'gave very satisfactory service and sometimes regarded themselves as being a "cut above" the voluntary workers', but there are also suggestions that wherever possible men opted for the better paid E.A.M.L.S. until recruiting was stopped, and the Labour and Native Affairs Departments both commented on the decreasing output and efficiency of all labour in the later war years.[58] This decline must have included conscription among its causes. The system lasted many months after the war had ended largely owing to the pressure of the Ministry of Supply who wished to continue the high production of sisal in East Africa and to the fear in the Colonial Office that the industry in the neighbouring colony of Tanganyika might collapse if conscription ended precipitously. Recruiting ceased only at the end of 1945. The last conscripted labourers, who were at work on sisal and essential food-stuff estates, were only finally released in September 1946.[59]

There were also attempts to control and to regulate the supply and cost of Asian artisans. In 1941 the government passed regulations setting the wages of Asian artisans in the Central, Rift and Coast provinces. The minima ranged from 72 cts. to 85 cts. per hour and the maxima from Sh. 1/- to Sh. 1/25, rates set by a wages board chaired by Isher Dass. In March 1942 the government moved to block the return of Asians to India by declaring that no one could leave the country without the permission of the Director of Man Power. The following month the government was empowered to register artisans, in effect to begin the civil conscription of skilled Asian workers. It also declared that employees in certain occupations which were of special importance to the war effort could not leave those posts without official approval. These restrictions led to protests and demonstrations by some of the Asian community in April and May. Isher Dass, the Director of Indian Man Power, was driven from the stage of the Playhouse Theatre when he tried to explain the new regulations to an Asian audience, and the Governor hinted in a despatch to London that Dass's strong arm methods may have been a factor in his subsequent assassination. Later in 1942 when the government announced its intention of introducing a form of *kipande* for Asian workers which would have involved compulsory trade testing and the issue of a certificate listing grade, wage and the name of employer, the Asian trade unions along with the Labour Trade Union successfully resisted and the regulations remained a dead letter. The Asians also won another old battle when in July 1942 the Railway agreed to admit six hundred artisans to the permanent establishment.[60]

Despite the conscription process, wage rates for voluntary African labour rose a few shillings in the war years. The signing on rate for unskilled labourers of Shs. 8/- to Shs. 12/- (with rations and housing) in 1940–1 rose to Shs. 10/- to Shs. 16/- by 1945; both of these rates covered a thirty-day ticket.[61] The government's rural labour gangs were generally receiving Shs. 14/- per ticket with food and housing by 1945. As has already been noted, the food supply improved notably in quality, and the last years of the war led a few estate employers also to improve their housing arrangements. The small cash increases, however, did not compensate for the rise in the cost of living and the minor increases in taxation and L.N.C. rates of the war years. More real increases occurred in the wages of domestic servants caused, in the words of the 1942 Labour Department report, by the presence of 'strangers in our midst with no knowledge of Africa or the

African'. Nairobi engagement rates for domestic staff in 1940 lay between Shs. 20/- and Shs. 80/- (with a house or hut but no food) according to skill, the nature of the employment (gardener, cook, etc.) and testimonials; by 1945 the comparable figures were Shs. 35/- and Shs. 90/-. This increase represented a considerable African gain; over 30,000 Africans were employed as domestic servants in 1945, nearly double the pre-war total and equivalent to a third of the total monthly paid agricultural workers, this despite restrictions imposed in 1944 on the number of servants in a household. The figures are strongly suggestive of the type of society which Europeans were creating in Kenya as well as of the drift by Africans to the cities and the shrewd appreciation by the unskilled of what were the best paying jobs.[62]

The high figure is all the more surprising in view of the general pattern of the war years—one of steadily worsening labour shortages. The 1944 and 1945 shortage created by the demands of the military were exacerbated by the expanding economy, the fleeting prosperity brought to some African reserves by remittances and the high price paid for meat and grain, and the acute shortage of consumer goods for Africans to buy. Even the twenty-four professional recruiters, now limited to Nyanza province, found that by 1945 they could only recruit just over 4,000 men (charging employers as much as Shs. 60/- per man) compared with the 10,000 recruited in the 1938–41 period. The 1944 labour census showed 255,030 men to be at work with a further 43,332 on squatter contracts. In 1945 when new light industries began to operate, the shortage worsened still further; one measure of the difficulty was the employment of 250 Rwanda men on a Kericho tea estate. Another, more serious indication was the continued use of juvenile labour; 40,000, or 11.7 per cent of the total male labour force, were at work on the 1944 census date. Many of these boys were attracted to the higher wage rates paid in Nairobi and Mombasa where they were found to be at work against their parents' will in poor or bad conditions, often in Asian stores or bazaars. The Labour Department officers returned these juveniles home where possible, and their position was also helped by the Employment of Servants (Amendment) Ordinance of 1943 which abolished penal sanctions in juvenile labour contracts. The Secretary of State had assumed that the legislation regarding juveniles passed in 1939 had been proclaimed and had so informed Parliament in August 1940. He was very annoyed to find that this was not so just at the moment when Britain was about to ratify the Penal Sanctions Convention and to issue a white paper. However, the tea and pyrethrum growers were opposed to the registration provisions of the 1939 ordinance, and a compromise was reached whereby penal sanctions were abolished but registration of juveniles remained inoperative.

The 1939 Resident Labourers Ordinance came into force in August 1940, but resettlement of the excess number of squatters proceeded very slowly. The 30,000 acres of land at Olenguruone set aside in 1942 for surplus squatters proved unpopular. The land was high and poor necessitating strict conditions governing rotational cropping, limitation of stock and control of grazing, which together with the use of the area for the resettlement of other communities created discontent. Only 450 squatter families had been resettled by 1945. In general the government took the view that the squatters had done well out of the war. It was argued that, for example, in the Nakuru area squatters' wages, together with earnings from the sale of produce, provided them with an average monthly income of Shs. 52/-, although it was accepted that the wages element may well have only been Shs. 6/- to Shs. 12/-. Those on decent land near to Nairobi could, in fact, do well producing commodities in high demand such as eggs and vegetables. Others profited from the black market caused by rationing. The administration came later to suspect that some post-war political and trade union careers were launched on the profits of such illegal trading. But at the time the government's view was optimistic.

Some European district councils were availing themselves of their powers to restrict squatters' stock and lengthen their obligatory period of work, justifying this on the grounds of soil conservation and efficiency; most councils tried to enforce the 240 days of obligatory work. The Aberdare council prescribed 270 days and a limit of one acre, fifteen sheep and two donkeys per working male, and the Trans-Nzoia council had reduced the permissible number of cattle to five per squatter by 1945. To supervise and implement these regulations a special section of the new Labour Department, the Resident Labour Inspectorate of three or four European officers, was instituted in 1944, commencing work in the Nakuru district. Their work was highly unpopular, often involving early morning raids on farms —'*ngombe*-counting' as it was referred to within the department. Farmers failed to realize that the removal of stock should have been, in African eyes, compensated by an increase of cash wages, and unrest and resentment increased, particularly on those farms where owners had previously applied few overt restrictions.

The number of squatter labourers remained fairly constant, the 1943 census noting 38,515, the 1944 43,332 and the 1945 42,183. There was, however, a very large increase in the squatting population, comparable to the colony's overall increase; the Labour Department later estimated over 200,000 dependants for a working squatter population of approximately 45,000 in 1946. A few farmers, notably Hector Munro at Dundori, appreciated the social problems caused by this rise and established a community and social service centre which also provided primary education. But these farmers were the exception; overall, for reasons both economic and social, the value of squatting for the Africans changed from a channel of modernization which it had been in the nineteen-twenties to a brake. Squatters as individuals may have continued to accept paternalism, but they had reached a stage at which they thought of themselves as an exploited and deprived class. Incentive to prosper was removed by the restrictions of farmers and by council orders, and many squatters relapsed into indifference and apathy. Administrative reports and occasional African evidence alike commented 'that the normal resident native labourer is less advanced than his brother in the Reserve'. Rumours of large-scale European settlement planned for the post-war period led to unrest and refusals to work among squatters in 1944. The grave consequences of these pressures and frustrations were to be seen in the open resistance to follow in the next few years.[63]

By late 1943 and during 1944 the government developed a new policy.

It was believed that there was not an absolute shortage of labour but a maldistribution. Percy (later Sir Percy) Wyn-Harris, the acting Labour Commissioner, estimated that agriculture was short of some 10,000 to 15,000 men but that there was both an excess in Nairobi and an accelerating drift to the towns. A labour review by Wyn-Harris based on the results of the Special Labour Census of 1943 was circulated to the Executive Council early in 1944 and many of its suggestions were adopted by the authorities.[64] The government took emergency powers to control labour in Nairobi and Mombasa; for this purpose special Labour Control Officers were engaged and attached to the newly formed Labour Department. Africans could not stay in Nairobi for more than thirty-six hours without employment, and attempts were made to enforce a 10 p.m. curfew with special evening passes for those at work. It was made illegal to employ a juvenile without a permit which was only given when the parents were resident. This measure, subsequently made permanent, greatly reduced the number of juvenile workers.[65] All engagements and discharges had to be made through a control office, a measure that had a marked stabilizing effect; non-resident unemployed men, nearly 3,000, were directed to work, conscripted or returned to their reserves.[66] The size of domestic staffs and certain large labour forces were reduced; for example contractors in Nairobi had to secure permits authorizing the number that might be employed in quarrying and construction. It was believed that many such firms were flagrantly inefficient, and the effect of the regulations, therefore, was to discourage reliance on migrant labour. The most significant action for the future, however, was the proclamation of a legal minimum wage of Shs. 28/- in May 1944. This wage, the colony's first legal minimum, permitted two deductions of Shs. 5/- for food and housing when they were supplied, but stipulated a minimum cash payment of Shs. 18/-. It was a triumph, albeit belated for the Labour Department.[67]

The New Labour Department and its Problems

In June 1940 the Labour Section had been elevated in status to that of the Labour Department by Moore as a consequence of the Willan Report, and the post of Labour Commissioner was created to which Allen was appointed. There were initially six labour officers with offices in Nairobi, Mombasa, Kitale, Kisumu and Nakuru. Wartime financial and staff difficulties prevented any considerable expansion until 1946; from 1940 to 1945 the only additions were two further labour officers for Eldoret and Thika, and five African sub-inspectors of labour (three in 1943 and a further two in 1945) together with the small Resident Labour Inspectorate and the labour control officers already noted. The exact status of the members of the department had provoked correspondence between Moore and Lord Moyne in 1941.[68] Moyne and Orde-Browne both considered that the department should be staffed with officers who were the equal of district and provincial commissioners and who could be interchanged with them while Nairobi preferred local people. Orde-Browne wrote gloomily: 'I feel distinctly distrustful of Sir H. Moore's suggestion that such posts should be used to reward deserving, if ill-educated returning soldiers.' Despite this,

Whitehall's views generally prevailed from then on. Allen retired in October 1944 and was succeeded until April 1946 by Wyn-Harris, an administrative officer, as a temporary appointment. In September 1945 another administrative officer, Meredyth Hyde-Clarke, was appointed Labour Commissioner but he was not released from his wartime duties as Director of Man Power until April 1946.[69]

The department's philosophy was a mixture of the British tradition of the minimum necessary interference by the government in the relations of employer and employee, combined with a measure of protective paternalism which stemmed from its sponsors, the Social Services Department of the Colonial Office.[70] The department's main work, as described in its annual reports in the first years of its life, consisted of a close supervision of the activities of the professional recruiters, prosecutions for illegal employment of juveniles, the arranging of compensation for victims of accidents at work (for which the Colonial Office model ordinance was used as a basis for assessment, apparently with success even if without legal sanction), the inspection of some 2,000 work sites per year, the supervision of transit camps at Nairobi, Kisumu and Mombasa, and the recovery of wages not paid by defalcating employers. Not everyone was enthusiastic about the work of the labour officers. Lieut.-Col. Kirkwood told the Legislative Council in 1941 that they:

> ... interfere with matters not their concern. I do not think that that on the whole they are very useful. They are the progeny of the Secretary of State, and nothing else. They are there to make themselves a damned nuisance to employers, and little use to the natives themselves. What else can be done about that I do not know.[71]

More and more, however, the spirit of the British war effort was directed towards creating an egalitarian society. The ethic of the home front was hostile to profiteering and special privilege. In East Africa this was reflected in more and more pressure from the imperial government to adopt the reforms suggested in the nineteen-thirties. For the first time London began to use meaningful sanctions. The Colonial Development and Welfare Act of 1940 was one example of this. In August 1941 Lord Moyne issued a despatch that was terse but to the point:

> ... the obligation to raise the standard of living of all those classes in the Colonial Empire whose standard is at present below the minimum that can be regarded as adequate. As I have already said it is an imperative duty to do all that is practically possible to fulfil this obligation even during the war. This is in no way inconsistent with the present necessity for restricting non-essential consumption by the better off.[72]

Inevitably the Labour Department would be much involved in any such policy. Such a role would make it impossible for the department to continue merely as a labour inspectorate; it would have to participate in the debate in Kenya over the future of labour policy, particularly in the urban areas. This, in turn, would bring it into disrepute among many Europeans although it was able, from 1943 on, to ally itself with certain liberal employers who were willing to see changes in the labour pattern of the colony. The department would also have to free itself from the myth that urban workers were only temporary migrants, a radical reappraisal as even the Labour Commissioner himself was telling the Nairobi Chamber of Commerce in 1941 that he was opposed to making cities more attractive to Africans. There was, he said, a need to keep Africans away from the towns and to restrict technical training to those already in employment who wished to better themselves.[73] Given this view from on high, it is not surprising that most Europeans refused to accept the permanence of the urban working class and the consequences that flowed from this. Very few were willing to consider urban problems on their merits although they repeatedly said that they were willing to do so. The tensions, shortages, and inflation caused by the war only served to deepen the gulf between the two nations.

Further, the Labour Department was to meet with a signal defeat almost at the beginning of its career. In January 1941 the Kenya government published a bill to amend the trade union ordinance in order to give the unions freedom from actions of tort. About the same time the imperial government announced that it was planning to appoint trade unionists as advisers in the colonies.[74] There was a strong reaction. Typical was a letter from Miss Violet Wainright of Thomson's Falls:

> ... the new section ... is most iniquitous, whether in Great Britain or any other country, as it puts Trade Unions above the law, making them unaccountable for their evil deeds ... under United Kingdom legislation, in times of peace, an employer of Trade Unionists ceases to be master in his own business ... In any case this legislation is obviously being introduced here to please the Labour Party at Home, who are singularly ignorant of our local conditions and should therefore refrain from interfering.[75]

A. J. Don Small of the East African Power and Lighting Company told the Nairobi Chamber of Commerce that such privileges should not be given until the unions '... prove their goodwill and ability for a substantial period'. He pointed out that 'the Trade Unions at home had gained considerable experience in labour matters before their present freedom had been granted to them'.[76] The Chamber of Commerce duly opposed the bill. But the major voice against it was that of Cavendish-Bentinck, who also spoke to the chamber and whose views were circulated by the government in an official memorandum. He believed that '... to protect such vague organizations as might be formed against actions of tort ... is madness until we have had more experience of the development of the Trade Unions movement in this country'.[77] Many Europeans were even ignorant of the legality of trade unions in Kenya and assumed that this was still an issue, a number of letters to the *East African Standard* urging the authorities to prevent the creation of trade unions. As a consequence of these pressures the government withdrew the bill and made no further effort to secure a trade union adviser.[78]

But urban labour problems could not be conjured away. In August and September 1941 the taxi drivers in Mombasa and Nairobi went on strike. In December the Nairobi firemen struck and late in the following year there were more persistent strikes in Mombasa and Nairobi. These led the government to prohibit strikes and lock-outs. Under the legislation of 1940, the government had created a special tribunal to settle labour problems, but it had remained inactive. When the strikes occurred in Mombasa, the tribunal was reconstituted with Judge J. A. Lucie-Smith as chairman.[79] The tribunal examined the situation in Mombasa and recommended an increase of Shs. 10/- (half in kind and half in cash) for the railway workers which was followed by most of the other major employers. The strikes spread to Nairobi, and the tribunal, after the addition of Alfred (later Sir Alfred) Vincent to its ranks, made an award of Shs. 6/50 in kind, not in cash. Cooke refused to sign either decision. Since the Nairobi award was substantially less than that at Mombasa, the railway workers went on strike again. They returned when threatened with dismissal, and when some eighty were in fact signed off trouble spread to other firms. Police broke up a strike at Unga Ltd. and arrested five leaders. This was Unga's fourth strike of the year. Finally the Chamber of Commerce recommended that its members pay the award but in cash.[80] Little more was heard of the tribunal until the end of the war, but in the annual report of the Labour Department, the Labour Commissioner commented, 'I have no hesitation in saying if it had not been for a strong Labour Department, Kenya labour troubles in 1942 would have been much more serious and critical'. Moreover, the euphoria which characterized some of the earliest of the department's annual reports was beginning to ebb. In 1942 it suggested that unrest in Mombasa was caused by 'food shortages and the apathy of certain employers to remedy legitimate grievances arising out of the war...'[81]

The bureaucratic inertia was difficult to overcome. Its triumph can be seen in three successive committees in 1942 whose titles reveal a saga of futility:

1. *The Fact Finding Committee 1942.* Appointed 'to inquire into and report whether the essentials of life are beyond the economic capacity of the Government and of the Kenya and Uganda Railways and Harbours, European, Asian, and African officers in the lower grades'.
2. *The Report of the Cost of Living Committee 1942.* 'To consider the Report of the Fact-finding Committee...'
3. *The Stronach Committee, December 1942.* On the 'practicability of applying the recommendations of the Relief Committee to the Arab and African employees of the Government'.

Late in 1942 the government, influenced by the Lucie-Smith awards and the report of the Fact Finding Committee, decided to pay a war bonus to the civil service. This was originally restricted to Europeans and Asians but granted to Africans in January 1943.[82] African civil servants had had grievances over salaries and terms of service for many years prior to this. Before 1927 there were only two classes of clerical civil servants—European and Non-European; in that year the Arab and African service was created with a lower pay scale than those for Asians. The Kenya African Civil Servants' Association as such, appears to have come into existence about this time. In 1933 the association submitted a memorandum to the Commission of Inquiry into the Administration of Justice in which it attacked the *kipande* and suggested that Africans should be able to become members of municipal councils, *wakils* practising in the courts, and the like.[83] In the later nineteen-thirties the association was dominated by Jimmy Jeremiah and restricted its activities to grievances which were more strictly those of the civil service.

The new Arab and African service was meant to be on an experimental basis for two years, but no review was undertaken. To most Europeans, the African clerk was a distasteful reminder that the world was not divided into European bureaucrats and African tribesmen. Furthermore, from its inception the civil service had relied on excellent Asian, particularly Goan, clerical support and feared the consequences of change. Even the some-time friend of the African, the missionary, was suspicious and unsympathetic. F. Cecil Smith, the secretary of the C.M.S. wrote to the Kenya Colonial Secretary in 1937 protesting that the railway, the post office and the customs paid disproportionally high salaries to African clerks and thereby caused disaffection among the teachers employed by the missionaries. 'We urge,' he wrote, 'the dangerous class distinctions which are bound to result when wages of the order of Shs. 150/- are the normal prize of education . . .' He argued that Africans could not be prepared for agriculture if clerical jobs paid so well and suggested that there should be a standard wage.[84] Brooke-Popham was impressed, but the Colonial Office was not. One of the officials suggested that it was ' . . . quite fantastic . . . to compare clerical rates with the sums earned by Africans on their farms, most of whom are quite poverty-stricken judged by any reasonable standards. Indeed I would go further and say that it is high time that the question of the Africanization of the Kenya Service was seriously tackled . . . [but] political forces are far too strong.' He believed that '. . . a reasonably educated and efficient African should have prospects of going beyond £7 10s. a month without having to wait for a special staff grade vacancy'. Finally, echoing Malcolm MacDonald's 1939 despatch on housing, he suggested that 'one of the main problems in East Africa is how to improve the African's purchasing power (not merely from an economic point of view but also to enable him to house and feed himself better) and Government alone can take the lead'.

But the government was certainly not prepared to do so. In 1938 Brooke-Popham reported that the recommendations of the Inter-Departmental Committee of 1930 concerning the African and Arab terms of service had been shelved pending the creation of local European and Asian services. One of the 1930 recommendations had been for retiring benefits for African civil servants. When the two new services were finally created in 1935. Brooke-Popham told Malcolm MacDonald:

> As you are aware economy was one of the main reasons which led to the establishment of Provident Funds for the European and Asian Local Civil Services and the objects in revising the terms of service both of Europeans and Asians were twofold viz. to bring those terms of service more into line with present-day conditions in the Colony and to effect ultimate economy in the pensions bill.
>
> In the case of the African Civil Service it was considered that the inauguration of an African Provident Fund would add to the cost of the Arab and African Service and although the increase in cost, from the Committee's Report, did not appear likely to be substantial, it was considered unwise to

introduce a measure of this kind until the financial position of the Colony was favourable enough to justify its inception.[85]

It is small wonder that the African Civil Servants' Association could complain to the Secretary of State in 1938 that 'various requests have since (1927) been made to Government, and in January of last year a deputation waited on the Honourable the Chief Native Commissioner in regard to the question of the improvement in the conditions of service, but it is with great regret that we have to report that those requests have been ignored, and our deputation was unsympathetically and somewhat brusquely informed that "nothing would or could be done".' The association then went on to demand equal pay with the Asian local service.[86] It had, however, to be satisfied with an inquiry into the terms of service which did not report until 1941 and was not accepted by the government until the beginning of 1943. 'You need not worry yourself unduly', wrote J. F. G. Troughton to C. A. Grossmith in the Colonial Office in May 1940, 'about the African Civil Service Association. It is not a particularly responsible body.' Since the report when it finally emerged did not recommend equal pay, the association was particularly angry. It is also significant that the new terms were not extended to the post office until 1945 because, in the view of that department, they were not attractive enough to get the best Africans.[87]

The civil servants in 1943 were thus enraged both by the war bonus and by the report on terms of service. Furthermore the Fact Finding Committee had confirmed in November 1942 that the essentials of life were, indeed, beyond the economic capacity of the lower paid civil servants.[88] At the annual meeting in February 1943 the association again petitioned the Secretary of State urging that the '... time has long arrived for Government to introduce a unified non-European Service for all subject races in Kenya without discrimination'. It urged a royal commission. This declaration was rejected by the Governor and brought out the most paternal in the *East African Standard* which called it 'immature' and showing that '... help is clearly needed, and kindly and understanding guidance'.[89] Cooke took the opposite view and wrote that the grievances were justified, that he favoured a unified service, and that the association would not postpone its demands until the end of the war because it did not trust the government. He had discussed the matter with some senior civil servants who were, in his view, 'out of touch with realities.[90] The government responded in 1943 by creating a specifically African service under an African Civil Service Board to formulate regulations and to give advice concerning appointment, promotion and transfer. On 1 January 1945 it finally created the long-awaited provident fund, and in the same year set up another inquiry into the local civil service.[91] It was not a very stirring response.

Nevertheless by 1943 there was a perceptible acceleration in the programmes of social welfare and in the development of labour legislation. The war had begun to turn decisively in Britain's favour. Funds were available under the Colonial Development and Welfare Act of 1940 but not until Kenya had changed its labour legislation to allow it to receive grants. Prosperity, only slightly dimmed by the food shortages of 1943, had returned to the European community in the colony. As a consequence taxes produced a yield which would have seemed extraordinary in the previous decade. So far as the ordinary labourer was concerned, the most visible result was in the field of housing.

Nothing had come of the scheme by which Nairobi was to raise £30,000 in 1939 for African housing except for a new lodging house in the location. In 1941 Martin, the Senior Medical Officer, and T. C. Colchester, the Municipal Native Affairs Officer, estimated that £150,000 should be spent in Nairobi on African housing. The same year the government created a committee under the chairmanship of the Commissioner for Local Government to investigate housing for government employees. Plague added a certain urgency to its discussions. As a consequence of its report, extensions were begun in 1942 to the government Nairobi housing project at Starehe. In these years the numbers without proper accommodation were growing steadily. Registration for food rationing confirmed that there were far more Africans in the city than the European establishment had thought possible. Martin and Colchester argued that the situation was similar to that in Mombasa in 1939 and might, by inference, produce the same results. They also favoured the creation of a permanent urban working class and pointed out that the housing situation militated against this. In 1942 there was another inquiry, and the following year the government created the Central Housing Board and a Housing Fund. The board joined with the Nairobi and Mombasa municipalities in joint housing schemes which were mainly financed under the 1940 legislation. In this regard Nairobi was more advanced than Mombasa. It had a higher rateable value, less of a problem of slum clearance, and a more significant group of European liberals in the administration and in the business world. Moreover, Nairobi was the capital and its problems, therefore, were both more visible to the government and more of a security risk.

These housing schemes also led the government to become more involved in social welfare in the African locations. In Nairobi the Municipal Native Affairs Officer (later Municipal African Affairs Officer) was appointed to administer the new housing estates and to be responsible for African welfare within them. Under Colchester this involved an increasing variety of activities, much of it in association with such tribal associations as the Luo Union. These associations provided a welfare function that might have been provided by trade unions had they been in existence. They were also sometimes involved in protest about general problems, some of which touched on labour such as low wages and the colour bar. Some also offered a number of benefits, particularly funeral and burial costs and sometimes access to tribal business associations. Furthermore tribal associations were easier to administer since there were no detailed regulations as in the case of trade unions. They were also favoured by the European location officers as a more natural form of African organization and one which might prevent united African protest under radical leadership. Such organizations, therefore, undermined the growth of trade unionism as, owing to the ethnic diversity of Nairobi and Mombasa, they could not provide a unifying voice for the working class.[92]

There was also some new legislation in 1943, and a few Africans were appointed to labour boards and committees. The government created a

Labour Advisory Board, the purpose of which was to be a sounding board for the policies and proposed legislation of the Labour Department; it was considered an important innovation by the Colonial Office and a number of M.P.s. Most of the members chosen were from the European or Asian establishment but one African, Anthony Akullo, and a single representative for the two existing trade unions, Arjan Singh Virdee, were also appointed, with Eliud Mathu replacing Akullo two years later. The board could only discuss those matters referred to it by the government, and it could not, therefore, raise issues itself. Nor did it meet very frequently in its early years but in time it became increasingly useful as a means of testing business opinion in relation to changes desired by the department.[93] The Central Wages Board was reappointed and enlarged in 1943. The next year two chiefs, Paul Mboya of South Kavirondo District, whose command of English at the time was rudimentary and Josiah Njonjo of Kiambu were appointed.[94] The choice was dictated by the involvement of the board with conscript labour and by the need to find English-speaking chiefs.

A new instrument of trade union legislation was also enacted—the Trade Unions and Trade Disputes Ordinance. This ordinance replaced that of 1937 and brought Kenya into line with Tanganyika. It, at last, specifically asserted that trade unions were not liable for actions of tort, and reasserted the 1937 protection against actions for conspiracy providing the activities were not criminal; it also specifically permitted peaceful picketing and narrowed and sharpened the definition of intimidation. The ordinance made no provision for inter-territorial trade unions or for a trade union federation but neither were forbidden by its provisions. It provided for appeals against a refusal of registration to the Supreme Court and not as previously to the Governor.[95]

By this time the trend of business support for such policies, noted in the last decade, was accelerating. More employers favoured a government policy to increase the standard of living of the Africans in the colony. Some were beginning to see that they would have to tolerate trade unions and that a common employer policy should be evolved. In 1943 the Joint East Africa Board recommended a variety of welfare measures ranging from improved health facilities and a better diet to the creation of urban housing with decent amenities based on the South African experience. All this was with the purpose, so the board stated, of improving labour efficiency.[96] In the same year a local businessman, George Tyson, spoke on the radio and printed a pamphlet along the same lines. The returned African soldiers, he said, '. . . will have been used, over a period of years, to regular feeding on a balanced diet; they will have been used to discipline; they have been well clothed and, when they needed it, they have received medical attention. Can any reasonable person assume that they are coming back merely to revert to the old pre-war state of affairs?' Tyson recommended public works to create jobs, a vigorous housing policy, training and a massive programme to pipe water to the reserves.[97] These proposals, however, could be seen within the context of imperial paternalism and hard business sense. The promotion of trade unions was another matter for it implied a degree of self-government—the creating of structures which would allow Africans to make some of the decisions. Neither the Joint East Africa Board nor Tyson mentioned trade unions.

George Nicol, the member for Mombasa and general manager of Smith Mackenzie, told the Legislative Council in 1943 that 'he would welcome [trade unions], because he had experience in trying to deal with strikes in Mombasa and disputes with labourers, and he knew how difficult it was to get somebody responsible to negotiate with . . .' At the same time, they wanted to be sure 'that unions here grew up on the right lines' and he suggested that it would be worthwhile to get an expert from home to advise them so that they started off properly[98] In October 1943 the annual meeting of the Association of Chambers of Commerce of Eastern Africa discussed the question of trade unionism. The meeting was told by its president, S. H. Sayer, that it should not hinder properly run trade unions but that it and the government should prevent the creation of general unions which had been, in his opinion, a disaster in West Africa. The chamber wanted to confine this privilege to craft unions and to dictate the terms under which these unions would operate. A. A. Lawrie of the Nairobi Chamber of Commerce moved:

> That the Executive be instructed to pursue inquiries with a view to assisting the formation of Trade Unions for skilled workers in order that uniform terms and conditions of employment can be laid down for craftsmen according to their assessed ability and thereafter to arrange that membership of the union shall be restricted to those who undertake an accepted form of training in the craft concerned on lines similar to those prevailing in Craftsmen's Trade Unions in the United Kingdom.[99]

There was some confusion in the minds of the association between trade testing, apprenticeship and trade unionism. There was also a unanimous belief that legislation and government action should be so arranged as '. . . to prevent exploitation of ignorant Africans by unscrupulous, self-appointed "leaders" '.[100] This view was widely held; Cooke said in the Legislative Council:

> There is also the question of trade unions, to which I think most people, including some prominent business people in this country, are now reconciled, and I hope that an assurance may be given that trade unionism is going to be put on the correct lines before it goes wrong.[101]

There remained many, of course, such as J. J. Hughes of the motor trade who were opposed to any concessions, but the leaders of the business community seemed to be prepared to concede trade union rights to the elite of the working class while remaining determined to prevent it becoming a serious mass movement.[102] Whether they were prepared to accept the high wage urban economy which was the natural corollary of this policy remained to be seen.

During 1944 the chambers of commerce took another step. S. H. Sayer told the Nairobi chamber that Kenya Europeans were ignorant of the way in which the trade union movement should be run. The members then supported a request to the authorities to arrange for a visit to East Africa by a labour expert to advise on trade unions, a suggestion that had already been made by Creech Jones in the British House of Commons in the previous month. In October the association went further than the Nairobi chamber and accepted a motion in favour of the appointment of a permanent trade union adviser.[103] All these moves, however, took place under special circumstances. There was, in fact, no effective trade union movement during these years; the discussions were, therefore, abstract, and their sincerity would not be tested until after the war when trade unions not only reappeared but actually went on strike. Then the business community would divide. It is likely that these 1944 resolutions represented the views of a minority of liberal businessmen, not of the chambers as a whole. Nor did they act as a very effective lobby for their views. Late in 1944 for instance, Oliver Stanley, the Colonial Secretary, sent his Labour Adviser, Orde-Browne to tour East Africa. He remained until March 1945, and among other things also recommended to the Kenya government the appointment of a trade union adviser.[104] Nothing, however, was done at the time.

The meeting of the Electors' Union in 1944 brought out all the old cliches in an atmosphere reminiscent of 1918. W. F. O. Trench from the Rift Valley attacked the mission schools who only taught the Africans not to work on Sunday. 'The first thing,' he said, 'to teach the African today, is to do an honest day's work. The whole root of the trouble is education.' Valpy, the representative from Trans-Nzoia recommended discipline, and Dr. Parsons told the meeting that Africans were not grateful. The Rev. Leonard Beecher disagreed and said that he disliked sweeping generalizations about ungrateful Africans. He urged the Electors' Union to realize that trusteeship was becoming partnership, but there were not many Europeans willing to listen. The following year saw many of the same complaints. Mrs. Bryan Shaw told the Union of the need for discipline. 'The Kipsigis,' she said, 'at one time, for example, had been good workers, but now the young men were virtually unemployable.'[105]

The old ways still had great vitality in European circles. When it looked as though the railway workers in Nairobi might walk out in the aftermath of the 1945 Uganda riots and strikes, the government replied with a draconian circular:

> The Kenya Government is determined that disorders such as have been experienced in Uganda shall not take place in Kenya. Government is aware that certain evilly-disposed persons put up a notice advising a strike in Nairobi and Government gives a firm warning that it will not tolerate illegal strikes . . .
>
> Next Tuesday (30.1.1945) a new law will come into force making it a criminal offence for any person to incite workers in essential industries to strike or leave work, and people doing so will be properly dealt with and suitably punished . . .

Even the *East African Standard* protested. 'We are,' its editorialist wrote, 'witnessing the stirrings of new thought in Africa, and are attempting to cope with the problems arising from it by antiquated methods and creaking machinery. Restrictive legislation may postpone trouble, but it offers no answer to living issues.[106]

APPENDIX III

Table 1

TOTAL NUMBERS OF AFRICANS AT WORK 1942–5

Date	Conscripts	Voluntary labour	Total
1 July 1942	2,595	228,066	230,661
1 Jan 1943	13,652	224,710	238,362
1 July 1943	6,310	225,642	221,952
1 Jan 1944	10,056	242,541	252,597
1 July 1944	16,003	241,627	257,630
1 Jan 1945	21,903	224,124	247,027

Table 2

OCCUPATIONS OF CONSCRIPTED LABOUR
SPECIAL LABOUR CENSUS—NOVEMBER 1944

Production of essential food & pyrethrum	4,394
Civil labour for urgent works	363
Sisal	10,265
Sugar	1,060
Rubber	931
Flax	51
Government & Local Government works	189
Lime burning	202
In Labour Camps	704
Total	18,159
Sick, off-duty	517
On leave	125
Absent without leave	1,668
Total:	20,469

NOTES

1. 1940 Annual Report, Elgeyo District.
2. R.A.F. stations at Nakuru and Gilgil, the Gas and Small Arms School at Nakuru, the Officer Cadet Training School at Njoro, the Royal Engineers at Eldoret, two P.O.W. camps in Nakuru district and one at Eldoret. 1941 Annual Report, Rift Valley Province; 1939 Annual Report, Uasin-Gishu District.
3. 1941 Annual Report, Thika District.
4. 1942 Annual Report, Kitui District. See also 1942 and 1944 Annual Reports, Fort Hall District for similar views.
5. *Colonial Office List, 1946*. For a more detailed examination of the pressures on the Colonial Office, see B. C. Roberts, *Labour in the Tropical Territories of the Commonwealth*, 1964, *passim*. 'Independent members' were also added to the committee; these included Rita Hinden of the Fabian Society and Professor W. M. Macmillan, both of whom were known critics of Kenya's labour situation.
6. *Sessional Paper No. 3 of 1945; The Times*, 10 July 1945; G. Bennett, *op. cit.*, ix; C.O. 533/537.

7. *Report on Native Affairs, 1939–45*, 1947; G. St. J. Orde-Browne, *Labour Conditions in East Africa*, 1946 (hereafter Orde-Browne), 12; *Kenya Gazette*, 16 Sept, 6 Dec 1939.
8. The right of appeal was sometimes overridden. 'We are informed cases have occurred of natives being press-ganged into employment by the tribal authorities without being able to settle their family affairs before being sent out of the district.' *Report on the Conscription of African Labour*, 1942.
9. Interview C. Pierce, 1969.
10. Orde-Browne, 120.
11. C.O. 820/37, Acting Governor to Secretary of State, 9 Jan 1940 and subsequent documents. The Germans, advised of this incident by the Italian consul, used it as propaganda, thus obliging the authorities in East Africa to admit that the incident had taken place. *E.A.S.*, 17 Jan 1940.

    For an interesting account on which the subsequent paragraphs are based, see D. M. Barber, *Africans in Khaki*, 1948, *passim.*
12. African corpses were a favourite selection of German engineers and pioneers when preparing booby-traps. Suggestions have been made also that German military medical care of Africans captured may have been inferior.

    In the campaign against the Italians the pioneers were used in moments of crisis as additional infantry, and almost invariably formed part of front-line formations. See, for example, N. Orpen, *South African Forces, World War II*, I, *East African and Abyssinian Campaigns*, 1968, 325.
13. Casualties: Sept 1939 to 31 Oct 1945:

	Europeans	Africans	Asians
Killed in Action	79	1,388	0
Died from wounds	2	128	0
Wounded	97	2,298	4
Died P.O.W.	1	20	4
Died disease	86	6,872	12
Died accident	64	1,232	34

    The large majority of the Europeans were British Army personnel not domiciled in Kenya. *E.A.S.*, 10 Nov 1945.
14. W. Itote, *Mau Mau General*, 1967, 27. However, R. H. Kakembo, a Muganda in the Army Education Corps, recorded his preference for the South Africans or the British rather than the Kenya whites in his memoir 'An African Soldier Speaks', Kampala, 1944. C.O. 822/118.
15. W. Itote, *op cit.*, i, iii.
16. *1945 Annual Report, Medical Department*

    '... it must be remembered that when the war is over many Africans on demobilization will return to Kenya as industrial labourers. During their army life they have become used to a balanced diet and in consequence ... they have felt fitter men. If they are suddenly put back on a single diet of maize meal they will begin to feel less fit and tend to become disgruntled.'

    Food Shortage Commission of Inquiry Report 1943, 1943 (hereafter Food Shortage Report).
17. For the N.A.T.D., *E.A.S.*, 17 July 1942; for censorship, interview Derek Erskine, 1963; for the visit of the chiefs, *E.A.S.*, 2 Nov 1945; for the views of the Europeans, *ibid.*, 2 Nov 1945, speech of General Sir William Platt in which he said, 'Whether the African soldier should or should not be educated was argued hotly by sections of a mixed and vocal British community ...', and speech of Lieut.-General Sir Kenneth Anderson, *ibid.*, 7 Dec 1945. A similar argument arose over the education of African police. *Report of the Committee on Police Terms of Service*, 1942.
18. *Post-War Employment Committee Report and Report of the Sub-Committee on Post-War Employment of Africans*, 1943. No Africans were appointed to this committee. *Kenya Gazette*, 3 June, 19 Aug 1941.
19. *Man Power, Demobilization and Reabsorption Report 1945*, 1946. The schemes could only absorb some of those who had received a little craft or

mechanical training in the army. The remainder found their opportunities for further training blocked by the increasing Asian population. For a collection of pamphlets on training, etc., see C.O. 822/118 and C.O. 533/534.

Two common disastrous forms of entrepreneurial activity by demobilized soldiers were the purchase of worn second-hand box-bodied lorries or buses, and the formation of co-operative enterprises by individuals lacking in any commercial or accountancy knowledge.

20. C.O. 533/503, circular telegram, Secretary of State, 15 Sept 1939, Kenya hoped to concentrate on the production of butter, cereals, seeds, bacon, sisal, sugar and tea and to investigate possible development of hides, wattle and wool. *The Times*, 4 Nov 1939.
21. Food Shortage Report.
22. The Emergency Powers (Defence) Act, 1939 passed into law in Britain on 24 Aug 1939 and applied with modifications to Kenya through the Emergency Powers (Colonial Defence) Order in Council, 1939 and the Emergency Powers (Colonial Defence) (Amendment) Order in Council, 1940.
23. *E.A.S.*, 2 Oct 1939.
24. *Report and Recommendations of the Registration of Domestic Servants Ordinance Committee 1939*, 1940. 'There is a strong feeling in the District for the retention and strict application of the Domestic Servants Ordinance.' 1939 Annual Report, Uasin-Gishu District.
25. C. J. Wilson, *One African Colony*, 1945.
26. *Kenya Debates*, 26 Nov 1941.
27. *1941 Annual Report, Labour Department.*
28. 'I have lived in this country a good many years and I must say that I have always got on very well with the Native. He is a good fellow so long as he is handled in the right way. A white man wants a leader, and a native wants a master.' *E.A.S.*, 17 Sept 1941.
29. *Ibid.*, 7 March 1941.
30. *Mombasa Times*, 11, 12, 26 Sept 1942.
31. *Kenya Debates*, 17 Nov 1943, 9 Jan 1945. In 1945 the Attorney-General, S. W. P. Foster-Sutton promised to press for an increase in the number of offences for which prisoners were liable for corporal punishment.
32. *E.A.S.*, 2 Jan 1941. This was opposed by the Chief Native Commissioner and by the provincial commissioner. An anonymous letter signed 'Old Guard' stated that officials disliked settlers and hindered labour recruitment. T. A. Budgen wrote that the officials at Nanyuki were helpful but opposed to labour conscription. Orde-Browne, 69–70.

    In Nyeri district, when recruiting began for the military labour corps '... the response was good but it had an unsettling effect on farms. Labour were attracted to the Corps by a higher rate of wages and rations which they could never expect on a farm'. 1940 Annual Report, Nyeri District.

    The Governor recorded his view in 1944: 'The hard facts are that in war time the African prefers soldiering to hard work, and after some four years of close observation of what soldiering in East Africa means, he has no hesitation in making his choice.' C.O. 822/117, Moore to Stanley, 5 Jan 1944.
33. *E.A.S.*, 7 Feb 1941.
34. *Ibid.*, 22 Aug 1941. The board also wanted an increase in the number of labour officers by two and a consideration of the use of P.O.W.s.
35. *Ibid.*, 9 Jan 1942.
36. *Ibid.*, 3, 4, 6, 8 Oct 1941.
37. *Ibid.*, 2 Feb 1942.
38. *E.A.S.*, 7 Jan 1941, anonymous letter from Thomson's Falls.
39. *Ibid.*, 17 Jan 1941.
40. 'We are told that there are labour difficulties in the country. There always have been; there always will be; because, as in the rest of the world, we cannot hope to establish in Kenya a perfect relationship between employers and employed; but considering the abnormal times they are far less now than we might have expected.' *Ibid.*, 21 Feb 1941. See *ibid.*, 7 Feb 1941, letter from

Muriel Howard-Williams, and *ibid.*, 2 Sept 1941 in which an anonymous letter urged improved rations and long-term contracts at higher wages so that the worker could be joined by his wife. A letter, *ibid.*, 9 Jan 1942 from B. W. Bampfylde protested against the abusive language of European letter writers; see also letters, *ibid.*, 24 Feb, 3, 12 March and 24 Sept 1941 including two from Africans, K. M. F. Kinyanjui and C. F. R. Sigungu.

41. *Ibid.*, 14 Feb 1941, anonymous letter from Limuru.
42. *Report on the Conscription of African Labour*, 1942; *E.A.S.*, 6 Feb 1942, speech of G. M. Rennie, Chief Secretary, at Barry's Hotel, Thomson's Falls on the failure of assisted recruiting; *Kenya Gazette,* 28 Oct, 25 Nov, 2 Dec 1941; also *E.A.S.*, 24 Oct 1941, 11 Feb–4 March 1942, *passim*; C.O. 533/525, Moore to Moyne, 20 Oct 1941 and subsequent correspondence, Watherston to Surridge, 3 May 1943 enclosing model ration scale.
43. 1941 Annual Report, Tambach District.
44. *Report on Native Affairs, 1939–45*; The Defence (African Labour for Essential Undertakings) Regulations 1942, *Kenya Gazette,* 3, 24 March 1942. The second list included the production of dairy products, slaughter cattle, pigs, sheep, forage crops, potatoes, pulses, vegetables, as well as bacon, meat, sisal product and wattle factories, flour mills, brick and tile works, work for the P.W.D. in connection with the Air Ministry, the Admiralty, roads, building works, water works and workshops, work for the municipal councils in the maintenance of roads and public health services, and work for district councils in the maintenance of roads. In determining wage rates, the Central Wages Board was directed to take into consideration 'the maintenance of a satisfactory standard of living . . . the increased cost of living arising out of war conditions, and to the average rate of wages . . . in the district concerned for natives . . .' For an example of regulations by the Central Wages Board, see *E.A.S.*, 29 Jan 1943; for the authority to conscript, see *Kenya Gazette,* 5 Sept 1939.
45. Orde-Browne, 700.
46. 1941 Annual Report, Nyeri District; 1943 Annual Report, Meru District.
47. *Manchester Guardian*, 26 March 1942. See also *ibid.*, 18 March 1942 where an editorial asked 'But what security is there that these provisions are adequate to protect the African labourer in a colony with Kenya's bad history and special circumstances?' and *ibid.*, I Apr 1942 in which it made its claim in respect of reforms. See also *New Statesman*, 28 Feb 1942 and letter from Leys, *ibid.*, 14 March 1942.

    The Times saw things differently: '. . . it is interesting to know that some of these conscripts recently swaggered on the sisal estates, looked down on ordinary voluntary labourers with some contempt, and announced that they, the conscripts, were His Majesty's land soldiers who had been sent to get on with the war job'. *The Times*, 29 June 1942.

    C.O. 533/525, Margery Perham to Cranborne, 17 March 1942 plus a file of protest letters. Cranborne to Margery Perham, 2 Apr 1942 explicitly rejected the notion of increasing production in the reserves. The government was also concerned about criticism in the United States which came predictably from the *Chicago Tribune* but also from the *Christian Century*, one of the organs of the eastern establishment. For the debate in the House of Commons, see *Parliamentary Debates, Commons*, 26 March 1942, Cranborne to Moore, 2 Apr 1942, *East Africa and Rhodesia*, 2 Apr 1942, *Economist*, 4 Apr 1942.
48. For the Total Defence Union see *E.A.S.*, 20 March 1942 and C.O. 533/530, Moore to Cranborne, 28 July 1942; for the Nakuru district council, *E.A.S.*, 15 Apr 1942.
49. *E.A.S.*, 6 Nov 1942. He used them for road building instead of tea production. The following month the resident magistrate in Nairobi, D. B. W. Good, ordered workers prosecuted by the district officer to be sentenced to P.W.D. road work and suggested that forty-two be sent to Major Buxton. This was quashed by Judge Lucie-Smith, *ibid.*, 10 Dec 1942.
50. *Mombasa Times*, 23 Sept 1942. For instance, if a worker completed thirty tasks in less than thirty days he had to be paid for the full thirty days.
51. Food Shortage Report, '. . . people were moved to go back by consciousness

of the shortage, and when we eventually started rationing by the fact that we were able to pick and choose whom we would ration'. Native Affairs Officer, testimony to the commission. *Kenya Gazette*, 13 27 Apr 1943; *E.A.S.*, 12 Feb 1943 (E.A.P. and S.C.), 8 Dec 1943; *The Times*, 13 March 1943; *ibid.*, 9 June, 1 July for the Chief Native Commissioner; *1943 Annual Report, Labour Department*; C.O. 533/530, 533/535.

52. *E.A.S.*, 24 Nov 1943, letter from J. W. Reid.
53. Rationing for non-Africans began on 8 March 1943. Essential Commodities (Control of Distribution) Regulations, 1943, *Kenya Gazette*, 19 Jan, 9 March 1943; The Control of Native Foodstuffs (Nairobi) Order No. 1., *ibid.*, 16 March 1943; *E.A.S.*, 26 Feb, 3–18 March 1943, *passim.* J. Ngugi refers to this period in a short story, 'Gone with the Drought', *Kenya Weekly News*, 2 June 1961: '. . . the "Famine of Cassava" as it was called because people ate flour made from cassava . . .'
54. The Defence (African Labour for Essential Undertakings) Regulations, 1944, *Kenya Gazette*, 29 Feb 1944; cancellation of eight notices, *ibid.*, 23 Nov 1943; *E.A.S.*, 22 Nov 1943; C.O. 533/526; C.O. 533/533, Rennie to Stanley, 11 Aug 1944; C.O. 822/117, Moore to Stanley, 7 Jan 1944, Seel to Houghton, 3 Feb 1944; 'Enquiry into the Compulsory Recruitment of Civilian Labour in Kenya and Tanganyika to secure the maximum production of essential foodstuffs and of certain raw materials vitally needed for the United Nations War Effort', 14 Dec 1944 (secret).
55. 1943 Annual Report, Kitui District.
56. 1942 Annual Report, Fort Hall District.
57. 1941 Annual Report, Fort Hall District. This was not however the view of the district commissioner in Nyeri, 1941–5 Annual Reports, Nyeri District. In 1942, for instance, P. Wyn-Harris reported that the Mount Kenya coffee crop was harvested only with the greatest difficulty. For an approximate comparison with the situation in the First World War, see *supra*, p. 192, n. 27.
58. *Report on Native Affairs, 1939–45.* The Information Office reported that as one consequence of conscription there were 6,000 more voluntary workers in September 1942 than in December 1941. *E.A.S.*, 26 Sept 1942.
59. *Kenya Gazette*, 27 Nov 1945; C.O. 822/117. For protests see Creech Jones to Stanley, 29 March 1945, Farringdon to Stanley, 9 Apr 1945.
60. Defence (Fixing of Wages) Regulations, 1940, reg. 3, *Kenya Gazette*, 21 Jan, 12, 18 March 1941; Defence (Artisans) Regulations, 1942, *ibid.*, 21 Apr 1942; Defence (Employment of Artisans) Regulations, 1942, *ibid.*, 13 Oct 1942; Makhan Singh, 111–15; *Colonial Times*, 9 May 1942; *Kenya Daily Mail*, 18 Nov 1942; C.O. 533/529, Moore to Dawe, 24 Nov 1942.
61. The Defence (Amendment of Laws No. 154) Regulations legalized, under certain conditions, verbal contracts up to 108 days and could require work agreed upon over a forty-two day ticket contract period to be completed in thirty-six days.
62. The schedule allowed a single European three domestic servants, *Kenya Gazette*, 25 Apr 1944.
63. *Report on Native Affairs, 1939–45*; R. M. Gatheru, *op. cit.*, 46. For an example of a district council order, see those of the Naivasha district council, *Kenya Gazette*, 3 Nov 1942.
64. C.O. 533/533, 'Labour Review', mimeo, 15 Feb 1944; *E.A.S.*, 29 Feb 1944.
65. Nairobi Municipality (Amendment) By-Laws, 1944, *Kenya Gazette*, 2 May 1944; for juveniles see the Employment of Servants (Written Contracts) Rules, 1944. These were made permanent by the Employment of Servants (Engagement of Unregistered Natives), Rules, 1945, *ibid.*, 12 June 1945.
66. Wyn-Harris told the Legislative Council in 1946 that the office in Nairobi dealt with 7,000 Africans in 1944–5, half being sent to essential industries or to approved employment and the remainder being sent home.
67. *Kenya Gazette*, 25 Apr 1944. See also the Minimum Wage (Nairobi Advisory Board) Rules, 1943, *ibid.*, 21 Sept, 12 Oct 1943. The board consisted of the

D.C., the Labour Commissioner and the Native Affairs Committee of the Nairobi municipal council.

68. C.O. 533/526, Moore to Moyne, 24 Feb 1941 *et seq.*
69. Ernest Meredyth Hyde-Clarke, *qui vivit.* Educated St. George's School, Harpenden, L.S.E. and Oxford; Kenya administration 1927–46; Labour Commissioner 1946; Gold Coast administration 1950; Secretary Overseas Employers' Federation 1953; Director Organisation of Employers' Federations 1957.
70. At times this paternalism assumed quaint forms such as football. In the *1945 Annual Report, Labour Department*, for example, the Labour Commissioner wrote, 'The Labour Department, in collaboration with the bigger sports outfitters, has managed to earmark a large proportion of balls coming into the country and has distributed them to employers.'
71. *Kenya Debates*, 28 Nov 1941.
72. *E.A.S.*, 15 Aug 1941; *ibid.*, 21 March 1941, anonymous letter stating that Kenya would not be able to isolate herself from the world after the war and would have to accept trade unions as 'an integral principle of the democracy for which we are fighting...'; *ibid.*, 14 March 1941, letter from J. Y. Martin of Nairobi urging that trade unions should be encouraged since Britain was not destroyed by them and they had proved their worth during the war; *Manchester Guardian*, 17 Nov 1943, editorial which referred to pre-war Kenya as '... one of the scandals of the Empire' and said: 'The war has stimulated British minds to think more freely about their Imperial responsibilities. The new temper has been inspired by the needs of the war, the emotions it excited, the new relationships it has created between rulers and ruled, and the atmosphere of world-wide discussion into which it has brought all colonial questions.'
73. *E.A.S.*, 22 Aug 1941.
74. *Ibid.*, 23 Jan 1941.
75. *Ibid.*, 7 Feb 1941.
76. *Ibid.*, 25 Feb 1941.
77. Cavendish-Bentinck Notes; Makhan Singh, 104–6; *E.A.S.*, 25 Feb 1941.
78. *E.A.S.*, 24 March 1941; *ibid.*, 14 March, 28 May, letters from M. S. H. Montagu welcoming the postponement of trade union legislation and hoping that the appointment of a trade union adviser would be similarly deferred; *ibid.*, 25 Feb 1941, letter from W. T. Shapley opposed to trade unions; *ibid.*, 11 March 1941, anonymous letter opposed to trade unions as a form of Naziism—'Let us rather go back to the dignity of labour...' A rare opposing view came from J. Y. Martin: 'Experience... has proved their value both as a means of arbitration for the worker and as a firm basis on which the employer can have confidence for the adherence of his employees to any agreement reached.' He suggested that craft unions might raise standards and that everyone else in Kenya was protected by associations of one kind or another. *Ibid.*, 14 March 1941.
79. The Defence (Trade Disputes) Regulations, 1942, the Defence (Trade Disputes) (Tribunal) Order, 1942, *Kenya Gazette*, 20 Oct 1942. The tribunal was originally set up in 1941 under the Trades Disputes (Arbitration and Inquiry) Ordinance of 1940. The chairman was the Director of Man Power and he had the right to co-opt others, *Kenya Debates*, 17 Apr 1941, *Kenya Gazette*, 15 Apr 1941; *Financial News*, 19 Oct 1942.
80. The Nairobi award to the railway workers was an increase of Sh. 1/- in housing allowance, Shs. 2/- in rations and Sh. 1/- in fuel and the issue of one bush shirt, one pr. shorts, and one shirt with Shs. 2/50, *E.A.S.*, 10 Nov 1942. Allen had already told employers to withhold wage increases until the tribunal reported and then to act in concert, *ibid.*, 30 Oct 1942. For the railway workers, *ibid.*, 13, 17 Nov 1942; for Unga Ltd., ibid., 13 Nov 1942.
81. Makhan Singh, 108–16; *1942 Annual Report, Labour Department*; for the taxi strike, *E.A.S.*, 13 Aug, 9 Sept 1941—there had been a number of fights with soldiers and the drivers demanded protection; *ibid.*, 23, 26 Aug 1943 for a

further strike by the taxi drivers over petrol allowances and government inspection.

82. *E.A.S.*, 31 Dec 1942, 29 Jan 1943. For Africans earning between Shs. 35/- and Shs. 165/- the bonus was Shs. 6/50 or the free issue of food.
83. Makhan Singh, 44–5.
84. C.O. 533/492, Brooke-Popham to MacDonald enclosing Smith to Kenya Colonial Secretary, 12 Nov 1937.
85. *Ibid.*, Brooke-Popham to MacDonald, 8 Aug 1938 and enclosures. In 1936 Pim had complained of the lack of African administrative officers, although he conceded that the need for education and the maintenance of standards would render progress slow. He also recommended a provident fund or contributory pension for Africans in the medical, posts and education departments. The pay scales at that time were:

Clerical Staff

	Learners	2nd Grade	1st Grade
African	£12–£36 p.a.	£38–£54	£57–£90
Asian	£30–£72 p.a.	£90–£240	£252–£330

European clerks grade C received £180 to £200 and Grade A £340 to £500. Seventy African Officers had salaries of £87 10s. or better; fifty had between £57 and £87. Pim Report.

86. C.O. 533/492, Brooke-Popham to MacDonald enclosing Kenya African Civil Servants' Association memorandum to Colonial Secretary, 18 July 1938.
87. *Report of the Committee on Arab and African Terms of Service*, 1941. The committee said that a unified non-European service would have to come but that it was premature. The government stated that it would accept the report with some variations and hoped to implement it by 1 Jan 1943, *Mombasa Times*, 17 Dec 1942; also testimony to Thacker Tribunal, *ibid.*, 19 Feb 1947. *The Report of the Committee on Police Terms of Service*, 1942, stated that the major grievance of the African police was the lack of a provident fund.
88. *Fact Finding Committee 1942; E.A.S.*, 10, 14 July, 18, 23, 27 Nov 1942.
89. *E.A.S.*, 6 March 1943. C.O. 533/530, Moore to Stanley, 20 March 1943. The Colonial Office was not pleased with the dilatory handling of this issue and the Under-Secretary of State wrote: '... the ultimate object should be to fuse Africans and Asians into one service in which there should be equal pay for equal work'. Devonshire to Moore, 10 Sept 1943. The leading figures in the K.A.C.S.A. in 1943 were D. M. Gikonyo (Eldoret), E. O. Josiah (Kisumu), H. G. S. Harrison, E. K. Binns, Ali Ahmed of the Arab Boys School (Mombasa), J. Jeremiah and S. O. Josiah (Nairobi), J. Jairo (Nakuru).
90. *Ibid.*, 15 March 1943, letter from Cooke.
91. African Civil Service Board, *Kenya Gazette*, 9 Feb 1943; Government Staff Provident Fund Ordinance, Ord 11 of 1944, *Kenya Gazette*, 14 May 1944. L. C. Hill was appointed to investigate the demands of the various civil service associations. The Europeans wished one European service, the Asians similarly sought an Asian service, while the Africans wanted a unified non-European service, and a single Asian M.L.C. one unified service, *ibid.*, 27 Feb 1945.
92. Martin–Colchester Report; interview T. C. Colchester, July 1970, C.O. 533/528.
93. The other members were: for the government, the Attorney-General and the Chief Native Commissioner, for the employers the General Manager of the Railways, W. H. Billington (Magadi), A. F. Dudgeon (a farmer), J. D. Kothari (a lawyer), and for the employees Rev. L. J. Beecher. The Labour Commissioner was executive officer, *E.A.S.*, 8 Oct 1943; *Kenya Gazette*, 5, 12 Oct 1943, 18 Dec 1945; *E.A.S.*, 15 May 1944, editorial considered the board too passive as it had only met twice.
94. *Kenya Gazette*, 19 Jan 1943. The Central Wages Board was appointed under the Defence (Fixing of Wages) Regulations, 1940. The original members in 1943 were J. F. G. Troughton (Chairman), the Director of the P.W.D., the Labour Commissioner, J. H. Baldwin, Shamsud-Deen, S. T. Thakore, Arjan Singh Virdee.

95. The Trade Unions and Trade Disputes Ordinance, Ord 1 of 1943, *Kenya Gazette*, 30 March 1943.
96. Joint East Africa Board, *Memorandum on Post-War Problems in East Africa*, 1943; Association of Chambers of Commerce of Eastern Africa, *Memorandum on the attitude of the Commercial Community towards the Economic advancement of the African population of Eastern Africa*, n.d.
97. George Tyson, *The Beveridge Plan as Applied to Kenya*, 1943. 'The days of Shs. 8 and Shs 10 per month, plus posho, must be regarded as past and the European producer must make his plans on the basis of substantially increased wages and improved living conditions of his African employees.'
98. *E.A.S.*, 23 March 1943; Makhan Singh, 117; *E.A.S.*, 30 Oct 1942 suggested that the 1942 strikes had shown the need for a regular and continuing committee to review the labour situation including availability, recruiting, housing, training, and 'the relationship of master and servant'; *ibid.*, 30 Nov 1942, suggested that the transformation from casual labour to permanent wage earning was further advanced than usually thought but 'it is equally true that, following age-long custom, employers believe that cheap labour is an essential condition if they are to prosper'. It recommended a labour advisory board.
99. *E.A.S.*, 6 Oct 1943; Makhan Singh, 117–18.
100. *Ibid.*, 8 Oct 1943; Associated Chambers of Commerce and Industry of Eastern Africa, *Memorandum on the attitude of the Commercial Community towards the Economic Advancement of the African population of Eastern Africa*, n.d., C.O. 533/530.
101. *Kenya Debates*, 6 June 1944.
102. *E.A.S.*, 6, 15 Oct 1943.
103. Makhan Singh, 119–20; *Parliamentary Debates, Commons*, 7 Dec 1943; *E.A.S.*, 21 Jan, 12, 24 Oct 1944. In October F. J. van Oldenborgh from Dar es Salaam said that unions were premature and that what was needed was an expansion of labour departments. C. H. Bird of Uganda supported this view and argued that union growth should not be forced 'at an unnatural pace'. But the president, S. H. Sayer, told the meeting that the post-war British government was likely to force the pace and there was a need to be prepared.
104. Orde-Browne, 87; C.O. 533/526, Moore to Gater, 22 Dec 1943 raising the question of a trade union adviser.
105. *E.A.S.*, 31 March 1944, 7 March 1945.
106. *Ibid.*, 26 Jan 1945; Makhan Singh, 122. The government did bring in legislation to prohibit strikes in essential services. The strike in Uganda began with the P.W.D. and spread to other unions. Eight were killed in the riots, *E.A.S.*, 18, 19, 22 Jan 1945; R. C. Pratt, 'Administration and Politics in Uganda 1919–1945', *Oxford History of East Africa*, II.

Chapter 8

THE RISE AND FALL OF THE AFRICAN WORKERS' FEDERATION: MOMBASA 1940–1950

I feel uneasy about the E.A. ports generally; there appears to be a prospect of serious difficulties after the war, and the machinery to deal with them does not seem likely to be evolved as matters stand.

Major G. St. J. Orde-Browne, Labour Adviser to the Secretary of State, Colonial Office Minute, November 1941.

I try to be a father to the employees.

The Port Manager, Mombasa, Capt, C. W. Hamley, reported in the *Mombasa Times*, 27 February 1947.

Poverty and Unrest, 1940–6

As we have seen, living conditions in Mombasa were among the worst in the colony. Between 1939 and 1947 there slowly emerged a class and race consciousness among the workers in Mombasa which culminated in the general strike of 1947. Only in the post-war years did this resentment take the form of overt political nationalism. Although there were repeated inquiries into the unrest in Mombasa, only a few Europeans other than the Labour Department saw the reality of the situation. Most believed that more repressive legislation would solve the problem. The annual report of the Labour Department in 1942 remarked on the lack of truculence among the workers even during strikes but stated that 'the African labourer is awakening to the fact that he is holding a very strong hand'[1] In the following year, the provincial commissioner, S. O. V. Hodge, told the Food Shortage Commission that 'labour is more touchy down here and is very ready to take concerted action.' Whitehall was well aware of the seriousness of the problem and tried to secure without much success the implementation of the proposals of the Willan Report. In December 1941 Lord Moyne had pressed on Moore the importance of converting casual labour in the port into a permanent work force and of amalgamating the stevedoring companies. A month earlier D. C. Watherston had minuted that the Governor's despatch had left him '... with an uneasy feeling that the war-time prosperity of the port had already effaced the memory of the strikes which occurred in 1939'. But the Governor had the whip hand as he could always plead the exigencies of the war as an excuse for inaction.[2]

During these years there were a series of strikes and inquiries which set the stage for the major struggle in 1947. The port was an important naval base and became even more so with the fall of Singapore and the threat to Ceylon. There was also a large army encampment. These together resulted in a considerable demand for labour. Shortages of food and consumer goods encouraged a flourishing black market, inflated prices and consequently demands for more pay.[3] The police had other priorities than enforcing the Shop Hours Law. The resistance to pay demands, particularly by the Landing and Shipping Company, was all the more extraordinary as its profits had been so high in 1941 that the Railway had forced a revision of the 1937 contract on a cost plus basis. This meant that profits could not be affected by successful wage claims. Nevertheless the company resisted both wage increases and decasualization with considerable success.[4] The housing situation, so graphically described by the witnesses before the Willan Commission, was aggravated by the wartime influx of many new workers. There were also problems on the nearby sisal estates. In July 1942 200 conscripted workers from the Gazi Sisal Estate marched on Mombasa to protest against their work loads. At meetings at the Likoni Ferry and in front of the Treasury Buildings they were told to return and were promised an investigation. The labour officer and the district commissioner considered they had no case.[5]

As the year 1942 progressed, there were more and more signs in Mombasa of the trouble to come. In July a committee on the cost of living reported an increase between December 1940 and April 1942 of 31 per cent for local goods and 51 per cent for imported ones.[6] Early in October there was a riot at Shimanzi involving the Pioneer Corps and the Railway employees. One Luo and one Arab were killed. The same month, the *Mombasa Times* noted a rapid decrease in essential foodstuffs for Africans, particularly maize. It criticized the military, the P.W.D. and the Railway for not feeding their employees. The municipal board set up a committee to inquire into wages and conditions of labour.[7] Then the railway workers and the monthly paid staff of the port struck on 15 October for three days. The crane operators came out in sympathy, and the port was virtually closed. Harragin, the Director of Man Power, and Reginald (later Sir Reginald) Robins, the General Manager of the Railways and Harbours, came to Mombasa. They found, as in 1939, that the 'strikers had no leaders with whom negotiations could have been conducted...' Robins spoke to the railway workers and told them: 'that he was satisfied that assistance was necessary for all Arab and African employees owing to the increase in the cost of living', that the form and the amount of the assistance would be determined by a committee to be appointed at once, and that the Railway would accept the recommendations and put them into force retroactively to the beginning of October.[8] But strikes and threats of strikes in the P.W.D., the Posts and Telegraphs, East African Light and Power and a number of smaller private concerns followed, although all remarked on the 'restrained' and 'commendably moderate' behaviour of the strikers.[9] At this point the government transformed the inquiry promised by Robins into the tribunal chaired by Judge Lucie-Smith, to which employers and employees made submissions. The tribunal recommended an increase of Shs. 10/-, Shs. 5/- in kind and Shs. 5/- in cash as a cost of living allowance; this raised the basic wage to Shs. 33/-. The tribunal also recommended price and rent control and the creation of state-controlled shops for African food supplies.[10]

Kenneth Cowley, the labour officer, considered the strike to be caused by food shortages, the increased cost of living, and the '... apathy of certain employers of labour to remedy legitimate grievances'.[11] The *Mombasa Times* thought it to be the fault of the government for not being responsive to African needs. It complained that there were no feeding arrangements or canteen facilities for Africans and that the African labourer was not getting his fair share of food. The section of the P.W.D. staff which struck received neither housing nor rations. The *Mombasa Times* also commented on the deteriorating housing situation which had first come to light with the Willan Commission. This was also noted by the M.O.H. and in the annual report of the Labour Department which pointed out that no action had been taken on the government's 1941 housing scheme. In 1941 the M.O.H. had reported that '... (African) housing accommodation is inadequate, unhealthy and very expensive', and in 1942 he commented that building was at a standstill despite the influx of African labourers and Asian artisans: '... kitchens, stores, in fact anything, suitable or unsuitable, that could be so used was used as living accommodation'. Overcrowding combined with under-nourishment to produce malnutrition and tuberculosis. The *Mombasa Times* felt that the grievances submitted to the tribunal were genuine especially in regard to food supplies and to the soaring cost of living, and that the reasonable behaviour of the strikers should encourage the authorities to remedy their grievances and to 'check rampant abuses in the commercial sphere'.[12] Cooke who refused to sign the tribunal's report as he objected to payment in kind, was more outspoken and told the Legislative Council:

> ... the General Manager had dealt with the labour troubles in the way he would have dealt with a troublesome mosquito—he brushed it aside. The Railway Administration, however, was to blame for the trouble that took place. The General Manager was warned by his own officers in Mombasa at the beginning of July that trouble was possible. He was also forwarded a petition by his African Staff, to which he replied in the language of a professor talking to a class of students. He talked about 'inflation' and all the other jargon. The Africans asked for bread and got a stone ... In my opinion the findings of the Tribunal were not founded on the evidence. If more sympathy had been shown these strikes would not have occurred.[13]

Cooke wanted a social and economic survey of Mombasa as a first step towards improving the 'deplorable living conditions of the African population'. The government refused.[14] The last flicker of the strike occurred in November when the Shell employees walked out and demanded an increase of Shs. 5/- over their basic wage of Shs. 33/-. Since the oil company employees were better off than most, the administration was unsympathetic. The strikers were addressed by the labour officer and by the superintendent of police but refused to return. Three hundred and one were then arrested and held for four days in Fort Jesus, after which they decided to return without a raise.[15]

There were some improvements. The Railway built a camp at Tudor and another was constructed by the naval dockyard; some food control was introduced in November, and the East African Civil Defence and Supply Council decided to select certain retail shops and to sell through them essential foodstuffs at rationed prices and in limited amounts.[16] There was also another predictable reaction—the municipality attempted to enforce a curfew on Africans between 9 p.m. and 6 a.m.[17] But the essential problem—that of the labour at the port—remained untouched. The testimony before the Thacker Tribunal which was later to investigate the general strike of 1947 revealed how total the stagnation had been. No food was supplied despite the ever lengthening hours. Mechanical handling was ignored. 'We have tried,' J. F. Stephens, the general manager of the Landing and Shipping Company, told Thacker, 'one or two things. As a general rule they have not been very satisfactory.' Symptomatic was the demand of one of the workers to the tribunal that there be extra pay for loads over 200 lb. There was little security and no provident fund for those earning less than Shs. 70/-. Stephens also told the tribunal that in twenty years of contracting, his company had never had discussions with the Railway about the housing of the employees.[18]

In 1943 there was a serious shortage of food throughout the colony, and the Food Shortage Commission visited Mombasa to inquire into the problems. The officials who testified were convinced that nothing could be done. The district commissioner, C. P. Norman, said that '... it was felt very strongly that if Government were to embark on registration [of African workers] the position would be very much worse than if Government had left well alone. The reason was that it was generally believed that immediately rationing was started, the Native would construe it to mean that he was going to get a regular ration.' The labour officer, Cowley, testified that it had been decided not to introduce either registration or rationing. The senior agricultural officer, Norman Humphrey, pointed out that there had been six periods of food shortage between 1917 and 1934, implying a fatalist resignation to this sort of problem. In the port, permanent employees received rations from the employers, casual labour only on the days they worked and then only for themselves and not for their families. The Mombasa Commodity Distribution Board preferred to try to solve the food shortage by the sale of 1½ lb. of maize per day per person through twenty controlled shops. This meant long queues formed every day rain or shine. There were also abuses. Since no one in Mombasa was registered the wives of permanent workers could buy maize at these shops and sell it on the black market. Africans from the mainland areas also patronized the shops thereby helping to ensure that they would frequently run out of maize before all the customers were served. Stephens pointed out that this system did not allow any food for dependants, and the M.O.H. did not think it possible for even a single man to have proper nutrition on the official diet.[19] Nevertheless, Hodge, the provincial commissioner, who still used the word 'boy' in his testimony, considered the shop system 'as satisfactory as it was possible to desire at the moment' although he admitted that registration was theoretically better.[20] In general the officials argued that action should not be taken owing to the absence of defined African locations and of statistics, the difficulty of identifying casual labour, and the lack of staff. 'We are not impressed,' wrote the Food Shortage Commission, 'by the weight of the difficulties raised ...' It pointed out that 30,000 Africans had been registered in two weeks in Nairobi; it recommended that the same be done in Mombasa.[21] This recommendation was finally carried out the following year. In September the Governor announced that he hoped to restore the 2 lb. issue of maize rations within the month, but until the short rains fell, $1\frac{1}{2}$ lb. would have to be maintained and mixed with cassava, *mtama*, and *wimbi*.[22]

There also appeared before the Food Shortage Commission the Mombasa branch of the Kenya African Servants' Association, which was virtually restricted to the clerks of the P.W.D. Two clerks, H. G. S. Harrison and Matthew Henry, presented a cost of living budget to the inquiry justifying their demand for higher wages.[23] This technique was to be repeated in 1947 when virtually every African appearing before the tribunal of that year was asked to include a budget in his submission. There were also complaints of discrimination in the larger amounts of food, particularly sugar, made available to non-Africans. When asked why he thought this happened, one witness replied, 'he thought that was because the African was just unfortunate'.[24] During 1943 the Railway administration provided three shops for food at controlled prices. The government promulgated two sets of regulations to control rents of houses and of single rooms. Rent control was however not very effective because the complainant had to put down Shs. 20/- before the government would investigate.[25] Much more significant was the start of construction of the Tononoka housing scheme for African civil servants and another for municipal employees although this took continuous prodding from London. Moreover, the development of public housing for African workers lagged behind that of Nairobi. As late as 1946 the government was relying on converted military and naval buildings, having just acquired the land for the first major public housing scheme at Tudor. It admitted that the 'shortage of housing for all classes and races continued with not more than moderate abatement'.[26]

In October 1943 there were signs of more labour trouble because the Railway had paid a war bonus to the more senior African staff only, thus causing discontent among the less well paid. As a consequence the provincial commissioner and the Employers' Advisory Committee agreed to recommend an inquiry. This was duly appointed by the Governor under the Trade Disputes Ordinance of 1940 with Warren S. Wright, a local resident magistrate, as chairman. He reported in the following year that casual labour could subsist on the existing wages but that there should be a minor adjustment in some monthly wages. As a consequence, the Railway increased its wages by Shs. 1/- to a total monthly wage of Shs. 35/-. He also strongly urged that the control of the casual labour pool recommended by the Willan Commission be put into effect.[27]

As a consequence of this inquiry, the government in April 1944 decreed that no African could enter the Coast Province without a written permit; this lasted until February 1946 although never very effectively. One purpose of the regulation was to prevent Africans from coming to Mombasa to avoid civil conscription. Legislation the previous December had also given the authorities the power to deport 'undesirable' persons from the city and 2,375 unemployed men, women and children were repatriated.[28] The Limitation of Labour Regulations were also applied to Mombasa making it an offence to remain forty-eight hours unemployed without reporting to the authorities.[29] In August 1944 the registration of casual labour began;

this measure might have been the basis for decasualization but it was not. By December 1944 there were about 6,000 men registered with about 3,600 working on any given day. In March 1945 there was a re-registration by which it was hoped to cut down the numbers, but the end of the war inevitably meant a relaxation in the enforcement of such regulations.[30] Despite all the inquiries during the war there had been no significant changes in government policy. Nor was the proclamation of a minimum wage in Nairobi followed by the same action in Mombasa. The core of the problem remained the unstable and corrupt system of casual labour in the port. Until this was remedied, Mombasa was bound to suffer labour unrest. An attendant problem was the lack of accurate information, particularly in the form of statistics. The Mombasa Employers' Association repeatedly asked the government for an African cost-of-living index for the city, but no action was taken.[31]

P. R. Morgan of the African Wharfage Company was one of the first in Mombasa to believe that the problem of casual labour could be solved. As early as September 1943, he had written a memorandum recommending a labour pool for the port because of 'the changes in the control and conditions of labour in the Port of Mombasa that must eventually be forced upon us by the Government and the Home Labour influences . . .' He suggested that a retaining fee be paid on the basis of a forty hour week. Morgan sought support outside the stevedoring industry. Inspector Childs of the local police force argued that the town could not be properly controlled until casual labour was eliminated. The local labour officer believed that the government would force such a scheme eventually and that the companies, therefore, would be advised to take action themselves to forestall this. But there was no progress. The Landing and Shipping Company would not accept the idea of a retainer. Others considered that it should not be undertaken because the times were abnormal and that it should be postponed until the end of the war.[32] Morgan made one last protest before lapsing into silence:

> The conditions under which our casual labour live and are employed are similar to the conditions of the London dock labourers many years ago when Mr. Ben Tillett came into the picture and created some of the biggest strikes in English history. In those days Mr. Tillett got little support outside his own strikers, but times have changed and if we do not make some improvements we may find ourselves in a hopeless position with every official and non-official opinion against us and the possibility of all work being taken from us. The casual port labour live and are employed under mediaeval conditions.[33]

No further action was taken until 1946.[34]

Meanwhile the years 1945 and 1946 saw a spate of strikes. In 1945, as previously noted, the news of the strike in Uganda spread along the railway line affecting the railway employees in Nairobi and Mombasa. In February and March there were two general meetings of the African staff, the second called by the Railway African Staff Union Committee, and two meetings of the Railway's African Welfare Committee at all of which the workers demanded an increase in wages and in the war bonus. Captain C. W. Hamley, the port manager, refused to consider any increase until after the war and pointed out that the war bonus was a matter for the central government, not for the Railway. Late in February Orde-Browne visited the city, and the Railway workers took the occasion to press their claims on him. Finally on 23 March another general meeting of the Railway staff shouted down the leaders of the staff association who were trying to report Hamley's views. The men demanded a wage increase and set a strike deadline of 2 April 1945.

The Labour Commissioner and the provincial commissioner for the Coast then agreed to call in two Nyanza chiefs, Chief Paul Agoi and Chief Amoth. They came to Mombasa and spoke to a meeting of some 2,000 men who were distinctly hostile both to the chiefs and to the government:

> Speakers abused the Chiefs and Government and many of the speeches were delivered with a great deal of bitterness. A young Mkamba addressed the meeting and was approved by a large number present. He said that they would strike on 2nd April, and if necessary die, in the same way as their compatriots had died in Burma. He blamed the Government for always putting them off with promises . . .[35]

The following day the chiefs tried a different tactic, Amoth discussing the issue with the Luo and Paul Agoi with the Baluhya. From their point of view, this method proved more successful, and a second general meeting, dominated by Jonathan Oredo of the Luo Union, agreed to suspend strike action. The staff association of the Railway then made a formal complaint to the Governor which resulted in the appointment of the Phillips Committee. There was also unrest among the employees of the Customs where seventy-five men signed a petition, and in the port where the monthly employees of the Landing and Shipping Company wrote a letter to the management complaining of the cost of living. However, there can be little doubt that most African workers in Mombasa were waiting for a lead from the Railway employees.

Arthur Phillips, a Crown Counsel, chaired the committee of inquiry and reported in June 1945, but the government refused to publish the report. This was not entirely surprising as Phillips and his colleagues concluded that the lower paid employees had a legitimate grievance concerning their wages. It therefore recommended an immediate increase of Shs. 5/- and the establishment of a minimum wage. But the report was much more subversive than those recommendations would suggest as it rejected previous inquiries such as that of Warren Wright because they based their conclusions on the assumption that urban work was done by migratory tribal labour. The Phillips Committee considered that a permanent urban proletariat was being created and that the wage structure should, therefore, reflect the needs of such men and their families. It suggested that the mechanism created by Professor E. Batson of Cape Town for determining such a wage might be suitable in Kenya. It also pointed out that urban Africans were not prepared to accept racial discrimination in salary scales.[36] Nor were they incapable of seeing that many others including senior Africans, traders and those living in certain reserves had profited considerably out of the war while their real wages were declining. It also uncovered a series of abuses ranging from the failure of rent control to exorbitant charges for water and fuel.[37] All this also effectively undermined the credibility of the chiefs and ensured that the workers would no longer be impressed by such tactics in the future.[38]

In 1946 there was a considerable increase in the number of strikes in Mombasa. There were four at Lime Burners Ltd., and the labour officer indicated his disgust with the company by telling the management that he would not mediate again unless they decided to follow his advice.[39] Among the railwaymen there were persistent but incoherent attacks on the welfare officer and the welfare committee. The newly formed staff association did not take the matter up, and it seemed to blow over. There were, however, two strikes in September over an allegedly harsh Sikh overseer. In the port the most highly skilled Africans, the crane drivers, demanded equal pay with the Asians.[40]

In March 1946 Wyn-Harris, the acting Labour Commissioner, reported that his department had raised the matter of the casual labour in the port with the Labour Advisory Board and that it was conducting negotiations with the stevedoring companies. He noted in his report that the board was 'not particularly sympathetic to the Labour Department's proposals in this matter on the grounds that they are not practicable. The Department will, however, continue to press for a pool even if started on an experimental basis.' In June 1946 the stevedoring companies agreed to the suggestion of the Labour Commissioner for such a pool for themselves, but excluding the Landing and Shipping Company because it was paying a lower wage and was generally hostile. In November a rotating pool of 800 was proposed with a retaining fee of Shs. 10/- per month and a guaranteed wage of Shs. 40/- a month. This was submitted to the Labour Commissioner who was requested to come to Mombasa in early December. By that time there were persistent rumours of a strike in the port. The stevedoring companies modified their original plan to meet the objections of the Landing and Shipping Company. They suggested a pool of 600 labourers who would be engaged on a monthly basis and would be guaranteed a minimum earning of Shs. 40/- per month as well as a good attendance bonus of Shs. 5/- per month. The Labour Commissioner, now Hyde-Clarke, returned to Nairobi to consult the General Manager of the Railways and Harbours and came back to Mombasa with a Railway representative. The latter's contribution was tartly summed up by the anonymous scribe of the African Wharfage Company:

> ... during the discussions here (he) asked why the proposals, in addition to improving the conditions of employment, showed a general increase of 5s. a month. He was told that it was in anticipation of labour trouble. He described this as 'panic'. Shortly after, the Strike broke out.

The Railway had effectively sabotaged the proposed arrangements.[41]

The fate of the report of the Phillips Committee was another example of this malaise. The Mombasa Employers' Association had recommended a tribunal with mandatory powers, but the government had turned this down. Nevertheless, Cooke was convinced that there was no reasonable doubt that an implicit understanding had been given to the workers that their grievances would be redressed if so recommended by the committee.[42] But the report was never published. The committee reported to the Labour Department directly rather than to the Executive Council as had been the case in the past. Between July 1945 and January 1947, the department submitted three reports on the implementation of the committee's recommendations; they reveal a strangulation of the administrative process. Part of these reports was concerned about the problems of casual labour but there were other suggestions.[43]

Typical was the handling of the suggested social survey of Mombasa which, it was hoped, would produce statistics and information to aid the government in deciding its policy. Professor Leo Silberman of the University of Witwatersrand was invited to the colony and submitted a report in 1946 on the methods of determining the effective minimum wage and recommending a survey of the city by a team of experts. Silberman, who had already been involved in the Mombasa town planning survey, offered his services in this connection. The government's Social Welfare Sub-Committee recommended to its parent body, the Development Committee, that such a survey be undertaken both in Mombasa and in Nairobi. The reply of the Development Committee indicated the suspicion of experts and civil servants so long prevalent in the colony:

> ... the committee takes the view that, while investigation into social conditions and economic circumstances in the towns of the colony will serve a useful purpose, such work should be carried out in the first instance on an experimental basis, taking full advantage of the knowledge possessed by those in close and continuous contact with the population of the centres mentioned.[44]

The Labour Commissioner was unimpressed and reported that the failure to make such a survey had rendered the task of setting the minimum wage exceedingly difficult owing to the absence of accurate data.[45]

The reason for the suppression of the Phillips Report and for the distrust of outside experts was the appalling situation which their work revealed. The Booker-Deverell Report estimated that the population of the city had almost doubled during the war from 55,068 in 1939 to 100,450 in 1947. The African population had grown from 30,194 to 56,000 and was in the view of the report increasing rapidly. The figures make clear the strain on working-class housing. The figures also show the great importance of migrant up-country labour in the city and the consequent social problems:

LENGTH OF STAY IN MOMBASA

	More than 6 years	Less than 6 years
Men	12,400	15,100
Women	10,300	3,700
Children	10,200	4,300

According to the labour census in 1946 about 75 per cent of the adult male population was working:

Males employed by	
Private employers	11,400
Government	2,900
Railway	3,600
Municipality	1,400
Total	19,300
Daily paid casuals	2,200
	21,500
Females	250
Juveniles	200
Total	21,950

The report estimated prices increased during the war between 60 and 100 per cent, rents by 100 per cent and clothing by 300 per cent. Imported cotton piece goods rose by 500 per cent while goods on the average went up 300 per cent. It concluded that the African cost of living had increased 100 per cent and considered that those who had received wage increases of 80 per cent or less were, therefore, justified in striking. The following table of wage increases suggested that all but the first category had suffered a decline in real wages:

Minima	1938	Jan 1947	Increase	
			Shs.	*Per cent*
Government and Municipality (monthly)	16/-	40/-	24/-	150
Railway (monthly with housing)	20/-	35/50	15/50	77
Shore labourers (monthly)	40/-	54/50	14/50	36
Shore labourers (casual—day)	1/50	2/-	0/50	33
Stevedores (casual—day)	2/-	2/50	0/50	25

These were, of course, minimum wages, but in Mombasa the minimum tended to become the maximum; the Booker-Deverell Report estimated that half the work force in the city was paid the minimum wage.[46]

The effect of the decline in real wages could be seen in the testimony to the 1947 Thacker Tribunal. The memorandum from six employees of the Landing and Shipping Company said that 'many years ago the pay for labourers was better than it is now, and now things are much dearer'. Alfani Musa the head *serang*, told the tribunal that he had been fourteen years with the company. He was on a monthly contract which had started at Shs. 70/- and was now Shs. 118/-. He was married and had two children and could not make ends meet on less than Shs. 150/- which, in terms of real wages, would be almost exactly the level at which he started. Furthermore, he complained, there was no security. Most of the African testimony to the Thacker Tribunal came from the monthly paid employees of the P.W.D., the Post and Telegraphs, and the Railway. It not only revealed the effect of inflation but also showed the increasing demand of urban Africans for consumer goods and a higher standard of living. Benjamin Agola, the probationary sub-postmaster at Kilindini, was criticized by the tribunal for his extravagant cost-of-living analysis which included two suits, dresses for his wife, cigarettes, the cinema and a servant. Tomwere Tumuyunge, an employee of the Landing and Shipping Company, said like many others he was unable to make ends meet on Shs. 40/- a month.[47] But the Booker-Deverell Report was based on the assumption that the wages in 1938 were adequate and it also specifically rejected the notion of a reasonable standard of living which could be found in the works of such social reformers in England at the turn of the century as Rowntree. This, the report argued, had only been possible in England by income redistribution. It was impossible, so the report said, to redistribute Kenya's income in any way which might increase appreciably the standard of living in the colony, adding also that it would be wrong to create a class of privileged urban employees—a view which would become an orthodoxy of the nineteen-sixties.

The report's statistics also assumed regular employment. In the case of the port, however, the authors showed just how insecure and inefficient the port labour system actually was. In 1937 the highest number of casual labourers employed in any one day was 2,900, and the average monthly employment was two-thirds of this. But 56 per cent of the casual labour was employed for nine days or less in the month. Such workers were not able to earn enough money to live. Furthermore, since none of them were housed, they had to contend with a 100 per cent increase in rents which had not been the case for some of the monthly labour whose employers provided housing. In terms of efficiency, the situation was appalling; approximately 44 per cent of the workers were doing 76 per cent of the work in the port while 33 per cent did only 7 per cent. The report concluded that efficiency had declined in the port and that the only solution was to pay a percentage of the casual labour a monthly retainer with a guaranteed number of days work.[48]

There were other abuses and complaints besides the cost of living. Water was secured at communal taps at a cost of 1 ct. a debbie and was resold to those who did not have the time to queue at 5 cts. Most of the employees in the Post and Telegraphs worked overtime without pay. This, according to an official amounted to about 120 hours each per year, the department also insisted that all complaints had to be in writing, thereby eliminating this possibility in the case of the illiterate.[49] The municipality admitted that some Africans worked 365 days a year.[50] Furthermore Dr. Rana, one of the more conservative Asian leaders, thought that half the African working class suffered from malnutrition.[51]

When the Thacker Tribunal of 1947 questioned a stonemason on whether grievances could have been settled without a strike, he replied, 'Yes, I would have thought so, but it must be admitted that we have made these grievances known for a long time without anything being done.'[52] George Brown, the acting provincial commissioner, substantiated this sense of frustration.[53] In January of the same year, the *Mombasa Times* carried an anonymous article about the rigidity of local society from someone leaving the city. 'It is amazing to us,' he wrote, 'that after a world war which has so changed the outlook and mode of living of almost every other country in the world, Mombasa should adhere so rigidly to old, worn-out standards . . . Mombasa is afraid of progress. There is a large percentage of die-hards in the town, who greet every new plan with the remark that such a thing has never been done before... The thing to realise is that Mombasa stood still for too long...'[54] The wonder is not that there was a major strike but that it took so long to come.

The 1947 Mombasa General Strike

Three events converted this unrest into the general strike of 1947.[55] It seems that the news of the successful strike of African dockers in Durban travelled along the East African coast. In Mombasa itself there were widespread and accurate rumours that the railway administration had forced the stevedoring companies to abandon a plan for a pool of labourers who would be paid a retaining fee. Finally, late in 1946, there appeared a leader to focus and to organize the discontent and unrest. This was Chege Kibachia, a Kikuyu from Nairobi.[56] He was a young man, aged twenty-eight, who commanded authority because of his education. He was a product of Alliance High School where he had secured the Cambridge School Certificate. In Nairobi he had operated a chicken and egg business, which he tried to expand to Mombasa but failed for lack of refrigeration facilities. He had been a member of the K.A.U. and editor of the *African Leader* but had resigned from the party over internal differences. Late in 1946 he moved to Mombasa where he took a job as a salesman for the East Africa Clothing Company.

Soon he was gathering workers together to form a new organization. He was assisted by two Kamba, Livingstone Kienza who worked at Shell and M. K. William, secretary of the Mombasa branch of the Akamba Union, a tribal association. The new body purposely kept apart from the local branch of the K.A.U. The labour officer in Mombasa was unsympathetic, but the Labour Commissioner met Kibachia on two occasions in the city and gave him some books and pamphlets on trade union organization. Later Kibachia told the Thacker Tribunal that he had read widely including the works of Karl Marx, but he did not have any theoretical or practical experience in trade union organization. He told the tribunal, for instance, that he favoured Whitley Councils but that their voting membership should be restricted to the workers. Kibachia's lack of experience did not prevent short-term success but did contribute to the difficulties he faced in sustaining the agitation.

Throughout December 1946 and January 1947 there were rumours of a strike. On 7 and 8 January, the labour officer and the welfare officer of the Railway met with 200 to 400 of the discontented. On Saturday the 11th, the Labour Commissioner arrived in Mombasa and spoke to a number of the leaders persuading them to present demands rather than to strike. The main complaints concerned married men with families who found it impossible to live on the existing salaries 'particularly on the agreed minimum wage of Shs. 40/- a month, without a house'.[57] But the leaders could not control a mass meeting held the next day, and they reverted to their original plans. The strike finally broke on the morning of 13 January and lasted twelve days. Kibachia resigned his job to become the full-time official of the committee which was christened the African Workers' Union (later the African Workers' Federation).[58] It had a central committee of twelve but little organization below that. It claimed 1,000 members when the strike commenced.

The strike started with the dockers and the railwaymen, and quickly spread to virtually all Africans including the houseboys and the sugar workers at Ramisi on the mainland. The Labour Department estimated that 15,000 men were involved. Kibachia has recalled that he received little support from the official leaders of the railway and civil service staff associations. The core of his support was in the port where a staff association for the employees of the Landing and Shipping Company had been founded in 1945 and recently recognized. The general manager dismissed the seven men who formed the executive of the association. In an angry interchange before the Thacker Tribunal he at first denied victimization and then admitted it.[59]

The strike was spread by word of mouth rather than by an elaborate organization which just did not exist. The African taxi drivers, who had walked off the job, drove carloads of union organizers about the city to persuade or if need be to force the workers to join the strike. But there was little need for intimidation. Both the *East African Standard* and the president of the Chamber of Commerce testified to the lack of violence. The latter remarked that 'intimidation was also more by propaganda than by actual physical force'. It must be admitted,' he went on, 'that the behaviour of the strikers was exemplary.'[60] There were a few cases of stone throwing but nothing serious. The strike also seems to have included both the higher and lower paid workers judging by the testimony at the Thacker Tribunal. A memorandum from six employees of the Landing and Shipping Company catches the atmosphere:

> 1. For some time we have found that the lowest paid workers had trouble purchasing food, clothing and housing—the higher paid were not able to get everything that their senior position entitled them to.
> 2. No complaint was made to the Company.
> 3. When the strike was talked about, we thought that because everyone thought as we did, that it was better not to come to work until we saw what would happen ... later threats were made against anyone working, and many were afraid to come to work.[61]

In the later stages of the strike the heads of fifteen African scabs were shaved in fantastic shapes before a crowd of some 6,000. The victims were told that the next time the shaving would be done with broken beer bottles. The district commissioner managed to disperse the crowd peacefully.

The government concentrated on trying to break the strike. On the fourth day a detachment from H.M.S. *Fal* marched through the streets, and seven lorryloads of the 4th King's African Rifles in battledress with steel helmets and with rifles and bayonets fixed, circled the city. The next day more troops arrived with three bren-gun carriers. Extra police were recruited from Nairobi. Almost 500 people were arrested; the Labour Commissioner thought that 90 per cent of them were held illegally. The provincial commissioner banned all news from all unofficial sources. The schools were closed on the advice of the superintendent of police. The city was showered with leaflets by the R.A.F. and toured by loudspeaker vans reminding the

Africans that the strike was illegal, that they were losing money, and that they might be dismissed from their posts. One pamphlet urged the people not to be deceived by the 'foolish advice of these people afar off'. Some employers joined the battle. The Railway issued its own leaflet as did the port manager, Captain Hamley.[62]

The authorities kept the port and the essential services operating with voluntary labour. Europeans, Asians, and Arabs were all prepared to scab. The least enthusiastic were the Arabs, and the *Liwali* gave an extremely ambiguous statement to the newspapers:

> ... the attitude of the Arabs is not to oppose the Africans in any way, as they sympathize with their legitimate demands, but at the same time they will take no part in the illegal strike.[63]

Europeans were enrolled as special constables and undertook such unusual services as the garbage collection in their own area. Italian prisoners of war who were awaiting a ship for Italy were supplied to the European bakery. On 16 January the Indian Association met with the two local Asian members of the Legislative Council, Rana and A. B. Patel. The meeting decided to co-ordinate the Asian community for garbage collection and other essential services and recommended the creation of a voluntary corps. The next day the administration formed a Central Man-Power Committee from all the non-African races. This committee was in charge of the distribution of voluntary labour throughout the remaining days of the strike. Meanwhile the port was building up a pool of labour which reached a thousand in number by the end of the strike and succeeded in turning around all the ships. At the same time the authorities, although they said they would not negotiate until the men returned, made a series of concessions.

The workers appealed to Archdeacon Beecher. He journeyed to Mombasa and told them that he would fight for their demands as soon as they returned to work. They, however, refused to do so.[64] Shortly thereafter Mathu, the single African M.L.C., intervened. He secured prior guarantees from the government of a tribunal with mandatory powers and of a review of the housing situation. He then came to Mombasa, spoke to some 10,000 of the strikers and to their leaders, and persuaded them to return to work.[65] The success of Mathu and the failure of Beecher, one of the more radical missionaries, was very much a sign of the times. The government did set up the promised tribunal under Judge Ransley Thacker and included an African member; it was this time given mandatory powers. The tribunal in two separate awards gave pay increases to both casual and monthly labour. It also recommended a permanent labour pool in the port of 600–800.[66] Thacker heard a great variety of opinion including that of Kibachia. The tribunal made considerable efforts to ensure that the Africans who appeared were representative. The Post and Telegraphs, for instance, was rebuked for choosing two Africans to appear rather than allowing the employees to pick their own representatives.[67] The same problem arose with the stevedoring companies.[68] Pressure was applied to the African witnesses to produce budgets with concrete figures. Some of these were ludicrous and some dishonest but, in total, they revealed that most Africans were not prepared to accept their pre-war status and were determined to share in the material benefits of the community. Inevitably the more literate and the more articulate secured a disproportionate hearing and there was at least one African, a labourer by the name of Murage, who protested against this. 'All the low paid people,' he testified, 'are very much against statements made by people who are highly paid. My food expenses are equal to those of a clerk.'[69]

The strike also broke the paralysis of administration. On 14 January the minimum wage order for Mombasa was gazetted: Shs. 40/- with deductions of Shs. 5/- for housing and Shs. 12/- for rations.[70] A Coast Labour Committee with an African representative replaced the Employers Advisory Committee; it was designed to provide advice for the Labour Advisory Board from the Coast.[71] Canteens and a dispensary appeared at the port, and government loud speakers toured the city urging Africans not to pay more rent for their premises than they had on 3 September 1939. A. S. Booker and Miss N. M. Deverell were hired from London, in Cooke's words 'by return of post', to carry out the long-delayed social survey.[72] The Landing and Shipping Company began looking for a new general manager.

The African Workers' Federation had shown that it was not necessary to have elaborate organization to paralyse the city for almost two weeks. Class and racial feelings ensured success. That feeling was evident in an angry and revealing letter from the federation to the *Mombasa Times* written after the strike was over and signed by Livingstone Kienige, presumably Kienza, and R. C. Kibocho, probably Kibachia.[73]

Kibachia wrote in a similar vein to the *East African Standard*. He claimed the motives behind the strike were:

1. Indifferences towards paying them equally with the other workers of other races who perform identical or same duties.
2. Partiality and disrespect shown to the African worker wherever he is employed.

He also listed the high cost of living and the lack of allowances for families which, he said, represented a conspiracy to keep Africans impoverished. The placing of equality as a first priority is significant.[74]

Yet the A.W.F. failed to capitalize on the victory it had secured. This can be attributed largely to its rudimentary organization and to the campaign of the government to destroy and discredit it. The government was now trying to promote what it considered legitimate trade unionism, that is unions whose activities were restricted to economic matters within a specific industry or trade. The A.W.F. was the enemy of this conception as the government's newly-appointed trade union adviser, James Patrick, recognized:

> When I arrived in Kenya two years ago (in 1947) an organisation calling itself the African Workers' Federation was very much to the fore. The Leader became such a danger to the maintenance of law and order he had to be deported. I personally had to discourage the growth of the Federation because I believed it would be completely impractical to administer. There was no restriction, limitation, or qualification on membership. You could be a baker, a tailor or a candle-stick maker, it didn't matter what your

occupation was, if you wanted to join, the African Workers' Federation would only be too pleased to accept you.[75]

It was a fair description of Kibachia's catch-all body, but ignored the ability of Africans to conduct strikes with minimal organization and finances. Kibachia was opposed to separate unions, and one of his lieutenants, Japhet Banks, told a meeting that with one union there would be two salary rates, one for the skilled and one for the unskilled. With more than one union, there would be many different scales.[76] In the first few months Kibachia found it impossible to deal with all the business himself and came to favour separate sections within the A.W.F. There were attempts to organize the houseboys, bakery workers, and sugar workers on this basis. He also tried to extend the union by including a women's section and various tribal groups. Banks called on the tribal associations to unite with the A.W.F. in the same manner as the associations in Nairobi merged with the K.A.U. Branches were formed outside Mombasa at Kilifi, Malindi, Kwale, and Msambweni.

Kibachia also tried to spread the union to other parts of the colony. In April there was a general strike in Kisumu and stoppages in other towns in the Nyanza province. The news of the successful strike at Mombasa no doubt travelled on the bush telegraph with the Luo going to and from Mombasa. It is likely that Kibachia hoped to channel this discontent into an effective organization. His main ally was Mwangi Macharia, the first secretary of the A.W.F. who had lost his job with the Railway and Harbours and had been deported from Mombasa. Meetings were held in Nairobi, and in July 1947 it was decided to form a Nairobi branch of the A.W.F. with Macharia as secretary. In August Kibachia came to Nairobi, met the leaders of the K.A.U., and formally opened the branch. He also met the leading trade unionists and spoke at Uplands and at Nakuru.[77] At a meeting of the federation on 24 September, after the arrest of Kibachia, it was decided to constitute itself as a central board to represent all Kenya workers and to open branches in all parts of East Africa.[78] But the arrest of Kibachia prevented this and reduced the A.W.F. once again to a Mombasa organization.

The biggest weakness of the federation was in accounting. The books were in chaos, ready-made for any official who wished to help himself. Ordinary members paid Sh. 1/- a month, but the cash book did not record individual contributions. Nor did it specify expenses except in the most general way. For instance, on 31 August 1947 Shs. 352/- was paid out for food for the office staff with no mention whether this was in lieu of wages or not. Asian lawyers received almost 25 per cent of the income. Shs. 384/- went for taxis during the visits of Mathu and Kenyatta. There were no auditors and no bank account. Kibachia told the Thacker Tribunal that he took no salary, only a food allowance which apparently amounted to Shs. 90/- a month. Despite all this, the federation had raised the impressive amount of Shs. 4,413/- (£220 13s.) by September 1947, it was able to put down Shs. 2,000/- for a house in Majengo, and had an office staff of five. There was also a more sinister side. Some minor officials of the union discovered that many Asian shopkeepers were easily frightened, and they developed a shakedown in which strikes and other troubles were threatened unless the A.W.F. organized the employees. If the employer agreed, union officials then allowed him to pay less than the minimum wage.[79]

The A.W.F. fought quite succesfully the first award of the Thacker Tribunal persuading two-thirds of the African workers to spurn the interim award. However it accepted the final award and attacked those firms which did not implement it. Enforcement remained a problem, and both the union and the Labour Department put pressure on the employers. In May the *East African Standard* reported that the owners of the Kenya Ice Factory were paying less than the minimum wage.[80] In July the Labour Department launched a campaign against employers who broke the law in Mombasa, convicting forty-one for employing juveniles without a permit and nine for paying workers below the minimum wage.[81] Later in the year some workers of the Landing and Shipping Company who were on monthly contracts complained of inaccurate calculation of their salaries. There was a brief strike and investigation showed that 190 were underpaid, twenty-one overpaid, and nine were correctly paid.[82] In December Sondhi Ltd. was fined Shs. 400/- for failure to pay the final award. During the trial G.A. Skipper, the district commissioner, suggested that the award had to be enforced thoroughly as conditions in Mombasa remained unsettled.[83]

Kibachia and many other Africans appeared before the tribunal, an experience which no doubt increased African sophistication in dealing with European employers. It also allowed for a rare confrontation of views. Hamley, for instance, testified that if public holidays occurred during the leave of an African, he received extra days off. The employees produced an official notice from the Railway which contradicted this. The tribunal restrained Hamley when, in his turn, he tried to browbeat the African witnesses. Africans cross-examined one of the European supervisors of the P.W.D., asking him why Asians were paid three times more than they were for the same work and disagreeing with his views on salaries and feeding arrangements. The testimony of R. V. Stone of the Landing and Shipping Company was interrupted by cries of dissent from the Africans present in the hall, who put up their own counterfigures.[84]

After the strike the A.W.F. relied on weekly meetings on the grounds of the Sakina Mosque to maintain enthusiasm. The colour bar remained one of the key issues. Early in August the A.W.F. applied for permission to hold a protest march displaying banners saying, 'Away with the Colour Bar' and 'Equal Pay for Equal Work'.[85] Kibachia wrote to the *Mombasa Times* that the:

> ... cultural and material well-being of the African is dwindling day by day, while the career of the capitalist is crowned with success at the cost of African sweat. Racial discrimination is at the bottom of the whole affair . . .[86]

But gradually the attendance at the meetings fell off. In May the owners refused the use of the grounds, and the police would not allow a brass band to stir up excitement.

Perhaps because of this the A.W.F. became more willing to work with the K.A.U. On 5 May 1947, Jomo Kenyatta, Peter Koinange, and Jesse Kariuki spoke at the weekly meeting to some 6,000 people. The federation was able to charge a special entrance fee of 10 cts. for this meeting. Later in the month James Beauttah, head of the Mombasa branch of the K.A.U., also attended a meeting. Then in June Francis Khamisi, editor of *Mwalimu*, returned from India and spoke at a Sunday meeting. On 26 July Kibachia was reported as telling a meeting that in the next strike, scabs would not only have their hair shaved off but also their ears—an allegation denied subsequently by him. He was arrested late in August, tried in secret and deported within the colony. Eighteen others were also arrested, including the secretary Hilton Mwandila and the assistant treasurer, Mohammend bin Mbwana.[87]

The leadership then fell into the hands of more radical men, Murene Wangara, Japhet Banks, and James Muchendo. References to the specific grievances of the Kikuyu became more frequent. Muchendo gave a very revealing speech in September:

> Last week I told you about Trade Unions . . . Those Trade Unions are just like religions; when religions were brought in this country Africans were induced to believe. Africans are believing religions now, and Europeans who knew religions better are going in good cars, aeroplanes, and everything good. Also the digging of trenches in reserve, if a man used to have 100 bags of maize, due to digging of trenches he will harvest only 50 bags. Those Trade Unions are just the same. He went on to say that if you agree with Trade Unions you shall have separate Trade Unions for instance like K.U.R. & H. will have theirs, and P.W.D. will have theirs too. We formed an African Workers' Federation to unite all Africans, why should we be separated? Do you agree that we should be separated like that?[88]

Muchendo was intent on exhorting the Africans to support a general protest movement and to oppose attempts by the Labour Department to divide the federation by creating separate unions. The next month Murene Wangara attacked the Christian missionaries and on 7 December opened the A.W.F. meeting with a Kikuyu prayer. Meanwhile the unrest in Mombasa had helped to inspire strikes in Zanzibar in late August and in Dar es Salaam in September. Although the A.W.F. had nothing to do with the organization of these strikes, they certainly created an atmosphere among Kenya Coast Europeans of concern for the power of labour leaders.[89]

Kibachia's successors, however, were not able to hold the union together. At the end of 1947 they quarrelled and Banks temporarily set up a separate body. More arrests followed which prevented a renewal of the general strike in December 1947 or January 1948 as some of the leaders had hoped. Thirteen members including the secretary and the assistant treasurer were sentenced for conducting illegal courts. About the same time a former official was convicted of embezzling the funds. The years 1948 and 1949 were a period of decline, although the authorities retained a respect for the potential power of the federation.[90]

The main thrust of the administrative response to this threat was to be found in closer administration and in the encouragement of alternative forms of African organization. The Municipal Native Affairs Officer was one of the key figures in this development. In 1947 he was instructed to give more attention to the tribal associations. By 1949 there were over 100 such bodies actively in existence in the city; the most important of these were the Luo Union and the Coast African Association. The latter had been formed in 1943; among those instrumental in its creation were Jimmy Jeremiah and H. G. S. Harrison, who had played an important role in articulating workers' grievances in the latter part of the war. The authorities also encouraged the development of the African Advisory Council which had been formed in 1945 and expanded in 1947. Unlike its Nairobi counterpart in this period, the Council, dominated by the Coast African Association, became the accepted form of African political discussion in the late nineteen-forties and fifties.[91]

Early in 1949 there was a brief revival of the African Workers Federation, perhaps because of the consolidation of the Thacker award into one sum and possibly because rumours had reached Mombasa of a series of strikes in the ports of Aden, Massawa, and Mogadishu. The authorities still had a healthy, and as it turned out, exaggerated respect for the memory of Chege Kibachia. One hundred special armed police and two armoured lorries were sent to Mombasa under the direction of a senior police superintendent.[92] The only strike, however, was on the mainland at the Vipingo Sisal Estate. Meanwhile the police tried to harass the remaining officials. Japhet Banks was arrested for embezzlement and intimidation. The case against another organizer for impersonating a labour officer was dismissed on a technicality. Finally in August 1949 Daudi Unda, the secretary of the A.W.F., was convicted for failing to pay the salary of the office boy. The A.W.F. lay in ruins.

Later in 1949 Makhan Singh, who had returned from India in 1947, took over the remains of the union and had it renamed the East African Workers' Federation. In a show of bravado the imprisoned Chege Kibachia was named president, but the union was largely a paper organization.[93] Rather than organize, Makhan Singh preferred to use the name of Kibachia as a stick with which to beat the administration. As a consequence when Fred Kubai tried to spread the Nairobi taxi strike to Mombasa in September 1949, there was little response. Nevertheless in January and February 1950 the authorities were alarmed lest the unrest in Dar es Salaam spread to the port. Japhet Banks proclaimed 25 January 'target date', and a company of police with armoured cars was despatched to Mombasa. A meeting to protest against the banishment of Kibachia was banned, and the police ordered to stand by.[94] Nothing, however, developed. In March Makhan Singh called a meeting at the Kaloleni Hall in Nairobi to start a monster petition for the freeing of Kibachia, but the authorities retaliated by arresting and imprisoning Banks. The cause of trade unionism in Mombasa seemed well and truly dead.[95] Nevertheless, despite this decline, the events of 1947 had shocked the colony, forced the government to consider seriously the causes of labour unrest and created a legend which later labour leaders could invoke.

APPENDIX IV

'Sir—We, the African Workers beg to draw your attention to our grievances and claims as follows:

1. *Grievances.* It is not unusual that the African workers have for many a time asked for higher wages on the basis of equal pay for equal work. We have also

claimed for allowances for our wives and children. The Authorities concerned have given unsatisfactory responses under the auspices of meagre small increments which do not come near satisfaction of our needs for a decent living. Sometimes we are given promises which when interpreted into their basic meaning are mere tantalisation. Now we have come to a point where we cannot keep patient any longer, but claim for what we think fair and just for us. Before we put down our claims, we would like to know how it is expected one with a family to live on a wage, let us say for instance, of Shs. 80/- (We quote Shs. 80/- because majority of us earn far less than that sum); while he has essentially to occur such expenses as food Shs. 40/-; sundry expenses (soap, water, paraffin, fuel, letters, etc) Shs. 15/-; House rent (average) Shs. 10/-, furnitures and utensils. Shs. 10/- per month. Clothes? Saving? Families at home who look upon workers for substantial help?

Rather than accidental, the giving of low salaries, so that one has nothing to save, is deliberate, so that there may not be ground for the African workers to refuse work. This fact is shown in the Press comment that the African workers' strike was not expected to continue long due to 'lack of money'. So it is clear that low salaries are intentionally desired to keep the African workers always at his work. What is one, then, who works without either a decent living or saving? Clearly a tool of exploitation. What is your explanation to that comment, Mr. Labour Commissioner?

2.*Claims.*

(a) (N.B.) The set form of salaries that you were given at the Railway Institute concerned only a particular section of workers, i.e. K.U.R. & H. and therefore did not represent public demand. The public, therefore, asks cancellation of that set form and adoption, for further reference of what the general public has recommended, as appended below.

(b) We also claim fair handling and treatment of the African workers by employers. We also wish to see kicking out of jobs in disrespectful ways stopped. Further, we wish to stress strongly that no longer are we regarded as low people who, as some presume, should be regarded as a working tool by superior exploiters. Henceforth, we appeal to you, we want to be regarded and treated equally with the other races, from the point of view of being able or capable of performing the same duties.

Expecting kind consideration and early reply.'

R. C. Kibocho, Livingstone Kienige.

Notes attached to the above

To be started with:

1.	All Labourers including sweepers and squatters.	100/- by 5/- per month.
2.	(Scales A of African Civil Services)	120/- by 7/50 per month.
3.	(Scales B of African Civil Services)	150/- by 10/- per month.
4.	(Scales C of African Civil Services)	200/- by 15/- per month.
5.	(Scales D of African Civil Services)	250/- by 20/- per month.
6.	(Scales E of African Civil Services)	450/- by 60/- per month.
7.	(Coast Ship Workers)	200/- by 15/- per month.
8.	Ayahs and Sisters	as 1. above.
9.	Daily Labourers Day 10/- per day. Night 15/- per night.	

NOTES

1. *1942 Annual Report, Labour Department.*
2. *Mombasa Times*, 23 July 1942; C.O. 533/526, Moyne to Moore, 17 Dec 1941; minute Watherston, 11 Nov 1941; memo Hamp, Acting General Manager K.U.R.H., 16 Jan 1942 rejecting Moyne's suggestions.
3. *Mombasa Times*, 17 March 1942, 10 Jan 1947.
4. Testimony of R. P. Walker of the Railways and Harbours Administration to the Thacker Tribunal. Walker claimed that the company had secured a 125 per cent profit in 1941 and that in 1943 it had made £11,360 on £40,000. *Mombasa Times*, 4 March 1947.

5. *E.A.S.*, 21, 24 July 1942.
6. *Ibid.*, 24 July 1942.
7. *Mombasa Times*, 2, 7, 8 Oct 1942.
8. *Ibid.*, 17 Oct 1942; *E.A.S.*, 16, 19, 23 Oct 1942; C.O. 533/526.
9. *1942 Annual Report, Labour Department; E.A.S.*, 22 Oct 1942; *Mombasa Times*, 21 Oct 1942. The M.O.H. reported unrest in his staff owing to the increased cost of food and rent and the shortage of food. This was met by increased wages. *1942 Annual Report, M.O.H. Mombasa.*
10. The award was an increase of Shs. 2/- in rations, Sh. 1/- in fuel, and Shs. 2/- in housing for a total of Shs. 5/- plus Shs. 5/- in cash as a cost of living allowance for those earning under Shs. 40/- and Shs. 7/50 for those between Shs. 41/- and Shs. 99/-; C.O. 533/526, Award of the Disputes Tribunal in the Dispute between the Kenya and Uganda Railways and Harbours Administration and its Arab and African Employees in Mombasa, 1942.
11. 1942 Annual Report, Labour Officer, Mombasa quoted in Report of the Committee of Inquiry into Labour Unrest in Mombasa (hereafter Phillips Report).
12. *Mombasa Times*, 17, 19, 21, 22 Oct 1942.
13. *Ibid.*, 16 Dec 1942. 'I was a member of the Willan Committee in 1939 and of two Tribunals in 1942. Incidentally I resigned my membership of the Tribunal owing to a successful effort of the Government to interfere with its findings. I regard a Tribunal as a quasi-judicial body which sifts the facts and bases its findings on those facts uninfluenced by political or other extraneous matters.' Cooke, Memorandum to the Thacker Tribunal, 24 Feb 1947.
14. *Mombasa Times*, 18 Dec 1942.
15. *Ibid.*, 12 Nov 1942; *E.A.S.*, 16 Nov 1942; testimony of the Shell employees to the Thacker Tribunal. *Mombasa Times*, 12 March 1947.
16. *Ibid.*, 5, 22 Nov 1942; *1942 Annual Report, Labour Department.*
17. The Mombasa Municipality (Control of Natives) By-Laws, *Kenya Gazette*, 15 Dec 1942.
18. *Mombasa Times*, 1, 4 March 1947.
19. 'If a Native were to get just the 1½ lb. of posho per day and nothing else he was going to become disgruntled, and one could hardly expect him to keep honest. The casual labourer, he thought, had the "thin end of the stick" ', testimony of J. L. Stephens, *E.A.S.*, 23 July 1943. Registered monthly labour was entitled to better rations including rice and sugar.
20. *Ibid.*, 23 July 1943.
21. Food Shortage Report. In 1940 the government passed the Employment of Servants (Casual Labourers) Rules which gave the authorities the power to register casual labourers but this was not done in Mombasa, *Kenya Gazette*, 21 May 1940. The Booker-Deverell Report in 1947 concluded that there were not enough Europeans in Mombasa to extend the system of controls without decreasing business efficiency. A. S. Booker and Miss N. M. Deverell, *Report on the Economic and Social Background of Mombasa Labour Disputes*, 1947 hereafter Booker-Deverell Report.
22. *E.A.S.*, 24 Sept 1943. *Mtama* is millet, *wimbi* another locally grown brown grain.
23. *Ibid.*, 23 July 1943. Harrison subsequently became president of the Coast African Association and Assistant African Municipal Welfare Officer in Mombasa. He also testified to the Thacker Tribunal. *E.A.S.*, 2 May 1947.
24. *Ibid.*, 20 July 1943. Cooke favoured equal distribution of sugar, *ibid.*, 23 July 1943.
25. The Defence (Control of Ground Rentals at Mombasa) Regulations, 1943; the Defence (Native Sleeping Accommodation) Regulations, 1942, *Kenya Gazette*, 9 March 1943; *Kenya Debates*, 15 Sept 1943; *E.A.S.*, 16 Sept 1943; testimony of George Brown, acting provincial commissioner, to the Thacker Tribunal. *Mombasa Times*, 21 Feb 1947.
26. *Kenya Colony Annual Report*, 1946, C.O. 533/526, memorandum Moore, 30 Sept 1941 *et seq.*
27. 'to examine the rates of wages and conditions of service of African employees in the Port Area at Mombasa . . .', *Kenya Gazette*, 2, 16 Nov 1943. Phillips Report.

There had been a Sh. 1/- increase by the Railway in February 1943 as a consequence of the rise in the price index. In 1944 there was a one-day strike of the Railway firemen in Nairobi and Mombasa. Makhan Singh, 121; *E.A.S.*, 25 Aug 1941; *1944 Annual Report, Labour Department.*

28. Phillips Report.
29. The Defence (Limitation of Labour) Regulations, *Kenya Gazette*, 2 May 1944 were applied to Mombasa, *ibid.*, 31 Oct 1944; the Defence (Limitation of African and Arab Travel to the Coast) Regulations, 1944, *ibid.*, 25 April, 28 Nov 1944; the Defence (Removal of Persons from Mombasa Area) Regulations, *ibid.*, 7 Dec 1943; *E.A.S.*, 28 Apr 1944; *1944 Annual Report, Labour Department; Mombasa Times*, 15 Feb 1947. The Phillips Report indicated that the committee thought that these regulations had solved the problem of casual labour in the port.
30. The Defence (Casual Labour Mombasa) Regulations, 1944, *Kenya Gazette*, 1 Aug, 7 Nov 1944; *E.A.S.*, 2 Aug 1944.
31. Cooke, Memorandum to the Thacker Tribunal, 24 Feb 1947.
32. Memorandum P. R. Morgan, 9 Sept 1943, Superintendent's File—Labour 1943–52, African Wharfage Company. He suggested a retainer of Shs. 4/- per week of forty hours, a 10 cts. cut for each hour the labourer was short, pay of 25 cts. an hour 7 a.m. to 7 p.m. and 30 cts. 4 a.m. to 7 a.m., four weeks' leave, double retainer when certified ill, issue of shorts, provision of soup kitchen by the employers, and the creation of the post of European labour superintendent. He favoured municipal rather than company housing: 'I do not suggest housing should be paid for by the employers, not only on account of expense, but because I believe it would incline to ruin the character of the labourer by relieving him of too much responsibility and also interfere with his individual freedom.' He considered that the existing arrangements for manning the port were not even economical. He also included some sugar coating: 'The inauguration of the scheme would seem a suitable time to put forward an increase in the basic stevedoring rate per ton...', memoranda Morgan, 9 Sept, 7, 9 Oct 1943.

    The scheme was rejected by Lunt as too costly and difficult, that the times were abnormal, that it was impossible to arrange for labour in peak periods of work; and that the government should house and register labour. It was also rejected by the General Manager of the Railway and by J. Stephens. The latter was opposed to a retainer but favoured registration, some form of guild, a central labour supply and a welfare committee. Memoranda Lunt, 8 Oct 1943, Stephens, Nov 1943. An undated, unsigned memorandum in the 1943 files catches the local flavour in its recommendation that there should be no welfare measures because it removed the African's backbone.
33. Memorandum Morgan, 9 Oct 1943.
34. The Labour Department failed to persuade the stevedoring companies to engage some of their labour on monthly terms, *1944 Annual Report, Labour Department.*
35. Report of Chiefs Paul Agoi and Amoth, quoted in Phillips Report.
36. The Coast African Association gave written testimony attacking racial discrimination in salaries and suggesting a unified non-European scale.
37. Phillips Report.
38. *1945 Annual Report, Labour Department*; Cooke Memorandum to the Thacker Tribunal, 24 Feb 1947; *Kenya Debates,* 3 May 1945 for a statement by the government in response to a question from Beecher as to why no African was appointed to the committee; for the Customs, *E.A.S.*, 21 March 1947; Phillips Report.
39. 1946 Annual Report, Principal Labour Officer, Coast Province. The title was later changed to Senior Labour Officer. In 1944 the Governor had reported that the lime burning company 'cannot recruit voluntary labour' and, therefore, had to rely exclusively on conscript labour. C.O. 533/533, Moore to Stanley, 3 March 1944.
40. 1946 Annual Report, Principal Labour Officer, Coast province.
41. Memorandum Morgan, 21 Nov 1946; memorandum of a meeting between

Morgan and L. M. Haynes, 22 Nov 1946; four undated memoranda, 1946. Superintendent's File—Labour 1943–52, African Wharfage Company. Notes in the file on decasualization suggested a system on the lines of the National Council of Dock Labour in Britain, that is, an independent organization to supply labour to the employers. A pool of 1,000 was suggested, the companies would have established a uniform wage and taken on certain obligations such as medical treatment, leave and housing. A pool of 800 was estimated to cost £5,000

42. Cooke, Memorandum to the Thacker Tribunal, 24 Feb 1947.
43. S.L.O., Mombasa, file concerning the Phillips Report.
44. *Ibid.*
45. *Ibid.*
46. Booker-Deverell Report. The report also suggested it was unreasonable to tell the African that his wage increases would be inflationary when prices paid for cotton were up 200 per cent, coffee and sugar 100 per cent and pyrethrum 50 per cent.
47. *Mombasa Times,* 18, 19, 20 Feb, 1 March 1947.
48. Booker-Deverell Report. There were 1,030 Africans in the port on monthly terms. The labouring wages ranged from Shs. 44/50 to Shs. 220/- plus Shs. 23/85 cost of living allowance. Clerks were paid from Shs. 40/- plus Shs. 14/50 to Shs. 280/- plus Shs. 14/50. There were 750 Africans at Shs. 40/-. An establishment was created in 1939 with incremental salaries for *serangs, tindals* and technical personnel only.
49. *Mombasa Times,* 17 Feb 1947; for the water problem see testimony of Hyde-Clarke, *E.A.S.*, 21 Feb 1947.
50. *Mombasa Times,* 8 March 1947.
51. *Ibid.*, 21 Feb 1947.
52. *Ibid.*
53. *Ibid.*
54. 'Mombasa as Others See It—Intolerant, Unfriendly, Unaware and Cliquish', *Mombasa Times,* 4 Jan 1947.
55. Information concerning the African Workers' Federation and the 1947 strike came mainly from an interview with Chege Kibachia, 1963, the files of the S.L.O., Mombasa, the testimony to the Thacker Tribunal, the files of the *E.A.S.* and of the *Mombasa Times.*
56. Chege Kibachia, *qui vivit.* Educated Alliance High School; trade union leader Mombasa 1945–7; deported to Baringo 1947–57; employed D.O.'s Office Maralal; Industrial Relations Officer Labour Department 1964; S.L.O. Mombasa 1964.
57. Hyde-Clarke spoke to two workers representing each of the larger firms, *Mombasa Times,* 10 Jan 1947.
58. The name was changed at the suggestion of Mathu in order to prevent confusion with the K.A.U. Makhan Singh, 143.
59. Kapwembe Zosia testified as president of the Kenya Landing and Shipping Company African Staff Union. He had joined the company in 1932. The union had been formed in 1945 but had lapsed when Zosia went on leave. The other members of the executive were Arthur Shems (Vice-president), Rouli Kahi (Secretary), Claudio Aduol (assistant secretary), Mzee Hasi, and Sidney Grant Ralph.

    Stephens had forgotten to sign off the *kipandes* so that they were still legally employees despite his dismissal of them.
60. Testimony of G. Coventry, director of Boustead and Clarke to the Thacker Tribunal, *Mombasa Times,* 21 Feb 1947.
61. Memorandum submitted by six representatives elected by the employees of the Landing and Shipping Company, *ibid.*, 1 March 1947.
62. *Ibid.*, 16 Jan 1947.
63. *Ibid.*, 18 Jan 1947.
64. *Ibid.*, 18, 20 Jan 1947.
65. *Ibid.*, 24 Jan 1947; Hyde-Clarke to S.L.O. Mombasa, 27 Jan 1947, noted the undertaking to Mathu. The *E.A.S.*, 7 Feb 1947, claimed that no undertakings were given prior to the return to work.

66. *Kenya Gazette*, 4 Feb 1947. The tribunal was composed of A Hope-Jones, F. T. Holden, Lieut.-Col. C. V. Merritt, A. H. Noormohammed, and John Silas.
The first award was made on 20 March for employees of the government, Railways, Landing and Shipping Company, the stevedoring companies, the municipality, Wilson Construction, and the oil companies. Those earning less than Shs. 54/50 received an increase of Shs. 6/75 and an increase in housing allowance of Shs. 3/25, for a total of Shs. 10/-. This did not cover casual workers or any other monthly workers. The final award was announced on 21 June 1947. This was a further increase of 75 cts. After five years' service, an employee was to get a raise of Shs. 7/50. Public holidays were to be paid holidays. Monthly workers were to receive twelve days' local leave with the right to accumulate to fifty. Casual labourers were to be paid Shs. 2/75 for eight hours; stevedores Shs. 3/25 rising to Shs. 3/75 if a pool were formed. *Thacker Tribunal Final Award*, 1947; *E.A.S.*, 21 June 1947; *Mombasa Times*, 21 June 1947; Makhan Singh, 114, 150.
67. *Mombasa Times*, 17 Feb 1942.
68. *Ibid.*, 6 March 1947.
69. *Ibid.*, 27 Feb 1947.
70. *Kenya Gazette*, 14 Jan 1947.
71. *Ibid.*, 11 Feb, 18 March 1947. The members were: Capt. C. W. Hamley (Chairman), the D.C. Mombasa, the Municipal Native Affairs Officer, the M.O.H. Mombasa, the Divisional Engineer of the P.W.D., the S.L.O. for the Coast province, the *Liwali* of the Coast, John Silas, and individual representatives nominated by the municipal board, the Landing and Shipping Company, the stevedoring companies, the oil companies, and the European and Indian Chambers of Commerce.
72. Cooke, Memorandum to the Thacker Tribunal, 24 Feb 1947; Booker, who was from the London School of Economics and had been working in the Gold Coast, was recommended by Professor Carr Saunders, Chairman of the Social Science Research Council in London, *Kenya Debates*, 4 Feb 1947. *The Times*, 14 Jan 1947, reported the government statement that changes were already in process of being taken when the strike occurred.
73. *Mombasa Times*, 25 Jan 1947, see Appendix IV at end of chapter for the full text.
74. *E.A.S.*, 21 Jan 1947. Also letters, *ibid.*, 1, 26 Feb 1947.
75. J. Patrick, Memorandum on Trade Unions—Development and Policy— Kenya, Labour Department, Nairobi, 1949.
76. *Mombasa Times*, 26 Sept 1947.
77. Makhan Singh, 154–5.
78. *Ibid.*
79. S.L.O., Mombasa, file concerning the A.W.F.
80. *E.A.S.*, 2, 23 May 1947.
81. *Mombasa Times*, 16 July 1947.
82. *Kenya Colony Annual Report*, 1947.
83. *E.A.S.*, 22 Dec 1947.
84. For questioning of I. H. Frost of the P.W.D. by Enoch Benjamin, *ibid.*, 28 Feb 1947; for Captain Hamley, *Mombasa Times*, 25, 26, 27 Feb 1947.
85. *Mombasa Times*, 2 Aug 1947.
86. *Ibid.*, 11 Aug 1947.
87. *Ibid.*, 28 Aug 1947; Makhan Singh, 157; *E.A.S.*, 26 Aug, 1, 10, 24 Sept, 2 Oct 1947.
88. S.L.O., Mombasa, file concerning the A.W.F.
89. For Zanzibar, see *Mombasa Times*, 7–18 Sept 1948, *passim*; for Dar es Salaam, see Iliffe, *op. cit.*; *Mombasa Times*, 9–27 Sept 1948, *passim.*
90. S.L.O. Mombasa, file concerning the A.W.F.
91. Files of the Municipal African Affairs Officer, quoted in R. Stren, 'Administration and the Growth of African Politics in Mombasa 1945–1964', *Makerere Institute of Social Research, Political Science Papers*, 1970.
92. *Cape Times*, 31 Jan 1949.
93. Makhan Singh, 246. In 1948 the campaign to free Kibachia had produced a

contemptuous response in the House of Commons from D. R. Rees-Williams, the Labour Colonial Office Parliamentary Under-Secretary:

> ... this man was rather a dangerous individual. In July, 1947, he threatened that unless people came out on a strike he proposed to call, they would have their ears cut off. (Laughter). The Government did not think this constituted good trade union practice. (Loud laughter). Until the man learned to behave himself he would be detained. (Laughter).

The Times, 26 Feb 1948.

94. *News Chronicle*, 21 Jan 1950; *Manchester Guardian*, 4 Feb 1950.
95. Makhan Singh, 252.

Chapter 9

BRAVE NEW WORLD, 1945–1952

With the cessation of hostilities the farming community looked to the future of agriculture and to their political security. The advent of a Labour government in England raised inevitable apprehension over the prospects of possible change of Colonial Office policy towards Kenya and white settlement, and it was with some relief that no immediate or drastic changes were noted.

1945 Annual Report, Uasin-Gishu and Trans-Nzoia Districts.

It is discouraging to have to report that an improvement of pay and conditions frequently results in insolence and insubordination on the part of the natives whose conditions of service it is sought to improve.

The Labour Officer for the Uasin-Gishu, quoted in the 1944 Annual Report, Uasin-Gishu District.

Welfare Colonialism

For the settlers the new era was to be the old writ large. Plans had already been laid during the war to facilitate large-scale white immigration. The war had saved the white farming class from the disaster of the Depression. The government had encouraged maximum food production at guaranteed prices and had given financial support to increase the amount of land in actual use by the farmers. Just as war broke out, the Colonial Office approved the creation of a Land and Settlement Board to assist white immigration. It was upon this structure that the colonists built.[1] As early as 1941 the Committee on Post-war Employment was concerning itself with white immigration and ensuring that jobs and land were available. In December 1942 Cavendish-Bentinck raised the question of white settlement in a debate in the Legislative Council and demanded an assurance that the government would honour its pledges in this matter.[2] The Governor gave that assurance and agreed to the appointment of a settlement officer. In June 1943 a special section of the Production and Settlement Board was created with fifteen settlers and two officials as members. At its first meeting Cavendish-Bentinck was able to announce that a scheme was in existence and that a special officer had been appointed.[3] Land, however, was something of a problem as the delineation of the highlands and of the reserves had fixed the amount of land available for Europeans, and most of it was in private ownership although considerable sections were undeveloped. A Land Control Board was, therefore, set up to acquire such unoccupied lands and re-distribute them to the new arrivals.[4] The land was to be made available with long-term loans by which the prospective immigrant could cover 90 per cent of the cost.[5] Egerton College, which had been founded at the beginning of the war for the training of white farmers, was to be used to provide agricultural education for those new colonists who needed it. The numbers of Europeans rose; by 1949 the total exceeded 30,000 and continued to increase until the emergency years.

The settlers were determined to build on the political advances they had made during the war. In fact, from 1945 to 1952 white nationalism grew very rapidly. It flourished in the post-war prosperity of the colony which, although it produced serious inflationary problems, gave great confidence to the European community. They planned to lead the unofficial majority (of all races combined) given to the Legislative Council in 1948 by the Governor, Sir Philip Mitchell.[6] As more and more officials retired in Kenya, the old animosities between the administrators and the settlers began to fade. Paternalism and white nationalism blended into each other, although the antagonism never entirely disappeared and was liable to flare up in moments of stress; there were to be, for instance, periodic mutinies by settler extremists like the Tigoni Tigers. So long as the Labour Party remained in power, there was bound to be a suspicion that the officials, no matter how sympathetic to the settler point of view, might have to carry out a policy dictated by the Labour left wing. Even a moderate politician such as Michael (later Sir Michael) Blundell could talk in terms of rebellion if sweeping political changes were made by the Labour government.[7] The old cry of self-government was renewed, and Blundell summed up the position of the colonists: 'I believe that there is only one constitutional advance that is any good for the European community in Kenya and that is self-government with a European predominance.'[8] Further, among the new settlers were some with more racist and more extreme views than those already established, perhaps because many thought of themselves as escaping a socialist Britain for a country where a man could still be a gentleman. The colour bar remained rigid throughout this period. It led the correspondent of *The Times* to remark concerning the decision of the left wing Labour M.P., Fenner (later Lord) Brockway, to stay with an African, ex-senior chief Koinange, during his visit to Kenya in 1950: 'Probably since the days of the early explorers few if any Europeans have done so in East Africa.'[9] It was the apogee of white dominance. More and more Europeans were looking to the Union of South Africa.[10] The columns of the local newspapers carried increasing amounts of news about South Africa and Rhodesia. A reporter from the *Cape Argus* noted in 1947 that 'the Europeans in East Africa look southward with a growing interest...'[11] Even in government circles, the apparent tranquillity and contentment of the South African scene was thought to be successful benevolent paternalism; when, for instance, the government rushed to investigate housing policy, it sent T. C. Colchester, a senior administrative officer, and Frank Carpenter, the Deputy Labour Commissioner, to South Africa and Rhodesia.[12]

There were, however, clouds. In July 1945 the ancient enemy of the settlers, the Labour Party, had come to power in Britain. The United Nations was born in San Francisco and gave an early indication that it would be more militantly anti-colonial than the League of Nations. The Pan-African Congress in Manchester in October 1945 heralded a new and more vigorous African nationalism. In the same year the World Federation of Trade Unions (W.F.T.U.) was created and took a strong anti-colonial stand. In September 1946 Jomo Kenyatta returned to Kenya from England and in 1947 took over the leadership of the main nationalist political party, the Kenya African Union (K.A.U.). Under his direction the tempo of the nationalist politics noticeably increased. A number of visitors to Kenya in the years immediately after the war noted the sense of unease among the Europeans despite their apparent total dominance. A reporter for the *Cape Argus* wrote in 1947 of the growth of African nationalism and of the European fear of democratic self-government.[13] In July 1948 Lieut.-Gen. H. G. Martin reported in the *Daily Telegraph* that the minds of Africans were being poisoned by 'misguided idealists or disgruntled nationalists'. He hoped that the clouds would pass but reckoned that they would not unless there was a firm paternal hand in charge.[14] The same month A. T. Steele wrote in the *New York Herald Tribune*:

> The early British settlers had visions of making Kenya a white man's country for all time, but the present generation of colonists is not so sure. Despite accelerated immigration, the whites are losing ground in the competition of numbers ... The growth of African nationalism, the Indian problem and the ambiguous colonial policy of the British government have raised uneasy doubts as to the country's future.[15]

There was also some disquiet over the attitude of returned African soldiers. 'They learnt a lot,' wrote General Martin, 'not all of it good.'[16] The previous year Vernon Bartlett had commented on 'the young African who has returned from the wars ... self-confident and ambitious in a way his father cannot understand. Not content with a pastoral life, he wants to drive an engine or to open a store.'[17] Mrs. Agnes Shaw, at the Electors Union Conference in 1946, attacked the Army Education and Welfare Department as subversive.[18] The chatter of the barber and the character of Boro in James Ngugi's novel, *Weep Not Child*, was precisely the frame of mind suspected and feared by many Europeans. The barber diverted his customers with stories of the pleasures, or lack of them, in sleeping with white women. Boro had returned from the war to find that there was neither work nor land for him nor could he find solace in his father's belief in prophecy. 'To his father, he said, "How can you continue working for a man who has taken your land? How can you go on serving him?" He walked out, without waiting for an answer.'[19]

No one among the Europeans really believed that the nationalists could win, but their presence added a touch of insecurity which gave an edginess to European politics. In 1947 Sir Alfred Vincent warned the Electors' Union about the pernicious influence of the United Nations. Since the proponents of equality, he argued, were in the majority, they were bound to attack South Africa, Australia and Kenya. It was a challenge '... to the position of western civilisation in Africa ...' for 'the application of the concept of an unqualified equality to all men would be disastrous at this stage for the development of Africa. It is essential that for many years to come the white man should continue to guide the destiny of millions of people in this continent.'[20] Sir Philip Mitchell, appointed Governor in 1944, was equally certain that European rule had to continue for the indefinite future. His autobiography, *African Afterthoughts*, shows how he considered Africans to have been totally without history or civilization and to be just emerging from a barbarous state of nature. In the past this common official view had led many to a paternalism which defended these supposedly innocent people from exploitation by white colonists. But the challenge of African nationalists was for some a presumptuous development which now hastened an alliance with the settlers.[21] Mitchell himself told a Caledonian dinner at Nakuru:

> ... people were going about today with fantastic ideas of the creation in Africa of an entirely African self-governing state. This was as practicable a proposition as it would be to set up in the United States an entirely autonomous, self-governing Red Indian republic ... Kenya was marching inevitably towards the creation—by leadership, friendship, co-operation and mutual confidence—of a new Dominion of the Commonwealth, in which British people for a very long time ahead would be the controlling and directing force.[22]

The major racial *cause célèbre* of the decade had exploded soon after the Labour Party came to power in 1945. The new Secretary of State provoked a confrontation with the settlers by issuing *Colonial Office Paper 191* which proposed the creation of an East African High Commission with equal representation of the races in the central legislature. It was ironical that the Europeans who had for so long demanded closer union should now judge their position to be menaced by the revival of this idea; it was truly Frankenstein's monster. The Europeans used every means of public and private pressure to force the imperial government to change its mind. Meeting after meeting and editorial after editorial denounced the Secretary of State. The imperial government, as a consequence of the gravity of its problems in Asia, decided to modify its position in Kenya, and by *Colonial Office Paper 120* of 1947 announced a retreat from racial parity. Not only had the colonists again demonstrated their power of veto, but the violent emotion of their agitation coloured the colony's politics for the rest of the decade.[23]

This was evident in two issues which were of more immediate concern to the African workers. The first of these was racial discrimination in the civil service. In July 1948 the report of the commission headed by Sir Maurice Holmes on the civil services of East Africa was published.[24] It provoked an immediate clamour among the colonists over its proposed increases in pay. Nothing could be more evident in this campaign than the residual dislike of the settlers for the civil service which had become the focus of their frustrations in the fight for dominion status. But the report was important for other reasons.

The Holmes Commission accepted the argument for racial scales and terms of service thereby entrenching, not only in the civil service but in the private sector as well, the traditional structure of European administrator, Asian clerk, and African labourer. The commission denied the racial nature of its scales, claiming that they rested 'not on racial but on other and more fundamental grounds'.[25] They suggested that equal pay implied equal quality of work which was, in their view, not true of the situation in Kenya. The style of the report was in the tradition of avuncular paternalism which so irritated precisely those few Africans who had managed to become subordinate members of the administrative civil service. The report, like Mitchell's autobiography, dwelt on how remarkable it was that a few Africans had escaped the bondage of tribalism and the stone age in such a short period of time. It also included a homily about education which included all the old bromides about education for character rather than for marks—the code phrase which signalled dislike of the mission school products without actually saying so. The report did raise another point which would become a significant issue much later—namely did equal pay for equal work mean that all civil servants should be paid a European salary? The commission feared the creation of a privileged elite but, in the context of the report, this fear seems more of an excuse for inaction than a discussion of a genuine problem. Such tepid liberalism led, moreover, to the same conclusion as that drawn by the more forthright settlers who considered all Africans barbarians, namely that racial barriers must be preserved:

> ... it would be true to say that, subject to individual exceptions, the African is at the present time markedly inferior to the Asian of the same educational qualifications in such matters as sense of responsibility, judgement, application to duty and output of work.

It should be remembered that this was the conventional wisdom of the time. Even a critical observer such as Vernon Bartlett wrote that the African was 'least trustworthy' and 'had not yet learnt to accept responsibility'. 'He is still quite likely to absent himself from his work for weeks at a time if some tribal celebration promises to be interesting.'[26] Furthermore the Holmes Report said, '... European civil servant surpasses the Asian in such matters as sense of public service, judgement and readiness to take responsibility'. The solution proposed was to open all posts to candidates of all races but to pay an inducement to Europeans who would not otherwise serve in Kenya. Open competition remained almost entirely theoretical until the nineteen-fifties, and the effect of the Holmes Report was to preserve the status quo, which suited the government; it accepted this section of the report and set non-European scales at three-fifths of that to be paid to induce Europeans to come to the colony.[27] The Legislative Council passed by 23 votes to 9 a resolution in support of the principle:

> This council agrees that all posts should be open to candidates of all races possessing the requisite qualifications and character but that the economic law of inducement and other consideration necessitate different rates of salaries for Europeans, Asians and Africans.[28]

Examples of the results of this policy were well known, especially to the victims. A first grade engine-driver was paid on the following scale—European £330, Asian £236, African £90.[29] The lowest grade clerk in the civil service received different rates of £150–£420 for Europeans, £90–£300 for Asians and £36–£54 for Africans.[30] In 1947 C. H. Northcott, however, had found the demand for equal pay widespread in the railway workshops and had concluded that '... the canons of efficiency require that each man shall get the wage which he is worth'.[31]

The Holmes Commission did recommend an increase in the number of African civil servants and their entrance into slightly higher grades, but the *East African Standard* attacked even this modest suggestion. African civil servants, it claimed, would be 'inadequately trained and with limited capacity and no tradition' and would be used 'simply to satisfy an ideological point of view'.[32] Blundell spoke against proposals to admit Africans by examination: '... one result ... would be that young Africans with a smattering of education, would enter the civil service on terms far higher than could be achieved by faithful old servants of the Government who had been at their jobs for thirty years'.[33] There was also opposition to Holmes's recommendation that the lowest government salaries be increased by 100 per cent. The government rejected this but said that it would make adjustments, 'In making these ... the Government will of course bear in mind the necessity of relating the emoluments of this group to those of similar employees of private concerns and local authorities'.[34] Private employers, as noted below, were none the less still dissatisfied. Finally, the government deferred Holmes's recommendation of a Whitley Council for the civil service.[35] After all the effort, only a mouse had been hatched.

Identity legislation was the second of the major racial issues. The African leadership in Kenya was determined that the end of the war would see the abolition of the *kipande*; in this they had an ally in the Labour Commissioner, Hyde-Clarke. In 1946 the problem was referred to a Labour Advisory Board sub-committee which included two Africans, Mathu and Khamisi, and the Labour Commissioner. The African and Asian members pressed for total abolition; the *East African Standard* claimed that the grievances of the Africans were being exploited by a few agitators.[36] The sub-committee and the board eventually decided that a non-racial system was necessary.[37] This reform was accepted by the government and four ordinances were prepared to implement the change.[38] Under this legislation citizens of all races would carry the same simple identity certificate and the labour record would become both a voluntary and a separate document. The Red book was also abolished and the registration of domestic servants made voluntary, as had been recommended in 1940.[39] At the time there was little European protest except over the Red Book.[40] The East Africans' Women's League tried to introduce an equivalent Brown Book, but the government advised that an employer could be sued for libel on account of any derogatory notations in the new book.[41] These ordinances, however, were not immediately proclaimed, and Africans were, therefore, still compelled to have a *kipande* although the terms were modified so that it could be signed off by administrative officers as well as by employers, and the requirement that it be carried at all times was limited. The government also ceased the large-scale prosecutions for *kipande* offences which had been such a feature of the pre-war decades.

After agitation by the reinforced African membership of the Legislative Council, the government decided to put the new legislation into effect. Immediately there were violent protests by the European community. Meetings were held, organizations formed, and pamphlets published which focused on the supposed injustice of fingerprinting innocent people. But basically the Europeans considered the *kipande*'s abolition an assault on their privileged position, and they could not accept legislation which implied the equality of all citizens. One speaker in Mombasa found the measure 'insulting and degrading to our race'. At Thomson's Falls another settler remarked, 'It is completely ludicrous that we who have advanced so far, should have to fall down to the level of people in the Stone Age.'[42] One pamphlet issued in Nairobi claimed that the government's plans were '. . . in pursuit of the Fabian-Creech Jones policy of appeasement of the African and the subordination of European interests. Exactly the same viewpoint is contained in the notorious UNO report in Tanganyika . . .'[43] Europeans also claimed that all Africans, except a tiny minority of malcontents, valued their *kipandes*. The harassed government then retreated and asked Sir Bertrand Glancy, a former Indian administrator, to inquire into the problem.[44] He recommended that the regulations concerning Europeans be relaxed, but the government decided to proceed on its original course. A few European civil servants were finger-printed, and then suddenly the government lost its nerve. The legislation remained on the statute book, but it was inoperative and the storm over registration in part led to Hyde-Clarke's resignation. Nevertheless the *kipande* was no longer obligatory for Africans, and a major labour grievance of the past quarter of a century had passed into history.

What could the civil service, the guardians of African interests, do in the face of such militant and obstructive white nationalism? What would be the response of the new Labour government in Britain? Many Europeans in Kenya believed that the Labour triumph in 1945 had brought to power those who wanted the immediate destruction of the colonial system. But Labour was much more concerned with decolonization in India than in Africa. Many of its leaders also shared the common view of the time that, while it might be argued that Asians were capable of self-government owing to their ancient civilization, it was most certainly not the case with Africans who would go on being wards of Britain for many years to come. Furthermore Labour had to rebuild a war-shattered Britain, one part of its strategy was to invest in the sterling area, particularly in Africa. At the meeting of colonial governors in 1947, Sir Stafford Cripps laid great emphasis on the need for increased production in the colonies, which had the double virtue of stimulating the production of raw materials needed by Britain and of conserving scarce dollars. To promote this strategy, a Labour junior minister, Hilary Marquand, visited Kenya and other East and Central African territories in 1948, with the message of Lugard and the Dual Mandate—production of raw materials in the colonies would benefit both the Africans in Kenya and the British in the United Kingdom. Marquand was even prepared to recommend the emigration to East Africa of hundreds, if not thousands, of white technicians. 'The Africans,' he said, 'themselves ask for them.'[45] The *Financial Times* was perhaps accurate in not taking Marquand's trip very seriously, but clearly Labour's preoccupation with development gave the white community important leverage in Whitehall for it could and did argue that development could not take place without white leadership and white political control.[46]

The Fabians, therefore, not the revolutionaries took over the Colonial Office. A Secretary of State such as Creech Jones did not think that independence was an immediate practical possibility. It was necessary in his eyes to make trusteeship a reality, the theme of the Fabian attack in the nineteen-twenties and thirties when they claimed that policies such as trusteeship were hypocritical in the hands of Conservatives but would be made a reality by a Labour government. In the Kenya context this philosophy meant an attempt to ensure that Africans would have a share of the post-war prosperity, that minimum standards of wages, safety, and social services would be enforced, and that the Labour Department, newly reorganized would be the agent and watchdog of these changes. In short, that there would be an effective countervailing power to that of the white settlers. These aims remained the policy of Labour throughout its period of office; even when Fenner Brockway and Leslie Hale made their famous descent on Nairobi after the declaration of the Mau Mau emergency in 1952, they did not preach instant independence but rather reform.[47]

The programme of social welfare for Africans had begun before Labour came to power. It had its legislative origins, as we have seen, in the Colonial Development and Welfare Act of 1940. From 1943 onward investment under the programme began to increase very rapidly. That year London announced a programme of £2,000,000 of development assistance, the largest amounts going to soil conservation and to African housing. The Kenya government planned to raise another £2,000,000 on the London market for construction projects.[48] Between 1943 and 1947 the government built housing in Nairobi for its own employees at Starehe, erected temporary housing at Marurani, and later built a number of permanent estates for African workers to be let at sub-economic rentals. By the end of 1946 £325,370 had been spent on housing in Nairobi—one half as a free grant and the other as a loan. About 10,000 to 15,000 were housed in the new estates; new housing was also built in Pumwani and a further 10,000 to 15,000 lived there and in Shauri Moyo. Parallel developments occurred in Mombasa although usually one step behind Nairobi. From the latter years of the war there had also been a growth in the social services, particularly within the housing estates. In 1944 a report was issued on African welfare, and in 1945 two officers were sent to South Africa to study modern welfare techniques. Municipal social halls and football stadiums began to appear, much of this financed by the profits on the sale of beer in the locations. By 1946 both Nairobi and Mombasa had Municipal African Affairs Officers, each with a small bureaucracy to administer housing and the social halls, to promote community activity particularly football and to deal with juvenile delinquency and other social problems.[49] These local government officers in practice were to usurp some of the powers and the grass-roots contacts of the colonial administration.

But there was never enough housing. Orde-Browne, although recognizing the progress made in Nairobi, commented in 1946 on 'the disastrous legacy from the past'.[50] As soon as the wartime restrictions were eased, the population of Nairobi rose rapidly, perhaps by as much as 40 per cent in the year and a half after the end of the war, and these pressures continued throughout this period. In 1951 the Labour Department remarked on the deterioration of the housing situation between 1949 and 1951 even though by then there were six housing estates in Nairobi. For many Europeans social welfare still remained '... the simple prewar remedy ... of giving the Natives sufficient amusements of a healthy type to afford an outlet for their energy and canalize it into fruitful and uplifting channels'.[51] Of the social services, the one most lacking in the locations and the absence of which was most resented, was adequate education facilities. The financing of urban projects remained a battle. There was not only the problem of the allocation of funds between the various racial groups, the Depression mentality remaining among many of the senior officials. The latter was reinforced by the widespread view that there would be a serious financial recession at the end of the war. Mitchell wrote in 1952:

> No doubt it is true that the foundations for human, social development were neglected, that we did not foresee nor provide against the consequences of a vast increase in production stimulated by undreamed-of price levels, by a sudden willingness to invest in new enterprises on a scale which would have seemed fantastic up to 1939—a scale running into hundreds of millions of pounds ... We have terrible arrears of urban housing to overtake ...[52]

The Railway was the leading paternalist in the country in this period, so much so that the Labour Department gradually became disenchanted with its stress on welfare.[53] The welfare policy had had its roots in the pre-war period when the Railway had built its own housing estates and created its own technical school; it also set a tradition of self-containment and isolation from other employers. In the latter years of the war, the Railway began to develop its welfare policies further. All the workers were housed, the majority in railway housing estates. It engaged a welfare officer, and in 1946 R. W. Osgathorpe was appointed as Staff and Welfare Assistant to the General Manager. When the extent of the food shortages was revealed in 1943, the Railway had helped to pioneer food shops in Mombasa, Nairobi and Eldoret where goods were sold at fixed prices. It appointed European supervisors to ensure that the system was not abused. Until 1947 it was also a partisan of payment in kind, particularly of rations, to the lowest paid workers—a government requirement for all employees earning less than Shs. 60/-. Most of the lower paid also received clothing and fuel allowances. There was free medical attention, welfare clinics and nursery schools, and the Railway even sponsored anti-malarial campaigns. It also increased its training section. By 1947 there were two schools, one in the transport department and the other in the chief mechanical engineer's department which were teaching 122 Asians, 182 Africans and 9 Europeans. The Railway had accepted the Phillips Report and was paying a minimum of Shs. 40/- for two years before it formal proclamation in Mombasa. It did not, however, agree to incremental scales because, as the General Manager told the tribunal, the Railway would only pay for increased output. 'In fact, it is common knowledge,' he asserted, 'and can no doubt be substantiated statistically, that the average output per head of African employees has steadily fallen ...' He did not, however, produce the statistics.[54] The welfare policy could, moreover, break down as it certainly did in Mombasa in 1947 where Hamley dominated the Railway Welfare Committee and was oblivious to complaints which did not come through the proper channels. One small incident was typical. Hamley complained that the African railway workers had boycotted a pilot midday meal experiment: 'I mention this to show you the atmosphere of suspicion in which we have to work. Will it ever be possible to get any industrial peace in this town when such an atmosphere exists?' Although Hamley had told the Thacker Tribunal, 'I try to be a father to the employees . . .' the Africans complained to the tribunal that the food was bad and Lieut.-Col. C. V. Merritt suggested that the prices were much too high.[55] After the Northcott Report, the Railway became much more interested in efficiency and output.[56] Robins was one of the strongest supporters of trade testing which he thought should have legislative force. He also increased the differentials considerably between the skilled and the unskilled and used the Railway's patronage to advance the cause of the former. The corollary of this was heavy emphasis on European supervision. Northcott also emphasized nutrition, but the Railway did not inaugurate a canteen for its Nairobi workers until 1950.

In the last years of the war the Railway administration had also decided to sponsor the creation of a staff association under a fatherly official eye. In 1946 this association became the Railway African Staff Union. It held its first annual meeting in 1947 electing Philip Muinde as secretary. But this union, as its title implied, was much more a staff association. Both Cooke and the Labour Department considered it unrepresentative, but within its guidelines it did some useful work for the African professional staff. It had strong support from the General Manager who allowed the leadership to use Railway facilities to visit branches and to hold meetings. He undoubtedly hoped that it would accelerate the process of creating a skilled staff. The union was not registered, partly because the management was reluctant to see the mass of its employees organized and partly owing to the jurisdictional confusion created by the amalgamation of the East African railways in 1948. It was not until 1952 that it was clearly and finally decided that each territory should have its own railway union and that there should not be one inter-territorial body. There was also a workshop committee in the Chief Mechanical Engineer's Department, but according to Northcott, this did not meet very frequently. The real thrust of Railway policy took place in the housing estates owned by the Administration. Village councils were formed on each estate. There was a representative from each tribe on the village council which, in turn, sent a delegate to the African Housing and Welfare Committee. After the Mombasa strike, more Africans were appointed to this latter committee and new welfare sub-committees were formed in various parts of the colony. An assistant welfare officer was appointed to Mombasa along with an African welfare assistant. In Mombasa three representatives of the R.A.S.U. met with Hamley in the chair. By 1948 there were three European assistant welfare officers and five African assistants in the colony as a whole. A colony-wide association football competition was inaugurated, and the Railway sponsored communal broadcasting in the locations both for entertainment and for education.[57] Nevertheless Northcott found in 1947 that there was serious over-crowding in the Nairobi estates. The style of building was that of rather old-fashioned barracks primarily designed for single men. Only a percentage of the married men could bring their families with them; the Railway aimed at a figure of 80 per cent although it was not achieving it in 1947. Most single men were living two, three or occasionally five to a room.

The testimony of the Railway officials to the Thacker Tribunal was very revealing; the tone is one of hurt surprise. A. Dalton, the Deputy Manager, told Thacker: 'We do not admit there are any legitimate grievances.'[58] Dalton said that there would be no negotiations until the men returned as the strike was illegal. Hamley argued that the strike was political rather than industrial.[59] The General Manager denied the allegations of his employees that there was a colour bar. '... The work performed by Africans', he argued, 'is not equal to the work performed by other races ...'[60] In the Railway's annual report the A. W. F. was denounced as a 'political group', and the staff union commended for denouncing the strike although 'they were not strong enough to keep the Railway section at work owing to intimidation'.[61] The annual reports of this period stress the growing sense of responsibility of the union leadership. In 1948 when the K.A.U. protested against the new schedule of Railway salaries resulting from the Holmes Report, the General Manager remarked that the leadership '... gave welcome evidence of a spirit of responsibility and was proof against the subversive efforts to undermine the good relations between the Administration and its staff'.[62]

The Railway certainly was a remarkable empire. The emperor, the General Manager, earned a salary of £3,150; the colony's Chief Secretary and Financial Secretary received only £2,600 and £2,150 respectively, even the Chief Justice earned only £2,700, and the Governor was the sole official to draw more from the taxpayer. The Railway and Harbours Administration was the most important employer in the colony. In 1948 there were 20,530 Africans employed by it in Kenya and Uganda. In 1950 the East African Railways and Harbours employed 42,326 spread over the three territories. Its policy of welfare capitalism was similar to that of the mines in Northern Rhodesia, in particular the stress on welfare societies. It prided itself on its commercial realism. 'The need to run the Railways as a business concern,' Hamley told the Thacker Tribunal, 'brings us down to earth as far as grandiose social service schemes are concerned.'[63] Before 1939 this view had led to a generally *laissez-faire* policy, but starting in the latter years of the war, the Railway created what it considered to be both an enlightened and practical attitude towards its employees. If success is judged by lack of strikes, then this policy was very successful between 1947 and 1960. But it did ignore the desire of the African worker to have some share in the decisions which concerned him, and the Railway was to pay for this lack in the late nineteen-fifties and sixties. It would also pay for the smugness and arrogance with which it ran its labour policy largely oblivious to the views of anyone else, notably the Labour Department. Nevertheless, it should also be borne in mind that the trend in labour policy since independence has seen a much greater stress on welfare than on industrial relations of the western type.

So far as the Labour Department was concerned, the blueprint for the post-war period was laid down by Orde-Browne. In general he believed that in most cases the existing labour legislation was adequate and that what was needed was administrative action to implement the laws which could only be done, in his view, by reconstituted and reorganized labour departments. So far as Kenya was concerned, he recommended that the Kenya government should continue to appoint a Labour Commissioner from the administration with the rank of a provincial commissioner. Under him he suggested a double hierarchy, one being the field inspectorate largely drawn from local officers with a practical knowledge of the people and their language, the other being the technical departments namely health, factory inspection, statistics, industrial relations, and legal services. The technical section, he thought, should be staffed by specialists, most of whom coming inevitably from Britain. He toyed with but did not pursue the notion that all district officers might be required, as in Malaya, to spend time as labour officers.[64]

In terms of policy Orde-Browne was concerned about such traditional matters as the increased use of female and child labour and the quality of housing, but he laid major emphasis on the need to remedy the inefficient use of labour and its lack of productivity. He considered that standards had declined during the war owing to labour shortages, forced labour, the lack of supervision and of consumer goods. He thought the return to peace-time conditions would remedy some of these problems, and he hoped that 'fear of the sack' might become at least an inconvenience if not a direct threat to the African worker, a fear which might persuade him to up-grade standards.[65] To the same end he strongly advocated practical education on the French model, notably in agriculture, and he urged that a system of trade-testing be inaugurated. In all this he wished to move cautiously towards the Katanga policy of the Belgians, but there were obvious differences between Kenya and Katanga, particularly the lack of an industry with such a large labour force and such profitability as Union Minière. In terms of size, the Railway was the only comparable employer, and it is significant that it was one of the few employers to embark on a full-blooded policy of welfare capitalism in the post-war period. Orde-Browne suggested that the problems of over-population and erosion in the reserves might be alleviated by secondary industry. He saw this in terms of the development of factories in or near the reserves, such as the war-time vegetable canning factories at Karatina and Kerugoya. '. . . it is unlikely,' he wrote, 'that the chronic shortage of workers will change to the extent of presenting any kind of unemployment problem . . .'

In other words, there were to be two African economies, one traditional and agricultural, the other modern and urban. The Labour Department was to assist, as far as possible, in the creation of the permanent and skilled African working class necessary for the urban economy. It was also to maintain its traditional role of guardian of the African working class, both urban and rural, against exploitation and abuse. With variations this remained the policy of the department throughout the nineteen-forties and fifties, when for a period it brought a much higher standard of living to many workers. At the time, however, it was not appreciated that the policy was based on certain characteristics of the economy which were not at all typical. For some years the post-war boom absorbed most of those who wanted to become urban workers. Furthermore in the nineteen-fifties the restrictions on the Kikuyu imposed as a consequence of Mau Mau were to limit the number of job seekers. Only in the sixties would it become fully clear that the urban economy would have such attractions and the rural such difficulties that many more Africans than could be absorbed would prefer urban destitution to rural destitution, though references forecasting the future can be seen in the Labour Department's annual reports in 1950 and 1951 which mention unemployment among 'untrained would-be clerks' or of 'unsatisfactory domestic servants'.

It was in this context that the new Labour Commissioner, Meredyth Hyde-Clarke, was chosen to head the Labour Department. He had been a district officer before the war, but between 1939 and 1945 he had held a succession of administrative posts in the secretariat which had brought him into contact with many leading figures of the government and had involved him in some of the crucial problems relating to labour. He was an acting Assistant Secretary (a Secretariat section officer) in 1941 and was later secretary to a number of important committees, notably the inquiry into labour conscription and the Kenya (later East African) Civil Defence and Supply Council. By 1944 he was personal assistant to Cavendish-Bentinck who was then Chairman of the Agricultural Production and Supply Council. In November 1944 he became the Civil Reabsorption Officer for Kenya and Director of Man Power. He was appointed Labour Commissioner in 1945 but did not take office until April 1946 when he was released from his wartime duties.

In *Sessional Paper No. 1 of 1945* the government announced Hyde-Clarke's appointment. A large staff was promised for the department including specialist staff from Britain owing to '. . . the development of new undertakings after the war, which must include modern Factory Legislation, an extension of the Trade Union Movement, Workmen's Compensation and so on . . .' *Sessional Paper No. 5 of 1945* revealed the details of the new posts involved. Provision was made for a Deputy Labour Commissioner; there was to be an increase in the number of senior labour officers from one to four and of labour officers from seven to nine. The government also authorized the appointment of a senior medical officer, a trade union adviser, and a boiler inspector. Hyde-Clarke also secured an increase in the number and status of the African inspectors (the prefix sub- being dropped at the request of Mathu); by the end of the decade the Labour Department led the way in the granting of executive duties to Africans. Furthermore, in the general reorganization of government, labour became a major department in its own right, and Hyde-Clarke secured a seat on the Legislative Council.

On the institution of the quasi-ministerial 'Membership' system in 1945 (i.e. membership of Executive Council), labour remained at first under the Chief Secretary and then was transferred to the portfolio of the Deputy Chief Secretary, who from 1950 was referred to as the Member for Education and Labour. The Member was responsible for policy, the Labour Commissioner and his department for the execution of that policy and for advising the Member. The Deputy Chief Secretary, i.e. the Member for Education and Labour, was a senior Colonial Administrative Service official; the Colonial Office was never prepared to concede these two vital subjects to a local European. Prior to 1950, with Hyde-Clarke as Labour

Commissioner, policy initiative lay with the Department. After Hyde-Clarke's departure and C. H. (later Sir Charles) Hartwell's promotion to Deputy Chief Secretary the position was to change.

In terms of policy, the government foresaw the continuation of the inspectorate system. It also expected the department to be concerned with trade disputes and labour unrest. The development of trade unions would be guided by an officer from Britain. Legislation would be presented concerning workmen's compensation, certain of the rules limiting and controlling the movement of labour would be retained, and a system of free labour exchanges established. The department would be charged with the consolidation and amendment of existing laws, particularly in relation to resident labour, juveniles and migrants. In general the government regarded '. . . the basis of its labour policy to be the promotion of good relations between the employer and the worker. Such relations can only subsist when the worker is employed under decent conditions and gives a fair day's work in exchange for a wage which enables him to maintain a decent standard of living.'[66] One speech in the council showed, however, that the new Labour Commissioner would not easily live down old prejudices. Mrs. Watkins, although approving the changes in principle, felt that 'for purely budgetary reasons I do rather regret the additional titles and corresponding salary increases'. She also expressed the hope that the new officers would '. . . go out among the labour and render its contentment greater than it is at present'.[67] To maintain the *status quo* while the new Labour Commissioner and other officials were beginning their jobs and considering their priorities, some war-time legislation was extended until the end of 1947. This included, among other matters, price and rent control, the trades disputes regulations of 1942, and the restrictions on casual labour, though any new orders under the Defence (African Labour for Essential Undertakings) Regulations were specifically prohibited.[68]

Throughout the period from 1946 to 1952 the inspectorate and social welfare functions of the department were primary, although Hyde-Clarke believed that industrial relations would gradually replace field inspection in importance. The field staff, therefore, continued its job of inspecting farms and factories attempting to ensure that the law was obeyed in relation to wages, contracts, sanitation and the like. The inspection from below indicates the variety of these tasks:

CONFIDENTIAL

A.
1. Labour Inspection Report No.
2. Estate/Firm/Employer.
3. Manager.
4. District.
5. Address.
6. Nature of work.

B. NUMBERS EMPLOYED
1. Written.
2. Ticket.
3. Monthly.
4. Casuals.
5. Others.
6. Women.
7. Juveniles.
8. Resident Labourers.
9. Period of agreement.
10. Stock allowed.
11. Cultivation.
12. Records kept.
13. Principal tribes employed.
14. Supply and Demand.
15. Is Muster Roll kept.
16. Are Labour Returns submitted.

C. WAGES
1. Men.
2. Women.
3. Juveniles.
4. When paid.
5. Other details, bonus, increments, etc.

D. RATIONS
1. Details of issue.
2. How cooked.
3. If supplemented from cultivation.
4. Issue to dependants.

E. HOUSING
1. Type.
2. General conditions.
3. Adequacy.
4. Present and future policy.

F. SANITATION
1. Are latrines provided.
2. Type.
3. Adequacy.
4. Female accommodation.
5. Sweepers employed.
6. General conditions.
7. Remarks on general cleanliness of camp.

G. WATER SUPPLY
1. Source.
2. Quantity available.
3. Condition of supply.
4. Proximity to camp.

H. MEDICAL CARE
1. Dresser.
2. Dispensary or Hospital.
3. Stocks of medicines.
4. Remarks on ability of dresser and condition of dispensary.
5. Number sick.
6. Health generally.
6. Deaths for year.
8. Records and registers.

I. SAFETY APPLIANCES
1. Type of machinery.

J. WELFARE AMENITIES
1. Schools.
2. Churches.
3. Clubs.
4. Sports.
5. Shops.
6. Other amenities.

K. TASKS
1. Work begins.
2. Average hours worked.
3. General remarks on output, etc.
4. Skilled labour.

L. SPECIAL FEATURES

M. OTHER GENERAL REMARKS

Inspecting Officer.................................... Date..........................

The department's field inspectorate was a mixture of men recruited locally and in Britain, some had previous commercial or farm experience and the large majority had held commissions in the armed services during the war. Only a very few were graduates; some specialist training was provided by the colonial labour officers' courses organized by the Ministry of Labour in Britain. Most officers approached their field inspection work with sympathy towards African labour and a general sense of vocation, though one or two held old-fashioned ideas on African status and the majority held reservations about the department's concern for the trade union movement, particularly at local branch levels.[69] Support for a trade union branch official could sometimes lead to difficulties with the local police and administration.

The department took a particular interest in two unrelated subjects, training and diet. We have already noted the training schemes for the demobilized African soldier and will later examine the department's further plans. The Labour Commissioner would have liked to have had the powers to prescribe diets since it was clear that the old European notion that one meal of *posho* a day was quite sufficient for an African worker was still widespread and as far off the mark as ever. Only in the case of road gangs did the department secure that authority, and so it had to content itself with printing recommended dietary regulations as an appendix to its annual report and urging employers, through the field staff, to implement them. The department also published a leaflet on minimum housing standards.[70]

A committee was appointed under the aegis of the department to consider revision of the legislation pertaining to children and juveniles.[71] Hyde-Clarke took the first steps towards reforming the *kipande* system with the results already noted. He also continued the policy, begun about 1943, of appointing Africans to most of the boards and commissions that were within the jurisdiction or the influence of the department. This was certainly tokenism rather than Africanization, but it was a policy far in advance of almost all other government departments.

New welfare legislation also reached the statute book in 1946—the Workmen's Compensation Ordinance and the Minimum Wage Ordinance.[72] The latter gave the government the power to set up an advisory board or boards, defined liability, required employers to keep records, and empowered officials to make inquiries in connection with the enforcement of the act. However, the government refused to make either of these laws immediately operative. The administration also refused to appoint the trade union adviser promised in 1945 or, as we have seen, to commission the Mombasa social survey. Furthermore the Railway was obstructing all attempts to decasualize port labour in Mombasa. It was also typical of the times that the Development Committee which was appointed in 1945 and reconstituted in 1946 did not have a single African on it, and in its report in 1945 had only one brief mention of labour, namely a restatement of the traditional view that everyone must work but within the guidelines of the Dual Policy. Output per head had to be increased although the committee did not give any formula for achieving this except through improved health facilities and education.[73] The government was, of course, hard pressed by the problems surrounding the return to peace-time rule and handicapped by its memories of the Depression. Others, however, particularly among the settler leaders, disliked all such legislation and were quite happy to see, in this regard, a return to the rather ineffectual pattern of the thirties when laws were discussed, sometimes passed, but rarely enforced. But notwithstanding these difficulties, a further important reform effected by Hyde-Clarke in 1948 was the revision of the 1938 Employment Ordinance when the word 'employee' was used in replacement of the terms of 'African' or 'servant"; even more significant was the removal from the ordinance of the 1910 panel provisions against employees, in accordance with I.L.O. requirements. Thereafter the only employees liable for arrest as criminals were men deserting after having been paid a recoverable advance.

Wyn-Harris, Hyde-Clarke and the department also had plans to deal with the problem of the squatters; Hyde-Clarke saw the problem as most urgent, but primarily one of land utilization rather than one of manpower or employer-employee relations. A committee of officials and farmers was appointed in 1947 with Cavendish-Bentinck as chairman to study squatters and an economic survey of squatter labour was also carried out. The department saw the solution to the squatter problem as one of transition towards a rural labour force divorced from its dependence on land and, instead, earning its livelihood in cash wages.[74] In a long memorandum Hyde-Clarke envisaged a transition in three stages. The first stage was to be one of 'crofters'; these crofters were to be less dependent on land than the squatters, deriving more of their income from wages. Hyde-Clarke wished that their land and stock be reduced to an acre, a few sheep and one or two cows only, with the employer able to pay a higher wage since the farm land, no longer spoilt by squatters, could be used more efficiently. Shops, tailoring and shoe repair stores were to absorb those redundant on the farms, and social services and schools were to be supplied in small villages. The next stage, 'cottage' labourers were to earn almost all their income from wages, their land being further reduced to small vegetable plots. From this stage Hyde-Clarke planned the transfer to the final one of 'independent workers', entirely wage-earning and living in properly planned and administered large villages.

The department realized that this change would take time and involve issues of African social custom. For the latter Hyde-Clarke argued for a planned reduction of bride-price in the reserves, enforced if necessary by a system of tribunals in the highlands, and the eventual provision of 'alms-houses' for the aged. As interim measures while the transition was being planned, he hoped for the adoption of an official ration scale for squatters, the distribution of which was to be properly supervised to ensure that it was distributed fairly among the squatter and his family and not sold at a profit to casual or monthly labourers; simpler agreements; fewer divergences between conditions permitted to squatters by different councils, and the transfer of squatter inspection to a department more concerned with land utilization than labour issues. But overall Wyn-Harris, Hyde-Clarke and the department saw a phased change of status as the only way in which large numbers of Africans could continue to live in the White Highlands. They accepted that the increased population in the reserves could no longer reabsorb the increased number of squatters, but they believed that a reduction of the dependence on land and its replacement by a good cash wage would, after a period of readjustment, lead to an efficient and contented rural labouring population.

This scheme of Wyn-Harris and Hyde-Clarke merits description, as it represents the most careful and considered proposal to solve the squatter problem in both its labour and land conservation aspects ever prepared by the colonial government, Unfortunately, however, it suffered from certain drawbacks. One of these was that although squatters might be removed from farm land, not all the farmers had the capital to develop the land vacated; they could not therefore, pay the higher wages. Another was that the proposed villages required land in the White Highlands. The suggestion that there might be Africans living in the White Highlands who were not there solely for the purpose of working for the European farmer was unacceptable to the European political leaders, notably, again, Cavendish-Bentinck who, as Member for Agriculture, was in a position to kill by procrastination. A careful scheme became, instead, a delusion; because the proposals were known and were being discussed by officials and settlers, these both felt that the squatter problem was being slowly tackled and life for the squatter would improve in time.

In reality the reverse was the case; the squatter problem was worsening to one of despair for the squatters themselves. The various district councils, 'politically elected bodies... almost exclusively representative of the interests of employers', periodically enacted fresh regulations reducing the acreage and stock permitted to squatters.[75] One of their objectives was to free land for increased white settlement. Another was to prevent Africans by sheer weight of numbers from establishing a moral and political claim to white farming land. This was particularly true in the Uasin-Gishu and Trans-Nzoia districts.[76] In 1946 Nairobi district council, for example, reduced cultivation per squatter to five acres, with ten head of cattle and ten sheep or goats; Naivasha district council reduced sheep from forty to fifteen and cultivation to two acres, at the same time increasing the required number of days to be worked from 240 to 270. The Trans-Nzoia and Uasin-Gishu councils planned to remove all squatter stock by annual reductions spread over four or five years, the former nearly succeeding. In the latter district, however, the numbers of stock were so great that the process had to be extended and was never completed; a further complicating factor being the sympathy of many farmers, particularly those who had served in the army, for their Nandi and Elgeyo squatters, and a consequent refusal to co-operate. The differences between what the various councils, or even one council in respect of different wards, permitted squatters heightened the confusion and resentment. So, also did the increasing number of inspections, particularly dawn raids by labour officers of the Resident Labour Inspectorate to count squatter stock; the inspectorate numbered three officers in 1946, by 1950 the number had risen to twelve (five in the Uasin-Gishu forming a special team and administering stock sales, and one in each of the other district council areas).

For the ordinary squatter on the farm the most serious problem was his overall loss of earnings. The 1953–5 East African Royal Commission compared the consequences of stock and acreage reduction in the case of Nakuru district resident labour in 1946 and 1953. In 1946 a squatter was permitted 2½ acres of land and fifteen sheep or goats; in 1953 in certain wards, he was reduced to 1½ acres and no stock:

> A sample census carried out by a labour officer in 1946 showed that those resident labourers and their families who derived their income from wages, the cultivation of land and the keeping of stock, obtained an annual average of Shs. 187 from cash wages, the equivalent of Shs. 358 in cash from cultivation and Shs. 198 from stock. The cash wage, therefore, represented about 25 per cent of the cash value of the total income of the family. The average cash wages of a resident labourer in 1946 in this area were approximately Shs. 12 a month, and we observe, from the report of the Committee on African Wages in 1954, that in 1953 the average cash wage of a resident labourer in the Nakuru District was Shs. 16 a month. The wages part of the income of a resident labourer's family had, therefore, risen by about one third. If we assume that with the enforcement of the 1953 order the quantity of produce from cultivation was reduced in proportion to the reduction in acreage, that is from 2½ acres to 1½ acres, and that the income from stock disappeared, it would appear that, whereas the 25 per cent of the total income

derived from cash wages was increased by one third, the 75 per cent of the total income attributable to cultivation and stock was reduced by more than one third on account of the removal of stock alone. The 1946 sample census showed that the produce of cultivation was consumed by the family to the extent of almost half its value. Consequently a two-fifths reduction in quantity under the 1953 order left only one-tenth of the total produce to be sold for cash as against a half in 1946. It would have required at least a five-fold increase in the cash values of produce over the period to leave the cash position of the labourer unchanged so far as his crops were concerned. Thus, even leaving out of account the general depreciation in the value of money, and despite the rise in cash wages, the resident labourer's income was materially reduced by the implementation of the 1953 orders.[77]

This pattern of wage reduction was repeated over the other districts of the White Highlands, with consequences more severe in those where the stock reductions were most drastic, and less severe in districts where limited stock could still be kept. Although many farms began to receive considerable capital investment by the early nineteen-fifties the pattern remained varied, and many others were as impoverished as in earlier decades; almost all farmers could, however, agree that wage levels should remain low, those investing large sums using this very investment as an additional justification. But wages were not the only physical tribulation that squatters faced. In the early post-war years before the overcrowding in the reserves was fully appreciated, surplus squatters and stock were returned there, 2,200 men and their families being so repatriated in 1946.[78] Prosecutions for excess or illegal stock or grazing also continued, 462 convictions being effected in 1951, with a further 98 for illegal residence and 51 for unbranded stock.[79]

The African squatter reaction to the evolving pattern developed from resentment to vocal protest, and then in despair to revolt. At first men refused to renew or sign squatter contracts on the new terms, shortages of squatters also being noted in the more tightly controlled districts. Refusal to renew the contract led to the removal of the squatter and his family, which 'often resulted in the loss of crops and a considerable loss of stock which could not be accommodated in the reserve areas'.[80] Sometimes there were spontaneous strikes. Occasionally squatter protest was led by officials of the K.A.U. In 1946, for instance, the labour officer in the Uasin-Gishu and Trans-Nzoia conducted a series of *barazas* for squatters to explain the reduction from ten to five in the number of cattle allowed. He found considerable opposition, most of it articulated by the president and secretary of the local branch of the Kenya African Study Union.[81] Two years later in the same area, some Nandi and Elgeyo squatters made an abortive attempt to form a Resident Labourers' Association. But this form of protest was premature, and discontent was expressed more usually through tribal societies or religious revival movements. In 1949 the district commissioner in the Trans-Nzoia noted the importance of the cult of *Dini-ya-Mswambwa* as an example to those who might think in terms of violent reaction to bad employers. But tribal associations were probably more significant. The earliest in this area were more active in the towns such as Eldoret and Kitale than in the strictly rural areas, but in 1949 the Kalenjin Union was founded on a broader base including civil servants and teachers but also with a direct interest in the squatter problem. There were also various Kikuyu societies, particularly in the towns and among the forest squatters. These associations tended to concentrate on welfare and protection for their members. By and large they avoided direct political or trade union activity since this would have brought down on them the wrath of the white officials, but ethnic nationalism, nevertheless, was bound to be implicitly anti-European and, therefore, opposed to the economic as well as to the political establishment. Sometimes this opposition was explicit. In 1948 one district commissioner noted that tribal associations particularly resented European males having sexual intercourse with African females. The Kikuyu Up-Country Fraternal Society, for instance, created a disturbance at the Pioneer Hotel where a European had his Kikuyu concubine. But it was difficult for such associations to do much that was practical for the squatter labourer other than to try to maintain or establish an ethnic base on particular farms.[82] In 1947 400 squatters from Nairobi and Nakuru districts invaded the grounds of Government House in protest, demanding to see the Governor. This demonstration was the most important peaceful protest by squatters prior to the Mau Mau uprising.[83]

Protest failing apathy returned, the 1949 Labour Department report commenting on the 'lackadasical attitude to work' among the younger generation. Squatter numbers fell as the system's stock and cultivation attractions declined; only the overall pressure of population in the reserves and the chance for a man to keep his family around him saved the system from collapse.[84] Below the surface Mau Mau was recruiting adherents, from 1950 onwards.

The Labour Department under Hyde-Clarke realized that the unrest was not due entirely to the popular bogy, the political agitator; since its major policy was blocked by procrastination the department turned to a few lesser reforms to try to ease the squatters' lot. Labour liaison committees were created to bring together employers, chiefs, and administrators. However, the European farmers generally regarded them as recruiting organizations. In the Uasin-Gishu and Trans-Nzoia area, for instance, the district commissioner allowed the committee to lapse for this reason and reverted to reliance on those employers he regarded as enlightened—in this case Major C. G. Parbury of Hoey's Bridge and J. F. Perkins of Teldet Estates, Kitale. The department's officers gained some slight improvement in squatter housing on a number of farms; they were most successful with the sisal estates where in 1946 the government operated a system of witholding Shs. 50/- per ton from the sale of sisal which was only paid on production of a Labour Department certificate in respect of employees' conditions. It tried, where possible, to ensure a fair price was paid for squatter stock that was to be removed on the introduction of a new order. The old penal provisions were removed from the Resident Labourers Ordinance. Less successfully, a co-ordinating committee to try to create some common pattern in district council legislation was set up at the instigation of the department, and the Labour Advisory Board considered the squatter problem in general terms from time to time. The system remained wastefully inefficient; despite all the settler pressure for reduced stock and more working days the squatter's actual hours at work rarely exceeded four to six per day.

One of the system's defenders was, curiously, another department of government, the Forest Department, which relied heavily on low wage squatter labour. Many of the Forest Department's squatters could live very comfortably planting between rows of young trees, breeding sheep (though goats were not permitted), producing charcoal for sale through fellow tribesmen in the towns, and remaining free from close daily supervision. The European district council boundaries included large areas of forest; technically the district council orders limiting stock applied to the forests, and the Forest Department lodged objections when the draft orders were published for comment. These objections were almost invariably overruled, but the remoteness of many of the forest areas meant that the orders were often ignored, a fact which soon came to the knowledge of the farm squatters, increasing their discontent.[85]

The Labour Department warmly encouraged the few farmers who tried to arrange community centres for labour from groups of farms on the lines of that of Munro at Dundori; these came to include stores, a dispensary, beer hall and teashop; others at Ndaragua, Saboli and elsewhere in the Highlands followed adding schools as funds permitted. It was, perhaps, the success of the Dundori scheme that led Carpenter, Hyde-Clarke's successor, a small farmer himself and a personal friend of Munro, to take a less realistic view of squatters.[86] Carpenter saw future development to the cottage stage only; as late as 1953 despite all the evidence of poverty and discontent he was still able to write paternally of the system: 'it is really popular with tribal Africans, particularly the relatively able and intelligent Kikuyu . . . The facts are that such a life is generally a carefree and happy one with all the family living together, often with primary education for the children in estate schools, free medical attention and comparative security of tenure.'[87] This mistaken view was also firmly held by Mitchell, who had himself purchased a farm with squatters and had consistently obstructed Hyde-Clarke's overall view of squatting as a land rather than a labour problem with which the Labour Department should not be concerned. It was also held by C. (later Sir Colin) Thornley, the Member for Labour (Deputy Chief Secretary) and E. W. Barltrop, the Labour Adviser to the Secretary of State for the Colonies in London.

The reality, however, was an accelerating trend towards a black rural proletariat. In 1948 W. H. Hale, the district commissioner in the Uasin-Gishu and Trans-Nzoia wrote that the white farmers in his area had done well out of the war but that 'this prosperity was not passed on to the African Agricultural Labourer'—a stricture that he repeated a year later. In 1946–7 Hale had noted wages as low as Shs. 8/- or Shs. 9/- in parts of the Trans-Nzoia. Moreover there was also a marked disinclination on the part of the Europeans to accept social welfare measures for Africans. 'Perhaps the general theme of political meetings was how to get increased services for Europeans without additional taxation and that Africans should pay more and more for their social services . . .' 'Prosperity', he wrote, 'built on such foundations cannot last.'[88] Six years later Carruthers Johnston, the provincial commissioner in the Rift Valley, gloomily noted that many farm wages were still below subsistence level.[89]

The plantations were the other major source of agricultural employment in the postwar period. The most volatile was the coffee industry because the vast majority of its employees were Kikuyu who were caught up in the nationalist enthusiasm created by the K.A.U. In that industry new, although not very modern, methods of settling wages were created. In Thika, Ruiru, Kiambu, Fort Hall and Nyeri the coffee farmers formed labour committees which grew out of the production committees of the wartime period. In these committees representatives of the farmers met with the chiefs and headmen, usually with the district commissioner present, in order to set the local wages in the traditional way. At Ruiru and Thika in 1947 the planters entertained the chiefs to tea. However, two members of the Kiambu Native Council also attended and sounded a more militant note: '. . . their contribution indicated the type of obstructive and political approach to problems which has become typical of the elected members of the Kiambu Council. They are not supported by the Chiefs and the Chairman was obliged to dispose of some of their suggestions with some directness.'[90] The planters also recruited labour from such areas as Meru. *Barazas* (discussion meetings) were held in the various divisions, but the Meru resisted employment until the wages were increased. In 1945, for instance, there were adverse comments on the wage rate at the *barazas* and at a later meeting of the Local Native Council, but by 1946 recruiters were able to secure the labour they wished.[91]

Wages, however, were low and there were periodic protests, usually led by local political leaders.[92] In September 1947 there was a strike by coffee pickers between the Chania and Ndarugu. The administration believed that the moving spirits were Solomon Memia, a local councillor, and Lawson Mbogwa, who had been active in the agitation against Chief Kibathi at Gatundu. The strike was stopped by direct action. In 1951 there was considerable unrest among the coffee pickers, no doubt reflecting the increasing strength of the K.A.U. and of the oath givers. There was a boycott of coffee picking by the Kikuyu of Gatundu, but it collapsed after a week when it became clear that the administration would import Meru to do the job.[93] Further afield such outbreaks were dealt with in a summary fashion; the 1952 annual report for Uasin-Gishu notes a strike of 200 employees at the Eldoret Wattle Estates, '. . . caused by one agitator, who was subsequently sentenced to six months' imprisonment'. In the early nineteen-fifties new types of organization began to appear as well. In 1951 the Nanyuki District African Labour Union was founded by Ayub Kingori Kariethi. The administration at first thought that its leadership might improve labour relations and combat Mau Mau; however, Kariethi was eventually convicted as an oath giver and the union disappeared.[94] The Emergency made the creation of further rural trade unions impossible until the end of the decade.

The squatter problem and coffee wages were not the only contentious rural labour problems in the postwar period. For some years the provincial administration had become more and more concerned with the ravages of erosion and destructive agricultural practices in the African reserves. Many feared that the more populated reserves might well be destroyed unless some action was taken. It seemed to most district officers that the solution lay in communal efforts to restore the land. If this could not be done by persuasion, it would have to be done by compulsion. After the war, compulsion was resorted to more and more frequently in the Kamba and Kikuyu reserves. In Kikuyuland the requirement was to work two mornings a week without pay; this involved both men and women.

Such work was very unpopular; in 1946 the ex-*askaris* who had returned to Fort Hall demanded to be excused from soil conservation work unless they were paid at the same rate as soldiers. Even such respectable figures as Harry Thuku protested, particularly over the use of women.[95] The K.A.U. found the terracing work a convenient target and began a sustained attack against it. In 1947 P. S. Osborne complained in Nyeri district that the politicians found a ready audience among the 'ignorant and idle' and reported that '. . . terracing work had slackened off or entirely ceased . . .'[96] But the major onslaught on terracing came in Fort Hall where Kenyatta spoke to an audience of some 10,000 in July 1947 and urged the women to cease communal work. This appeal was so successful that compulsory communal terracing had to be abandoned; it was replaced by regulations requiring each individual to terrace his own land. Attempts to enforce this latter policy by fines resulted in a demonstration and near riot by the Fort Hall women at the local court house in 1948.[97] The following year the women at Meru invaded the local township to protest against the soil conservation measures.[98] By 1950 it appeared as though the practice was dying out, at least in Kikuyuland, but it was to be revived during the Emergency.

Communal labour was not, of course, restricted to the Kikuyu reserve. In Ukambani, for instance, there was a determined effort by the administration to save the Machakos and Kitui areas from erosion after the disastrous destocking episode of 1938. This involved terracing and planting grass much of it by communal labour in which the Kamba women played a significant part. This labour was usually turned out by the chief and did not technically fall under the ordinance concerning compulsory labour although these powers were invoked from time to time. In 1940 some 500 women at Iveti rioted against the soil conservation measures.[99] But by 1945 the district commissioner could report some progress on terracing, grass planting, and building dams although the results were not very evident to visitors in the years immediately after the war.[100] Although a few areas were reclaimed, most of Ukambani remained an object lesson in soil destruction, and famine relief continued throughout the forties and early fifties.[101] In November 1950 the K.A.U. held a meeting at Kitui where Tom Mbotela attacked excessive communal labour; as a consequence terracing in the area came to a halt. The following year the K.A.U. was active in Machakos opposing communal work, cattle inoculations and sales.[102]

The campaign against terracing more than most actions persuaded the administration of the fundamental bad faith and irresponsibility of the Kikuyu politicians. Subsequent events, however, have shown that the K.A.U. leaders regarded this simply as part of the struggle for power. As Kenyatta himself said twenty years later when visiting a local self-help scheme in Meru: 'This showed what independent people could do for themselves. If they had been forced by a colonial master to do such things they would not have been so willing . . . During colonial days . . . there was no co-operation between the administration and politicians, but now the two groups were one.'[103]

Wages, Productivity and Trade Unions

The event which shocked the colony and forced the government to allow the Labour Department to proceed with many of the innovations for urban labour desired by Hyde-Clarke was the Mombasa strike in 1947. The immediate response of the administration to the strike was to ring the changes on the themes of law, order and conspiracy. The Attorney-General S. W. P. (later Sir William) Foster-Sutton had told the Legislative Council that the labour situation in Mombasa at the beginning of the year had '. . . appeared to be calmer and more satisfactory than had been the case for a considerable time'. He drew the only reasonable conclusion one could from this premise, namely that 'it is believed that the suggestion of a strike did not originate in Mombasa'. 'Throughout the strike,' he continued, 'we had clear evidence that a considerable number of workers were out of sympathy with it, and would have returned to their work had it not been for the fact that a systematic and underground plan of intimidation was in operation.'[104] The annual report of the Labour Department reflected, without much conviction, this official point of view:

> The view of Government authorities is that the strike was actually political in character, as many of the economic grievances, which were genuine enough, were in progress of correction at the time of the strike. The strike was in fact an attempt to coerce the Government into raising the standard of living of the labourer beyond the economic capacities of the country.[105]

The *East African Standard* warned the government to repress such challenges to its authority. 'Failure to do so,' it said, 'is equivalent to abandonment of the rule of law.'[106] The *Mombasa Times* was convinced that the strike was part of a large-scale conspiracy. 'Its very orderliness and the apparent excellence of its organization make that clear.' It claimed that the strike was based on a system of cells, that the local leaders were mere catspaws, and that no one knew who the real leaders were:

> There is a major political issue behind this strike and it cannot be emphasised too strongly that all members of the community must stand together to show these leaders, who may be hundreds of miles away even from East Africa, that the strike does not pay as a weapon and that however much the advancement of the African may be wished, the country's economy cannot stand the fantastic demands he is making.[107]

Scores of Africans were arrested but none for conspiracy. The only serious charge was brought against Haroon Ahmed, the editor of the *Daily Chronicle*, who was sentenced to six months for making a false statement likely to cause fear and alarm. The publisher was also fined £200. Ahmed was charged with writing that the police had instructions to fire on the strikers but had been delayed by bad weather at Nairobi airport.[108]

The European establishment was concerned that the strike might be part of a general subversive movement supported by the Soviet Union to challenge their power. Vernon Bartlett reported to the London *News Chronicle* some months later that '. . . the recent Negro strike at Mombasa —most probably only the first of a series—was an alarming reminder that an African need not be literate to be politically organized'.[109] Some saw the challenge in class terms. There was, for instance, a widespread rumour among the European community in Mombasa that the strike had been started by sixteen former *askaris* who were demanding the same standard of living as British workers—'good clothes, cigarettes, perfume, lipstick and dances'—and saying 'Africans who occupy more important posts should be able to afford their own motor cars and other luxuries'.[110]

In the sense that the strike was a challenge to European authority and a demonstration of African power it was part of the nationalist protest against European rule. But the strike, it must be emphasized, grew out of the economic discontent of the working class in Mombasa. It was not primarily political in the sense of being organized by nationalist politicians for political ends. The movement gradually became such after the strike but only for a few years. The *Liwali* told the Thacker Tribunal that there was no attempt to enforce a political ideology during the strike, the workers were doing what people did elsewhere, and that there was no evidence of agitators from outside the city although some of the leaders had not been long in Mombasa.[111] 'It was,' wrote Negley Farson, 'one of the most bitter, all-embracing, heart-felt protests that the African has ever staged against his low wage and working conditions.'[112] Others, such as the correspondent of *The Times* saw this as well. On the first day of the strike both the Labour Commissioner and V. M. McKeag, the provincial commissioner, stated that the trouble stemmed from the high cost of living, particularly with regard to housing, for men who had to maintain families. 'There are,' said McKeag, 'certain things which will definitely have to be put right.'[113] But statements such as this merely reiterated the warnings of successive commissions and repeated promises made in Mombasa since 1939 which had produced no results. Hyde-Clarke was determined to ensure that this would not be the case again. European business and political leaders, shocked and confused by these events, were prepared to acquiesce in considerable innovation on the part of the Labour Department, both in legislation and in practice, in 1947 and 1948. By no means all the enemies of the department remained silent but the weight of the big battalions tended to counteract the publicity of the traditionalists.

Joelson, for instance, in *East Africa and Rhodesia* castigated the government for its failure to act on the warnings which had come from Mombasa: '. . . every businessman . . . from whom we have heard on this subject in the past couple of years has expressed the opinion that the ruling rate of wages was too low'. Nor was Joelson prepared to accept the argument of the backward sloping supply curve—that if wages rose, Africans would need to work fewer days to secure their requirements.[114] The *East African Standard* was also critical of the government's failure to act in Mombasa and complained that the Africans had been 'fobbed off for many years'.[115] Concern and confusion could be seen in an interview conducted by the *Mombasa Times* shortly after the strike. Six businessmen were interviewed.

Of these only K.A. Adcock of Mitchell Cotts was prepared to say that the cost of living had increased but wages had not. Others such as A. W. Henry of Baumann and Company felt the need for a channel of information about African grievances from the government to the local chamber of commerce. W. Read of Dalgety thought the source of the trouble was the black market. Most of them would probably have agreed with M. R. Prodger of the Kenya Farmers' Association that quick action was needed although agreement on the type of action was unlikely. One, who preferred to remain anonymous, recommended Whitley Councils but not trade unions. Only Gordon White of Express Transport was entirely negative. Although he recognized the poverty of the Africans, he dwelt on the difficulty of doing anything about it: '. . . (the) African was trying,' he said, 'to go ahead too quickly, legitimate though some of his grievances may be'.[116]

One of the few businessmen who publicly favoured the drastic change to a high wage economy was Adcock. He told the Thacker Tribunal that it was necessary to ensure a higher wage for Africans so that they could secure adequate food and clothing. He believed that the increases had to come first and that it was silly to argue that the Africans must first deserve them. He thought higher wages would lead to more efficiency and that companies which could not pay did not deserve to be in business:

> One of the main troubles in this country is that many organizations expect to make far too high a profit in comparison to the risk involved—and the amount of capital outlay. If the profit ration were reduced to compare with other countries employing similar labour, there would be no question whatsoever but that the African could receive a higher wage, without the necessity of increasing the cost of living.[117]

That was the voice of big business, although there were still many others both in government and in commerce raised against it. Behind the scenes Adcock's views were shared by two increasingly influential figures—E. A. (later Sir Ernest) Vasey and Hartwell. From humble origin in Britain, Vasey had become a very successful Kenya businessman as well as one of the more active and intelligent aldermen on the Nairobi Council. Hartwell was an administrator, but by temperament and background differed from the other senior administration officers who had served in Kenya for twenty years or more. Hartwell had come to Kenya in 1947 from the Ceylon Service. His first taste of East Africa had been as deputy to Sir Alan Pim in his pre-war inquiry into the administration of Kenya. Throughout this period he was Director of Establishments, and in 1947 he had been appointed Chairman of the African Civil Service Committee. In Mombasa Captain G. R. Williams, the new manager of the Landing and Shipping Company, also raised his voice in favour of high wages and more efficiency. Nor were Kenya officials as isolated as before the war. Inter-territorial meetings of labour commissioners and international gatherings of colonial officials increased in number during these years and allowed the conscientious to compare their policies with other parts of the empire or with the French or the Belgians. In 1948, for instance, representatives of the three colonial powers met at Jos in Nigeria and, among other matters, agreed to the principle of voluntary collective bargaining on wages and conditions of work.[118] In 1949 there were two meetings of the East African labour commissioners concerning problems associated with trade unionism, and the following year a more general conference at Elisabethville.

The immediate results in Mombasa have already been noted—the appointment of the Thacker Tribunal with mandatory powers, the proclaiming of a local minimum wage, the appointment of the Coast Labour Committee and of the Booker-Deverell inquiry. Hyde-Clarke ensured that the strike would not be regarded as a local incident but as one with repercussions for the whole colony. Private rather than public pressure was applied within the government to ensure that long-delayed projects would come to fruition. A minimum wage of Shs. 31/- was proclaimed for Nairobi.[119] This example was followed some months later by another minimum wage of Shs. 28/- for Kisumu.[120] Next the Minimum Wage Ordinance was put into effect, and a Central Minimum Wages Advisory Board was created under Judge W. K. (later Sir William) Horne.[121]

Two Africans, S. O. Josiah and J. C. Njeroge were appointed. Meanwhile as soon as the Thacker Tribunal awarded wage increases in Mombasa, the government made similar decisions elsewhere without waiting for action from the Central Minimum Wages Advisory Board. The Nairobi minimum rose to Shs. 38/-.[122] The award in Mombasa also spurred employees to demand higher wages. A case in point was the demand made on the Nairobi council by the African Local Government Servants Association.[123] The Trades Disputes Tribunal handled the complaints of the police and the prison warders and raised pay accordingly.[124]

For welfare legislation also the dam was being breached. This aspect of the department's work was much less glamorous than industrial relations but perhaps just as significant. From 1947 to 1951 there was a steady stream of such legislation.[125] The Workmen's Compensation Ordinance was proclaimed on 1 May 1947.[126] One long battle fought by the Colonial Office and by the Labour Trade Union was over. There was a steady increase in the number of labour exchanges, which had had their origin in assisting soldiers who had received post-war craft training to find employment. By December 1947 there were exchanges in Nairobi, Mombasa, Nakuru, Fort Hall, Kiambu, Thika, Kitale and Thomson's Falls. There were as well Civil Reabsorption Offices in four other towns. All these offices also handled applications from ex-servicemen for training at Kabete.[127] The Labour Control Office continued in existence in Nairobi. It was regarded as the department in which '... an attempt is made to safeguard the African and ensure that adequate conditions of living are being provided'. An Asian and an African sub-inspector inspected buildings. Their work was 'closely allied' to that of the medical specialist. Two Europeans dealt with the permits and with complaints from Africans 'who are becoming increasingly house conscious'. There was also attached to the Nairobi Labour Office an inspector of quarries whose job was to improve conditions of work, increase quality, and to make the workers 'more conscious of personal hygiene'.[128] This war-time office lasted until pre-war protective legislation was overhauled and brought into line with the current I.L.O. conventions. New legislation was passed concerning the employment of women, young persons and children. The Employment of Servants Ordinance was amended to provide firmer recruiting rules and a clearer definition of the obligation of the employer in the case of sickness. The following year new rules were adopted under the ordinance for medical examinations and for sanitation. Legislation legalized contributory provident funds and safeguarded their accounts.[129] In 1948 the department produced a report on the housing of the P.W.D. which it found inadequate. The Labour Advisory Board recommended immediate action, and labour officers were instructed to pay particular attention to the housing of government employees. No doubt it was hoped that such strictures would be heard not only in government but also in private industry.

In 1946 the department had begun the consideration of a comprehensive factory code. There were many delays before this became law, partly because the department lacked a qualified factory inspector until the appointment of W. R. C. Keeler in 1949.[130] A draft ordinance was circulated in 1947 but at first no legislation was forthcoming. Intensive discussion began again late in 1949, and the legislation was duly passed in 1950 by the Legislative Council. The Factories Ordinance, as the legislation was called, came into force in 1951. It was drafted to cover a very wide range of installations and after a massive survey, 4,000 premises covering 60,000 workers were registered under the ordinance, many of them very small. The ordinance was administered by the Factories Committee of the Labour Advisory Board.[131]

In the late nineteen-forties the Labour Department was also much concerned about the problem of productivity on which Orde-Browne had laid great stress in his report in 1946. Hyde-Clarke believed that economic development depended on work undertaken by Africans outside the reserves. It remained as necessary to persuade Africans to become wage-earners as it had been before the war, but it was now equally important to ensure the highest possible productivity when they did come to work. In 1947 Hyde-Clarke wrote in the annual report of the department of the need to find the proper incentives to induce Africans to work harder and at a higher level of skill, but the tone is one of perplexity—'The chief difficulty is to bring home to the African, not merely that increased cash benefits are only to be derived from greater efforts on his part, but also that increased cash is in fact worth working for at all.'[132] There was, in his view, little fear of dismissal as there was a shortage, particularly of skilled workers, and most still had in any case ties with the reserves to which they could return if jobs were not available. He also suggested that bonuses and profit-sharing had been tried without much success. In 1948 he wrote that population pressure might in time provide the necessary incentive.

Meanwhile in London Orde-Browne was pursuing this and related problems. In 1944 he had put forward a number of proposals for research in connection with labour in the tropical colonies to the Colonial Social Science Research Council. While these were under discussion, Robins had suggested that a pilot study might be made of the employees of the Kenya and Uganda Railway. This was accepted, and Dr. C. H. Northcott, formerly Labour Manager of Rowntree and Company, was commissioned to undertake a study of the 7,000 employees of the Railway based on Nairobi. The inquiry was welcomed by the *East African Standard* which, however, could not forbear to remark that. 'They will find, however, that a great deal of most valuable work has been done by capable enthusiasts . . .' It hoped that Northcott's work would recapture the 'good comradeship and understanding' that Europeans and Africans had achieved during the war.[133] The work was accomplished in some six months in 1947. As a consequence of the short period of time, the report was tentative and incomplete and was regarded, in the event, by the Railway as a waste of time.[134] Northcott was not impressed by the European conventional wisdom concerning the inefficiency, if not incompetence, of African workers. He suggested that the wage scale was a legitimate source of complaint. His statistics showed that most Africans were at the bottom of the scale but, more significantly, that almost all Africans, except those paid the absolute minimum had suffered a loss in real wages since 1939 as a consequence of inflation. Northcott also recommended that as many as possible of the special bonuses be consolidated into one cash wage so that employees could see exactly what they were getting. In July 1947 both the Railway and the Railway African Staff Union successfully petitioned the Trades Disputes Tribunal to modify the 1942 award so that those who wished could have cash instead of rations and clothing.[135] Northcott also emphasized the importance of improving the quality of supervision. In general he believed that backwardness on the part of African workers was caused by handicaps which could be removed, in particular, improper nutrition and the lack of education. He laid stress on the need to improve and to increase technical education and on the importance of the teaching of English '. . . as the vehicle through which modern scientific, economic and political ideas can become factors in promoting the efficiency of East Africans'—precisely the reasons why so many Europeans had opposed the teaching of English in the past. He also urged more consultation between European management and African staff, and recognized that industrial relations was part of a more general problem. 'As an impression,' Northcott wrote in his summary, 'the view is recorded that African confidence in the European is slipping. This is probably a gradual movement and may be due to changes in African sentiment to which the European has not adjusted himself.'[136]

The Labour Department certainly agreed with Northcott's views on the need for higher wages, consolidation of payment, and better supervision. As early as January 1946, Hyde-Clarke told the Electors Union of a pilot agricultural scheme at Machakos to see if high wages and good food increased productivity.[137] He justified the creation of the Central Minimum Wages Advisory Board in these terms:

> During inflationary periods there is likely to be a time lag in keeping pace with prices before wages are increased; consequently the real share of the national income will decline. Some way had to be found to protect labour during these periods and generally to provide compensation for its weak collective bargaining position.[138]

In this connection the department strongly favoured the strengthening of the statistical branches of the government, and the first official annual African cost of living indices came into existence. In 1948 the Holmes Report allowed for another general increase despite the caution of the government in accepting the salary scales for the lower paid employees. Consolidated salary scales were proclaimed for the various levels of government, and private employers perforce had to follow suit. Hyde-Clarke noted that there had not been much notice to the private employers which '... created a good deal of adverse comment', and where industry had not raised wages, there were strikes.[139] In Mombasa the government and Railway were exempted from the Thacker award owing to the increases and gradually all the major employers followed suit.[140] These scales had to be approved by the Coast Labour Committee and by the Labour Commissioner.[141]

But one of the main agencies for wage changes remained the minimum wage. Between 1948 and 1952 in Mombasa it rose from Shs. 35/- with Shs. 5/- housing allowance to Shs. 52/25 plus Shs. 8/25. In Nairobi the increase was from Shs. 35/- plus Shs. 5/- to Shs. 50/- plus Shs. 6/50. Similar increases were recorded in the seven other towns to which minimum wage coverage was extended. The increases were based on the Mombasa African Retail Price Index which showed an increase of 64 per cent between 1947 and 1952. The rise in the minimum wage, therefore, kept pace with the rise in the cost of living, but, in the view of the Committee on African Wages in 1954 the index itself was based on a defective sample of goods necessary for an urban African.[142] The minimum wage was based on a formula worked out by Professor Batson of the University of Cape Town. It saw the minimum wage in terms of the barest minimum for food, clothing, fuel and light with a percentage addition to allow for petty expenses such as beer or a bus ticket. In the case of Kenya, the addition was one-third to form the 'effective minimum level', although both Batson and the Phillips Report had recommended 50 per cent. The Central Minimum Wages Advisory Board considered the minimum wage to be a 'social safety net' and based the rate on the expenses of an unmarried adult male employee. However, the minimum wage usually became, as the Carpenter Committee later noted, the actual wage paid, and most Africans were married, not single, both of which ensured that the effect of the minimum wage would not be that originally planned. In 1954 the Carpenter Committee could say: 'We have found very few witnesses prepared to say that the present minimum wage is adequate to cover the cost of living of a single man living under urban conditions.'[143] The housing allowance, at best, paid for a bed-space in a crowded room.

There was also much concern within the Labour Department concerning technical training. There were two aspects to this problem, one was the place of technical education in the school curriculum which was the responsibility of the Education Department, and the other involved training within industry or specific schemes to upgrade African artisans. Experience taught the department that apprenticeship was not the solution to the problem of technical education for apprentices deserted as soon as they had enough skill to get a decent job at a regular wage.[144] The department decided to stress trade testing. This seemingly innocuous decision was to plunge it into controversy with the trade union leadership. In 1947 the department announced a scheme of trade tests for certain groups of artisans, particularly in the building trade. Testing was to be by application from workers who had spent a required period of time in the trade. There was to be a central employment bureau with trade testing panels on which there would be representatives of employers and of the department.[145] In the course of the following year, the government began to think of making these tests compulsory. A scheme of tests was worked out by the Overseas Food Corporation which together with the Railway pressed for such a measure. The Railway saw this as one means of carrying out the recommendations concerning efficiency in the Northcott Report; the scheme was circulated to the interested parties and publicized in the *East African Standard*.[164] The East Africa Trade Union Congress (hereafter E.A.T.U.C.) strongly opposed the compulsory nature of these tests, arguing that it was a scheme which would peg maximum rates and thus undercut collective bargaining, and the government abandoned these plans.[147] In 1951 Dr. F. J. Harlow, the Assistant Adviser on Technical Training to the Secretary of State, visited the colony, and fresh plans for trade testing were drawn up. It was decided to start a pilot trade testing scheme in the motor industry and to appoint a trade testing and apprenticeship officer, but the Mau Mau crisis delayed the full implementation of these projects until the later nineteen-fifties.

Within the Educational Department also there were some important changes in regard to technical education. In 1948 the department opened a new trade school at Thika, and in 1949 took back the two training centres at Kabete from the army. In conjunction with the Labour Department a four-year course was prepared leading up to standard trade tests; short courses for adults were also offered. Similar facilities were also created at the Muslim Institute in Mombasa.[148] It was, however, very difficult to persuade Africans to take these courses, partly because of the status of clerical jobs, partly owing to an unfavourable scale for artisans compared with clerks, and partly because technical work seemed to some Africans taking Europeans, particularly officials, as a reference group, to condemn them to subservience to Europeans or Asians.[149]

Wages and productivity remained at the root of the labour problem. Most employers preferred to pay low wages and would not consider raising them unless there was a prior increase in productivity. Yet there could be no increase in productivity until higher wages allowed the African a measure of stability and increased his desire for consumer goods thereby tying him to his job. Nor could there be such an increase in productivity until increasing wage costs forced the European employer to use his labour more efficiently. Wyn-Harris had pointed to the dilemma of this circular problem in a speech to the Nairobi Rotary Club in 1946.[150] It was reiterated by the *East African Standard* at the time of the Mombasa strike. The paper knew well that the permanent African urban worker was more numerous in Mombasa than elsewhere, yet it could not see its way to approval of higher wages without a prior increase in productivity. Nevertheless it supported the Thacker award and saw it as one more step on the way to urban self-sufficiency.[151]

In this connection the Labour Department was committed to a high wage policy, to be implemented by legal minimum wages. Another part of its strategy was to encourage trade unionism. The case for this was most clearly put in a pamphlet, *Trade Unionism in African Colonies* written by

R. E. (later Sir Richard) Luyt who was then an officer in the administration in Northern Rhodesia but who would eventually become Labour Commissioner in Kenya in the mid nineteen-fifties.[152] This pamphlet was well regarded in the Kenya Labour Department and was required reading for new recruits. Luyt argued that trade unionism was a *fait accompli* since Britain had supported the relevant I.L.O. resolutions. He also saw the development of trade unions as a feature of the '... integration in the world economy' of the trade and industry of Africa. Repression would only produce revolutionary unions associated with the communist cause. It would be better to accept, as Julius Lewis had recognized in *The Colour Bar in the Copperbelt* in 1941, that 'Africans are fumbling after the technique of collective bargaining and, with suitable guidance would adopt it with advantage to themselves and their employers alike'. Luyt suggested that employers would benefit because a high wage economy would force more efficient use of labour. The working force would become stabilized in the urban areas which in turn would lead to a higher standard of skills. Unions would allow a better and more efficient contact between management and employees and, in total, would increase the contentment of the working force. Luyt envisaged simple unions built from the ground up, led by a leadership drawn from the traditional elders and the new intelligensia, which would be primarily industrial and non-political, although he recognized that there were bound to be international contacts and influences. He saw this development as part of the Secretary of State's policy to stimulate local self-government, and he suggested that the colonial bureaucracies should welcome the new leadership as it emerged. It was time for European well-wishers to step back and allow the African to organize so that he could help decide priorities. Furthermore, it was clear in most colonies that the Labour Department would never have the manpower to administer a quasi-welfare state. Nor did Luyt hesitate to apply this policy to farming, which he thought could only survive by mechanization. This was, however, a policy which in its logical conclusion would sacrifice inefficient small businesses and farming to the interests of the major companies and of the strategic interests of the great powers. Inevitably it would bring vigorous controversy among settler communities in Africa. Kenya was no exception as can be seen in the controversy over the Mombasa strike and the Thacker award. Furthermore many officials maintained their traditional belief that they were much more qualified than African trade unionists to defend the interests of African workers. They suspected that such leaders might abuse their power for personal gain, and they were most reluctant to see a fading of their authority in such matters.

The higher wages policy was very unpopular with certain employers. An Asian, G. K. Ishani, wrote to the *East African Standard* that the smaller employer could not even pay the Thacker award, and he recommended an end to sentimentality in dealing with the Africans.[153] J. F. G. Troughton, the Financial Secretary, told the tribunal that he was opposed to any wage increases because they could not be confined to Mombasa and would ultimately spread to the rural areas. He felt that an increase could only be justified on the grounds of a prior increase in productivity. Under questioning he was prepared to relent a little and to approve small increases, paid in kind, to the poorest workers. Nor had the speakers and letter-writers lost any of their venom. E. A. Aubrey wrote from Limuru protesting against the meetings that were being held to discuss an increased cash payment on the coffee farms from Shs. 12/- to Shs. 15/-. He complained:

> The effort is part and parcel of the general idea that if we go on pumping fodder into the tummies of our labour and filthy lucre into their pockets they are going to work like 'little niggers'—or should it be 'the devil'... And the sooner we recognize that the psychological factor—the will to work —must first be established then the sooner will the physical factor—the ability to work be found establishing itself.[154]

When the Rift Valley Electors' Association produced a questionnaire on the introduction of minimum wages, Blundell, Scott and Lady Sydney Farrer all joined in denouncing such a possibility. Blundell said he was opposed in principle, particularly in agricultural areas, because '... I believe it is faulty to give advanced social thought or action to backward peoples'. He would, however, concede the minimum wage in the towns because of the high cost of living and the danger of communism. Lady Sydney Farrer and Scott were even more emphatic although the former was prepared to see a minimum wage for African artisans trained at the N.I.T.D.[155] Protests came from a variety of settler and Asian organizations—Naro Moru Association, Nanyuki District and Farmers Association, Nanyuki Indian Association, Mount Kenya Association, Nyeri Township Committee, Nyeri Indian Association, Aberdare Electors Organization, Ngobit Association, and Mount Kenya branch K.N.F.U. Wages Co-ordinating Committee.[156] Hyde-Clarke promised that the ordinance would not be applied to the agricultural industry.[157]

This negative attitude was particularly pervasive at the level of the European manager or of the foreman. The following interchange took place between the members of the Thacker Tribunal and an official of the Posts and Telegraphs:

> Hope-Jones: Have you ever considered whether the wage your boys receive is sufficient for them to live on
> Hobbs: I have never given it a thought.
> Merritt: Is there anybody in your Department who takes an interest in whether they get enough to live on?
> Hobbs: No.
> Thacker: Well then, let us put it this way—do you think your Africans are paid adequately for the work they do?
> Hobbs: I think they get more than enough for what they do.

Thacker then asked whether the employees could live decently on the wages paid, and Hobbs replied '... that he had no knowledge of the African's living conditions, but it had occurred to him that he spent far too much money on clothing—why, for instance, did he have to wear boots?' Nor did he think that Africans should have money to go to the cinema.[158]

Testimony in regard to trade unionism to the Thacker Tribunal was also distinctly cool. J. S. Nelson of the Posts and Telegraphs thought that unions were premature, as did his colleague Hobbs.[159] The dialogue between

Thacker and E. H. Robins, a former engineer of the P.W.D., was typical:

Robins: I see great dangers. I do not think our trade unions in England have proved themselves.
Thacker: Trade unions in England have surely been the means of effecting a better standard of living?
Robins: Definitely sir. But if the employer and the employee get together, there is obviously no need for trade unions.[160]

Even such a moderate witness as C. H. G. Coventry believed in the 'family baraza' rather than in trade unionism.[161]

The Thacker Tribunal disagreed:

Much inconvenience and delay was caused by the problem whether or to what extent their so-called representatives were, in fact, speaking on behalf of their fellow workers. The Tribunal is of the opinion that there is nothing inherently wrong in trade unions, but that it is necessary, *inter alia*, to progress by gradualness and as it appears that the African can be influenced and swayed to a marked degree by advisers who may not always be the best counsellors it is essential that the leaders should be men of responsibility.

Trade unionism of a kind has already come to Kenya and will undoubtedly develop further either along sound or unsound lines. It behoves all concerned to continue progressively to guide and assist in implanting a concept foreign to the African rank and file so that it may grow to be an instrument for his welfare and development and not for his undoing.[162]

The *East African Standard* was already a convert to this point of view. It saw trade unionism as a device to maintain a skilled labour class. 'The good worker,' it wrote, 'is constantly at the mercy of the unskilled intruder.' Such workers needed security. As a consequence there should not only be trade unionism but also proper negotiating machinery and the setting of professional standards.[163]

The Labour Department had, therefore, to tread warily. Prior to the Mombasa strike, it had been pressing without success for the appointment of the trade union adviser promised in 1945. The Governor had little sympathy and considered that strikes 'were fomented by the usual type of sorry rogue masquerading as Trade Union organizers'.[164] Thacker's remarks added to the department's pressure, and the government duly appointed James Patrick, a Scottish trade unionist. Nonetheless Hyde-Clarke told the Legislative Council in 1948 that development had been 'advisedly slow' and would only continue 'with the utmost circumspection'.[165] Patrick was one of a number of trade unionists appointed to various African colonies by the British Labour government. This was a policy strongly backed by the T.U.C.; in 1946 the Southport Conference passed a resolution favouring colonial trade unions 'with the same rights and privileges as British trade unions' and requesting the executive to give assistance to such unions.[166] The post was a particularly difficult one; the adviser was an employee of the local government which was itself the major employer in the colony and on whose councils were represented many of the more important private concerns. It was not, therefore, easy for the trade union adviser to establish a genuine independence in the eyes of the Africans although Patrick did his best. Patrick was also much more of a bureaucrat than a rabble-rouser, and this trait made it impossible for him to work with the more militant trade unionists. He accepted the views of the government and of the T.U.C. that the functions of unions were purely industrial, and that his job was to encourage proper structures and attitudes so that unions could by industrial action help to enforce protective labour legislation and to secure a higher standard of living for themselves on a vertical pattern, each within its own industry. This made him an enemy of the A.W.F. and later of the E.A.T.U.C., who were regarded by the Labour Department as incorrect and dangerous 'horizontal' or occupational associations.

Patrick toured the country meeting employers and employees. In Mombasa, for instance, late in 1947 he had thirty-one meetings with employers and twenty-eight with employees in order 'to encourage closer liaison'.[167] He urged the employers to accept modern industrial practices including Whitley Councils and trade unionism, and he regarded the council set up by the Mombasa municipality as one of the more successful in the country. He gave lectures for trade unionists in Nairobi, Mombasa, Kisumu and Maseno, and prepared simple pamphlets in English and Swahili on the structure and use of unions entitled *What is a Trade Union?*, *The Organization of a Trade Union*, and *Trade Union Rules*.[168] Examinations were held, and certificates were given for merit.[169] Patrick gave direct assistance and counsel to certain unions, notably the Transport and Allied Workers' Union, one of the few unions almost completely African and one which Patrick hoped would become a model. He secured a scholarship to Ruskin College for the union's secretary, Meshach Ndisi, thereby inadvertently assisting the much more radical Fred Kubai to entrench himself in the leadership.[170]

In September 1947 Carpenter, the Deputy Labour Commissioner, made a statement to amplify the department's position on trade unions. He said that the government favoured the establishment of unions 'but it must be satisfied that the people who wish to form them know what they are about; that the purposes are, in fact, the proper ones for trade unions and not for some semi-political body'. On these grounds, he claimed, the A.W.F. 'could not possibly be recognized as a trade union'. Patrick had been hired, so he argued, precisely to ensure a proper development of unions.[171] In September 1948 Hyde-Clarke told the Mombasa Rotary Club that he hoped for self-government in industry but that it would have to come gradually. He warned his audience that the riots in Accra had shown how nationalism complicated industrial relations, and he argued that equitable pay must be given or economic unrest would be exploited by the communists.[172] The matter of politics was, of course, the nub of the problem. In 1948 Hyde-Clarke wrote in his annual report:

> Considerable difficulty has arisen over the misconception in the mind of the African of the true purpose of a trade union, partly due to a growing political consciousness on his part; action has therefore had to be taken to guide certain African associations formed chiefly from political motives, but calling themselves trade unions, into a more formal channel of trade union practice.[173]

Legislation between 1948 and 1950 reflected the uncertain and ambiguous view of the Labour Department and of the interplay of political forces within the government. A number of bills were brought forward. One was a simple updating of the legislation pertaining to arbitrations and inquiries. The new ordinance repealed that of 1940 and added the concept of conciliation to those of arbitration and inquiry. The Labour Commissioner was empowered to initiate conciliation proceedings and, if successful, to endorse the results as if they were a formal award. This was an important piece of legislation for it gave a greater range and sophistication to the work of the labour officers.[174] The other proposed ordinances were more controversial. One was clearly aimed at the general unions—the A.W.F. and the Labour Trade Union. It clarified and enlarged the reasons for refusal if (*a*) the principal purposes of the union were not in accord with the definition of a trade union, and (*b*) if the union represented more than one trade or calling without 'suitable provision for the protection and promotion of their respective sectional industrial interests'. The legislation as revised effectively prevented the A.W.F. from ever securing registration, and was a distinct threat to the Labour Trade Union when in 1949 all unions which had come into existence prior to this ordinance were compelled to re-register.[175] New legislation also gave the Registrar the right to call for accounts from unions and to inspect the books, membership lists and other documents This was an important power but was much curtailed in practice by the lack of manpower to enforce it.[176] The more radical unions also heartily disliked some other legislation passed in 1949. One ordinance was the so-called 'spivs' bill; few ordinances so perfectly represented majority European feeling concerning urban Africans. It gave labour officers the power to order the unemployed, 'the idlers and stiffs', to specific jobs, but it does not seem to have been much used.[177] Makhan Singh had particular reason to fear the new legislation authorizing the deportation of either foreign or immigrant British subjects for conducting themselves 'so as to be dangerous to peace, good order, good government or public morals' or 'in a manner calculated to raise discontent or disaffection among His Majesty's subjects . . .'[178]

In 1948 the government introduced legislation which seemed to point away from reliance on trade unions. This was a bill to replace the Minimum Wage Ordinance with legislation of a much wider scope. It proposed wages councils with considerable powers to fix wages and conditions of work in particular areas or specific occupations. This concept was much too radical for the employers and so the legislation failed. It was, however, to be revived when at the end of the decade trade unions had fallen into disrepute in the eyes of the authorities.[179]

The issues looked a little different from the other side of the fence. In this period of heightened tensions between 1945 and 1952, it was not possible for many urban Africans to accept that politics and industrial relations could exist in two separate compartments. Those who disliked colonial rule usually protested against the effects of that rule, notably low wages and the colour bar and, in some cases, this made them both politicians and trade union leaders. It is nevertheless striking that the tradition of non-political trade unionism began to emerge in this period. Both the Railway African Staff Union and the Kenya African Civil Servants' Association by and large pursued their own ends within their professions and disassociated themselves from the more radical trade unionists. From time to time they might send representatives to various meetings or occasionally join in protest but, in the main, they pursued internal rather than politico-industrial aims. In both cases the unions were dominated by their professional members rather than by the mass of the semi-skilled workers. The African Civil Servants' Association was primarily concerned with the Holmes Commission and the agitation concerning the colour bar in the Civil Service which led to the investigations of the Lidbury Commission in 1953–4. The status of the union was recognized by the appointment of Jeremiah to the Legislative Council.

Other unions, more directly linked to the semi-skilled, came into existence after the war.[180] The most important of these was the Transport and Allied Workers' Union. It had its origins in the association of Nairobi African taxi drivers who had gone on strike several times during the war and had formed a union in 1943 with John M. Mungai as president. About the same time Douglas Mbugwa formed the Thika Motor Drivers' Association. Its president, Chenge s/o Kiseite, and its vice-president were among those who testified to the committee concerning *kipande* legislation in 1946. After a certain amount of friction between the two groups, they amalgamated in 1947 as the Kenya Road Transport and Mechanics' Union. Their headquarters at Kiburi House became the centre for Nairobi trade unionism. John Mungai remained president and Fred Kubai became general secretary.[181] There were five branches outside Nairobi. The union leaders were associated with Mwangi Macharia in the increased union activity in Nairobi following the Mombasa general strike. As a consequence the government looked on the K.R.T.M.U. as a political organization, and Patrick intervened to attempt to direct it into purely industrial action. In 1948 Ndisi became secretary and Kubai organizing secretary. The number of branches grew to nine, and the first annual conference was held. A year later, at the next annual conference, the name was changed to Transport and Allied Workers' Union. It had by this time, in the eyes of Patrick, proper accounts and a book membership of 1,138. Ndisi then took up a scholarship at Ruskin College, and Kubai became the dominant force in the union.

There were other unions as well coming into existence. The African Painters' Association, the forerunner of the future Building and Construction Workers' Union, was formed in 1944. Although it inspired several strikes in 1948, it was unable to decide during this period whether it wished to be an association of sub-contractors or of workers and as a consequence was not particularly successful. In 1946 the Kenya Houseboys' Association was formed. Three years later it became the Domestic and Hotel Workers' Union but was not registered until 1951. Two more unions were formed in 1948. One was the Kenya Night Watchmen, Clerks and Shopkepeers' Union, the predecessor of the Distributive and Commercial Workers' Union, but it was not particularly active between 1949 and 1952. The other union brought together various groups of tailors as the Tailors, Tent-Sailmakers and Garment Workers' Union. It was registered in 1948 and two years later secured an agreement with the Nairobi Master Tailors' Association which it found almost impossible to implement. Other unions were more Asian than African, notably the Shoemaker Workmen's Union and the

Typographical Union. The latter was formed in 1941 but did not attract Africans in any numbers until its successful strike in 1950. There were as well a variety of staff associations and also a proliferation of special interest groups which could hardly be called trade unions. In September 1947, for instance, the treasurer of the Jaluo Houseboys' Association was sentenced to six months imprisonment and a fine of Shs. 335/- for stealing the funds of the association.[182]

When Patrick first arrived in Kenya, he was not particularly impressed by the quality or strength of these unions. Events were to prove that it was not necessary to have an elaborate structure to provoke militant agitation—this had already been demonstrated in Mombasa by Chege Kibachia. The arrest of Kibachia did not, however, restore tranquility because in the same year Makhan Singh returned from India.[183] The immigration authorities had intended to refuse him admittance but failed to do so owing to inefficiency in Mombasa. As soon as the government realized that he was again in the country, it declared him a prohibited immigrant but it failed to maintain the validity of this in the courts. A year later the government tried again, but Judge (later Sir Marie) Nageon de Lestang held that he was entitled to remain since he was a permanent resident. The trials showed that no quarter and no co-operation could be expected.[184]

At first Makhan Singh involved himself in political activities. He worked with the Indian Congress in the election of 1948, but he was never trusted or accepted by the hierarchy of the Congress which was powerful enough to keep him to the fringes of the movement. Nor does he seem to have associated too closely with the young and radical Asian intellectuals and journalists who were much involved in the *Daily Chronicle*. So he revived the Labour Trade Union in 1948 and devoted his full time to it.

It would seem that he tried to make the Labour Trade Union once again an all-embracing general organization for the workers of Nairobi. For some time he was a one-man secretariat. He won publicity for the union by press statements concerning some of the government's legislation such as the Workmen's Compensation Bill, the Trades Union and Trade Disputes Bill, and the Wages and Employment Bill.[185] He also attacked what he considered the inadequacy of the Holmes Commission Report on the civil service salaries.[186] Since this was a fertile time for legislation, he found such tactics very successful in securing publicity. He was reported extensively in the *Daily Chronicle* and fairly frequently, although with disapproval, in the *East African Standard*. In September 1948 he called a conference on the cost of living.[187] His records indicate that there were thirty representatives present from seven groups including the Railway African Staff Union, the Shoemakers' Union, and the Typographical Union. About half those present were Africans. It seems that the real purpose of the meeting was to create a committee to co-ordinate union activity. But the move was premature as the Africans already involved in trade unions were unwilling to submerge their identity. As a consequence a new form of organization was needed.

The moment for this arrived early in 1949 when Patrick called trade unionists together at the Labour Department to discuss the draft bill on wages and conditions of employment. At the end of the third meeting,

Kubai suggested that a formal federation should be considered. On 12 February the leaders called a meeting at the Indian Institute which approved the idea of a federation and called on the member unions to ratify the decision by the end of March. Five unions did so—the Labour Trade Union, the Transport and Allied Workers' Union, the Shoemaker Workmen's Union, the Tailors and Garment Workers' Union, and the Typographical Union. Later in 1949 the Kenya Houseboys' Association changed its name to the Domestic and Hotel Workers' Union and joined the E.A.T.U.C., as did the E.A. Workers Federation, and the E.A. Seamen's Union, and in 1950 the East Africa Painters' and Decorators' Union. But three Asian unions refused to join, and the Railway African Staff Union and the African Civil Servants' Association also stood aloof. The formation of the new body was announced on May Day at a public rally where the K.A.U. leaders, Kenyatta, Mathu and P. M. Koinange gave their blessing. It was called the East Africa Trade Unions Congress, and it was to have a short but stormy life.[188]

The organization of the congress was sketchy. Formally it was composed of five representatives from each of the member unions. Kubai became president and Makhan Singh secretary. In fact it was a very informal body with a small group of active members dominating the structure. There was little bureaucratic differentiation beyond the fact that Makhan Singh looked after the records and the correspondence. It had a small office but no paid staff. The annual conference met only once but on that occasion the executive seemed in full control, perhaps because it had introduced the system of card voting.[189]

In theory the congress got its money from dues, Shs. 25/- from each union and 10 cts. per member over 500.[190] But neither the congress nor its affiliates was ever able to organize a satisfactory system for collecting subscriptions. Paid collectors were used from time to time with little success. Much of the money stuck to their hands. The police and the employers were hostile while the workers were too poor and, when immediate results were not obtained, too fickle. During Makhan Singh's subsequent trial at Nyeri, he testified that all new members had filled out forms: 'We consider them as members and they occasionally pay their membership fees.' Most of the money came from collections at public rallies. Makhan Singh also admitted that at the time of his arrest there was Shs. 55/- in the account of the Transport and Allied Workers' and Shs. 48/- in the Tailors and Garment Workers' Union.[191] Money was, however, of less immediate significance than in the western world; nevertheless the congress did seek support from the British T.U.C. and from the W.F.T.U. but received no material aid from either body.

The 1950 Nairobi General Strike

Both Fred Kubai and Bildad Kaggia regarded the E.A.T.U.C. as a ginger group to prod the K.A.U. into more dynamic political action. In practice this meant that the congress in the first four months of 1950 issued a stream of press releases and sponsored some twenty-five to thirty meetings, the tenor of which became more and more radical. It also meant that the congress supported three important strikes in 1949 and initiated a political demonstration early in 1950 which culminated a few months later in a general strike in Nairobi.

The first strike occurred before the congress was officially born. The shoemakers struck on 12 April 1949 and stayed out over a month.[192] At first the Indian Shoemakers' Association refused to negotiate until the union apologized for the press campaign against it. But Patrick eventually brought the parties together and concluded a settlement favourable to the union. Working hours were reduced from sixty-three to forty-nine, an interesting indication of the degree of exploitation prevalent among the Asian employers.[193] In September the congress supported a strike of the servers in the Indian sweetmeat shops. Only 100 Africans and Asians were involved, but they won a wage increase.[194] A few weeks later the government appointed a board of inquiry, composed of Cooke, Osgathorpe and Horne to look into a dispute between the Labour Trade Union and the United Motor Works regarding the dismissal of six employees.[195] The hand of Makhan Singh can be seen in most of these disputes for they primarily concerned Asians.

But these were overshadowed by the decisions of the Transport and Allied Workers' Union to call a strike to protest against the new taxi by-laws in Nairobi which had been designed to raise standards and to fight crime. This dispute had been in the air since 1946 when the city first considered the new by-laws. The union felt these were unduly restrictive, unfair to those who already had licences and would impose unreasonable financial demands on the poorest African taxi drivers. It also feared that its source of drivers would vanish with the new regulations. Kubai called out all the taxi drivers in Nairobi and arranged a sympathy strike at the Kenya Bus Company. The strike lasted sixteen days despite repeated threats by the bus company and by the city that they would dismiss all strikers. But efforts to spread the strike were a failure. The workers in Mombasa voted 54–6 against the union after hearing the local labour officer denounce the strike as illegal.[196] Only at Thika was there a partial success. Ultimately Mathu persuaded the strikers to return after Kubai had declared his inability to do so. The Labour Department refused to intervene on the grounds that proper notice was not given and that the strike was directed to political rather than to industrial ends. The government issued leaflets attacking the strike, and the city council passed the by-laws but allowed a right of appeal to the Attorney-General—a concession of little interest to the union.[197]

Four months later in February 1950 Makhan Singh and other leaders of the congress called a meeting at Kaloleni Hall in Nairobi to urge a boycott of the visit of the Duke of Gloucester to the city. The Duke was to present a charter giving Nairobi official city status. Kubai and Makhan Singh denounced the celebration on the grounds that the oppressed and downtrodden had nothing to rejoice about; they demanded instead far-reaching social and economic as well as political reforms. Makhan Singh said '. . . that if people will not attend, the King's son will observe that Africans are not happy in these celebrations, because some people are not happy and he will also observe that there is slavery and that there are slaves'.[198] The congress leaders also believed that the charter was a prelude to the expansion of the city at the expense of Kikuyuland. The boycott was, whether by design or accident, a move that could not fail to enrage the ultra-conservative and passionately monarchical settlers.[199]

But it also divided the K.A.U. The action of the congress was repudiated in the name of the K.A.U. by a group of moderates, Eliud Mathu, Tom Mbotela, and Joseph Katithi. They were, in turn, attacked by Kenyatta in an interview sympathetic to Makhan Singh which he gave to the *Daily Chronicle.* But on 15 March Kenyatta was persuaded to heal the rift in the K.A.U. by telling a mass meeting that he was opposed to the boycott and accusing Makhan Singh and Kubai of harming African unity. None the less the congress was determined to go ahead, but the police banned the proposed demonstrations. Action had to be confined to the wearing of black armbands and the issuing of a vigorous circular.[200]

The trade unions, in turn, divided. In March 1950 Ndisi, who had returned to Kenya three months earlier, resigned as general secretary of the Transport and Allied Workers Union because the 'policy of the union is influenced by persons outside it who are supporters of the Communist-dominated World Federation of Trade Unions'.[201] On 27 March he issued a statement saying that he would 'try his very best' to start a trade union movement on British lines to oppose the E.A.T.U.C. He explained that he had no quarrel with the members of his own union 'but I have found that anything I propose has first of all to have the approval of a group outside it who are influencing its policy . . . I am expected to be completely subservient to their wishes and demands.'[202] In April Ndisi was appointed to the Central Minimum Wages Advisory Board, and later in the year he joined the Labour Department.

On 23 April Makhan Singh and Kubai participated in a dramatic meeting of the K.A.U. at the Kaloleni Hall. There was a lengthy resolution moved by A. B. Patel and Tom Mbotela protesting against the current political demands of the settlers. The leaders of the E.A.T.U.C. successfully proposed an amendment in favour of complete independence and sovereignty. During the course of the debate, Makhan Singh declared: 'Yes, I am a Communist. I am fighting for the freedom of all countries in the world.'[203] He repeated this statement at his trial.[204] When Makhan Singh described himself as a communist, he probably meant that he was a generally Russian-oriented Marxist, not a disciplined member of a communist structure since there does not appear to have been any formal communist organization in Kenya at the time. Nor does the E.A.T.U.C. seem to have received any practical support from the W.F.T.U. or from other communist bodies.[205] He had the worst of both worlds. He alienated many Asians and Africans by his declaration and gave the Europeans an effective handle with which to beat the labour movement without securing any practical advantage for himself or for the E.A.T.U.C. The government turned down a request for a May Day parade but it allowed a meeting at the Desai Hall which reiterated the pledge in favour of independence. It was also announced at the meeting that attempts would be made to organize the railway and agricultural workers.

On 15 May 1950 Makhan Singh and Fred Kubai were arrested.[206] The control of the union fell into the hands of Chege Kiburu and Mwangi

Macharia who called a general strike which the government declared illegal under the recently proclaimed Essential Services Ordinance.[207] Kiburu was arrested and Macharia disappeared but was later picked up.[208] The strike took place without the official leaders and lasted eight days. A contributing cause was a strike in the Asian printing trade which started the same day after lengthy negotiations had collapsed.[209] Over 6,000 workers were involved in the general strike at its peak, and Mathu and Jeremiah were booed when they tried to mediate. It spread to the Bata Shoe factory, hotels, and schools in Limuru but not apparently beyond that. About 1,000 were on strike in and around Limuru, and it required a police baton charge on 20 May to disperse a crowd of some 1,500 to 2,000.[210] In Nairobi a perpetual fire was kept burning at Shauri Moyo. The P.W.D. and the city administration were among the most seriously affected. The employees of the central government and the Railway were involved but to a lesser extent. For a few days the enthusiasm of the strike brought a great sense of solidarity to the African locations. 'If others strike,' Wariegi s/o Korunja told the resident magistrate, 'I must strike also.'[211] Patrick O'Donovan reported to the *Observer* that at first there had been a holiday amosphere in Pumwani but that this quickly vanished and was replaced by 'sullen resentment'. If asked why they were on strike, Africans replied 'The strike is for the "black men" or "I am striking because others have, and I must" '; '. . . there are thousands,' he wrote, 'who wheel and flee . . . at the smallest police gesture, and yet gather again and again to listen to some individual cry for immediate self-government, or cheaper maize, or higher wages'.[212] Over 100 strikers were arrested and sentenced including Kiburu who received eleven months. Police enrolled the Luo as special constables since they were frequently the victims of the strikers, '. . . itching to get even with their Kikuyu assailants'.[213] The strike also saw the first use of tear gas in Kenya although it was not particularly effective.[214] Gradually the leaderless workers drifted back to work as they ran out of money and as it appeared unlikely that the government would release its prisoners.[215] A provincial commissioner could conclude that, 'in a trial of strength the Government won, and was seen to have won'.[216]

Makhan Singh was brought to trial before Judge Thacker who found him an undesirable person within the meaning of the Deportation (Immigrant British Subjects) Ordinance.[217] The Governor ordered him to be interned in a remote part of the colony, an exile which was to last until 1960. On the day of Thacker's decision Makhan Singh faced two further charges of perjury arising from testimony in his earlier immigration cases. In June he was sentenced to three months on one of the counts, a decision that was reversed on appeal.[218] During the same month both Makhan Singh and Kubai were charged with failing to dissolve an illegal union after registration was refused. The resident magistrate found the E.A.T.U.C. to be a union operating illegally because despite its lack of registration it was, according to rule three of its constitution, trying to regulate the relations of workmen and employees. Both men were fined each a token Shs. 110/-, but the significance for the government was that the illegality of the congress had been established.[219] Kubai was immediately re-arrested and charged with the attempted murder of Councillor Muchohi Gikonyo and with an attempt to buy a pistol without a permit.[220] He was acquitted in 1951 although the judge clearly thought him guilty. He was subsequently tried and sentenced with Kenyatta at Kapenguria in 1952.

The congress was in ruins. It is true that in retrospect its leaders could claim that it facilitated the rise of such young nationalists as Kubai and Kaggia. It was also a training ground for future trade unionists, and it made trade union issues current in the colony. But it did collapse, and in the two years between its demise and the declaration of the emergency, Kubai and Kaggia turned more and more to party politics, although they continued to take an interest in some labour questions. They took over the executive of the Labour Trade Union in order to continue the spirit of the E.A.T.U.C. But they now also held important posts in the Nairobi branch of the K.A.U., and Kaggia was editing two newspapers for the party. Kenyatta seems to have urged Kubai to choose between trade unions and politics. However after the destruction of the congress, there was no choice for an ambitious man. Some of the member unions continued a shadowy existence; they were brought together by a young Baluhya, Aggrey Minya of the T.A.W.U., who decided to co-operate with the Labour Department and with the International Confederation of Free Trade Unions (I.C.F.T.U.). Kubai opposed these decisions which increased the gap between him and the other unions.[221] By 1952 the government was prepared to recognize the formation of the Kenya Federation of Registered Trade Unions with which neither Kubai nor Kaggia had any connection and which did not include the Labour Trade Union.

For most of the period between 1945 and 1952 trade unions were of little account politically. But during the twelve months from May Day 1949 to the middle of May 1950 the East Africa Trade Union Congress was able to mount an increasingly vigorous campaign which received more and more publicity. Its leaders were attacking the white oligarchy in a practical way. It seemed entirely possible that the E.A.T.U.C. might force itself into the councils of the K.A.U. But as soon as the government moved against the congress it collapsed. Why? The congress was inexperienced and no match for the government as the registration controversy showed. Its most important leader was an Asian who was vulnerable to racial attacks, a fact not overlooked by Mathu, Mbotela and other African critics of the congress.[222] It was not prepared to embark on revolution and it had prepared no plans for going underground. It had developed no bureaucracy—no money, no cells or cadres of followers, no press and no significant overseas support. In the short run it did not matter, but it was no preparation for a political siege.

It is ironical that both the K.A.U. and the settlers were suspicious of the E.A.T.U.C. Between 1946 and 1952 neither Kenyatta nor the other K.A.U. leaders envinced much interest in trade unions or in labour questions other than the *kipande* and the colour bar. In the wake of the riots and deaths at Uplands in 1947, Kenyatta and W. W. W. Awori had urged a moderate and business-like approach. Awori told a meeting at Thika that strikes should not be started on the spur of the moment and that it was more practical to collect money to train Africans in Britain.[223] Kenyatta told a meeting at the Kaloleni Hall:

Write your demands on paper, give them to your employers, give them notice of intention to strike and then strike if need be—that is the proper way. But lightning, illegal strikes, without notice and without the people really knowing what they are about or what they want are useless.[224]

Kenyatta seems to have been willing to associate with Kibachia or with Kubai and Makhan Singh so long as their organizations were subordinate to the K.A.U. The party was a coalition of many political views, and Kenyatta as leader had to try to hold it together. This sometimes involved rather complicated shifts in policy as with the agitation over the Duke of Gloucester's visit. The moderates in the party were even more outspoken. At the meeting in Kaloleni Hall on 23 April 1950 when Makhan Singh declared that he was a communist, the treasurer of the K.A.U., Ambrose Ofafa, joined with the Asian leaders in attacking him.[255] In June Mbotela denounced the E.A.T.U.C. in much stronger terms at a K.A.U. meeting in Nakuru:

... Africans ought to learn to strike in a civilised manner and not in the ridiculous way of the recent strike. The disturbance had brought trouble to many and had led to large numbers losing their jobs which, in turn, would bring trouble to their wives and children and cause them to turn to a life of crime. He strongly criticised those who had played a leading part in the disturbance because they had refused to take the advice of people who knew better and had followed a Sikh who had claimed to know everything. He wanted to see strikes organised in accordance with the law as is the practice in Britain and other civilised countires.[226]

The fate of the E.A.T.U.C. must be seen, however, in the context of European fears over the rise of Mau Mau and the hardening of the government's policies between 1950 and 1952. Many things contributed to this. One was the disturbances in Uganda in 1949; '... there must be an end to the policy', wrote the *East African Standard*, 'which neglects to stamp at the earliest stage on the type of trouble-maker we have seen at work in Uganda'.[227] The authorities in Kenya were sufficiently perturbed to order large-scale exercises involving the police reserve and the riot squad.[228] The same year the police services were modernized, in particular by more intensive anti-riot training.[229] The increased tensions of the Cold War also affected local opinion. The government banned a number of left-wing periodicals and books and the possibility of communist infiltration became a part of official oratory.[230] In May 1950 the government sought powers to suppress seditious publications and to prohibit organizations 'trained and equipped to usurp military or political power, or which seek to influence political life by displays of violence'. These were described as measures to outlaw communism.[231] The Member for Law and Order, for instance, justified the arrest of Makhan Singh by arguing that 'in this country today certain not too well-educated deluded persons, mainly Africans, are being seduced from their own way of life by an Asian brand of Communism. They remind me of animals confronted by a snake—mesmerized, bemused and swaying to the rhythm ...'[232] European instransigence went hand in hand with the increasing militancy of the nationalist movement.

Officially the policy of the government remained that of multi-racialism based on European leadership, but it did not seem to differ very much in practice from the old forms of white rule. There was some attempt by the Governor to develop multi-racial politics in the Legislative Council, but the position of the Europeans was made clear by the publication in September 1949 of the Kenya Plan by the Electors' Union. The title of the brochure which accompanied it, *We Are Here to Stay*, summed up the contents.[233] The Europeans also continued to seek closer ties with the south. In May 1949 Vincent told the Nairobi Rotary Club of the need to take steps which would lead to the federation of East and Central Africa and then to a link with South Africa.[234] Four months later Eric Louw, the South African Foreign Minister, made an official visit to Kenya where he gave a number of speeches warning of the communist peril and urging closer association between the white governments of eastern and southern Africa. He also visited the Afrikaans community of Eldoret whose increasing prosperity was made evident by the construction of a new Afrikaans elementary school.[235] In 1950 three settler leaders visited Rhodesia. There was great interest among the Europeans in Kenya in the development of the Federation of Rhodesia and Nyasaland. Lord Malvern and Sir Roy Welensky became heroes in the white community for doing in Rhodesia what the settlers would have liked to do in East Africa—to create an English-speaking white dominion in black Africa. The Electors' Union Notes in the *Kenya Weekly News* recorded the following appreciation:

> Lastly the sane and healthy liberalism of Sir Godfrey Huggins himself was a tonic. It is a liberalism in the finest tradition of the Empire, boldly and courageously seeking the good of all men. It is, however, a manly liberalism and quite different from the flabby sentimentality of the Fabians. Sir Godfrey looks facts straight in the face and deals with problems in a spirit of absolute reality. It is an attitude which we in this Colony could do very well to emulate.[236]

This was directly related to increased white fears of African nationalist politics in the colony from 1950 onwards. In that year the correspondent of *The Times* noted that the European community was shocked by the development of anti-European feeling. The months before this comment had seen a clash with the Suk members of *Dini Ya Msambwa* in which three Europeans were killed and also the first mention of Mau Mau in connection with a trial of Kikuyus arrested near Naivasha. Between 1950 and 1952 there was a steady increase in terrorism which, although ignored by Mitchell, had a profound effect on the politics of the European community.

In 1951 Mitchell and the settlers were able to persuade James Griffiths, the new and even more cautious Secretary of State who had succeeded Creech Jones, to postpone any significant constitutional change until 1956. The same year the Labour Party was defeated, the Conservatives came back to power, and 1956 looked much less menacing. None the less to the settler leadership Mitchell was much too complacent in the face of the rising militancy of the K.A.U. and of the terrorism which was developing in the Central Province and in Nairobi. Furthermore, Lyttleton, the Colonial Secretary in the 1951 Conservative government, appeared to be unaware of any economic conditions that might lead to unrest. Even when he visited the colony as Secretary of State after the Mau Mau revolt had begun, he held the view that it was due to a few powerful and lustful men and that there was no economic background to it whatsoever.[237] The settlers, led by Blundell, wished to sweep away Mitchell's vaguely liberal multi-racialism, declare a state of emergency, and arrest the Kikuyu leadership. On 20 October 1952 after violence against Europeans had commenced they got their way. The new Governor, Sir Evelyn Baring, signed the declaration of an emergency and ordered the arrest of Kenyatta and ninety-three others.

The effect of this unfolding drama had been to force the Labour Department on to the retreat and greatly increased the influence of the more right-wing settlers and officials. The signs of the counter-attack were clearly visible in 1949. There was a most revealing confrontation in January at the Thika Club between Patrick and various of the settler leaders. Although Patrick told the 100 guests present that he was '... trying to preach the gospel of content and friendliness' and quoted the Joint East Africa Board in favour of unions, he was the victim of a ferocious attack by Major J. Delap, an up-country farmer. Delap denounced the Joint East Africa Board as 'people who do not live here or have not lived here for a great many years and who don't understand very much about it'. He asked with heavy irony how the government could accept the advice of someone who had only been in the country a year as against that of settlers who had been there for decades. He argued that trade unions were '... the most fearful threat of all to our one industry—agriculture'. He claimed that he had no differences with his labour and did not want '... my relations with them altered in any way'. 'I think,' he said, 'Mr Patrick is about 500 years premature ...' Then came an interchange which would haunt Patrick for the rest of his career in Kenya:

Major Delap: Has Mr. Patrick met one African capable of being a real Trade Union official in this country?
Patrick: Honestly—no ...

W. B. (later Sir Wilfrid) Havelock, the M.L.C. for Kiambu, claimed that the whole question arose from the Mombasa strike. He argued that it would be better '... to have employees controlled by Mr. Patrick than by Mr. Stalin ...' Lady Shaw also supported Patrick, but the meeting brushed these views aside and passed a resolution denouncing trade unionism 'for many years to come'.[238] In October 1949 the *East African Standard* concluded that the taxi strike showed trade unionism to be 'premature'.[239] E. H. Hanson wrote from Limuru that the strike showed '... the obvious necessity of recognising that the post of trade union adviser has served no useful purpose ...' and should be terminated immediately.[240] In April Blundell spoke in favour of proper unions and negotiating machinery, but denounced the manifesto of the E.A.T.U.C. as 'clap-trap'. He urged that those who misused free speech to promote bitterness and hatred 'must be dealt with and they must be dealt with firmly'.[241]

The next month the *East African Standard* recommended staff associations instead of unions and suggested that only suitably qualified persons should be allowed to hold office in unions.[242] Stanley Ghersie, in his election address, was prepared to go further and recommended 'vetting' of trade union leaders 'or a system whereby committee members were nominated by Government'—a notion which would later re-emerge under rather different circumstances.[243] In January of the following year the Government made a vigorous attack on subversion in the labour movement.[244] The annual reports of the Labour Department for 1949 and 1950 reflect this. In 1949 Hyde-Clarke reported that Africans were finding it extremely difficult to organize unions and that a simpler form such as staff associations might be preferable. He noted that there were six recognized staff associations, four in Nairobi and two in Mombasa. He argued that if trade union leaders did not have the basic knowledge of trade unionism, the movement could become 'a very dangerous menace... The organization in the mass of immature and illiterate people makes the possibility of exploitation by political extremists an easy matter, and there is ample evidence that such a situation exists in Kenya.' The following year the Labour Commissioner noted that trade unionism was 'at a very low ebb' owing to the influence of 'a small clique of Asian and African agitators', but he suggested industrial relations greatly improved after the arrest of Kubai and Makhan Singh. In 1950 the government, alarmed by the industrial situation, passed an essential services ordinance to provide for compulsory arbitration.[245] The legislation was available to help combat the general strike, and a number of Africans were charged under it.[246] The list of essential services grew and the lack of major strikes in the next few years seemed to suggest that it was a success. However, the question which remained unanswered was that posed by Luyt in his pamphlet on trade unions—what would the government do if large numbers of African workers went on strike despite the ordinance? Would they arrest all the dock workers in Mombasa? The Essential Services Ordinance was passed at the same time as a Public Order Ordinance which was directed against organizations'... usurping the functions of the police or the armed forces...' or organized to display physical force in promoting political objects.[247]

Hyde-Clarke resigned on 26 May; he did so in frustration at the failure of his attempts to rid the Labour Department of the administration of the worsening squatter system, his failure to persuade Mitchell to increase government employees' wages and enact orders improving other minimum wages, and also in resentment against the blame attributed to him over the unpopularity among Europeans of the new non-racial identity card.[248] With his departure the department lost some of its influence and status for several critical years. In a farewell statement in July, Hyde-Clarke admitted that industrial relations in Kenya had been a failure because neither side had been sufficiently well organized. Although the Labour Department was still committed to trade unionism, it would be necessary to 'go about it another way and much more slowly'. This meant in the rural areas wage discussions with the K.N.F.U., the farmers' associations and the production sub-committee in which the Labour Department represented the workers. About ten such agreements were already in force. In the urban areas the ministry would develop staff associations and wages councils.[249] New minimum wage legislation was introduced in July 1950.[250] Hyde-Clarke thought these new arrangements would take the place of unions 'for a long time'.[251] The new Labour Commissioner, Carpenter, was determined to prevent any revival of the E.A.T.U.C. by carrying out these policies as firmly as he could. At this time the government also decided to establish a Central Whitley Council for the civil service, on the staff side four members each were nominated by the European, Asian and African civil servants' associations. The government intended departments to establish their own Whitley Councils but set its face against arbitration.

Local trusteeship was once again the orthodoxy of the moment. The attempt to introduce unions, wrote the *East African Standard*, was 'well-intentioned' but had largely failed. No one realized that the Mau Mau rebellion was about to break out and that in the cauldron of revolution not only would new local leaders and policies emerge but the imperial government would also assert its right to direct rule, with results that few could imagine in 1952.

APPENDIX V

EMPLOYMENT IN CERTAIN TRADES AND TOTAL EMPLOYMENT FIGURES

Year	Agriculture	Government	Domestic Service	Building and Construction
1947	106,551	81,261	24,184	9,920 (4%)
1948	110,754 (37%)	85,779 (29%)	22,896 (8%)	11,163 (4%)
1949	189,168 (48%)	92,657 (24%)	38,762 (10%)*	16,171 (4%)
1950	201,941 (48%)	95,054 (23%)	38,528 (9%)	16,287 (4%)
1951	203,158 (48%)	93,361 (23%)	34,575 (8%)	12,696 (3%)
1952	202,688 (47%)	101,568 (23%)	39,914 (9%)	15,582 (4%)

* Hereafter described as others including domestic service.

Year	Total Employed
1947	281,857
1948	296,454
1949	394,917
1950	420,783
1951	412,416
1952	434,539

1947-52 Annual Reports, Labour Department

NOTES

1. *Daily Telegraph*, 18 May 1939. A committee had been set up in 1937 which reported in 1939; its report, the *Kenya Land Settlement Committee Report*, 1939 was the basis of the settler argument. *Kenya: White Man's Country?*, 1943.
2. *E.A.S.*, 18 Dec 1942; *Kenya: White Man's Country?*, 24.
3. *E.A.S.*, 18 June 1943; *Kenya: White Man's Country?*, 24.
4. *The Times*, 30 Oct 1943.
5. *Manchester Guardian*, 24 Nov 1943, 12 June 1944, letters from Rita Hinden.
6. *The Times*, 19 June 1948.
7. M. Blundell. *So Rough a Wind* (hereafter Blundell), 1964, 82.
8. *E.A.S.*, 3 May 1948.
9. *The Times*, 9 Sept 1950.

10. See Blundell, vi, viii and x, *passim*, especially 85, 121, '... appeals to Malan reach me constantly', and 152.
11. *Cape Argus*, 12 May 1947.
12. E. A. Vasey, *Report on African Housing in Townships and Trading Centres*, 1950; also *Cape Times*, 8 Feb 1950, *Johannesburg Star*, 25 Jan 1950; *E.A.S.*, 12 March 1949, report by Carpenter.
    South Africa's low cost housing was at the time the most advanced in anglophone settled Africa.
13. *Cape Argus*, 12, 13 May 1947.
14. *Daily Telegraph*, 16 July 1948.
15. *New York Herald Tribune*, 25 July 1948.
16. *Daily Telegraph*, 16 July 1948. Most of the Mau Mau terrorists in J. Ngugi's novels are depicted as returned soldiers. See, for instance, Boro in *Weep Not Child* and General R. and Koinandu in *A Grain of Wheat*.
17. *News Chronicle*, 17 Apr 1947.
18. *E.A.S.*, 28 Jan 1946.
19. J. Ngugi, *Weep Not Child*, 10–11, 30.
20. *Johannesburg Star*, 10 March 1947.
21. For an example see C. J. Wilson, *One African Colony*, 1945.
22. *E.A.S.*, 2 Dec 1948.
23. For the reaction of the K.A.U., see, for instance, *E.A,S.*, 8 Aug 1947. Africans in Uganda and Tanganyika were also opposed but for other reasons.
24. *Report of the Commission on the Civil Service of Kenya, Tanganyika, Uganda and Zanzibar*, 1947–48, hereafter Holmes Commission Report; *E.A.S.*, July, Aug 1948, *passim*.
25. *E.A.S.*, 16 July 1948.
26. *News Chronicle*, 29 Apr 1947.
27. *Sessional Paper No. 2 of 1948.*
28. *Mombasa Times*, 2 Sept 1948.
29. *News Chronicle*, 29 Apr 1947.
30. Holmes Commission Report, 1948. Both examples are of scales prior to the Holmes Commission Report.
31. *African Labour Efficiency Survey*, ed. C. H. Northcott, 1949.
32. *E.A.S.*, 30 July 1948.
33. *E.A.S.*, 5 Aug 1948.
34. *Sessional Paper No. 2 of 1948.*
35. *Ibid.* See W. J. Haimes, *Report on Whitley Councils*, 1950. Whitley Councils were a British name for civil service negotiating bodies.
36. *E.A.S.*, 4 May 1949; see also, *E.A.S.*, 27 Sept 1947, letter of Buck Ryan.
37. Report of the Sub-Committee of the Labour Advisory Board appointed to examine any suggestions submitted to it for the revision of the present Native Registration System and to make recommendations as to any modifications considered desirable; *E.A.S.*, 4, 5 June 1947.
38. The Employment of Servants (Amendment) Ordinance, Ord 31 of 1947; The Native Registration (Amendment) Ordinance, Ord 32 of 1947; The Registration of Persons Ordinance, Ord 33 of 1947; The Domestic Employment (Certificate of Registration) Ordinance, Ord 34 of 1947; *Kenya Gazette*, 1 July 1947.
39. *Report and Recommendations of the Registration of Domestic Servants Ordinance Committee 1939*, 1940; see *supra*, p. 236.
40. *E.A.S.*, 26 June 1948, Electors Union Conference.
41. *E.A.S.*, 22 Dec, 1948.
42. *Mombasa Times*, 4 June 1949; also 3–31 May, *passim*, 4, 17 June, 4 July 1949; *The Times*, 7 May 1949.
43. Society for Civil Liberties, *Fingerprints—Why?*, 1949. Motor-car stickers denounced 'Kipande-Mitchell' and 'Thumb-Print-Hyde-Clarke'.
44. *Kenya Gazette*, 11 Oct 1949.
45. *The Times*, 13, 27 Jan 1948; *Yorkshire Post*, 10, 13 Jan 1948; *Daily Mail*, 16 Feb 1948; *Daily Herald*, 3 May 1948; *Manchester Guardian*, 30 Aug 1944,

letter quoting Sir Edward Bennett, 'It would take the Africans some generations to become factory hands.'

46. *Financial Times*, 9 Feb 1948.
47. See for example, Fenner Brockway, 'Report on Mau Mau', *Daily Herald*, 17, 18, 19, 20 Nov 1952.
48. *Manchester Guardian*, 10 Nov 1943.
49. Mary Parker, Political and Social Aspects of the Development of Municipal Government in Kenya with special reference to Nairobi, unpublished Ph.D. thesis, Univ. of London, 1949.
50. Orde-Browne, 75.
51. *East Africa and Rhodesia*, 29 Dec 1938.
52. Sir P. Mitchell, 'Kenya in Perspective: Progress and Promise', *Daily Telegraph*, 10 Oct 1952.
53. This section relates strictly to the Railway employees, not those employed by contractors as in the port of Mombasa.
54. *Mombasa Times*, 6 March 1947.
55. *Mombasa Times*, 27 Feb 1947.
56. See *infra*, p. 318.
57. 1943–47 *Reports of the General Manager of the Railways and Harbours, Kenya and Uganda Railways and Harbours* (hereafter *Annual Report, K.U.R. & H.*). *1948–52 Reports of the Commissioner for Transport and the General Manager on the administration of the East African Railways and Harbours* (hereafter *Annual Report E.A.R. & H.*).
58. *E.A.S.*, 17 Jan 1947.
59. *Mombasa Times*, 28 Feb 1947.
60. *Ibid.*, 25 Feb, 6 March 1947.
61. *1947 Annual Report, K.U.R. & H.*
62. *1948 Annual Report, E.A.R. & H.*
63. *Mombasa Times*, 26 Feb 1947.
64. Orde-Browne, 35; see also *E.A.S.*, 22 Feb 1945, speech of Orde-Browne at production conference in Kenya.
65. In 1946 the Governor visited the Uasin-Gishu and Trans-Nzoia Districts and warned the European farmers that 'fear of the sack' must replace penal sanctions. 1946 Annual Report, Uasin-Gishu and Trans-Nzoia Districts.
66. *Sessional Paper No. 5 of 1945.*
67. *Kenya Debates*, 11 Jan 1946.
68. The Emergency Laws (Transitional Provisions) Act, 1946, the Emergency Laws (Transitional Provisions) (Colonies, etc.) Order in Council, *Kenya Gazette*, 23 Feb 1946. Food rationing, for instance, lasted until June 1948. *E.A.S.*, 10 June 1948.
69. One officer as late as 1950 kept a small cane in his office with which he meted out punishment when he felt the allegations of an employer against an erring employee were justified.
70. *1946 Annual Report, Labour Department.*
71. *Kenya Gazette*, 2 Apr 1946.
72. The Workmen's Compensation Ordinance, Ord 54 of 1946; the Minimum Wage Ordinance, Ord 55 of 1946; *Kenya Gazette*, 31 Dec 1946. The Secretary of State had expressed some exasperation at the dilatory handling of workmen's compensation in 1945. See C. O. Stanley to Edmonds, 14 May 1945 in which he says, 'In November last, the Governor of Kenya was told of the importance attached to the introduction of workmen's compensation legislation and the hope was expressed that the Governor would shortly be able to report that progress was being made in the preparation of an Ordinance for enactment in Kenya.' C.O. 533/537.
73. *Interim Report on Development*, 1945; *Kenya Gazette*, 19 March 1946.
74. Memorandum on 'The Resident Labour Problem' prepared by the Labour Department; dated 3 March 1947.
75. *East Africa Royal Commission 1953–1955 Report*, Cmd. 9475 of 1955 (hereafter Dow Commission Report).
76. 'The reason is really a political one. The Farmers are convinced that the

presence of cattle eventually will give the resident labourer a right—a moral if not a legal one to the land he grazes.' 1946 Annual Report, Uasin-Gishu and Trans-Nzoia Districts.

77. Dow Commission Report. See also the *1946 Annual Report, Labour Department*, which noted the case of a squatter whose income amounted to Shs. 300/- per month, of which only Shs. 25/- was in cash, for another example of the small percentage of a squatter's income that lay in wages. The Labour Department, however, was apt to be dazzled by sudden revelations of the wealth of individual squatters into assuming that such wealth was common.
78. *1946 Annual Report, Labour Department*; see also 1947–9 Annual Reports, Rift Valley Province. In each year the provincial commissioner, D. L. Morgan, expressed doubts about the repatriation of squatter cattle to the reserves.
79. *Ibid.*, 1951.
80. *Ibid.*, 1946.
81. 1946–9 Annual Reports Uasin-Gishu and Trans-Nzoia Districts, 1949 Annual Report, Rift Valley province, 1950 Annual Report, Baringo District. Some of the tribal associations, such as the Swahili protection societies in this area, were exotically titled—the Royal Guard of the Simba Scotch and the Arabian Congo Union.
82. 1946, 1948 Annual Reports, Uasin-Gishu and Trans-Nzoia Districts. For an earlier example of such ethnic bases see T. Aubrey, 'Labour', *E.A.S.*, 29 Aug 1941; mixed labour forces were however the general rule.
83. See also the rural strike fomented by the K.A.U. in J. Ngugi's novel, *Weep Not Child*, 58–9, 64–7.
84. Precise squatter numbers are difficult to assess as the official statistics were not always collected on the same basis; the Dow Commission appeared to judge them all to be under estimates. The Labour Department's 1946 report estimated 45,000 squatters with 200,000 dependants. The 1948 report noted 27,914 at work on the census date, 5,774 on strength but not at work, and 6,665 old men given squatting rights, with in addition 8,739 female members 6,697 juvenile members of squatter families at work. The total number of male squatters had fallen to 33,802 by 1951.
85. See *Kenya Debates*, 26 July 1945, debate on the Resident Labourers (Amendment) Bill, in which the government introduced and then withdrew a bill to include the forest squatters within the jurisdiction of the local council orders. The government argued that it could achieve the same result by administrative direction. The Commissioner for Lands and Settlement estimated that there were 3,500 employed by the Forest Department and 15,500 by private contractors.

    We are grateful to A. T. Matson for the information concerning the charcoal industry.
86. Frank Wingate Carpenter, *qui vivit.* Educated Dean Close School and Cambridge; Nigerian administration 1928–40; military service 1940–5; district officer Kenya 1945; Deputy Labour Commissioner 1947; Labour Commissioner 1951–4.
87. *1952 Annual Report, Labour Department.*
88. 1946–7 Annual Reports, Uasin-Gishu and Trans-Nzoia Districts.
89. 1952 Annual Report, Rift Valley province.
90. 1947 Annual Report, Kiambu District.
91. 1945,1946 Annual Reports, Meru District; 1947 Annual Report, Nyeri District.
92. In 1947 the price was raised from 20 to 25 cts. per *dhebbie,* ultimately reaching 50 cts. by 1951.
93. 1947 Annual Report, Kiambu District; 1951 Annual Report, Thika District.
94. 1952 Annual Report, Central Province; F. D. Corfield, *Historical Survey of the Origins and the Growth of Mau Mau,* Cmnd. 1030 of 1960.
95. Rev. L. J. Beecher to P.C., Central Province, 6 May 1944, relaying complaints from Harry Thuku and the Kikuyu Provincial Association. Thuku had opposed communal labour before the Second World War. Thuku to P.C. 5 Aug 1937. Central Province papers, K.N.A.

96. 1947 Annual Report, Nyeri District. See also 1947 Annual Report, Meru District; L. S. B. Leakey, *Defeating Mau Mau*, 1954, 30–1.
97. 1947, 1948 Annual Reports, Fort Hall District; M. P. K. Sorrenson, *Land Reform in the Kikuyu Country*, 1970, 75.
98. 1949 Annual Report, Meru District.
99. 1940 Annual Report, Machakos District.
100. 1945 Annual Report, Machakos District; Elspeth Huxley, *The Sorcerer's Apprentice*, 1948, 44–8; Creech Jones quoted in 1946 in Elspeth Huxley, *A New Earth*, 1960, 188–9.
101. Between 1946 and 1955 A.L.D.E.V. spent £2.4m. on reconditioning African lands and for African settlement. One-third of this went to the Machakos district.
102. 1950 Annual Report, Kitui District; 1951 Annual Report, Machakos District.
103. *E.A.S.*, 2 Feb 1968 quoted in D. C. Savage, 'Kenyatta and the Development of African Nationalism', *International Journal*, XXV, 3 (1970).
104. *Kenya Debates*, 28 Jan 1947.
105. *1947 Annual Report, Labour Department; Kenya Colony Annual Report, 1946.*
106. *E.A.S.*, 15 Jan 1947.
107. *Mombasa Times*, 25 June 1947.
108. *E.A.S.*, 14 Feb 1947.
109. *News Chronicle*, 17 Apr 1947.
110. *Mombasa Times*, 18 Jan 1947.
111. *E.A.S.*, 28 Feb 1947.
112. N. Farson, *Last Chance in Africa*, 1949, 24.
113. *Mombasa Times*, 14 Jan 1947; *The Times*, 14 Jan 1947. McKeag had been one of the six Kenya officers who had attended the first colonial labour officers' course in London.
114. Farson, *op. cit.*, 23.
115. *E.A.S.*, 21 June 1947.
116. *Mombasa Times*, 4 Feb 1947.
117. *Ibid.*, 21 Feb 1947.
118. *E.A.S.*, 9 March 1948.
119. *Kenya Gazette*, 14 Jan 1947.
120. *1947 Annual Report, Labour Department; E.A.S.*, 23 July 1947.
121. *Kenya Gazette*, 1 Apr 1947.
122. *E.A.S.*, 24, 29 Apr 1947.
123. *Ibid.*, 26 May 1947.
124. *Ibid.*, 31 July, 1, 8 Aug 1947.
125. *Kenya Debates*, 24 Nov 1947, speech by Carpenter in which he urged the need for a social policy and pointed out that increased education and improved health created material wants, which in turn could cause commercial prosperity.
126. *Kenya Gazette*, 29 Apr 1947; *E.A.S.*, 24 Apr 1947.
127. *E.A.S.*, 20 Dec 1947.
128. *Ibid.*
129. *Kenya Gazette*, 19 Feb 1950.
130. Walter Richard Cubitt Keeler, *qui vivit*. Educated Great Yarmouth Grammar School, Imperial College of Science; Inspector of Factories Home Office and later Ministry of Labour 1938–46; Inspector of Labour Palestine 1946–9; Chief Inspector of Factories Kenya 1949; Deputy Labour Commissioner 1954; Labour Commissioner 1957–63.
131. The Factories Ordinance, Ord 38 of 1950, *Kenya Gazette*, 28 March 1950.
132. *1947 Annual Report, Labour Department.*
133. *E.A.S.*, 15 March 1947.
134. *African Labour Efficiency Survey, 1947*, ed. C. H. Northcott, 1949.
135. *E.A.S.*, 5, 8 July 1947.
136. *African Labour Efficiency Survey.*
137. *E.A.S.*, 1 Feb 1946.
138. *1947 Annual Report, Labour Department.*
139. *1948 Annual Report, Labour Department.*

140. *Mombasa Times*, 30 Sept 1948.
141. See *ibid.*, 4 Nov 1948 for the municipal board; and also *E.A.S.*, 30 Sept, 1 Oct 1948, where editorials attacked the new wage scales as inflationary and unjustified. *Kenya Gazette*, 21 June 1949.
142. *Report of the Committee on African Wages*, 1954 (hereafter Carpenter Committee Report).
143. *Ibid.*
144. The Employment (Amendment) Ordinance of 1950 provided for no standard form of apprenticeship agreement but required that they be approved by the Labour Commissioner, *Kenya Gazette*, 14 Feb 1950.
145. *Mombasa Times*, 11 July 1947.
146. *E.A.S.*, 21 July 1949.
147. Makhan Singh, 210–12.
148. *E.A.S.*, 27 Aug 1948, 24, 28 Jan 1949.
149. A Uganda example of the frustration experienced by informal apprenticeship to small-scale Asian employers is provided in J. Okello, *Revolution in Zanzibar*, 1967, 50; Okello quickly found his 'employer insisted that I learn only one day a week, and spend the other days making button-holes; we disagreed. I had requested to be allowed three or four days a week learning, and since I wanted to be more than just a maker of button-holes, I gave up my job with him in order to learn masonry.' Another African view of apprenticeship is seen in J. Ngugi, *Weep Not Child*, 23, 48, 54.
150. *E.A.S.*, 12 Jan 1946.
151. *Ibid.*, 15, 27 Jan, 21 March, 21 June 1947.
152. Richard Edmonds Luyt, *qui vivit*. Educated Diocesan College, Rondebosch, Cape Town and Oxford Universities; Cadet Northern Rhodesia 1940; military service 1940–5; D.O. N. Rhodesia 1946; seconded Labour Officer 1946; Senior Labour Officer 1949; Deputy Labour Commissioner Kenya 1953; Labour Commissioner 1954; Permanent Secretary 1957; Chief Secretary Northern Rhodesia 1962; Governor and Governor-General British Guiana 1964; Vice-Chancellor, University of Cape Town.
153. *E.A.S.*, 14 Feb 1947.
154. *Ibid.*, 9 July 1947, also *ibid.*, 3 Sept 1947, letter from E. A. Aubrey.
155. *Ibid.*, 3 May 1948.
156. *Ibid.*, 2 July 1948.
157. *Ibid.*, 2 July 1948.
158. *Mombasa Times*, 17 Feb 1947.
159. *Ibid.*, 17, 19 Feb 1947.
160. *Ibid.*, 18 Feb 1947.
161. *Ibid.*, 21 Feb 1947.
162. *Thacker Tribunal Final Award*, 1947; *E.A.S.*, 27 June 1947.
163. *E.A.S.*, 15 Jan 1947.
164. Sir P. Mitchell, *op. cit.*, 242.
165. *Kenya Debates*, 19 March 1948.
166. *1946, 1947 Annual Reports, T.U.C.*
167. *E.A.S.*, 8 Nov 1947.
168. Makhan Singh, 169–70. *E.A.S.*, 13 Jan 1948. Patrick gave a series of ten lectures on trade unions at Pumwani Memorial Hall, *ibid.*, 15 Jan 1948.
169. *E.A.S.*, 31 July 1948.
170. Meshach Ayako Okelo Ndisi, *qui vivit*. Educated C.M.S. School, Maseno and Alliance High School, Kikuyu; general secretary Transport and Allied Workers' Union 1948; Ruskin College, Oxford on T.U.C. scholarship 1948–9; returned and resigned as general secretary, appointed Member Labour Advisory Board and appointed Assistant Industrial Relations Officer, Labour Department, all 1950; promoted Labour Officer 1956; Senior Labour Officer 1961; Assistant Labour Commissioner 1962; Permanent Secretary Ministry of Labour and Social Services 1963; Eastern and Southern Africa Area Director I.L.O. 1967; Regional Director for Africa 1969.
171. *Mombasa Times*, 16 Sept 1947; Makhan Singh, 158–9.
172. *Mombasa Times*, 29 Sept 1948.

173. *1948 Annual Report, Labour Department.*
174. The Trade Disputes (Arbitration and Inquiry) Ordinance, Ord 71 of 1948, *Kenya Gazette*, 21 Sept 1948.
175. The Trade Union Registration Ordinance, Ord 35 of 1949, *Kenya Gazette*, 27 Sept 1949; *E.A.S.*, 13 Apr 1949; *Kenya Debates*, 12 Aug 1949. It was opposed by Mathu, A. B. Patel and C. B. Madan.
176. The Trade Unions and Trade Disputes (Amendment) Ordinance, Ord 33 of 1948, *Kenya Gazette Supplement*, 27 Apr 1948.
177. The Voluntary Unemployed Persons (Provision of Employment) Ordinance, Ord 39 of 1949, *Kenya Gazette*, 27 Sept 1949; *Kenya Debates*, 10, 19 Aug 1949. It was opposed by Mathu and Jeremiah.
178. The Deportation (Immigrant British Subjects) Ordinance, Ord 37 of 1949, *Kenya Gazette*, 27 Sept 1949.
179. The Wages and General Conditions of Employment Ordinance, 1948, *Kenya Gazette*, 3 Aug 1948.
180. Interviews, M. A. O. Ndisi, 1960, 1963; Makhan Singh, *passim*; files of the Labour Department concerning the origins of particular unions.
181. Fred Kubai, *qui vivit*. No formal education; E.A. Posts and Telegraphs 1931–46; organizer African Workers Federation 1946; organizing secretary Kenya African Road Transport and Mechanics Union (later Transport and Allied Workers Union) 1947; acting general secretary 1948; president East Africa Trade Union Congress 1949; arrested and acquitted 1950; chairman Nairobi branch K.A.U. 1951; editor *Sauti ya Mwafrika* 1951; arrested, tried and convicted with Jomo Kenyatta 1952–3; released 1961; M.N.A., Parliamentary Secretary Ministry of Labour and Social Services 1963; Assistant Minister 1969.
182. *E.A.S.*, 10 Sept 1947.
183. The section on the E.A.T.U.C. is based largely on an interview with Makhan Singh, 1964 and papers in his possession.
184. *Colonial Times*, Nov 1947, Jan, Oct 1948, *passim.*
185. *E.A.S.*, 15 March 1948.
186. *Ibid.*, 19 Aug 1948.
187. *Ibid.*, 11 Sept 1948.
188. *Ibid.*, 6 May, 27, 31 Aug 1949.
189. *Ibid.*, 8 June 1949.
190. *Ibid.*, 31 Aug 1949.
191. *Ibid.*, 29 May 1950.
192. This union had evolved from an Asian social organization, the Surat District Mochi Karigar Mandal, under Makhan Singh's direction.
193. *E.A.S.*, 30 March, 11, 14, 20 Apr, 6, 20 May 1949.
194. *Ibid.*, 14 Sept 1949.
195. *Ibid.*, 30 Sept 1949; *Kenya Gazette*, 27 Sept 1949.
196. *E.A.S.*, 6 Oct 1949.
197. *Ibid.*, 4–23 Oct 1949, *passim;* The Nairobi Municipality (Taxicab) (Amendment) By-Laws, 1950, *Kenya Gazette*, 13 May 1950; The Nairobi Municipality (Taxicab) By-Laws, 1947, *ibid.*, 27 May 1947.
198. Testimony of Constable Mwangi Musau, transcript of the trial of Makhan Singh.
199. *Daily Chronicle*, 7, 21, 25 March 1950.
200. Makhan Singh, 253–4, full text; *Manchester Guardian*, 22 March 1950.
201. *E.A.S.*, 6 March 1950.
202. *Manchester Guardian*, 28 March 1950.
203. *E.A.S.*, 25 Apr 1950; Makhan Singh, 260–2.
204. *E.A.S.*, 27 May 1950.
205. At Makhan Singh's trial, the Crown alleged that, according to secret information, he worked for communist causes, requested to be sent to Moscow, was sub-editor of a communist paper in the Punjab between 1943 and 1947, and received communist publications from India in 1948–9. The papers were the *Communist*, the *Labour Monthly, The African Newsletter,* and the *People's Age. E.A.S.*, 24 May 1950. He testified that the Anglo-American imperialists

planned to destroy the Soviet Union and that there was no guarantee that they would not attempt to reconquer India, having bases in Africa. *E.A.S.*, 27 May 1950.

Letters to Makhan Singh from S. Rostovsky and Louis Saillant of the W.F.T.U. were produced at the trial, the first asking for '... any information you may possess on the trade union organization activity and the economic and social situation of the countries bordering on Kenya, particularly Tanganyika. We ourselves have only very vague information, for example about the Dar-es-Salaam dockers strike which seems to us of considerable importance.' The second merely sent a May Day manifesto and urged publicity. (Transcript of the trial of Makhan Singh.) Makhan Singh also sent three letters to the W.F.T.U., one listing the unions affiliated to the E.A.T.U.C. and two containing protests about labour legislation and the internment of Chege Kibachia. (*Ibid.*)

206. *E.A.S.*, 16 May 1950.
207. The government had anticipated the strike. 'In May it was decided to take action against Makhan Singh and other officers of a body called the East Africa Trade Unions Congress and to obtain a decision in the Courts as to the illegality or otherwise of the Congress. It was expected that the Congress would attempt to call a general strike in protest, as it did ... It was essentially political in origin and intent, claims for higher wages being tacked on as an afterthought ...' 1950 Annual Report, Central Province.
208. *E.A.S.*, 17 May 1950.
209. *E.A.S.*, 16 May 1950; *Colonial Times*, 17 June 1950.
210. 1950 Annual Report, Kiambu District; 1950 Annual Report, Central Province

   A fictional account possibly based on this incident can be found in J. Ngugi, *A Grain of Wheat*, 205. It also suggests that the local women played a significant role in the strike.
211. *E.A.S.*, 20 May 1950.
212. *Observer*, 21 May 1950.
213. 1950 Annual Report, Central Province. 'For some months rumours were kept alive in the Location as to what the Kikuyu were going to do to the Luo for breaking the strike ... The Luo Union gave great assistance to the District Commissioner both during and after the strike in controlling the Luo in the locations at a time when feeling against the Kikuyu was running high and might easily have led to serious fighting.'
214. *The Times*, 19 May 1950; 1950 Annual Report, Central Province.
215. *E.A.S.*, 16–27 May 1950, *passim*.
216. 1950 Annual Report, Central Province.
217. *E.A.S.*, 29 May 1950.
218. *Ibid.*, 27, 28 May, 3 June, 8, 10, 28 July 1950.
219. *Ibid.*, 15–21 June *passim*, 22 July 1950; *Kenya Debates*, 17 July 1945, question by Cooke; 8 Jan 1948, speeches by Cooke and Wyn-Harris.
220. *E.A.S.*, 20 May 1950.
221. The executive of the Labour Trade Union became B. M. Kaggia, president; F. Kubai, vice-president; J. D. Kali, second vice-president, and P. C. Mula, general secretary. The union presented a memorandum in opposition to the proposed trade union bill. See B. M. Kaggia and E. Githuku, Memorandum to the Select Committee of the Legislative Council of Kenya on the Trade Union Bill, 7 March 1952. Fabian Society Papers. The union was banned on 20 May 1953.

   Aggrey Minya, *qui vivit*. Official of Transport and Allied Workers Union; general secretary of Kenya Federation of Registered Trade Unions, 1952–3; area secretary of Central Organization of Trade Unions, 1966–7; area secretary Plantation and Agricultural Workers Union 1967.
222. *E.A.S.*, 6 Sept 1949, letter of F. M. Ruhinda.
223. *Ibid.*, 9 Sept 1947. In 1946 the K.A.U. submitted to the government a comprehensive statement of its position entitled, 'The Economical, Political, and Social Aspects of the Africans in Kenya Colony'. Under labour it did not refer to trade unions but did speak of the difficulties of three groups of

workers—(i) civil servants, teachers and railway workers, (ii) the labourers who needed minimum wage legislation, balanced diet, housing, workmen's compensation, etc. and (iii) squatters who had inadequate social services. The document also recommended more labour officers and more African assistants. C.O. 533/537, Rennie to Secretary of State, 17 Aug 1946, and enclosures.

224. *Ibid.*, 12 Sept 1947.
225. *Ibid.*, 24 Apr 1950.
226. *Ibid.*, 12 June 1950.
227. *Ibid.*, 2 May 1949.
228. *The Times*, 29 June 1949.
229. *Ibid.*, 23 May 1950.
230. *Daily Herald*, 18 May 1950, banning of G. Padmore, *Africa: Britain's Third Empire.*
231. *Manchester Guardian*, 6 May 1950.
232. *The Times*, 10 May 1950; *Manchester Guardian*, 28 March 1950, statement of General C. C. Fowkes, president of the Electors' Union that 'the Government was well aware of the great danger to Kenya from the Communist-influenced union movement and was able to deal with it'.
233. George Bennett, *Kenya: A Political History*, xii.

The Rev. W. Scott Dickson of the Church of Scotland and secretary of the Christian Council of Kenya (C.C.K.), in an interview in the United Kingdom, rejected the demand of the settlers for permanent white domination but in these terms: 'Permanent European domination was an impossibility. There was room for European leadership for many years to come . . .', The *Scotsman*, 29 March 1950.

234. *Mombasa Times*, 7 May 1949.
235. *Johannesburg Star*, 6, 8, 9 Sept 1949.
236. *Kenya Weekly News*, 24 March 1950.
237. Blundell, 104. See also Elspeth Huxley, 'The Roots of Mau Mau Go Deep', The *Straits Times* and other newspapers, 15 Dec 1952. Mrs. Huxley also downgraded the economic circumstances of the revolt. 'But the Mau Mau outbreak goes down to something deeper. It is a sign of social maladjustment which must be dealt with, not on the economic but on the psychological plane.' In a letter to the *Daily Telegraph*, 1 Nov 1952, she argued that Kenyatta was '. . . in some respects a small-scale African Hitler . . . An overweening personal ambition is the base. Added to this is that mysterious ability to compel others to believe and follow . . . There are grievances, of course. Germany had grievances too. Appeasing Hitler did not cure them; nor will appeasing the Kikuyu, so long as they nourish the Mau Mau.'
238. *E.A.S.*, 14 Jan 1949, full text in Makhan Singh, 190–6.

Patrick was denounced for these remarks in Britain. See, for instance, *1949 Annual Report, T.U.C.*, speech of A. L. Cohen, Union of Shop, Distributive and Allied Workers; Derek Kartun, 'Employers would pay for Unions like this', *Daily Worker*, 20 Sept 1951.

239. *Ibid.*, 5 Oct 1949.
240. *Ibid.*, 21 Oct 1949.
241. *Ibid.*, 22 Apr 1950; see also *ibid.*, 13 Apr 1949, speech by Blundell saying '. . . in other parts of the world, trade unionism appeared to be a method of blackmailing more reasonable members of the community'.
242. *Ibid.*, 31 May 1950.
243. *Ibid.*, 3 May 1950.
244. Makhan Singh, 249–50; Sir P. Mitchell, *op. cit.*, 242.
245. The Essential Services (Arbitration) Ordinance, Ord 4 of 1950, *Kenya Gazette*, 14 Feb, 16, 23 May 1950.

Under the ordinance, the Labour Commissioner was allowed no discretion as to whether he should attempt conciliation in a dispute in an essential service, he was obliged to do so. If conciliation failed, the Member could order compulsory arbitration by tribunal. Persons in essential services were forbidden from taking part in strikes or lock-outs. The original schedule to the ordinance covered a wide range of undertakings, road and rail transport, docks, posts and telegraphs, aviation, hospitals and medical supply services, fuel oils, milk and perishable foodstuffs.

246. *E.A.S.*, 17 May 1950. After the strike, seen by the government as politically inspired, the list of essential services was extended, in the words of the Labour Department Annual Report to '... discourage agitators from precipitating action by workers before opportunity is given for Government to see how it can help in settling the dispute ...'

247. The Public Order Ordinance, Ord 26 of 1950, *Kenya Gazette*, 27 June 1950.

248. *E.A.S.*, 26 May 1950; interview E. M. Hyde-Clarke, 1970.

249. *E.A.S.*, 14 July 1950, statement E. M. Hyde-Clarke. For a detailed examination of these associations and councils see *infra*, pp. 369–70.

250. See *infra* pp. 369–70.

251. *E.A.S.*, 14 July 1950.

Chapter 10

THE SQUATTERS' REVOLT

> . . . when Mau Mau atrocities and violence are identified with opposition to Government, when honest criticism is in danger of being treated as sedition, and when even the shamba boy who wants a raise in pay is apt to be accused by his employer of Mau Mau sympathies—then the wise man keeps quiet.
>
> 1954 Annual Report, Machakos District.

Political Developments

The declaration of the Emergency on 20 October 1952 and the arrest of the K.A.U. leadership had profound effects both on the colony and on its nascent labour movement. Two main themes can be discerned. The first theme, mostly at the national level and in particular in Nairobi and the Central province, was the gradual creation of the military and administrative structure designed to contain and destroy the revolt. This led to the appointment in 1953 of General Sir George Erskine as Commander-in-Chief and to the appointment of a series of committees culminating in 1954 in the creation of a small War Council composed of the new Governor, Sir Evelyn Baring, his deputy, the Commander-in-Chief, and the leader of the European community, Blundell. The inclusion of Blundell was mistakenly seen in some quarters as a return to an older style of Kenya politics when the settlers secured significant political advances through their representation on similar committees. There was certainly no lack of settler spokesmen who hoped to utilize the Emergency in this manner. However, it transpired that the colonial establishment co-opted Blundell, rather than the reverse. Blundell not only wanted the efficient prosecution of the military campaign but came to believe that Mau Mau could only be killed by social reform and ultimately that the future for the Europeans lay in a multi-racial Kenya—views that were shared by many of the senior officials of the colonial establishment. This liberalism gradually led to an estrangement between Blundell and the majority of his European supporters which resulted in the creation of a series of right-wing settler political parties, and finally in a bitter election campaign against Cavendish-Bentinck in the Rift Valley in 1961.

At the local level the theme was represented by a drastic increase in the number of district officers to ensure the closer supervision which the War Council desired. Local co-ordinating committees of the district administrators, police and military, frequently with a settler as executive secretary, were formed to co-ordinate the battle plans. This augmentation of the provincial and district administrations was to have profound short-term and long-term effects on Kenya politics.[1] The focus of government became once again the traditional field service; this stress inevitably meant that the newer specialized services such as the Labour Department would have temporarily to take a back seat to the provincial administration. The effect could be seen both in terms of the decline of the influence of the Labour Department in the counsels of the government between 1952 and 1954 and the subordination of local labour officers to the provincial administration. To some Europeans the outbreak of the insurrection justified their previous sceptical views about the department as an agency of subversion.

Closer administration also involved a host of new regulations and restrictions, particularly aimed at the Kikuyu, Embu and Meru. Most of these were regulations issued under the Emergency Powers Order in Council of 1939 rather than new legislation. They multiplied in number so quickly that they were eventually codified in a local handbook.[2] Politically the most significant was the banning in 1953 of the K.A.U. and of all African political parties. Such action was not, however, extended to African trade unions; these enjoyed a measure of protection through the influence of the T.U.C. and the Labour Party in Britain and of Hartwell, now the Member for Labour in Kenya. There were also bans on the possession of weapons, some restriction on trade, powers to confiscate property and to restrict or detain without trial. The death penalty was imposed for a wider variety of offences. In order to cope with the increased number of legal cases, Emergency assizes were established. Collective punishments, usually in the form of seizures of cattle and goats, were used between 1952 and 1956 when this was superseded by a policy of fines. The land of known terrorists was confiscated. The police forces were expanded from 7,000 to some 15,000 full-time and 6,000 part-time members in 1953, the Special Branch reorganized, and African Home Guard units established. This latter organization had enrolled 10,000 men by January 1953 and was eventually to reach 25,000. The British military establishment was also increased reaching a maximum of eleven battalions in 1953. Local Europeans and Asians were called up, though not in large numbers, but many more performed part-time duties for the police or the administration.[3]

There were successive round-ups of Kikuyu in Nairobi in 1952 (Operation *Jock Scott*) and 1954 (Operation *Anvil*), the latter involving some 30,000 of whom 16,538 were detained and 2,416 of their dependants returned to the reserve. By the end of 1954 67,000 people were either in prison or in detention on charges relating to Mau Mau, and a total of nearly 90,000 were detained before the Emergency came to an end.[4] Strict controls on the movement of Kikuyu were also established.[5] In the Rift Valley and in other rural areas frightened European farmers attempted to drive their Kikuyu resident labour back to the reserve. Perhaps as many as 100,000 Kikuyu returned to their homeland as a consequence of this campaign.[6] The implications of these developments for the Kenya labour force will be discussed later.

Strict control of the Kikuyu, Embu and Meru was established through the use of a new pass system. In January 1953 the Labour Department was directed to produce a 'History of Employment' card for all Kikuyu labour; this card recorded a man's particulars, his fingerprints and photograph with a record of employment.[7] The department resisted pressures for the insertion of wage rates, but some employers added them notwithstanding; they echoed a European political cry of the time, 'Bring back the *kipande*'. In 1954 the more elaborate Kikuyu, Embu and Meru passbook system was introduced although again wage rates were not included.[8]

Resistance focused on the photographing of the Kikuyu. Mau Mau organizers urged their followers not to allow such photographs to be taken. They were, of course, able to capitalize on the distrust of new gadgets in a conservative rural community. In the Wanjohi and Kipipiri areas for instance, there was a mass refusal to co-operate since, according to the district commissioner, Mau Mau '... threatened death to anyone who had their photographs taken, and informed labour that photography would result in binding the taker to work in the Settled Areas for life and the forfeiture of their lands in the Reserve'.[9] As a consequence the work was suspended for some months but completed by the end of the year. Pressure was exercised by a regulation which ordered employers of labour who refused to be photographed or fingerprinted to pay outstanding wages to the local senior labour officer, who would hold it in suspense accounts subject to any fines that the worker may have incurred.[10]

The Emergency, however, also opened up, at least temporarily, many new jobs for Africans in the security forces. In 1953 the provincial commissioner in the Southern Province noted: 'Recruiting parties for the Army, the Kenya police, the prisons, and farm guards etc. continued unabated through the year. The demand on the Akamba for service in these traditional spheres of activity was necessarily very heavy in view of their considerable expansion consequent on the Emergency.'[11] The expansion of the police forces has already been noted. At the same time the staff of the Prison Department grew from 43 to 457 Europeans and from 1,100 to 14,000 Africans.[12] Occasional examples of unrest occurred; in the Suez Canal zone where East African labour was still employed in the British Army's Pioneer Corps, labourers threw stones at their officers during small local demonstrations, almost certainly at the instigation of the Kikuyu amongst them.

But the second major theme of the Emergency was the assertion of control by London and the gradual insistence by the Colonial Office that social and political reform must accompany repression. Between 1952 and 1960 successive Conservative Secretaries of State were determined to keep power in their hands and to end the *de facto* veto of the Kenya administration by the settlers. If the British taxpayer was going to spend vast sums on a military campaign in Kenya, his representatives in the British cabinet would have the ultimate say.[13] Furthermore each Secretary of State in his turn made it quite clear to the settler leaders that they would not tolerate a general claim for increased European privilege under the guise of fighting Mau Mau. Even Oliver Lyttelton, who was not prepared to concede that any genuine grievances lay behind the Mau Mau uprising, told the settler leaders in 1952 in Nairobi that '... rule by a small minority was over, and that political advance, when it took place, must embrace all the races in the country'.[14] The Conservative government also had to consider, at least until 1955, its small majority in the House of Commons, the considerable body of British public opinion opposed to adventures in Kenya, and the anti-colonial views of the Americans and of the United Nations. During the decade it slowly became convinced that it did not wish to fight a protracted colonial war in Kenya and that the price of this was gradual concessions to the nationalist cause. This led inexorably through the Lyttelton constitution of 1954 which conceded Council of Ministers posts to two Asians and one African, and the first direct African elections in 1957, to the Lennox-Boyd constitution of the same year, and ultimately to the decision of Iain Macleod to concede majority rule in 1960. In the first half of the nineteen-fifties, few thought the process would accelerate as quickly as it was to do. Assurances were given to the settlers that Britain intended to stay.[15] Imprecise and muddled views of multi-racialism became the rhetoric both of Whitehall and of those settlers such as Blundell who were associated with the regime, a state of mind which half accepted the inevitability of African control and half hoped that it would not take place. One reason for this optimism was the generally favourable economic circumstances, at least in the early nineteen-fifties; the symbol of this was the building boom in central Nairobi which ushered the capital into the era of steel and glass. Even as late as the beginning of 1960 the Governor, Sir Patrick Renison, could assure a British army visitor that independence was ten years away although Beecher, now Archbishop of East Africa, considered ten months more likely.[16] The failure of the European community to recognize the march of events, particularly after the Suez crisis and the rise of Harold Macmillan, can be measured by the violence of their reaction to the Lancaster House proposals of 1960. What was especially galling to the right-wing was that this process took place under the aegis of the Conservative Party, not under that of their traditional enemies, the Fabians. As Blundell himself said: 'The Tories are far colder and more dangerous fish. Centuries of government have taught them the value of ruthlessness, especially when their own interest are concerned.'[17]

One consequence of the revived power of Whitehall was a determination, as Lyttelton said in 1952, '. . . to discharge . . . responsibilities within the rule of law and the general humanitarian principles of Great Britain'.[18] Gradually there was an increasing stress on practical social reforms to secure the political momentum for the guerrillas in the forest and their allies elsewhere. Better housing, higher wages and land reform were three of the major objects. In the villages there was a stress on social welfare, amenities such as sports fields, and rudimentary technical and agricultural education. Such policies commanded widespread support in the British press, notably in a lengthy article in *The Times* by its Nairobi correspondent, and in two series of despatches, one by Patrick Monkhouse in the *Manchester Guardian* and the other by Fenner Brockway in the *Daily Herald*.[19] One of the consequences was the revival after 1954 of the influence of the Labour Department and the social service agencies.

Important influences were also at work in the employer community. Although agriculture had remained the chief industry of the colony after the Second World War, secondary manufacturing had flourished, particularly in the building and associated trades and those catering to the new African market in clothing, furniture, beer, soft drinks, cigarettes and the like. A very large proportion of these firms were British rather than local.

Many were accustomed in Britain and in other parts of the empire to ordering their labour relations efficiently through trade unions and regularized bargaining procedures. Prior to Mau Mau the voice of such companies was heard from time to time to the effect that Kenya was backward in regard to industrial relations, the new form of expression of the more progressive business attitudes first noticeable before the war. Most, however, had been prepared to accept the domination of politics by the local European farmers and small businessmen. But Mau Mau shocked the expatriate business community and eroded its faith in the traditional European establishment.

Led by the London-based Overseas Employers' Federation where Hyde-Clarke had become secretary, the expatriate firms gradually decided to accede to a modern system of industrial relations in Kenya, partly to ensure that welfare capitalism rather than radical socialism triumphed in the colony and partly to allow co-operation with labour in a form which might mitigate the colour bar by transforming the local relationship from race to one of economic bargaining.[20] But these policies were not fully reflected in Kenya until Mau Mau was on the wane. In 1956 the major expatriate firms created the Association of Commercial and Industrial Employers (A.C.I.E.), later the Federation of Kenya Employers (E.K.E.) which they judged to be a better instrument than the stuffy and old-fashioned chambers of commerce. P. J. (later Sir Philip) Rogers, a business man with West African experience who was director of the British and American Tobacco Company in Kenya became the first president of the A.C.I.E. and a link between expatriate industry and the Labour Department.[21]

It was on ground not wholly unreceptive, therefore, that the Colonial Office and the Kenya government were able to appoint a series of commissions to signpost the way to economic development and to a higher standard of living, particularly for the Africans. Between 1953 and 1955 the Whitehall-appointed East Africa Royal Commission reviewed the economic circumstances and prospects of East Africa. Its views were, in the words of Carey Jones, 'the pure milk of Adam Smith'—perhaps more accurately the liberal capitalism of contemporary western Europe. The commission wished to banish traditionalism and paternalism in so far as it was possible to do so and to introduce into East Africa the modern economic arrangements and practices of the western world. It hoped to do this by eliminating the so-called dual economy and by integrating Africans into the European sector.[22] Most of the general strategy of the Dow Commission had however already been accepted by the government of Kenya by the time the report was published; the nineteen-fifties saw other local inquiries and reports designed to make the necessary adjustments. The most important of these were the Carpenter Report which dealt with African wages, the Lidbury Commission Report on the civil service, the Dolton Report on social security, and the Swynnerton Plan for African agriculture, all of which will be examined in detail later.[23] The government did not seem to realize how fundamentally subversive some of these ideas were; in time the creation of a single economy was likely to make European settlement redundant and to create in Kenya a situation similar to West Africa, where the large commercial organizations such as Unilever and Imperial Tobacco were already making the necessary adjustments for African rule.

Rural Developments

The Dow Commission recognized that development in East Africa depended on the growth of the agricultural industry. To induce this growth its major recommendations were to sweep away, as much as possible, tribal and other restrictions on land and convert the African population to land consolidation and freehold titles. It argued that in the past the only real security that the tribal system offered for the problems of increasing population or of famine was either to move or to annex new land. Since these options were no longer open, the traditional system, in the view of the Commission, condemned the Africans to perpetual poverty based on subsistence agriculture. Furthermore it suggested that urban wages depended fundamentally on the health of the agricultural industry and that wages would only increase in so far as there was an increasingly profitable farming base to the economy.

The Dow Commission recognized that steps towards freehold tenure had already commenced with the Swynnerton Plan. This was made possible by the emergency powers granted the government under which the rural Kikuyu were forced to live in villages, thereby making land consolidation, the prerequisite of the plan, a practical possibility. In line with the commission, the government expected that the combination of freehold tenure, markets and technical assistance would produce a class of successful middle-class African farmers, participating in the same economy as the Europeans, and forming a bulwark against Mau Mau and radical nationalist politicians. It was recognized that one of the consequences of this plan would be a firm division in Kikuyuland between the landowners and the landless. It was hoped, nevertheless, that the rural areas as a consequence of improved farming practice would absorb some of the landless, partly as workers on the farms and partly in village industries. The more sanguine saw the Kikuyu reserves ceasing to be a labour-exporting area. Between 1952 and 1960 land consolidation was therefore carried out with evangelical enthusiasm; the programme for the entire area was practically completed by the end of the Emergency. However, the long-term results did not justify the early optimism—at least in terms of the capacity of the Kikuyu reserve to absorb the landless into employment.[24] This failure was to be of crucial importance when the reserve had to face the unprecedented employment difficulties of the late nineteen-fifties.

One of the continuing problems of the rural areas remained the position of resident labour. The outbreak of Mau Mau led to a major upheaval for the Kikuyu squatter and his employer.[25] The majority of the Kikuyu working in the white settled areas were willing or unwilling adherents of Mau Mau in 1952 and 1953. Frequently the farm headman emerged as a Mau Mau leader, and Mau Mau recruiters and oath administrators toured the Rift Valley, Thika and Nyeri areas persuading squatters either to active violence or, at least to supply food and clothing. Farm owners and managers could sense the atmosphere of strain and tension, divided loyalties and fear among their labourers, and their own fears worsened, often leading to intolerance and panic. Labour from other tribes not affected by Mau Mau but frightened by the charged atmosphere, sometimes, particularly in the early years of the crisis, left for home leaving the employer with even greater problems. Some saw this as a form of inter-tribal labour war by which the Kikuyu hoped to secure a monopoly position for themselves: 'on the farms, they attacked and murdered a number of non-K.E.M. tribes with the clear intention of driving out the non-Kikuyu'.[26]

The only solution seen by the administrator and by the farmer alike was the removal of Kikuyu labour, total removal in some areas, and its replacement by men from other communities, a policy which produced demands for compulsion in traditional terms from those settlers affected. Early in 1953 the Labour Department's staff were organizing transit camps for squatters, some of whom returning of their own choice, others with contracts terminated or not renewed by their employers, or others simply ordered to move by the administration under emergency regulations. The removals continued into 1954 culminating in an almost total mass deportation of Kikuyu, Embu and Meru from the Rift Valley. They were carried out in overcrowded trains or P.W.D. lorries, and the camps presented a depressing picture of wretched, confused and frightened humanity. Several hundred Kikuyu were also repatriated from Uganda and Tanganyika. In 1953 alone Kiambu received about 37,000, Nyeri and Fort Hall some 20,000 each.[27] Those Kikuyu who returned to their overcrowded reserves found the life and atmosphere quite foreign to them, some could not even remember their place of origin; their presence was always unwelcome, and little or no land was available. A number of former Rift Valley squatters turned to violence in the Kiambu and Fort Hall districts. F. A. (later Sir Francis) Loyd reported that in Kiambu 'they were mostly bitter landless and penniless persons who joined the passive wing but owing to their poverty it was difficult to take retaliatory action and many had to be employed in paid gangs'.[28] In Embu it was believed that 90 per cent of those returned were Mau Mau sympathizers; one report noted the return of a group of 268 who engaged in '... continuous singing of subversive songs en route'.[29] Only large-scale screening operations regarded as successful by the administration prevented similar mass removals in the Nyeri and Nanyuki areas. One example of this was the work of confession teams with the resident labour on the farms at Limuru: 'It was found that some farms were completely under the control of Mau Mau and it was necessary in these cases to remove the entire labour force. The men were immediately replaced with other screened labour from the reserve. This method had the double advantage of completely removing all Mau Mau contact on the estate, and of making it clear to labour on other farms that unless they confessed they too would lose their jobs and would return to the reserve.'[30] Police raids, military operations and anti-Kikuyu prejudices when men sought local work or promotion added to the general misery.

Ironically as soon as the Kikuyu were in the process of repatriation, the district and provincial administration began to receive complaints from the European farmers that the new workers were not as good as the old. Some tried to keep their Kikuyu labour.[31] By 1954 most of the Rift Valley farmers had concluded that their new non-Kikuyu labour was inferior, and in the following year there were strong demands for the replacement of the Kipsigis by screened Kikuyu. There were also demands from employers in the Athi River area to import Kikuyu owing to 'the abuse by Kamba labour of their Emergency created monopoly...' It was gradually becoming clear that the colony could not function properly without a Kikuyu work force.[32]

Owing to the removals and detentions, the problem of suitable work for the Kikuyu became one of the major difficulties of the period. In the case of the detainees, it became clear when the government interned large numbers of Kikuyu that it could not keep them restricted indefinitely nor did it think it wise to leave them perpetually idle. The early camps had work projects associated with them; at Manyani and Lodwar, for instance, the detainees built the local airfields. But gradually it was decided that the prerequisite to release would be a period spent in a specific work camp where '...the emphasis was on hard work together with a complete confession...'[33] It was also decided that there would be a gradation or pipeline of camps which would lead the detainee back to his own location. In the early stages some of the detainees refused to work arguing that they were prisoners of war or political prisoners and exempted from such labour by the Geneva Convention. However, the vast majority perforce accepted the work arrangements, and the government avoided problems under the Convention by paying its detainee workers a small salary and depositing it in a Post Office account.

One of the public projects on which many detainees worked was the Yatta Furrow, an irrigation project in Ukambani which involved digging a furrow 10 feet wide, 16–18 feet deep and 40 miles in length.[34] Others were engaged in the Mwea-Tebere irrigation scheme in Embu by which it was hoped to provide both work and ultimately new land for some 10,000 landless families from the Kikuyu reserve. Still others worked on the Perkerra irrigation scheme near Lake Baringo and at Embakasi, Nairobi's international airport.[35] At times, as Elspeth Huxley has said, it seemed as though officialdom would revive every plan suggested for land reclamation in the past generation in order to keep the detainees at work.[36]

Josiah Kariuki has given a vivid picture in his book, *Mau Mau Detainee*, of the strategies of obstruction, resistance and survival in some of these camps. Resistance inevitably led to retaliation on the part of the prison staff and consequently to charges of brutality and torture. The most celebrated confrontation took place at Hola Camp. Here there were two detention schemes; one was for those detainees who would agree to cooperate, work and accept a salary, the other for the recalcitrant. On 3 March 1959 a group of the latter were made to march to the irrigation site and when they refused to work, the warders beat them with batons leaving eleven dead. This scandal was the subject of bitter parliamentary criticism in Britain, profoundly affecting the colonial authorities, causing a reorganization of the prison structure, and resulting in a considerable speeding up of the rate of release of the hard-core detainees.[37]

Within the reserve it was necessary to start public works projects with paid gangs to absorb the destitution and landless from the Rift Valley. These gangs were put to work on road building, terracing and betterment schemes. In 1954 there were sixty-seven relief gangs at work in Nyeri district; by the middle of 1955 12,000 were working on such projects in the Kiambu district although the number had dropped to half by the end of the year. Famine relief was also necessary; most villages in Nyeri district maintained communal soup kitchens for the children and for the elderly.[38] Forced communal labour was also revived for terracing road repairs, water supplies, fencing, bush-clearing, grass planting and for such Emergency projects as clearing the Mile Zone and digging the fifty-mile defensive ditch.[39] This was seen to be as much a punishment as a productive enterprise; it remained as unpopular as ever.[40] In 1952 the provincial commissioner in the Central province remarked on the exodus of young men when communal labour had to be done but also commented on the success of the 'reversion to communal labour' in the Fort Hall area. By 1956 the number of required days had dropped to twenty-eight in the Kiambu area, but it continued to be used in all parts of Kikuyuland throughout the Emergency period. In 1957 communal labour was stopped in Nyeri for certain periods during the year to enable the people to plant the maximum possible food. According to the district commissioner, this 'paid a handsome dividend.'[41] When Josiah Kariuki was released in December 1958, his '... first free night's sleep was abruptly interrupted at dawn by a confused trumpeting noise like the roaring of a lion. When I asked Wangui what on earth it was, she told me it was a human voice, shouting through a megaphone and calling the people of the village to forced communal labour.' He reports that he worked four consecutive days and then feigned illness; it seemed to him that 'the whole country [was] ... in detention with the village as the compound and the works camps as the small cells. We were not released from anything.'[42]

Communal labour in Ukambani, however, took a rather different course in the late fifties. From late 1956 land reclamation became a consuming passion in the area. It was carried out, usually by women, grouped in clans called *mwethya.* Between 1957 and 1960 some 450 dams were constructed in the Kitui area alone, the bigger ones by A.L.D.E.V. (African Land Development) machinery and the rest by communal labour. In Machakos, terracing, grass planting and closure to stock worked miracles in regenerating the reserve. Here again most of the work was carried out by communal effort. The results were so successful that Elspeth Huxley, who had seen nothing but desiccated hills in 1947, could in 1960 entitle one of her chapters, 'Machakos Miracle'. Previous investment was at last beginning to pay off. Furthermore the power of the chiefs had been temporarily restored by the Emergency, and in many cases this was used to further soil conservation. The presence of African officials lent credibility to the schemes, and, at least for the women, there was an immediate impetus in terms of convenient supplies of clean water as a consequence of building the new dams.[43]

One of the consequences of the arrest of so large a number of Kikuyu men was to shift the wage-earning function in many families to the women. Kikuyu women had for many years worked seasonally as coffee pickers. These arrangements continued and, as in the nineteen-forties, wages were set between the chiefs, headmen and the settler labour liaison committees, with the district commissioner acting as umpire. But the situation for many of them now was much more critical. Mumbi, one of the central characters in James Ngugi's novel, *A Grain of Wheat,* took daily employment on a European plantation in order to keep her family alive and to avoid forced communal labour. In 1956 D. J. Penwill, the district commissioner, reported that in Kiambu some 27,000 women were crossing the reserve boundary daily to work on the European farms. The reason was not difficult to find as the gathering of the Kikuyu into villages had revealed a rate of malnutrition among the children ranging from 15 to 50 per cent.

Penwill considered that this was caused by the appalling conditions resulting from the Emergency and from the repatriation of Kikuyu families. He noted that 'since the standard wage for women is from Shs. 20/- to Shs. 25/-, with rations extra; since many of the women have several children in the Reserve and no husbands; and since it is hard to see how any human being can be adequately fed on less than Sh. 1/25 a day; the reasons for some of this distress are obvious'. However, Penwill noted, '... it is the Kikuyu who caused the Emergency'. In the early days of the uprising, Mau Mau guerrillas attempted to stop this movement but they were unsuccessful. Women began to move into other jobs as well, notably in Thika. In 1953 Kenya Canners replaced their men with women at Shs 2/50 per day, one meal and clothing. They found the women more efficient except that the recorded music '... sometimes leads to exuberance accompanied by dancing'. Two years later in the same town East African Bag and Cordage began employing considerable numbers of women.[44] In 1955 the Labour Department appointed a special woman Labour Officer with exchange and inspection responsibilities for the increasing number of women at work. The Labour Exchange services were also considerably expanded during the decade, broadcasting being used on occasions. In 1956, for example, 62,828 Africans were placed in employment.

In the Rift Valley and in those parts of the Central province where Europeans had settled, police and other operations had revealed that virtual '... African settlements had grown up in the remoter part of large farms, and on temporarily unoccupied farms ...', a familiar theme from the past; the answer was again thought to be closer control and supervision.[45] Despite the Emergency and the unpopularity such measures caused, the white-dominated district councils, promoted to county council status in 1953, continued to issue orders limiting stock and cultivation, believing often wrongly that such orders would produce the required control. Resident labour inspectors continued to enforce these orders and to prosecute offenders. However, in 1955 the Council of Ministers vetoed a scheme by the Nakuru County Council to eliminate squatter status and replace it by a cottage and wage-earning scheme.[46]

Some farm owners were as reluctant as ever to co-operate. In the case of Kamba squatters in the Central province, farmers considered that it was the government's duty, not theirs, to see that the number of stock conformed to local regulations. In 1953 one farmer at Thika was fined £100; nevertheless in the following two years the annual report for the district commented on the continuing problem of squatter stock. The same situation occurred in Kiambu. In Nanyuki in 1954 the senior labour officer reported that resident labour remained popular with the employers in that area

'... chiefly due to its stability compared to casual labour'.[47] As late as 1956 the Labour Department, despite the criticism of the squatter system by the Dow Commission, persisted in the Carpenter view that Africans preferred the squatter status to all other forms of agricultural labour and that the squatters were the best rewarded farm workers.[48]

The Labour Deparment did however take the opportunity of the Emergency to use its influence and to put pressure on some farmers to improve their squatter housing. For security reasons the housing frequently had to be concentrated in lines. In the initial rush to consolidate, quality sometimes deteriorated. But such labour lines eventually led to better supervision and consequently improved hygiene, the provision of primary schools, and some instruction in a more modern world for many African women. However, housing continued to be better on the plantations; and during the Emergency the Anglo-French coffee and sisal estate, for instance, carried out experiments with new types of rural housing.[49]

The Luo, Baluhya and Kamba labourers who were brought in to replace the Kikuyu squatters also created new problems. Their services were secured in some cases by old-style 'encouragement' by district commissioners and chiefs, an 'encouragement' made easier by the severe overpopulation and erosion in their home areas. The Kamba were already accustomed to the system of squatting in their own area—an institution which continued to flourish on a small scale throughout the nineteen-fifties, notably in Thika and Kilima Kiu.[50] But a large number of these replacement men were hired on monthly terms rather than on squatter contracts; others were engaged on squatter contracts which provided for no stock and so little cultivation as to amount to a monthly rate with a small garden. The wages paid rose in value by Shs. 10/- to Shs. 15/-; the labour shortage led inevitably to wage increases, a trend accelerated by the practice of the non-Kikuyu labourers moving on to a new employer if he paid a few shillings or so more. But despite the increases the labour shortage lasted into 1956, and Loyd, the provincial commissioner in the Central province, thought that '... employment conditions ... bear unfavourable comparison with those obtaining or projected elsewhere in the Colony, and that further trouble can be expected unless steps are taken to improve rural wage scales and other conditions of rural employment'.[51] The actual rates over the whole territory were as shown in the table on p. 358.

Certain unpopular rural jobs, notably sisal cutting, experienced particularly severe shortages of labour. As the industry's workers, traditionally Luo, went in search of better paid jobs on the farms, in Nairobi, or at the Coast, the owners wrestled with the problem of maintaining their labour and of increasing productivity but without much success. The rival attractions of Nairobi and Mombasa (and the security forces) also had adverse effects on the Kamba betterment scheme in Machakos which, even before Operation *Anvil*, was only reaching 60 per cent of its monthly target of 568 miles of terracing. Labour shortages also held down production at the district council sisal factory, and in general farm labour was very difficult to obtain in Ukambani perhaps one of the reasons for the continued popularity among employers of the long-term resident labour.[53]

RURAL WAGES—1955[52]

	1 Average cash wage Sh.	2 Value of rations inc. in 3 Sh.	3 Average total emoluments Sh.
Colony	36	23	64
Laikipia and Naivasha	42	27	76
Nakuru	34	27	64
Trans-Nzoia	30	17	52
Uasin-Gishu	28	17	54
Nyanza	39	24	68
Central and Nairobi	38	25	72
Southern	36	21	67
Coast	37	20	60

The Emergency opened up a variety of jobs for the non-Kikuyu peoples in the cities, particularly after the *Anvil* operation which removed many Kikuyu from Nairobi and the earlier Mombasa removals. An acute short-term labour shortage especially of skilled Africans was created. The Railway for instance was forced to hire more Asian tradesmen to replace those Africans who were detained. A more lasting and more important consequence was to undermine seriously the Kikuyu domination of the labour market in Nairobi and to cause an influx of men from other tribes, notably the Kamba, Baluhya and Luo. By 1954 there were 30,000 Kamba in Nairobi and 13,000 in Mombasa '. . . in search of the high wages that any Kamba can command now that Kikuyu are a difficult market'.[54] Many of the newly arrived found it difficult to get decent accommodation and to avoid exploitation by certain employers. The authorities were particularly concerned at the large number of Kamba juveniles seeking work and living in deplorable conditions. The district commissioner in Machakos tried to enforce regulations whereby those under eighteen would not get registration certificates and would be forbidden to leave their locations. Many juveniles disregarded these orders and slipped away without the proper papers, thus making themselves even more vulnerable to unscrupulous employers. 'Recently there were 60 young Kamba found working for one firm', wrote the district commissioner, 'not one of whom had a Registration Certificate.'[55] Passes were also introduced for the Kitui Kamba who wished to go to Mombasa. In order to meet the social problems caused by this migration to the cities and also to channel Kamba politics into approved channels, the authorities supported the creation of the Akamba Association.[56] In 1955 the Kamba chiefs visited their people in Mombasa, and a half-hearted attempt was made by the authorities to invoke the power of the chiefs in connection with the strike in the port. Chief Uku Mukima, senior chief of the Machakos district, and Joseph Mutiso, president of the Akamba Association, sent telegrams welcoming the end of the strike and urging the Kamba to return to work so as to retain the good name of the Kamba people.[57] Nor was this migration to Nairobi and Mombasa a temporary phenomenon: the new arrivals had every intention of staying in the cities. In 1955 the labour officer in Machakos reported that '... contrary to the Kamba custom in the past, the vast majority of those who have taken up employment out of the District are remaining outside in their employment.'[58]

Many non-Kikuyu were also employed in the security forces; in Naivasha district alone for example, the government enrolled and paid some 1,400 special farm guards. Some interesting and typical problems arose from the creation of this force which received some three weeks training at Naivasha but was essentially under the control of the local European farmers. Some farmers disliked the guards because they received higher pay than the agricultural labourers and squatters. Others attempted to exploit them; in 1956 the district commissioner noted that 'although divisional D.O.'s made every effort to ensure that Farm Guards were treated properly a considerable number were employed as day herds in addition to their night duties and moreover it was not always possible to make certain that they were receiving their full scale of rations from employers.' In the end, the district commissioner concluded, morale was high where the local farmer was a good employer—otherwise it was very poor.[59]

Conditions in Nyanza, Trans-Nzoia and Uasin-Gishu were much less affected by the Emergency, in some cases not at all. There the old-fashioned paternalism remained for a final decade, except in Nyanza wage-levels remaining low, the squatters growing maize, millet and sorghum on their reduced plots and living in their conical mud, wattle and grass huts. The men now often wore cast-off clothes of the farmer and tended to pierce and twist their ear-lobes less, although the women remained far more conservative. Witchcraft and magical beliefs persisted, as did the killing of twins and, among the Kikuyu, female circumcision. The campaign to rid the Uasin-Gishu of squatter stock proved to be only temporarily effective.[60] In 1954 the Labour Department '... set about in earnest to enforce the forty head-per-farm rule, and to remove the large numbers of excess stock to the Nandi and ... Elgeyo reserves'.[61] The government, however, vetoed the total abolition of squatter stock, at least until 1956; it considered such a move politically unwise before the end of the Emergency.[62] The European population of the area was as divided as ever on the merits of total abolition. and the district commissioners in the reserves warned of the disastrous folly of exporting large numbers of cattle to already overgrazed reserves. As a consequence it was decided in 1956 not to proceed with total elimination; by 1959 the district commissioner could report: 'The squatter problem and the grazing of illegal stock is still much in evidence in spite of intensive activity by the Labour Department...'[63]

Old-style discipline also persisted; as late as 1957 Mrs. Cherry Lander, writing of the work of the small labour tribunal of elders on her farm, described the punishments awarded—for example ten strokes of a light whip on a bare back for theft, a sentence executed before a crowd so as to ensure the maximum hurt of pride, and a punishment as illegal as those advocated by Lord Cranbrook fifty years earlier. Mrs. Lander also described her provision of medicine and of the farm's school—starting with a home-made blackboard and fencing posts as benches, but developing into a recognized primary school receiving an Education Department grant and teachers. But these provisions all operated within the context of heavy paternalism; a typical Kenya farmer, Mrs. Lander wrote in surprise as well as disgust that all the squatters' children wished to be clerks and that her attempts to provide a midday meal largely failed because the men still insisted that this should be prepared by the women of their own tribe.

Although by the middle of the decade conditions in the rural areas appeared to be returning to normal, this 'normalcy' was only to last a very brief span. The new Kamba and Baluhya labour were settling down, farmers were paying better wages and employing fewer men, and there were not as many disturbing police raids. A Kenya civil servant and newspaperman could even recall buying a farm at Molo in 1959 and staffing it in the time-honoured way by hiring a good headman and telling him to find the labour.[65] But this 'normalcy' proved an illusion as the gradual release of detainees built up impossible pressures in the Kikuyu reserve. A small number of Kikuyu were gradually allowed back into the Rift Valley; the first were some 5,000 loyalists in 1955. Then came the less reliable and the detainees. Transit camps were set up, and all discharges were made through these camps. Farmers could ask for particular individuals under a 'Nominated Persons Scheme', and gradually the numbers increased. At first the Kikuyu could work only on monthly terms, but provision for squatters was made in 1956.[66] In 1957 5,000 adult Kikuyu males and 20,000 dependants moved into the Rift Valley, and the district committees laid down wages for them between Shs. 24/- and Shs. 30/-. There was, however, a sinister side to the European enthusiasm for the return of Kikuyu labour. The provincial commissioner first noted and then crossed out of his annual report the following comment: 'They [Kikuyu] are particularly popular with farmers as they were under discipline and restraint of a nature far greater than the normal run of farm labour. For this very reason, great care had to be exercised that they were not exploited by the bad employers only too thankful to have Government recruit for them.'[67]

But by 1958 the trickle had become a flood. Serious unemployment was reported by almost all the district commissioners except in the most remote areas. F. R. Wilson, the provincial commissioner in the Central province, wrote:

> This was especially serious in Fort Hall District which before 1952 sent large numbers of workers to Nairobi and the Rift. Up to the end of 1957 it was possible to export labour on sponsored schemes in numbers approximately equivalent to those being released from detention, but in 1958 the number exported dropped to a trickle, whereas the numbers released increased to a flood. Efforts to improve the situation were made doubly difficult by the economic recession.[68]

Moreover conditions had changed, and farmers had learnt to prefer intensive farming with a small labour force. They could now offer monthly terms only and still maintain a stable labour force. A further factor was the beginning of uncertainty over the future of white farming, an uncertainty reflected in an absence of expansion, and consequently reduced prospects of employment. The position began to resemble that of the nineteen-thirties, with gangs of lean men touring the farms looking for work that was not there.

The Mau Mau crisis had focused attention on land and squatters; debate and controversy continued but little policy definition emerged. The Dow Commission Report noted that many squatters had no land in the reserve; it saw efficient productivity as the solution, recommending that the government purchase land in the settled areas for squatter villages, where squatters might live in a house with a small family-size plot on a long lease, freed from the worries of a tied cottage and administered by an appropriate local authority. The report also recommended some leasing of suitable land to tenants by white farmers. But once again these proposals met with European opposition; Blundell, Havelock and L. R. Maconochie-Welwood, the three elected European ministers flatly forbidding any such proposal and only Hartwell and Vasey supporting the proposals among the officials in the Council of Ministers.[69]

In the formal despatch sent by the government of Kenya to the Colonial Office commenting on the Dow Commission Report, the Governor argued against squatter villages on the grounds of 'the loss of the personal connection between employer and worker on which so much depends' (the code phrase for paternalism), distances between villages and work place, the costs of building and supervising the villages and the loss of farming land. The government's alternative proposals were the provision of further social centres, a vague reference to the long-term replacement of squatters by monthly labourers and an even more vague reference, providing no details, to provision for retired workers. Even the commission's reference to the inefficiency of migrant labour was qualified by the government, who also firmly rejected the proposal for a radical change in the Forest Department's squatter system.[70]

Discussion over minimum wage fixing in agriculture remained almost equally fruitless. The Carpenter Committee had noted the very real difficulties in such wage-fixing, difficulties occasioned by differences in type and hours of work and the provision of housing and rations, but recommended that a Rural Wages Advisory Board with area committees be established to create minima where possible, a proposal later supported by the Dow Commission. The government was however faced with particularly hostile and emotive settler criticism over this recommendation, some farmers even threatening to withdraw from their workers the rations and hut-building material essential on remote farms. These difficulties weakened the position of Hartwell and the sessional paper on the Carpenter Report therefore only noted that agricultural wages would need special study by a further committee.

This further committee reported late in 1955; the government found both its theme and its detailed recommendations so acutely embarrassing that the report, although printed in quantity, was never actually published. It returned to the old theme of productivity and efficiency before an increase of wages or improved conditions. In arguments almost identical to those of the Barth Commission of 1912–13 it even recommended a return to an employment history record differing little from the former *kipande*—a recommendation furiously criticized in a bitter minority note written by the two African members of the committee, John Muchura of the Labour Department and J. K. Ole Tipis. A minimum wage at an ungenerous level was proposed but the wage was to be limited to those who signed six month contracts and was to be conditional on the introduction of the employment record. It is a remarkable commentary on colonial Kenya after sixty years of colonial rule (and with independence, little foreseen, only eight years away) that a committee chaired for most of the deliberations by R. G. (later Sir Richard) Turnbull, one of the colony's most senior officials about to be promoted to Chief Secretary, and including an experienced field labour officer and a district commissioner among its members, could arrive at such retrograde conclusions, so much at variance with those of the Carpenter Committee and the subsequent official policy for urban workers.[71] The whole performance delayed more constructive study of rural wages and it was only in 1957, following a visit from representatives of the Plantation Workers International Federation (P.W.I.F.), that the government announced that it was intending to take powers to fix minimum wages in agriculture. However, it was not at all clear how a statutory minimum wage could be enforced in a period of slumping prices, political confusion, and almost certain evasion. The year 1959 was spent in deciding how the powers should be taken; 1960 saw discussion of these powers by the Labour Advisory Board. But by 1961 conditions and circumstances had changed. Agricultural unions were by then in existence, and moreover, many considered that the priorities were the retention of more men in work than paying those in work more money. Nevertheless in December 1962 the government finally enacted legislation to provide for statutory minimum wages in agriculture, and a wages council for the industry was created in the following year.[72]

In agriculture the last years of colonial rule were of such uncertainty that employer and employee suffered alike. The official end of the Emergency in 1960 led to yet more Kikuyu, Embu and Meru entering the Rift Valley in search of employment; many not finding employment settled on corners of farms and refused to leave. Conditions were worsened by famine in 1961. Although this was a calamitous farming year, many settlers retained employees on their farms even though there was little or no work; this led to friction between those fully employed and those underemployed. Contracts were now usually for one year only, expansion had come to a virtual standstill and a variety of new problems had appeared. These were essentially political and centred over the control of land, in particular resentment by other tribes at the return of the Kikuyu and the reaction of the Kikuyu to this resentment which took the form of oathing and secret protective associations. There was also friction between those landless and unemployed whom the government wished to resettle on a departing European farmer's estate and squatters already there claiming prior rights. On occasions the squatters attempted to seize land for themselves. For the farmer employer the situation was one of uncertainty, unrest, a great increase in stock, crop or property theft with diminished chance of recovery or compensation, and sometimes personal intimidation; the latter was more often intended to drive the settler away so that his land might be divided rather than to pose any serious threat of assault, although there were a few murders of Europeans usually by violent robbers. In 1960 the provincial commissioner in the Central province remarked that 'as fast as Emergency Detention camps were closed they were reopened as prisons'.[73]

Finally in 1962 the whole legal basis of the squatter system was removed when the Resident Labourers Ordinance was repealed, a repeal to become effective in 1963. So. in law, ended the squatter system, though many former squatters stayed on as tenants, employees or small entrepreneurs dealing in wood, charcoal or produce, and were provided with a piece of land as part of their reward.[74] The Dow Commission's estimate of 250,000 men, women and children resident on farms (a total which included monthly labourers, some with small plots) may perhaps have been exaggerated, but if so the exaggeration was not great. In 1955 the Labour Department recorded 44,970 men (including working dependants) on squatter contracts in agriculture, some 20 per cent of the total agricultural labour force. By 1961 the figure had dropped to 24,260, or 9.7 per cent. Even allowing for the different basis of calculation, it is evident that the squatter system was giving way to the more modern and efficient pattern of monthly labourers who also received a garden. This relationship, moreover, constituted an apparently permanent African penetration of the White Highlands.

NOTES

1. For a discussion of this, see Cherry Gertzel, *The Politics of Independent Kenya 1963–8*, 1970, *passim*; Blundell, 118–19, 140–1, 162–3, 174.
2. *Emergency Regulations made under the Emergency Powers Order in Council, 1939*, 1953.
3. F. Majdalany, *State of Emergency*, 1962, 153, 157, 188.
4. F. Majdalany, *op. cit.*, 204; C. G. Rosberg and J. Nottingham, *The Myth of Mau Mau,* 1966, 325; Margery Perham in J. M. Kariuki, *op. cit.*, foreword.
5. The Emergency (Movement of Kikuyu) Regulations, 1953, *Kenya Gazette*, 5 Feb, 5 May, 17 Nov 1953. These regulations allowed the Member for Agriculture and Natural Resources (later the Member for African Affairs) to order any Kikuyu either to remain in or to vacate a certain area. Kikuyu were forbidden to leave the Central province and were specifically prohibited entry in the Coast, Nyanza and Northern provinces and the Maasai E.P.D., The Emergency Regulations Orders, *Kenya Gazette*, 21 Oct, 25 Nov, 9 Dec 1952, 24 March 1953. In 1953 Kikuyus were restricted to their districts of origin within the Kikuyu reserve unless permission to leave was granted, *ibid.*, 10 March 1953. No African on a farm in the Nanyuki, Thika, Nairobi, Nakuru, Naivasha or Laikipia areas could leave the farm without a permit, *ibid.*, 2, 16 Dec 1952. In 1953 provincial commissioners in designated areas were required to ensure that any Kikuyu who left employment was removed to a labour transit camp and that all hiring of Kikuyu would be through these camps, The Emergency (Control of Kikuyu Labour) Regulations, *ibid.*, 13 Jan 1953. Specific regulations also applied to particular districts.
6. D. H. Rawcliffe, *The Struggle for Kenya*, 1954, 60, suggests this figure which does not seem an exaggeration.
7. The Emergency (Kikuyu History of Employment) Regulations, 1953. *Kenya Gazette,* 13 Jan, and amendments 17 Feb, 10 Nov 1953. These were extended by the Emergency (Meru and Embu History of Employment) Regulations, *ibid.*, 1 Sept, 10 Nov 1953. See also the Emergency (Kikuyu Female Domestic Servants) Regulations, *ibid.*, 21 March 1953 and the Emergency (Meru and Embu Female Domestic Servants) Regulations, *ibid.*, 13 Oct, 17 Nov 1953. All other Kikuyu, Embu and Meru were required to have identity cards, *ibid.*, 1 Sept 1953.

8. One beneficial service rendered by the department was a careful collection of records of outstanding wages owed to employees removed under compulsory orders. Over £26,000 out of approximately £30,000 deposited by employers was paid out to labourers as they could be traced.
9. 1953 Annual Report, Naivasha District.
10. The Emergency (Kikuyu History of Employment) (Amendment) (No. 3) Regulations, *Kenya Gazette*, 7 July 1953.
11. 1953 Annual Report, Southern Province.
12. *Report on the General Administration of Prisons and Detention Camps in Kenya*, 1956.
13. The official cost in cash was £55,585,424—half of it borne by the Kenya government. F. Majdalany, *op. cit.*, 221.
14. Blundell, 115.
15. *Ibid.*, 64–5; N. S. Carey Jones, *The Anatomy of Uhuru*, 1966, 87–8.
16. A. Clayton, *Canadian Journal of African Studies*, v, I (1971).
17. Blundell, 83.
18. *Ibid.*, 115.
19. *The Times*, 3 Dec 1952; *Manchester Guardian*, six articles, Nov 1952 esp. 24 Nov; 'Report on Mau Mau', *Daily Herald*, 17–20 Nov 1952. See also *News Chronicle*, 17, 22 Sept, 15 Nov 1952.
20. 'The purpose of the Federation is primarily to represent the interests of overseas employers at international conferences, particularly where those conferences have a strong left-wing bias and are likely to impose conditions on employers that are not in the best interests of the economies of the territories concerned.' O.E.F. letter of Sept 1954, quoted A. H. Amsden, *International Firms and Labour in Kenya, 1945–70*, 1971 (hereafter Amsden), 54.
21. See Amsden for a much fuller discussion which, however, in our opinion underestimates the influence of the Labour Department and the trade unions.
22. Dow Commission Report.
23. Carpenter Report; *Report of the Commission on the Civil Services of the East African Territories and the East Africa High Commission 1953–1954*, 1954 (hereafter Lidbury Commission Report); *Report of the Social Security Committee*, 1957 (hereafter the Dolton Report); R. J. M. Swynnerton, *A Plan to Intensify the Development of African Agriculture in Kenya*, 1954.
24. M. P. K. Sorrenson, *Land Reform in the Kikuyu Country*, 1967, *passim*.
25. See the *1952–1962 Annual Reports, Labour Department*; N. S. Carey Jones, *op. cit.*, *passim*; M. P. K. Sorrenson, *op. cit.*, *passim*.
26. 1954 Annual Report, Kiambu District; see also 1953–4 Annual Report, Thika District.
27. 1953 Annual Report, Central province.
28. 1954 Annual Report, Kiambu District. 'From these repatriates the gangs obtained a number of recruits and they accentuated the difficulties for the Administration; since many had no ties in the Reserves their numbers, together with those evacuated from the Mile Zone, added to the pressure on land which could be cultivated.' See also 1953 Annual Report, Central Province; J. M. Kariuki, *op. cit.*, 42.
29. 1953 Annual Report, Central Province.
30. 1955 Annual Report, Kiambu District.
31. 'European Farmers at Thomson's Falls whose Kikuyu labour has been herded back to the reserves appear to be none too pleased...' *Manchester Guardian*, 1 Dec 1952.
32. 1953 Annual Report, Naivasha District; 1954 Annual Report Central Province; 1956 Annual Report, Machakos District.
33. 1955 Annual Report, Central Province.
34. J. M. Kariuki, *op. cit.*, vi; Elspeth Huxley, *A New Earth*, 1960, 184–7.
35. Elspeth Huxley, *A New Earth*, 28–30.
36. Sometimes the plans went astray. Liliaba Camp was built to supply labour for the laying of a pipeline and the making of a cattle trough for the Northern Grazing Area Scheme; Mbeu Works Camp for the Thura-Nkabune Tse-Tse Fly Clearing Scheme. The wages to be paid the detainees were Shs. 1/95 a day,

but it proved to be more economical to hire local labour at 50 cts. a day. As a consequence the detainees were employed in building their own camps and in making bricks. 1955 Annual Report, Meru District. These camps were authorized under the Emergency (Detained Persons) Regulations, *Kenya Gazette*, 5 May 1953 which laid down a maximum of eight hours work per day and payment ranging from Sh. 1/- to Shs. 2/- per day.

37. *Record of Proceedings and Evidence in the Inquiry into the deaths of eleven Mau Mau detainees at Hola Camp in Kenya*, Cmd. 795 of 1959. *Documents relating to the deaths of eleven Mau Mau detainees at Hola Camp in Kenya*, Cmd. 778 of 1959; *Further documents relating to the deaths of eleven Mau Mau detainees at Hola Camp in Kenya, Cmd.* 816 of 1959. See also *Administrative Enquiry into Allegations of Ill-treatment and Irregular Practices against Detainees at Manyani Detention Camp and Fort Hall District Works Camp*, 1959.
38. 1952 Annual Report Central Province; 1954 Annual Report, Nyeri District; 1955 Annual Report, Kiambu District.
39. 1955 Annual Report, Meru District. The authority for this was the Emergency (Communal Services) Regulations, *Kenya Gazette,* 19 May 1953 which allowed communal labour for up to ninety days in '... any circumstances... which endangers the existence of the well-being of the whole or any part of the inhabitants of the district...' or '... that is necessary or desirable for the maintenance of the health, safety and well-being of such inhabitants or for the good rule and government of such district...' The work could be paid or unpaid.
40. The 1954 Annual Report for Fort Hall notes that communal labour was rigorously enforced in 'bad' areas like Rwathia.
41. 1952 Annual Report, Central Province; 1956 Annual Report Kiambu District; 1957 Annual Report, Nyeri District.
42. J. M. Kariuki, *op. cit.*, 144–5.
43. 1958 Annual Report, Southern Province; Elspeth Huxley, *A New Earth*, xi, xii.
44. J. Ngugi, *A Grain of Wheat*, 166; 1952, 1956 Annual Reports, Kiambu District; 1953 Annual Report, Thika District; 1955 Annual Report, Central province.
45. *1953 Annual Report, Labour Department*.
46. 1955 Annual Report, Rift Valley Province.
47. 1953–5 Annual Reports, Central Province; 1954 Annual Report, *Kiambu* District.
48. For a hostile view of the system, see Solomon Kagwe, 'To a Farm in the White Highlands', *Origin East Africa*, 1965, 119–22.
49. 1953 Annual Report, Central Province; 1953 Annual Report, Thika District Such consolidation of housing could be required by the Member for Agriculture under the Emergency (Farm Resident Labourers) Regulations and the Emergency (Forest Area Resident Labourers) Regulations, *Kenya Gazette*, 7 Jan, 16 May 1953.
50. In 1956 the district commissioner in Machakos wrote that he did not foresee any change in the squatter system in the near future. 1956 Annual Report, Machakos District.
51. Annual Report, Central Province.
52. This survey was carried out in July 1955 for the Rural Wages Committee, but was published in the *Report of the Social Security Committee*, 1957. The survey examined wages paid in non-African agriculture, and the many sawmills situated in the White Highlands. The apparent discrepancies between the figures given in columns 1 and 2, and the total in column 3, is accounted for by including in the latter such items as free fuel, medical attention, blankets and other articles which became the property of the worker, the rental value of land cultivated by the worker, and free grazing for squatters with stock. Not included in the total emoluments were the cost of free housing and water, which on a Colony basis averaged Shs. 50/- and Shs. 8/- per annum respectively at the time. For further details see n. 71.
53. 1953–4 Annual Reports, Machakos District.
54. 1954 Annual Report, Machakos District.

55. *Ibid.*
56. 1954 Annual Report, Southern Province.
57. *Mombasa Times*, 10 March 1955; 1955 Annual Report, Southern province.
58. 1955 Annual Report, Machakos District.
59. 1956 Annual Report, Naivasha District. District commissioners were empowered to direct farm owners to employ farm guards if in the administration's opinion the security situation warranted it. The Emergency (Farm Guards) Regulations, *Kenya Gazette*, 14 Apr 1953.
60. In 1950 21,607 head of cattle and 10,000 sheep were returned to the Nandi district.
61. 1954 Annual Report, Uasin-Gishu District.
62. 1954 Annual Report, Rift Valley Province.
63. 1956, 1959 Annual Reports, Uasin-Gishu District.
64. Mrs. Cherry Lander, *My Kenya Acres*, 1957, ix, xi, xiii, 108–9.
65. 'First Year As a Farmer', *Kenya Weekly News*, 17 Feb 1961.
66. 1955 Annual Report, Rift Valley Province; 1956 Annual Report Naivasha District; *1956 Annual Report, Labour Department.*
67. 1956 Annual Report, Rift Valley Province. In 1956 510 ex-detainees were sent to the Athi River Cement Factory; they lived in a barbed wire camp under strict control, conditions which perhaps explain in part why the employers at Athi River were so anxious to replace Kamba by Kikuyu labour. See also 1956 Annual Report, Southern Province.
68. 1958 Annual Report, Central Province. 19,913 detainees were released in 1958.
69. Hartwell had persistently and stubbornly defended the interests of African labour in Executive Council and in the Council of Ministers; this was to result in his transfer to Uganda as Chief Secretary rather than promotion in Kenya—in the tradition of Hollis, Ainsworth, Tate and McGregor Ross.
70. *Despatches from the Governors of Kenya, Uganda and Tanganyika, and from the Administrator, East Africa High Commission, commenting on the East Africa Royal Commission 1953–1955*, Cmd. 9801 of 1956.

    The Kenya government also preferred only to recommend that the ticket contract system (which provided for the completion of thirty days work over a forty-two-day period) be amended to require the work to be completed in thirty-six days rather than to abolish it altogether as the commission had recommended.
71. The committee noted, from the 1954 census, that 135,000 men, 48,900 women and 38,100 children were in employment in agriculture, earning a total of Shs. 5,621,800/-. In addition there were 26,300 male squatters, 21,900 female and 28,300 children. It foresaw a worsening labour shortage (the reverse was to be the case); to meet immediate needs it approved measures already in hand to import labour from Rwanda and Burundi. On the basis of the E.A. Statistical Department's researches, it noted a colony average rural cash wage of Shs. 36/- per month, average total emoluments of Shs. 64/- and an average value of Shs. 23/- for rations supplied, the balance being made up of land and hut values etc. Wages were lowest in the Uasin-Gishu (cash element Shs. 28/-) and highest in the Rift Valley (Shs. 42/-) on account of the Emergency. Tea paid best, mixed farms and ranches least. The colony average rates of wage and hours worked were 38 cts. per hour (of which 21 cts. were in cash) for a thirty-nine-hour week. The committee produced much evidence of low productivity, making unfavourable comparisons with labour elsewhere, it noted a high rate of labour turnover on the plantations and a low rate on mixed farms but, overall and in contrast to the Carpenter Committee, it attached little importance to a stabilized labour force fearful, perhaps, of the political implications. It deplored private recruiters' recruiting methods (noting that a colony average of 16 per cent of men at work in agriculture were still recruited), and the massive number of desertions, 27,000 per year, of which some 12 per cent deserted before commencing work. The employment record (to include tax receipts), it was argued, would protect the good employee; without it the committee's proposed minimum wage (Shs. 57/- plus a meagre ration scale for eight hours work in a six-day week, on a written contract of not less than six

months), was not justifiable, other employees were not 'useful members of society'. Improved housing was to be secured by income tax relief. Casual labour in the Highlands towns was to be registered and controlled. A Rural Wages Board was to be established and the squatter and ticket systems slowly abolished.

The committee justified its stance principally on the grounds of the uncertainty of world market prices.

We are grateful to Dr. John Weeks of the University of Sussex for drawing our attention to the fact that this report was actually printed, and for the loan of a copy of the University of Michigan microfilm of the document.

72. The Regulation of Wages and Conditions of Employment (Amendment) Ordinance, Ord 46 of 1962, *Kenya Gazette*, 31 Dec 1962; The Regulation of Wages (Agricultural Industry Wages Council Establishment) Order, *Kenya Gazette*, 10 Dec 1963.
73. 1960 Annual Report, Central Province.
74. The Resident Labourers (Repeal and Transitional Provisions) Ordinance, Ord 47 of 1962, *Kenya Gazette*, 31 Dec 1962.

Chapter 11

THE AGE OF TOM MBOYA

It is simply that we have learned to live with the world as it is and set out from there to remould it in a practical manner.

Tom Mboya, *The Challenge of Nationhood.*

Government Policy and the Labour Department, 1950–6

In 1950 the new Labour Commissioner, Frank Carpenter, was determined to prevent any revival of the East Africa Trades Union Congress by carrying out the revised policies of the department as firmly as he could. He was by nature more cautious and conservative than Hyde-Clarke, and the events of the previous two years had convinced him of the folly of attempting to introduce western industrial relations into the colony except by the slowest and most gradual methods. In any event the growth of subversion and terrorism ensured that neither the government nor the settlers would be in any mood to listen to radical revisions of labour practice, and Carpenter both by temperament and by the fact that he was a small landowner himself was in sympathy with more moderate settler opinion. In this he found himself at some variance, both with Hartwell, the new Deputy Chief Secretary and Member for Labour, and his own acting Deputy Labour Commissioner, Ian Husband, whom the Colonial Office had transferred to Kenya from Sierra Leone in an effort to modernize the Kenya labour scene. In 1953 the Colonial Office also transferred R. E. Luyt from Northern Rhodesia to become substantive Deputy Labour Commissioner in 1954. Although Luyt had earned a very progressive reputation as a consequence of his pamphlet, *Trade Unionism in African Colonies*, and for his work in labour relations on the Copper Belt, the Mau Mau insurrection made it impossible for him to secure major changes until the security situation changed in the government's favour.

The basis of Carpenter's policy remained the slow but steady escalation of the minimum wage of which he wrote in 1950 that it formed '... the platform upon which the wage structure in urban areas is based. It is really an agreement rate for unskilled labour. Labour rarely stays on these rates for very long, for employers recognize the need for giving increases when labour is working well.'[1] He pointed to the practice of the government of hiring at the minimum wage but ensuring that the worker became a minor employee on a wage scale after twelve months. Most observers, however, were much less sanguine and considered that the minimum wage usually became the maximum wage, particularly in private industry and that by and large the rate was not adequate to meet the simplest requirements of the workers, a view held by Hartwell, who favoured a substantial early increase.

In 1950 the East Africa High Commision Statistical Department carried out a survey which showed that food, lodging and other essentials consumed almost all the income of those earning the minimum. Most spent half as much again on food as the minimum wage formula allowed and many had little to eat for the last few days of the month.[2] The Committee on African Wages, appointed in 1953, was to find that little had changed in the situation. It concluded that the minimum wage had become 'very much a real wage' and that 'for many others [it] . . . has acted like a magnet to hold down wages'. Nor did it think that the wage had adequately covered the cost of living of single adult males. As a consequence it found 'discontent and frustration' among the Africans.[3] Both the Dow Commission and various left-wing commentators concurred in this point of view.[4]

There was also the problem of enforcement since the government never had enough labour officers and inspectors to carry out the task in every corner of the country and also since it was reluctant, at least prior to 1954, to encourage trade unions which might themselves act as enforcement agencies. In 1952, for instance, the Labour Department admitted in its annual report that only about 10 or 11 per cent of the wage earners earned the barest statutory minimum. Furthermore between 1946 and 1954 minimum wages were based in part on the assumption that the government could and would hold down prices and rents through regulations and subsidies. This policy was a costly failure as prices rose so precipitously throughout this period that even the Europeans demanded an inquiry.[5]

New minimum wage legislation was introduced in July 1950 and passed the following year as the Regulation of Wages and Conditions of Employment Ordinance.[6] This new legislation provided for a new Wages Advisory Board which took over from the old Central Minimum Wages Advisory Board. The old legislation had provided only for a universal basic minimum in each of nine towns. The new ordinance retained this provision, but also allowed the Member for Labour to set up wages councils in particular industries where there was no effective machinery for the regulation of wages. These were patterned on the British trade boards system. Employers, employees and independent members nominated by the Labour Department sat on these councils and were empowered, subject to the approval of the Member, to set a variety of wages within the industry; these rates were then published as a proposal and after the consideration of any objections they became legal rates for particular skills, non-payment of which was a punishable offence. Details of the rates were to be displayed on work-places and the Labour Department's officers, increased by a number of new African inspectors, ensured a measure of compliance.[7] Although this legislation was partly introduced for political reasons, it nevertheless served a useful function, particularly in those industries where there was a horde of small employers who were more likely to be coerced by law than by an ineffective trade union. Nor were European employers necessarily opposed since they believed, with some justification, that the legislation could have the effect of increasing the wages paid by their Asian competitors.

The first of these councils was created in 1952 for the tailoring industry and covered some 3,000–4,000 workers throughout the colony. The following year three orders were issued to cover various aspects of that industry:

tent-making, soft furnishings such as curtains and bedspreads, and bespoke tailoring.[8] The rates were increased in 1954 and in 1955.[9] But the growth of these councils was slow, owing to inexperience on the part of labour and employer members, the low overall wage levels discussed and the difficulties of defining skills, and also to the suspicion of the trade union leaders—a not unfounded suspicion since Carpenter made it clear that he regarded wages councils as a form of industrial relations which could operate without trade unions, although in practice employee representatives were mostly union nominees. In 1953 a second council was created for the road transport and haulage industry but the first rates were not proclaimed until the following year. This order covered some 1,500 workers in the Nairobi area. In 1954 the council for the hotel and catering trades industry was established and adopted its first rate schedule in 1955.[10]

The shock and alarm caused by the Mau Mau insurrection led the government to revive Hyde-Clarke's proposal for a special committee to investigate African wage levels.[11] The committee was chaired by Carpenter himself, its members included all types of employers, and employee representatives, one of whom was Harry Thuku.[12] Perhaps, the decisive personality, however, was the secretary, Keeler, the Chief Inspector of Factories, who was to become Labour Commissioner from 1958 to 1963. The committee's main theme was to suggest that not only was the minimum wage inadequate for a single person but that the calculation of the formula on the basis of a single man should give way to one based on the need to support a family. The Carpenter Report had a very significant impact on the Labour Department but its implementation belongs more to the period when Luyt had succeeded Carpenter as Labour Commissioner.

The other major aspect of Carpenter's policy was his determination to clip the wings of the trade union movement if he could possibly do so. His suspicions can be seen quite clearly in his 1950 annual report when he wrote of '. . . the policy that the trade union movement should be encouraged to develop slowly.'[13] However, it took three years to move the proposed trade union legislation from the planning stage in 1949 to the statute book in 1951 and 1952. The groundwork had been laid at a meeting of the labour commissioners of the three East African territories in 1949 at which the Kenyan experience was a major subject of discussion. The commissioners agreed to press for certain amendments to the trade union acts. These were mostly in the direction of more control and supervision including probationary status, suspension for misconduct, and stronger powers for the registrars who, it was hoped, would become members of the labour departments. They also wished to press for amendments whereby all officers of a union would have to come from the trade concerned, for the banning of general unions, and for representative strike votes presumably supervised by labour officers. They also talked of a 'simpler form of organization' and urged the creation of employers' federations.[14]

These ideas took form in Kenya in two pieces of legislation, the Regula- of Wages and Conditions of Employment Ordinance which, as we have seen, was prepared in 1950 and passed in 1951. The second was the Trade Unions Ordinance which was proclaimed in 1952. This latter ordinance was scrutinized by a committee of the Legislative Council and by the Colonial

Office, the latter after representations from the British T.U.C. which had been critical of earlier drafts. The Trade Union Ordinance was also opposed by the remnants of the E.A.T.U.C., notably by Kaggia in the name of the Labour Trade Union.[15]

Despite criticism from some African nationalists and from some European employers, these two ordinances became the legislative basis for government policy for the remainder of the decade. They made clear what the labour commissioners had meant in 1949 by simpler forms of organization, namely structures less formal than a trade union. They recognized a pyramid of negotiating levels within an industry by providing for works councils, which were a type of joint grievance committee within a particular firm, and for joint industrial councils which were internal negotiating bodies for an entire industry. Agreements could be reached through such structures and registered by the Labour Commissioner. If there were no bargaining procedures in the firm or in the industry, the employers could present to the Labour Commissioner a statement of their terms and conditions of employment and, if he approved, this would be given the imprimatur of the department and would have the force of an agreement. These the department found very difficult to enforce. The new ordinances recognized staff associations and other similar groups which were bodies of employees with the right to negotiate but without the rights of a union in terms of strike action and the collecting of money. These associations could be represented on works councils and on joint industrial councils. By the end of 1951 twenty-two agreements were registered and a number of works councils were set up. However, the unrest of this period seems to have inhibited the growth both of works councils and more particularly of joint industrial councils. For some time the J.I.C. for the port of Mombasa, which was created in 1952, remained the only such body in operation.

The Trade Union Ordinance also provided certain of the safeguards demanded in 1949, although the original bill was much modified by the Colonial Office. It did incorporate provisions for a probationary status of from three to twelve months, deferred registration, and permitted the refusal of registration where 'any other trade union already registered is sufficiently representative'. It did allow, however, for the general secretary of the union to come from outside the trade. The justification for this was that the ordinance also insisted that such an official had to be literate in English or Swahili which, in practice, meant English as it was the language of discourse in government and the language in which the forms pertaining to the act were printed. It was believed that in certain trades it would not be possible to find a leader literate in English and it would, therefore, be necessary to choose someone from outside. The same provisions applied to the treasurer. There can be little doubt that these requirements contributed to the rise of a class of trade union leaders drawn from clerical rather than labouring ranks. The trade union legislation also provided for more stringent control of funds. Moreover it was possible to remove registration if the union engaged in activities not condoned by its constitution. This was regarded as an important safeguard against the politicization of the trade union movement since no union would be registered which had explicitly political aims.

Carpenter considered the new forms of organization and bargaining which he had introduced to be more suited to the capabilities of the Africans working in industry and, of course, much less prone to political manipulation. He also directed that the efforts of the department should be in the direction of promoting these new forms of bargaining in industries covered by the Essential Services Ordinance, where the workers could not in any event legally adopt strike action. This philosophy of bureaucratic paternalism was clearly expressed in his 1951 report:

> It has been found advisable to exercise a great deal more supervision over the existing trade unions and nascent organizations of employees than would be necessary in more developed countries, owing to the almost complete lack of understanding of the primary purposes of trade unionism by the vast majority of African workers in East Africa, and their susceptibility to the influence of educated or semi-educated persons, who may have ambitions of a political or purely pecuniary nature.

However, these rather cautious and conservative developments were overcome by events in 1952. The complacency of the years between 1950 and 1952 gave way to fear at the rise of terrorism and revolutionary nationalism in the shape of Mau Mau. The consequent revival of the power of the Colonial Office noted in the last chapter meant, after the initial military phase, an increase in the influence of the Labour Department, Hartwell and Luyt being the important figures in this development. Changes in labour policy and practice took place on a number of fronts. There was, for instance, a distinct change in the tone of the department. Luyt was able to strike up a working relationship with Tom Mboya who was establishing his power in the trade union movement at this time; this understanding was one of the essential ingredients in keeping the trade union movement alive in the midst of the Mau Mau uprising. Both Luyt and Mboya were prepared to try to make effective the ideas outlined in Luyt's pamphlet of the nineteen-forties.

The government as a whole at last came to recognize the inadequacy of the urban wage structure. As we have seen, the Carpenter Report recommended a change in the minimum wage formula so that a man could maintain his family on a permanent basis in the city. The Carpenter Committee considered detribalization and the creation of a stabilized urban working population essential to the creation of an effective labour force. 'We cannot hope to produce', they wrote, 'an effective African labour force until we have first removed the African from the enervating and retarding influences of his economic and cultural background.'[16] The only way that this could be done was to pay a sufficiently high wage so that the African worker could acquire material goods and hence a vested interest in the western industrial system ('... the production of human material best calculated to respond to incentive schemes ...'), and also so that the worker could maintain a family in the city free from obligations and traditions in the countryside. Writing in the plainest terms the committee reported that '... approximately one half of the urban workers in Private Industry, and approximately one quarter of those in the Public Services are in receipt of wages insufficient to provide for the basic needs of health, decency and working efficiently...' for life as a single man, and further that the wages were inadequate in relation to the work performed. Of the 59,000 workers in towns, 26 per cent were earning less than Shs. 65/-.[17] Higher wages, the committee thought, would force employers to use their manpower more effectively, thus eliminating what the committee considered a reckless indulgence in so-called cheap labour; employers should furthermore reduce both their labour force and their profits. It would also make the loss of a job a matter of much more concern to the worker—an echo of Orde-Brown's and Hyde-Clarke's views concerning the fear of the sack.

Specifically the Carpenter Report recommended two new minimum wages. The first of these was to be calculated on a slightly more generous formula, allowing more money for food, clothing and contingencies, and calculated on actual prices costed by the East African High Commission Statistical Department rather than on the official controlled prices. The house allowance was also to be increased to the actual sum of a bed-space rent. The rates at the new formula (which were calculated to represent an increase of Shs. 16/50 plus Shs. 5/- housing in Nairobi) were to be introduced on 1 January 1955; in the meantime an immediate increase of Shs. 10/- was recommended. The rates were to be applied to the original nine towns only. To implement its theme of labour stabilization the committee recommended a 'family' minimum wage at a rate of two and a half times the 'bachelor' rate and designed to support a man, his wife and two children; this 'family' minimum wage was to be accompanied by a similar increase in house allowance. The 'family' rate was to be applicable only to those over the age of twenty-one with a record of thirty-six months continuous employment outside a reserve. It was to be introduced from 1 January 1956 by means of 15 per cent additions to the minimum wage over a ten-year period.

The report also recommended weekly wage payments, the extension of wage-negotiating machinery in industry, a state-operated provident fund (with contributions payable by both employer and employee) and old-age settlements, and the amendment of legislation to provide for voluntary notice clauses and also requiring the thirty days work of a ticket contract in thirty-six (and not forty-two) days. The committee emphasized the urgent necessity for a large housing programme, and urged that in the meantime government and local authority housing subsidies be maintained; it favoured tenant-purchase and neighbourhood housing schemes and stressed the need for a priority extension of African education services in the towns, with English being taught at the lowest feasible level. Drawing on Northcott's views on labour efficiency it stressed the need for the training of African supervisors and recommended a Training Within Industry specialist be appointed to the Labour Department. Finally the committee proposed that the Minister be given powers to prescribe ration scales where necessary, that the Wages Advisory Board be given powers to enquire into and advise on any subject which it thought fit, that systematic sociological research into African urban conditions be undertaken, and most controversially of all, that minimum wage protection be extended to agriculture.

The government's sessional paper on the report accepted the principle of labour stabilization noting only that migrant labour might sometimes be necessary, and approved both the calculation of the basic minimum wage, which it renamed the 'youth' rate, on the revised formula and the immediate proclamation of an increase of Shs. 10/- and improved housing allowances. For the future the government preferred a lower aim, that of an 'adult' minimum wage at a rate of 1.67 of the 'youth' rate, designed to be sufficient to enable a man to support himself and his wife, and to be attained in five years. The sessional paper considered the 2.5 target to be too severe a strain for the country's economy to support. The housing allowance for the 'adult' was also to be limited to a rate twice that for the 'youth'. The government proposed that the Wages Advisory Board should decide the size of each year's increase, and firmly dropped the concept of linking the higher rate to a period of employment.[18] The recommendations in respect of supervisors, T.W.I., the Wages Advisory Board's powers and sociological enquiries were all accepted, as was, subject to staff, the extension of education services. The government decided to defer the proposals for notice, ticket contracts and weekly wage payments for further study and warned that the housing programmes must depend on available finance and the views of local authorities. On provision for old age, and the highly controversial issue of minimum wages in agriculture, the government took refuge in the rapid appointment of two further special committees.[19] Of these the fate of the Rural Wages Committee Report has already been noted and that of the Social Security Committee is examined later.

But all in all the Carpenter Report and the government's sessional paper represented a summation of the views of the Labour Department since the Second World War. This was true of its emphasis on the minimum wage as the essential tool of government to increase the economic well-being of the workers and the placing of well-being before output and efficiency. It can also be seen more generally in the committee's desire to see the functioning of the western industrial and commercial system in Kenya through high wages, high productivity and increased consumer demand. It was a manifesto for the high wage system. It put these issues boldly before the colony, just at the moment when both government and industry were most receptive to such changes owing to their need to find alternative policies to combat Mau Mau and just when a new and vigorous trade union leader, Tom Mboya, was beginning to take control of the labour movement in Kenya. The spirit of the Carpenter Report was very much in accord with that of the Dow Commission which hoped to break what it considered the shackles of paternalism and tribalism in order to establish a modern economic order, although the commission was more cautious in its specific recommendations. These were also the views of Luyt, the new Labour Commissioner.

Nevertheless the report provoked a great deal of criticism. Some senior officials and expatriate company directors might have convinced themselves of the merits of the new welfare capitalism but they had left many of their followers, both in the provincial administration and in the chambers of commerce, far behind. One member of the Carpenter Committee, F. T. Holden, of Unga Ltd. and an influential Nairobi business man, rejected the high wage view in a lengthy minority report. He argued that the report would create 'high wage zones', drive investment elsewhere and ruin African agriculture. Holden's arguments were warmly commended in the press and in Legislative Council by the many business and agricultural interests opposed to paying higher wages.[20] It was as a consequence of this opposition that the government felt compelled to water down the committee's proposals, but it did accept stabilization in principle and that the aim of the minimum wage should be a rate adequate for a man and his wife to live in an urban area. And as further evidence of intention it agreed to an annual review of all salaries (including those outside the nine towns) in the public sector. This was intended to become an annual adjustment in the basic minimum and, therefore, an important factor in creating a high wage urban economy. The general policy of the Carpenter Report and of the Labour Department has also been much criticized in later years, largely on the grounds that it created a privileged elite of urban workers and that it did not foresee unemployment and the consequent demand for labour intensive industry which emerged in the nineteen-sixties. The phrase 'high wages' is, perhaps, in this connection somewhat misleading since in 1956 in Nairobi this meant a rate of Shs. 82/50 a month plus Shs. 17/50 housing allowance. This problem is discussed further in the final section of this chapter.

Of perhaps even more importance was another commission set up by the imperial government and chaired by Sir David Lidbury, a retired assistant director-general of the British postal services, dealing with the salaries of civil servants in East Africa. In Kenya this involved directly a force of some 7,000 although the indirect effect would inevitably involve a much greater number. Whitehall had already decided that officially sanctioned racial salary scales had to be abolished. The Colonial Secretary had informed the House of Commons on 16 December 1952 of his opposition to the three-fifths rule which had been supported by the Holmes Commission in 1947–8, and of his hopes for a non-racial scale with some form of expatriate allowance. In April 1953 the Governor of Kenya had told the African Civil Servants' Association that racial scales in the clerical civil service would be abolished. Lidbury was instructed to make these ideas operative. Perhaps because of the East African perspective of his commission, the report was much more forthright in its proposals than many in Kenya had expected. It recommended the abolition of salary differentials between local African, Asian and European civil servants. 'The essential principle', noted the report, 'is that for the future there shall be no barrier in any part of the service which is in fact (even though not in name) one of race', an observation clearly directed at the so-called 'A', 'B' and 'C' salary scales in Kenya, although these were technically non-racial. 'Grading', the report continued, 'by race rather than by responsibility, where it exists at present, should disappear. The limit of advance of any serving member of a service must be set solely by his qualifications and proved ability.'[21] One of the main justifications offered for this stance was that many more qualified Africans were becoming available for the civil service than had been the case in 1948. This was a consequence of changes in the educational system, the expansion of Makerere and the award of overseas scholarships.[22]

The commission, however, concluded that the educational system was not producing enough highly skilled manpower to justify an immediate policy of localization. As a consequence it recommended a variable expatriate allowance for overseas civil servants. However, the commission saw this as a temporary expedient and made one of the guiding principles of its report '. . . the assumption . . . that we are to provide for a service ultimately to be recruited wholly within East Africa'.[23] It was this assumption combined with the non-racial salary scales which made the Lidbury Report so revolutionary in the Kenyan context, for it implicitly recognized that Kenya was not going to remain a white man's country on the South African model but rather would be treated as a colony similar to those in West Africa where expatriate civil servants were gradually giving power over to the local Africans. Furthermore the report recognized the need for accelerated training of Africans and recommended for this purpose a training grade which would be the precursor of the programmes of the early nineteen-sixties designed to produce rapid Africanization.[24]

The government of Kenya outlined its response to the Lidbury proposals in *Sessional Paper No. 17 of 1954*.[25] There was a certain lukewarmness in this response along with an attempt to water down the effects in so far as they related to local Europeans and to certain senior Asians. Nevertheless the government did accept the major principle of a public service '. . . staffed by the people of the country', although it added the caveat that '. . . there should be no lowering of standards in the services'. This latter phrase could have become a code word to indicate effective sabotaging of the proposals for racial equality, but events in Kenya occurred much too rapidly for this to be the case. Some in the government evidently hoped to evade the consequences of Lidbury's recommendations by insisting that all those recruited in the United Kingdom by the Secretary of State or by the Crown Agents would receive the expatriate 'inducement' pay regardless of their place of birth and upbringing; thus the best of the Kenya Europeans, who normally received their advanced education in Britain, could be recruited in this manner and would, therefore, still have a superior wage scale as compared with local Asians and Africans. Those Kenya Europeans, however, who came on these terms would inevitably be placing themselves in the position of temporary expatriates rather than a permanent locally-based white civil service; this device was not practicable for posts other than the provincial administration and senior professional appointments. Lidbury, then, was the end of the old dream of Cavendish-Bentinck and the settler leaders to make Kenya safe for white settlement by substituting local European civil servants for expatriates.

The principles of the Lidbury Report became the guide-lines for changes in staff policy both in the High Commission corporations such as the Railway and the Posts and Telegraphs, and in a number of private companies. The consequences of such reforms, such as for example the end of racial housing zones on government estates, and their replacement by housing allocations to grades irrespective of race, were followed through logically if somewhat slowly. Perhaps more than any other single legislative measure, Lidbury began to change the face of Kenya. Enlightened officials began to invite as guests to social gatherings all colleagues of particular grades without regard to race, new spending patterns of wealthier Africans attracted business men's attention and also their hospitality, the former racial civil service staff associations slowly began to reform themselves to represent different grades rather than races—for many, hope replaced frustration. On the other hand, Lidbury marked a major step in the creation of an expensive African social elite. Carey Francis, the headmaster of the Alliance High School, Kenya's leading African school, in memorandum which he submitted to the commission wrote:

> ... Kenya cannot afford European salaries ... Europeans should be replaced as soon as possible, not by Africans who take over their salaries, but by local men who receive, say, a quarter of their salaries and make possible a corresponding extension of the social services concerned ... *At a time when all over the world the tendency is to draw rich and poor together, in Kenya the Civil Service Salaries drag them apart.*
>
> [Carey Francis's italics][26]

In many ways the Carpenter Committee, the Lidbury Commission, and the Dow Commission provided in these middle years of the nineteen-fifties the framework for much of government policy until the formal end of colonial rule. Nor should it be forgotten that the first steps in the constitutional developments which would lead to independence were taken in 1954 with the Lyttelton Constitution. However, the veneer and for a few years much of the substance of settler rule remained, particularly much residual racial discrimination which took time to disappear and so effectively fuelled nationalist fires. It would require African leadership to grasp the opportunities presented by the decline of the Emergency and by shifts in imperial policy.

A New Leader

One of the first Africans to appreciate and seize the new opportunities was Tom Mboya. Mboya was twenty-two when the Emergency was declared. He was the son of a headman of Sir William Northrup MacMillan's sisal estate near Thika although his family originated on Rusinga Island in South Nyanza. He was educated in a series of mission schools including St. Mary's School, Yala in Central Nyanza, and then at the Holy Ghost College at Mangu which he left in 1947 when his father was incapable of financing his education further. He was not a great scholar, but he liked singing, acting and debating. He also acquired a lasting dislike of the European church establishment which frowned on politics in the school and favoured the *status quo*; throughout his career he remained both Catholic and anti-clerical. After he left school, he moved to Nairobi where he joined classes leading to the Royal Sanitary Institute Joint East African Examination Board's sanitary inspector's certificate; the courses were free and were given at the Kenya government's Jeanes School. There he was elected head of the student council, in which capacity he had a number of clashes with the principal, Tom Askwith, whom Mboya suspected of trying to whittle away the rights of the students. However, he qualified and then joined the staff of the Nairobi city council in 1951.

Mboya was a young man in a hurry. He was able and ambitious and immediately began looking for the best way to exercise his talents. This was clearly not going to be in the Nairobi sanitary department where he was exposed to racial insults from the European public, paid about one-quarter of the salary of European sanitary inspectors, and expected to wear a uniform and ride a bicycle while the Europeans had cars and no uniforms.[27] He attended nationalist meetings, heard Jomo Kenyatta speak and joined the K.A.U. in 1952. Mboya, no doubt owing to his association with Walter Odede, became director of information and later acting treasurer. But these were ephemeral jobs as the party had been effectively destroyed by the events of October 1952 and was banned the following year.

So Mboya's attentions turned to the organization closest at hand; he became an enthusiastic member of the municipal staff association. He was soon secretary and rapidly transformed that body into the core of a new union, the Kenya Local Government Workers' Union (K.L.G.W.U.). The union was not to be officially recognized until 1955 but nevertheless Mboya represented the workers in connection with day-to-day issues such as lateness, sickness and supervisor problems. For these activities he was dismissed by the city council who considered him a trouble-maker, but he immediately became the full-time secretary of the union. Mboya's early success showed the characteristics on which his climb to power would be based. He had great intelligence and he worked long hours. He knew how to organize, and the K.L.G.W.U. soon became the only African union other than the Railway African Union to possess an efficient office. He had a fine command of English which he could and did use to impress Europeans. He also spoke several African languages and rapidly developed an effective platform presence.

Mboya took his union into the K.F.R.T.U. and immediately set his eye on the top position. In 1953 Minya ran into difficulties while he was away for an I.C.F.T.U. meeting in Europe. He was suspended and in September of that year, Mboya was elected general secretary. At the same time he retained his base as secretary of the K.L.G.W.U., necessary as the federation was in bad shape financially, but also an indication of the wary, shrewd caution which would stay with Mboya throughout his trade union career. He would not lightly give up one post until he was absolutely secure in a new one. Mboya found the federation to be in a state of chaos when he took over. In 1951 an I.C.F.T.U. mission had reported that the movement was 'badly disorganized'.[28] The federation consisted of five unions: the Transport and Allied Workers' Union; the Tailors, Sailcloth and Tent-makers' and Garment Workers' Union (in 1959 changed to Tailors and Textile Workers' Union); the Domestic and Hotel Workers' Union; the East African Federation of Building and Construction Workers' Union; and the Nightwatchmen, Clerks and Shopworkers' Union (in 1954 changed to the Distributive and Commercial Workers' Union.) Mboya considered that outside assistance was essential if he was to maintain the trade union movement through the difficulties caused by the Emergency. As a consequence he developed and strengthened the relationship between the federation and the I.C.F.T.U.

The I.C.F.T.U. had been formed in 1949 by the leading western trade union federations as a result of the increasing domination of the World Federation of Trade Unions (W.F.T.U.) by the Soviets and their allies. As a consequence, throughout the late nineteen-forties and fifties, the policies of the I.C.F.T.U. were very much motivated by the course of the Cold War. To the American unions this was the primary justification for the existence of the I.C.F.T.U., and they were prepared to accept money secretly from their government as well as more publicly from their labour movement for the I.C.F.T.U. in order to achieve these ends. The Americans were especially anxious to extend the activities of the I.C.F.T.U. into the Third World where they feared that W.F.T.U. affiliates might easily take over. An International Solidarity Fund was raised to finance this work, although by the last few years of colonial rule the Americans were increasingly prepared to bypass the fund and to deal directly with the unions in East Africa.

The Americans correctly saw that such an extension of activity would inevitably have to be associated with nationalist movements in Africa, Asia and Latin America if it was to have any credibility. This anti-colonialism brought them into constant conflict with the British T.U.C. which preferred to work in a Fabian spirit with the Colonial Office, in the first instance for improved living conditions in the colonies, and later, for an orderly and tranquil movement toward independence under the aegis of the British. The T.U.C. was supported by many Europeans who thought Cold War politics distracted from the real task of creating viable unions and better conditions of employment, and there can be little doubt that decisions made on the basis of the Cold War situation were not always the most sensible in terms of the growth of the trade union movement. Furthermore American, British and other European trade union officials were not always well versed in the difficulties of creating trade unions in the Third World. Nevertheless, many individual trade unionists, even though they personally disagreed with the extreme American position, were prepared to serve the I.C.F.T.U. with considerable dedication in the field because they saw the opportunity to assist Africans to secure a better standard of of living. They faced the same dilemma as colonial civil servants in that they had to decide whether it was better to work within the organization for practical reforms or to stand outside and denounce the system in its entirety.

A curious rhetoric development around this split in the I.C.F.T.U. whereby the T.U.C., in a stand rather different from that practiced in the British Isles, argued that African unions should be insulated from politics and built 'from the ground up' while the Americans, despite the tradition of Sam Gompers and his descendents, insisted that political involvement was inevitable and that this must involve strong support for the creation of national trade union centres affiliated with the I.C.F.T.U. Both the T.U.C. and the I.C.F.T.U. gave assistance to the newly formed Kenya Federation of Registered Trade Unions, but in the nineteen-fifties the cautious style and paternalism of the T.U.C. did not appeal to Kenya's trade union leaders, particularly to Mboya who considered the British too close to their own government. As a consequence the federation became quite intimately associated with the I.C.F.T.U., and this connection lasted throughout the remainder of the colonial period. The T.U.C. leaders resented this lack of gratitude and considered Mboya a cheeky young know-it-all with an overweening ambition.[29]

The I.C.F.T.U. had first moved into East Africa in 1951 when it sent a delegation headed by G. H. Bagnall of the T.U.C. to investigate the trade union situation. The committee was very suspicious of the attitude of the Labour Department which it characterized as believing 'that the African is not ready for trade unionism' and consequently encouraging other forms of worker representation. It urged the I.C.F.T.U. to make a 'determined effort . . . to reverse the attitude of the Kenya government . . .' which it feared would influence the governments of Uganda and Tanganyika as well. Representations were made through the T.U.C. to the Colonial Office which in the view of the I.C.F.T.U., resulted in some satisfactory changes in the pending legislation.[30] The delegation also recommended that an I.C.F.T.U. representative be appointed for British East Africa to be centred in Nairobi. This latter recommendation was not acted on immediately.[31] While in Nairobi, the delegation met with Minya and other leaders of the K.F.R.T.U. Subsequently the federation requested assistance from the I.C.F.T.U., particularly after the declaration of the Emergency, and as a consequence Bagnall and David Newman were sent to Kenya in July and August 1953, where amid the preoccupation of the Emergency the Labour Department regarded them as a nuisance.

However they met Baring and had six meetings with Hartwell at which they requested the government to cease harassment of the unions under the guise of anti-Mau Mau activities; the worst of the harassment was that of local police and administrative officers acting in disobedience to and the subsequent disapproval of Nairobi. In particular they urged a relaxing of restrictions on dues collectors and on trade union meetings, and they asked that union officials be given passes for travel without too much red tape. They complained of the intimidation by members of the local European-staffed Kenya Police Reserve and the home guard, and of the illegal seizure of union documents. They also attempted unsuccessfully to interview those union leaders who had been detained and not yet brought to trial. In general Bagnell and Newman believed that the situation for trade unions had improved between the I.C.F.T.U. visit in 1951 and the declaration of the Emergency but that a considerable regression had taken place after October 1952. Finally the delegation reiterated the proposal for an I.C.F.T.U. area representative in Nairobi. This latter recommendation was now accepted by the I.C.F.T.U., and Jim Bury, a Canadian trade unionist, was sent to Nairobi in December 1953. This turned out to be a very significant appointment as Bury's free and easy style and rather aggressive politics appealed to Mboya and to many of the other trade union leaders. The trust he established combined with the efforts of the I.C.F.T.U. to assist the unions in the dark days of the Emergency and to help finance the K.F.R.T.U. marked the primacy of the I.C.F.T.U. over the T.U.C. Ironically Bury was just as committed to self-help and to the creation of unions 'from the ground up' as any member of the T.U.C.[32]

Mboya and Bury worked together to try to bring order into the affairs of Kenya's trade unions and thereby ensure that they would have some power. There were many difficulties to overcome. Minya remained the head of the Transport and Allied Workers' Union and attacked the new leadership of Mboya with increasing bitterness. Gradually Mboya undermined Minya's position; the clash came to a head in September and October 1954 when Mboya insisted that all member organizations of the K.F.R.T.U. should pay their dues. Minya objected and temporarily led eight unions out of the fold. However, he did not have the strength to sustain this defection, and gradually the unions returned as Mboya and Bury prediced they would. The last to do so was the Transport and Allied Workers' Union which reaffiliated in August 1955. By making his stand on a point of trade union procedure, Mboya also ensured that any appeal from Minya either to the I.C.F.T.U. or to the T.U.C. would fall on deaf ears, however many private doubts might be entertained in these quarters about Mboya.[33]

More serious was the chaos within the unions themselves. Bury considered that they had little idea of the basic job of a trade union and that they were primarily interested in securing numbers rather than in formulating policy and negotiating with the employers. He considered this to be a legacy from the days of the A.W.F. and the E.A.T.U.C.[34] Walter Hood of the T.U.C. concurred in this view and wrote in 1953 that the unions were '... experiencing all the difficulties and problems similar to the majority of Colonial trade unions in this early phase of their development'. He ascribed this to '... lack of knowledge of the techniques and practices of trade unionism'.[35] Bury considered the leadership good and devoted people, eager to learn and to equip themselves under the most trying circumstances. Nor did he think that imposed reforms were likely to be very effective unless they were grounded on a real move toward equality for the Africans.

The only two unions to conduct their affairs with efficiency were the Railway African Union which joined the K.F.R.T.U. in 1954 and the K.L.G.W.U. which was already a member. The latter, for instance, had a very successful annual meeting in 1954 and kept minute and account books at a reasonable standard of efficiency. The R.A.U. had evolved out of the staff association formed by the management in the nineteen-forties and was dominated by the African clerical staff and skilled workers. Since the union leaders had railway passes, they could and did foster their branches in a manner which could not be rivalled by any other union; they conducted business-like negotiations in the normal way with management. But they were handicapped by the refusal of the government to allow inter-territorial unions despite the fact that there was a unified management for all of East Africa. Furthermore the union leadership was unrepresentative of the mass of workers who were employed as manual labourers, and Bury considered them too close to the industrial relations officers of the Railway. Nevertheless this leadership group managed to maintain control until the railway strike in 1960 and to play an important moderating role in the K.F.R.T.U. The Kenya African Civil Servants' Association had a very similar although even more cautious attitude and refused to join the K.F.R.T.U. in this period, thereby depriving the federation of the services of a significant part of the African elite in the colony.[36]

In the other unions and in the federation itself there was little attempt made at keeping records or financial books. Mboya and Bury gave classes to the local union leaders to teach them these bureaucratic skills. In this connection Bury worked with the Labour Department, notably with Luyt and Patrick, who were interested in establishing trade union courses at the Jeanes School. The department placed Mboya and David Njomo, the president of the K.F.R.T.U., on the organizing committee for these courses, but then balked at allowances for the students, thus almost ending the scheme. But despite all the difficulties created by the Emergency, two courses were offered in late 1954 with fifty trade unionists present. These courses were vigorously attacked in the Legislative Council. An idea of the difficulties facing the government can be gained from the *Kenya Debates* of June 1955. Group Captain Briggs, supported by other European elected members, launched a violent criticism of the Kenya government's trade union policies in a debate which had to be adjourned for half an hour on account of the feelings aroused. Supported by the African members Hartwell so vigorously defended the government's policies, the trade union movement and the right of the K.F.R.T.U. to comment on political issues that Briggs concluded by saying that he wondered '... whether I was sitting here in Legislative Council in Nairobi or whether I was in the Kremlin'.[37]

Bury was firmly of the opinion that all such training should take place in Africa and was opposed to scholarships to Europe. He assisted the I.C.F.T.U. in arranging that same year for two Kenya trade unionists to attend a labour course in the Gold Coast. Mboya also urged the I.C.F.T.U. to consider creating an organization in East Africa which could undertake such training and which would be controlled by the unions and not by the government; this suggestion was eventually realized by the later foundation of the I.C.F.T.U. Labour College in Kampala. He also requested scholarships to Ruskin College at Oxford.[38] In the following year Bury and Mboya organized a two day course in Mombasa for fifty-five officials from six unions. Other courses were held the same year at Eldoret, Kisumu, and Kericho. The basis for these seminars were three leaflets on trade union practice produced by the I.C.F.T.U. Labour College in Calcutta and translated into Swahili.[39]

The primary need was to secure formal recognition of the unions from the employers so that they could operate in the light of day. Mboya's strategy was to focus on local government authorities where he secured recognition for the union in Kisumu and Mombasa. However, it would take a full-scale confrontation with the Nairobi Council in 1955 before such developments were accepted in the capital.[40] Analagous to this was the struggle to secure trade union representation on government boards. Africans, of course, had been appointed in small numbers to such boards since the Second World War, but Mboya wanted them to be nominated by the K.F.R.T.U. The T.U.C. had pressed this matter on the Colonial Office in 1953, but '... the Minister's reply was by no means satisfactory'.[41] Gradually Mboya ensured that federation members were appointed to the Wages Advisory Board, the Labour Advisory Board and other statutory bodies. For instance, Saidi Mohamed, an officer of the Transport and Allied Workers' Union and Leonard Gichui of the Railway African Union were appointed to the Wages Advisory Board. However, there was still resistance in some quarters to these appointments, and Mboya protested against the African nominees on the Social Security Committee. The Minister of Labour replied: 'These people had been known to the Labour Department for some time for the experience and ability to act as such and that they had great respect from employers who had recommended them highly.'[42]

It was also essential in Mboya's view to secure union representation on wages councils and on joint industrial councils. The government generally complied in respect of wages councils although it was much criticized for so doing; some in authority elsewhere preferred Africans picked by a benevolent bureaucracy rather than by the workers themselves even though the employers picked delegates from their own associations. Again some progress was made, but the principle was not established in a major joint industrial council until a further strike in Mombasa in 1955 persuaded the dock employers of the merits of this position.

Another important part of Mboya's strategy was to try to form unions on an industrial rather than a craft basis, a move which did not please the T.U.C. although it was acceptable to Luyt in the Labour Department because it seemed likely to be efficient and because it hindered the growth of general unions. This decision undoubtedly stemmed from Bury's experience of Canadian trade unions and from Mboya's desire to avoid fragmented and weak organizations. It also fitted in with the K.F.R.T.U.'s decision to concentrate on local government, the Railway, the docks and the oil industry, all large areas of employment where demarcation was fairly obvious. It was, however, more difficult to define for unions such as the Transport and Allied Workers' Union and the Nightwatchmen, Clerks and Shopworkers' Union, whose members worked for numbers of small employers. The older style of trade unionist tended to believe that members were paramount and the trade of those involved of little matter. Minya shared this view, and it remained an area of conflict between him and Mboya.

Mboya also wished to create trade councils in areas outside Nairobi. The Labour Department was opposed to this, but such bodies were set up nevertheless in Kisumu and Mombasa although they did not function very effectively. It was hoped that through this mechanism something could be done to assist the branches of the unions, many of which had been swept away in the Emergency. Mboya, Minya and Bury visited Mombasa in January 1954 and spoke to the municipal workers and then later to a mass meeting of trade unionists. The following month, with the assistance of the Labour Department, they made a safari to thirteen towns and trading centres in the Central, Nyanza and Rift Valley provinces. At the core of most of their meetings were the local African tailors, some of whom complained that the Asian employers paid them less than the minimum wage but forced them to sign a paper saying that they had received full payment. In Kitale the district commissioner cancelled the meeting, arguing that it had to be confined to union members and, since there were no union members in Kitale, there could be no meeting; similar difficulties were met at Kisii. However, the delegation was particularly impressed by the work of Geoffrey Frere, the Labour Department officer in Kisumu.

Publicity was another concern. The K.F.R.T.U. was too poor to have its own newspaper. For a while the federation had a page in a Swahili newspaper published by Awori, one of the African members of the Legislative Council, but this paper collapsed in 1954. Thereafter Mboya had to rely on a mimeographed bulletin, entitled the *K.F.L. Newsletter*, edited by Arthur Ochwada and others.[43] Mboya also sought out the opportunity to speak whenever and wherever he could, but this was not easy as there were drastic restrictions on meetings as a consequence of the Emergency. He also looked on travel and participation in meetings abroad as another means of creating publicity and establishing the credibility both of the federation and of himself. In June 1955 he made a two week visit to Tanganyika on behalf of the I.C.F.T.U. In Dar es Salaam he gave lectures, spoke to a public meeting, and discussed the possible co-ordination of union work in the East African ports. The following month he went to Uganda, once again as a representative of the I.C.F.T.U. There he met with government and union officials, toured the plantations, and spoke to the students at Makerere.[44] In August he was a member of the Kenya delegation at the fourth International African Labour Conference in Beira.[45]

Many of the problems faced by the unions stemmed from lack of regular finances. Since practically none of them were recognized by the employers, it was not feasible to consider a shop steward system. Nor would many of the trade union officials themselves collect money from members as they considered this would diminish their status. As a consequence, they used paid collectors, mostly Kikuyu women who would attempt to secure dues from the members on pay day. The results were not very successful. In January 1954 the Domestic and Hotel Workers' Union claimed about 11,500 members but could only get about 2,000 of these to pay dues. In March 1954 the Nightwatchmen, Clerks and Shopworkers' Union collected Shs. 1,800/- at a cost of Shs. 800/- From the government's point of view, this practice was doubly objectionable. It first of all offended the Labour Department's view of the proper functioning of trade unions in terms of western bureaucratic notions of efficiency and of a somewhat Victorian morality which stressed the desirability of self-sacrifice on the part of union leaders. It also offended Carpenter, who told Newman and Bagnall that these women were prostitutes and some were the mistresses of the local union officials. Carpenter informed the I.C.F.T.U. delegation that he was anxious to see that the trade unions did not fall into disrepute because of these women collectors. In this he was given strong support by Hood of the T.U.C.[46] However, there was another and more serious reason for the response of the administration since it was widely assumed that these collectors diverted some of the trade union money to Mau Mau organizations and acted as couriers for the revolutionaries. As soon as the Emergency was declared, there was a general clampdown. Since the collectors were the employees of the trade unions, these unions had to apply to the Nairobi district commissioner for passes to allow them to continue to work. The police referred these requests to the Labour Department which uniformly rejected all of them.[47] However, the K.L.G.W.U., the R.A.U. and the newly formed Dockworkers' Union all developed alternative, if rudimentary, systems of collecting through their own officers.

But most of the unions were chronically broke, and control of finances was the despair of the Labour Department and of the representatives of the

T.U.C. and the I.C.F.T.U. In 1954, for instance, the International Transport Workers' Federation gave £200 to the Transport and Allied Workers' Union, money which rapidly disappeared with little or no accounting. Bury was reluctant to see the I.C.F.T.U. take over the financing of the unions, but he did think that select and judicious support should be given from time to time to particular unions and to the federation. This advice was followed, and apparently caused some difficulties since Minya had promised Shs. 200/- a month indefinitely to each union after his return from the I.C.F.T.U Stockholm Conference. In 1958 an I.C.F.T.U. delegation interviewed the African assistant industrial relations officer in Mombasa and was shocked by what he revealed. Between March and July 1957, for instance, the general secretary of the Dockworkers' Union admitted to misappropriating Shs. 3,300/-; another Shs. 2,000/- was found to have disappeared in late 1957 or early 1958. Nevertheless the same individual had recently reappeared as branch secretary in Mombasa of the Kenya Petroleum Oil Workers' Union.[48]

It was commonplace in some government and settler circles to use these undoubted facts to paint a picture of an enfeebled and corrupt trade union movement led by half-educated and dishonest clerks. The government had, of course, ensured that the trade unions would be led by clerks rather than by men working in the industry by insisting on a command of English. Such officials had to deal with the government in a second language which many imperfectly understood or wrote. There was a predilection in some European circles, even amongst those who denounced the products of the mission schools, to equate command of English, dress and the social graces with virtue, intelligence and efficiency. Most of the union officials had very little experience or education; they could not rely on the wisdom of their predecessors as most of these were in detention. They were carving a career out for themselves and it is not surprising that their methods were rough and ready, rewarding their friends in a crude way and buying off their enemies. They also had to meet the many obligations imposed on an African by his family and relatives. All this had to be done on a very limited salary which, in turn, depended on the success of collectors and later of minor union officials. Furthermore between 1952 and 1955 such a career involved constant suspicion and the threat of arrest since many in government equated trade unionism with the Mau Mau uprising. It was not a life of ease and comfort. But the style of such leaders, however reprehensible in the eyes of Europeans, was more appealing to the rank and file than that of the grey and cautious bureaucrat. Nor was it really necessary to have much in the way of formal organization to declare a strike and make it operative as had been demonstrated in Mombasa in 1939 and 1947 and as would be shown again in 1955. In the long term, however, such haphazard methods were likely to lead to the eclipse of the unions in the face of more powerful organizations. It was here that Mboya, by his organizational genius and by his ability to play the European bureaucratic game better than most Europeans, simultaneously laid the groundwork on which the union movement could continue to exist in the future and also forced the white establishment to take notice of the union movement.

However, the catastrophic situation in the finances of most of the member unions meant that the majority paid nothing to the central body. Bury decided that some practical support in terms of securing an office and furniture was necessary and paid for these from I.C.F.T.U. funds. An office in Nairobi's Victoria Street was taken and served both the K.F.L. and the I.C.F.T.U. regional representative. He also successfully sought assistance from the United Auto Workers in the United States who agreed to send a jeep station wagon. But the basic problem remained, and Hood concluded after a visit to East Africa in March and April 1954 that the K.F.R.T.U. was dead, although in this case the wish may have been father to the thought.[49]

The effects of Operation *Anvil* made the situation even more difficult. Mboya told the I.C.F.T.U. that the revenue of the Transport and Allied Workers' Union had dropped from Shs. 900/- per month to Shs. 100/- and that of the K.L.G.W.U. from Shs. 800/- to Shs. 98/-. It was in this context that the reorganization of the federation, already mentioned, took place. At a meeting on 18 September 1954 three resolutions were passed decreeing that all member unions must make a regular contribution to the federation, that if they were incapable of paying they should open their books to the federation, and that those unions who refused to pay by 15 October 1954 would be expelled.[50] It was a stormy meeting with Minya in opposition and the leaders of the K.L.G.W.U. and the R.A.U. strongly favouring the proposals which passed thereby causing the walkout of Minya and his friends. The failure of that walkout and the consequent victory of Mboya enormously enhanced his prestige within the labour movement in the colony.

Mboya and Bury were convinced that one of the remedies to the financial situation was the development of the shop steward system and of the check-off. Luyt was prepared to back shop stewards and to maintain a benevolent neutrality on the matter of the check-off, a development which he and Mboya thought most likely in municipal government and in the Railway. He was also prepared to allow Patrick to assist in the development of a shop steward system. Mboya and Bury discussed this matter with a number of town clerks on their up-country safari in 1954. On the whole they found the officials sympathetic if cautious; relations were particularly good at Kisumu and Mombasa. But in Nairobi and certain other centres there was resistance, and the African affairs officers used their influence to try to prevent unionization.[51] However, certain of the larger private firms were interested in these developments, and shortly after Bury arrived in Kenya, he was invited to discuss the shop steward system with the East African Tobacco Company, whose managing director, Rogers, held exceptionally modern views, noted earlier, on higher wages and trade unions.

In Mboya's eyes, Bury's main function in Kenya was to act as a defender and representative of the unions in the white community during the tense days of the Mau Mau uprising. This was an exceedingly difficult, complicated and discouraging task. There were close connections between some of the unions and the banned K.A.U.; Mboya himself had been an official of the K.A.U. in its dying days. Three unions, the Transport and Allied Workers' Union, the Domestic and Hotel Workers' Union, and the Night-watchmen, Clerks and Shopworkers' Union had shared space in Kiburi House with the Nairobi branch of the K.A.U. before it was banned. Since some of those in the K.A.U. who were directly associated with Mau Mau were members of the Nairobi branch, it is not surprising that the revolutionaries found support in these three unions. Bury, for instance, was satisfied of the genuineness of the evidence against certain of the Kiburi House unionists. The Transport and Allied Workers' Union, as a consequence of its membership of taxi drivers, was particularly well placed to assist both legitimate and secret political activities. The police Special Branch considered both this union and the Domestic and Hotel Workers' Union to be the centres of the conspiracy and set out to destroy them. A total of nineteen officials of these two unions were arrested as well as some from other unions; the two most prominent were the Kikuyu president and treasurer of the K.F.R.T.U., David Njomo and Daniel Ngethe.[52] Corfield considered that by the end of 1954 the power of these two unions had been destroyed.

Mboya was, of course, an ardent nationalist but he did not sympathize with the violence of the Mau Mau insurrection. Furthermore he was a Luo and, therefore, somewhat apart from the clannish politics of the Kikuyu. It is also true that within the trade union world those who objected to Mboya's leadership tended to come from Kiburi House. Mboya saw from the beginning that since the trade unions had been exempted from the ban on African political organizations, it was essential for him to maintain a strict dividing line between himself and those who might be involved in Mau Mau. Gradually he began to use the K.F.R.T.U. as a more general vehicle of African political, social and economic protest which, of course, in turn enhanced Mboya's own future political prospects.[53] It was impossible to separate demands for better wages, housing and education from a more general nationalist position, and the K.F.R.T.U., for instance, opposed the Lyttelton constitution on the grounds that it provided for inadequate African representation. Mboya also protested against the continuation of an exclusively White Highlands and demanded legislation to end the colour bar. He accepted the decision of the government to offer surrender terms to the forest fighters, but he coupled this with a statement deploring the failure of the government to state a policy concerning the future of the detainees and attacking the irresponsible oratory of the settlers.[54] This became a favourite tactic whereby Mboya would establish his credibility with the government by agreeing to a moderate policy but would simultaneously demand more reforms; there was always the unspoken hint that if some of the reforms did not materialize Mboya might in the future be unwilling or incapable of pursuing moderate policies.

The Emergency both hampered the functioning of the unions and simultaneously placed new demands on them. As Mboya told J. H. Oldenbroek, the general secretary of the I.C.F.T.U.: 'due to the Emergency a lot of progress that might have otherwise been made has proved very slow if not impossible. We are all the time coming up against emergency regulations rather than doing real constructive work.[55] Workers beseiged the individual unions and the K.F.R.T.U. with complaints that their 'green cards', the Kikuyu history of employment record, were being cancelled by the Nairobi district commissioner without justification. In January 1954 the federation was asked to take up 150 cases of which they considered seventy-one legitimate. Of these they managed to secure renewals for thirty-nine. In the early part of 1954 Mboya and others spent a good deal of time on these cases; Bury considered that Arthur Small, the district commissioner, could only foresee a solution to the security problem in Nairobi in terms of removing all Africans or, at least all the Kikuyu. Mboya and Bury managed to secure Labour Department representation at the hearings which mitigated the situation somewhat. They also saw the Member of Labour and the Member for African Affairs (another Colonial service official) to protest against the misuse of the power of cancellation. In addition they wrote to the Governor but could not secure an interview with him. In February the *Sunday Post* printed an interview with Bury in which he complained about the harassment of the unions and pointed to the I.C.F.T.U. as a bulwark against communism and terrorism.[56] Mboya also considered the possibility of urging all Nairobi residents to throw away their cards or of calling a general strike. He was, however, dissuaded from these drastic measures, largely by the feeling that they would be ineffective. Moreover, he did receive sympathy and support from Luyt and others in the Labour Department whom he considered did their best but had little influence at that moment.[57]

Mboya believed that many officials in the government wished to use the Emergency as a means of destroying both him personally and also the trade union movement. Desmond O'Hagan, then provincial commissioner at the Coast, told Bury that only fear of international trade union repercussions prevented the government from arresting Mboya early in 1954. The main spokesman for this point of view was the district commissioner in Nairobi who had warned Mboya in a manner which suggested that he would do well to leave the union movement. Bury, for his part, was followed by the police most of the time he was in Kenya and although he protested, no changes occurred other than to make the shadowing somewhat less conspicuous and more efficient. Employers also took the opportunity to threaten union officials. When Mboya and Bury went to see the M.O.H. in Nairobi about a grievance, he peppered his reply with sentences such as, 'Any more of this nonsense and you Tom Mboya know where you will end up', 'Any African is here to obey and that is all there is to it', and 'I have no confidence in the workers or their leadership'. Mboya made a point of not losing his temper under such circumstances which no doubt infuriated those concerned even more, although Bury did complain to Patrick and to Luyt. Many Africans were frightened by such events and were, therefore, reluctant to participate in union work. Bury found union officers who were not even certain whether it was legal to belong to a trade union. It was certainly not easy to keep up morale when the shadow of the war in Kikuyuland fell on all events in Nairobi. Moreover the federation leaders feared that Small was doing his best to encourage tribal associations at the expense of trade unions and other groups. In a newsletter in March 1955 they accused one of his assistants of telling African audiences that they should only pay dues to tribal associations.[58]

Then on 24 April 1954 came Operation *Anvil* which drastically changed the situation for the worse. The original plan had been to repatriate all the Kikuyu in Nairobi, but it was eventually recognized that this would paralyse the city. The sweep was, therefore, restricted to 16,500 but even so this inevitably meant the disappearance of many trade union officials. Although Labour Department officials were brought in from all over Kenya and special instructions issued to give trade union officials priority where possible in the screening process, the weight of the security machine prevailed. By the end of the operation a total of forty-five officials were picked up; Mboya, himself, was detained for a few hours but released. The police raided the K.F.R.T.U. offices where they shot and wounded one man, Jonathan Njanga s/o Kagari.[59] They also raided the offices in Kiburi House leaving only Minya and one other free as they were not Kikuyu. Mboya and Bury had an interview with Luyt who agreed to see what he could do about those who were innocent but warned that the matter was entirely in the hands of the security forces who were not going to be overly concerned at a few mistakes in an operation of the scope of *Anvil.* Mboya felt immensely discouraged; he had '... been told in no uncertain terms to lay off', and he began to think of moving the federation to Mombasa, a *démarche* strongly opposed by Luyt. Bury considered that the operation had completely crippled the unions in Nairobi with morale dropping to zero. 'The members remaining outside the barbed wire', Mboya wrote, 'are living in a state of fear and uncertainty, so much so that they are not willing to come forward to do anything for the movement lest they are noticed and arrested.'[60] Members would not attend meetings, show their cards or pay dues.

Meanwhile the Labour Department was continuing in its efforts to obtain priority in screening for the trade union officials; Patrick and Ndisi were sent to tour the camps to identify trade unionists and to speed up the screening process. They wrote a damning report for the department, alleging that they were told at Manyani that all trade unionists would naturally be categorized as recalcitrant or, in the quaint terminology of the camps, 'black', since the trade union movement was semi-communist and all associated with it were bad. Patrick, therefore, concluded that by making inquiries about particular men, the Labour Department was in a sense condemning them. Mboya and Bury saw J. M. (later Sir John) Stow, the Minister of Labour, to urge on him that the effect of the sweep would be to deliver the unions into the hands of the inexperienced, thereby producing more chaos.[61] They argued that those released without any charges being laid should receive back their jobs and houses while those detained should receive any wages, gratuities or provident fund payments owed to them. Mboya also protested to the I.C.F.T.U. about the conditions of the camps, particularly the mass camps at Manyani, Langata and Mackinnon Road, and urged that pressure be put on the Colonial Office. He also questioned the wisdom and humanity of sending the families of the detained back to the reserves when, in some cases, they had little or no contact with their traditional homeland. Mathu raised the question of the detained trade unionists in the Legislative Council but, despite assurances, nothing was done until June. Then the Minister for Labour assured a meeting of the African members of the Council and the K.F.R.T.U. that all trade unionists would be rescreened.[62] Meanwhile Mboya was growing bolder in his criticism. He held a press conference in early September to denounce the screening system.[63] Stow replied that the government had not rescreened but had merely given priority in screening to trade unionists, the consequence of which was the release of four and the continued detention of thirteen. He also announced that the government would rehire any of those found to be innocent and that it would seek to persuade private employers to do the same.[64]

Mboya also wished to send a delegation to England, but Bury was opposed to this until all channels had been exhausted in Kenya. Meanwhile Bury urged Oldenbroek at the I.C.F.T.U. to put pressure on the Colonial Office through Tewson at the T.U.C. to which Oldenbroek complied; it would appear that T.U.C. pressure was one factor in preventing the extension of an employment record to all African employees, under consideration at the time as an 'Emergency' measure and advocated later by the Rural Wages Committee. The T.U.C. had already made representations to the Colonial Office in 1953 about the arrest of trade unionists and had made clear that '. . . the T.U.C. could not tolerate any attempt to smash the trade unions as if they were looked upon as an adjunct of the Mau Mau.'[65] However, Tewson was much swayed by the Colonial Office view of Mau Mau and its allegations of trade union complicity in the insurrection. He and others at the T.U.C. accepted the premise that the war had to be won since Mau Mau, in their view, represented a retreat to barbarism. This inevitably meant some restrictions. It is likely, however, that T.U.C. pressure, particularly after Operation *Anvil*, helped to persuade the Colonial Office to issue strict instructions that detained trade unionists were to be processed quickly and were not to be restricted unless there was a concrete case against them. Mboya and Bury also made contact with certain Labour M.P.s such as Ronald Williams and James Griffiths who visited Kenya in 1954 as part of the parliamentary delegation; in addition they corresponded with the Fabian Colonial Bureau.[66] They also saw from time to time the Indian Commissioner, Shri Aba Pant, who was very unpopular in European circles owing to his militant anti-colonial views. Finally Mboya, irritated with what he considered procrastination on the part of the I.C.F.T.U., took advantage of an offer from Moral Rearmament of an aircraft ticket to Switzerland and departed for Europe in July. From Switzerland the I.C.F.T.U., *faute de mieux,* paid his way to Brussels where he discussed the Kenya situation with Oldenbroek. Mboya also hoped that M.R.A. would give him some respectability in government circles although he had no intention of joining the movement. Later Bury visited England on leave and saw Tewson, urging on him the necessity of some action concerning the detainees; he also visited some of the officials at the Colonial Office.

Meanwhile the I.C.F.T.U. in Brussels was keeping up propaganda concerning the detained trade unionists; Bury considered that this was more effective than any other action in securing their rescreening. The release of some trade unionists in fact led a few of the sharper inmates of the camps to come forward with resounding but spurious trade union titles. In time Mboya decided to carry the battle to the world congress of the I.C.F.T.U. in Veinna despite threats from the T.U.C. 'to raise hell' if colonial issues were brought forward at the meeting. The K.F.R.T.U., which had changed its name to the Kenya Federation of Labour in May 1955, sent four resolutions:

(*a*) That the I.C.F.T.U. should resolve to continue and even increase its assistance to the Trade Union Movement in Kenya and East Africa.
(*b*) That the I.C.F.T.U. Congress instruct its Secretariat to contact the people in the proper places with a view of seeking to better the conditions of African workers in agriculture in Kenya.
(*c*) That the Congress approach the International Labour Organization requesting them to look into the problems of detention of Africans without trial and forced labour in Kenya.
(*d*) That the I.C.F.T.U. Congress instruct its Secretariat to approach the British Government with a view of removing conditions now existing in Kenya and which in our opinion have contributed to frustration among Africans, that has been the root of Mau Mau and acted as fuel to its continuation.

The evidence cited for this latter proposition was the unbalanced state of the races in the Legislative Council, the existence of the White Highlands, and the freedom accorded to European but not to African politicians.[67]

Perhaps most significant of all for the future were events in Kenya in the early part of 1955, two dramatic industrial victories scored by Mboya which consolidated his hold on the trade unions in the colony and made him a political personality to reckon with. These triumphs also triggered differing reactions in the European community. Mboya excited a great hatred in some Europeans who feared his power and loathed his arrogance. His industrial successes no doubt explain the attempts on the part of some of these Europeans, notably Group Captain Briggs, to secure his detention ostensibly because of his political utterances. But many of the leaders of the industrial and commercial community were also alarmed by the technique through which Mboya had secured his victories, namely by means of committees of inquiry, and they decided that they would prefer to tolerate an increase in trade union strength and industrial bargaining to avoid this becoming a standard form of settlement.[68]

The first of these victories was Mboya's successful intervention in the Mombasa dock strike of March 1955. He took over this strike, negotiated first the means of and then the settlement itself. These events demonstrated for all to see his versatility, public personality and command of tactics. The details of this struggle in Mombasa are discussed in the following section. The second success was the securing of recognition of the Kenya Local Government Workers' Union after a bitter struggle with the Nairobi council. Between 1949 and 1953 negotiations had taken place in a joint staff council, the employees' representatives being chosen at least from 1951 onwards by the African Local Government Servants Association. In 1953 the association transformed itself into a branch of the K.L.G.W.U. and there followed a deadlock over recognition for nearly two years. The city government tried hard to promote other and more docile forms of negotiation but without success since as the 1955 tribunal remarked, '. . . all those employees who are interested at all in organized representation have refused to consider any negotiating machinery in which the Union is not represented . . .'[69] The union then declared a trade dispute early in

1955 and demanded an inquiry. The city fathers entered the inquiry in a state of great complacency. They did not prepare their case very effectively, and they found their position rapidly torn to shreds by Mboya who personally represented the union. The report of the tribunal was released in the middle of May and proved to be almost as categorical as Mboya himself. It dismissed most of the arguments of the council as a smokescreen for political objections to the rise of African trade unions. It categorized the council's paternalism as sincere but foolish and dismissed it with a rather contemptuous summary: '... the Council entertains a genuine apprehension that this Union, and perhaps the trade union movement generally in East Africa, is being used, and will increasingly be used, as a political weapon, to the ultimate detriment of all concerned, not least of the misguided African employee himself, who needs to be protected in his own interest, by a wise and benevolent City Council, from becoming entangled in the snare of trade unionism of any kind'.[70]

The tribunal then went on to recommend that the council recognize the union in the same manner and form as in Mombasa.[71] It was a great personal triumph for Mboya since he had successfully carried the war into the heart of the enemy's camp. The Nairobi city council, much more than the Mombasa port employers, represented smug and entrenched European power and the symbolism of this victory could not be more telling. Even the suspicion that the Labour Department had assisted by agreeing to the tribunal with alacrity and by nominating sympathetic commissioners could not dim Mboya's personal triumph. He was now secure enough to take up an offer which had been stimulated by Hood of the T.U.C. and Edgar Parry, the Deputy Labour Adviser at the Colonial Office, to attend Ruskin College at Oxford. This had been suggested in 1954, but Mboya did not feel secure enough to take it at the time. He left for Britain in October 1955 and remained there for a year where he was much influenced by the anti-colonial wing of the Labour party. He would return to become a full-fledged politician as well as a trade union leader.

Industrial Relations in the Port of Mombasa 1950–60

Although the K.F.R.T.U. did not move to Mombasa, it did decide to make unionization of the docks a top priority of the federation.[72] When Mboya and Bury visited Mombasa in 1954 to promote such a union, they found a situation much changed since 1947. This was largely due to the work of Captain G. R. Williams, who had been appointed general manager of the Landing and Shipping Company after the 1947 strike, and of Peter Wilson, who was for some time senior labour officer in Mombasa. Williams was determined to run an efficient and modern operation, and he was prepared to listen to the Labour Department and to learn from mistakes. In 1951 the company signed a new contract with the Railway administration which made it a single company in charge of all shorehandling in the ports of East Africa but eliminated the cost plus arrangements in favour of payment according to tonnage handled. It also gave the Railway a shareholding interest in the company. The contract meant that the company still had to secure the agreement and co-operation of the Railway to any material changes at the port. There were constant battles between the Railway, which tended to conservative and penny-pinching management and which regarded the ports as a secondary operation, and the more flamboyant Williams. 'I have maintained', Williams wrote in his 1955 annual report, 'that we, as Contractors, having been advised by the Administration the end to be achieved, must be free to determine the means to that end . . .'

In 1952 Williams made a trip to the United States and came back convinced that he should introduce modern handling and tallying techniques. Between 1952 and 1955 there was a mechanical revolution in the port. The most important of these early innovations was to place all outgoing cargo on pallets which could then be handled by fork-lift trucks. Much back-breaking labour was eliminated by this development. In the last year of this programme the number of machines at Kilindini other than cranes and scammels increased from forty-four to 100 despite the many and surprising difficulties of operating this equipment in the tropics.[73] The Railway was very suspicious of the cost of these developments, and Williams was only able to get the scheme started by persuading the Robin and Moore/McCormack Lines to donate the initial machinery. The renovating of the port continued throughout this period. New docks and sheds were built, heavier cranes were installed, a Merton Overloader was ordered to handle coal at Mbaraki, and instack tallying began in the second half of the nineteen-fifties. All this took place in its earlier stages at a time of chronic congestion in the port as goods flowed in to sustain the postwar prosperity. Between 1952 and 1956 the port had to operate a special phasing arrangement to mitigate the situation.

So far as labour was concerned, Williams came to believe in the necessity of consultation and in the merits of a high wage economy based on skilled labour, but it took some time before he was in a position of sufficient authority to implement these views. By the mid nineteen-fifties and early sixties he had become a moving force among employers in Mombasa in securing these goals. He expected that with higher wages combined with better equipment, he could demand high productivity, reduce the size of the work force, and increase pay to a level which would allow for the growth of a permanent skilled labour force. The later nineteen-forties, however, were a period of little action. The companies were prepared to subsidize a certain amount of welfare activity, notably football teams and, in the fifties, track meets—the docks produced some of Kenya's notable international athletes. However, the companies resisted any attempts to make them supply housing although eventually in the fifties they did lease and then rent space to individual workers at the Changamwe housing estate. They found this to be the worst possible arrangement as they had no control over the rents charged by the municipality but were, of course, blamed for the increases. To some of the employers, however, one of the virtues of casual labour was that they did not need by law to supply housing. In the key areas of wages, the companies maintained the legally correct procedure between 1947 and 1955 of matching the increases in the government's minimum wages, a policy which did nothing toward increasing the standard of living or of stabilizing the labour force. In 1949 the casual labour rules promulgated in 1944 under the defence regulations were made permanent.[74]

All casual labour had to secure from the Labour Office a Casual Labour Registration Certificate which included the normal particulars and a photograph; nevertheless, the system remained inefficient and corrupt. It was fairly easy to forge the registration certificates, and it was still possible for the *serangs* and *tindals* to influence the employment of labour and thereby secure kickbacks from the men involved. Moreover the periodic swoops on the labour force to check certificates were much resented, particularly since the town merchants took to demanding these documents as surety on payments.

Little, therefore, was accomplished until the new contract of the Landing and Shipping Company was signed in 1951. In that year there were some 5,000 casual labourers employed at the docks working an average of thirteen to fourteen shifts per month. The Labour Department persuaded the employers to set a minimum of fifteen shifts in order to weed out those who were only working part-time in the port. It anticipated that in time 2,000 men could be eliminated from the casual labour pool who, it was thought, could be absorbed by the sugar and sisal industries in the Coast province. At the same time the employers agreed to the formation of a J.I.C. composed of five representatives from each side with an impartial chairman. The following year joint staff committees came into existence for clerical and non-clerical staff. When the I.C.F.T.U. delegation to Kenya in 1951 visited the port, they urged the need for a trade union to represent the workers in this structure, a suggestion rather curtly dismissed in the general manager's annual report of that year. There can be little doubt that Williams was strongly influenced on this matter by the 1950 dock strike at Dar es Salaam which he considered irresponsible and which had resulted in the deregistration of the union. A wage increase for the lowest monthly paid labour of Shs. 5/- in 1952, moreover, deflected any overt criticism of the structure in Mombasa.

In November 1953 casual labour in Mombasa was divided into two pools, one for the city and the other for the port, with 700 and 4,800 respectively. Furthermore the J.I.C. agreed to increase the number of required shifts in the port from fifteen to twenty. This was accomplished in the first six months of 1953. In 1954 it was also agreed that joint committees of labour and management would advise on the operation of the pool and that there would be an appeals tribunal to hear grievances. By the end of the year the strength of the pool stood at 3,472 a reduction of nearly 700 in twelve months. The Labour Department hoped to persuade the employers to introduce a system of guaranteed minimum payments. To this end new premises were built in 1955 for the labour pool, new registration certificates introduced which it was hoped were proof against forgery, and the pool was split into stevedoring and shorehandling sections. The effect was to decrease the numbers in the pool and to give greater security and higher salaries to those who wished to make a living as casual labourers in the port. It was not however, until the end of the decade that the port made a serious effort to give these workers weekly or monthly status.

There was in 1954, moreover, still no union to represent the labour. The workers' representatives on the J.I.C. were picked at elections on the docks supervised by the African welfare officer and by the tribal headmen. They were supposed to report to the members of the pool, but the system worked ineffectively nor did it provide any muscle for the workers' position. In practice Williams and the Labour Department had established a benevolent dictatorship in the docks, dispensing efficiency and social welfare with a minimal participation by the recipients. It was in this context that Mboya began to organize the Dockworkers' Union. This immediately provoked another clash with Minya who wanted these workers to fall under the jurisdiction of his union, the Transport and Allied Workers' Union. Another jurisdictional problem was avoided by making Francis Thiongo, the local head of the Nightwatchmen and Clerks' Union a member of the union organizing committee which also included all the African members of the J.I.C. The I.C.F.T.U. financed the immediate needs of the union in terms of office rent, printing membership cards and the like although Bury expected the union to become self-financing in a short period of time. Luyt was in favour of these developments provided they did not disrupt the J.I.C., and Wilson told Mboya that he would not stand in the way of a proper union. Patrick and Bury assisted the interim committee in drafting a constitution, and the union was duly registered in October 1954. Dues of Sh. 1/- were established, and some money begun to flow into the treasury. The leading figures in these developments were Israel Jacob Okoth, Sammy T. Omar, and Kombo Mohamed. However, the remaining months of 1954 and early 1955 saw little action on the part of the employers in terms of recognizing the union as an integral part of the J.I.C. machinery. Nevertheless the union members on the J.I.C. pressed for certain changes on the part of the employers, notably for dirty money and for protective clothing when dealing with such cargoes.[75] In this they received assistance from the International Transport Workers' Federation but little response from the employers. They also met the Minister for Labour, Stow, when he was visiting Mombasa, and questioned him about some of the things they did not like such as surveillance of union officials.

Matters came to a head in March 1955 when the dockers went on strike. There were a number of grievances in the air. The Railway administration, acting on the Carpenter Report, had decided to increase salaries retroactively and had paid their employees a lump sum of Shs. 250/- in January. The Landing and Shipping Company had paid this increase on a monthly basis from March 1954, but it was less spectacular than that of the Railway and cut two months off the award which was only legally binding on the government and the Railway. Moreover the dockers in Tanga had received a substantial raise as a consequence of an arbitration award in 1954, and the cost of living, particularly rents and tea had increased considerably. There had also been some difficulty between the port labour officer and the casual workers over a check of certificates, and Omar thought that the strike originated with those affected by this inspection. Then men also complained of the insulting language used by the Mombasa branch manager of the Landing and Shipping Company.

On 26 January Okoth and others warned the J.I.C. of unrest in the port; Omar stated, rather optimistically as it turned out, that the union representatives would not be responsible for what happened since the employers would not discuss the cost of living issue until the next regular meeting.

The deputy chairman replied rather complacently: '. . . should there be trouble, then we should face it when it comes'.[76] The union did not, in fact, present any grievances at the next meeting on 24 February, partly because the organization of the union had declined somewhat and partly because they had written to the East Africa Statistical Department on 3 February only to be told that the relevant statistics would not be available until April. There was, however, considerable discussion of an anonymous letter which had appeared at the port and of notices that were chalked on the walls. The letter read:

> To all Africans working in Kilindini M.B.S. even those who are working in the port on 3.3.55, everybody will go on strike, clerks, askari, drivers, casual labourers, new and old employees, if you go on work this is your shauri if you die. We are will stay at home, at Kisauni, Magongo, Changamwe, Mtongwe, and Likoni. We are all must stand in one hand. Nobody can be allowed to leave his home. We are the labourers.[77]

No leaders were visible which was not surprising as the docks fell under the Essential Services Ordinance and any strike was, therefore, illegal. The union leaders agreed to attempt to counter this propaganda, but the employers refused permission for a mass meeting at the port to explain labour policy on the grounds that it would encourage the men to consider the strike a serious possibility. Bury arrived in Mombasa the same day and found that considerable pressure was being put on the union leaders to join the strike movement. He encouraged them to try to take charge of the situation by simultaneously urging the men to stay at work and also submitting a detailed claim to the companies. On 1 March Omar presented a budget on behalf of the union to the meeting of the J.I.C. to persuade the employers of the merits of a wage increase since real wages were dropping as a consequence of the rise in the cost of living. The union also issued three pamphlets urging the workers to follow legal and constitutional channels.[78] The reply from the anonymous strike leaders was immediate:

> We have seen your reply, but we do not agree. We have sent our representatives many times and we did not receive any reply except when we wrote our letter we received your reply. But just now we want reply before the 3rd March 1955, and if we do not receive reply before 3.3.55 we do not want to fight with you or Indians or Arabs, We shall stop work, we Africans, and this letter is for all Africans who are working in Kilindini Harbour, Mombasa and Kisauni, Changamwe, Motongwe and everybody who is working in Kilindini.

However, the employers would not consider an increase until a government study of the cost of living had been completed and refused another meeting until 16 March. The strike broke out on 3 March; it was immediately 80 per cent effective and began spreading sporadically to other industries and businesses in the city.

The union leaders wired Mboya for assistance, and he came to Mombasa immediately. Mboya and Bury feared, as a consequence of their experiences in Nairobi, that a strike would provoke drastic retaliation from the government. In fact the authorities did produce the usual show of force—Royal Inniskilling Fusiliers with bayonets fixed marching through the streets,

R.A.F. aircraft flying low over the city, lorryloads of *askaris* moving about the city while European and Asian volunteers worked the port. One sign of the times was that the Arabs, who had assisted in strike-breaking in 1947, promised to do so again but failed to turn up. The Port Employers' Association threatened to dismiss the strikers, and the city was very tense. Bury and the Labour Department, however, persuaded the P.E.A. to resume discussion in the J.I.C. despite the strike. When Mboya arrived, he hired a loudspeaker van and called a meeting which drew 8,000 to the football grounds. He urged the strikers to go back and put their demands through the union and the J.I.C. Just as he was speaking, Africans began distributing Swahili leaflets from the employers warning the men that they would be dismissed and punished if they did not go back to work by 5 March. The meeting broke up in disorder with union officials and Luo workers surrounding Mboya and whisking him away. Okoth and Omar were roughed up, stones thrown at the loudspeaker van and attempts made to break in to it as Mboya and the others were departing.[78] Bury considered this *démarche* sheer criminal stupidity on the part of the P.E.A. The men lost all confidence in the union leaders, the executive of which stepped down.

Mboya informally got together a negotiating committee from among the strikers, which was not easy to do as many feared they would be victimized. At first the P.E.A. told Mboya that he could attend the J.I.C. but not speak, an offer which Mboya accepted on 5 March.[80] That meeting proved entirely fruitless, and Mboya told the *Mombasa Times* that the employers had made his position impossible.[81] The senior labour officer, Dundas Bednall, then put pressure on the P.E.A. to remove the chairman of the J.I.C., George Usher, M.L.C. On 7 March the district commissioner agreed to preside at an *ad hoc* meeting of the employers and the strike committee which reconstructed the J.I.C. and elected Williams as chairman. This meant that, on the employers' side, power had moved decisively into his hands from the old guard. Mboya then gave a masterful presentation of the union's case. The meeting proceeded for some six hours, and gradually the employers' position softened. They offered an immediate increase of 50 cts. plus binding arbitration and the withdrawal of the dismissal notices. The union asked for Shs. 2/- and deadlock ensued. Meanwhile talk of a general strike was becoming louder in the city, and the police repeatedly broke up crowds of stone-throwing youths. The government threatened to bring in troops to man the docks and, at that point, Mboya, with the concurrence of the strike committee, agreed to the settlement.[82] The strike committee then toured the locations with the sound truck and called the men to a meeting on 8 March which ratified the arrangements and the men returned to work the following day.[83]

The arbitration was conducted by Judge (later Sir Ralph) Windham and was a complete victory for Mboya. He prepared a lengthy memorandum which rehearsed the grievances of the workers and defended this before the tribunal.[84] The minimum wage was raised about 30 per cent from Shs. 101/- to Shs. 130/-. By this award Windham fixed an industrial differential between the wages paid in the docks and the minimum wage which would remain part of the pay structure in Mombasa from that time on. It was accepted by Francis Thiongo, the new president of the union, despite rumours that there would be a second strike.[85] Later the port employers asked Mboya for suggestions on a new J.I.C. which would allow for representation by the union. A draft was presented at a meeting on 20 May by Mboya, and the employers concurred, the pact being ratified three days later by the J.I.C.[86] An agreement covering general terms of service of dockworkers was negotiated in the J.I.C. and came into force on 1 October 1955. More than any single event the strike and the results he secured for the workers established Mboya's real power.

Despite teething problems the union registered some important gains between 1955 and 1958. Guaranteed minimum payments had been first suggested to the union in 1954; however, at the time, nothing came of the idea because the union considered it a dodge to avoid paying a higher salary. But in 1956 there was a considerable fluctuation in employment in the port as consequence of the ending of phasing and of the Suez crisis, and the union began to take an interest in such a scheme. It went before the J.I.C. which eventually agreed on a system of attendance benefits which came into effect at the beginning of 1957 with payment of Shs. 3/- for casual labour. But in June and July the port was exceptionally quiet and the costs rose to £8,000. Eventually the employers and the union, rather than reducing the size of the pool which was legally impossible for them to do unilaterally, agreed that the casuals would be laid off for one day a week.

The unions also took full advantage of the refusal of the authorities to allow interterritorial unions, in this case, one union for all the East African ports. As a consequence each port negotiated separately, and from 1955 on there was increasing co-operation between the leaders. One of the reasons for pressing all disputes to arbitration was to keep alive a system of leap-frog awards by which the workers could use the gains in one port to justify their own increases. In this context arbitration awards had more prestige than mutually agreed settlements. Moreover, like most unions in Kenya at the time, the Dockworkers' Union did not possess the check-off, and it had, therefore, to demonstrate its presence whenever possible. This was frequently done by implicitly or explicitly supporting unofficial stoppages which usually arose from a local quarrel or difficulty in one section of the port or another. The other technique of the union which particularly annoyed the European management was to present extravagant demands, push them until deadlock was reached in the J.I.C., and then demand arbitration. This was sure to produce some gains for the workers and allowed the union to transfer the onus of blame for not securing all that was desired on to the tribunal.

A strike, for instance, occurred without warning on 8 and 10 November 1957 over payments to winchmen for a shift worked the previous night. An assembly of dockworkers then took up the cry for increased wages. The dockers were joined by 1,500 construction workers in the port, and a further 6,000 in nearby undertakings. Mboya persuaded the men to return to work and to submit their demand for Shs. 20/- to conciliation. Conciliation failed when the employers refused to make any offer, and the result was the creation of the Edmunds Tribunal. This gave a 5 per cent increase along with changes in shifts and improvements in certain fringe benefits. In 1958 there were three minor strikes in January, February and June.[87]

This unrest came to a head in September with a wildcat strike. The employers dug their heels in and withdrew recognition from the union leaders, thereby automatically suspending the operation of the J.I.C. In order to break the strike, the government introduced convict labour into the port, a move opposed by Williams who considered that if such measures were deemed necessary, the work should be done either by volunteers as in 1947 or 1955 or by the army. Since all these strikes were illegal as had been all previous strikes in the port, and since it was impossible to arrest 4,000 strikers, the employers recommended that the docks cease to be an essential service, a recommendation which came into effect in December 1958. That year also saw the arrival of Denis Akumu as general secretary of the union and his militant stand was undoubtedly part of a strategy to entrench his leadership and to deflect criticism of the appointment of an outsider and a Luo, for in this period the Coast people were beginning to assert their rights to employment in the port more vociferously than before.[88] In time Akumu secured a firm grip on the union so that by early 1959 the J.I.C. was reconstituted with a new recognition agreement and by the early nineteen-sixties he had secured the respect both of Williams and of Kenneth Harrap, the senior labour officer, so much so that the three of them virtually ran the labour relations of the port and of the city.

Meanwhile in these years Williams had pushed on with his programme of efficiency and welfare, securing the support of the union where he could and imposing the changes where he could not. Non-racial salary scales were introduced in 1955, and a company medical scheme in 1957. Africans were appointed to the clerical grade in increasing numbers. This particularly affected the Asians who dominated this grade and maintained their own protective society, the Harbour Asian Union, to the end of the colonial period. The African clerks resented this union, refused to sit on joint staff committees with the Asians, and joined the Dockworkers' Union. It was thus necessary for management to establish a separate African clerical joint staff committee. There were nevertheless continuous difficulties between Asian and African clerks concerning pay, seniority and the like. The company also found that it had to introduce some training facilities for clerks since it was very difficult to hire Africans with the appropriate training on the open market. However, the supervisory grade remained exclusively European, a lack of judgment for which the company would pay dearly in the nineteen-sixties.

Williams was also very interested in various efficiency schemes. In 1957 he imported consultants to do a time and motion study. The consulting company did not produce the desired results but certain of its recommendations were implemented notably a permanent works study or research group. Williams also persuaded the employers to give £600 towards the Mombasa social survey which had been commissioned through the government sociologist, Dr. J. C. Wilson. He was also anxious to improve the quality of the European supervisors, one of the points strongly stressed by Wilson in his report. He offered better terms and amenities in the hope of getting better supervisors. Throughout the nineteen-fifties he lamented in his annual reports that there was no place in East Africa to train such supervisors, but by the end of the decade he had arranged for such training at the Jeanes School and had made Swahili mandatory for all those who wished to join at the supervisory level. Many of these changes involved altercations with the Railway, particularly over financing. Every year, for instance, the union and the company complained of inadequate toilets, water outlets, and canteens on the docks and every year these were ignored, thereby increasing pollution, losing many man hours and provoking demands by the employees for long lunch breaks so that they could go home.

Williams and the Labour Department also pressed on with plans to make the work force more permanent and improve the local labour machinery. In 1956 the Labour Department began negotiations with the employers to change the structure for hiring and assigning casual labour. It felt that this should no longer be within the department's jurisdiction, partly because the employers were perfectly capable of doing it themselves and partly because it hampered the work of the labour officers in terms of inspection and conciliation. In addition the government sociologist had reported that there was still considerable corruption in the way the system worked, and the department considered that this would only be ended by the transfer of increasing numbers to monthly terms. As a consequence of these discussions, the employers created a new agency, the Mombasa Port Labour Utilization Board (M.P.L.U.B.) which took over the attendance records from the labour officer in the port. Some 750 men were transferred to monthly contracts with more doing so in 1958. Some, however, resisted as they could earn good wages as casual labour profiting from overtime, extra shifts and attendances, and dirty money. The effects of the new system can be seen from the following table:

NUMBER OF DOCKWORKERS ON MONTHLY/DAILY BASIS[89]

As at 31 December	1953	1955	1957	1958	1959
Monthly contracts	1,683	2,614	3,079	3,077	4,432
Daily (casual)	4,800	4,254	2,268	1,783	1,030
Total	6,483	6,868	5,347	4,860	5,462

Salaries also rose throughout this period, the minimum monthly wage for casual labour moving from Shs. 101/- in 1954 to Shs. 130/- with the Windham Award and to Shs. 152/55 in 1958. Salaries for senior head *serangs* rose more slowly, going from Shs. 340/- in 1954 to Shs. 370/- in 1958. In fact Wilson had criticized the company for failure to give adequate recompense to the foreman class and, as a consequence, Williams introduced a new foreman grade with better salary in the late nineteen-fifties. There was constant sniping at the salaries paid in the docks on the part of the settler press which tended to present an image of dockers living a life of well-paid ease while the price of everything imported into the colony went up as a consequence. Fortunately those in authority were prepared to disregard these attacks and to continue the policy of trying to make the port a place where a man could earn a decent standard of living.

In 1959 Sir Ian Parkin conducted an exhaustive inquiry into all aspects of dock labour in East Africa other than wages. The report was very detailed and had a profound effect on the industry.[90] Canteen and sanitary facilities were improved. New shifts and overtime arrangements (including double-time for the new night shift, Sundays and holidays) were established. Finally by the end of 1959 both sides had agreed to a new weekly contract system for casual labour which was introduced early in 1960.

The Development of Policy, 1956–63

This period began with a determined effort on the part of some settlers and officials to restrict the activities of Mboya who was creating a certain international reputation for himself while at Oxford through his associations with political critics of British colonial policy in the Fabian Society and in the Africa Bureau. What particularly irritated the settler leaders was that the Kenya government had given Mboya financial assistance to supplement his Sir William Bowen scholarship; it had done so in order that he would not have to seek financial support from what it considered to be undesirable political quarters.[91] After his year at Oxford, he had visited West Germany, the United States and Canada. In the latter two he had articulated the anti-colonialist view with great effect both in speeches and on television and had met with George Meany, Walter Reuther and David Dubinsky of the A.F.L.–C.I.O., thus creating an *entente* which would last for many years. These activities infuriated many Europeans in Kenya who, led by Group Captain Briggs, were determined to cut him down to size even before he returned home to restrict the K.F.L. to purely industrial matters.[92]

Two incidents seem to have brought the matter to a head. Early in 1956 Mboya spoke at a press conference in London arranged by the Labour Party, and on 20 February the K.F.L. issued a pugnacious statement in Nairobi which, among other things, promised that it would launch a newspaper at the beginning of March. This paper would be financed by the I.C.F.T.U., a body which as already noted had inflamed the settlers by the resolutions concerning Kenya passed at its Vienna congress and which the more extreme European M.L.C.s considered to be led by communists and fellow-travellers. The government could do nothing about Mboya as long as he was abroad; however, it seriously considered revoking the registration of the K.F.L. and arresting Mboya on his return. At the end of February the K.F.L. was called upon to show why its registration should not be cancelled on the grounds that its political activities were beyond the scope of its constitutional objects as a registered society under the Societies Ordinance of 1952. The federation was registered as a society in order to give it legal status but to prevent it from calling strikes.[93] Once again Mboya appealed to his allies overseas, and Tewson intervened directly to throw his influence against any such step. Tewson and Hood flew to Nairobi to assist the K.F.L. In the event, and after several days of negotiations involving reference to the full Council of Ministers this proved to be decisive. The government accepted the argument that a measure of political activity was legitimate, chose not to enforce the emergency regulation prohibition on any nation-wide political activity and maintained the registration of the federation. It was the last time that colonial government officials would think seriously of taking such action against Mboya or the K.F.L.; it was clear that any such action was most unlikely to be supported by the Colonial Office in London. As a sop to the settlers, the government passed amendments to the Trade Union Ordinance which tightened some of the controls by the registrar on the unions, in particular restricting the reasons for which a union could be formed to those which were purely industrial.[94]

As soon as Mboya was back in Kenya, he resumed his post as general secretary of the K.F.L. and plunged into local Nairobi politics. By 1956 the British were entirely confident that they could contain the remnants of the Mau Mau insurrection, and, as a consequence, they had begun to ease the restrictions on political activity although only permitting parties organized on a local basis. This made it less necessary for Mboya to continue to use the K.F.L. as a vehicle for airing nationalist opinion, but the federation nevertheless remained an essential part of his own political machine. It was however Clement Argwings-Kodhek, Kenya's first African barrister who initially exploited these new constitutional developments by forming the Nairobi District African National Congress in 1956. Mboya challenged Argwings-Kodhek for the leadership of the party, and in the following year Mboya defeated him and was elected to the Legislative Council. He then formed his own party, the Nairobi Peoples' Convention Party (N.P.C.P.) which rapidly overtook the N.D.A.N.C. The same year he led the African elected members in a concerted attack which resulted in the breakdown of the Lyttelton Constitution and the imposition of a new one by Lennox-Boyd which gave the Africans six more members. His fame spread beyond Kenya, and in December 1958 he was elected chairman of the All African Peoples' Conference in Accra.[95]

Mboya continued this dual role of trade union and political leader from 1956 to 1963 to the despair of many in the Labour Department. However, the trade union apparatus remained a vital adjunct to Mboya's political machine. He was well aware that the political situation of the mid nineteen-fifties in Nairobi was extremely artificial since the Kikuyu were still banned from political activity in any numbers. He knew that the day would come when these restrictions would be removed, and he would be at a disadvantage as a Luo in a Kikuyu city. Nor could he seriously contemplate retreating to a rural Luo constituency in Nyanza province since all his connections were in the urban areas and since his rival, Oginga Odinga was clearly becoming the dominant political personality in that province. The trade union movement allowed him to appeal beyond tribal lines. It also provided a city-wide and a colony-wide structure on which to build his political fortunes. Men could be switched back and forth between the trade union and the party structures to suit the convenience of the moment. One of the most notable of these was Akumu who worked with the N.P.C.P. and then was projected by Mboya into the general secretaryship of the Dockworkers' Union in Mombasa in 1958. The trade unions could informally provide manpower for electioneering, and the post of general secretary of the K.F.L. ensured that Mboya was always in the public eye. Finally it was a source of power because it was a source of funds. Mboya was able to tap American unions and such other sources in the United States as the American Committee on Africa and the Kennedy family. The A.F.L.–C.I.O., for instance, contributed $35,000 for the building of a new headquarters for the K.F.L., which Mboya wisely situated in a working-class area of Nairobi and which was opened with pomp and ceremony in 1960. This building became a symbol of the type of power he could command. So was the air lift of students to the United States. As a consequence the overwhelming majority of trade unionists in Nairobi belonged to the N.P.C.P. until it was superseded by K.A.N.U. in 1960 and continued to support Mboya politically at least until 1961 or 1962. Three top labour leaders, Clement Lubembe, Akumu and Minya became respectively the chairman, general secretary and vice-chairman of the N.P.C.P. However, his association with the A.F.L.–C.I.O. and the enthusiastic support he received from a section of the western press proved a liability as well as an asset since it contributed to the alienation of the other major politician of the time, Odinga.[96] The struggle between Mboya and Odinga, as we shall see later, was fought out not only in the party political arena but also within the structure of the K.F.L.

Throughout this period Mboya worked closely with the Labour Department. The department had opposed the deregistration of the K.F.L., and the failure of the settler attack set the stage for it to develop its ideas and policies both in connection with industrial relations and with social security free from any serious possibility that these would any longer be inhibited by the European members of the Legislative Council. There was, of course, still strong criticism from time to time, particularly during the debates on the estimates, but there was no likelihood that the British government would countenance any serious disruption of the policies of the department. Furthermore the leaders of the business and financial community had come to accept Luyt's views of industrial relations and became closely associated with the department in making them operative. Finally the gradual withdrawal of the British from Kenya meant the downgrading of the influence of the provincial administration which had grown so rapidly during Mau Mau and an increase in the influence of the specialized departments. The dominant official figure in this period was Luyt, who became Permanent Secretary to the Ministry of Education, Labour and Lands in 1957 and four years later Secretary to the Cabinet and Permanent Secretary in the Governor's office. W. R. C. Keeler, the former Chief Inspector of Factories and secretary of the Carpenter Committee became Labour Commissioner. He was a cautious and rather shy administrator with in public an exaggeratedly British self-depreciation. He was not at ease in his relations with Mboya who disliked him but recognized that the majority of his policies were in the best interest of the labour movement. It was widely assumed that the much more ebullient Deputy Labour Commissioner, Husband, would succeed Keeler, but this was precluded in the eyes of the Colonial Office by his marriage to the daughter of a leading Kenya settler.

Keeler presided over a rapid development of those social security, inspection and training policies whose origins can be found in the nineteen-thirties and late nineteen-forties and which became of increasing importance after independence. In the Labour Commissioner's former domain, there was slow but steady progress. The main necessity was the recruitment of sufficient inspectors to make the elaborate legislation of the early part of the decade operative. It had been difficult to find such people during the height of Mau Mau, but in the first few years of this period the numbers increased, although there was a decline after the 1960 Lancaster House conference.[97] The Labour Commissioner could report in 1957 that it had become possible, for the first time, to carry out factory inspections on a systematic basis; meaningful statistics had begun to be assembled the previous year. The increase in establishment and in numbers also allowed the section to develop new techniques and regulations. Special rules to deal with explosive cellulose solutions, safety devices in the woodworking industry, and regulations for the docks at Mombasa were all adopted between 1957 and 1963. Since Kenya was not a country with any heavy industry, it did not possess the dark satanic mills of nineteenth-century England. But nevertheless there were some 5,000 establishments registered under the ordinance, and it required constant vigilance to keep them up to standard, particularly the smaller ones. It was only in 1960 that the inspectorate could undertake a systematic check of the smaller premises in Nairobi, a survey which unearthed some very dismal conditions.

The main thrust of the Factories section, however, was to ensure that the larger premises were properly maintained in terms of health and safety. It contracted with private individuals or firms to carry out many of the technical inspections required under the ordinance, and gradually through this period it developed manuals and a general expertise among its contractors which had been lacking in the early nineteen-fifties. It also decided to associate the more progressive employers with the department in attempts to raise safety standards. To this end it created advisory bodies in the sisal and tea industries which issued reports and suggestions for improved safety standards. The section was able to exploit the fact that it was in the interest of the larger international companies, which maintained reasonable safety and health standards as a matter of course, to force their competitors to adopt the same standards and to prevent them from price-cutting based on inadequate investment in these facilities. The inspectorate also worked closely with those investing in new plant in Kenya, attempted to ensure that their plans took into account safety and health factors and tried to prevent the introduction, particularly from Japan, of machinery with sub-standard safety devices. During this period there was only one major industrial disaster when in 1960 an explosion in a pyrethrum extracts factory in Nairobi caused the death of three workers and serious injuries to a further nineteen. The inspectorate also maintained the litany of complaint begun in the nineteen-thirties concerning the lack of proper sanitation in many rural concerns.[98]

Compensation for accidents occurring as a consequence of employment was dealt with under the Workmen's Compensation Ordinance of 1948. The department sought no basic change in this legislation during this period. As both Tanganyika and Uganda had essentially the same ordinances, the three territories had been participating since 1951 in a joint standing committee on workmen's compensation. This committee suggested changes in 1954 in certain of the procedures established by the ordinance and also an increase in benefits. The necessary legislation was drafted in 1955 and became effective at the beginning of 1956. Maximum benefits for death were raised from £700 to £1,200, for permanent incapacity from £1,000 to £1,700 and for periodical payments from Shs. 320/- per month to Shs. 450/-. Other adjustments were made including raising the maximum permissible income level for coverage from £500 to £840. Additional administrative procedures were established during this period, in particular the practice of medical officers reporting industrial accidents treated by them to the local labour officer. The department continued to publicize the work of the Registrar of Workmen's Compensation, but it would appear that Kenya had reached a plateau of coverage by the middle of the nineteen-fifties, with compensation paid out by employers amounting to some £50,000–£73,000 per year. A greater total, £84,135 was reached in 1962 when wage rates were higher. The government did not choose to make operative section 26 of the ordinance which provided for compulsory insurance, instead labour officers put pressure on employers to take out accident insurance. Between 1948 and 1951 there had been an increase in such premium income by the members of the Kenya Accident Insurance Association from £32,908 to £128,575, but it would appear that insurance coverage had also stabilized by the latter half of the nineteen-fifties. Most of the larger businesses took out accident insurance as part of group insurance plans which were becoming popular in this period. In 1962 Kenya acceded to article 5 of the I.L.O. Convention 17 and inaugurated a system whereby payment under the Workmen's Compensation Ordinance would be paid by instalment through the Post Office Savings Bank nearest to the home of the recipient, with the principal earning interest at the standard rate.[99]

The department was, however, much more concerned to try to develop an adequate scheme of old-age security. It followed from the Carpenter Report and the Dow Commission that the government would have to strive to create a stable work force. The more urbanized this work force became, the less the traditional means of social security would apply. Normally the extended African family in the rural areas was expected by tradition to look after the elderly by providing a hut, perhaps food or the land on which to grow it. If the views of the Carpenter Report and the subsequent sessional paper were to be implemented, a necessary corollary was a state system of pensions to replace these traditional methods. In 1953 both the European Elected Members' Organization and the K.N.F.U. had also urged an inquiry into the pension question. The following year the Legislative Council supported a motion of Humphrey Slade, a leading European elected member, to create such a commission, a demand duly acceded to by the government with the creation of the Dolton Committee which was to enquire into whether a pension scheme was feasible and, if so, the most appropriate for the colony. At the same time the government made it quite clear that it expected to create such a system on a contributory basis, thus causing the resignation of one of the members of the committee who thought the matter prejudged.

Nevertheless the committee continued its work. Public hearings were held, and a questionnaire distributed. The K.F.L. appeared, as did the Kenya African Civil Servants' Association, the Railway African Union, the Kenya Local Government Workers' Union branch in Mombasa, and the Mombasa Dockworkers' J.I.C. The list is suggestive of the degree of organization of unions in 1954 and of the awareness of such issues at pensions.

The union representatives were far outnumbered by private and public employers and by members of the Labour Department. The committee also sought expert advice in a three week tour of England in 1955. Traditionally private employers had been hostile to the notion that Africans should have either provident or pension fund schemes. If employers were concerned, the most the majority were prepared to give was a lump-sum gratuity for long service. This, in turn, reflected the long-standing view that Africans were casual and not permanent labour and, if permanent, were retainers rather than workers with rights. In 1953 only 35,000 employees (including 11,000 Europeans and Asians) out of a work force of 500,000 had either pension plans or provident funds.[100] Nothing could more clearly indicate the racial character of employment in Kenya than a survey of pensions and provident funds undertaken by the Labour Department in 1956 of some 25,000 workers in 30 large undertakings.[101]

PERCENTAGE OF LABOUR FORCE COVERED

Race	Pension	Provident fund	Terminal grant
European	57.25	14.58	0.18
Asian	21.55	41.92	—
African	9.10	14.93	30.77

The Dolton Committee did not report until 1956, and the government delayed publication until the following year as it was embarrassed by the recommendations. Despite this it made the provision of social security for the aged a part of its statement of policy in 1956.[102] The committee suggested a state pension scheme of a contributory nature for non-agricultural workers which would involve a shared contribution of Shs. 4/- a month, resulting in a basic pension of Shs. 60/- a month after ten years. There was to be the possibility of enhanced pensions through higher contributions, and the government was to bear the full cost of creating and administering the scheme. Finally the proposal was to complement rather than to supersede existing private schemes.[103] It was not until May 1958 that the government finally announced its decision; the Minister for Local Government, Health and Town Planning told the Legislative Council that the government would not accept the report because the proposals were too costly and because the colony lacked the necessary vital statistics.[104]

As soon as the government made clear its position, the Labour Department began to press private employers to secure pension or provident fund coverage from the insurance companies, and after 1960 the trade unions also began to add their voices. As a consequence, between 1958 and 1963 there was a very general increase in this type of coverage. For instance 16,000 employees were added between 1961 and 1962 even though the work force declined by some 10,000. There were also more traditional ways explored; in 1962 the General Agricultural Workers' Union and the K.N.F.U. concluded an agreement, one part of which was to provide old-age security through the provision of land on the employer's farm. The department also waged a battle to reopen the question of a state pension; however, matters pertaining to pensions tended to move with glacial slowness. In December

1959 it recommended that the decision of the government concerning the Dolton recommendations be reversed. The following year it secured jurisdiction in this area from the Ministry of Local Government, Health and Town Planning, and it requested expert advice from the Colonial Office to assess the recommendations of the Dolton Committee. In 1961 two experts were finally secured through the Colonial Development and Welfare Fund; this in turn led to a further recommendation in 1962 that the social security plans of Nigeria and Malayasia be examined before any steps were taken in Kenya, a task which was also funded by London. However, the inauguration of such a scheme was left to the new African government which took over in 1963.[105]

The department continued its concern in the area of juvenile labour. The Emergency had both aggravated the problem and had slowed down consideration of remedial action. In 1952 the government had enacted the Employment of Juveniles (Hours of Work and Welfare) Rules specifying a six-hour day and requiring the appointment of a special supervisor if the business employed more than fifty juveniles. In the same year a committee chaired by Slade recommended a tightening of the laws pertaining to child and juvenile work. Furthermore the existing legislation needed to be brought up to date in relation to the I.L.O. Convention. However, the demands of the Emergency precluded the department from undertaking this, and the Emergency itself caused, as noted earlier, a rapid increase in the number of illegally employed juveniles. In 1955 Luyt noted in his annual report that:

> The illegal employment of children continues to be a problem, particularly difficult to combat when, as is often the case, the employer, the child and its parents are all in league to defeat the purposes of the law.

The latter part of the nineteen-fifties saw an attempt by the department to take action in this area. In 1956 amendments were passed to the Employment of Women, Young Persons and Children Ordinance incorporating many of the suggestions of the Slade Committee and bringing the legislation into harmony with the I.L.O. Convention. Children were defined as being under sixteen, the previous age-limit being fifteen. Young persons were defined as between sixteen and eighteen, and everyone under eighteen was defined as a juvenile. Stricter rules were passed concerning the employment of children in industry, the control of children living away from home, and the amount of permissible night work. The following year the department adopted new rules to cover the employment of juveniles in the tea industry, this being the single largest employer of juveniles in the colony. In both these years a series of prosecutions was launched against some of the worst offenders, employers who, for instance, were paying as low as Shs. 10/- a month with little or no food. These actions undoubtedly curbed some of the abuses, particularly in Nairobi. However, the years between 1960 and 1963 saw a decline in the economic situation in the colony, an increase in unemployment and continued widespread violation of such laws as people became more and more desperate for jobs.[106]

The department was concerned not only with the social security net and the prevention of gross abuses but also with the whole question of training. For years it had been anxious to promote greater productivity in the African work force, and its policy of high wages was directed to this end. This point of view led the department to encourage various types of incentive schemes which grew in variety and scope in the latter part of the decade, and in addition to stop a move by the Tailors and Textile Workers' Union in 1957 to end piecework. But between 1956 and independence it also invested much of its time and effort in the direct training of Africans. Apprenticeship had never been a very successful way of doing this since apprentices could secure reasonable wages long before their contracts had expired and, as a consequence, usually disappeared unless they were in boarding schools which were expensive to maintain. Furthermore it was difficult for apprentices outside the government to secure proper industrial training until the Technical Institute was opened in 1954 in Nairobi as an adjunct of the Royal Technical College. As a consequence apprenticeship tended to be restricted to the trade schools of the government, the Railway, and the Posts and Telecommunications. The department had, therefore, to adopt different techniques to meet the local situation.

Trade testing was one of these. Prior to 1954 all trade testing was carried out by officers of the trade schools and was mostly confined to the students of those schools. In 1954 the government authorized the hiring of five testing officers by the Labour Department. They became the nucleus of a strong push in this area between 1956 and 1963. Initially the testing was carried out at the Technical Institute or on the premises of the employer. However, in 1956 the department opened a trade testing centre in Nairobi's industrial area which gradually grew in terms of staff, equipment and space. The statistics indicate the change. In 1953 there were 318 trade tests; in 1962 2,317. The gradual development of employment in the urban areas allowed employers to demand higher standards from their workers, and more and more these were determined by the Labour Department's trade tests. This meant that although the tests were never legally compulsory, they were becoming much more so in fact. An industrial training bill was drafted, published in 1959, and became effective in May 1960. In it the government rejected compulsory training and opted for two types of learning contracts —apprenticeship and indentured learners, the latter being a less exacting grade. The purpose of the ordinance was to encourage both governmental and private schemes and to ensure that the Labour Department would regulate any such contracts and the terms and conditions of employment of the juveniles involved.[107] All these activities came under the Trade Testing and Apprenticeship Section of the department.[108]

Another important development was the decision to promote Training Within Industry for supervisors, in accordance with the recommendation of the Carpenter Committee. This was launched in 1956 with the education of twenty-one trainers, the inauguration of a number of training courses plus a barrage of propaganda in terms of booklets and a magazine called *Kenya T.W.I. Topics.* The government considered that it was no longer possible to expect that all training could be handled in government schools and that it was essential for industry and for agriculture to play an important part. The Labour Department was also convinced that proper supervision was one of the most important ingredients in increasing productivity. The significance of this to the government can be seen by the fanfare surrounding the conference, 'Focus on Jobs', which was held at the Royal Technical College in 1957. It was opened by Baring, and presided over by the Minister for Labour with delegates from sixty-four organizations. The general and committee reports of the conference along with the major lectures were all published. T.W.I. grew substantially from then on.

In its first years the T.W.I. section was primarily concerned with the inculcation of proper supervision as a method of modern management. But in the last few years of colonial rule, this role changed drastically. As soon as it became apparent at Lancaster House in 1960 that Kenya would become in the near future an independent African state, panic struck both government and private industry over the lack of trained African supervisors and executives. In May 1961 in government alone there were only 500 Africans among the 8,000 on the C (Executive) Scale, only nine Africans out of ninety-three in the grades between Assistant Secretary and Permanent Secretary, and only fifty-one Africans out of 228 officers in the provincial and district administration; lower in the hierarchy there were no African personal secretaries or stenographers. The situation in private business was worse.[109] From 1960 the T.W.I. course grew in number and scope and became an essential part of the government's response to the demand for immediate Africanization. In 1958 466 people took T.W.I. courses while by 1962 the number had increased to 3,671; the number of instructors in the department grew from nine to twenty-nine. Much of this work was done in conjunction with the Kenya Institute of Administration which replaced the Jeanes School in July 1961 and became the primary device of the colonial government in attempting to ensure an orderly policy of localization at the supervisory and administrative levels. The variety of courses at the K.I.A. were astonishing by comparison with earlier years and ranged from the training of office supervisors to farm headmen. The work was heavily subsidized by American A.I.D. through building grants and by a contract with Syracuse University. The Labour Department also collaborated with private industry in creating additional training programmes outside the government structure; the private sector, for instance, founded and maintained the East African Institute of Management. One of the most publicized of these was the training scheme adopted by East African Oil Refineries Ltd. to train 119 employees between 1961 and 1963 for the operation of the new oil refinery in Mombasa.[110]

A third section of the department was concerned with aptitude testing. This unit was first created as part of the response to Mau Mau, in particular to solve the problem of how to apportion detainees to particular kinds of training. In this capacity the unit was part of the Prisons Service. However, in 1959 it was transferred to the Labour Department where it grew at an astonishing rate in the next few years. Once again this was largely due to the rush towards independence and the demand by government and private industry for some means of assessing the aptitude of Africans for higher supervisory and management posts. By 1962 this section was carrying out 3,000 tests per year, not only in Kenya but for the other East African governments as well.[111]

Although the development of public housing was not an official concern of the Labour Department, it was nevertheless vitally interested in the success of the government's plans. The Central Housing Board was the responsible authority; it administered a fund which had been created in 1953 and which had reached the following totals in 1960:

£400,000 free grant from the Kenya government
£2,000,000 loan from the Colonial Development Corporation
£787,000 loan from the Kenya Development Fund
£47,000 from the Emergency Fund
£244,709 loans prior to 1953

The contribution from the Kenya Development Fund increased to £1,621,767 by 1963 when the American A.I.D. began to assist public housing in Kenya. Proper housing had been one of the major cries of the reformers during Mau Mau, and the Central Housing Board saw its work in this light: '... the Board considers', the annual report stated in 1960, 'that the possession of their own homes has a stabilizing influence on people ...' Despite the admirable aims of the government and the success of some of the schemes, it still remained impossible to cope with the flood of people coming to the cities. Between 1948 and 1962 the official population figures for Nairobi rose from 118,976 to 226,794 and those for Mombasa from 84,746 to 179,575. Most African housing was drastically overcrowded. In 1964 a United Nations survey team found that 52 per cent of the rooms in Nairobi housed three or more people and 74 per cent had two or more. Squatter towns grew up, and the authorities could do little about it since they could not offer alternative accommodation. The United Nations report found the public housing in Kenya on the whole adequate, in some cases excellent, but insufficient in quantity.[112]

The cornerstone of the Labour Department's protective policy, however, remained the control of minimum wages. These were increased every year between 1955 and 1963, although not at the rate projected in the government's 1954 sessional paper. The Nairobi wage increases went as follows:

	Male employees over 21		Other employees	
	Basic miminum	*Minimum housing*	*Basic minimum*	*Minimum housing*
Year	Shs.	Shs.	Shs.	Shs.
1 Jan. 1956	82.50	17.50	75.00	13.00
1 Jan. 1957	85.00	20.00	75.00	13.00
1 Jan. 1958	85.00	22.50	75.00	13.00
1 Dec. 1958	90.00	22.50	75.00	13.00
1 Jan. 1960	95.00	24.50	73.00	13.00
Dec. 1960	102.00	26.00	74.00	13.00
Dec. 1961	107.00	26.00	74.00	13.00
Dec. 1962	115.00	26.00	79.00	13.00

1956–62 Annual Reports, Labour Department

This represents a percentage increase in the total wage packet of 41 per cent. The average engagement rate in Nairobi showed a considerably higher increase; this rose by 103 per cent between 1954 and 1961. A wage earners' index of consumer prices was, however, only kept from October-

December 1958; this showed an increase of 8 per cent between that time and December 1962. From 1954 to 1962 total employment of Africans rose only from 492,551 to 525,351 (after a peak year in 1960) and that of adult males from 390,949 to 430,793. When these statistics are viewed in the light of a rapidly increasing population, it is clear that the policy of creating a stable labour force was becoming more and more successful.

The other method of minimum wage controls was through wages councils. In December 1955 two new wages councils were created, one for the motor engineering trade and the other for the baking, flour confectionery and biscuit-making trades. The development of wages councils, however, was halted in 1956 by a boycott on the part of the trade unions concerned arising from the government's refusal to make such orders applicable in rural areas. This, in turn, reflected the power of the European farming lobby which had always been fearful that minimum wages would be extended to the agricultural industry. The boycott ended in 1957, and in the same year the government decided to inaugurate such a council in the building industry, a move successfully resisted by the union until 1960; the K.F.L. was generally hostile to the development of more councils on the grounds that it undercut the union movement. As a consequence wages orders were not promulgated in the two councils created in 1955 until 1958, and no new councils were added until the period 1960–3 when those for the building, laundry trades, knitting mills, footwear and distributive trade, were created.[113]

All this reflected a continued faith in a high-wage economy, and this orthodoxy probably reached its peak at the joint meeting of ministers of labour of East Africa at Kampala and Dar es Salaam in 1962. At Kampala the ministers, prompted by Mboya, stated:

> The Ministers noted that in the past East African wages policy had been based on a low wage economy. This had been due to the absence of strong trade unions and to the weak bargaining position of the workers; it had for a long time been believed that a low wage economy was in keeping with the undeveloped status of East Africa. In some cases no effort had been made to move away from this low wage economy, but rather to consolidate it and make it the basis for the future. There had been arguments that increases in wages might lead to contraction in investments and even to greater unemployment. Having reviewed all the economic arguments and possible implications the Ministers agreed that the future policy must be based on a high wage economy, and that each East African Government should review its wage structure aiming at a minimum wage that would provide a worker and his family with a reasonable standard of life.

The ministers then went on to say that as much as possible this should be achieved through collective bargaining but that 'government would still, however, continue to have overall responsibility...', a policy reaffirmed at the meeting in Dar es Salaam in November.[114]

Unemployment was the Achilles heel of this policy. It was discussed in Kampala but only in terms of possible methods to register the unemployed. But at Das es Salaam the consequences of a high wage policy were both discussed and accepted. It was assumed by the delegates that 'automation and mechanisation... would be closely associated with such policy. It was felt that such developments were inevitable in the modern scientific world and must therefore be accepted.' The delegates also recognized, in a more general sense, that:

> Unemployment was a constant threat which had to be taken into account when deciding the pace of movement towards a high wage economy. It must not, however, be used to stop any such movement since it was felt in the long run it was better to have a smaller but satisfied and efficient labour force rather than a large, badly paid and frustrated labour force.

However, between 1959 and 1963 Kenya had increasingly to deal with the problem of unemployment, where the government argued dubiously that the cause lay in underemployment or lack of development in the African reserves, but was off-set by social customs in those reserves. But *Hapana kazi hapa* said more and more signs on businesses in Nairobi and Mombasa and the issue could not so easily be wished away. On the whole, however, both the government and Mboya still held to the high wage position, and Mboya reiterated this when he joined the coalition government in 1962 as Minister for Labour.[115] There was nevertheless a certain amount of wavering, and in 1960, for instance, both Blundell and Lord Portsmouth had urged on the Legislative Council the merits of labour intensive methods, particularly in road making and harvesting. Rogers was appalled at this deviation from economic orthodoxy. However gradually after 1962 Kenya began, *de facto*, to move away from a rigid high wage policy.[116] This culminated after independence in the Tripartite Agreement of February 1964 by which the government persuaded both public and private employers to take on more staff even though there was no need in terms of efficiency. The government hoped in return to secure a wages standstill and a ban on strikes from the unions, but this was, in the event, an illusion.[117] Unemployment, also, however, undermined minimum wage policy in another very serious way, namely through evasion. As unemployment grew, unscrupulous businessmen, particularly in the smaller businesses and trades, began to take advantage of their employees. The most common form of this was to demand a kickback on wages which could and sometimes did place the worker below the minimum wage. Such evasion was talked about in labour circles in Mombasa, for instance, in 1960 but appeared to have become chronic in certain areas such as the distributive trades by 1963.[118]

Industrial relations remained the most publicized work of the department. Roy Damerell joined the department in 1957 as Patrick's successor in the post of Industrial Relations Officer. He was a university graduate, had served with the Royal Air Force during the Second World War, and had been the general secretary of one of the smaller civil service unions in Britain. He was chosen in the hope that this background would appeal to both trade unionists and to employers. Damerell was much more stable in this post than his predecessor, and he was able to carry out the industrial relations policies of the department efficiently and with a minimum of fuss. From 1960 onwards the African members of the department came to have a gradually increasing influence in this area. This was particularly true of Ndisi, Christopher Malavu, and J. W. Owuor. Nevertheless as late as 1961 there were only three African labour officers in an establishment of thirty-two although there were eight Africans listed as labour officers (supernumerary). But the department was able to draw on experienced men from the wages and labour inspectorate grades which had always been African and it was only a matter of a short period of time before these Africans moved into the senior positions.[119]

One of the features of industrial relations in this period was the strong support given by the department to the creation of an effective employers' organization, free to concentrate on industrial relations problems and not dominated by the local European farming interest. As early as 1949 Parry, Assistant Labour Adviser to the Colonial Office, and Hyde-Clarke had spoken to the Nairobi Chamber of Commerce urging that the strikes of that year showed the necessity for better organization by the employers. 'I think', said Parry, 'the first move should be the establishment of a first-class organization of employers throughout the territories, and you should see what can be done about it.'[120] Nothing much came of this intervention, but we have seen how certain key employers such as Rogers became convinced by the events surrounding the Emergency of the need for the larger expatriate employers to form their own organization and to create a system of industrial relations on the western model in order to assure their survival.

The Association of Commercial and Industrial Employers (A.C.I.E.) came into existence in Nairobi in 1956 with a lawyer, Ian Duthie, as executive officer. It did for Nairobi what the Mombasa and Coast Province Employers' Association had already done in the Coast province; the two organizations merged in January 1959 to form the Federation of Kenya Employers (F.K.E.). Duthie was one of the principal architects of this development. It meant that many of the leading firms were predisposed to treat with the K.F.L. or, at the very least, to tolerate its existence. But growth remained slow and uneven. Certain important business figures such as Peter King, the chairman of the Kenya Meat Commission, never accepted ideas of this nature. Others, such as the owners of the stevedoring companies, gave only lip service. Local European and Asian businessmen remained, by and large, suspicious. Nevertheless the A.C.I.E. (and later the F.K.E.) was able to create a climate of opinion, particularly in expatriate circles, in which the ideas of Luyt, Hartwell and others could flourish.

Employers were concerned not only about the effects of the Emergency but also about the development of compulsory arbitration. The major corporations were horrified by the precedent set in 1955 by the Mombasa award and foresaw the possibility that the control of the cost of their labour force might pass out of their hands through this device. In 1957 the A.C.I.E. listed the following drawbacks to compulsory arbitration:

1. An employer is compelled to leave conditions in a particular industry to the judgment of an outsider who may have little expert knowledge of that industry's particular problems.
2. An employer may be compelled to accept the verdict of an arbitrator appointed by the government although he may consider the arbitrator unsuitable.
3. Arbitrators tend to have the preservation of industrial peace as their first

objective. Their inclination to play for safety at the expense of the employer's pocketbook is intolerable.[121]

As a consequence the A.C.I.E. came to favour free collective bargaining over compulsory arbitration. Some corporations had as well other motives for supporting this stand. The Europeans in the engineering trade hoped, for instance, as in the past, to eliminate the competitive margin of Asian employers by standardizing wage rates.

In 1957 the A.C.I.E. prepared a 'Joint Consultation Report' in which it outlined its approach to collective bargaining. Although there was a deferential bow to works councils, the major corporations were determined to secure a system of bargaining by industry. This would simultaneously inhibit general strikes and prevent private settlements by individual employers. Such multi-employer negotiations would also give the A.C.I.E. secretariat the opportunity to influence in a very direct way the general tenor of wage settlements. The specific device was to be through joint industrial councils. The report also attempted to lay down certain guidelines for the recognition of unions (membership of 40 per cent, for instance) and for deciding what were bargaining issues and what were not. In this latter regard it opposed the check-off. However, the notion of bargaining by industry or by the use of joint industrial councils was hardly an invention of the employers. Both Luyt and Mboya had been committed to this model for some years although they had failed to curtail the two major general unions, the Distributive and Commercial Workers' Union and the Transport and Allied Workers' Union.

What was new was the interest in industrial bargaining by a large number of major employers and their acceptance of another recommendation of the report, namely that there should be a meeting between the employers and the K.F.L. This meeting took place in November 1957 and was chaired by the Minister for Labour, both the K.F.L. and the Labour Department welcoming the general position of the employers. Mboya, however, successfully argued against stringent rules for the recognition of unions and secured agreement on a general and rather meaningless phrase to the effect that would-be unions must be able to ensure that agreements would be kept. Both sides also agreed on the industrial basis for collective bargaining. It has been suggested that the K.F.L. was reluctant in its acceptance of the industrial basis, but this hesitation was probably more tactical than real as Mboya was already in favour of such a move; he had however to consider the role of the general unions in the K.F.L. The Labour Department assumed much more than a neutral chairmanship at this meeting, pressing the F.K.E. to make their proposals more flexible and the K.F.L. to accept the agreement. There then followed in May 1958 a further meeting between the employers and the K.F.L. which led to a demarcation agreement. This set the structure for the organization both of employers and of workers for the remainder of colonial rule and for the first decade of independence. Industrial unions became the pattern; where general unions existed, it was agreed that they would have distinct sections with separate bargaining procedures.[122]

Both the employers and the unions were pressing for a modification of the Essential Services Ordinance. In October 1957, for instance, the K.F.L. addressed a series of demands to the Colonial Secretary which included an attack on the ordinance as a violation of I.L.O. conventions.[123] The following year the government decided to reduce drastically the list of such services, retaining only water and electricity supply, health, hospital and sanitary services, air traffic control and civil aviation, and telecommunications, meteorological and fire services as well as the transport to make these services operative. The reduced list represented a substantial reduction from the original ordinance; it omitted the railways, docks, bus services, and posts and telecommunications and showed the government's commitment to collective bargaining.[124]

The strength of the A.C.I.E. (and particularly of the F.K.E. when it was formed in 1959) came from informal rather than constitutional provisions. The federation successfully incorporated the few existing employers' associations such as the K.N.F.U. and the Port Employers' Association and encouraged the growth of many more. By June 1960 there were fourteen registered associations affiliated to the F.K.E. Since the trade union legislation allowed for the creation of employers' unions, most of these took on this status. There were also sub-groups, particularly among the members of the Distributive and Allied Industries Association. Gradually the requirement that the members should seek the advice of the F.K.E. before making a wage settlement became a firm rule.

The F.K.E. was able to respond to its members' needs because its dues were sufficiently high for it to be able to afford a growing staff, headed throughout this period by David Richmond as chief executive officer. The larger associations were also able to afford their own executive officers who were sometimes former members of the Labour Department. The F.K.E. staff offered its services during negotiations, issued a stream of press releases on all aspects of collective bargaining including a monthly newsletter, and often served as secretaries of the less wealthy employers' associations. They met with business leaders frequently, and they issued guidelines and suggestions to enable employers to meet the unions with a well-informed and reasonably united front. They vigorously recruited the smaller businesses in the colony although the large corporations continued to dominate the organization through their hold on the Board of Management. One of the major successes in 1958 and 1959 was to persuade, through its Rural Management Committee, many of the leading figures in the farming community of the inevitability of rural collective bargaining although the point was not finally driven home to the rank and file until the outbreak of strikes in 1960.

However, all was not smooth sailing between 1957 and 1960, particularly in the relations of R. J. Hillard, the founding president of the A.C.I.E., with Tom Mboya. Hillard resigned at the annual meeting of the F.K.E. in January 1960 and vigorously attacked Mboya and the K.F.L. He opposed a statement of Mboya's favouring political action by the unions. This was nothing new on the part of Mboya as the K.F.L., for instance, had applauded the decision of the African elected members of the Legislative Council to refuse ministries under the Lennox-Boyd constitution until self-government was guaranteed. Hillard said that the F.K.E. might have to advise the government to withdraw recognition from the K.F.L. He also lamented the American pattern of trade unionism which, he argued, would lead to dictatorial practice. He deplored the rise of intimidation, particularly the calling of strikes to attack European or Asian supervisors which he considered a form of racialism. Finally he told the annual meeting that the F.K.E. had tried hard to work with the K.F.L. but with meagre response. This speech voiced many of the fears and resentments of Europeans resident in the colony on the eve of the crucial Lancaster House conference. On the one hand the employers, like most of the white colony, feared the rise of African political power. On the other they had had many difficulties since 1957 in dealing with the new unions with their largely inexperienced leadership which were frequently divided by faction fights, tribal or otherwise. The speech also showed that Hillard was losing touch with political realities, as it was absurd to think that the government would withdraw recognition from the K.F.L. in 1960. The annual meeting then proceeded to adopt a resolution deploring political activity by the unions as well as the tendency to undemocratic methods and to intimidation.[125] Mboya was quick to reply. He considered the speech 'negative and dangerous' combining paternalism and threats, both of which were out-of-date. He found it hard to understand how Hillard, who had tried to put into effect the F.K.E./K.F.L. agreements, could make such a statement, and he insisted that the real need was for positive action to raise the standard of living of the workers. Furthermore he alleged that the F.K.E. was unable to control its own members, citing laggard negotiations as the cause of a recent bus strike and pointing out that the Railway, one of the biggest employers in the colony, had successfully frustrated meaningful negotiations for years.[126]

G. C. Clarke, a director of the Metal Box Company was then elected as president and had to guide the members away from the dangerous shoals created by his precedessor. He was followed by Sir Colin Campbell who led the organization through independence and throughout the nineteen-sixties. Campbell was a perfect spokesman for the major international corporations. He held a large number of directorships including one in Consolidated Holdings which owned the *East African Standard* and was in turn controlled by Lonrho Ltd., one of the most aggressive British companies in Africa in the nineteen-sixties. As soon as it became apparent that Kenya was indeed shortly going to be independent, most of the laggards joined the F.K.E. hoping that the good sense and pragmatism of G. C. Clark, Sir Colin Campbell and David Richmond would see the business community through the perils of the moment. That hope was by no means in vain.[127]

The Flowering of the Trade Unions

Meanwhile Mboya and his allies were exploiting to the full the situation created by the decline of Mau Mau, the return to normalcy and the willingness of the employers collectively to accept modern industrial relations. The consequence of these events and of the demarcation agreement with the A.C.I.E. led over the next few years to a rapid expansion in the number of registered trade unions affiliated with the K.F.L.:

1. Posts and Telecommunications African Workers' Union (1957)
2. Brewing and Bottling Workers' Union (1958)*
3. Kenya Petroleum Oil Workers' Union (1958)
4. Kenya Chemical Workers' Union (1958)
5. Electrical Power Operators' Union (1958)
6. Kenya Dyers, Cleaners and Laundry Workers' Union (1958)
7. Kenya Timber and Furniture Workers' Union (1958)
8. East Africa National Union of Seamen (1958)
9. Kenya Engineering Workers' Union (1959)
10. Tea Plantation Workers' Union (1959)†
11. Kenya Civil Servants' Union (1959)‡
12. Kenya National Union of Teachers (1959)
13. Sisal Plantation Workers' Union (1959)†
14. Kenya Motor Engineering and Allied Workers' Union (1960)
15. Kenya Union of Sugar Plantation Workers (1960)
16. Kenya Shoe and Leather Workers' Union (1960)
17. Kenya Quarry and Mine Workers' Union (1961)
18. General Agricultural Workers' Union (1961)†
19. Tobacco Workers' Union (1961)
20. Kenya Customs Workers' Union (1962)

(The date in brackets is the date of registration)

* Originally the Tobacco, Brewing and Bottling Workers' Union.

† In 1961 the sisal and coffee unions joined to form the Sisal and Coffee Plantation Workers' Union and in 1963 sisal, coffee and tea unions federated to form the Plantation and Agricultural Workers' Union.

‡ Joined the K.F.L. in 1962.

At the same time methods of fee collecting improved somewhat and gradually the employers were persuaded, particularly in the last few years of colonial rule, to accept the check-off in the interest of creating a stable trade union situation. In 1959 the following accounts were submitted by the unions to the Registrar's office:

INCOME OF AFRICAN TRADE UNIONS—31 DEC 1959 (TO THE NEAREST POUND)

Unions	Income £	Expenditure £	Assets £
Typographical Union	269	292	27
Tailors and Textile Workers' Union	7,407	7,398	59
Transport and Allied Workers' Union	1,480	1,274	241
Domestic and Hotel Workers' Union	1,143	1,054	213
Building and Construction Workers' Union	1,478	1,113	500
Distributive and Commercial Workers' Union	1,645	1,100	660
Kenya Local Government Workers' Union	1,935	1,778	785
Railway African Union*	859	881	270
Dockworkers' Union	2,275	2,652	3
Posts and Telecommunications African Workers' Union	885	635	436
Kenya Petroleum Oil Workers' Union	625	590	45

INCOME OF AFRICAN TRADE UNIONS—31 DEC 1959 (TO THE NEAREST POUND) contd.

Unions	Income £	Expenditure £	Assets £
Tobacco, Brewing and Bottling Workers' Union	353	215	188
Kenya Dyers, Cleaners and Laundry Workers' Union	91	66	28
Electrical Power Operators' Union	282	183	251
Kenya Chemical Workers' Union*	190	24	166
East Affica National Union of Seamen	351	381	11
Kenya Timber and Furniture Workers' Union	24	12	12
Tea Plantation Workers' Union	726	255	524
Kenya Engineering Workers' Union	218	167	51
Coffee Plantation Workers' Union	421	102	319
Sisal Plantation Workers' Union	88	—	88

* Information as of 31 Dec. 1958.
It should be noted that some unions functioned before registration.

The finances of the Distributive and Commercial Workers' Union reveal very clearly the advance in revenue around 1957 and the spectacular increase as the check-off became more common in the nearly nineteen-sixties:

Year	Income Shs.	Grants	Subscriptions Shs.
on registration 1953	5,411.10		630.00
1953	222.75		—
1954	5,974.77		5,371.00
1955	3,273.45	440 (K.F.L.)	2,065.00
1956	5,841.48		4,459.00
1957	24,915.34		13,250.00
1958	23,267.87		20,674.00
1959	32,891.85		19,536.85
1960	83,935.27	7.980 (I.C.F.T.U.)	69,584.00
1961	107,759.69	11,831	87,321.00
1962	209,435.08		119,020.00

Other examples of this trend can be seen with the Railway African Union which increased its revenue from Shs. 4,845/63 to Shs. 16,827/94 between 1954 and 1955 and had a further increase from Shs. 16,253/59 in 1961 to Shs. 94,595/29 in 1962, the latter including a grant of Shs. 5,400/- from the International Transport Workers' Federation.
The Petroleum Oil Workers' Union increased its revenue more than sevenfold in four years:[128]

Years	Income Shs.	Fees and subscriptions Shs.	Grants
1958	12,194.30	10,402.00	
1959	12,501.00	12,497.00	
1960	20,682.77	12,243.00	
1961	31,054.85	28,623.00	1,800.00
1962	84,695.65	31,908.00	21,294.75

None of these figures should be taken as exact, but they do reveal the general trend between 1957 and 1963. These funds were normally used to add to the number of officers and organizers on the payroll of the union. Undoubtedly a certain amount of 'brotherization' took place; however, the central offices of a number of the unions, both new and old, gradually became more effective although the management of the branches remained a chronic source of difficulty for most unions. New leaders gradually emerged, men who would play an important role in labour relations over the next decade. Among these were Ochola Mak' Anyengo, one of the founders of the Petroleum Oil Workers' Union and its general secretary for many years, Peter Kibisu, general secretary of the Posts and Telecommunications African Workers' Union and later acting general secretary of the K.F.L., Clement Lubembe, the president of the Distributive and Commercial Workers' Union and later general secretary of the K.F.L. and of its successor C.O.T.U., Walter Ottenyo, who moved from the Petroleum Oil Workers' Union to the Railway African Union and was an officer of the K.F.L., Were D. Ogutu, longtime secretary of the Chemical Workers' Union, and S. J. Kioni of the Kenya National Union of Teachers.

There were, however, many problems involved with the sudden creation of so many unions. Most of the new leaders, along with their opposite numbers in management, were inexperienced. It was one thing to favour modern industrial relations; it was quite another to make them work. One of the first to discover this was Rogers of the East African Tobacco Company. The Tobacco, Brewing and Bottling Workers' Union was formed in 1958 with, in theory, three separate sections. The East African Tobacco Company was almost immediately faced with a strike, which was ended by an agreement to study the various grievances which had emerged during the strike. Negotiations dragged on until 1 June 1959 when the workers went on strike again. It would appear that in the interval between the strikes negotiations to create proper procedures became inextricably tied up with negotiations on particular grievances so that, in fact, very little progress was made on either front. The first sign of trouble was an ultimatum by the union on 16 May. This was followed four days later by an unofficial strike over a foreman which everyone assumed was provoked by the union and then on the 1 June by a strike officially called by the union leadership. The strike was called without a vote as required by the constitution, but nevertheless it was fully effective. The management suspected that Mboya was using the strike to advance the political fortunes of the N.P.C.P. and were furious to discover during the strike that East African Breweries, one of the largest employers organized by the same union, had settled for a Shs. 35/- increase with a bonus of Shs. 20/- without any consultataion with the other employers.

A board of inquiry was set up headed by K. Bechgaard. Mboya, as was frequently the case in such disputes, represented the union. The board recommended that *ad hoc* procedures be adopted to deal with the immediate problems and that the negotiating procedure should then be refined in consultation with the Labour Department so that the responsibility of each level was clear. The board considered, however, that the strike was prompted more by questions of status than of pay, particularly by complaints about racial discrimination and the searching of employees as well as by demands of concern to the permanent employees of the company such as provident funds, leave, monthly payment and the like. The board also thought that there had been insufficient consultation by the two parties with the Labour Department and that such discussions might have prevented the impasse which led to the strike. These events showed that experience was necessary before even one of the more enlightened employers and the union could learn to deal satisfactorily with each other. It also suggested that some of the groupings of workers which had been created in 1958 in order to ensure the viability of the new unions were rather unreal. Eventually the tobacco workers seceded and formed their own organization despite fears in the K.F.L. that this might produce a company union.[129]

There were other employers who were just obdurate. One of these was King, the head of the Kenya Meat Commission who had worked with conspicuous success with Blundell when the latter became Minister for Agriculture to build up the meat industry in Kenya and to secure export markets. But the K.M.C. had little interest in industrial relations or personnel policy and King considered that his entire responsibility was to the meat producers, despite strictures to the contrary by Rogers during the debate when the commission had been set up in 1957.[130] A brief strike in March 1959 was a prelude to the major confrontation of the following year. The K.M.C. dealt with the 1959 strike by dismissing all the workers although it was eventually forced to negotiate with Mboya and Sammy Muhanji, the union's general secretary. The K.M.C. management had nothing but contempt for the Distributive and Commercial Workers' Union and for Muhanji whom they considered to be a scruffy troublemaker and a writer of illiterate letters. But Muhanji was not alone in feeling this contempt; a later report referred to King's 'tactless and extravagant comments' regarding the African employees.[131]

In 1960 the union began organizing workers at the plant at Athi River and provoked a strike which was effective though technically illegal since no union had been recognized. The major complaint was housing, which a commission of inquiry found to be inadequate. It also considered that 'reasonable amenities' were 'sadly lacking'.[132] King insisted on taking complete charge of the strike situation and demanded an inquiry despite the suggestion of the Labour Commissioner that such an action by the K.M.C. might be unwise. But the K.M.C. persisted, the union leapt at the opportunity, and a committee of inquiry was set up chaired by Professor W. C. Rodgers, the head of the faculty of commerce at the Royal Technical College, a faculty not known for its radical politics. The union had the good sense to request Mboya to make their case, and he proceeded, in one of his most brilliant performances by ruthless cross-examination, to demolish the K.M.C.'s position and the arguments of their lawyers. The result was a report which condemned the management for its 'mediaeval approach' and 'absolute irresponsibility' towards labour relations at Athi River. It characterized the K.M.C.'s policy on labour relations as one which '... appears to be dismissal of any individual who becomes a nuisance on union matters and, in the event of a strike, to dismiss the entire labour force'. It suggested that personnel management could no longer be left to retired army officers—a hit at a very common practice in Kenya—and recommended that the K.M.C. appoint a fully qualified specialist.[133] The real sign of the times, however, was the acceptance and support of the report by the editors of the *East African Standard*.[134] But the troubles of the K.M.C. were by no means over; it rejected the Rodgers Report and ignored many of its recommendations.[135] In 1961 the executives of the K.M.C. had a spectacular and public falling out over administration; the government removed King and enforced most of Rodgers' recommendations.[136]

In other state and para-statal enterprises unions and management were groping for new methods of negotiation. In July 1960 the central government established a J.I.C. for the manual and industrial staff with a provision for compulsory arbitration. But elsewhere there were many difficulties. Kenya's 21,500 African teachers, for instance, found themselves in a most disadvantageous position. The central government had prevented for many years the creation of a unified teaching service. It had, however, contributed two-thirds of the cost to L.N.C.s and guaranteed a reasonable parity in teachers' salaries. The councils and the boards of mission and secondary schools remained the legal employers of the teachers. The system began to collapse in the early nineteen-sixties when many African councils found it more and more difficult to collect taxes to pay for their third of the cost of education while the missions were equally hard-pressed financially. The only solution was to fire teachers in large numbers. Furthermore many teachers resented the control of the missionaries and desired a secular state system directly under the control of Africans, which among other matters could abolish the privileges of Europeans and Asians. The colonial government was not prepared to concede such arrangements although it attempted on an *ad hoc* basis to deal with the periodic crises over the staffing of schools, modified somewhat the racial structure, and in 1962 created a free pension paid from the Consolidated Fund. But the teachers had to wait until 1966 for the formation of the long-desired Teachers' Service Commission which began its operations in the following year.

Other unions, particularly those involved in the East Africa High Commission, faced inherited jurisdictional problems. The two most significant of these were the Posts and Telecommunications and the Railway. In 1954 as a consequence of the Lidbury Report, it was decided by the East African governments that salaries for subordinate staff in Posts and Telecommunications would follow the pay structures of the governments in each of the three territories. This meant in practice a veto on the salaries that they could be offered by the administration. It also meant that they would be regulated, like other civil servants' salaries, by periodic commissions of inquiry in the manner of Holmes and Lidbury. However, in 1958 the management created a Joint Staff Council representative of the nine racial unions in the three territories. Within a year the African unions were becoming restive at these arrangements and began to demand direct negotiations. A strike in Tanganyika in 1959 prompted the administration to take the first steps toward creating normal bargaining procedures in each territory early the following year.[137]

This, however, did not prove to be the case with the Railway where there was a series of tumultuous and difficult strikes in 1959 and 1960. The Railway, as we have seen earlier, had for many years run a paternalistic empire remarkably free from major strikes and as a consequence contemptuous of outside advice. However, the Railway African Union had been pressing for a long time for bargaining on an East African rather than a territorial basis since management was organized in this way. These demands began to gather force in the late nineteen-fifties, particularly after the Railway was removed from the scope of the Essential Services Ordinances in Kenya and in Tanganyika in 1958. In 1957 the retiring General Manager, Sir Arthur Kirby, had criticized the failure of the governments involved to develop negotiating procedures on an East African basis, but the only response of management and of government was to inaugurate in the same year an All-Line Joint Staff Advisory Council which was ignored for the most part by the African unions because it was purely advisory. The following year there was a salary award by Judge Abernathy which was rejected by all the African unions, and there were rumours of a strike in Kenya.[139] It was clear that the traditional leadership of the union was under increasing pressure from the rank and file to produce better results for the membership. Management, however, was blind to these developments. Furthermore in the late nineteen-fifties the railway unions began to receive significant attention and financial support from the British T.U.C., the International Transport Workers' Federation (an affiliate of the I.C.F.T.U.) and from the I.C.F.T.U. itself. This in turn led to charges of outside interference and provocation; however, the causes of the strikes to come in 1959 and 1960 were almost entirely indigeneous.

In August 1959 all three African unions withdrew from the Joint Staff Advisory Council. In the following month the leaders met at Mwanza, probably planned the strategy for a strike, christened themselves the National Congress of Railwaymen, and issued a bellicose statement of no confidence in the General Manager of the Railway, Sir James Farquharson. J. B. Ohanga, the new general secretary of the R.A.U. in Kenya said that he had a 'lack of sympathy, bias and a racialist approach'.[140] The three leaders demanded structural reforms so that regional issues would not have to be referred to Nairobi while inter-territorial issues could be negotiated by a central body. However, the speed of Africanization soon became one of the key issues as matters developed in the next few months. But the planning of the union leaders did not prove to be very effective. The strike broke out first in Kenya in November and lasted sixteen days. The workers in Uganda did not strike until shortly afterwards and those in

Tanganyika not until early the following year. As a consequence the management was able to deal with the unions one at a time and to keep the trains running with European and Asian scab labour.

Nevertheless the situation gradually became more intractable. In December the Tanganyika union filed a claim, and at the end of the month the full-time officials of the three unions met once again to co-ordinate their action. Discussion in Tanganyika broke down in January 1960, and the workers went on strike on 9 February. The strike proved to be particularly lengthy, much more so than the authorities had dreamed possible. The workers either secured support from their families or returned to their homelands to subsist for the duration of the strike. Claims but not strikes followed in Kenya and Uganda, and Christopher K. Tumbo, the Tanganyika leader, attacked the Kenyans for not keeping their word regarding strike action.[141] During this period the unions received considerable aid from the I.C.F.T.U., both in terms of assistance in negotiations and direct financial grants. The R.A.U. in Kenya, for instance, received £2,500 from the I.C.F.T.U.

All this made the Railway management extremely bitter. Osgathorpe wrote that 'it does seem to be a tragedy that these Unions, which are really Unions in name only, are to be backed in their attitude of irresponsibility by British and International organization . . . I am quite certain that any support, either moral or financial, from outside organizations to continue this strike in Tanganyika is against the best interest of the workers themselves, and the principles of Trade Unionism. Indeed such support will merely build up an anarchy.'[142] Finally in March 1960 a conciliator proposed a raise of Shs. 10/- and the appointment of an independent inquiry into structures. The union leaders met in March and April. The gravity of the situation can be measured by the presence of Mboya at the first of these meetings and of the I.C.F.T.U. representatives at each of them. The latter meeting authorized the I.C.F.T.U. advisers to mediate officially. The Railway reluctantly accepted the main recommendations of the original conciliator but then decided to apply the award solely to Tanganyika workers. A month later the raise was extended to Uganda and two months later to Kenya—a gesture guaranteed to create the maximum of ill-will. The Railway also appointed M. A. Whitson, a British Ministry of Labour conciliation officer, to conduct an independent inquiry into the industrial relations machinery. As a consequence of his report, a Central Joint Industrial Council was formed in 1962 with an independent chairman and twelve representatives from each side. Territorial councils were also created to deal with territorial matters other than pay and conditions of employment and local staff committees where there were fifty or more employees. However, political events overtook the Whitson Report and ensured that separate unions in the three territories would continue to exist.[143]

One reason for Osgathorpe's bitterness was the violent dissension which plagued the Railway African Union in Kenya during this period. This was not unknown in other unions, but the R.A.U. was one of the more spectacular examples of the disease. In 1959 J. B. Ohanga seized control of the union from Philip Muinde, Hilary Oduol and the traditional leadership of clerks which had been in control throughout the nineteen-fifties. There then followed a bitter struggle for the control of the union in the course of which Ohanga dissipated most, if not all, its funds and seriously compromised the R.A.U. during the critical strike period between November 1959 and April 1960. In January 1960 Oduol and his allies repudiated Ohanga's strike notice, but towards the end of the month Oduol felt it necessary to resign as president of the union as he was powerless to prevent statements being issued under his name without any consultation.[144] At the same time a spate of anonymous letters appeared in the *East African Standard* accusing Ohanga of high living at the expense of the union.[145] Gradually the ousted officials struck back with the assistance of the K.F.L. In August the Nairobi branch voted Ohanga out of office, but he refused to go. At this point the C.I.D. began to probe into the financial affairs of the union. Ohanga's reply to these developments was categorical: 'I am going to remain in the Railway Union office until I die or until the world ends.'[146] In October the K.F.L. suspended both Ohanga and Muinde along with all the executive and seized the union's van. The final confrontation came in November when Ohanga walked out of the K.F.L., threatening to create his own union, the National Union of Railwaymen, but the registrar indicated that he would not approve a second union and that he might also cancel the registration of the R.A.U.[147] All this took place in the glare of publicity which did nothing to inspire confidence in the union. Eventually Ottenyo, one of the officials of the K.F.L., became the new general secretary, and the I.C.F.T.U. gave considerable financial backing to support his leadership because they feared that Mboya's enemies might take over the union.[148]

There were, of course, divisions in other unions as well, and these provided much of the gossip in labour circles in Nairobi during these years. Some were simple struggles for power or just plain opportunism; others reflected ethnic differences. The Emergency had provided the opportunity for the non-Kikuyu to move into the trade union leadership, and one of the most successful groups in this regard were the Baluhya. It was widely assumed that Mboya favoured the Baluhya and hoped to create both a trade union and a political alliance with them even though one of his major rivals, Ochwada, was a member of the same ethnic group. As the Emergency began to fade the old leadership of the unions re-emerged and frequently insisted on restoration to office. One such was Makhan Singh who returned proclaiming his communism. 'I was a Communist and I am a Communist,' he said, 'but my first duty is to Kenya and East Africa.'[149] There was inevitably some friction since few of the incumbents were prepared to move. However, in those trades in which the Kikuyu were much involved such as tailoring, it was inevitable that a Kikuyu leadership would emerge although when it did it involved both the new and the older generation. The Kikuyu were also much involved with two of the newer unions, the Coffee Plantation Workers' Union and the General Agricultural Workers' Union. But most of the detainees were pensioned off with sinecures and were content with that. It would be a mistake, therefore, to think that union leadership between 1956 and 1963 was in a constant turmoil and flux. The records of the registrar in 1963 revealed the following statistics:

Union	No. of years that records kept by Registrar	No. of Gen. Secs.	No. of Presidents	No. of Treasurers
Transport and Allied Workers' Union	11	8	4	8
Domestic and Hotel Workers' Union	12	7	8	8
Distributive and Commercial Workers' Union	11	4	5	7
Dockworkers' Union	9	5	5	7
Kenya Chemcial Workers' Union	5	1	3	3
Kenya Local Government Workers' Union	10	2	3	3
Kenya Engineering Workers' Union	4	1	2	1
Kenya Timber and Furniture Workers' Union	5	2	2	1
Tailors and Textile Workers' Union	13	5	2	4
Electrical Power Operators' Union	5	4	2	4
Post and Telecommunications African Workers' Union	6	4	6	4
Kenya Dyers, Cleaners and Laundry Workers' Union	5	2	4	3
Kenya Quarry and Mine Workers' Union	4	2	2	2
General Agricultural Workers' Union	3	1	2	3
Sisal and Coffee Plantation Workers' Union	2	9	7	7
East Africa National Union of Seamen	5	3	4	4
Railway African Union	11	6	3	6
Kenya Union of Sugar Plantation Workers	3	1	2	3
Tea Plantation Workers' Union	4	3	4	4
Printing and Kindred Trades Workers' Union	11	4	7	7
Kenya Shoe and Leather Workers' Union	3	7	5	2
Petroleum Oil Workers' Union	6	1	4	6
Kenya Motor Engineering and Allied Workers' Union	4	4	2	2
Tobacco Workers' Union	3	3	2	3
Building and Construction Workers' Union	11	9	7	10
Kenya Civil Servants Union	5	3	4	5
Kenya Customs Workers' Union	1	1	1	1
Kenya National Union of Teachers	5	1	3	4

The instability of the Transport and Allied Workers' Union and the Domestic and Hotel Workers' Union can be attributed, in large part, to the difficulties of the Emergency and those in the plantation unions to the peculiar problems of that industry which are discussed below. One or two of the smaller unions, such as the Kenya Shoe and Leather Workers' Union, were the constant prey of adventurers while a few others, such as the Kenya Motor Engineering and Allied Workers' Union seemed incapable of curing internal divisions.[150] Otherwise the table shows a relative stability which is surprising in a period of civil tension and rapid change, and indicates that a professional trade union leadership was emerging in the urban areas.

But what was true of the urban areas did not seem at the time to be the case on the farms and plantations. Here the K.F.L. between 1959 and 1961 scored some of its biggest gains, creating four new unions and enrolling many thousands of workers. But the result seemed to many observers to be chaos and to some Europeans the beginning of a revolution, coming as it did at the time of the decline of the squatter system, as already noted. A few scattered rural unions had existed prior to 1952, but these were mostly based on towns such as Nanyuki or were within commuter range of Nairobi in areas such as Kiambu and Thika. There was some discussion in the K.F.R.T.U. in 1952 and 1953 concerning the creation of an East African Agricultural Workers' Union but this proved to be premature.[151] All such organizations were, however, obliterated by the Emergency. In Thika in 1954 P. E. Walters, the district commissioner, wrote that 'most of the union officials were arrested or detained and the movement has become moribund'; in 1956 Penwill noted the formation of the first union branch in Kiambu since the declaration of the Emergency.[152] The revival of the unions was confined at first to these periurban areas, and strictly agricultural unions were not allowed to make a public appearance until 1957.

During that year the provincial and district administrations began to see signs of the emergence of a union for the plantation and agricultural workers.[153] The K.F.L. had considered such work in 1955, but it did not get off the ground until the P.W.I.F. and the I.C.F.T.U. began to offer some assistance in 1957.[154] In that year the K.F.L. drafted a constitution for the proposed Kenya Plantation Workers' Union. Jay Krane of the I.C.F.T.U. objected to this procedure as it effectively prevented the agricultural workers from having any say in the making of the constitution and gave all real power to a central committee rather than to the delegates' conference. He recommended the pattern adopted in Tanganyika where the general council of the Tanganyika Federation of Labour had set up a small committee to supervise an organizer in the field prior to the creation of a union and the adoption of a constitution. These objections seem to have had some impact, and during that year John B. Abuoga was assigned by the K.F.L. to organize the plantation workers but made little progress.[155] Later that year Tom Bavin, the Director of Organization of the P.W.I.F., visited East Africa, found the A.C.I.E. willing to discuss the possibility of agricultural unions, and recommended starting in the tea industry.

In March 1958 Bavin wrote to Mboya recommending that David Barrett be sent from his work in Tanganyika to assist in the creation of a similar union in Kenya.[156] There was some in-fighting within the K.F.L. about this as Ochwada, the deputy general secretary, hoped to secure this area as a power base for himself. Despite this, Abuoga continued his work and with the assistance of Damerell and the new I.C.F.T.U. representative, Albert Hammerton, drafted a model constitution which met with the approval of the registrar although no formal move for registration was made at that time. Barrett began his work in Kenya, and Ochwada went to the United States on a scholarship. Early in 1959 Jesse Gachago was appointed to organize the plantation workers in conjunction with Barrett and the P.W.I.F.[157] Gachago was a former health inspector in Nakuru where he had also been a member of the K.L.G.W.U. and secretary of the district trades council before becoming organizing secretary of the K.F.L. in January 1959. He was articulate, popular and a Kikuyu—the latter an asset with the Kikuyu coffee and farm workers but a distinct liability in the tea, sisal and sugar plantations.

The Europeans were divided over these developments. The provincial administration considered most of the rural unions ineffective and corrupt. The Nyeri district commissioner described them as '. . . rather shady societies and unions which manage to get themselves registered.'[158] The administration also believed that the unions were trying to take away powers that legitimately belonged to the bureaucracy. 'A further disturbing feature of local trade unionism', wrote the district commissioner in Thika, 'is that these local officials appear to think that they are in a position to usurp the functions of both the Labour Department and the Administration.' They were imposed from the top, he wrote in the cliché of the time, by irresponsible young men stirring up trouble 'where no trouble ever existed before'.[159] Nor were these views particularly secret; Robin Wainwright, the provincial commissioner in the Rift Valley, was quoted in the press in opposition to the unionization of agricultural labourers.[160]

Many individual farmers and plantation managers were equally strongly opposed and became increasingly bitter as the unions started establishing themselves. It was particularly difficult for employers who had, according to their own lights, practiced a humane and reasonable paternalism on their estates to deal with the challenge of the new unions. The tea industry, as has been noted, had a long history of concern for the welfare of its employees. The Kiambu Coffee Growers' Association had levied between 1946 and 1961 a cess on coffee production to pay for certain welfare items for Africans, particularly in the field of medicine. The fund raised £7,500.[161] Many sisal estates had become self-contained communities where the management provided housing, plots of land for growing crops, football equipment and transport to play teams on other estates, monthly films and church buildings. Long-service employees received railway fares for their leaves, and many of the elderly were looked after on the estates. Nor were the tasks in the field especially onerous; the work could usually be done in three or four hours. The new dispensation would require a formalization of these privileges, but, much more disturbing to the Europeans, a sharing of management's power with the local Africans. The manager of the Ridge Estate at Ruiru, for instance wrote to Godwin Wachira, the general secretary of the Coffee Plantation Workers' Union, in August 1960:

> I am sorry but I can find no reason for you to visit this Estate. None of my workers belong to it, and in my opinion there is no need for them to belong to it. We have worked very happily for many years, they are well treated and fairly paid. I am also sorry, but I have laid down the rule that any stranger found on my Estate will be treated as a Trespasser.[162]

The more recalcitrant simply refused to join the employers' associations which they considered feeble, weak and flabby in the face of militant trade unionism. Such a move meant that they were not bound by the agreements. Among the most obdurate were a minority of sisal plantation owners who were, in the view of the district commissioner at Thika '... out of touch with the pace of events in the more politically mature parts of the Colony...'[163]

However, the F.K.E. through its Rural Management Committee, as we have seen, recognized the inevitability of rural unions and persuaded the leaders to accept this although it remained extremely difficult to keep the rank and file in line. 'Nothing on earth', Hilliard warned the farmers at Limuru, 'can stop the march of trade unionism in Kenya...'[164] The K.N.F.U. was one of the strongest supporters of the new policy albeit in a somewhat schizophrenic way. In 1957 it had simultaneously supported demands for the restoration of the *kipande* and given qualified approval to the organization of rural trade unions 'provided the machinery for consultation with employers is fully adequate'.[165] In 1960 its labour committee even recommended the check-off so that the union could be more stable and in order to render unnecessary the type of strike that was solely designed to raise subscriptions. Although this did not receive much immediate response from the members, leaders of the K.N.F.U. such as Lord Delamere, Blundell and Major J. P. Lucas worked closely with Herman Oduor, the founder of the General Agricultural Workers' Union; they considered him to be a responsible and reasonable leader, attributes that would eventually lead to charges which were never proved of honeymoon agreements.[166] By 1962 the K.N.F.U. had created joint consultative machinery at the local and national level; any member suggesting this ten years earlier would have been branded a communist, if not a lunatic.[167]

But the employers also wished to drive a bargain. They wanted to prevent a single union for plantation and farm workers and they wanted to stop any rural minimum wage legislation. They hoped to argue with the government that trade unionism made minimum wage regulation unnecessary.[168] They were temporarily successful on both fronts. An agreement to create separate plantation and agricultural unions was signed by the K.F.L. and the F.K.E. on 25 June 1959, and Hilliard made much of this in his speech at Limuru in October. The major employers were equally determined to negotiate favourable agreements within their particular industries, and they had formidable powers peculiar to the rural situation to strengthen their hand. The most important of these were the draconian regulations governing access to estates which had been an important part of the government's war against Mau Mau and which had not been altered with the end of the Emergency. They also had traditionally greater control of their work force than was customary in the cities. In the tea industry, for instance, which was the first target of the K.F.L., the employers resisted an access agreement for the better part of the year and only signed in March 1960. They wanted to exclude from the recognition agreement all the monthly paid staff as was the case in India, but Mboya insisted that this should apply only to managerial staff with disciplinary powers. On the sisal estates, management, with in this case the support of the Labour Department, hoped to secure higher productivity as a *quid pro quo* for recognizing the union.

The K.F.L. publicly launched a major drive to organize the plantation and agricultural workers late in 1959. This was done in conjunction with the P.W.I.F. and with the assistance of a grant of £1,500 from the I.C.F.T.U.[169] The first three unions were registered in that year—the Tea Plantation Workers' Union, the Coffee Plantation Workers' Union, and the Sisal Plantation Workers' Union. The Kenya Union of Sugar Plantation Workers followed in 1960 and the General Agricultural Workers' Union in 1961.[170] Even the squatters employed by the Forest Department in Kiambu joined the Kenya Civil Servants' Union, and several urban unions, notably the Distributive and Commercial Workers' Union, tried to muscle in to the rural areas but without much success. Rural unions outside the official purview of the Labour Department and of the K.F.L. also made a brief and transitory appearance—unions such as the Nyeri African Workers' Union and the Kenya African Landless Union.[171] By 1961 there were joint industrial councils in the tea, sugar and sisal industries, and such a council was formed for general agriculture the following year. The results were an overall movement toward monthly contracts rather than the ticket system, a parallel movement towards a consolidated wage incorporating housing and all other allowances into one wage payment, and explicit opposition to the squatter system under which it was practically impossible to operate a union.[172]

These were the years when there was a general relaxation of the restrictions on rural life which had characterized the Emergency. The consequence was a flowering both of political parties and of trade unions; nowhere was this more obvious than in the Central province and in the Rift Valley where the lid had been held on the tightest. 'Generally speaking', wrote G. V. H. Grimmett, the district commissioner in Kiambu, 'the rise of Trade Union interest was largely a result of the re-awakening of Kikuyu political consciousness.'[173] The result was an unprecendented number of rural strikes in 1960 including one in the tea industry where 35,134 workers struck from sixteen to nineteen days until the dispute was referred to arbitration, the largest strike in a single industry that the colony had yet experienced.[174] Threats of strikes imperilled the coffee harvest, and wildcat strikes occurred in farms and plantations throughout the Central and Rift Valley provinces. In May 1960 Keeler told Barrett that there had already been forty strikes in the Thika area alone that year and that politics was seriously affecting the trade union situation; the matter was also raised in the Legislative Council where Luyt told the members that there had been thirty-seven strikes in the Thika area involving 11,200 men and concluded by remarking without elaboration: 'I also know unfortunately that there are other reasons that are affecting the outbreak of strikes.'[175]

In such a fluid situation it was not always easy to distinguish a trade union from a political party or even a tribal association since they all used the word 'union'. Grimmett noted this in Kiambu and wrote that '... considerable work had been done by Government officers to try and make this distinction clear'.[176] However, despite the effects of the government, divisions in the leading nationalist party, the Kenya African National Union

(K.A.N.U.) were reflected in the agricultural unions. The Kenya Union of Sugar Plantation Workers, for instance, was strongly influenced by Odinga since that union was centred in Nyanza where his power was paramount. Some of the ex-detainees such as Babu Kamau saw the agricultural unions as a means of securing power in the union movement—a power which was denied the Kikuyu in the urban areas by the Luo and Baluhya establishment in the K.F.L.[177] Also involved was the struggle surrounding the political position of Mboya as Kenya moved toward independence and the older political leaders were gradually released.[178] All this represented a jockeying for power in a confused and uncertain situation.

But other manifestations of the strike situation seriously alarmed the Europeans and the more conservative Africans. The 1960 rash of wildcat strikes at Thika were prompted by Jesse Gachago and directed against headmen who were either loyalists or non-Kikuyu.[179] A similar pattern occurred in Kiambu where unofficial strikers on the coffee estates demanded the dismissal of the headmen and clerks who would not join the union.[180] The same year the resident labour working for the Forest Department in Kiambu held secret meetings and defied government officers.[181] These strikes reflected the waning of European power and were, in part, attacks on those Africans who had associated with European economic development. But above and beyond this, many feared revolution either from the new works councils which were growing up on the estates and which frequently refused to accept any traditional authority either African or European, or from new secret societies such as the *Kiama Kia Muingi* or the Land Freedom Army which the government believed to be the successors of Mau Mau. The *Sunday Post*, for instance considered the coffee strikes at Ruiru, Thika and Mitubiri to be the work of Mau Mau leaders.[182] One coffee estate manager spoke bitterly about these developments:

> My estate is run by three African union officials. They tell my labour when to work, how to work, when to go slow, when to get up in the morning and when to go to bed . . . How would you like to sit in the middle of tens of square miles of coffee with 200 African labourers just following you around with their glares whenever you move about your farm? . . . I tell the labour to clear a field and they just stand and stare. Then one of the union men will swagger over, look me up and down, turn to the waiting labour and, then, depending entirely on how he feels, tell them to get on with the work or else inform me that they can't work unless they get more posho or more pay.[183]

The Minister for Internal Security and Defence, A. C. C. (later Sir Anthony) Swann, spoke on several occasions both inside and outside the Legislative Council about the deteriorating security situation, and referred to '. . . a general spirit of lawlessness and a feeling that it is no longer necessary to observe the law with the coming of freedom . . .' These fears were heightened in the latter part of 1960 by the horrendous stories coming from the Congo. But revolution was contained and orthodox trade unionism triumphed even though European fears continued.[184] One reason for this was the firm action of Mboya in resisting revolutionary chaos and supporting traditional trade union practice; Apolo Owiti, for instance, was sent by the K.F.L. to settle the strikes caused by Gachago in the Thika area.[185] Mboya himself was very active trying to settle the coffee disputes, and when the growers refused the union's wage demands and precipitated a crisis later in 1960, the district commissioner in Thika recorded that 'it is almost certain that no agreement would have been reached, had it not been for the influence exerted by Mr. Tom Mboya'.[186]

The agricultural unions, moreover, faced all the usual problems of such new organizations—how to find competent leaders, how to set up an efficient structure, and how to win the support of the workers. Financial chaos threatened a number of these unions, notably the Coffee Plantation Workers' Union. First of all, it was difficult to collect dues owing to the scattering of the potential membership and to the poverty and suspicion of the rural workers. In 1960 the union claimed 1,586 paid members although it was estimated that 12,000 had joined.[187] Furthermore there were constant allegations of financial mismanagement. It was alleged that the union spent Shs. 150,000/- in one year and was Shs. 30,000/- in debt. In 1960 an officer of the union at Kiambu was convicted of theft, and in the same year the general secretary faced similar charges. The union was finally deregistered in 1961.[188] It was equally difficult to keep track of the activities of other minor union officials scattered over large areas. The G.A.W.U., for instance, although it had secured training for a number of its officials and had good relations with the K.N.F.U., found it necessary to issue public warnings to some of its organizers for violations of the access agreement and for wildcat strikes.[189]

But above and beyond these problems, many of the agricultural unions found themselves at birth in impossible economic circumstances. The sisal plantations, for instance, were unionized just at the time when sisal prices had slumped so seriously that the future of the industry in Kenya was dubious. In 1962 a tribunal found in favour of the employers, mainly owing to low productivity and declining profitability.[190] In the coffee and tea industries, the government was vigorously encouraging smallholder production; by 1968 small farm output had tripled the value of its production at independence and had surpassed that of large farms.[191] Furthermore African farms proved to be much more difficult to unionize than those of Europeans, partly because of size and partly because of the difficulty of determining who were employees and who were members of the family.

Hardest hit by these problems was the General Agricultural Workers' Union. It concentrated on organizing labour on the European mixed farms precisely at the moment when many such farmers were considering leaving the country and were not prepared to spend any more than was necessary on their farms. 'It is perhaps unfortunate', wrote the general secretary, Oduor, 'that the Union should have been born during a political upheaval when everyone tends to be suspicious of everyone else, when faith has been lost on both sides, confidence has dwindled, new investments in the country threatened, and when the older farmers are reluctant to plough back their profits into the land and so open more opportunities for unemployed people.'[192] Moreover by the time the union was registered, the government was converting some European farms to African ownership, mainly on the basis of small holdings.[193] Mervyn Hill argued that such schemes would increase unemployment as agricultural labourers would be dismissed to make way for smallholders; Blundell, the Minister for Agriculture, disagreed, saying that the Board 'will do its utmost to avoid operating in areas where this might happen. It is recognized that the great majority of farm labour are casual workers moving from job to job. Where farm labouring families have been employed for a considerable period on the land to be purchased, the Board will take special steps to settle them within a scheme.'[194] In that same year the G.A.W.U. and the K.N.F.U. reached agreement on a minimum wage: Shs. 55/- with half an acre and Shs. 60/- with no land. It was signed by Lord Delamere and George Kanya, and the low wages faithfully reflected the weakness of the union's position.[195]

These weaknesses together with political and ethnic differences made it very difficult to create one unified structure among the plantation and agricultural workers, even supposing the government and the employers decided to relent in their policy in this regard. It was also rumoured that the K.F.L. leadership was less than enthusiastic over the creation of one union which could have more members than all the others in the federation put together and could rival the K.F.L. itself. The coffee and sisal unions came together only to split in 1960 with an unseemly squabble over the control of finances. They joined again in 1962 in a rather shaky alliance which was recognized by the registrar. During the same year the K.F.L. failed in an attempt to create one union under its control, but in 1963 a loose federation finally emerged with separate sections for each industry. Only the sugar workers refused to join, largely because of the distrust of their leaders for Mboya and the K.F.L. Oduor became the first general secretary; that choice ensured that the new developments would take place within the ambit of the K.F.L.[196]

The Triumph of Mboya

Mboya, himself, was always the centre of controversy, and this became much more marked in the period between the 1960 constitutional conference at Lancaster House and independence. There were a series of plots to dislodge him from the leadership of the federation. These were partly personal as Mboya was contemptuous of the less able among the union leaders and highly suspicious of those who might be capable of taking over from him. The plots and manoeuvring also involved a good deal of jockeying for political position in the aftermath of the Lancaster House discussions, particularly during the formation of the K.A.N.U. in 1960. But this was more than intrigue; it also involved different conceptions of the role of trade unions and the government. Mboya's critics were never very precise. However, they all wished to curtail the influence of the Americans and of the I.C.F.T.U. in the interests of a purely national movement. Some favoured the Tanganyika pattern of state control. Others wished the unions to push for a more militant policy line in regard to nationalization and to foreign policy. It was, perhaps, for many in the trade unions more a question of style and patronage than of substance, but few doubted that a triumph for Odinga would mean substantial changes in the working of industrial relations in Kenya. As a consequence both the role of trade unions and the question of their leadership became key political issues in the next few years.

A caretaker government had been established early in 1960 with a substantial increase in the number of African ministers, including Ronald Ngala as the first African and the first political (as opposed to official) Minister for Labour; it had, however, a mandate only until the first elections to be held under the new constitution which were scheduled for the early part of 1961. K.A.N.U. excluded itself until Kenyatta was released, but there were strong rumours that the government nevertheless had offered Mboya the portfolio of commerce which he had refused.

At the same time investment declined almost to a standstill, the economy stagnated and large amounts of money were transferred to safer quarters outside the colony. The ranks of the unemployed grew along with the number of strikes, thereby increasing the unease in many parts of the country. The 1961 election proved to be inconclusive. The British refused to release Kenyatta and K.A.N.U. in consequence maintained its refusal to join or form a government, even though it was the largest party in the legislature. The shadow of the chaos in the Congo fell over these intrigues and splits in the nationalist movement and magnified both local and British concern. Finally the Kenya African Democratic Union, K.A.N.U.'s rival, formed a government with Ngala at its head and Teita arap Towett as Minister for Labour; K.A.N.U. went into opposition until the release of Kenyatta and his return as the member for Fort Hall in March 1962. With this decision, the confusion and uncertainty in Kenya politics began to ebb. A coalition K.A.D.U.–K.A.N.U. government was formed in 1962, a second constitutional conference was held in London, and the elections of May 1963 swept K.A.N.U. into power and allowed it to guide the colony to independence in December of that year. This period was a testing time for Mboya as both Odinga and Dr. J. G. Kiano led Luo and Kikuyu attacks on him and hoped to drive him from the front ranks of the K.A.N.U. Kenyatta gave covert support to this endeavour until 1965 when he switched his support from Odinga to Mboya. Odinga, however, had moved into the trade union field to try to exploit the differences in the K.F.L. and to undermine Mboya's power base. This in turn led both sides to seek support from the East and West and involved the K.F.L. in the cold war struggle for the control of the trade union movement in Africa. The unrest within the K.F.L. reached a crescendo when Mboya entered the coalition government in 1962 as Minister for Labour.

Ochwada, the head of the Building and Construction Workers' Union and the deputy general secretary of the K.F.L., had been one of the first in the union movement to make a serious move to oust Mboya. He disliked Mboya's involvement in politics, and as a consequence in 1957 Mboya had supported an offer made to him of a scholarship at Harvard to ensure that he would be out of the way. When he returned from the United States, he began a campaign to replace Mboya. He complained to the I.C.F.T.U. about Mboya's political role and his frequent absences from trade union duties. He tried, as we have seen, to secure control of the nascent organizing committee for plantation workers in order to provide himself with a proper base for a formal attack on Mboya's leadership. He promoted but did not sign a petition sharply critical of Mboya, but the K.F.L. chose to vote confidence in their general secretary by a margin of 80 to 15 and to expel six members. Finally in September 1959 Ochwada openly launched an assault on the leadership. This attack, however, failed and Ochwada walked out of the K.F.L. to form a rival federation, the Kenya Trade Union Congress (K.T.U.C.). Ochwada thought that he had the support of six unions, but Mboya's counter-attack was so well organized that only two unions formally supported the K.T.U.C.—Ochwada's own union and the Printing and Kindred Trades Union under Wilson Makuna who some months later returned to the K.F.L. fold.[197] Most of his individual support came from members of his own Baluhya tribe. Typical of the confusion, however, was the decision of Ndungu Marigi first to accept, and then to renounce, the presidency of the K.T.U.C. Ochwada commented that Marigi '. . . chose the position of president himself, and the excuse he gave for withdrawing his support was that his own union would dismiss him if he insisted on joining the T.U.C.'[198] Other leading supporters of the K.T.U.C. were expelled from their unions. The Distributive and Commercial Workers' Union, for instance, dismissed J. J. Mugalla, their branch secretary in Mombasa, when he was appointed assistant secretary of the K.T.U.C.[199] Mboya also successfully attacked Ochwada's own base by detaching the quarry and mine workers, the real core of the Building and Construction Workers' Union, and forming a new and separate union.[200] It was the opinion of the Labour Department that Ochwada's union had always been one of the more ineffective in the colony and that the secession of one of its more important elements turned it into a paper union.[201]

Ochwada then sought support in Eastern Europe and in China and seems to have secured sufficient financial assistance to sustain both the K.T.U.C. and his own union for the next two years. During this period the K.T.U.C. became the springboard for Ochwada's own move into nationalist politics. In March 1960 he assisted in the attempt to form a nationalist party, the Uhuru party, which would have excluded Mboya. Mboya, however, successfully maintained a powerful position in the negotiations and manoeuvring which led to the demise of the Uhuru party and the formation of K.A.N.U. He was elected general secretary of K.A.N.U. and Ochwada became deputy secretary, an uneasy alliance at the best of times. These political deals also brought Ochwada into an explicit alliance with Odinga which became manifest at the latter's famous press conference in January 1961 when he denounced both Mboya and Gichuru.[202]

Such bickering not only fractured K.A.N.U. but had serious repercussions in the K.F.L. The colonial government having transferred the subject of labour to African political initiative, conflict was now to centre around the form that initiative should take and who would direct it. One early result of the bickering was the decision of Akumu to support the ginger group in K.A.N.U. which was critical of Mboya's and Gichuru's promise to pay compensation for land in the White Highlands. Although Mboya persuaded Akumu not to stand and divide the K.A.N.U. vote in Mombasa, these differences set in train a series of events which progressively alienated Akumu from Mboya and was to culminate in the formation of the Kenya Federation of Progressive Trade Unions in 1964 as another serious rival to the K.F.L. A second split opened when Mboya and the K.A.N.U. leadership early in 1961 decided to back their demands for the release of Kenyatta by calling a general strike without first consulting the trade union leadership. Even Mboya's friends were offended by this inept move, and the strike threat collapsed ignominously when it was opposed both by the K.F.L. and by Odinga.

But the most spectacular confrontation occurred with Gideon Mutiso, who had replaced Ochwada as deputy general secretary of the K.F.L., and with Gachago. During 1960 Mboya became increasingly suspicious of Mutiso's and Gachago's politics and had also come to the conclusion that Gachago was more of a menace than an asset in his work with the plantation workers. At the beginning of January 1961 he suspended both of them and launched an inquiry into their activities under Philip Muinde. Mutiso promptly attacked the K.F.L. as being under American influence and the the victim of imperialism. He announced that he would join the K.T.U.C. and that Ochwada was expecting assistance from Ghana in the struggle with the K.F.L.[203] He also plunged into the election campaign and spoke for Mboya's opponent, Dr. Munyua Waiyaki, in the election in Nairobi East where he praised Odinga and referred to Solidarity House as the place where secrets were hatched to sell Kenya to the Americans.[204] Mboya however, buried Waiyaki by a vote of 31,407 to 2,668. Meanwhile Ochwada stood in Nakuru Town as one of the three K.A.N.U. candidates for the two seats. He also suffered a humiliating defeat, losing his deposit and coming at the bottom of the poll behind the former European mayor.

In his campaigning Ochwada had been gradually shifting the public battleground to the struggle surrounding the creation of an all-African trade union federation. Mboya had of course always been prominently associated with the work of the I.C.F.T.U. in Africa; that organization had held its first regional conference on the continent in 1957 and had created, at least on paper, a regional body to represent the affiliated centres in Africa. This regional body operated through area committees, and in 1958 Mboya had become chairman of the East, Central and Southern Africa committee and later an executive member of the I.C.F.T.U. in Brussels. It had been the I.C.F.T.U. which had posted Bury and then Hammerton to Nairobi, and which in 1958 had started the labour courses in Kampala that eventually grew into the I.C.F.T.U. Labour College. This facility fulfilled a long-standing desire of Mboya's and a considerable number of Kenya trade unionists went to the college whose second principal was J. Odero-Jowi, a close associate of Mboya's.[205] Mboya had been grateful for the assistance of the I.C.F.T.U. during the Mau Mau insurrection and afterwards and for its anti-colonial stand.[206] He also found the practical good sense of the individual I.C.F.T.U. representatives in East Africa to his taste, as he was not really at home with political ideologues and theoreticians and considered that radical trade unionists would merely provoke governmental restrictions. Although he favoured the alliance of labour and nationalism particularly in the colonial period, he had made his reputation in the first instance as a trade union leader and he remained concerned that the unions should be reasonably free of state control. He used his influence after independence to prevent the more crude attempts to nationalize the

K.F.L. and tried to work out modalities whereby the state and the K.F.L. and later the Central Organization of Trade Unions (C.O.T.U.) could work together without the former destroying the latter. He always considered, however, that this was a reciprocal arrangement and that the unions had to operate sensibly and moderately, had to make demands based upon facts, and had with independence to search out new ways of serving their members, perhaps along the lines of Histadrut in Israel. If the unions refused, the alternative, he warned, would be more and more state control. To this extent he shared the views of his American and West European allies in the I.C.F.T.U.

However, the I.C.F.T.U. also remained an important source of financial support for the K.F.L. throughout this period as it was still very difficult to persuade the member unions to pay their fees at least until the check-off became fairly common. In late 1959 the K.F.L. was receiving £750 a month from the I.C.F.T.U.[207] The K.F.L. also received money directly from the A.F.L.–C.I.O. through Irving Brown who provided, for instance, Shs. 28,000/- in the early part of 1961.[208] Mboya was not unaware of the anti-communist purposes of the A.F.L.–C.I.O. and of the I.C.F.T.U. and he shared their dislike of eastern totalitarianism. He was prepared to put up with the cruder manifestations of American policy because he believed that he was master in his own house, that the I.C.F.T.U. and the A.F.L.–C.I.O had become over the years more fearful of offending him than the reverse, and that the money was being used to create a viable union movement in Kenya which would one day dispense with all foreign aid. There was always a Machiavellian streak in Mboya—a fact of which his allies in Brussels and Washington were uncomfortably aware. He was also understandably cynical about those who professed to see moral superiority in the funds which came to Odinga from the East.

In December 1958 the All African People's Conference at Accra had passed a resolution favouring an all-African trade union organization. Mboya had been, of course, one of the chairmen of the conference. The I.C.F.T.U. at its regional conference in 1959 supported such a move provided that the individual trade union centres in each country were free to affiliate with international bodies if they so desired. It gradually became clear that the issue of affiliation would become the major point of conflict between the I.C.F.T.U. and the dissident unions led by Ghana. The W.F.T.U. wisely stood aside, at least in public, and supported the activities of the Ghanaians from behind the scenes. Nevertheless Mboya met with John Tettegah of the Ghana T.U.C. in Kenya to try to sort out their differences prior to the founding meeting of the All-African Trade Union Federation (A.A.T.U.F.). They agreed that A.A.T.U.F. should not be affiliated to any international body but that the national trade union centres could if they so wished.[209]

When, however, the A.A.T.U.F. congress was convened at Casablanca in May 1961, this compromise broke down and A.A.T.U.F. went on record as opposing all such affiliations save by the federation itself, thus causing the I.C.F.T.U. unions to walk out. Although Mboya was elected *in absentia* to the executive of A.A.T.U.F., he declined the honour and ensured that the K.F.L. did not accept membership. He considered A.A.T.U.F. to be under the thumb of the Ghanaians, too willing to interfere with national autonomy, and much too closely associated with the W.F.T.U. The I.C.F.T.U. responded to the challenge of A.A.T.U.F. and sponsored the creation of a rival organization, the African Trade Union Confederation (A.T.U.C.) which was founded in Dakar in January 1962. Thus the split between the Casablanca and Monrovia powers was paralleled in the organization of African trade unions, and these unions became publicly and overtly a battleground between Russia and the United States in their search for influence on the African continent.[210] The *Ghanaian Times* called Mboya 'an imperialist stooge, under the thumb of America', and Tettegah declared war on those who opposed A.A.T.U.F.: 'We shall isolate them, break them, enter their countries and form A.A.T.U.F. unions there. It's as simple as that—total war.'[211]

The K.T.U.C. sent Gachago and Minya as delegates to the founding conference of A.A.T.U.F.[212] Meanwhile in Kenya, Mutiso proclaimed that A.A.T.U.F. would give the K.T.U.C. assistance while Vicky Wachira, the K.T.U.C.'s assistant general secretary, attacked the K.F.L. for failing to associate with the new pan-African federation.[213] Although Mboya seemed to have been placed in the difficult position of opposing pan-Africanism, he once again out-manoeuvred his opponents. In July the K.F.L. organized a strike at the Ramogi Press in Kisumu which was controlled by Odinga who replied in the best Victorian manner: 'I shall strongly recommend that the men be dismissed'.[214] The K.F.L. had great fun with this response. Lubembe warned: 'Mr. Odinga has said that he believes in equality and true socialist principles but I do not think he always understands what he shouts about.'[215] Peter Kibisu told Odinga that even the foreigners had to obey the labour laws.[216] But this was a *divertimento.* The end of this phase of the life of the K.T.U.C. (but not of the attacks on Mboya) came in October when Mboya announced that the K.F.L. would honour 20 October, the date of Kenyatta's arrest, as Labour Day. Ochwada denounced this and was trapped as Mboya announced that there would be a rally in Nairobi and that the invited speakers would be Kenyatta, four other Kapenguria defendants, Ngei, Oneko, Kaggia, and Kubai—and himself. For once Mboya had clearly associated himself with the Kenyatta cult to the disadvantage of his opponents. Ochwada gave in and told the rally that the K.T.U.C. would be dissolved although Wachira and others tried to keep it going.[217] The K.L.F. then moved to solidify this new alliance with the old guard by making Fred Kubai the director of organization and by welcoming Makhan Singh back to the fold.[218] In the event neither was to remain a member for very long.

The year 1962 turned out to be one of the most tumultuous in the history of the K.F.L. with Kubai back at the centre of the storm. The number of strikes escalated dramatically from 167 in 1961 to 285; the number of workers involved rose from 26,677 to 132,433 and the number of individual days lost from 120,454 to 745,709. Six years earlier in 1956 there had been only 38 strikes involving 5,713 men with 28,230 days lost.[219] The strikes hit their peak during and immediately after the formation of the coalition government on 7 April 1962 when Mboya became Minister of Labour. A number of different strands can be discerned. Some of the K.F.L. leaders, particularly Peter Kibisu who had become acting general secretary when Mboya entered the cabinet, were beginning to fear the possible domination of the unions by K.A.N.U. through the agency of Mboya who refused to resign his post as general secretary of the K.F.L. Kenyatta, for instance, in June condemned the wave of strikes as did others in K.A.N.U.[220] Kibisu was also fearful of the resurgence of Kikuyu power and was personally and understandably furious with Mboya for denying him the general secretaryship. To the south in Tanganyika there was unmistakable evidence that the new African government was intending to curtail the traditional rights of the Tanganyika Federation of Labour.[221] These fears led to attacks on Mboya personally and to suggestions that the workers might be better served by an independent labour party. Although such a party never actually came into existence, a number of trade union leaders stood as independent candidates for the National Assembly in 1963 when they were roundly defeated.

This pattern was further confused by the persistence of the split between Odinga and Mboya and the continued attempts of Odinga to undercut his rival by eroding his trade union base. Kubai, who had been defeated by Kibisu for the acting general secretaryship by only one vote, eventually succeeded Ochwada as the leader of the dissidents although as late as May 1962 the K.F.L. reported its satisfaction with Kubai to the the I.C.F.T.U.[222] Kubai now, of course, had the prestige of having been Kenyatta's fellow prisoner. He and Kibisu quarrelled bitterly in the latter part of the year and fought each other for control of the K.F.L. The break-away K.T.U.C. continued a rather shadowy existence under Wachira until it was declared illegal by the registrar in November, but not before Kubai had made an attempt to revive it as a vehicle for his attack on Mboya and Kibisu. Kubai and Wachira both received support from A.A.T.U.F. as well as from Odinga while the K.F.L. had as yet evolved no formula for sharing with individual unions the receipts from the check-off system. These events were in turn further complicated by tribal differences. Babu Kamau, for example, was supported by the K.T.U.C. in his attempts to frustrate the merger of the coffee and sisal workers' unions.[223] But his real strength came from the Kikuyu coffee workers who did not wish to see themselves dominated by the Luo sisal cutters. It should not be assumed, however, that all the disputes were motivated by political and sectional interests. Many workers simply saw the period before *uhuru* as the moment when the holders of power were weakening and it might, therefore, be possible to secure sizeable gains by industrial action.[224] Even during the strike wave, Mboya stated that the problems were essentially industrial although he obviously considered that politics had complicated the issues.[225] For instance, one of the major confrontations of that year, the conflict between the Local Government Workers' Union and the Nairobi City Council, had its roots in the traditional and old-fashioned management practices of the city.

The strike in Nairobi had been brewing for some time, the city provoking the final showdown by dismissing some of the union leaders from their jobs. The strike then began on 13 March and quickly spread throughout the city administration. The council alleged that the strike was a violation of the Essential Services Ordinance and was being enforced by the union through intimidation. Gordon Nyawade, the general secretary, and Jacob Ochwino, the organizing secretary were both arrested, the former for violating the ordinance and the latter for intimidation. The arrests further inflamed the situation, and the strike began spreading to other councils in the colony. The K.F.L. leadership threatened to call a general strike despite the opposition of Mboya to this move. At this point K.A.D.U. entered the picture and denounced the idea of such a general strike; the head of the Coast branch of the party, J. J. Mugalla, also attacked the wave of illegal strikes and linked them to K.A.N.U. Later on Ngala made the same allegations.[226] Eventually the interested parties were brought together by the Labour Department, William Lawrence of the P.S.I. and E. K. Welch, the representative of the I.C.F.T.U. who had succeeded Hammerton. A settlement was reached on 27 March, and the workers returned on the 29th. Both Nyawade and Ochwino were acquitted.[227]

But there was a persistent suspicion that the spreading of this strike and the eruption of many others at about the same time reflected an attempt by Odinga and his supporters to bring down Mboya.[228] In March the Kericho branch secretary of the K.F.L. deplored the infiltration of communists and those who were opposed to the K.F.L. into the Tea Plantation Workers' Union. He alleged that the K.F.L. had just recently beaten off an attempt to subvert the Union of Sugar Plantation Workers in Nyanza and that now a similar pattern was developing in Kericho. 'I am against', he said, 'those who run to Communist countries for assistance and then return to oppose the Kenya Federation of Labour.'[229] These allegations were denounced the next day by Kubai, but the tea and sugar unions remained battlegrounds between the factions in the K.F.L. throughout the year.[230]

The war of words escalated in May when Kibisu attacked the lavish spending of Ghana to try to split the K.F.L., and was brought to a head by the impending visit of Tettegah to Kenya. 'We shall treat the visit', said Kibisu, 'as one aimed at intensifying the dirty activities already engaged in by Ghana.' Nor could the K.F.L. which strongly supported trade union freedom, have 'friendship of any degree with governments, people or autocratic Heads of State who do not preach and practice the same principles as ourselves'.[231] A week later Kibisu attacked Odinga over the question of foreign assistance to the unions and alleged that he was receiving vast amounts of money from Russia.[232]

By the beginning of June it was clear that the wave of strikes was receding and Mboya began to assert his own position. He told the unions that he was in favour of self-government in industry but that such a system could only be maintained if neither side abused its freedom. He informed them that the government would not tolerate disorder, industrial strife and indiscipline which would adversely affect the economy and the development programme by giving a poor image overseas; nevertheless he knew full well the problems of the unions and promised to promote a universal check-off to ensure financial stability which would eventually mean that they could forego foreign assistance. He also committed himself to increase the training available to union leaders, to reorganize the industrial relations branch of the ministry to provide more expeditious service, to revise the law so that there could be an industrial relations court, and to create an agricultural wages board for the rural areas.[233]

A week later he turned on Odinga:

> Mr Odinga has said that while he supported the workers, Mr. Mboya and his Ministry were responsible for the workers' grievances.
>
> It is not my intention to descend to this level to seek publicity or to exploit these kinds of incidents . . . I feel that Mr. Odinga has been using and exploiting the workers for his own ends and for political popularity.[234]

At the end of June and the beginning of July Mboya met with the leaders of the K.F.L. and the F.K.E. These meetings were preliminary to the enunciation of a general government policy on labour relations which would take shape later in the year as the Industrial Relations Charter.[235] Mboya also took the opportunity to reiterate his warnings to the unions on a number of occasions during the remainder of the life of the coalition government; furthermore he saw to it that one of his closest allies, Lubembe, was elected to the Executive Board of the I.C.F.T.U.[236]

In the middle of June Kibisu spoke at the annual meeting of the Nyanza branch of the K.F.L. in Kisumu. He attacked Mboya for his threatening language during the strike period and urged that the K.F.L. stand free of the political machinations of ministers of the government.[237] Towards the end of the month Kibisu denied that the strikes were a challenge to Mboya but renewed his charges concerning foreign money, possibly communist, possibly African, designed to overthrow the K.F.L. and agrravated by the rivalry of the politicians in K.A.N.U.[238] Both Lubembe and Mak'Anyengo attacked Kibisu's allegations about communist infiltration, the latter saying that the major problems were unemployment and bickering politicians.[239] Odinga then made a speech at Miwani attacking Kibisu and the K.F.L. He said that Kibisu was like a record playing his master's voice and that the K.F.L. was '. . . being made purely into an imperialist organization, being used by the Americans'. 'There are', he said, 'strikes in the country because the workers have no say in the huge profits that the employers make—although they contribute the labour while the employer only contributes the capital.'[240] Ngala responded by warning of subversion of the unions and claimed that £100,000 had come into the country for this purpose. He quoted Swann, the British colonial service minister in charge of internal security, as saying earlier in the year that £40,000 to £50,000 had been received particularly by one individual, whom everyone assumed to be Odinga.[241] Odinga denied that he was furthering unrest with communist money and claimed that he had been neglecting the unions but would assist if asked.[242] Meanwhile Odinga went to visit Moscow and there were renewed charges that he was pouring money into the sugar workers' union to cause its disaffiliation from the K.F.L.[243]

Then in August came a different turn of events. Seven of the trade union leaders headed by Kibisu attacked no less a person than Kenyatta for 'ugly, irresponsible and destructive' statements at a K.A.N.U. rally. Kenyatta had referred to the issue of foreign money and had described those who were bought as 'insects'. Kibisu demanded to know when Kenyatta would produce a development plan and condemned the calling of the rally without consulting the Nairobi branch of K.A.N.U., which was headed by Mboya.[244] Kibisu returned to the attack a few days later reiterating his demand for a K.A.N.U. economic plan and complaining that Kenyatta had failed to consult with the K.F.L. He also attacked Kiano alleging that his policies as a minister were unimpressive and that he was biased against labour.[245] These were tactical errors of the first magnitude and they eventually cost Kibisu his job. It was, to say the least, foolhardy to attack both Kenyatta and Odinga and to alienate Mboya all at the same time, and there was an immediate but unsuccessful counter-attack the next day when fourteen trade unionists demanded Kibisu's resignation.[246]

On 25 August Kibisu and his associates met to consider whether the K.F.L. should create an independent labour party, a project which had been under consideration for some time. In February the *East African Standard* had printed a story from its reporter in London that the labour leaders were considering contesting the next election; the story quoted Akumu as demanding that the European farms should be sequestered and that the government should adopt collectivism on the Israeli model.[247] Akumu and some of the trade union leaders had gone to London in order to try to persuade the government to allow them to participate in the second constitutional conference as trade union delegates. This had been refused, and one of Akumu's arch-rivals in Mombasa, Juma Boy, was quoted as saying that Mboya would represent all the workers as general secretary of the K.F.L. In April the K.F.L. had formally discussed the role of Mboya in the federation, eventually deciding to allow him to retain the general secretaryship with an unpaid leave of absence and to make Kibisu the acting general secretary. During the wave of strikes, several union leaders had attacked Mboya's moderation. One was Ottenyo who resented the refusal of the Ministry of Labour to accept a dispute in which the R.A.U. wished to press for immediate Africanization of all posts on the Railway.[248] There was talk of 'rubber stamps' of the government and the like; one letter to the *East African Standard* stated that: 'Hearsay has it that the present trade union movement in Kenya is allowing itself to be run from the Government Secretariat.'[249]

Kibisu was clearly fed up with the K.A.N.U. leadership and desired an independent party. However, the others wavered. The key figure was probably Mak'Anyengo who would not commit himself other than to say 'the time has come when we should watch vigilantly all political parties'. There then followed parallel meetings of the K.F.L. and of the K.A.N.U. leaders. Although Mboya publicly opposed the creation of an independent labour party, he used that explicit threat to sustain his position in K.A.N.U. against those who wished to purge him. After he had won the battle in K.A.N.U., he urged the K.F.L. to abandon the idea of creating such a party. There were also rumours that Kibisu was really in league with K.A.D.U. which undermined his credibility, particularly since there were indications that K.A.D.U. was thinking of forming regional trade unions.[250] In the end the K.F.L. opposed the creation of a labour party and chose instead to recommend a watchdog political committee with Mak'Anyengo as chairman. Mak'Anyengo in turn stated that the K.F.L. would be neutral in politics and condemned 'malicious and fabricated' stories about the possibility of K.F.L. support for a labour party.[251] On 29 August Akumu also spoke of the neutrality of the K.F.L., denied that there was any split and referred to Kibisu's remarks on Kenyatta as 'personal'. Many of the trade unionists, however, considered that they had been used by Mboya in this struggle and had been made scapegoats. This further alienated them from his political leadership.[252]

The last few months of the year saw yet another round in the struggle within the K.F.L. In late August the registrar asked the K.T.U.C. to furnish proof of its existence or be dissolved. The congress could only allege support from the Building and Construction Workers' Union and the National Seamen's Union and a number of branches within other unions.[253] In the same month members of a K.A.N.U. mission in Cairo claimed at a press conference that the I.C.F.T.U. was sending a mission to try to oust Kubai from the K.F.L. Kubai had spent some time abroad that summer; he had been given leave by the K.F.L. to attend the World Muslim Conference in Cairo but had, in fact, gone with Odinga to the World Peace Conference in Moscow and spent three months in Eastern Europe. When he returned in late August, he challenged Kibisu to answer for his 'disastrous stewardship' of the K.F.L. He demanded that Kibisu apologize to Kenyatta and to Tettegah, particularly since both Tettegah and Ghana deserved credit for leadership in the pan-African movement. Finally he alleged that there was a plot to oust him from the K.F.L.; he also decided to use the K.T.U.C. as the major vehicle for his attack.[254]

The same day the *East African Standard* published a very detailed article by Colin Gibson describing the alleged tactics by which the K.T.U.C. hoped to break the K.F.L. by causing the disaffiliation of its constituent members. Kubai had to secure control of at least two unions in order to ensure registration for the K.T.U.C. According to Gibson, this plan was to be financed by £20,000 from Ghana and East Europe and to start in the Nyanza and Coast provinces in the sugar, tea and dockworkers' unions. He alleged that in Nyanza Otieno Oloo, a close friend of Odinga's and a graduate of Leipzig was organizing the campaign. Gibson claimed that Oloo was assisted by three paid organizers with loudspeaker vans, including the chairman of the Central Nyanza branch of the K.A.N.U. Youth Wing. He also alleged that Msanifu Kombo had been approached to head the movement on the Coast and that Kubai would become general secretary of the congress.[255] Finally he stated that Wachira was in Cairo after having received training in Ghana.

In early September Kubai denied that he had received money while in the socialist countries and reiterated his attack on Kibisu.[256] There then followed a series of demands by minor K.F.L. officials for Kubai's resignation.[257] Kubai issued a broadsheet, *Kubai na K.F.L.: Mwito Kwa Wafanyi Kazi*, denouncing the I.C.F.T.U. in the strongest terms, attacking the K.F.L. for its decision to seek outside support in 1952, and favouring neutrality. He reiterated his charges in a speech at Kericho later in the month and alleged that the K.F.L. had received £1,500 from the I.C.F.T.U. with strings attached.[258] Then at the beginning of October he announced that he would open his own office to assist the workers without I.C.F.T.U. support.[259] More and more it became clear that Kubai was associating with the

K.T.U.C. even though he did not resign from the K.F.L. The battle raged through October and November and convulsed some half dozen unions.[260]

The K.T.U.C. made a fresh application for registration in October, and the allegations and counter-allegations continued unabated.[261] The registrar finally refused registration in late November; Kubai then declared total war on the K.F.L.[262]

But it was already too late. Mboya had seized the initiative through the Industrial Relations Charter. The K.F.L. met on 1 and 2 December and passed a radically left-wing policy statement advocating sweeping nationalization and collective farming, thereby undermining some of the appeal of the K.T.U.C.[263] It would also appear that Kenyatta put pressure on Kubai to cease and desist in return for a K.A.N.U. nomination. The first few months of 1963, in fact, saw a great increase in the discipline and efficiency of K.A.N.U. and a strengthening of Kenyatta's leadership in preparation for the election in May. The K.F.L. leadership made one last attempt to intervene directly. On 9 February 1963 the Executive Committee decided to sponsor its own labour candidates but it was talked out of this by Mboya at the end of the month.[264] K.A.N.U. swept to power by a large majority and became, therefore, the party to guide Kenya to independence. Mboya was returned in Nairobi Central by 16,084 to 8,049, Odero-Jowi in Lambwe in Nyanza Province by 20,222 to 13,495, Kubai in Nakuru East by 32,675 to 10,169 and Lubembe to the Senate for Nairobi by 68,798 to 35,110; all were official K.A.N.U. candidates. Kibisu, Akumu and Nyawade all ran as independents in Vihiga, Mombasa South and Nairobi East and were defeated receiving respectively 5,809, 212 and 21 votes. The defeat in Vihiga spelled the end of Kibisu's career in the K.F.L.; he resigned in July and took a post with the Shell Company. Lubembe took over and then defeated Akumu 148 to 125 for the general secretaryship which Mboya had finally decided to relinquish. Kubai and Odero-Jowi both became parliamentary secretaries to the Ministry of Labour, the one neutralizing the other.

But the constant bickering and divisions between 1961 and 1963 had certainly seriously handicapped the K.F.L. One casualty of the incessant political manoeuvring was the K.F.L. newspaper, *Mfanyi Kazi: Sauti Ya K.F.L.* The K.F.L. had long wished to have its own newspaper, and eventually in 1962 James Karebe made arrangements with West German and American sources to finance such an endeavour.[265] The idea was to donate a printing press to the K.F.L. with the understanding that it would be used for union and for some commercial printing as well as for the new weekly newspaper, *Mfanyi Kazi*, thus hopefully breaking even. Initially an American and an African were appointed editors, but eventually the latter, Said Kadhi, became solely responsible. The paper started on 30 May 1962. But the business side was not well managed; it was difficult to attract advertising and the control of sales was haphazard. Furthermore Kibisu used the newspaper as a vehicle for his attacks on Kenyatta.[266] The financial difficulties led to a series of complicated negotiations involving Mboya and the original founders in the United States and West Germany. The consequence was the sale of the machinery to the East African Institute of Social and

Cultural Affairs where it was used to produce, among other things, the *East Africa Journal*. *Mfanyi Kazi* then ceased to exist.[267]

The newspaper was not the only failure of the K.F.L. Mboya had seen it as one of a number of enterprises which the K.F.L. might sponsor, thus giving it a new rationale and deflecting it from a disastrous concentration on urban wages and on politics. An agreement was signed with Histadrut to create a joint development corporation which would establish consumers' co-operatives and a construction company. One shop, the Kenbir Trading Company Limited, was opened in Nairobi. These enterprises, however, suffered a fate similar to *Mfanyi Kazi*. The K.F.L. possessed neither the managerial skills nor the desire to make them work.[268]

However, the real beneficiary of the divisions and weakness within the K.F.L. leadership and within that of its enemies was paradoxically Tom Mboya. As Minister for Labour, he had first to weather the wave of strikes in the early part of 1962. None of his rivals, neither Ochwada, Odinga nor Kubai were able to establish a significant foothold in the labour movement for any period of time. As soon as it was clear that he was going to be able to control the situation in 1962, he moved to formalize his view of trade union operations in Kenya. He resisted the attempts of his colleagues in K.A.N.U. to ban the unions or to nationalize them on the Tanganyika pattern. 'I believe', he told Swedish trade unionists, 'in a free trade union movement and I believe that this freedom should be retained after independence has been gained.' 'On the other hand', he continued, 'I do not believe that our trade unions must necessarily be copies of the trade union movements in other countries. We must create organizations which are suited to the situation as it is in Africa'.[269]

As we have seen, he met with the K.F.L. and F.K.E. leadership in late June to start work on solutions for the widespread industrial unrest of the previous few months. He chaired a joint meeting in early July which agreed in principle to create an industrial relations charter. Ogutu, Kubai and Makhan Singh were among the representatives of the K.F.L. Discussions continued and a further meeting on 15 October 1962 ratified the document. The Industrial Relations Charter received a great deal of publicity, much of it well-intentioned but misguided. Although Mboya and others claimed that it was a novel African way of dealing with labour relations, it was really a restatement of the Fabian views of Mboya, a development of the traditional position of the Labour Department and a codification of existing practice. It set down a model recognition agreement and proposed guidelines for the actions of employers and of unions, including statements on intimidation and publicity. It dealt with the check-off which eventually became sufficiently universal for the K.F.L. to end its formal dependence on the I.C.F.T.U. in 1965. It guaranteed the right to strike but it set down procedures for handling disputes including the Joint Disputes Commission created in 1961 to which the parties could voluntarily refer disputes if negotiations broke down in a particular industry. The Joint Disputes Commission became the Industrial Court in 1964. The purpose of both the commission and of the court was to enforce a style of industrial relations whereby a premium would be put on orderly and rational discussion of the issues within the existing free enterprise system. It also provided a means of restraining wage demands by the unions and of preventing them from taking up political issues, although this latter was more effectively formalized with the creation of C.O.T.U. to replace the K.F.L. in 1965. The real significance, therefore, of the Industrial Relations Charter was not its novelty but its non-revolutionary symbolism, for it clearly indicated the triumph of Mboya's views on industrial relations in Kenya—a system which was to continue with only minor modifications for the next decade.[270]

NOTES

1. *1950 Annual Report, Labour Department*; Amsden, ii. By 1953 the rates had risen as follows:

Town	Monthly minimum	Housing allowance payable if no housing supplied
	Shs.	Shs.
Nairobi	52.50	7.00
Mombasa	54.75	8.25
Nakuru	50.00	7.00
Nyeri	51.00	5.00
Thika	50.50	5.00
Nanyuki	51.50	7.00
Eldoret	49.00	8.00
Kitale	51.00	6.00
Kisumu	47.00	5.00

2. *The Pattern of Income and Consumption of African Labourers in Nairobi, October-November 1950*, 1951.
3. Carpenter Report.
4. Dow Commission Report; articles by Fenner Brockway, *Daily Herald*, 17–20 Nov 1952; see also Amsden, ii.
5. *Report of the Cost of Living Commission*, 1950.
6. *Kenya Gazette*, 11 July 1950.
7. These inspectors were to provide many of the first full African labour officers in the next decade.
8. The Tailoring, Garment-Making and Associated Trades Wages Council (Establishment) Order, *Kenya Gazette*, 17 June 1952; the Wages Regulation (Tailoring, Garment-making and Associated Trades) Order, *ibid.*, 31 March 1953; the Wages Regulation (Soft Furnishings) Order, *ibid.*, 23 June 1953; the Wages Regulation (Bespoke Tailoring for Men and Boys) Order, *ibid.*, 23 June 1953 and subsequent orders.
9. *Kenya Gazette*, 8 June 1954, 29 March 1955.
10. The Transport and Road Haulage Wages Council (Establishment) Order, *ibid.*, 5 May 1953 and subsequent amendments; the Wages Regulation (Road Passenger Transport and Road Haulage) Order, *ibid.*, 2 Feb 1954 and subsequent orders; the Hotel and Catering Trades Wages Council (Establishment) Order, *ibid.*, 7 Sept 1954; the Wages Regulation (Hotel and Catering Trades) Order, *ibid.*, 6 Sept 1955 and subsequent orders.
11. Blundell, 120, claims that the appointment of this committee was the result of the initiative of European elected M.L.C.s, but the origins were in fact much earlier. It is possible that the colonial officials allowed the initiative to appear to lie with Blundell in 1953 for political reasons. The terms of reference covered the most suitable terms of employment to provide industry and efficiency, the calculation of wage-levels and the possibility of extending minimum wage legislation beyond the towns.

12. The full membership of the committee was Carpenter as chairman, E. J. Petrie (Treasury Secretary), J. H. Symonds, Lieut.-Col. C. V. Merritt, Harry Thuku, Solomon Adagala, Chanan Singh, S. Duckett, J. L. Claridge, and F. T. Holden. J. G. Njoroge served briefly prior to departure overseas.
    Chanan Singh in a note of protest objected to the Eurocentric style of the final report.
13. *1950 Annual Report, Labour Department.*
14. *Ibid.*
15. See also R. Millner, 'Unions by Kind Permission', *Daily Worker*, 28 Apr 1952.
16. Carpenter Report.
17. The committee's report, on the basis of Nov 1952 figures, noted 434,739 Africans at work of which 101,568 were in government service, and of which 351,568 were men, 40,354 women and 42,817 children. In respect of turnover 48 per cent of labour in Nairobi and 40 per cent in Mombasa worked for less than a year at a time and many workers only survived the first month of work by borrowing money, often thus placing themselves in a recurrent monthly cycle of debt.
18. This reduced aim was however not achieved, the government in 1959 stating that economic conditions precluded attainment. The rates proclaimed for 1 Jan 1960, the end of the five-year period, were:

	Male employees aged 21 and over		Other employees	
	Basic minimum	*Minimum housing allowance*	*Basic minimum*	*Minimum housing allowance*
	Shs.cts.	Shs.cts.	Shs.cts.	Shs.cts.
Eldoret	92.00	22.50	71.00	12.00
Kisumu	94.00	18.50	71.00	10.00
Kitale	88.00	18.50	68.00	10.00
Mombasa	93.50	27.00	71.00	15.00
Nairobi	95.00	24.50	73.00	13.00
Nakuru	93.00	21.50	71.00	12.00
Nyeri	87.50	22.50	67.00	12.00
Thika	94.00	22.50	72.00	12.00
Nanyuki	91.00	22.50	70.00	12.00

19. *Sessional Paper No. 21 of 1954.*
20. Carpenter Report, minority report by F. T. Holden.
21. *Report of the Commission on the Civil Service of the East African Territories and the East African High Commission*, 1954 (hereafter Lidbury Commission Report).
22. Some of these officials had, in fact, been placed exceptionally on the B (or Asian) scales and a very few, including Ndisi, on the A (or European) scales. The Labour Department under Carpenter had set a lead in these arrangements.
23. Lidbury Commission Report.
24. In relation to actual salaries, Lidbury generally accepted Holmes's scales but revised them according to the increase in the cost of living: 1939—base, Nov 1947—165, Dec 1953—237. In the case of the large number of subordinate employees, Lidbury opted for higher wages, higher productivity and a reduction in numbers.
25. The negotiations with the civil service over the Lidbury Report had provided the newly formed Central Whitley Council (on the staff side of which sat four representatives from each of the three racial civil service associations) with valuable experience. Although in general each association had particular points to press for its own members, each also supported the others' arguments. The Kenya government had proposed to backdate the increased awards by the commision to 1 July 1954, a date six months later than that agreed by the Uganda and Tanganyika governments. At the end of the negotiations the

entire staff side of Kenya's Central Whitley Council walked out in protest; the government armed with this evidence of unity in dissatisfaction was unable to persuade those ministers who had opposed 1 Jan 1954 that the earlier date would be necessary. The issue provided fuel for the later arguments over civil service arbitration procedures.

26. L. B. Greaves, *Carey Francis of Kenya*, 1969, 130–4.
27. T. J. Mboya, *Freedom and After*, 1963, 19–22.
28. Report of the I.C.F.T.U. Delegation to Egypt, the Sudan and East Africa, 13 March 1952, mimeo.
29. Interviews W. Hood, Marjorie Nicholson 1960; T. J. Mboya 1960 *et seq.*; B. C. Roberts, *Labour in the Tropical Territories of the Commonwealth*, 1964, vi. One reason for the T.U.C.'s conservative stance was the unfavourable impression created by certain college-educated Far Eastern trade unionists with keen political ambitions which they hoped to achieve by manipulation of the trade union movement.
30. W. Hood, Memorandum on the Kenya Trade Union Bill, mimeo. Fabian Society papers.
31. Report of the I.C.F.T.U. Delegation to Egypt, the Sudan and East Africa, 13 March 1952, mimeo.
32. T. J .Mboya, *Freedom and After*, 29, 35, 256–61.
33. Jay Krane of the I.C.F.T.U. Brussels office considered that Bury was much too close to Mboya, and that he should maintain neutrality in the quarrel between Mboya and Minya.
34. J. Bury, Report to the I.C.F.T.U. for the period January 1954 to October 1954.
35. Hood to Marjorie Nicholson, 10 Sept 1953 enclosing notes on Kenya and Gold Coast trade unions prepared for the T.U.C. (hereafter Kenya Trade Union Notes, 1953). Fabian Society papers.
36. The Kenya African Civil Servants' Association was faced with the difficulty that both its president, John Muchura, and its secretary, Luke Musiga, were officials of the Labour Department.
37. *Kenya Debates*, 14 Oct 1954, 2 June 1955.
38. Mboya to J. H. Oldenbroek, general secretary of the I.C.F.T.U., 15 June 1954.
38. K.R.F.T.U. Newsletter No. 6, 16 March 1955, mimeo.
40. See *infra*, pp. 725–6; J. Bury, Report to the I.C.F.T.U. for the period January 1954 to October 1954; J. Bury, Report of a Safari to the Rift Valley, Central province and Nyanza province, 1954.
41. W. Hood, Kenya Trade Union Notes, 1953.
42. Quoted in Mboya to Oldenbroek, Aug 1954.
43. Arthur Aggrey Ochwada, *qui vivit*. Educated Maseno, Advanced Management Course Harvard University 1958; K.A.R. Burma campaign 1943–6; general secretary E.A.F.B.C.W.U.; deputy general secretary K.F.L. 1955–9; general secretary K.T.U.C. 1959–61; I.C.F.T.U. executive board 1957; deputy general secretary K.A.N.U. 1960; M.N.A. 1963; vice-president Industrial Court 1964–7.
44. K.F.L. Newsletter, 23 June 1955, mimeo; Mboya to Krane, 29 June 1955; T. J. Mboya, Report on Uganda Visit, 7–20 July 1955; K.F.L. Newsletter, 25 July 1955, mimeo.
45. K.F.L. Newsletter, 9 Aug 1955. In Beira Mboya was shown plans of new housing by the Portuguese authorities, but when he went on a stroll to examine African housing for himself he was taken into custody. After explanations and apologies he was released.
46. Interview W. Hood, 1960.
47. Report of the I.C.F.T.U. Mission to Kenya, July-Aug 1953, mimeo.
48. The assistant industrial relations officer also reported that in Mombasa in 1957–8: Shs. 1,500/- was missing from the Distributive and Commercial Workers' Union, Shs. 1,600/- from the Building and Construction Workers' Union, Shs. 500/- from the Mombasa Trades Council and Shs. 240/- from the Domestic and Hotel Workers' Union, while the general secretary of the Shoemakers Workmen's Union had absconded with all the books and ledgers.

None of the unions were prosecuted. Report of the I.C.F.T.U. Mission to East and Central Africa, March–Apr 1958, mimeo.

49. Report on the Northern Rhodesia, Southern Rhodesia, and Kenya, T.U.C., 1954, mimeo.
50. Mboya to Oldenbroek, 28 Sept 1954.
51. K.F.R.T.U. Policy Statement, 1955.
52. F. D. Corfield, *op. cit.*; in interviews in 1960 Daniel Ngethe denied any connection with Mau Mau other than support for its political aims while Aggrey Minya, a Mluhya, claimed to have been an active participant.
53. See for instance the K.F.R.T.U. resolutions on home rents and on the rise in prices, 1955, mimeo; K.F.R.T.U. Policy Statement, 1955, mimeo.
54. T. J. Mboya, Statement on the New Surrender Terms, n.d., mimeo.
55. Mboya to Oldenbroek, 15 June 1954.
56. *Sunday Post*, 14 Feb 1954.
57. Mboya to Oldenbroek, Aug 1954.
58. K.F.R.T.U. Newsletter, No. 5, mimeo.
59. Bury tried and failed to secure compensation for Njanga and also failed to secure an inquiry, even though Njanga was clearly an innocent bystander.
60. Mboya to Oldenbroek, 15 June 1954.
61. On the introduction of the Lyttelton Constitution in 1954 the Member for Labour became the Minister; the portfolio still included Education. Stow held the Ministry while Hartwell acted as Chief Secretary in 1954–5. The portfolio remained in official hands until 1960, the Ministers being W. (later Sir Walter) Coutts from 1956 to 1958 and W. A. C. Mathieson, a Whitehall Colonial Office (as opposed to Colonial Service) official from 1958 to 1960. After Hartwell's departure and the arrival of Luyt, policy initiative in general reverted to the department. Other names occasionally appear as Member or Minister for Labour in gazette notices; these represent acting appointments while the substantive office-holder was on leave.
62. Mboya to Oldenbroek, 15 June, Aug, 1954.
63. *E.A.S.*, 2, 4 Sept 1954.
64. Government Press Office Handout No. 1126, mimeo.
65. W. Hood, Kenya Trade Union Notes, 1953.
66. Mboya to Marjorie Nicholson, 20 Jan 1955. Fabian Society papers; *Report to the Secretary of State for the Colonies by the Parliamentary Delegation to Kenya*, Cmd. 9081 of 1954, which supported urban and agricultural trade unionism and the family minimum wage.
67. T. J. Mboya, press release, 27 July 1955. The resolutions were modified under pressure from the British T.U.C. but a protest was made, *Report of the Fourth World Congress, I.C.F.T.U., 20–28 May 1955*, 1955, 417, 423–4.
68. See *infra*, p. 769.
69. *Report and Recommendations of a Board of Inquiry appointed by the Minister to inquire into a trade dispute between the Kenya Local Government Workers' Union and the Nairobi City Council*, 1955.
70. *Ibid.*
71. *Ibid.*; Government Press Office Handout No. 523.
72. This section is based on the *1947–62 Annual Reports, Labour Department*; 1951–9 Annual Reports, General Manager, Landing and Shipping Company; interviews J. D. Akumu, T. J. Mboya, G. R. Williams, 1960 *et seq.*; K. D. Harrap, S. T. Omar, J. Bury, 1960; an unpublished manuscript by J. Bury.
73. For instance, the Oldham batteries which powered the fork-lifts mysteriously ceased to operate long before they should have needed recharging.
74. The Employment (Casual Labour) Rules, *Kenya Gazette*, 28 Dec 1949.
75. The cargoes specified were clinker, cement, Magadi soda and coal.
76. J.I.C. Minutes, 26 Jan 1955.
77. *Ibid.*, 24 Feb 1955.
78. The union members of the J.I.C. were Juma Mohammed, Kadenga Mulewa, S. T. Omar, Kombo Mohammed, Francis Owoko Nyapola. J.I.C. Minutes, 1 March 1955.
79. *Mombasa Times*, 7 March 1955, editorial critical of the employers' leaflet.

80. J.I.C. Minutes, 5 March 1955.
81. *Mombasa Times*, 7 March 1955.
82. Minutes of an *ad hoc* meeting, 7 March 1955; minutes of a meeting of the employers' representatives and the newly elected employees' representatives, 7 March 1955; minutes of an extraordinary meeting of the newly constituted Dockworkers J.I.C., 7, 8 March 1955. Three old members of the J.I.C. were members of the strike committee: Kombo Mohammed, Kadege Mulewa, Juma Mohammed. The new members were: Hilfrid H. Stephens, Oyugi Nyabute Opotson, Japhet Ngoloson, J. M. Musebi, Adbulrahmani bin Hassani, Jesse Ph Mbima. See also K.F.R.T.U. Newsletter No. 6, 16 March 1955, mimeo, for the position of the K.F.R.T.U.
83. *Mombasa Times*, 8, 9 March 1955.
84. Memorandum for Submission to the Arbitration Tribunal appointed in the terms of the Essential Service (Arbitration) Ordinance in connection with an industrial dispute at Mombasa.
85. K.F.R.T.U. Newsletter No 8, Apr 1955, mimeo.
86. Mboya to Oldenbroek, 27 May 1955.
87. 11 Jan over shift hours; 1 Feb the watch and ward staff over the rotating day off and a demand for a forty-five hour week; 20 June over the dismissal of an African clerk. For the 1957 arbitration see *Kenya Gazette*, 3 Dec 1957. The members were E. A. J. Edmonds, R. G. Ngala, and C. W. Hamley.
88. James Denis Akumu, *qui vivit*. Educated Onjiko Secondary School, Central Nyanza 1947–9, Aggrey Memorial High School, Uganda 1950–2, Medical Training School, Nairobi 1952–4; lab. technician East African Breweries 1955–7; district organizer K.L.G.W.U. 1957; chairman K.F.L. Coast province 1958; secretary-general Dockworkers' Union 1958–63; asst. national general secretary K.F.L. 1963; general secretary P.C.W.U. 1965; deputy general secretary C.O.T.U. 1965; founder member People's Convention Party 1957; director of organization African Workers' Congress 1964–5; general secretary C.O.T.U. 1969.
89. *1959 Annual Report, Labour Department.*
90. *Report of a Board of Inquiry*, 13 Apr 1959; *1959 Annual Report, Labour Department.*
91. *Kenya Debates*, 16 Feb 1956.
92. *Ibid.*, 14 Oct 1954, 2 June, 21 Oct 1955, 16, 23, 28 Feb, 5 June, 18 July 1956; *Observer*, 4 March 1956; see also Conservative Commonwealth Council, 'The Future of Trade Unions in East Africa', 1955, mimeo.
93. *Kenya Debates*, 23 Feb 1956.
94. *Ibid.*, 14, 28 Feb 1956, and *Africa Digest* Dec 1972, letter from Marjorie Nicholson; there were some rumbles from the authorities in 1960 but these were meant for effect rather than action; the Trade Union (Amendment) Ordinance, Ord 11 of 1956, *Kenya Gazette*, 27 March 1956; see also the Regulation of Wages and Conditions of Employment (Amendment) Ordinance, Ord 34 of 1956, *ibid.*, 28 Aug 1956.
95. T. J. Mboya, *Freedom and After*, 74–98; T. J. Mboya, 'Turning Point in Kenya,' *The Progressive*, Oct 1957.
96. R. Sandbrook, 'Patrons, Clients and the Unions: The Labour Movement and Political Conflict in Kenya', *Journal of Commonwealth Political Studies*, March 1972; see also *Time*, 7 March 1960.
97. In 1958 at its greatest extent in the colonial period the department's establishment consisted of the Labour Commissioner, Deputy Labour Commissioner, two Assistant Labour Commissioners, six Senior Labour Officers, thirty-five Labour Officers, three Resident Labour Inspectors, six Senior Labour Inspectors, twelve Labour Inspectors, eleven Wages Inspectors, the Industrial Relations Officer and four Assistants, a Specialist Medical Officer, a Registrar of Workmen's Compensation, a Trade Testing staff of seven officers and a T.W.I. officer. Almost all posts were filled. Apart from one Labour Officer (Ndisi) Africans at this time were limited to the Labour and Wages Inspectorate and the Industrial Relations and Factories Assistants. Only in 1961 was serious provision made for the training of Africans for Labour Officer and more senior posts.

In 1959 9.716 full inspections, 3,976 partial inspections and 11,213 visits were carried out at the 12,000 places of employment (exclusive of domestic staff) known to the department.

98. *1955–63 Annual Reports, Labour Department*; some illustrative examples of the type of accident dealt with by the Factories Inspectorate appear in the 1955 report.
99. *Ibid.*
100. *1953 Annual Report, Labour Department*; Dolton Report, 1957; in 1954 the figure was 39,700 of whom 83 per cent were in government service.
101. *1956 Annual Report, Labour Department.*
102. *Report on the Government's Eighteen Point Statement of Policy: Achievements and Future Policy*, 1956.
103. Dolton Report, 1957.
104. *Kenya Debates*, 22 May 1958.
105. *1954–63 Annual Reports, Labour Department*; *E.A.S.*, 15 March 1961; A National Provident Fund was announced in 1964. *E.A.S.*, 8 June 1964.
106. The Employment of Women, Young Persons and Children (Amendment) Ordinance, Ord 12 of 1956, *Kenya Gazette*, 27 March 1956; see also the Employment of Juveniles (Hours of Work and Welfare) Rules, *ibid.*, 10 June 1952. In 1958 the number of African children (i.e. under 16) at work was officially 40,485. Thereafter the numbers declined for a variety of reasons of which adult unemployment was the most important. In 1962 only 14,056 were at work, almost all seasonally in agriculture but these figures did not include park boys and others working casually but unofficially in the cities. See J. G. Nderitu, 'The Problem of Kenya's Youth', *Kenya Weekly News*, 21 Apr 1961. For a fictional account of the terrors of casual juvenile employment, see W. Mativo, 'The Park Boy', *East Africa Journal*, Sept 1967.
107. The Industrial Training Ordinance, Ord 48 of 1959, *Kenya Gazette*, 17 Nov 1959; *E.A.S.*, 11, 12 May 1960; see also the Trade Testing Rules, 1951, *Kenya Gazette*, 8 Jan 1952.
108. *1952–63 Annual Reports, Labour Department.*
109. *Report of the Committee of Review into the Kenya Institute of Administration*, 1965; *Kenya Weekly News*, 13 Jan, 20 Oct 1961.
110. *1958–63 Annual Reports, Labour Department.*
111. *1959–63 Annual Reports, Labour Department*; for a hostile view of this vocational training as being too British and of aptitude as being South African and too hastily conceived, see J. Anderson, *The Struggle for the School*, 80.
112. *1958–63 Annual Reports, Central Housing Board*; L. M. Bloomberg and C. Abrams, *United Nations Mission to Kenya on Housing*, 1965.
113. The Road Transport Wages Council (Establishment) Order, *Kenya Gazette*, 30 Nov 1954, 26 Nov 1957; the Motor Engineering Trades Wages Council (Establishment) Order, 1955, ibid., 3 Jan 1956; the Bakery, Flour, Confectionary and Biscuit Making Trades Wages Council (Establishment) Order, 1955, *ibid.*, 3 Jan 1956; for the wages orders in 1958 see *ibid.*, 28 Jan, 29 Apr 1958; the Laundry, Cleaning and Dyeing Trades Wages Council (Establishment) Order, *ibid.*, 6 Dec 1960; the Knitting Mills Wages Council (Establishment) Order, *ibid.*, 11 Sept 1962; the Regulation of Wages (Footwear Industry Wages Council Establishment) Order, *ibid.*, 5 March 1963; the Regulation of Wages (Wholesale and Retail Distributive Trades Wages Council Establishment) Order, *ibid.*, 18 June 1963.
114. Minutes of the meeting of Ministers for Labour in Kenya, Uganda and Tanganyika held at Kampala on 20 Aug 1962, mimeo; *E.A.S.*, 22, 23, 24 Aug 1962; see also 'This is Our Stand', K.F.L., 1960, mimeo; Minutes of the Tripartite Labour Conference held in Dar es Salaam on 15 and 16 Nov 1962, mimeo; *E.A.S.*, 14 Nov 1962.

The urban minimum wage continued to be increased to meet rising food and housing prices, and four new towns were covered from 1 Jan 1962. At independence in December 1963 the rates had risen to:

	Male employees aged 21 years and over		Other employees	
	Basic minimum wage per month Shs.cts.	*Minimum housing allowance* Shs.cts.	*Basic minimum wage per month* Shs.cts.	*Minimum housing allowance* Shs.cts.
Nairobi	115.00	35.00	79.00	17.00
Mombasa	115.00	35.00	79.00	17.00
Eldoret	109.00	26.00	75.00	13.00
Kericho	109.00	36.00	75.00	13.00
Kisumu	109.00	30.00	75.00	15.00
Kitale	109.00	30.00	75.00	15.00
Machakos	109.00	30.00	75.00	15.00
Naivaisha	109.00	30.00	75.00	15.00
Nakuru	109.00	26.00	75.00	13.00
Nanyuki	109.00	26.00	75.00	13.00
Nyeri	109.00	26.00	75.00	13.00
Thika	109.00	26.00	75.00	13.00
Thomson's Falls	109.00	26.00	75.00	13.00

1963 Annual Report, Ministry of Labour and Social Services

115. *Kenya Debates*, 14 July 1962. See also A. G. Dalgleish, *Survey of Unemployment*, 1960; *Sessional Paper No. 10 of 1959/60*; *Kenya Debates*, 17 Nov, 11 Dec 1959, 26, 31 May, 16, 20, 21 Dec 1960, 17 July 1962; W. Elkan, 'Urban Unemployment in East African', *International Affairs*, July 1970.

In the E.A. Statistical Department's *Reported Employment and Wages in Kenya 1948–1960*, 1961, 560,882 Africans were reported to be in employment on 30 June 1960 of which 503,000 were estimated to be adult males. In the private sector the largest number were 263,275 reported in employment in non-African agriculture. Other large numbers were wholesale and retail trade 22,808, building and construction 18,234 and as in the past domestic service 24,952. The total for the private sector was 420,179. The total in the public sector was 140,703 of which 88,001 were employed by the government and 21,870 by the Railway. The estimated annual wage bill for African employees was £38,302,000 of which £23,931,000 came from the private sector. The African population at this date was between 6¾ and 7 million. These figures probably represent the peak of the colonial economic structure.

116. *Kenya Debates*, 26, 31 May 1960. A man convicted of armed robbery, Mwangi Karanja, provided a graphic illustration of the reasons for this move when he told the court that '. . . if I don't get employment when I come out I will do it again . . . it is the Europeans who made me do this. They eat and sleep in good beds.' 'Security and Unemployment', *Kenya Weekly News*, 28 July 1961; 'The Spectre of Kenya's Unemployment', *ibid.*, 3 Feb 1961.
117. *1964 Annual Report, Labour Department.*
118. Interviews senior labour officers and trade union leaders, Mombasa, 1960, 1963, 1964. A labour inspector in Mombasa was charged with receiving £5 from an employer as an inducement not to lay a charge, and with corruptly soliciting £5 for the same purpose. *E.A.S.*, 66 Apr 1961.
119. The technical services were much slower to Africanize and suffered a shortage of personnel in the early sixties as a consequence.
120. Minutes of the Management Committee, Nairobi Chamber of Commerce, 11 Sept 1949, mimeo.
121. F.K.E., Memorandum on the Essential Services (Arbitration) Ordinance from the Employers' Point of View, 1958, mimeo, quoted in Amsden, 72.
122. Amsden, 64–6; K.F.L. Circular Letter, 30 Sept 1957, mimeo.
123. Statement of the K.F.L. to the Colonial Secretary, 17 Sept 1957.
124. *Kenya Debates*, 3 Dec 1958; the Essential Services (Arbitration) (Amendment) Ordinance, Ord 48 of 1958, *Kenya Gazette*, 23 Dec 1958; see also the Essential Services Ordinance, Ord 22 of 1963, *ibid.*, 27 Aug 1963 which increased penalties for violations.

125. *E.A.S.*, 9 Jan 1960.
126. *Ibid.*, 13, 15 Jan 1960.
127. Amsden, ii, iii; D. Richmond, 'Looking Inside an Employers' Federation', *East Africa Journal*, Aug 1964.
128. Files of the Registrar of Trade Unions. In 1964 the annual reports of the Labour Department began listing the revenues and expenditures of trade unions. See also C. K. Lubembe, *The Inside Labour Movement in Kenya*, 1968, 177 for contributions to C.O.T.U.
129. *Report of a Board of Inquiry Concerning a Strike in the East Africa Tobacco Company Ltd.*, 1959 interviews personnel manager, East African Tobacco Co. Ltd., 1960, L. Obo, general secretary T.B.B.W.U. 1960; *Sunday Post*, 14, 21 June 1959; for formation of the new union, *E.A.S.*, 7 June 1960.
130. *Kenya Debates*, 24 Apr 1957.
131. *Report of the Commission of Inquiry into the Administration and the Staff Relations of the Kenya Meat Commission*, 1961; *Kenya Gazette*, 14 March 1961—the members were T. A. Dennison, R. E. Luyt, and E. T. Jones.
132. *Ibid.*
133. *Report of a Board of Inquiry appointed to Inquire into a Trade Dispute at the Athi River Premises of the Kenya Meat Commission*, 1960 (hereafter Rodgers Report); *Kenya Gazette*, 21 June 1960—the other two members were R. G. Datoo and C. S. Kabetu; submission of S. Muhanji to the board of inquiry, 1960, mimeo.
134. *E.A.S.*, 30 Aug 1960; for a contrary view see A. Moor, 'Whipping Boy of the Athi River Strike', *Kenya Weekly News*, 9 Sept 1960; *Kenya Debates*, 16 June 1960; report of S. Muhanji to the annual meeting K.D. and C.W.U., 1960, mimeo.
135. For the rejection, see *E.A.S.*, 1 Sept 1960.
136. *Report of the Commission of Inquiry into the Administration and Staff Relations of the Kenya Meat Commission*, 1961; *Sessional Paper No. 7 of 1961*; *Kenya Debates*, 5 Dec 1961; interviews J. I. Husband, W. R. C. Keeler, W. C. Rodgers, T. J. Mboya, S. Muhanji, 1960.
157. Mboya to Barrett, 26 March 1959. The Plantation Workers' International master-General, 21 Jan 1960, mimeo; memorandum submitted to the East African Salaries Commission by the Posts and Telecommunications African Workers' Union, Kenya, 9 Aug 1960; *Report of the Commission on the Public Services of the East African Territories and the East Africa High Commission*, 1960 (hereafter Flemming Report); H. A. Whitson, Report on Industrial Relations with the East African Posts and Telecommunications Administration, n.d., mimeo; interview acting establishments officer E.A.P. and T., 1960; interviews P. Kibisu, 1960, 1963; *E.A.S.*, 25, 28, 29 Dec 1959, 9 14 Apr 1960.
138. The Railway was never scheduled as an essential service in Uganda.
139. *Sunday Post,* 23 March 1958.
140. *Ibid.*, 15 Nov 1959.
141. *E.A.S.*, 9 Feb 1960.
142. R. W. Osgathorpe, unpublished document concerning the I.C.F.T.U. and the I.T.F., 1960.
143. R. Scott, *The Development of Trade Unions in Uganda*; C. K. Lubembe, *op. cit.*; *Sunday Post*, 15, 22, 29 Nov, 20 Dec 1959; *ICFTU Information Bulletin*, 1 Dec 1959, 1–15 March, 1–15 Apr, 1, 15 May, 1, 15 June, 15 Sept 1960; Osgathorpe to W. J. P. Webber (Transport Salaried Staff Association U.K.), 5, 27 Apr 1960; I.C.F.T.U. memorandum, 27 Apr 1962.
144. *E.A.S.*, 23, 28 Jan 1960.
145. *Ibid.*, 14, 16 Jan 1960.
146. *Daily Nation*, 28 Aug, 20 Oct 1960.
147. *Mombasa Times*, 31 Oct 1960; *E.A.S.*, 7 Nov 1960.
148. Mboya to C. Millard, 19 Feb 1960; K.F.L. Press Statement: Railway African Union, Nov 1960, mimeo; interviews T. J. Mboya 1960 *et seq.*, W. Ottenyo, 1963.
149. *E.A.S.*, 24 Oct 1961.

150. *Report of a Board of Inquiry appointed to inquire into the relations between the Kenya Motor Engineering and Allied Workers' Union and the Motor Trades and Allied Industries Employers' Association*, 1962.
151. Report of the I.C.F.T.U. Mission to Kenya, July–Aug 1952, mimeo.
152. 1954 Annual Report, Thika District; 1956 Annual Report, Kiambu District.
153. 1957 Annual Report, Central province; 1957 Annual Report, Kiambu District; 1957 Annual Report, Thika District.
154. J. H. Gaya, Report on Plantation Research Kenya, K.F.L., 1955, mimeo. Gaya wrote that 'the hostility of the plantation employers towards Trade Unionism requires no elaboration' and forecast difficulties of access.
155. K.F.L. Circular Letter, 5 May 1957.
156. Bavin to Mboya, 5 March 1958; *ICFTU Information Bulletin*, 1 Dec 1957, 15 March 1958 announcing the appointment of Barrett as an organizer in Kenya, Uganda and Tanganyika.
157. Mboya to Barrett, 26 March 1959. The Plantation Workers' International Federation (P.W.I.F.) merged with the International Landworkers' Federation (I.L.W.) to form the International Federation of Plantation, Agricultural and Allied Workers (I.F.P.A.A.W.) on 1 Jan 1960.
158. 1961 Annual Report, Nyeri District.
159. 1959 Annual Report, Thika District.
160. *Sunday Post*, 28 June 1959.
161. *Kenya Weekly News*, 14 Apr 1961. Its last act was to erect a plaque to Senior Chief Waruhiu at the Kiambu District Hospital.
162. Manager Ridge Estate, Ruiru to Wachira, 25 Aug 1960. C.P.W.U. papers.
163. 1960 Annual Report, Thika District.
164. *Sunday Post*, 18 Oct, 1 May 1959.
165. 1957–8 Annual Report, K.N.F.U.
166. K.N.F.U. Circular, 21 Apr 1960; undated circular, 1960, mimeo; 'Trade Unions and Agriculture', *Kenya Farmer*, July 1960.

    Herman A Oduor, *qui vivit*. Educated Ambire School and Siriba College as veterinary assistant; assistant to veterinary surgeon for three years; farm manager for four years; founder of General Agricultural Workers' Union 1961; first general secretary Plantation and Agricultural Workers' Union 1963; labour officer, Labour Department 1965; member Labour Advisory Board, Kenya Economic and Development Planning Commission, Commerce and Industry Advisory Board; studied trade unionism in West Germany.
167. *1961–2 Annual Report, K.N.F.U.*
168. K.N.F.U. Circular, 21 Apr 1960, mimeo.
169. *Coffee Plantation Worker*, Feb 1960; announcement by T. J. Mboya, *Sunday Post*, 29 Nov 1959.
170. *1959–61 Annual Reports, Labour Department.*
171. 1958 Annual Report, Nyeri District; 1961 Annual Report, Fort Hall District.
172. 1961 Mid-Year Report, G.A.W.U., mimeo.
173. 1960 Annual Report, Kiambu District.
174. *1960 Annual Report, Labour Department*; *Report of the Tea Dispute Arbitration Tribunal in the matter of a dispute between the Kericho branch of the Kenya Tea Growers' Association and the Tea Plantation Workers' Union*, 1960 (Nihill Award); *Kenya Gazette*, 4 Oct 1960.
175. Kenya Debates, 6 May 1960. Interviews T. J. Mboya, 1960 et seq., J. Gachago, 1960.
176. 1960 Annual Report, Kiambu District.
177. Interview B. Kamau, 1960. Kamau flirted with the K.T.U.C. but eventually became general secretary of the Sisal and Coffee Plantation Workers' Union in association with the K.F.L.
178. For further details, see *infra*, pp. 803–27.
179. 1960 Annual Report. Thika District.

    Jesse Mwangi Gachago, *qui vivit*. Educated Government African School, Kagumo and Kahuria Intermediate School; qualified as public health inspector 1952, employed Nakuru municipality; I.C.F.T.U. course Accra 1955; national organizing secretary K.F.L. 1958; helped form K.T.U.C. 1961; representative

I.F.P.A.A.W. East Africa; secretary Kenya African National Traders and Farmers Union; K.A.N.U. M.N.A. 1963; Assistant Minister for Education 1964; Assistant Minister Lands and Settlements 1965.

180. 1960 Annual Report, Kiambu District.
181. *Ibid.*
182. *Sunday Post*, 24 Apr 1960.
183. *Ibid.*, 27 March 1960.
184. *Kenya Debates*, 5 May 1960. See also 'Security and Unemployment', *Kenya Weekly News*, 28 July 1961; statements of A. C. C. Swann and H. H. Mainprice, Assistant Superintendent of Police, *ibid.*, 3 Feb 1961.
185. 1960 Annual Report, Thika District.
186. *Ibid.*; the Coffee Growers' Association signed an agreement concerning wages and conditions of service with the C.P.W.U. in January, an agreement which was to run for thirteen months. Kenya Coffee Growers' Association, circular 17, 18 Jan 1961.
187. *1961 Annual Report, Labour Department*; 1960 Annual Report, Kiambu District.
188. 1961 Annual Report, Nyeri District; 1960 Annual Report, Kiambu District; *1961 Annual Report, Labour Department.*
189. *Kenya Weekly News*, 6 Jan 1961 concerning an unofficial strike at White Rock Farm.
190. *Report of the Board of Inquiry into the Wages of Workers employed in manual occupations pertaining to the growing of sisal and the manufacture of sisal fibre and the arrangements existing within the sisal plantation industry for determining wages and other conditions of employment by voluntary collective bargaining and agreement*, 1962 (Matthews Award); *Kenya Gazette*, 20 Feb 1962.
191. G. K. Helleiner, 'Agricultural Development Plans in Kenya and Tanzania, 1969–1974', *Rural Africana*, 13 (1971).
192. H. A. Oduor, 'Aims of the Farm Workers' Union', *Kenya Weekly News*, 19 Aug 1960.
193. 'Splitting up the Kenya Highlands', *ibid.*, 20 Jan 1961.
194. *Ibid.*, 15, 22 Sept 1961.
195. *Ibid.*, 20 Jan, 24 Feb 1961; 1960 Annual Report, Rift Valley Province; 1961 Annual Report, Labour Officer, Kiambu.
196. *E.A.S.*, 27 Aug 1963.
197. *Ibid.*, 28 Sept 1959; 'The formation of K.T.U.C. was unnecessary and it was motivated by jealousy, personal animosities and its struggle for power because Mr. Ochwada was dismissed from the Deputy General Secretaryship of the K.F.L.'. J. G. Nderitu, 'The Kenya Trade Unions', *Kenya Weekly News*, 31 March 1961.
198. *E.A.S.*, 3 Oct 1959.
199. *Ibid.*
200. The Kenya Quarry and Mine Workers' Union, which was registered in 1961.
201. This view was reflected in the decision to inaugurate a wages council for the industry in 1960. The Labour Department held that the union, and Ochwada himself, represented small contractors rather than employed labour, and that a few of these small contractors were actually employers themselves.
202. G. Bennett and C. G. Rosberg, *The Kenyatta Election: Kenya 1960–1961*, 1961, 37–40, 132.
203. *E.A.S.*, 2 Jan 1961; for Akumu see E. Rodwell, 'The Coast Africans and the Elections', *Kenya Weekly News*, 3 Feb 1961; for a latter statement by Akumu of his position, see *E.A.S.*, 27 May 1963. A previous attempt to use the strike weapon for direct political purposes in 1960 had also failed. See R. Sandbrook, *op cit.*; *E.A.S.*, 14, 15, 16, 18 Apr 1960; *Kenya Weekly News*, 3 Feb 1961.
204. *E.A.S.*, 6 Feb 1961.
205. *Free Labour World*, Oct 1964.
206. T. J. Mboya, *Freedom and After*, 256–61.
207. Millard to Mboya, 25 Sept 1959; I. Davies, *African Trade Unions*, 1966, 212 states that this had become £12,000 a year by 1962. R. Sandbrook, *op. cit.*,

states that in 1963–4 the total amount was £12,600 paid at Shs. 21,000/- per month.

208. Auditor's Report, 24 May 1961. The A.F.L.–C.I.O. had maintained a separate presence in Africa for a number of years through its Department of International Affairs headed by Jay Lovestone. The department expressed the militantly anti-communist views of George Meany. In 1957 the A.F.L.–C.I.O. refused to contribute to the I.C.F.T.U. International Solidarity Fund and in 1960 Meany once again refused to make the American contribution which came to $220,000 because of insufficient urgency on the part of the I.C.F.T.U. in the fight against communism and because of his dislike for O. Becu, the general secretary. As a consequence more money was available for direct grants from the United States. An open rift within the I.C.F.T.U. was to follow in March 1965. I. Davies, *op. cit.*, ix; *Observer*, 18 Dec 1960; *A.F.L.–C.I.O. News*, 10, 17, 24 Dec 1955. For the C.I.A. see *New York Times*, Jan-Apr 1967.

209. Joint Declaration on behalf of the Ghana T.U.C. and the K.F.L., 21 Nov 1960, mimeo; see also 'A Joint Declaration on behalf of the T.U.C. of Nigeria and the K.F.L.', 22 Nov 1960, mimeo; *E.A.S.*, 19, 22 Nov 1960. At the K.F.L. annual meeting, the federation stated its belief in independent trade unions, the autonomy of each country in relation to affiliation, non-alignment and 'occasional or regular Pan-African trade union conferences . . .' [with] a loose organisation to co-ordinate . . .'
K.F.L. Press Statement, June 1960. 'This is Our Stand', K.F.L., 1960, mimeo.

210. D. Nelkin, *Pan-African Trade Union Organization*, Cornell Reprint Series, 1967; I. Davies, *op. cit.*, ix.

211. *West Africa*, 10 June 1961 quoted in Nelkin, 45.

212. *E.A.S.*, 27 May 1961.

213. *Ibid.*, 27 May, 25 July 1961.

214. *Ibid.*, 7 July 1961.

215. *Ibid.*, 8 July 1961.

216. *Ibid.*, 12 July 1961.

217. *Ibid.*, 21 Oct 1961.

218. *Ibid.*, 2 Dec, 1 Nov 1961. Kubai had become a member of M.R.A. and had spoken at an M.R.A. rally in Brazil. *Ibid.*, 9 Dec 1961.

219. *1956, 1961–2 Annual Reports, Labour Department.*

220. *E.A.S.*, 13 June 1962.

221. See for instance editorials in *Mfanyi Kazi*, 22 Aug, 21 Nov 1962, 9 Jan 1963.

222. 'Review of the Trade Union Situation in Kenya', K.F.L., May 1962, mimeo; Ochwada was arrested in July on eleven charges of forgery and theft in connection with his union and convicted in October on all counts and sentenced to fourteen months' imprisonment. *E.A.S.*, 27 July, 28, 29 Aug, 15, 22 Sept, 22 Oct 1962; R. Sandbrook, *op. cit.*

223. *E.A.S.*, 19 June 1962.

224. See for instance the agitation for a *uhuru* bonus in late 1963 which brought a major confrontation between the unions and Kenyatta's government when the latter flatly refused to pay it. *Reporter* (Kenya), 12 Oct, 2, 9, 16 Nov 1963.

225. *E.A.S.*, 9 June 1962; interview T. J. Mboya, 1963.

226. *E.A.S.*, 22 Mach, 7, 8 June 1962.

227. 'A Strike in Nairobi', *Free Labour World*, June 1962.

228. See for instance articles in *E.A.S.*, 22 June, 28 Aug 1962.

229. *Ibid.*, 12 March 1962.

230. *Ibid.*, 13 March 1962. See also statement by Ben Opar Mboya, *ibid.*

231. *Ibid.*, 8 May 1962.

232. *Ibid.*, 16 May 1962.

233. Speech at Solidarity House, *ibid.*, 2 June 1962.

234. *Ibid.*, 9 June 1962.

235. *Ibid.*, 29 June, 4, 6, 12, 16 July 1962.

236. See for instance *ibid.*, 19 July, 20 Oct 1962; *ICFTU Information Bulletin*, 15 July-1 Aug, report of the Berlin conference of the I.C.F.T.U.

237. *E.A.S.*, 18 June 1962.

238. *Ibid.*, 23 June 1962.
239. *Ibid.*, 26 June 1962.
240. *Ibid.*, 26 June 1962.
241. *Ibid.*, 27 June 1962.
242. *Ibid.*, 29 June 1962. See also attacks on Odinga by M. Muliro, *ibid.*, 30 June 1962, W. Odede, *ibid.*, 16 July 1962.
243. See statements by J. O. Anyango, president of the union, *ibid.*, 5 July 1962 and B. Opar Mboya, *ibid.*, 23 July 1962.
244. *Ibid.*, 16 Aug 1962.
245. *Ibid.*, 20 Aug 1962.
246. *Ibid.*, 21 Aug 1962.
247. *Ibid.*, 1 Feb 1962.
248. *Ibid.*, 2 June 1962.
249. Letter from M. D. Odinga, *ibid.*, 18 June 1962.
250. For Mak'Anyengo see *ibid.*, 24 Aug 1962; for K.A.D.U. see *ICFTU Information Bulletin*, 15 Apr 1962. K.A.D.U. did not oppose Kibisu when he stood for election in Vihinga in 1963.
251. *E.A.S.*, 27 Aug 1962.
252. *Ibid.*, 30 Aug 1962; R. Sandbrook, *op. cit.*
253. *E.A.S.*, 21 Aug 1962.
254. *Ibid.*, 28 Aug 1962.
255. Kombo later became mayor of Mombasa.
256. *E.A.S.*, 8 Sept 1962.
257. *Ibid.*, 10, 11 Sept 1962.
258. *Ibid.*, 24 Sept 1962.
259. *Ibid.*, 2 Oct 1962.
260. The Tea Plantation Workers' Union, Union of Sugar Plantation Workers, the Quarry and Mine Workers' Union, the Motor Engineering Workers' Union, the Dyers, Cleaners and Laundries Workers' Union, and the Transport and Allied Workers' Union.
261. *E.A.S.*, 4 Oct 1962.
262. *Ibid.*, 26, 27 Nov 1962.
263. K.F.L. Press Release, 3 Dec 1962.
264. C. Sanger and J. Nottingham, 'The Kenya General Election of 1963', *Journal of Modern African Studies*, II 1 (1964); Sandbrook, *op. cit.* At the same time Makhan Singh was expelled from the Printing and Kindred Trades Union on the grounds that he was an employer. *E.A.S.*, 11 Dec 1962. See also 'A Man in the Shadows', *Daily Nation*, 22 July 1963.
265. International Feature Services, Peace with Freedom, and World-Wide Partnership; *E.A.S.*, 31 May 1962.
266. See, for instance, *Mfanyi Kazi*, 22 Aug 1962.
267. Lubembe, 150–3.
268. *Daily Nation, E.A.S.*, 2 July 1963; *International Federation of Building Workers Bulletin*, Apr 1962. Some Africans were opposed. See the statement of the Kenya African National Traders' and Farmers' Union, *E.A.S.*, 21 Aug 1962. A similar development but with government initiative took place in Tanganyika.
269. T. J. Mboya, 'Africa Today and Tomorrow', *International Transport Workers Journal*, XXII, 2 (Feb 1962).
270. *1962 Annual Report, Labour Department*; T. J. Mboya. *Freedom and After*, x, appendix; Lubembe, 162–9; *I.C.F.T.U. Economic and Social Bulletin*, xi, 1 (1963).

CONCLUSION

Colonial Kenya, then, was a period of some sixty-five years during which a region of Eastern Africa, peopled by African communities of very different origins and hitherto living on a largely subsistence economy, underwent traumatic economic development through the imposition of a structure of capital, property-ownership and labour. Development by peasant production was judged to be impracticable and it was at work for foreign farmers and businessmen that black men came to think of themselves firstly as Africans and then later as Kenyans. The majority of the consequences of this structure have been examined in the preceding chapters, but a few are best viewed from the perspective of the colonial period as a whole.

It is premature finally to pronounce on whether the experience of work for an alien master, in a town or on a farm, had as a consequence the increase or the reduction of the sense of tribal identity. Although new loyalties of class and occupation began to appear, Kenya's migrant labourers did not lose sight of themselves as members of their original ethnic group; indeed at the end of the colonial period it seemed that these traditional loyalties had been considerably strengthened. At work men, and if they were accompanied their families also, wished to communicate with their fellow workers. But many Kenya employers deliberately employed a mixed labour force. Men and women therefore communicated initially with those to whom they could communicate; in the process a common consciousness was stimulated. Friction between employees of different tribes over tasks, rations, huts, women, stock and wages were frequent on the farms. In towns, particularly in Mombasa, competition for employment between local Coastal men and others from inland, notably the Luo, also led to friction, resentment and occasionally riots.[1] Sometimes the nature of the work, the supposed aptitudes of particular communities for it and marked employer preferences for men of the appropriate community also contributed to pride in local origin.[2] Songs sung at work might boast claims to superiority or emphasize characteristics of one tribe or another.[3] In the larger towns tribal welfare associations were formed under the leadership of tribal notables, work people in the towns forming the vast bulk of the membership. These associations performed useful social service work, but they also strongly reinforced tribal identities with all the added emphasis of the exile. The Kikuyu also found that their large absentee squatter population often clung to superstitions discarded in Kikuyuland.[4] Even in sport and relaxation local ethnic loyalties received massive support on the urban football fields, the inter-district Remington Cup matches attracting large crowds of local supporters. In the final decade of colonial rule ethnic factors played, and were seen to play, a large part in trade union affairs. The overall rise of population and its uneven distribution (a further consequence of the structure) also increased tribal feeling, particularly as the peoples which increased the most were those concentrated in overcrowded reserves, the concentration itself adding to the feeling.

In the slow process of fragmentation and reformation that form the histories of most African communities, the labour system therefore played a part. One group of several small communities in particular was affected, the peoples of North Nyanza, from whom a new ethnic identity as the Baluhya was to emerge during the colonial period—in marked contrast to the absence of a comparable cohesion among similar groups across the border in Uganda. The labour imposition, the resentment it aroused and the common experiences of work (including membership of urban associations initially district or smaller but later merging into one Baluhya association) were factors contributing to this unification, but it would be an overstatement to assert that labour was the only cause or even a major one. The most important causes were fear of domination by the neighbouring Luo, and a generally similar cultural and linguistic heritage.[5] Other significant causes were a common traditional opposition to the colonial-imposed Wanga chiefs, circumcision (which the Luo did not practice), the district borders and administration and later, the L.N.C. established with no particular thought to labour supply, trading, social and educational contacts that needed a common language and orthography. Another factor contributing to a wider local pride was football, although the North Nyanza people provided separate teams in the colonial period they were collectively the best football players in Kenya.[6] Elsewhere the labour system was one factor preventing the emergence to a full separate tribal identity of the smaller communities on the fringes of Kikuyuland now known as the Embu and Meru, but in the early years of colonial rule known by separate local names for each small community such as Tharaka and Igoji; here also more important factors were at work.[7]

In opposition to these trends of increasing tribal identity, however, can be set the diffusion of Swahili as a consequence of labour needs, government education policy related to those needs, and the movement of labour. The diffusion took place despite two disadvantages, firstly that Swahili had been the language of the slave-owner and was therefore regarded with suspicion, at times hatred, by many Africans, and secondly that Swahili or a bastard version of it was spoken by European and Asian employers. But work, wages, conditions, legislation, medical and social matters were all explained to employees by their employers in Swahili, albeit badly or through an indifferent interpreter.[8] Crafts and trades had to be taught in Swahili, food purchases often had to be made in Swahili, and military service in the two world wars and police service spread the language even further. More important still, Swahili quickly became:

> . . . the language of the towns, especially Nairobi where people from all parts of the country found it a convenient bulwark against the loneliness of city life as well as a ready tool to exploit the attractions which the city offered.[9]

It may perhaps be tentatively asserted that Kenya's first step towards an African national language was growing familiarity with Swahili during employment, a step unlikely to have occurred had the country developed by peasant production.[10]

The other major consequence of months or years spent in employment, was drastic modernization, of almost Stalinist severity, for traditional societies and individuals. To draw a balance, to judge whether or not the price paid in terms of aliens' profits, the suffering caused by rapid and harsh social changes, disease and death outweighs the gains in terms of this modernization (not all aspects of which were of unquestionable benefit), is both premature and beyond the scope of this work. But within sixty years scores of thousands of Africans became accustomed to regular work for a regular wage, modern means of transport, wages paid in coin and arrangements for personal saving, modern communications media, modern medicine, social services and housing (of varying standards), public health facilities and clean water, craft and trade training, and consumer goods, many of value though some worthless. Many Africans, consciously or unconsciously emulating European families for whom they had worked as domestic servants, aimed at a westernized bourgeois small-family style of life, at white collar status and retirement to a small country home. For almost all, there were new horizons of religion or ideology to replace old fears and superstitions. The early settlers were not entirely without justification when they spoke of the educative effect of work although few were aware of the implications of all that was learned.

One development of which the full consequences have yet to be seen is the arrival, from the early years of the century, of Africans in the former European farm areas as labourers resident, seen by Europeans as a work force but by the Africans themselves as tenant land-users. Although in the latter years of colonial rule the number of squatters fell, the numbers of monthly-paid labourers who received a small plot of land to subvent an inadequate cash wage rose considerably. The combined totals may represent a large-scale and lasting invasion of the capitalist production regions of Kenya by men and families chiefly preoccupied with subsistence, and may prove a trend parallel to the post-independence high-density resettlement schemes and the sharing or division of the consolidated plots of land in Kikuyuland. The urban worker, too, seeks wherever possible to retain a family holding, or a stake in one, and remains more peasant than proletarian. Both processes constitute a form of industrial response to capitalist development.

Another possible future development may well prove to be the use of women of their increased domestic bargaining position. There is almost no evidence to suggest that in the colonial period the wife of the migrant labourer, left behind to till the family patch, appreciated the power which the production of so large a part of the family's income gave to her. The migrant labour pattern, however, remains and the next generation of women may seek some rearrangements.

The British colonial system was based on a belief in the merits of entrepreneurial capitalism, with for preference a British entrepreneur, either a farm or plantation-owner, a trading company or a banker. Concepts other than this were not considered; reforms desired by humanitarians had to conform to the system. But this system cannot be dismissed as unrestrained capitalist control with colonial officials simply willing or unwilling agents. As we have seen the system, in its widest sense and including all its varied pressure groups, provided some considerable protection for Kenya's African labour. Despite the communication problem (particularly the lack of knowledge among responsible British officials in London and among British public opinion) the system provided certain checks and balances; these after a slow start and with occasional breakdowns worked to make the system tolerable. The poverty of Africa, reflected *inter alia* in the inefficiency of labour, was the system's main enemy; the relatively close attention paid to Kenya's affairs in Britain was the system's most useful asset, if not always so recognized. Unrestrained commercial exploitation would have been a catastrophe for an African territory, but a number of important restraints on total exploitation can justly be claimed. The British colonial system and its results are at least subjects on which historians can argue opposing points of view.

Many consequences of the British system were to survive after independence with much less alteration in the early years than in some other former British territories. Despite all the hardships borne by many in the colonial period, the Kenya of the nineteen-sixties saw no rejection of the belief in the merits of the private entrepreneur, a fact which cannot be explained solely in terms of the need to occupy the large numers of unemployed. One of the reasons was the ability of certain pressure groups such as the trade unions and the employers successfully to reorganize themselves in the nineteen-fifties to face the uncertainties first of civil war and then of independence. Both had a commitment to the western industrial and commercial system through the device of collective bargaining. It is unlikely, however, that this development would have taken place either so successfully and or in the form in which it did without the involvement of the Labour Department. This *troika* of government, labour and management wielded a good deal of power in the dying days of colonial rule and in the early years of African rule. The continuity was in part due to the peculiarities of politics in a pre-independence situation in which neither the British nor the Africans were fully in control; it stands in contrast to the eclipse of the influence of the Labour Department and the emphasis on administration during the early days of the Mau Mau crisis. It was also due to a form of guardianship of the mysteries for labour relations throughout this period which was developing into a specialized exercise where amateurs more and more frequently found themselves unwanted by any of the parties.

The advent of the Kenyatta government led to a curtailment but not an abolition of the trade unions. The government moved slowly, its main object being to prevent the unions from becoming a quasi-political party in opposition to the authorities. This was achieved by transforming the K.F.L. into the C.O.T.U. with a direct role for the Kenya President in naming the leading officials of the federation. However, it was not the intention of the government to eliminate collective bargaining. This was preserved partly by Mboya within the government and partly by the F.K.E. from without. Nevertheless the bargaining power of individual unions was restrained by the creation of an Industrial Court which, in effect, set limits to wage claims and enforced a certain technique of industrial relations. The organization of the unions remained mainly industrial with the exceptions already noted. Elaborate union-organized welfare and benefit schemes of the Israeli pattern which had at one time been planned were discarded, the initiative being left to the government whereas in colonial days the influence of the officials remained great. Emphasis in government circles gradually switched from industrial relations to social services, thus reviving another thesis of colonial labour policy which had been most marked when Carpenter was Labour Commissioner. Welfare capitalism rather than socialism was to remain the major characteristic of government policy. The 1965 statement on African socialism clearly and deliberately allotted an important role to the private sector. The large property-owners and wide differences of living standards between employer and employee remained. The successor elite, drawn mainly from the people who had suffered the most, the Kikuyu, showed few inhibitions over wide differences in standards *per se*, although devoting considerable political activity and skill to preventing disruptive consequences and to promoting black capitalism. Kenyatta had never preached revolution during his long political career, and this conservative style both in politics and in industrial relations was entirely consistent with his oratory and his actions since the nineteen-twenties. But there remained a shadow over this seeming tranquility—would it be possible for the system to solve the problems of land, employment and population and to contain the potential of revolution that was clearly involved?

NOTES

1. See *supra*, pp. 220–21, 331, 399.
2. The Kamba from early times exhibited mechanical aptitude, they and the Nandi preferred uniformed work, police, the K.A.R., administration *askaris*, etc. Nandi girls were preferred by Europeans as ayahs, Luo and Baluhya as domestic servants.
3. A K.A.R. marching song, for example, set out in Swahili the characteristics of various peoples in stanzas repeated in solo and chorus: 'Wajaluo wanapenda samaki . . . wapenda samaki . . . Wabaganda wanapenda matoke . . . wapenda matoke . . . etc. [The Luo like fish . . . The Baganda like bananas]. A famous Kamba porters' song, sung to the tune of *John Brown's Body* ran 'Watu wa Nairobi wanaishi na raha, Watu wa Kisumu wanakufa kwa njaa, Watu wa mashamba wanapenda kushiba, Ila watu Wakamba! Simileni tunakuja [thrice], Wanafunzi Wakamba!' [The people of Nairobi live in comfort, the people of Kisumu are dying of hunger, the people of the highlands like to eat too much, except the Wakamba! Out of the way we are coming! The Kamba boys!]
4. See for example, R. M. Gatheru, *op. cit.*, 46. 'Apart from the differences in dress and figures of speech I found out, too, that the Kikuyu people who lived in the Kikuyuland were less afraid of the so-called "witch-doctors" and magic than were the Kikuyu "Squatters" in the European settled areas . . . Kikuyu "Squatters" were much more superstitious than their brothers in the Kikuyu Country.'
5. C. G. Rosberg and J. Nottingham, *op. cit.*, 162–3, note the emergence of the North Kavirondo Central Association in the nineteen-thirties as a Baluhya opposition group to Archdeacon Owen's Kavirondo Taxpayers' Welfare Association. The name Luhya, they also note, was selected by the North Nyanza branch of the K.T.W.A. as early as 1929; 'abalimi' (the cultivators) was rejected in favour of 'avaluhya' (kinship). The origin of this word lay in 'oluyia', the fireplaces around which clan elders congregated.
6. For an outline account of these factors see *Oxford History*, II, 373–8.

7. These other factors included district demarcations (including an important reorganization in 1932–3), provincial joint meetings of L.N.C. delegates, markets, standard vernaculars and, again, sports.

   The Ndia, particularly those from the Sagana area, supplied night-soil sweepers to Nairobi and other Kenya towns, an arrangement believed to have been originated by the persuasion of Indian sweepers in the early years of the century. A situation in which one tribe or community supplies men for this distasteful work is met with elsewhere, notably the Balavale in Zambia and Hindu Untouchables in pre-revolution Zanzibar. One factor which influenced the Ndia, who came from a port area and appear to have been despised by other Kikuyu, may have been some half-conscious realization of the importance of their unpleasant occupation, though their own lack of opportunity at home and a pre-colonial tradition of travelling to a city (Mombasa) also played a part.

8. A minor but interesting example is a song used to teach Swahili numbers and agreements, a Swahili version of the English song 'One man went to mow, went to mow a meadow, one man and his dog went to mow, went to mow a meadow, two men went to mow, etc.' In Swahili this ran 'Mtu mmoja alienda, alienda kulima shamba, mtu mmoja na mbwa yake walienda kulima shamba, watu wawili walienda, etc.'

9. W. Whiteley, *Swahili—The Rise of a National Language*, 1969, 67.

   See also *Journal of African Languages*, III, iii, 1964, 'Problems of a Lingua Franca: Swahili and the Trade Unions', in which Professor Whiteley notes in a study of Tanganyika and Kenya trade unions that Swahili was the language used for union meetings, minutes, pamphlets and news-sheets. He notes also that the origin of the word *chama* (*chama cha wafanyi kazi*, a trade union) is obscure but 'probably cognate with *njama*, a secret meeting', and his article suggests other connotational problems arising from the translation of complex economic and industrial concepts. One immediate example provided is that *chama* is also used for an association or party in the political sense.

10. The role of the Europeans, insisting on communication with their labour in Swahili, can be compared with the pre-colonial diffusion of Swahili by the coastal Arab and Swahili slave-dealers and traders in mainland Tanzania.

SELECT BIBLIOGRAPHY

This bibliography is restricted to a selection of original and secondary sources, most of which are available for general reading. It is neither a complete list of the works consulted by the authors nor a complete list of all the press and parliamentary references to, or publications touching upon, labour questions in Kenya.

1. Unpublished sources

Administration Provincial and District Reports, Kenya National Archives.

Foreign Office Archives, F.O. 107 (Zanzibar) and F.O.2. (Africa) Series, Public Record Office.

Colonial Office Archives, C.O. 533 and C.O. 544 series, Public Record Office.

Papers of Dr. J. W. Arthur, Edinburgh University Library.

Papers of Dr. J. H. Oldham, International Missionary Council, Edinburgh House, London.

Papers of Mr. H. B. Thomas, Royal Commonwealth Society Library, London.

Papers of the Kenya Federation of Labour made available to Dr. D. C. Savage by the late Mr. T. J. Mboya.

An unpublished manuscript written by Mr. J. Bury, of the International Confederation of Free Trade Unions, made available to Dr. D. C. Savage.

Certain papers made available to Dr. D. C. Savage by Mr. Makhan Singh, the Mombasa Office of the Kenya Labour Department, the Dockworkers' Union, the Mombasa Chamber of Commerce and the Kenya Landing and Shipping Company.

Papers of Elspeth Huxley, Rhodes House, Oxford.

2. The United Kingdom Parliament

(i) United Kingdom *Parliamentary Debates, Lords* and *Commons*, Fourth and Fifth Series, 1895 to 1962.

Prior to 1920 references to affairs in Kenya are indexed under 'Africa' or 'Africa, East'; a few references also appear under 'Zanzibar' in the early years. In 1920 the index contains references under both 'Africa East' and 'Kenya'. Thereafter 'Kenya' is used for Commons volumes but occasionally 'East Africa' appears in the Lords index. The indexing is generally accurate but there are some errors and omissions.

(ii) *United Kingdom Parliamentary Papers: Annual Reports.* Command series: C.8683 (1897); C.9125 (1899); Cd. 769 (1901); Cd. 1626 (1903); Cd. 2331 (1905); Cd 2684 (1906); Cd. 3285 (1907); Cd. 3279 (1908); Cd. 4448 (1909); Cd. 4964 (1910); Cd. 5467 (1911); Cd. 6007 (1912–13); Cd. 7050 (1914); Cd. 7622 (1914–16); Cd. 8172 (1916); Cd. 8434 (1917–18); Cmd. 1–11 (1919); Cmd. 1–36 (1919). 1920–1960, Annual Reports for Kenya Colony.

Special subjects

Papers Relating to British East Africa; House of Lords, 158 of 1907.

Correspondence respecting the recent Rebellion in British East Africa C.8274 of 1895.

Report on the Progress of the Mombasa-Victoria (Uganda) Railway, C.8435 of 1897.
Correspondence respecting the abolition of the Legal Status of Slavery in Zanzibar and Pemba, C.8858 of 1898.
Report on the Uganda Railway by Sir Guilford Molesworth, K.C.I.E., C.9331 of 1899.
Report by the Mombasa Victoria (Uganda) Railway Committee on the Progress of the Works 1898–99, C.9333 of 1899.
Correspondence respecting the Status of Slavery in East Africa and the Islands of Zanzibar and Pemba, C.9502 of 1899.
Correspondence respecting Slavery and the Slave Trade in East Africa and the Islands of Zanzibar and Pemba, Cd. 593 of 1901.
Correspondence respecting the Uganda Railway, Cd. 670 of 1901.
Report on Slavery and Free Labour in the British East Africa Protectorate, Cd. 1631 of 1903.
Final Report of the Uganda Railway Committee, Cd. 2164 of 1904.
Reports relating to the Administration of the East African Protectorate, Cd. 2740 of 1906.
Correspondence relating to the Flogging of Natives by Certain Europeans in Nairobi, Cd. 3562 of 1907.
Correspondence relating to Affairs in the East Africa Protectorate, Cd. 4122 of 1908.
Despatch to the Governor of the East African Protectorate relating to Native Labour and Papers connected therewith, Cmd. 873 of 1920.
Papers Relating to Native Disturbances in Kenya, 1922, Cmd. 1691 of 1922.
Kenya Compulsory Labour for Government Purposes, Cmd. 2464 of 1925.
Report of the East Africa Commission, Cmd. 2387 of 1925.
Kenya, Tours in the Native Reserves and Native Development in Kenya, Cmd. 2573 of 1926.
Colonial Office Conference 1930, Summary of Proceedings, Cmd. 3628 of 1930.
Report of the Financial Commissioner (Lord Moyne) on Certain Questions in Kenya, Cmd. 4093 of 1932.
Report of the Kenya Land Commission, Cmd. 4556 of 1934.
Report of the Commission Appointed to Enquire into and Report on the Financial Position and system of Taxation in Kenya, Col 116 of 1936.
Labour Supervision in the Colonial Empire, 1937–43, Col 185 of 1943.
Labour Conditions in East Africa, Col 193 of 1946.
Report to the Secretary of State for the Colonies by the Parliamentary Delegation to Kenya, Cmd. 9081 of 1954.
East Africa Royal Commission 1953–1955 Report, Cmd. 9475 of 1955.
Despatches from the Governors of Kenya, Uganda and Tanganyika and from the Administrator, East Africa High Commission, commenting on the East Africa Royal Commission 1953–1955, Cmd. 9801 of 1956.
Historical Survey of the Origins and the Growth of Mau Mau, Cmd. 1030 of 1960.

3. Kenya Government Publications

(This section also includes E. A. High Commission and other local official publications.)

The Zanzibar Gazette, 1894–1900.
The East Africa Protectorate and, from 1920, Kenya *Official Gazette*, 1901–63.
Laws, Ordinances, etc., of the East Africa Protectorate and Kenya; Legislative Council Minutes (to 1925), Debates 1925–63, Sessional Papers, 1945–63.

(There are a number of series of these works which it is impossible to list in detail here.)
Departmental Annual Reports, especially Native Affairs Department (1919–45), Labour Department (1940–62), Education Department, Medical Department.
Reports of the Uganda Railway, later the Kenya and Uganda Railway and the East African Railways and Harbours.
Native Labour Commission 1912–13, Evidence and Report, 1913.
Standing Orders and Regulations for the Forces in B.E.A. 1915, 1915.
Military Labour Bureau Handbook, 1917.
Economic Commission Final Report, Parts I and II, 1919.
Report of the Labour Commission, 1927.
Memorandum on Native Progress, 1928.
Report of the Committee on the Working of the Resident Native Labourers Ordinance, 1925, 1935.
Report on Native Taxation, 1936.
Report of the Employment of Juveniles Committee, 1938.
Report of the Commission of Inquiry appointed to Examine the Labour Conditions in Mombasa, 1939.
Kenya Land Settlement Committee Report, 1939.
Report and Recommendations of the Registration of Domestic Servants Ordinance Committee, 1940.
Report of the Committee on Arab and African Terms of Service, 1941.
Report by the Senior Medical Officer and the Municipal Native Affairs, Officer on the Housing of Africans in Nairobi, 1941.
Report on the Conscription of African Labour, 1942.
Report of the Committee on Post-War Employment, 1943.
Food Shortage Commission of Enquiry Report, 1943.
Post-War Employment Committee Report and Report of the Sub-Committee on the Post-War Employment of Africans, 1943.
Man Power, Demobilization and Reabsorption Report, 1945.
Report on the Economic and Social Background of Mombasa Labour Disputes, 1947.
African Labour Efficiency Survey, 1947.
Report of the Commission on the Civil Services of Kenya, Tanganyika, Uganda and Zanzibar, 1947–48, 1948 (also Col 223 of 1928).
The Pattern of Income and Consumption of African Labourers in Nairobi, October–November 1950, 1951.
Report of the Cost of Living Commission, 1950.
Report of the Committee on African Wages, 1954.
Report of the Social Security Committee, 1957.
Report of the Commission on the Civil Services of the East African Territories and the East African High Commission, 1954.
Report and Recommendations of a Board of Enquiry appointed by the Minister to inquire into a trade dispute between the Kenya Local Government Workers' Union and the Nairobi City Council, 1955.
Report of a Board of Inquiry Concerning a Strike in the East Africa Tobacco Company Ltd., 1959.
A Survey of Unemployment, 1960.
Report of a Board of Inquiry appointed to Inquire into a Trade Dispute at the Athi River Premises of the Kenya Meat Commission, 1960.
Report of the Commission on the Public Services of the East African Territories and the East Africa High Commission, 1960.
Report of the Tea Dispute Arbitration Tribunal in the matter of a dispute

between the Kericho branch of the Kenya Tea Growers' Association and the Tea Plantation Workers' Union, 1960.

Reported Employment and Wages in Kenya, 1948–1960, 1961.

Report of the Commission of Inquiry into the Administration and Staff Relations of the Kenya Meat Commission, 1961.

Report of a Board of Inquiry appointed to Inquire into the relations between the Kenya Motor Engineering and Allied Workers' Union and the Motor Trades and Allied Industries Employers' Association, 1962.

Report of the Board of Inquiry into the Wages of Workers employed in manual occupations pertaining to the growing of sisal and the manufacture of sisal fibre and the arrangements existing within the sisal plantation industry for determining wages and other conditions of employment by voluntary collective bargaining and agreement, 1962.

4. The International Labour Office

International Labour Office, *Minimum Standards of Social Policy in Dependent Territories*, Montreal, 1944.

International Labour Office, *Social Policy in Dependent Territories*, Montreal, 1947.

5. Newspapers and Periodicals

(i) The United Kingdom

The Times
Scotsman
Manchester Guardian
Daily Telegraph
News Chronicle
Daily Herald
Observer
The Anti-Slavery Reporter
The Church Missionary Intelligencer
The Contemporary Review
New Statesman
East Africa and Rhodesia

(ii) Kenya

The East African Standard (*The African Standard* to August 1905)
The Leader of British East Africa
Kenya Weekly News
Mombasa Times
Sunday Post
Mfanya Kazi
Reporter
Daily Nation

(iii) Elsewhere

ICFTU Information Bulletin
A.F.L.—C.I.O. News
Free Labour World

6. Books

Altrincham, Lord, *Kenya's Opportunity*, London, 1935.

Amsden, Alice K., *International Firms and Labour in Kenya; 1945–70*, London, 1971.

Anderson, A. G., *Our Newest Colony*, Nairobi, 1910.
Bache, Eve, *The Youngest Lion*, London, 1934.
Barber, D. M., *Africans in Khaki*, London, 1948.
Blixen, Karen, *Out of Africa*, London, 1937.
Blundell, Sir M., *So Rough a Wind*, London, 1964.
Buell, R. L., *The Native Problem in Africa*, 2 volumes, New York, 1928.
Buxton, M. Aline, *Kenya Days*, London, 1927.
Carey Jones, N. S., *The Anatomy of Uhuru*, Manchester, 1966.
Church, A. G., *East Africa, A New Dominion*, London, 1928.
Churchill, W. S., *My African Journey*, London, 1908.
Cranworth, Lord, *A Colony in the Making, or Sport and Profit in British East Africa*, London, 1912 and 1919 editions.
Davies, I., *African Trade Unions*, London, 1966.
Dilley, Miss M. R., *British Policy in Kenya Colony*, New York, 1937.
Dinesen, I. (K. Blixen), *Shadows in the Grass*, London, 1960.
Dundas, Sir C., *African Crossroads*, London, 1955.
Eliot, Sir C., *The East Africa Protectorate*, London, 1903.
Elwin, M., *The Life of Llewelyn Powys*, London, 1946.
Farson, N., *Last Chance in Africa*, London, 1949.
Fearn, H., *An African Economy, A Study of the Economic Development of the Nyanza Province of Kenya, 1903–1953*, London, 1961.
Fendall, Brig.-Gen. C. P., *The East African Force, 1915–19*, London, 1921.
Gatheru, R. Mugo, *Child of Two Worlds*, London, 1964.
Goldsmith, F. H., *John Ainsworth, Pioneer Kenya Administrator, 1864–1946*, London, 1955.
Greaves, L. B., *Carey Francis of Kenya*, London, 1969.
Grogan, E. S., *From the Cape to Cairo*, London, 1900.
Harlow, V. and others, *History of East Africa*, Volume II, Oxford, 1965.
Hailey, Lord, *An African Survey*, London, 1938, and revised 1956, 1957.
Hill, M. F., *Permanent Way*, Volume I, Nairobi, 1950; *Magadi*, Birmingham, 1964.
Hindlip, Lord, *British East Africa, Past, Present, and Future*, London, 1905.
Hobley, C. W., *Kenya from Chartered Company to Crown Colony*, London, 1929; *Notes on Caravan Equipment, Organization and Procedure*, Mombasa, 1894.
Hordern, Lieut.-Col. C., *Military Operations—East Africa*, Volume I, London, 1941.
Hotckiss, W. R., *Then and Now in Kenya Colony*, London, 1937.
Huxley, Elspeth, *White Man's Country*, 2 volumes, London, 1935; *Red Strangers*, London, 1939; *The Flame Trees of Thika*, London, 1959; *The Mottled Lizard*, London, 1962; *A New Earth*, London, 1960.
Huxley, Elspeth and Perham, Margery, *Race and Politics in Kenya*, London, 1944.
Huxley, J. S., *Africa View*, London, 1931.
Jackson, Sir F., *Early Days in East Africa*, London, 1930....
Jeffries, Sir C., *The Colonial Office*, London, 1956.
Jones, W. Lloyd, *K.A.R.*, London, 1926.
Kariuki, J. M., *Mau Mau Detainee*, London, 1963.
Kenyatta, J., *Kenya, The Land of Conflict*, London, n.d.; *Facing Mount Kenya*, London, 1938.
Lander, Cherry, *My Kenya Acres*, London, 1957.
Leakey, L. S. B., *White African*, London, 1937.
Leys, N., *Kenya*, London, 1924.

Lubembe, C., *The Inside Labour Movement in Kenya*, Nairobi, 1968.
Lugard, Sir F. D., *The Dual Mandate in Tropical Africa*, London, 1922.
Lytton, Earl of, *The Stolen Desert*, London, 1966.
McDermott, P. L., *British East Africa or IBEA*, London, 1895.
Maclean, Rev. N., *Africa in Transformation*, London, 1913.
Makhan Singh, *History of Kenya's Trade Union Movement to 1952*, Nairobi, 1969.
Mannoni, O., *Prospero and Caliban*, London, 1956.
Mbotela, J. J., *The Freeing of the Slaves in East Africa*, London, 1956.
Mboya, Tom, *Freedom and After*, London, 1963.
Meinertzhagen, Col. R., *Kenya Diary*, Edinburgh, 1957; *Army Diary, Edinburgh*, 1960.
Mitchell, Sir P., *African Afterthoughts*, London, 1954.
Mockerie, P. G., *An African Speaks for his People*, London, 1934.
Mungeam, G., *British Rule in Kenya, 1895–1912*, Oxford, 1966.
Nelkin, D., *Pan-African Trade Unions*, Cornell, 1967.
Ngugi, J., *A Grain of Wheat*, London, 1967; *Weep not, Child*, London, 1969.
Oginga Odinga, *Not Yet Uhuru*, London, 1967.
Oliver, R., *The Missionary Factor in East Africa*, London, 1952.
Olivier, Sir S., *White Capital and Black Labour*, London, 1910.
Orde-Browne, G. St. J., *The African Labourer*, London, 1933.
Patterson, Lieut.-Col. J. H., *The Man-Eaters of Tsaro*, London, 1907.
Perham, Margery, *Lugard: The Years of Authority*, 1898–1945.
Philip, Dr. H. R. A., *God and the African in Kenya*, London, 1935.
Powys, L., *Black Laughter*, London, 1925; *Ebony and Ivory*, London, 1929.
Reid, C. Lestock, *An Amateur in Africa*, London, 1926.
Roberts, B. C., *Labour in The Tropical Territories of the Commonwealth*, London, 1964.
Roper, J. I., *Labour Problems in West Africa*, London, 1958.
Rosberg, C. G. and Nottingham, J., *The Myth of Mau Mau, Nationalism in Kenya*, New York and London, 1966.
Ross, W. McGregor, *Kenya From Within*, London, 1929.
Smith, H. Maynard, *Frank Bishop of Zanzibar 1871–1924*, London, 1926.
Sorrenson, M. P. A., *Land Policy, Legislation and Settlement in the East Africa Protectorate, 1895–1915*, Nairobi, 1968.
Stewart, Margaret, *Britain and the I.L.O.*, London, 1969.
Thuku, Harry, *An Autobiography*, Oxford, 1970.
Tomblings, D. J. and Keane, G. J., *The African Native Medical Corps*, London, undated.
Ward, H. F. and Milligan, J. W., *A Handbook of British East Africa, 1912–13*, London, 1912.
Watt, Mrs. E. S., *In the Heart of Savagedom*, London, 1912.
White, S. E., *African Camp Fires*, London, 1913.
Whiteley, W., *Swahili, The Rise of a National Language*, London, 1969.
Wilkinson, L., *The Letters of Llewelyn Powys*, London, 1943.
Wymer, N. G., *The Man from the Cape*, London, 1959.

7. Unpublished Theses

Clayton, A., 'Labour in the East Africa Protectorate, 1895–1918' (St. Andrews University, Ph.D., 1970).
Parker, Miss M., 'Political and Social Aspects of the Development of Municipal Government in Kenya with special reference to Nairobi' (London University, Ph.D., 1949).

Zwanenberg, R. van, 'The Labour Question in Kenya, 1919–1938' (Sussex University, M.A., 1968).

8. ACADEMIC JOURNALS

Ogot, B. A., 'British Administration in the Central Nyanza District of Kenya', *Journal of African History*, iv, 2 (1963).

Richmond, D., 'Looking Inside an Employers' Federation', *East Africa Journal*, August 1964.

Savage, D. C. and Munro, J. Forbes, 'Carrier Corps recruitment in the British East Africa Protectorate', 1914–1918, *Journal of African History*, vii, 2 (1966).

Temu, A. J., 'The role of the Bombay Africans on the Mombasa Coast, 1874–1904', *hadith* 3 (Proceedings of 1969–70 Conferences of the Historical Association of Kenya).

Tignor, R. L., 'The Maasai Warriors: pattern maintenance and violence in colonial Kenya', *Journal of African History*, xiii, 2 (1972).

Sandbrook, R., 'Patrons, Clients and the Unions: The Labour Movement and Political Conflict in Kenya', *Journal of Commonwealth Political Studies*, March 1972.

INDEX